BEGINNING
ASP.NET FOR VISUAL STUDIO® 2015

BEGINNING

ASP.NET for Visual Studio® 2015

BEGINNING

ASP.NET for Visual S

William Penberthy

WITHDRAWN

Beginning ASP.NET for

Published by
John Wiley & Sons, In
10475 Crosspoint B
Indianapolis, IN
www.wiley

Copyrigh

Publi

wrox™
A Wiley Brand

Visual Studio® 2015

c.

oulevard

46256

com

© 2016 by John Wiley & Sons, Inc., Indianapolis, Indiana

shed simultaneously in Canada

SBN: 978-1-119-07742-8

ISBN: 978-1-119-07712-1 (ebk)

ISBN: 978-1-119-07723-7 (ebk)

Manufactured in the United States of America

10 9 8 7 6 5 4 3 2 1

For general information on our other products and services please contact our Customer Care Department within the United States at (877) 762-2974, outside the United States at (317) 572-3993 or fax (317) 572-4002.

Wiley publishes in a variety of print and electronic formats and by print-on-demand. Some material included with stan- dard print versions of this book may not be included in e-books or in print-on-demand. If this book refers to media such as a CD or DVD that is not included in the version you purchased, you may download this material at http://book-support.wiley.com. For more information about Wiley products, visit www.wiley.com.

Library of Congress Control Number: 2015955845

ABOUT THE AUTHOR

 **WILLIAM PENBERTHY** has specialized in the Microsoft software development stack since the initial deployment of .NET, performing client, service, and web development in C# and VB.NET. He has directly participated in the development of over 135 applications, ranging from records retention management software to e-commerce storefronts, to geographic information systems, to point-of-sale systems and many applications in between.

ABOUT THE TECHNICAL EDITOR

DAVID LUKE is a graduate of Rutgers University who is an adaptable software/product developer with over 23 years of full life cycle experience. He has held positions with large companies and has also been a serial entrepreneur. David currently is working as the CTO for TravelZork, a travel industry startup.

CREDITS

Senior Acquisitions Editor
Kenyon Brown

Project Editor
Ami Frank Sullivan

Technical Editor
David Luke

Production Editor
Barath Kumar Rajasekaran

Copy Editor
Luann Rouff

Manager of Content Development & Assembly
Mary Beth Wakefield

Production Manager
Kathleen Wisor

Marketing Director
David Mayhew

Marketing Manager
Carrie Sherrill

Professional Technology & Strategy Director
Barry Pruett

Business Manager
Amy Knies

Associate Publisher
Jim Minatel

Project Coordinator, Cover
Brent Savage

Proofreader
Nancy Bell

Indexer
Nancy Guenther

Cover Designer
Wiley

Cover Image
©amaze646/Shutterstock

ACKNOWLEDGMENTS

KUDOS TO YOU, THE READER, for deciding to learn something new. As you work on software development you will find that you are learning something new almost every day; that is the nature of the beast and one of the things that make it such a rewarding practice.

Combining both MVC and Web Forms into a single project is simple: That's one of the features of the new Visual Studio. However, combining them both into a single beginning book proved to be difficult; giving enough information about each in a logical fashion meant that both approaches to ASP.NET, MVC and Web Forms, were not completely covered. While not completely covered, I think they have been covered in enough depth so that you can take the next step and go deeper into one or both of these technical approaches as you may deem necessary.

I would also like to take this time to thank Ami Frank Sullivan and Luann Rouff who had the unenviable job of helping turn my tortured prose into something that makes sense; I have never seen so many polite ways of saying "This is gibberish!" Many thanks also to David Luke, the technical reviewer, who spent a lot of effort to validate the various steps and code snippets and keep me on the straight and narrow.

Lastly, none of this would be possible without the support of my wife Jeanine, who allowed me to spend way too much of our free time working on this project.

ACKNOWLEDGMENTS

CONTENTS

INTRODUCTION

IT WAS ESTIMATED IN JUNE 2015 that 45 percent of the world's population has accessed the Internet. That's over 3 billion users, and the number is growing every day. This is a vast, connected market that can reach any content you decide to make available, be it a simple web page or a complex web application.

There are a lot of ways that you can make a simple web page available online. There are a lot fewer approaches when you are trying to build a web application. One of these web application technologies is ASP.NET from Microsoft.

ASP.NET is a framework that supports the building of robust and performant web applications. Think of it as the structural support for a car. You can add a couple of different body designs on top of this structure: ASP.NET Web Forms and ASP.NET MVC. These two approaches both rest on ASP.NET and depend on common functionality that is made available through ASP.NET.

Visual Studio 2015 is the primary tool used when creating and maintaining ASP.NET web applications. It will help you easily work with every aspect of your web application, from the "look and feel" all the way through to deployment of your application—and skipping none of the steps in between. In addition, because Microsoft is committed to supporting ASP.NET developers, it is available in a fully functional free version!

This book is an exploration of both ASP.NET Web Forms and MVC. As part of this exploration you will become familiar with all of the various components of a functional web application, creating a sample application as you go through the different parts of the development process. You will learn how the two frameworks do things, with some approaches being very similar while others are completely different. No matter the style of approach, however, it is always clear that they both rest on the same framework.

WHO THIS BOOK IS FOR

This book is designed for anyone who wants to build robust, performant, and scalable web applications. Although the development tools run in Microsoft Windows, you are free to deploy the application onto virtually any current operating system; therefore, even organizations that don't have Microsoft servers have the capability to now run ASP.NET web applications.

If you are new to software development you should have no problem following along, as the book has been structured with you in mind. Those of you who are experienced developers but new to web development will also find many different areas of interest and use, especially if C# is not your current programming language.

Lastly, experienced ASP.NET developers should also find many topics of interest, especially if your experience is mainly related to either Web Forms or MVC, but not both. This book will give you experience in both approaches as well as demonstrate how to integrate the two approaches into a single application.

WHAT THIS BOOK COVERS

This book teaches you how to build a fully functional web application. You will have the opportunity to build a complete site using both ASP.NET MVC and ASP.NET Web Forms approaches so that you can develop an understanding of, and build a comfort level with, the complete ASP.NET set of functionality. Each chapter takes you a step further along the development process:

➤ **Chapter 1: Getting Started with ASP.NET 6.0**—You will get an introduction to ASP.NET as a general framework and specifically with Web Forms and MVC. You will also download and install Visual Studio 2015.

➤ **Chapter 2: Building an Initial ASP.NET Application**—In this chapter you create the initial project, including configuring it to support both Web Forms and MVC.

➤ **Chapter 3: Designing Your Web Pages**—This chapter introduces you to HTML and CSS so that you can build attractive and understandable web sites.

➤ **Chapter 4: Programming in C# and VB.NET**—ASP.NET is a developmental framework with which you can use different programming languages, including C# and VB.NET. This chapter provides an introduction to using them.

➤ **Chapter 5: ASP.NET Web Form Server Controls**—ASP.NET Web Forms offers many different forms of built-in functionality that it provides as server controls. These controls enable you to create complex and feature-rich web sites with very little code. This chapter covers the most common controls.

➤ **Chapter 6: ASP.NET MVC Helpers and Extensions**—Whereas ASP.NET Web Forms have server controls to provide features, ASP.NET MVC offers a different type of support through the use of helpers and extensions. This chapter describes that different support.

➤ **Chapter 7: Creating Consistent-Looking Websites**—You will learn how ASP.NET enables you to use master pages and layout pages to create a consistent look and feel throughout your web application.

➤ **Chapter 8: Navigation**—In this chapter you learn the different ways to create menus and other navigation structures. You also look at the different types of links that you can build in both Web Forms and MVC.

➤ **Chapter 9: Displaying and Updating Data**—When you want to use a database with ASP.NET, there are no better options than SQL Server. In this chapter, you install SQL Server, create your initial database schema, and incorporate the creation and display of data into your application.

➤ **Chapter 10: Working with Data—Advanced Topics**—Advanced topics include pagination, sorting, and using advanced database items such as stored procedures to retrieve special sets of information from the database. You will also learn how you can speed up responsiveness by storing data in various places.

➤ **Chapter 11: User Controls and Partial Views**—ASP.NET offers server controls and helpers to provide built-in functionality. Learn how to create your own items to provide common functionality across multiple pages.

➤ **Chapter 12: Validating User Input**—A large part of your site's functionality is defined by the data that users input into your application. This chapter shows you how to accept, validate, and process user input using tools for both Web Forms and MVC.

➤ **Chapter 13: ASP.NET AJAX**—AJAX is a technology that enables you to update parts of your page without making a full-page call to the server. Learn how to do this for both Web Forms and MVC.

➤ **Chapter 14: jQuery**—Everything covered up until this point has been based on doing work on the server. In this chapter you are introduced to using jQuery for work on the client, without having to call back to the server.

➤ **Chapter 15: Security in Your ASP.NET Website**—This chapter adds the concept of a user, demonstrating how you can identify your visitors by requiring them to log in to your application.

➤ **Chapter 16: Personalizing Websites**—Here you will learn how to customize the user information you are using to get the information needed to ensure that users feel welcome at your site. Capturing information about the user's visit also helps you better understand what they want when they visit your site.

➤ **Chapter 17: Exception Handling, Debugging, and Tracing**—Unfortunately, it's very difficult to write code that is totally problem-free. Learn how to manage these problems, including finding and fixing them as well as ensuring that when they happen, users are given the relevant information as to why their actions were not successful.

➤ **Chapter 18: Working with Source Control**—Working within a team is an important aspect of being a professional developer. Source control provides a way for you to share code among users. It also manages backing up your source code with saved versions.

➤ **Chapter 19: Deploying Your Website**—After completing all the work to build your application, the last step is getting out onto the web where your users can visit it!

HOW THIS BOOK IS STRUCTURED

The primary instructional approach in this book is a set of detailed hands-on steps that walk you through the process of building a complete application. These "Try It Out" activities, which demonstrate whatever topic is under discussion, are followed by a "How It Works" section that explains what each step accomplishes. Each of the "Try It Out" sections builds on what was done previously, so they should be followed sequentially.

Exercise questions at the end of the chapter enable you to test your understanding of the material, and answers are available in the appendix. Some questions are specific, others more general. Together they are designed to help reinforce the information presented in the chapter.

A lot of information is presented in this book; it covers two technological approaches that sometimes seem completely different. Additional sources of information are included in the chapters if you want more detailed information about a particular approach or product.

WHAT YOU NEED TO USE THIS BOOK

In order to follow along with the chapter and its hands-on activities, you will need the following:

➤ Windows 7, 8, or 10 or Windows Server 2008 or 2012

➤ The minimum requirements for Visual Studio 2015, including RAM and hard drive space

CONVENTIONS

To help you get the most from the text and keep track of what's happening, we've used a number of conventions throughout the book.

TRY IT OUT

This is a hands-on exercise you should work through, following the text in the book.

1. They consist of a set of steps.

2. Each step has a number.

3. Follow the steps with your copy of the database.

How It Works

This section explains in detail the code from each "Try It Out" activity.

> **WARNING** *Boxes like this one hold important, not-to-be forgotten information that is directly relevant to the surrounding text.*

> **NOTE** *These are tips, hints, tricks, or asides to the current discussion, offset and placed in italics like this.*

As for styles in the text:

➤ We *highlight* new terms and important words when we introduce them.

➤ We show keyboard strokes like this: Ctrl+A.

➤ We show filenames, URLs, and code within the text like so: `persistence.properties`.

We present code in two different ways:

```
We use a monofont type with no highlighting for most code examples.
We use bold to emphasize code that's particularly important in the present
context.
```

SOURCE CODE

As you work through the examples in this book, you may choose either to type in all the code manually or to use the source code files that accompany the book. All the source code used in this book is available for download at `http://www.wrox.com/go/beginningaspnetforvisualstudio`. You will find the code snippets from the source code are accompanied by a download icon and note indicating the name of the program so you know it's available for download and can easily locate it in the download file. Once at the site, simply locate the book's title (either by using the Search box or by using one of the title lists) and click the Download Code link on the book's detail page to obtain all the source code for the book.

> **NOTE** Because many books have similar titles, you may find it easiest to search by ISBN; this book's ISBN is 978-1-119-07742-8.

After downloading the code, just decompress it with your favorite compression tool. Alternately, you can go to the main Wrox code download page at `http://www.wrox.com/dynamic/books/download.aspx` to see the code available for this book and all other Wrox books.

ERRATA

We make every effort to ensure that there are no errors in the text or in the code. However, no one is perfect, and mistakes do occur. If you find an error in one of our books, such as a spelling mistake or a faulty piece of code, we would be very grateful for your feedback. By sending in errata you may save another reader hours of frustration, and at the same time you will be helping us provide even higher quality information.

To find the errata page for this book, go to `http://www.wrox.com` and locate the title using the Search box or one of the title lists. Then, on the book details page, click the Book Errata link. On this page you can view all errata that has been submitted for this book and posted by Wrox editors. A complete book list, including links to each book's errata, is also available at `www.wrox.com/misc-pages/booklist.shtml`.

If you don't spot "your" error on the Book Errata page, go to `www.wrox.com/contact/techsupport.shtml` and complete the form there to send us the error you have found. We'll check the information and, if appropriate, post a message to the book's errata page and fix the problem in subsequent editions of the book.

P2P.WROX.COM

For author and peer discussion, join the P2P forums at `p2p.wrox.com`. The forums are a Web-based system for you to post messages relating to Wrox books and related technologies and interact with other readers and technology users. The forums offer a subscription feature to e-mail you topics of interest of your choosing when new posts are made to the forums. Wrox authors, editors, other industry experts, and your fellow readers are present on these forums.

At `http://p2p.wrox.com` you will find a number of different forums that will help you not only as you read this book, but also as you develop your own applications. To join the forums, just follow these steps:

1. Go to `p2p.wrox.com` and click the Register link.

2. Read the terms of use and click Agree.

3. Complete the required information to join as well as any optional information you wish to provide and click Submit.

4. You will receive an e-mail with information describing how to verify your account and complete the joining process.

> **NOTE** *You can read messages in the forums without joining P2P but in order to post your own messages, you must join.*

Once you join, you can post new messages and respond to messages other users post. You can read messages at any time on the Web. If you would like to have new messages from a particular forum e-mailed to you, click the Subscribe to This Forum icon by the forum name in the forum listing.

For more information about how to use the Wrox P2P, be sure to read the P2P FAQs for answers to questions about how the forum software works as well as many common questions specific to P2P and Wrox books. To read the FAQs, click the FAQ link on any P2P page.

1

Getting Started with ASP.NET 6.0

WHAT YOU WILL LEARN IN THIS CHAPTER:

➤ A brief history of ASP.NET and why it supports both Web Forms and MVC

➤ About the two frameworks, Web Forms and MVC

➤ How to install and use Visual Studio 2015

➤ The sample application that will be used throughout this book

CODE DOWNLOADS FOR THIS CHAPTER:

The wrox.com code downloads for this chapter are found at www.wrox.com/go/ beginningaspnetforvisualstudio on the Download Code tab. The code is in the chapter 01 download and individually named according to the names throughout the chapter.

The Internet has become a critical part of life to millions of people across the world. This growth in the use of the Internet has been accelerating since the 1990s and will continue as technology and access becomes more affordable. The Internet has become the go-to source for shopping, leisure, learning, and communications. It has helped to both build new businesses and give revolutionaries the capability to spread their message to the rest of the world.

This growth means that there will be a long-term demand for people with the skills to build and maintain the next generation of web applications. As an increasing percentage of the world's business is accomplished with web applications, learning how to work on these applications is an obvious career move.

AN INTRODUCTION TO ASP.NET vNEXT

The Internet started off as a set of sealed, private networks designed to share information between research institutions across the United States. The primary users of this system were the research scientists in those labs. However, as the usefulness and flexibility of this information-sharing approach became obvious, interest grew exponentially. More and more institutions became involved, resulting in the evolution of standards and protocols to support the sharing of additional types of information. The initial networks quickly expanded as commercial entities became involved. Soon, Internet service providers were available, enabling regular, everyday people to access and share the burgeoning content of the Internet.

In the early days of the Internet, most content was created and stored statically. Each HTTP request would be for a specific page or piece of stored content, and the response would simply provide that content. Early application frameworks changed that model, enabling the dynamic generation of content based on a certain set of criteria sent as part of that request. This enabled content to be built from databases and other sources, exponentially increasing the usefulness of the Web. It was at this point that the general public, rather than only scientists, really started to take advantage of the Internet's enhanced usability.

ASP.NET is one of those early web application frameworks, with the first version of the .NET Framework released in 2002. The ASP part of the name stands for "Active Server Pages," which was Microsoft's initial web application framework that used server-side processing to create browser-readable HTML pages. The original ASP, now called "Classic ASP," allowed the developer to use VBScript to add scripting code to HTML. However, the code and the HTML were all intermingled together in a single file.

ASP.NET was considered a major enhancement at the time because it allowed for a much cleaner separation of the code-behind, the code that handles the processing and markup, the code handling the building of the display, than any of the other frameworks available at that time. There have been improvements to this initial ASP.NET framework with every new release of the .NET Framework.

In 2008 Microsoft introduced a new framework that supported a different approach to content creation and navigation: ASP.NET MVC. MVC stands for Model View Controller, and references a software design pattern that provides a more complete separation between the user interface and the processing code. The original framework became known as Web Forms. Even as the Internet content-creation technologies evolve, the way that the Internet runs stays surprisingly unchanged. The movement of the information from the server to the client follows a very simple protocol that has barely changed since the beginning of the Internet.

Hypertext Transfer Protocol (HTTP)

Hypertext Transfer Protocol (HTTP) is the application protocol that acts as the foundation for communications within the Internet. It defines the interaction between the client machine and the server as following a request-response model whereby the client machine requests, or asks for, a specific resource and the server responds with, or sends a reply about, the information as appropriate.

This request can be very simple, from "show me this picture," to something very complex, such as a transfer between your bank accounts. Figure 1-1 shows the outcome of that request—whether it is displaying the picture for the first, simple request or whether it is displaying the receipt for the bank transfer from the second, more complex request.

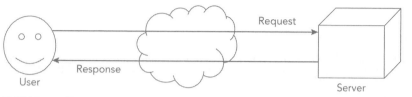

FIGURE 1-1: Request response

The HTTP protocol also defines what the requests and responses should look like. It includes methods, also known as verbs, which describe what kind of action should be taken on the item being requested. These verbs are not really used that much in ASP.NET Web Forms, but they are especially important in ASP.NET MVC because MVC uses these methods to identify the actions being taken on the requested object. The major verbs are listed in Table 1-1.

TABLE 1-1: Most Frequently Used HTTP Verbs

NAME	DESCRIPTION
GET	A GET is a request for a resource. It should retrieve that resource without any other effect resulting from taking that action. You should be able to GET a resource multiple times.
POST	A POST indicates that there is information included in the request that should create a new version of the resource. By definition, any item posted should create a new version, so passing in the same information multiple times should result in multiple instances of that object being created.
PUT	A PUT indicates that the information included in the request should change already existing items. The definition also allows the server to create a new item if the item that is expected to be changed has not already been created. This is different from the POST verb because a new item is only created when the request includes new information.
DELETE	The DELETE verb indicates that the specified resource should be deleted. This means that upon deletion, a GET or PUT to that resource will fail.

An HTTP request includes the following:

➤ A request line. For example, `GET/images/RockMyWroxLogo.png HTTP/1.1` requests a resource called /images/RockMyWroxLogo.png from the server.

➤ Request header fields, such as `Accept-Language: en`

➤ An empty line

➤ An optional message body; when using either the POST or PUT verbs, the information needed to create the object is generally put in this message body

An HTTP response includes these items:

➤ A status line, which includes the status code and reason message (e.g., `HTTP/1.1 200 OK`, which says the request was successful)

➤ Response header fields, such as `Content-Type: text/html`

➤ An empty line

➤ An optional message body

The following example shows a typical response:

```
HTTP/1.1 200 OK
Date: Thur, 21 May 2015 22:38:34 GMT
Server: Apache/1.3.3.7 (Unix) (Red-Hat/Linux)
Last-Modified: Wed, 08 Jan 2015 23:11:55 GMT
ETag: "xxxxxxxxxxxxxxxxx"
Content-Type: text/html; charset=UTF-8
Content-Length: 131
Accept-Ranges: bytes
Connection: close

<!DOCTYPE html>
<html>
  <head>
    <title>I'm a useful title to this page</title>
  </head>
  <body>
    <p>I'm some interesting content that people can't wait to consume.</p>
  </body>
</html>
```

The status codes, such as 200 OK in the preceding example, provide details about the request. The most common types of status codes are the 4XX and 5XX codes. The 4XX codes are for client errors, with the most common being a 404, which denotes that the resource being requested does not exist. The 5XX codes are for server codes, the most common of which is 500, or an Internal Server error. Anyone who does much web development will quickly become accustomed to the dreaded 500 errors.

These verbs are needed because, by definition, HTTP is a stateless protocol. That is why nothing in the request identifies any previous request; instead, each request-response is expected to act completely independently.

Much of this communication happens behind the scenes and is handled by the user's browser and the web server. However, the information being sent and received affects your web application. As you continue developing your knowledge and skills about ASP.NET, you will find cases where digging in deeper to the different values in either the request or the response becomes important. You may need to set request and/or response headers to ensure that some contextual information (such as an authorization token or the client's preferred language) are properly set.

Microsoft Internet Information Services

Microsoft Internet Information Services (IIS) is an application that comes with Microsoft Windows that is designed to support HTTP (known as a web server). It is included with all current versions of Windows, although it is not installed by default. When you develop an ASP.NET application, either Web Forms or MVC, the work of processing and creating the content that is returned to the client is done by IIS.

HTML 5

Whereas HTTP is the process of communicating between a client and a server, HTML is the core markup language of the Internet. HTML (HyperText Markup Language) is used for structuring and presenting content on the Web, and is a standard from the W3C (World Wide Web Consortium). HTML 5, finalized in October 2014, is the newest version of this standard. The previous version, HTML 4, was standardized in 1997.

As you can imagine, the Web went through some dramatic evolution during the 17 years between HTML 4 and HTML 5. While this evolution provided some advantages, especially to users, it also created some problems for website developers. One of the primary problems was that web browser companies tried to differentiate their products by providing a set of browser-specific enhancements, especially related to multimedia. This made developing an interactive website problematic because each browser had different specific development requirements.

HTML 5 was designed to help solve the problems caused by this fragmentation. Improvements include the following:

➤ Additional support for multimedia, including layout, video, and audio tags

➤ Support for additional graphics formats

➤ Added accessibility attributes that help differently abled users access the web page content

➤ Significant improvements in the scripting APIs that allow the HTML elements to interact with JavaScript (you will learn more about this in Chapter 14, "jQuery")

HTML Markup

HTML documents are human-readable documents that use HTML elements to provide structure to information. This structure is used to provide context to the information being displayed. A web browser takes the context and content into account and displays the information accordingly. These elements can be nested, meaning one element can be completely contained within another element, making the whole page basically a set of nested elements, as shown here:

```
<!DOCTYPE html>
<html>
  <head>
```

```
      <title>I'm a useful title to this page</title>
    </head>
    <body>
      <p>I'm some interesting content that people can't wait to consume.</p>
    </body>
  </html>
```

Each layer of elements acts to group related content. As each element is parsed by the browser, it is evaluated as to where it belongs within the logical structure. This structure is what gives the browser the capability to relate content based upon its proximity and relationship to other elements within the structure. In the preceding example, the `title` element is a child of the `head` element.

Note also the expectation of both open and close tags. This fits in with the concept that an element can be contained within other elements. Only those elements that cannot contain other elements do not need to be closed. The open tag is a set of angled brackets `<>` around an element `html`, while the close tag is a set of angled brackets `</>` around the same `element` name but prefaced with a slash `/html`. This enables the browser to identify each section appropriately. Some browsers may support some tags that are not properly closed, but this behavior is inconsistent, thus care should be taken to close all elements. The only item that does not follow this standard is the `<!DOCTYPE html>` declaration. Instead, this identifies how the content that follows should be defined. In this case, the content is defined as `html`, so the browser knows that the content should be parsed as HTML 5.

Some of the more useful elements available in HTML 5 are listed in Table 1-2. This is not a complete list! Visit the W3C site for a complete list of HTML elements and a full description of their usage at `http://www.w3.org/TR/html5/index.html`.

TABLE 1-2: Commonly Used HTML Elements

ELEMENT NAME	DESCRIPTION
html	Identifies the content as HTML code.
head	Defines the content as the head section of the page. This is a high-level section containing information that the browser uses to control the display of the content.
title	An item within the head section, this element contains the content normally displayed in the browser's title bar.
body	Defines the content as the body section of the page. This section contains the content that is displayed within the browser window.
a	Anchor tag that acts as a navigation link to other content. It can redirect the user to another location on that same page or to a completely different page.
img	This tag places an image onto the page. It is one of the few elements that does not have a closing tag.

ELEMENT NAME	DESCRIPTION
form	The `form` tag identifies the contained content as a set of information that will be submitted together as a block. It is generally used to transfer information from the user to the server.
input	This element plays a lot of roles within a form. Depending upon the type (much more on this later!) it can be a text box, a radio button, or even a button.
span	A way to delimit content inline. This enables you to give a special format to one or more words in a sentence without affecting the spacing of those words.
div	Like the `span` tag, this tag acts as a container for content. However, it is a block element, and different in that there is a line break before and after the content.
audio	An HTML 5 feature that allows you to embed an audio file into the page. The types of audio files supported may differ according to browser.
video	An HTML 5 feature to embed video files into the page so that the browser will play the content inline.
section	An HTML 5 addition that identifies a set of content as belonging together. Think of it as a chapter in a book, or areas of a single web page such as introduction and news.
article	Another HTML 5 addition that defines a more complete, self-contained set of content than the section element.
p	A paragraph element that breaks up content into related, manageable chunks.
header	Provides introductory content for another element, generally the nearest element. This may include the body, which means the content is the header for the entire page.
h1, h2, h3	An element that enables content to be designated as header text. The smaller the number, the higher it appears in the hierarchy. An `h1` element would be similar to a book title, `h2` could be chapter title, `h3` section title, and so on.
ul	Enables the creation of an unordered, bulleted list.
ol	Enables the creation of an ordered, generally numbered list.
li	The list item element tells the browser that the content is one of the items that should be included in a list.

Attributes in HTML

An attribute is additional information that is placed within the angle braces of the opening element. This attribute provides detail so that the browser knows how to behave when rendering or interacting with that element. An example is the anchor element, which provides a navigational link to other content:

```
<a href='http://www.wrox.com'>Awesome books here!</a>
```

The `href` is an attribute that tells the browser where to send users after they click the "Awesome books here!" link.

All elements support attributes of some sort, whether they are implied required items such as the `href` attribute in an anchor tag, or optional tags such as `name`, `style`, or `class`, which can be used to control the identification and appearance of the attributed element.

HTML Example

The code in Listing 1-1 is a sample HTML page that contains almost all of the elements in Table 1-2.

LISTING 1-1: An example HTML page

```
<!DOCTYPE html>
<html>
    <head>
        <title>Beginning ASP.NET Web Forms and MVC</title>
    </head>
    <body>
        <!-- This is an HTML comment.  The video and audio elements are not
displayed.-->
        <article>
          <header>
            <h1>ASP.NET from Wrox</h1>
            <p>Creating awesome output</p>
            <a href='http://www.wrox.com'>
                <img src='http://media.wiley.com/assets/253/59/wrox_logo.gif'
                    width='338' height='79' border='0'>
            </a>
          </header>
          <section>
            <h2>ASP.NET Web Forms</h2>
            <p>More than a decade of experience and reliability.</p>
            <ol>
                <li>Lots of provided controls</li>
                <li>Thousands of examples available online</li>
            </ol>
          </section>
          <section>
            <h2>ASP.NET MVC</h2>
            A new framework that emphasizes a <div>stateless</div> approach.
            <ul>
                <li>Less page-centric</li>
                <li>More content centric</li>
            </ul>
          </section>
```

```
      </article>
      <form>
        <p>
          Enter your <span style='color: purple'>email</span> to sign up:
          <input type='text' name='emailaddress'>
        </p>
        <input type='submit' value='Save Email'>
      </form>
    </body>
  </html>
```

Microsoft's Internet Explorer renders this HTML content as shown in Figure 1-2. All other HTML 5 browsers will also render this comment in a very similar way.

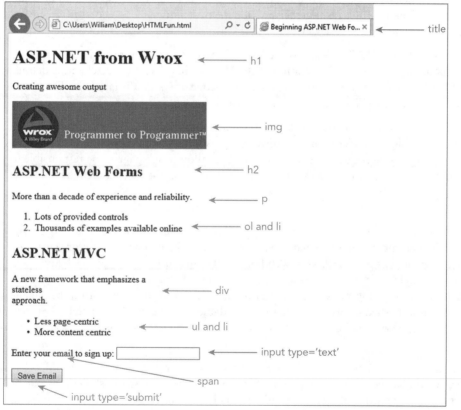

FIGURE 1-2: HTML rendered in the browser

As you can see, HTML provides some simple layout to the content. However, when you look at various sites on the Web, you will likely not see anything that looks like the preceding example. That's because HTML provides layout, but there is another technology that provides more control over the user experience (UX) by enhancing design. This technology is Cascading Style Sheets (CSS).

> **REFERENCE** *CSS is explained in more detail in Chapter 3, "Designing Your Web Pages."*

ASP.NET Web Forms

ASP.NET Web Forms have been part of the .NET infrastructure since its initial release. Web Forms generally take a page-based approach whereby each web page that may be requested is its own unique entity. During development there are two physical pages in the file system that make up each viewable page: the .aspx code, which contains the viewable markup, and the .aspx.cs or aspx.vb, which contains the code to do the actual processing, such as creating the initial content or responding to button clicks. These two pages together provide the code and markup necessary to create the HTML that is sent to the browser for viewing.

The main benefit of ASP.NET Web Forms is the level of abstraction that it provides compared to the request/response approach and the creation of the HTML that is sent to the client. A detailed knowledge of HTML is less critical than a detailed knowledge of C# or Visual Basic. The framework itself hides a lot of the HTML generation by doing it for you.

The primary model for communications between the client and the server is an approach called the *postback*, whereby a page is rendered in the browser, the user takes some action, and that page is sent back to the server using the same resource name. This allows each page to be responsible for both the creation of the page content and responding to changes in the page content as necessary.

ViewState

This response to change in the page content is enhanced through the use of ViewState. Because HTTP is a stateless protocol, anything that needs state needs to be managed in a more customized approach. ViewState is how ASP.NET Web Forms take this customized approach and transfer state information between the browser and the server. ViewState is a hidden field `<input type="hidden" name="_VIEWSTATE" value="blah blah">` that is included within the page. The entity's value contains hashed information that is unreadable by humans. Fortunately, ASP.NET is able to parse the information and get an understanding of the previous version of the various items on the page.

It is important to understand view state because of the significant role it plays in how ASP.NET Web Forms do their work. Say you are working on a page that has several postbacks. Perhaps one of the postbacks changes the value of a label. If the label had a default value from the first rendering, every initialization of that control on each new postback will reset that value to the default value. However, the system then analyzes the view state and determines that this particular label has a different value that should be displayed. The system now recognizes that it is in a different state and will override the default setting to set the label to the newer, changed version of the text.

This is a powerful way to persist changes between multiple postbacks. However, the more items that change and need to be tracked, the larger the set of view state information, which can be problematic. This information is passed both directions, from server to the client, and then back to the server. In some cases the amount of information being transferred as part of the view state can slow down the download/upload time, especially in those cases where network speed or bandwidth is limited.

By default, the use of ViewState is enabled on every control. However, as the developer you can override those settings as necessary, such as when you know that you won't need to know the previous state of the control. You can also use the view state programmatically. Imagine a large list of data that has both sorting capabilities and paging. If you are going to sort before paging, then the sorting criteria needs to be stored somewhere so that it is available to the next postback. The view state is one place to store this information.

ASP.NET Web Forms Events and Page Lifecycle

One of the strengths of Web Forms is the ability it gives developers to plug into the various events in the page lifecycle. The ASP.NET lifecycle allows the developer to interact with information at various points in the HTML creation phase. As part of the flow, the developer can also use event handlers to respond to events that may happen on the client, including clicking a button or selecting an item in a dropdown list. For developers who are coming from a traditional event-driven development approach, such as Windows Forms, this approach will be very easy to pick up. While the lifecycle process gives a lot of power to a developer, it also adds to the complexity of the application—the same code can result in a different outcome depending on when it is called during the lifecycle.

The steps in the lifecycle are shown in Table 1-3. Some of these items may not make any sense to you at this point, but as we move through the process of creating an interactive web site, you will start to see how this all comes together.

TABLE 1-3: ASP.NET Page Lifecycle Stages

STAGE	DESCRIPTION
Request	This stage happens before the page-calling process starts. It is when the system determines whether run-time compilation is necessary, whether cached output can be returned, or whether a compiled page needs to be run. There are no hooks into this stage from within the ASP.NET page itself.
Start	The page starts to do some processing on the HTTP request. Some base variables are initialized, such as `Request`, `Response`, and the `UICulture`. The page also determines if it is a postback.
Initialization	During this phase, the controls on the page are initialized and assigned their unique IDs. Master pages and themes are applied as applicable. None of the postback data is available, and information in the view state has not yet been applied.
Load	If the request is a postback, control information is loaded with the information recovered from view state.

continues

TABLE 1-3 *(continued)*

STAGE	DESCRIPTION
Postback event handling	If the request is a postback, all the various controls fire their event handlers as needed. Validation also happens at this time.
Rendering	Before the rendering stage starts, ViewState is saved for the page and all of the controls as configured. At this time, the page output is added to the response so that information may start flowing to the client.
Unload	This happens after the content was created and sent to the client. Objects are unloaded from memory and cleanup happens.

The steps in the lifecycle are exposed through a set of lifecycle events. A developer can interact with a lifecycle event as necessary. You will learn more about this interaction as you develop the sample application. These events are listed in Table 1-4.

TABLE 1-4: Lifecycle Events for ASP.NET Pages

EVENT	DESCRIPTION AND TYPICAL USE
Preinit	Raised after the start stage is complete and before the initialization stage begins. Typically used to create or recreate dynamic controls, setting master pages or themes dynamically (more on this later). Information in this stage has not yet been replaced with the ViewState information, covered earlier.
Init	This event is raised after all the controls have been initialized. It is typically used to initialize control properties. These initializations do not affect view state.
InitComplete	Only one thing happens between `Init` and `InitComplete`, and that is the enabling of view state for the controls. Changes applied in this event and after will impact view state, so are available upon postback.
PreLoad	Raised after the page manages the view state information for itself and all controls. Postback data is also processed.
Load	The `OnLoad` method is called in a page, which then recursively calls that same method on every control. This is typically where the majority of your creation work happens, initializing database connections, setting control values, etc.
Control Events	These are specific control-based events, such as the `Click` of a button, or `TextChanged` on a text box.

EVENT	DESCRIPTION AND TYPICAL USE
LoadComplete	This event is raised after all the event handling has occurred. Doing anything here would generally require all of the controls to be loaded and completed.
PreRender	After all the controls have been loaded, the `Page` object starts its Prerender phase. This is the last point at which you can make any changes to the content or the page.
PreRenderComplete	Raised after every databound control has been bound. This happens at the individual control level.
SaveStateComplete	Raised after view state and control state have been saved for the page and for all controls. Any changes to the page or controls at this point affect rendering, but the changes will not be retrieved on the next postback.
Render	This is not an event. Rather, at this point in the process, the `Page` object calls this method on each control. All ASP.NET Web server controls have a `Render` method that writes out the control's markup to send to the browser.
Unload	This is used to perform special cleanup activities, such as closing file or database connections, logging, etc.

The work that you will be doing in the sample application only takes advantage of a few of these events. However, understanding that they may occur gives you an idea of how ASP.NET Web Forms works under the covers. Web Forms enable you to tap into each of these events as needed, both at a page level and a control level. While you will likely encounter entire application projects that don't require anything outside of the Load and Control Events sections, Web Forms provide you with the power to do so as needed.

Some of the more powerful controls have their own sets of events, which you will learn about when you start to work on the sample application.

Control Library

One of the benefits of ASP.NET Web Forms is a powerful set of built-in server controls that give developers a boost in development speed and enhance rapid application development (RAD). Using these controls turns the development process into one that's more about configuration than development, providing an out-of-the-box experience that will likely satisfy many developers who need the most common default behavior. In addition, because of the maturity of this approach, an extensive set of third-party controls are available as well as rich and powerful support within Visual Studio.

These ASP.NET server controls are items that a developer places on an ASP.NET web page. They run when the page is requested, and their main responsibility is to create and render markup to the browser. Many of these server controls are similar to the familiar HTML elements, such as buttons and text boxes. Other of these server controls allow for more complex behavior, such as a calendar control that manages the display of data in a calendar format and other controls that you can use to connect to data sources and display data:

There are four main types of controls:

➤   HTML server controls

➤   Web server controls

➤   Validation controls

➤   User controls

HTML Server Controls

HTML server controls are generally wrappers for traditional HTML elements. These wrappers enable the developer to set values in code and to use events, such as a textbox control firing an event when its text display value has been changed. You will be working with many different HTML server controls as you work through the Web Forms part of the application.

Web Server Controls

A web server control acts as more than a wrapper around an HTML element. It tends to encompass more functionality and be more abstract than an HTML server control, because it does more things. A calendar control is a good example of a web server control; it enhances UI functionality by providing a button that enables users to access a grid-like calendar to select the appropriate date. The calendar control also provides other functionality, such as limiting the range of selectable dates, formatting the date being displayed, and moving through the calendar by month or year.

Validation Controls

The third type of control is the validation control. This control ensures that the values entered into other controls meet certain criteria, or are valid. A textbox that is expected to only capture money amounts, for example, should only accept numbers and perhaps the comma (,) and period (.). It should also ensure that if the value entered contains a period, then there are no more than two numbers to the right of the period. The validator provides this support on the client side and on the server. This ensures that the data is correct before being sent to the server and then ensures that the data is correct when it gets to the server.

User Controls

The last type of control is a user control. This is a control that you build yourself. If a set of functionality needs to be available on multiple pages, then it is most likely that you should create this functionality as a user control. This enables the same control to be reused in multiple places, rather than copying the code itself into multiple pages.

These controls can do a lot of very useful things for you, but they come at a cost. By using these controls, you may lose some control over the finished HTML, which may lead to bloated output or HTML that does not quite fit what the designer may desire.

ASP.NET MVC

Earlier, you learned that ASP.NET Web Forms is a page-based approach to designing a web application. ASP.NET MVC is a different architectural approach that emphasizes the separation of concerns. Whereas Web Forms are generally made up of two sections, markup and code-behind, MVC breaks the concerns into three parts, model, view, and controller. The model is the data that is being displayed, the view is how the data is being displayed to the user, and the controller is the intermediary that does the work of ensuring that the appropriate model is presented to the correct view. Figure 1-3 illustrates the interaction between the different parts.

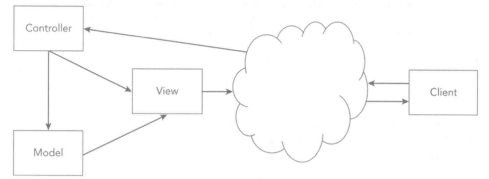

FIGURE 1-3: Model-View-Controller (MVC) design

A key difference between ASP.NET Web Forms and MVC is that MVC presents views, not pages, to the client. This is more than simple semantics, it indicates a difference in approach. Web Forms take a file system approach to presenting content; MVC takes an approach whereby content is based on the "type of action" that you are trying to perform on a particular thing, as shown in Figure 1-4.

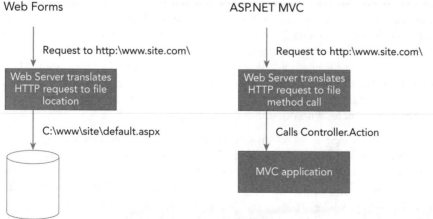

FIGURE 1-4: Different Approaches Between MVC and Web Forms

> **NOTE** *This kind of approach may be less intuitive for developers who are coming from a more event-driven background. However, developers who have experience with other MVC approaches, such as Ruby on Rails, will find the MVC pattern to be comfortable and a good fit with their previous experience.*

The key reason for the MVC pattern's success is the degree to which it helps developers create applications whose different aspects can be separated (input logic, business logic, and UI logic), while still providing a relatively loose coupling between these elements. A loosely coupled system is one in which each component has very little to no knowledge of the other components. This enables you to make changes in one of the components without disturbing the others.

In an MVC application, the view only displays information; the controller handles and responds to user input and interaction. For example, the controller handles query-string values, and passes these values to the model, which in turn might use these values to query the database. Because of this separation, you can completely redesign the UI without affecting the controller or model at all. Because of the loose coupling, the interdependency is much less rigorous. It also enables different people to assume different roles in the development of the application, by disassociating the HTML creation from the server that creates the data to be displayed.

The MVC pattern specifies where each type of logic should be located within your application. The UI-specific logic belongs in the view. Input logic, or the logic that handles the request from the client, belongs in the controller. Business logic belongs in the model layer. This separation helps you manage complexity when you build an application because it enables you to focus on one aspect of the implementation at a time.

Testability

An important consideration when using an MVC approach is the valuable increase in testability it offers. Unit tests are re-runnable items that validate a particular subset of functionality. This is important in modern development because these unit tests enable the developer to refactor, or make changes to, existing code. The unit tests enable developers to determine whether any negative side effects result from the change by running the already created unit tests. An ASP.NET Web Forms application is difficult to unit test for precisely the same reasons that it works so well as a RAD approach: the power of the built-in controls and the page lifecycle. They are very specific to the page of which they are a part, so trying to test discrete pieces of functionality becomes much more complicated because of the dependencies with other items on the page.

ASP.NET MVC's approach and separation means that controllers and models can be fully tested. This ensures that the behavior of the application can be better evaluated, understood, and verified. When building a very simple application this may not be important, but in a larger, enterprise-level application it becomes critical. The functionality it provides to the business might be essential, and it will likely be managed, maintained, tweaked, and changed over a long lifetime; and the more complex the code, the more risk that a change in one area may impact other areas. Running unit tests after a set of changes provides assurance that previously created functionality continues to work as expected. Building unit tests on new functionality verifies that the code is working as expected and provides insurance against future changes.

You won't be specifically building unit tests as part of the process in building the sample web application. However, the available source code does have a unit test project and some tests will be created as you work through the development process, especially for those areas that are using ASP .NET MVC.

Full Control over Output

ASP.NET MVC does not have the same dependence upon controls that ASP.NET Web Forms do, thus it does not have the same risk of becoming bloated HTML output. Instead, developers create the specific HTML that they want sent to the client. This allows full access to all attributes within an HTML element rather than just those allowed by the ASP.NET Web Form server control. It also allows for much more predictable and clearly understood output. Another advantage in having full control over the rendered HTML is that it makes the inclusion of JavaScript much easier. There is no potential for clashes between control-created JavaScript and developer-created JavaScript; and because the developer controls everything that is rendered on the page, using element names and other attributes that may have been commandeered by the generated HTML becomes easier.

Of course, this additional flexibility comes at some cost: Developers are required to spend more time building the HTML than otherwise may have been necessary with the Web Form controls. It also requires that developers be more knowledgeable about HTML and client-side coding, such as JavaScript, than was necessary with Web Forms.

Web Forms and MVC Similarities

It is important to understand that Web Forms and MVC are not opposing approaches but rather different approaches that have inherently different strengths and weaknesses. They each address different concerns and are not mutually exclusive. A developer can create unit tests in Web Forms; it just takes more work and requires the developer to add abstraction where the framework does not provide any by default. Just as with virtually any other development problem, there are multiple potential solutions and approaches. A well-designed application will be successful, regardless of the approach taken.

Fundamentally, as both Web Forms and MVC are designed to solve the same base requirement—creating HTML content that will be provided to the client user—there are a lot of similarities between the two. Properly architected applications will be much the same, especially in terms of backend processing. Accessing databases, web services, or file system objects will all be the same regardless of approach. This is why many developers can become proficient in both.

Choosing the Best Approach

As described earlier, each of these frameworks has its own set of advantages and disadvantages. You need to evaluate your requirements against these concerns and determine which is the most important to your project. This means that there is no right answer; some projects would be best implemented via Web Forms, whereas others might be better served by taking an MVC approach.

There are additional concerns when determining the appropriate development approach, including the background and experience of the developers who will be doing the work and how much information is being shown the same way on multiple pages.

Fortunately, with the advent of Visual Studio 2015 and ASP.NET 5.0 you no longer have to make an either/or choice. With a little bit of maneuvering, you can create a project that uses both approaches as necessary, enabling you to determine on a case-by-case basis which approach to use, instead of using a site-by-site determination.

This case-by-case approach is used in the sample application, which uses both ASP.NET Web Forms and ASP.NET MVC to solve various business problems presented.

USING VISUAL STUDIO 2015

Microsoft's Visual Studio is the primary integrated development environment (IDE) used to create ASP.NET sites and applications. The most recent version is Microsoft Visual Studio 2015, which includes quite a few enhancements. There are also new versions of both C#, version 6.0, and VB.NET, version 14. ASP.NET 5 is also an important release because it can now run on OS X and Linux with Mono installed.

Mono is a software platform designed to enable developers to easily create cross-platform applications. It is an open-source implementation of Microsoft's .NET Framework that runs on non-Windows operating systems. This is a tremendous game changer; because until now, every ASP.NET application, either Web Form or MVC, needed to be deployed to and run on a Microsoft Windows server.

Versions

Several different versions of Visual Studio are available for web developers:

➤ **Visual Studio Community Edition:** A free version of Visual Studio that is designed to help hobbyists, students, and other non-professional software developers build Microsoft-based applications

➤ **Visual Studio Web Developer Express:** Another free version of Visual Studio, supporting only the development of ASP.NET applications

➤ **Visual Studio Professional Edition:** A full IDE for use in creating solutions for the Web, desktop, server, cloud, and phone

➤ **Visual Studio Test Professional Edition:** Contains all the features of the Professional Edition, with the capability to manage test plans and create virtual testing labs

➤ **Visual Studio Premium Edition:** Contains all the features of the Professional Editions with the addition of architect-level functionality related to analyzing code and reporting on unit testing and other advanced features

➤ **Visual Studio Ultimate Edition:** The most complete version of Visual Studio, including everything needed for development, analysis, and software testing

The sample application will use the Community Edition because it provides a complete Visual Studio experience.

Downloading and Installing

Downloading and installing Visual Studio is straightforward. The following Try It Out takes you through the various steps involved, from downloading the correct edition, to selecting appropriate options, and completing the install.

TRY IT OUT Installing Visual Studio

1. Go to http://www.visualstudio.com/products/visual-studio-community-vs. You will see a site similar to what is shown in Figure 1-5.

FIGURE 1-5: Visual Studio site to download Community Edition

2. Select the green Download button to run the installation program. Running the download will give you the screen shown in Figure 1-6.

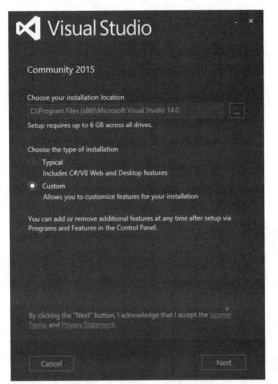

FIGURE 1-6: Installation screen for Community Edition

3. You can select the Custom radio button and see the screen as shown in Figure 1-7, or you can choose Typical and start the installation process.

4. Leave the default settings and click the Install button. You will likely get a User Account Control acceptance box to which you must agree before continuing, after which the download and installation process begins. This may take a while. When the installation is completed you will see a window like the one shown in Figure 1-8. Once completed you may need to restart your computer.

5. To launch the application, click the Launch button. This will bring you to the login screen shown in Figure 1-9.

6. For now, skip the login. This will bring up the Development Settings and Color Theme selection screen shown in Figure 1-10.

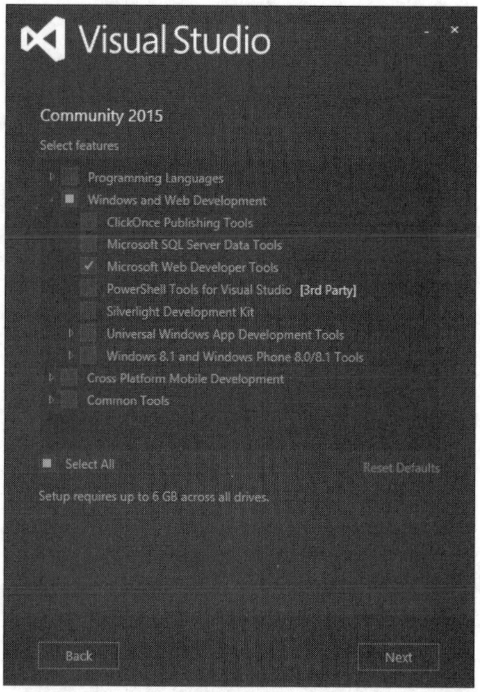

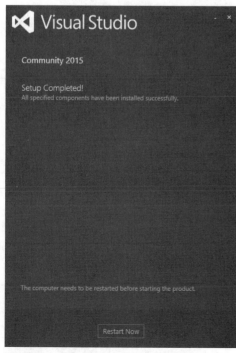

FIGURE 1-7: Select items to install

FIGURE 1-8: Setup Completed window

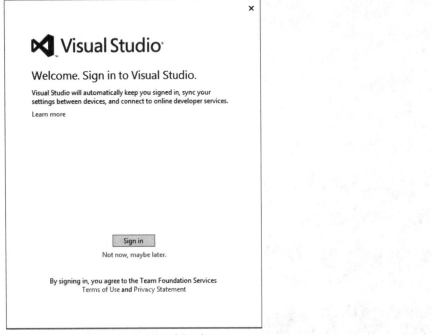

FIGURE 1-9: Login screen in Visual Studio

FIGURE 1-10: Initial configuration of Visual Studio

7. Select the Web Development option, and whichever set of colors you prefer. After configuring these preferences, the application will open, as shown in Figure 1-11.

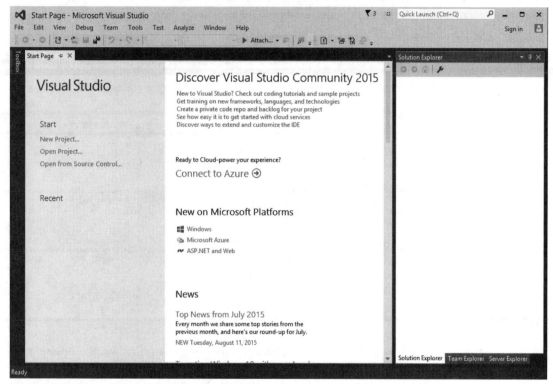

FIGURE 1-11: Start Page for Visual Studio

How It Works

You have completed installing Visual Studio. It is a relatively straightforward installation process, with the only unusual aspect being that Visual Studio now gives you the opportunity to link your installation to an online profile. This enables you to share source code repository information and some system settings between different installations of Visual Studio

If you have not used Visual Studio before don't worry; you will be spending a lot of time going through it as you build the sample application.

THE SAMPLE APPLICATION

The best way to learn how to do something, such as build an Internet application, is simply to do it. With this in mind, you will be building a real application as we go through each functional area of ASP.NET. We will be developing an application called RentMyWrox that acts as a loaning library.

Because this app supports both ASP.NET Web Forms and ASP.NET MVC, there will be some duplication of code and/or effort to show critical features in both frameworks. For some functionality you will be able to do this in two different pages; with other functionality you will have to replicate the same functionality both ways, basically replacing one version with the other version.

The requirements for this application are as follows:

➤ The site owner (administrator) can create a list of items that are available for rent or borrowing.

➤ The items contain pictures and text.

➤ Users can create and register an account online that will give them secure access to the application.

➤ Users can log in and select one to many items that they want to check out.

➤ The listing of items can be filtered.

➤ Users can complete their reservation through a type of checkout process.

These requirements will give you the opportunity to go over the design of the look and feel of the website, getting and saving information in a database, and handling user account creation and authentication using both ASP.NET Web Forms and MVC approaches.

SUMMARY

Microsoft has provided many different web application frameworks over the years. Before the .NET Framework was introduced, there was an approach that provided the capability to incorporate HTML5 markup with business processing. This approach, now known as "Classic ASP," was innovative at the time and enabled developers to quickly and relatively easily build complex business applications.

ASP.NET follows in those footsteps by providing developers with a framework on which to balance all development work. When ASP.NET was introduced, only a single development framework was supported: ASP.NET Web Forms. This framework took a page-bound approach, tying together a specific page and a resource name that would be called. There were two physical pages to each resource page: one page containing the HTML markup that would be returned to the client, and another page that provided all the processing. This allowed for a separation of concerns that Classic ASP did not address.

However, after several years Microsoft released another framework: ASP.NET MVC. This approach allows even more separation of concerns, and greatly enhances the capability to test the business processing in an automated fashion. This is important because it dramatically increases confidence in the correctness of the code.

All of these frameworks are designed to do one single thing: provide HTML from the server to a client. HTML is the language of the Internet—it incorporates the layout and markup of everything that you would see on a web site. The creation of this HTML is primary. Obviously, other processing is going on in the background, but every representation of this work back to the requesting client will be HTML.

EXERCISES

1. What is the difference between HTML and HTTP?

2. Why is ViewState important when you are working with ASP.NET Web Forms?

3. What are the three different architectural components of ASP.NET MVC?

4. What is Microsoft Visual Studio and what are we using it for in this book?

▶ **WHAT YOU LEARNED IN THIS CHAPTER**

Attributes	Extra information you can put in an HTML element that may change how that element interacts with the browser or with the user.
Elements	A section of HTML that defines a set of content. The elements define the content because there is an opening tag `<p>` and a closing tag `</p>` around the content.
HTML	Hypertext Markup Language, how content is identified on the Internet so that browsers know how to handle and display the information.
HTTP	Hypertext Transfer Protocol, the definition that handles the request/response behavior which delivers information from the client to the server and back.
IDE	Integrated development environment, a collection of tools and aids that help developers build programs and applications.
MVC	An architectural pattern that separates the responsibilities of a website into three different components: models, views, and controllers. Each of the sections takes responsibility for part of the process of building a user interface.
Web Forms	An approach to building web applications that is based on a page approach, so each set of functionality is its own page, responsible for both its rendering and business logic.

2

Building an Initial ASP.NET Application

WHAT YOU WILL LEARN IN THIS CHAPTER:

- ➤ The differences between web site projects and web application projects in Visual Studio

- ➤ The project types available in Visual Studio and what they mean to our sample application

- ➤ How to create a new ASP.NET site in Visual Studio

- ➤ File types and directory structures in both ASP.NET Web Forms and MVC

- ➤ The differences between ASP.NET Web Forms and MVC

CODE DOWNLOADS FOR THIS CHAPTER:

The wrox.com code downloads for this chapter are found at www.wrox.com/go/ beginningaspnetforvisualstudio on the Download Code tab. The code is in the chapter 02 download and individually named according to the names throughout the chapter.

Now that you have installed Visual Studio and have an understanding of the requirements for the sample application, it's time to get started building it. Visual Studio makes the creation of the application shell (the initial directory structure and commonly used files) very straight-forward if you are using either ASP.NET Web Forms or ASP.NET MVC. Creating a project that enables you to do both, as we will do here, is not quite as easy because it is not a traditional approach. However, there is no better way to see the two different approaches than by doing them side by side.

This chapter covers the different aspects of each approach, ASP.NET Web Forms and MVC, including file type and directory structure, as well as the differences that you will see as you work through the two different frameworks. Finally, the chapter explains in detail how to make a project that supports both ASP.NET Web Forms and ASP.NET MVC.

CREATING WEBSITES WITH VISUAL STUDIO 2015

Visual Studio 2015 is a very powerful integrated development environment (IDE). You can develop web applications, web services, mobile applications, and desktop applications with the same tool, using the same designer interfaces and many of the same development approaches. Because of this power, it is easy to make a misstep as you determine the approach that you want to take for designing and building your application. Luckily, however, starting over again is as simple as deleting your problem project and its directories.

Available Project Types

A project is Visual Studio's way of identifying a different approach to building an application. A project acts as a container for organizing source code files and other resources. It enables you to manage the organization, building, debugging, testing, analysis, and deployment of your application. A project file is either a .csproj or a .vbproj file and contains all the information necessary to manage all of the preceding relationships. When creating a site that will be accessed online, you can use two types of projects: web site and web application.

In Visual Studio, a web site project is treated differently than a web application project. Figure 2-1 shows how they are created differently.

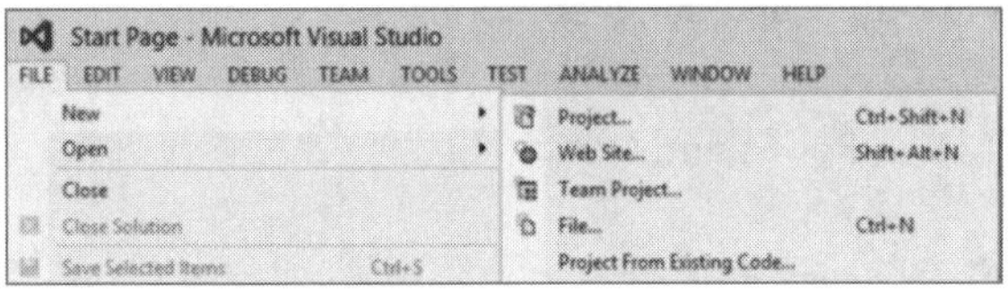

FIGURE 2-1: Creating a project or web site

There are a lot more differences between the two approaches than how they are created, however, as you will see in the following sections.

Web Site Project–Based Approach

The web site project is a less enterprise-type approach toward managing and deploying a web site. The markup (.aspx) files are copied to the server and called during the request. The code-behind files are compiled on the server and saved as temporary .dll files during the first call to the server. This process, where compilation is done during the execution of a program, at run time, rather than needing to be done before the program is run, is called just-in-time compilation. There is no project file as part of the project. Instead, each of the files and directories are treated individually.

As you can imagine, this makes it easy to work with a website. There are no special installations that have to be run on the server; all you need to do to get the site running is to copy the entire folder to a machine running Microsoft Internet Information Services (IIS). Adding and removing files from the web site is as simple as removing them from the directory, although once they are removed from the server they will not be reachable so it is important that any links to the page be edited as well!

However, this very flexibility in approach comes with some limitations. The limitation that impacts us the most for this project is that you cannot create an ASP.NET MVC application, because MVC applications require full compilation. You can only create ASP.NET Web Forms and other projects that do not require full compilation. Figure 2-2 shows the New Web Site dialog that appears after selecting New ➪ Web Site from the menu.

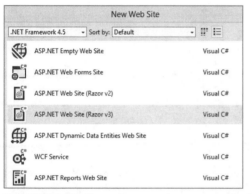

FIGURE 2-2: Options when creating a new web site

While there are many different options when creating a web site, note that they do not include an MVC application.

Web Application Project

Web applications are a much different approach to creating an application than web sites. The web application treats the project more as a true application than a simple grouping of files. This means that everything you may want to do with the site, such as adding an image file or other supporting item, should be done using the IDE. You also have to compile the application before deployment. While this requires a bit more work during the deployment phase, it also enables you to avoid deploying source code to the server. In addition, it speeds up the response time for your application, as your users do not have to wait for the just-in-time compilation to occur before their content can be created.

Because ASP.NET web sites do not allow for the creation of an ASP.NET MVC site, and that is one of the main requirements, you need to use a web application project as the approach to build your application.

Creating a New Site

The first step in creating the sample application is to create an appropriate project in Visual Studio. By selecting File ➪ New Project you will get the New Project dialog shown in Figure 2-3.

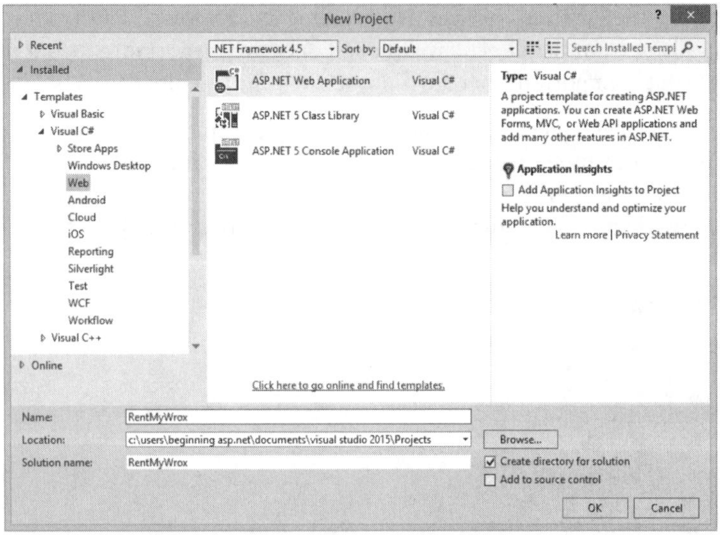

FIGURE 2-3: Creating a new project in Visual Studio

Select the ASP.NET Web Application project type, give it your desired name, and select your preferred location to store the project files. By default, Visual Studio is configured to save your files into directories under "My Documents." You can also select the .NET Framework version that you want to use in your application. Your filled-out screen should look something like what is shown in Figure 2-3. Once you select the ASP.NET Web Application projects and click the OK button, you will get the dialog shown in Figure 2-4, which shows the available templates from which you can choose. This tells the IDE what type of ASP.NET project you wish to create.

Selecting one of these templates will create the appropriate file structure and most commonly used files for that particular template. Each of these available templates is covered in detail in the following sections.

While Creating a Project

There are several other sections of the New ASP.NET Project window that you need to know because they impact the way the project is created. The template section is in the upper-left area of the window. The upper-right area of the window contains the selection for the type of authentication that your application will support "out of the box." The lower-left section of the window contains settings for "folders and core reference files" and unit tests, while the lower-right corner of the window allows you to manage deployment of your project to Microsoft Azure if you so desire.

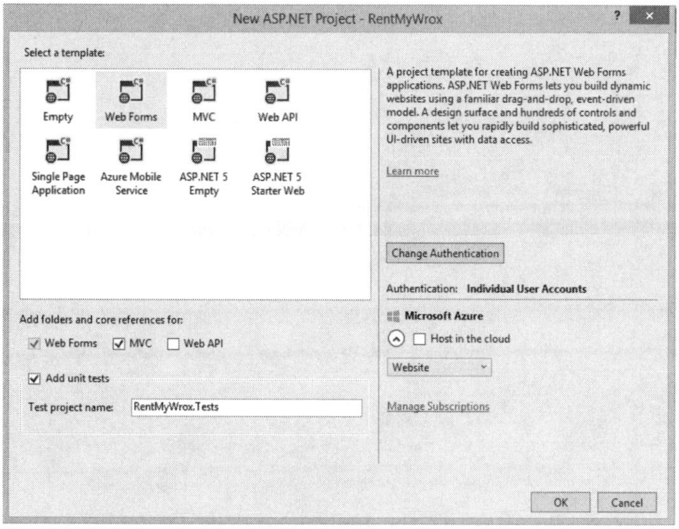

FIGURE 2-4: Selecting the appropriate ASP.NET template

Authentication Options

Authentication is an important consideration for every application that you will build, which is why it appears in the project creation window. As you likely know, authentication is the process of evaluating whether or not users of your application are who they say they are. If your application needs to be able to identify the user as a specific person, then the use of authentication is required. The most common way to verify that a person is who they say they are is through the use of a username and password. The username identifies the user while the password confirms that the person is who they say they are.

> **NOTE** *You should always understand your authentication needs from the very beginning. "Plugging in" security partway through the development process can be problematic because it can easily lead to security holes in your application due to missed retrofitting. It is always easier to remove security if you determine that you do not need it as you go forward than to add it after development is underway.*

The project templates have built-in support for four different settings for authentication, as shown in Figure 2-5:

➤ No authentication

➤ Organization Accounts

➤ Individual User Accounts

➤ Windows Authentication

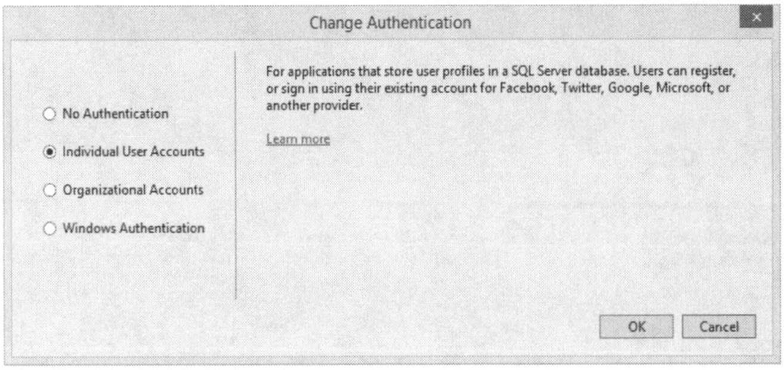

FIGURE 2-5: Authentication options for a new project

No authentication is pretty straightforward; it means that the application does not do any authentication out of the box. This could be used for sites for which the individual user doesn't matter—such as an informational website or a product site that does not support online ordering, or sites for which authentication will be handled differently than one of the built-in default approaches.

The Organization Accounts authentication option implies that you are using a third-party system to handle authentication. These third-party systems are generally on-premise Active Directory, Active Directory in the cloud (such as Microsoft Azure Active Directory), or Office 365. Other approaches are also supported if they follow some authentication standards.

Windows Authentication is a special feature only supported by Microsoft Internet Explorer. In this approach to authorization, the browser includes a special user token that the server can use to determine and identify the requesting user. This eliminates any username/password requests. However, it requires that the user has already logged into an Active Directory domain and that this information is available to the browser. This is different from the Organization Accounts approach mentioned previously, because that approach requires the user to enter a username and password that is then authenticated against the network, whereas this approach simply sends along an identifier and an acknowledgment that the user has already been authenticated.

Individual User Accounts is the default authentication setting, used for those cases where you need to determine who the user is and you do not want to use an Active Directory or Windows Authentication approach. When using this approach, you can use a SQL Server database to manage users, as well as other approaches, such as letting other systems (Windows Live or Facebook, for example) handle authentication of the user. You will be using this setting for your project.

> **REFERENCE** There is much more than this selection that goes into the configuration of security and authentication for a web application. Chapter 15, "Security in Your ASP.NET Website," covers application configuration, but there is still more! The server that you will use to host your application also needs to be configured to ensure that it supports the same authentication approach that your application will be using. This aspect is covered in Chapter 19, "Deploying Your Website."

Folders, Core Reference Files, and Unit Tests

The lower-left section of the New ASP.NET Project window provides two different configuration settings. The first is a selection of the folders and core references that you want added during creation of the new project. The options are Web Forms, MVC, and Web API. The items that will already be checked vary according to which template you select; thus, if you chose an ASP.NET MVC template, the MVC checkbox will already be selected. This section is shown in Figure 2-6.

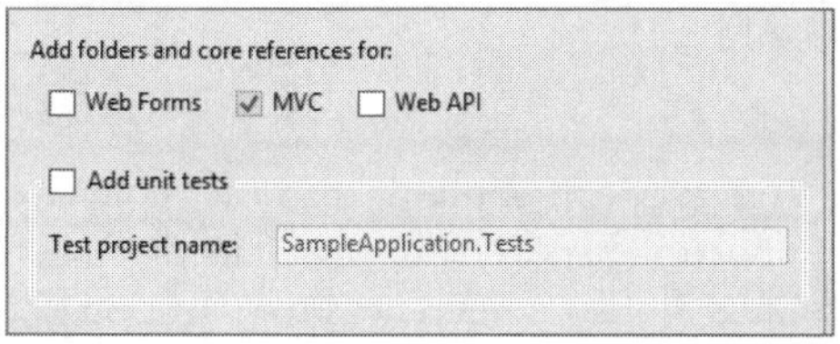

FIGURE 2-6: Adding directories and unit tests

Adding additional folders and core reference files does just that; it creates the folder structure and any default files, but it will *not* change any of the application creation from the template. For example, if you use a Web Forms project but select to add MVC folders, all the MVC folders are created for you, but they will have no content.

The other selection in this quadrant specifies whether you want to create a Unit Test project. A unit test is generally a way to test the smallest possible unit of functionality in a replicable, automated manner—a check to ensure that a particular method or function works as expected. Unit testing is the process of creating re-runnable tests that validate a particular subset of functionality. A Unit Test project is a Visual Studio project that manages the creation, maintenance, and running of unit tests. It enables a developer to run previously created unit tests against the application to ensure that changes have not negatively impacted other parts of the application.

If you were creating a true line-of-business application, then creating a unit test project is imperative. Unit tests give you assurance that your code is performing as expected by enabling you to provide known sets of data to parts of the application and then comparing the actual results from the application to the previously identified and expected results. This enables you to recognize when a change that may be needed in one part of an application can break another part of the application.

> **NOTE** *Because the proper design and implementation of unit tests is a topic warranting a book of its own, creating unit tests is not covered during our building of the sample application. However, the finished sample application available online includes unit tests, so you can see what they look like in order to get an understanding or to see how unit testing can help enhance the stability and correctness of your application.*

Hosting Your Project in Microsoft Azure

Microsoft Azure enables you to deploy web sites into the cloud rather than directly onto servers that you control. In this instance, it's a cloud computing platform used to build, deploy, and manage applications through a global network of Microsoft-managed data centers. Azure enables applications to be built using many different programming languages, tools, and frameworks, after which they can be deployed into the cloud.

As part of the project creation process, you can specify whether you will be deploying your application in Azure and configure how the deployment will be managed. Because we will not be deploying our example application into Azure, you can leave this checkbox empty and not worry about entering any configuration information.

Empty Template

An empty template creates just that, basically an empty directory compared to the other templates that create a sample application. There are some base-supporting files added, as well as those items you selected from the lower-left quadrant in the "Add folders and core references for" section. When you choose the Empty template, none of the "Add Folders" options are selected by default.

The outcome of not selecting any of these options becomes obvious pretty quickly. Figure 2-7 shows how an empty template creates a project with no folder and only a single file, the configuration file, "Web.config."

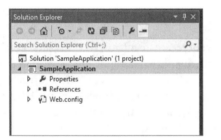

FIGURE 2-7: Creating a project using the Empty template

This is an empty template because no content is created. Attempting to view the output in a browser will result in an error, as there is nothing to display to the user.

PROPERTIES AND REFERENCES

Two additional items appear to be part of the project created from an empty template: Properties and References. These two items play special roles in a project. The Properties item has a wrench icon and is used to maintain information about the project, such as the version numbers for the .dll. This won't be part of our sample application.

The References section is different in that it contains all of the other libraries that your application uses. Figure 2-8 shows an expanded version of this item.

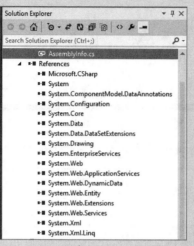

FIGURE 2-8: References created for an empty template

Although there are no working files created in this template, there are already some references. That's because all of ASP.NET is based on different areas of the .NET Framework. Each of the items shown in Figure 2-8 references a specific subset of functionality that the project assumes you need to build even the simplest of web applications. As you look through the various namespaces that are listed, these assumptions begin to make sense, as items such as `Microsoft.CSharp` (for C# projects) or `System.Web` will play a role in successfully building your application.

Web Forms Template

The Web Forms template creates a web site project with a few sample files so that you can get an initial start on your project. Some of the functionality that is added through this template includes user registration and the capability to log in to the application. These are some of the more complex parts of a web application, yet the template is created with this already working out of the box. Shown in Figure 2-9, this working application contains information about using ASP.NET and contains pages for Home, or default, About, and Contact.

The pages listed as menu items are all created as starter pages so that you can get an understanding of how applications of this type are built, especially when using authentication, which involves complex configuration.

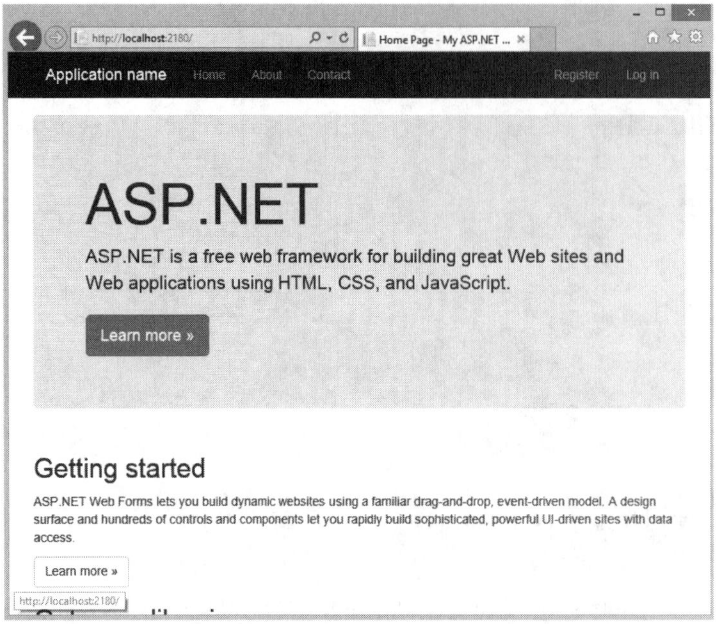

FIGURE 2-9: Running a newly created default Web Forms project

MVC Template

The MVC template takes the same approach as the Web Forms template by creating a small set of functionality, including the capability for a user to create an account and then log into the application. It contains the same Home page, About page, and a stubbed-in, empty Contact page as the Web Forms template. The look of the application when running is even identical, but the directory and file structures are completely different. We will cover more of the specific differences later in this chapter. When running the output of this template, however, you will see an application that is indistinguishable from that shown in Figure 2-9.

Web API Template

The Web API is an approach to developing RESTful web services that is based off of ASP.NET MVC; it was initially called ASP.NET MVC Web API. The conventions that it follows and the way that it is built will be very familiar to ASP.NET MVC developers. Once you complete the sample application you will also understand how you would write a Web API application.

Web services have become much more important in the Internet, as they enable two machines to communicate online. It follows the HTTP approach whereby one machine requests a resource from another through a well-defined locator, or URL. Whereas a user's browser would most likely ask for, and get, an HTML file, a web service will instead return information. Asking a web site for information about a product may return a nicely formatted HTML file with a picture, and perhaps other ancillary information about that product such as ratings. However, the web services would just return you any data about that product, formatted as either an XML or json file. These two formatting types are covered in more detail in Chapter 13, "ASP.NET AJAX."

RESTful web services are those web services that follow the representational state transfer (REST) architectural style to provide information over the Web. This style is highly representative of the HTTP process as mentioned earlier—including the HTTP verbs. The use of services in the sample application is covered in Chapter 13.

Although the concept of REST services means that there are no HTML files supporting them, this template does create two pages: a home page and an API Help page. The API Help page is the start of documentation for the types of information that your web service will understand and work with. Figure 2-10 shows the default API Help page.

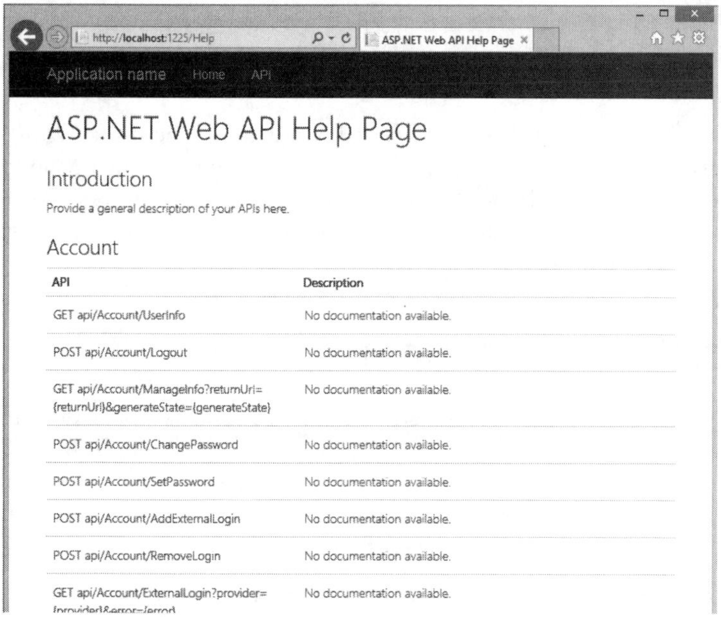

FIGURE 2-10: API Help page in a Web API project

While you will not be directly working with a Web API project as part of the sample application, there are a lot of similarities between the project and some of what you will be doing with services later as you build the sample application.

Single Page Application Template

Unlike the standard MVC and Web Forms approach, the Single Page Application template takes a different approach to building a web application. Rather than have different views and/or web pages, it is instead a single web page with the goal of providing a more fluid user experience akin to a desktop application. This means that there is one initial download of HTML and JavaScript files and then the application runs in that single page, fetching information and re-displaying either data or parts of the screen, sometimes even the entire visual screen as necessary.

The single-page approach means that most of the work is done either on the client, where the data is fetched from the server and then parsed through a client-side template, or on the server, where complete HTML-formatted snippets are returned to the client and replace various sections of the loaded page as necessary. The key difference is that the entire page is never called from the server again, only portions of the page are called. This eliminates several traditional problems: the flicker of a page in the web browser as it is completely replaced in memory by the newly downloaded page, the obviousness of waiting for an entire page to travel both ways to and from the server, and the necessity of moving all of the data both ways, thus requiring lower bandwidth and offering higher performance.

This approach takes advantage of the AJAX (Asynchronous JavaScript And XML) approach to use client code to call web services for information. Chapter 13 covers the use of AJAX in a web application. Creating a single-page application is an extension of that approach. In most cases, a single-page application will be working with RESTful services to get the data that needs to be displayed.

Azure Mobile Service Template

This project template is specifically for creating a Web API–based backend for Microsoft Azure Mobile Services. There are many different aspects to Azure, with one of them being their Mobile Services offering, which enables a developer to host a .NET or node.js (JavaScript on the server) backend to provide data to mobile consumers. Although mobile development is a rapidly growing development area, the sample app does not use this template.

WORKING WITH FILES IN YOUR APPLICATION

Just as in all other work on a Microsoft Windows computer, all of the work that you will do comes down to the individual files and the roles they play in the overall construct that is your web application. Because we are taking the web application approach rather than the web site approach to building an ASP.NET application, each of the files that the sample project uses will be either compiled into a single .dll file or copied over as a separate file to the web site.

Anything having to do with the server-side work is compiled into the .dll file. Anything that is going to be sent to the client, such as an image, JavaScript, or CSS files, is left intact and copied to the output folder on the server. This enables changes in design and client-side functionality to occur without having to do a complete web site deployment if so desired.

Because Web Forms and MVC each have a different implementation pattern there are different file types for each, stored in somewhat different folder structures.

File Types of an ASP.NET MVC Application

An ASP.NET MVC application is an implementation of the MVC pattern, or model, view, controller. This means that there will be three different types of files in the project to support this approach—one that will support the view, one that will support the model, and one that will support the controller. It will also contain supporting files that will be used for various other purposes such as configuration and client-side support.

The main file types for a basic MVC application are shown in Table 2-1.

TABLE 2-1: ASP.NET MVC File Types

FILE TYPE	FILE EXTENSION(S)	DESCRIPTION
View file	.vbhtml .cshtml	Used for creating the HTML output that makes up the view portion of the MVC application
JavaScript file	.js	JavaScript file that the browser uses to manage execution of code on the client side
Code file	.vb .cs	Anything that is compiled, executes and runs; both models and controllers are stored as code files within the project
Style sheet	.css	Gives the browser instructions on how to style the appearance of the web page
Configuration file	.config	Contains configuration information that is used by the application, such as a database configuration string, shown later
Application event file	.asax	Used by Microsoft IIS web server to handle application and session-level events such as creating routes
Web file	.html	A static web file that does not do any server-side processing yet presents HTML to the browser for rendering

Each of the files has a different kind of content. You can tell the type of file from both the extension and the content. A view file, for example, will have content that looks like the code in Listing 2-1.

LISTING 2-1: Example of the content for the `Account/Register.cshtml` file

```
@model WebApplication3.Models.RegisterViewModel
@{
    ViewBag.Title = "Register";
}

<h2>@ViewBag.Title.</h2>

@using (Html.BeginForm("Register", "Account", FormMethod.Post,
```

continues

LISTING 2-1 *(continued)*

```
            new { @class = "form- horizontal", role = "form" }))
{
    @Html.AntiForgeryToken()
    <h4>Create a new account.</h4>
    <hr />
    @Html.ValidationSummary("", new { @class = "text-danger" })
    <div class="form-group">
        @Html.LabelFor(m => m.Email, new { @class = "col-md-2 control-label" })
        <div class="col-md-10">
            @Html.TextBoxFor(m => m.Email, new { @class = "form-control" })
        </div>
    </div>
</div>
```

The HTML elements covered in Chapter 1, such as <h4> and <div>, should be somewhat familiar. Several different elements in there, however, are not HTML. Those are Razor commands, which you will spend a lot of time learning about going forward.

Another type of file created in the ASP.NET MVC application is the code file. Listing 2-2 shows an example of C# code from one of the controller files. None of the context in the file will be familiar to you yet, but by the end of the sample application you will have created controllers very similar to the example.

LISTING 2-2: Example of code from the Controller/AccountController

```
[HttpPost]
[AllowAnonymous]
[ValidateAntiForgeryToken]
public async Task<ActionResult> Register(RegisterViewModel model)
{
    if (ModelState.IsValid)
    {
        var user = new ApplicationUser { UserName = model.Email,
                                         Email = model.Email };
        var result = await UserManager.CreateAsync(user, model.Password);
        if (result.Succeeded)
        {
            await SignInManager.SignInAsync(user, isPersistent:false,
                                            rememberBrowser:false);

            // For more information on how to enable account confirmation and password
            // reset please visit http://go.microsoft.com/fwlink/?LinkID=320771
            // Send an email with this link
            // string code = await UserManager.GenerateEmailConfirmationTokenAsync(user.Id);
            // var callbackUrl = Url.Action("ConfirmEmail", "Account",
            //       new { userId = user.Id, code = code }, protocol: Request.Url.Scheme);
            // await UserManager.SendEmailAsync(user.Id, "Confirm your account",
            //       "Please confirm your account by clicking <a href=\"" + callbackUrl +
            //       "\">here</a>");
```

```
                    return RedirectToAction("Index", "Home");
            }
        AddErrors(result);
    }

    // If we got this far, something failed, redisplay form
    return View(model);
}
```

The rest of the files have their own specific internal design because they play very specific roles in the building and running of a web application. This specificity means that most of them are copied to the server as individual files so that they can be directly downloaded to the user's browser as required.

File System Structure of an ASP.NET MVC Application

When creating an ASP.NET application, some folders are created for both MVC and ASP.NET applications. These folders are listed in Table 2-2.

TABLE 2-2: ASP.NET General Folders

FOLDER	DESCRIPTION
App_Data	A folder used for data storage. It generally holds any SQL Server .mdf file that may be used in the web application. This is covered in more detail in Chapter 10, "Working with Data—Advanced Topics."
App_Start	The App_Start folder contains many of the configuration files used by the application. You will learn more about the different files throughout the book, as they are related with behaviors such as bundling JavaScript files, authentication, and URL construction or routing.
Content	The content directory is designed to hold items that will be sent to the client. By default, the Cascading Style Sheets (CSS) created as part of the initial application templates are stored there.
Fonts	This directory holds some of the glyph-fonts used in the default application. Normally you probably won't be using fonts like this, but you do have the capability.
Models	The Models folder is used to hold the models that were created as part of the template process. The models that are added as part of the project creation process are all related to authentication.
Scripts	This folder is used to store the JavaScript files that are sent to the client's browser to perform client-side processing.

When you create an ASP.NET MVC from the template, the folders shown in Figure 2-11 are also created as part of the process.

FIGURE 2-11: Installed folders with ASP.NET MVC

The extra folders added as part of the MVC template are for the views and controllers. You have already taken a brief look at how views and controllers fit into the framework, so now you'll take your first look at how these all come together in the template application.

Figure 2-12 shows the expanded folders for Controllers and Views. You should be able to see some similarities between the two, mainly in terms of how the different controller files have a corresponding view sub-folder that is named the same as the Controller file, without the text "controller" at the end. There's a views folder rather than a single file, as with the Controller, because each views folder generally contains multiple files.

FIGURE 2-12: Details under the Controllers and Views folders

If you look at the names of the files in the Account sub-folder, you will be able to identify a pattern whereby each file represents an aspect of user account management, from registration, as shown by Register.cshtml, to logging in, as shown by Login.cshtml, to handling a forgotten password, ForgotPassword.cshtml, to resetting a password and getting a confirmation that your password was reset, ResetPassword.cshtml and ResetPasswordConfirmation.cshtml.

All of the folders covered so far are folders created by default when adding a project from the ASP .NET MVC template. When you look at an ASP.NET Web Forms structure, you will see that it matches the directories listed in Table 2-2. This initially may seem surprising, but the approach when building a web application with Web Forms is different because the template and processing files go together, not like in an MVC application where they are separated into different directories.

File Types of an ASP.NET Web Forms Application

There are some shared file types between ASP.NET MVC and Web Form projects. Table 2-3 provides a list of the common file types in an ASP.NET Web Forms project.

TABLE 2-3: File Types of an ASP.NET Web Forms Application

FILE TYPE	FILE EXTENSION(S)	DESCRIPTION
Web Form page	`.aspx`	The individual pages that are viewed by your users
Web User Control	`.ascx`	A set of files that act as a single part of the UI; a user control is a set of reusable application parts
Code-behind	`.aspx.cs/.vb` or `ascx.cd/.vb`	The page that contains the processing code; the `.aspx` and `.ascx` files contain the markup, and its corresponding `.cs` or `.vb` files contain the code that manages the processing
Master page	`.master`	Enables you to create a template that is used for multiple pages, such as the navigation structure
Style sheet	`.css`	Gives you the capability to style and design your application
HTML file	`.html`	HTML page within the application
Configuration file	`.config`	Contains information that the application uses to perform other work
SiteMap	`.sitemap`	Contains an XML listing of the files in your application
JavaScript file	`.js`	Contains JavaScript that can be run on the client's computer; this is identical to the JavaScript files in the MVC application
Skin file	`.skin`	Holds design information for some of the ASP.NET controls that you may use in your application

The only file types that are the same are the configuration files, `.config`, and the files that are sent to the client side, the `.html`, `.js`, and `.css` files. The configuration files, as you saw when you were looking at the structure created when creating a project using the "empty template," are a default, and included with every ASP.NET application. This is because Microsoft IIS, the web server, uses the configuration files to determine how it needs to manage the web application.

The files that are sent to the client side are the same because that is how the client is expecting them. Your HTML page tells the browser which file it needs to fetch based on different aspects, such as styling or scripting, so you are not required to use a .js extension for your JavaScript files. However, using the appropriate extension is the standard approach and will make the content of the file more obvious to other developers. An extension of .js clearly identifies the content as being JavaScript.

Just as you can tell the type of MVC file both by the extension and by the content, you can do the same with the ASP.NET Web Form files. As you look at the following code listings, think about the similarities and differences between the samples shown previously and these, starting with Listing 2-3.

LISTING 2-3: `Register.aspx` **code snippet**

```
<%@ Page Title="Register" Language="C#" MasterPageFile="~/Site.Master"
        AutoEventWireup="true" CodeBehind="Register.aspx.cs"
        Inherits="WebFormsTemplate.Account.Register" %>

    <asp:Content runat="server" ID="BodyContent"
            ContentPlaceHolderID="MainContent">
        <h2><%: Title %>.</h2>
        <p class="text-danger">
            <asp:Literal runat="server" ID="ErrorMessage" />
        </p>

        <div class="form-horizontal">
            <h4>Create a new account</h4>
            <hr />
            <asp:ValidationSummary runat="server" CssClass="text-danger" />
            <div class="form-group">
                <asp:Label runat="server" AssociatedControlID="Email"
                    CssClass="col-md-2 control-label">Email</asp:Label>
                <div class="col-md-10">
                    <asp:TextBox runat="server" ID="Email" CssClass="form-control"
                        TextMode="Email" />
                    <asp:RequiredFieldValidator runat="server"
                        ControlToValidate="Email" CssClass="text-danger"
                        ErrorMessage="The email field is required."/>
                </div>
            </div>
            <div class="form-group">
                <asp:Label runat="server" AssociatedControlID="Password"
                        CssClass="col-md-2 control-label">
                    Password
                </asp:Label>
                <div class="col-md-10">
                    <asp:TextBox runat="server" ID="Password" TextMode="Password"
                        CssClass="form-control" />
                    <asp:RequiredFieldValidator runat="server"
                        ControlToValidate="Password" CssClass="text-danger"
```

```
                                ErrorMessage="The password field is required." />
                    </div>
                </div>
        ...
```

Again, you can see HTML elements in this file so you know that it contains the markup, the beginning of the information that will be sent to the user's browser. Listing 2-4 shows a snippet of the code-behind file.

LISTING 2-4: Snippet from the `Registration.aspx.cs` code-behind file

```csharp
using System;
using System.Linq;
using System.Web;
using System.Web.UI;
using Microsoft.AspNet.Identity;
using Microsoft.AspNet.Identity.Owin;
using Owin;
using WebFormsTemplate.Models;

namespace WebFormsTemplate.Account
{
    public partial class Register : Page
    {
        protected void CreateUser_Click(object sender, EventArgs e)
        {
            var manager = Context.GetOwinContext()
                    .GetUserManager<ApplicationUserManager>();
            var signInManager = Context.GetOwinContext()
                    .Get<ApplicationSignInManager>();
            var user = new ApplicationUser()
            {
                UserName = Email.Text,
                Email = Email.Text
            };
            IdentityResult result = manager.Create(user, Password.Text);
            if (result.Succeeded)
            {

    // For more information on how to enable account confirmation and
    // password reset please visit
    // http://go.microsoft.com/fwlink/?LinkID=320771
    //string code = manager.GenerateEmailConfirmationToken(user.Id);
    //string callbackUrl = IdentityHelper
    //          .GetUserConfirmationRedirectUrl(code, user.Id, Request);
    // manager.SendEmail(user.Id, "Confirm your account",
    // "Please confirm your account by clicking
    // <a href=\"" + callbackUrl + "\">here</a>.");
            }
        }
    }
}
```

Listing 2-4 is pure C# code. There is no HTML in it, so it is obvious that it is the processing portion of the file. While these are different files, playing completely different roles, they work together to create a single HTML file that is returned from the server to the user.

MVC AND WEB FORM FILE DIFFERENCES

When you look at the prior code listings, you may be struck more by their similarities than their differences. Yes, the contents of each file look somewhat different, but in the end you have two examples for each approach: one containing markup and the other containing the processing code. Therefore, conceptually, the approaches are very similar. The primary difference between the two approaches is not how the files are built, but how they are assembled.

ASP.NET Web Forms makes a very firm linkage between the markup file and the applicable processing file. You can tell by looking at them that they are related; Visual Studio even shows them together in the Solution Explorer. ASP.NET MVC is different. There is no automatic one-to-one relationship between the files. Instead, as shown by Figure 2-13, there are multiple View files to a single Controller file approach. In this case, there are 12 separate View files that all relate to a single file, the *AccountController*.

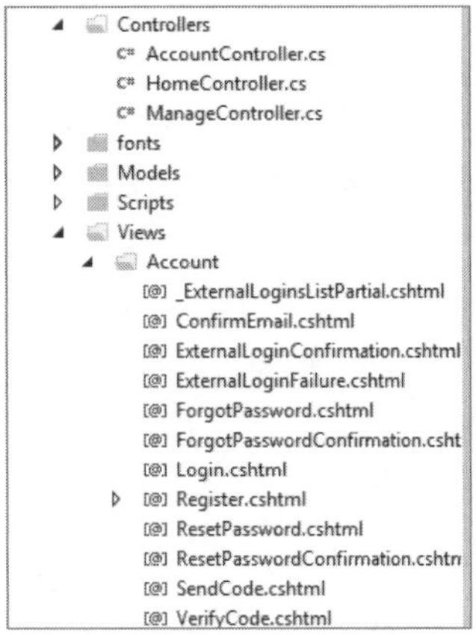

FIGURE 2-13: Relationship between View files and Controller files in an ASP.NET MVC application

The one thing that we haven't yet covered is the model, the "M" part of the MVC architectural pattern. That's because it is not a new concept. While the MVC pattern calls out the model as a separate entity, a well-architected Web Forms application embodies the same concept. This is demonstrated by how the Model directory was created for both the ASP.NET MVC template application and the ASP.NET Web Forms template application.

Looking back at the multiple View files for a single Controller file shows the primary difference between the two approaches. Whereas Figure 2-13 shows that 13 files are part of the account management process in ASP.NET MVC, 12 View files and one Controller file, when you look at the same set of functionality in ASP.NET Web Forms, you see something different, as shown in Figure 2-14.

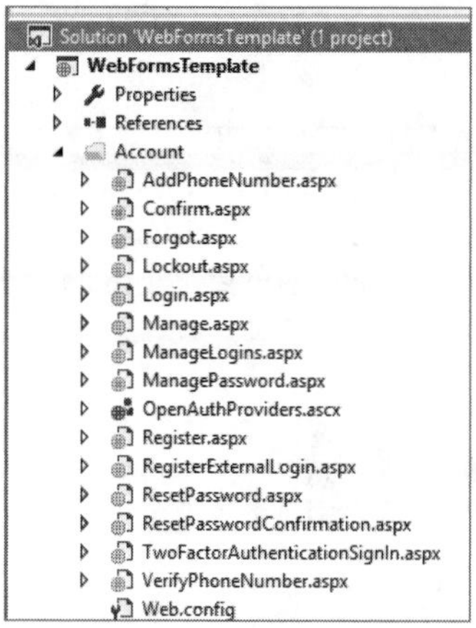

FIGURE 2-14: Account management functionality in Web Forms

In this case, you see at least 15 files listed in Solution Explorer. Also, because each of the files is actually the combination of .aspx and .aspx.cs files, there are 30 files in the directory that manage the same processes supported by the 13 files in the MVC system. That demonstrates the main difference between the two—the complete separation between processing and view. Yes, ASP.NET Web Forms provide some separation, but there is always the expectation of a linked processing file. MVC takes a much more flexible and better separated approach.

CREATING THE SAMPLE APPLICATION

So far, you have learned about various templates that are available when you create a new application, but not how you're going to start the application. What you do know:

➤ You want to support both ASP.NET MVC and ASP.NET Web Forms in the same application.

➤ The ASP.NET Web Forms list of directories is a subset of the directories created by the ASP.NET MVC template.

➤ ASP.NET Web Forms does not have a convention whereby separate folders are created.

Looking at these various points, it would seem to make the most sense to create the sample application using the ASP.NET MVC template, because that provides everything that you need. Go ahead and create the initial shell of the application by using the MVC template. You should also select the

Web Forms additional directory checkbox. Making this change doesn't add any additional folders or files, but it does add the necessary references for both ASP.NET MVC and Web Forms. The following Try It Out walks you through the steps of creating the project.

TRY IT OUT Creating the Initial Project

1. Open Visual Studio and select the File ⇨ New ⇨ Project menu item.

2. In the template section on the left-hand side of the screen, select the language that you want to work in (Visual Basic or C#). Then, in the Web listing, select the ASP.NET Web Application project template. Your window should look something like Figure 2-15. Be sure you give it the appropriate name at the bottom of the window.

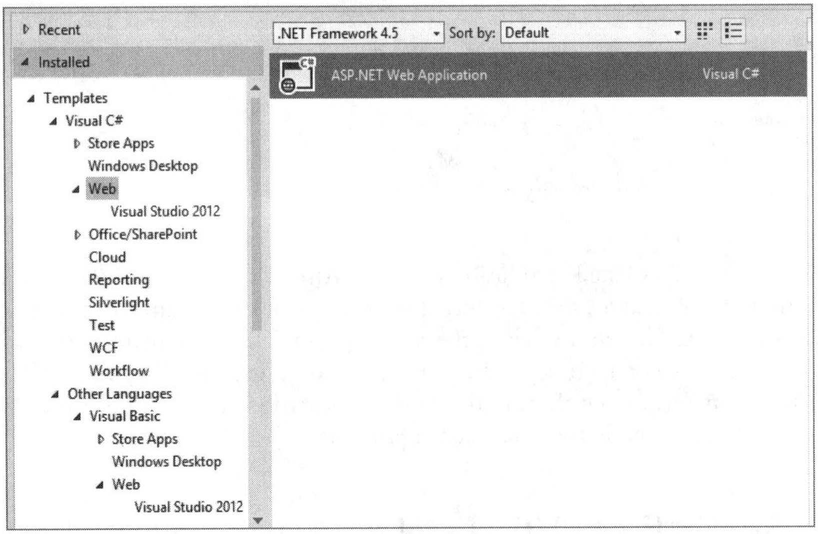

▷ Recent	.NET Framework 4.5 ▾ Sort by: Default ▾	
▲ Installed		
▲ Templates	ASP.NET Web Application	Visual C#
▲ Visual C#		
▷ Store Apps		
Windows Desktop		
▲ Web		
Visual Studio 2012		
▷ Office/SharePoint		
Cloud		
Reporting		
Silverlight		
Test		
WCF		
Workflow		
▲ Other Languages		
▲ Visual Basic		
▷ Store Apps		
Windows Desktop		
▲ Web		
Visual Studio 2012		

FIGURE 2-15: Creating your initial project

3. Select the MVC template, also ensuring that you check the box labeled Web Forms under the "Add folders and core references for:" section. Click the OK button to create the project.

4. Clicking the green arrow in the Visual Studio toolbar will compile this initial template and run it in the browser listed next to the arrow. The page that is displayed should look like Figure 2-9, shown earlier.

How It Works

The preceding process uses a Visual Studio feature called ASP.NET *scaffolding*. Visual Studio uses a set of templates to generate code files and build new content. You will see that the project name and the layout of the folder structure is based on information that you entered during the simple setup process.

If you look closer at the folders that are created, you will see that they include a set of views and controllers, as well as a model. Many of these views and controllers are there to support the user and account management process, some of which will be used out of the box for the application.

Some of the other views simply provide example information. Many of these will be replaced by your own content as you build your application. These initially built files will remain; you just change them to better suit your needs.

You were easily able to open the site in the browser by clicking the green arrow. However, you didn't do anything to "install" the application on a web server. This worked because Visual Studio installs a local version of Microsoft Internet Information Services Express (IIS Express). IIS Express is a small, lightweight web server that is suitable for running your application so that you can interact with it at runtime. Because IIS Express is running locally, you can do some very useful things such as debugging and tracing. If your web project is still running, you should be able to see an icon for IIS Express in the notification area of your Windows taskbar.

SUMMARY

Visual Studio and ASP.NET provide two different approaches to building ASP.NET applications. The first is through the use of a web site. A web site approach enables you to create an application that's easy to manage and deploy. It is handled differently during the deployment of the site because the files only need to be copied to the server, which then compiles the code-behind files as required. This makes the deployment process very straightforward. Unfortunately, this approach is only available for ASP.NET Web Form applications. You cannot create an MVC application as a web site.

The web application takes a more traditional application-based approach in that it requires that the application be compiled before being copied to the server. The large number of templates that are available in Visual Studio when you want to create an ASP.NET web application project indicates how popular web development is within the Microsoft development community.

The two templates that matter for the sample application are the ASP.NET MVC and the ASP.NET Web Forms templates. Both create an initial application that looks and works identically although they are built completely differently. Web Form files come in sets, with a markup file and a processing file, whereas MVC files come with Views and Controllers files.

EXERCISES

1. There are two approaches in Visual Studio to creating a web-based application. What are they, and what are their main differences?

2. What is a project template?

3. Compared to an ASP.NET Web Forms project, several extra folders are created in an ASP.NET MVC project. What are these extra folders and what purpose do they serve?

▶ WHAT YOU LEARNED IN THIS CHAPTER

Code File Types	Files that are created during the ASP.NET MVC project creation process with .vb or .cs file extensions are code files. These files are either the Controller or the Model files; you can tell which is which by the file filters that the code files are in.
MVC Template	The MVC Project template is used to create an ASP.NET MVC project. Depending upon choices made during the creation process, the template may create some base pages as well as integrate authentication into the project.
Project Types	Project types are how Visual Studio defines the type of output that will be created when a project is created. This output then determines what the project will look like when it is compiled, such as a web application, a desktop application, web services, or many other different types.
View File Types	The file extensions for views in an ASP.NET MVC application are .vbhtml and .cshtml. These contain the HTML that will eventually be sent to the client.
Web Application	A web application project is one that is accessible over the Internet. Code files are compiled and deployed to the server where Microsoft Internet Information Services (IIS) takes server requests calls and creates HTML content to respond to the user.
Web Form Template	A project template that is used to create an ASP.NET Web Forms application. Depending upon choices made during the creation process, the template may create some base pages as well as integrate authentication into the project.
Web Site	A web site project is an approach to creating a set of files that can be copied to a web server to provide Internet content. The source files are copied to the server, where IIS compiles them just before making the method call.

3

Designing Your Web Pages

WHAT YOU WILL LEARN IN THIS CHAPTER:

- ➤ How HTML and CSS work together
- ➤ Using CSS to add a design
- ➤ Adding and referencing CSS in your pages
- ➤ How to best manage styles

CODE DOWNLOADS FOR THIS CHAPTER:

The wrox.com code downloads for this chapter are found at www.wrox.com/go/ beginningaspnetforvisualstudio on the Download Code tab. The code is in the chapter 03 download and individually named according to the names throughout the chapter.

In many ways, modern websites are quite similar, regardless of their purpose. They tend to be functional, responsive, and attractive. Having a website that looks good is as important to getting and retaining visitors as the site's functionality. Very few sites can minimize the design elements and remain effective. However, all sites—regardless of content, design approach, and business needs—provide the same type of information to the user, who downloads one or more HTML documents, some styling information, and perhaps some imagery and even videos.

This chapter covers how all these aspects of a site come together, especially HTML and styling information, otherwise known as CSS. You won't become a design expert, but you will become familiar with CSS and learn how you can take advantage of Visual Studio tools to make working with CSS easier. You also work out the overall design of the sample application and review the strategies available to build a style dictionary.

HTML AND CSS

Chapter 1 talked about HTML and explains how it is the default language of the Internet, designed to provide context to content—especially with HTML5, the newest version. Earlier versions of HTML supported some styling-specific elements that allowed for some control over presentation on the screen. For example, there was an element for controlling the size, color, and font face of text contained within the element called *font*:

```
<font color="purple" face="verdana" size="4">
    I am large purple text
</font>
```

While these kinds of tags give you some ability to control the look and feel of your page, they have one major limiting feature: They are all embedded in the HTML and are not flexible. For example, suppose you wanted to change all the "large purple text" to "medium-size orange text." You would have to manually edit every page that used it, changing each instance. This means that even a relatively minor change in design can be both time-consuming and risky, because every page may require some changes. This is why CSS was born; it provides a more robust and powerful way of managing design.

Why Use Both HTML and CSS?

HTML is the language of the markup, and that is what it does best. HTML does a great job of helping you identify, delineate, and markup content, but it does little about controlling the appearance of the content. You can confirm this yourself with Figure 3-1, which shows the browser's rendition of the traditional HTML shown in Listing 3-1.

LISTING 3-1: HTML for a simple web page

```
<!DOCTYPE html>
<html>
  <head>
    <title>Beginning ASP.NET Web Forms and MVC</title>
  </head>
  <body>
      <article>
        <header>
           <h1>ASP.NET from Wrox</h1>
        </header>
        <section>
           <h2>ASP.NET Web Forms</h2>
           <p>More than a decade of experience and reliability.</p>
           <ol>
              <li>Lots of provided controls</li>
              <li>Thousands of examples available online</li>
           </ol>
        </section>
      </article>
      <form>
        <p>
           Enter your email to sign up:
```

```
                 <input type='text' name='emailaddress'>
            </p>
            <input type='submit' value='Save Email' class='button'>
        </form>
    </body>
</html>
```

As you can see in the figure, virtually no styling is applied to the content. Some default fonts are selected, and different levels of headings provide different font sizes, but everything is shown as a plain black font on a plain white background.

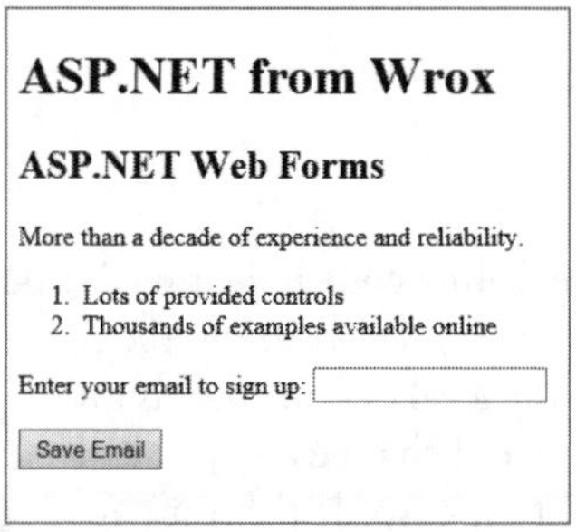

FIGURE 3-1: HTML without any CSS styling

CSS enables you to exert much better control over the presentation of your content. Simply adding 21 lines of CSS code (including whitespace) results in something considerably different, although you won't see the full effect in Figure 3-2, because it doesn't show the color you added. The CSS code to achieve this, shown in Listing 3-2, is added right below the opening <body> tag.

LISTING 3-2: Styles added to the HTML file

```
<style type="text/css">
    header {
        background:gold;
    }
    body {
        background:#F5EAA6;
        margin-top:0px;
        font:1.2em Futura, sans-serif;
    }
    ul  {
        color: red;
    }
    ol   {
        color: green;
    }
    .button {
        border: 1px solid #006;
        background: Green;
    color: white;
    }
</style>
```

Granted, this page may not be attractive yet, but it effectively demonstrate how a small amount of CSS can alter the appearance of a page, and how this styling differs from the old HTML approach to styling.

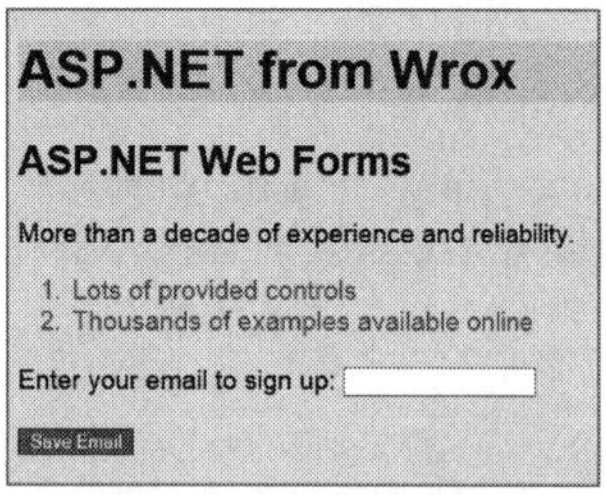

ASP.NET from Wrox

ASP.NET Web Forms

More than a decade of experience and reliability.

1. Lots of provided controls
2. Thousands of examples available online

Enter your email to sign up:

Save Email

FIGURE 3-2: HTML with some simple styles added

You will go over this in much greater detail later in this chapter, but the styling code in Listing 3-2 does two things. First, it sets the default look for every body, header, `<ul>`, and `<ol>` element on the page. Second, it sets the look for a particular style called "button." Consider the level of control this gives you over the `<font>` element mentioned earlier. Instead of having to find and change every one of the affected elements, you can instead change one instance and have it affect, or cascade to, every applicable element. CSS provides an elegant way to abstract out the control of the look and feel of your website.

> **ABSTRACTION**
>
> Abstraction is a technique that allows you to control more complex systems. It enables you to create a version of that system that is usually simpler and easier to control and maintain. Just as everything in VB.NET or C# is an abstraction of the work being done deeper in the system (you do not have to worry about copying the contents of one section of memory to another), CSS is an abstraction that gives you control of each page element, enabling you to make one change, in one place, and have it affect the entire site without additional risk.

Combining HTML and CSS allows you to separate the content from its display. Just as Web Forms and ASP.NET MVC both offer some separation of concerns in terms of displaying the information and creating the information, CSS and HTML enable you to separate the definition and display of the content on the page; it basically provides an additional separation of concern within the UI itself. In other words, whereas HTML tells the browser *what* it should display, CSS defines *how* it should be displayed.

An Introduction to CSS

If you look at CSS as a separate language, you will find that it is relatively easy to learn; each of the concepts by itself is pretty straightforward and clear. However, what becomes more complex is how the language elements may interact with each other and how to best use a particular approach to solve a specific problem.

We'll start by having you add some styling to the website. In the following Try It Out, you add a new page to the site and then add some content and styling to that page. You will learn about the different aspects of what you are doing as you go through the process.

TRY IT OUT Styling Your First Web Page

In this example you create a new page and then enter some CSS code by hand so that you can see how it affects the appearance of your content. The CSS tools included in Visual Studio are introduced later in the chapter.

1. Open the web application project that you created in the last chapter. Select the project within the Solution Explorer window. Add a new Web Form page from the top menu by selecting Project ⇨ Add New Item. Select Web Form and name the file **IntroToCss.aspx**. This exercise uses a Web Form page because it is a lot easier to see immediate results. The overall process of styling content is identical for both MVC views and Web Form pages. Creating this page creates code that looks like what is shown in Figure 3-3.

FIGURE 3-3: New ASP.NET Web Form file

2. Locate the closing head element `</head>` and press the Enter key right before it to add a blank line. If you begin by typing in the `<st` for the style element, the Visual Studio IntelliSense feature will automatically provide some help by popping up a dropdown menu of available elements. By the time you complete the "t" you should only have "style" available. Clicking the Tab key will cause IntelliSense to finish the text for the initial tag. Entering the closing bracket `>` will cause IntelliSense to close the element for you.

> **INTELLISENSE IS YOUR FRIEND!**
>
> IntelliSense is a Visual Studio feature designed to improve your productivity. Its primary feature is AutoComplete, whereby IntelliSense examines the context of what you have entered and is able to "guess" what you are trying to type, whether it is Visual Basic, C#, or HTML code. While this may negatively impact your ability to remember the names of classes, methods, or parameters outside of IntelliSense, it gives you rapid access to all the code support information you need right in the development environment, as you are writing the code.

3. Type the following code in between the style elements that you just added:

```
body {
    color: orange;
    font-size: 20px;
    font-weight: 800;
}
```

4. Ensure that you are in Split mode, where you can see both *Design* and *Source* modes in Visual Studio. Most likely you are currently in Source mode. Click the Split button on the bottom of the page in the right-hand side of the window to switch the window to the multiple mode window as shown in Figure 3-4.

FIGURE 3-4: Selecting Split mode displays both design and source code information.

IDE VIEWS OF WEB FORMS IN VISUAL STUDIO

Two different views are available when working within an .ASPX page: Design mode and Source mode. In Source mode, you can see and edit the code on the page—in this case, the HTML and CSS style you are working on. Design mode shows how the code is going to be rendered and displayed by the user's browser. Split mode enables you to see both Design mode and Source mode at once. As you change information or content in one area, you may be prompted to refresh to see it in the other. Running in Split mode enables you to see how the output changes as you make your changes in Source mode.

5. Once you are in Split mode, enter some text directly below the `<body>` tag and then refresh the Design mode. You will be able to see both your code and the rendered version of the text you entered. It should look something like Figure 3-5.

6. In Step 2 you added some default settings for all text that is entered into the HTML body. Now you will expand the style for the body section by including a colored background. In the styles area you created, add the following line:

```
background-color: lightblue;
```

Refreshing your Design mode view will show that the background color has changed. Also, note how IntelliSense helped you select the appropriate value!

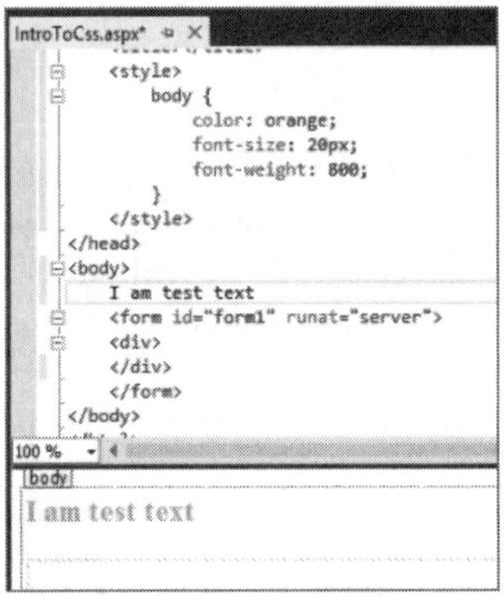

FIGURE 3-5: Code window with display of text

7. Create another style by adding the following code right below the closing bracket of the body style:

```
h1 {
    color: red;
```

```
        font-size: 26px;
    }
    .special {
        color: black;
        font-size: 16px;
    }
```

8. Alter your body text to the following:

```
<body>
    <h1>Introduction to CSS</h1>
    I am test text
    <div class="special">
        And I am special text!
    </div>
</body>
```

FIGURE 3-6: Design mode view of style and HTML content

This will give you output that looks like Figure 3-6.

7. Perform a Ctrl+F5 (Run without Debugging) to view the output in the browser. You will see that the output in your browser is identical to the view in your Design mode screen.

How It Works

The work that you performed seems relatively simple, but the changes that you made completely changed the appearance of your page. The first thing that you did was add the `<style/>` tags. This informed the browser that everything contained within those elements should be considered as it renders the content of the page. This is also why these were put into the `<head/>` section of the HTML page; the browser goes through this section first before it starts to analyze the content of the body page. Note that putting the styles in the header like this is not the best way to build a flexible site. You are taking this approach to be able to easily see how the styles and the elements work together.

There are two different approaches to how the styles were identified. The first used an element name, so did not start with any special characters. Any time you create a style in that fashion you are setting the default style for all items contained within that kind of element. With the second style that is defined here the defining name starts with a period. This means that only items marked with a particular class will pick up this styling.

Keep in mind how styles "code" is put together. One of the more confusing aspects of CSS is the lack of the "equals" sign; instead, items are defined by name: value, where the name/value delimiter is a colon (:). It is also important to remember that each internal line needs to have a semicolon (;) at the end, indicating the end of that property setting. As the browser builds the page, it links the styles that are defined in the styles tags with the HTML that is in the page, and renders that content using this relationship between element and style. When you consider the processing that has to go on in the background as the browser makes this analysis, it will be apparent why you want to keep your styling approach simple and consistent. The next section covers in more detail how the various styles interact with each other as elements with multiple applicable styles are rendered by the browser.

MORE CSS

You just saw how styling can affect the look and feel of HTML code. In this section you will examine the sections of the style and learn what each part means, including how it defines what kind of content it should be applied against, and what kind of styling should be applied. A selector defines the relationship between the element to be styled and the style to be applied.

Selectors

First consider one of the styles that you added earlier:

```
h1 {
    color: red;
    font-size: 26px;
}
```

The entire preceding snippet is known as a *rule*. The h1 is the selector of the rule, as it defines to what the rule should be applied. It is how the browser can determine which elements should have this style assigned to that element's content. You can have multiple selectors in a rule. There is no effective limit to the number of selectors that can be part of your rule. Changing the rule as shown in the following snippet creates a group of items to which this rule will be applied:

```
h1, h2 {
    color: red;
    font-size: 26px;
}
```

Thus, adding a comma between multiple selectors means that the browser will interpret the selector group as an OR. In the preceding case, the browser will apply this rule if the element it is creating is an "h1" element OR an "h2" element.

You can also separate selectors with a space, as shown here:

```
h1 .special {
    color: black;
    font-size: 16px;
}
```

As you can probably guess, this implies a different relationship between these two selectors than using a comma. Whereas the comma implies an "OR" relationship between the selectors, the space indicates an "AND" relationship. That means these rules are applied only to those elements that fulfill all the selectors in the list. Also, using a space indicates that these selectors are inheriting—thus, "h1 .special" means that the style will be applied to content within an element of class ".special" where that element is also contained within an h1 element. This can be a confusing concept, but more details are provided later in the chapter. There is no limit to the number of selectors that you can link together using a space to indicate the AND relationship.

You can also use both approaches at once, as shown here:

```
h1, h2 .special {
    color: black;
    font-size: 16px;
}
```

The preceding snippet will cause the browser to apply the rule to those elements that match the "h1" selector OR those elements that fulfill both the "h2" and ".special" selectors.

Type Selector

As shown previously, the rule used in the last example is applied to all of the "h1" HTML elements on the page, and it will be applied to every element of this type on the page. This type of selector is known as a *type selector* because it applies specifically to HTML elements. In addition, because HTML elements are not case sensitive, type selectors are not case sensitive either.

If you group a type selector with another selector, the browser will apply that style to all elements of that type that also match the other selector(s).

Class Selector

In the preceding example you had a selector that was prefaced with a period—.special. This type of selector is a *class selector* and it differs from the type selector in that it is applied to every element that is labeled with that class, regardless of the type of element.

The following ruleset will make every element that is selected red:

```
.special {
    color: red;
}
```

The browser is able to determine the appropriate style(s) because the HTML style has the class attribute set to the same value as the ruleset's selector. The first line of the following example turns a section of a sentence red:

```
I am not red text <span class='special'>but I am</span>.

<h1>I am not a red header</h1>
<h1 class='special'>But I am a red header</h1>
```

The second section of the preceding code snippet shows how the class selector is independent of the type of element, because both the span in the first section and the header in the second section match the rule, so the content will be displayed in the browser as red text.

The class selector is also different from the type selector in that it is case sensitive: The text you enter as the selector in the rule has to perfectly match the element's class value.

Id Selector

Whereas the type selector references the HTML element and the class selector is linked to the class attribute in an HTML element, the id selector references the id attribute of an HTML element. An Id selector is created using the hash symbol (#):

```
#mainArticle {
    color: red;
}
```

> **WARNING** *A page should only have one element with the same Id value. This rule of not reusing an id on a page is an HTML and a jQuery/JavaScript expectation. All the major browsers will still display all page elements regardless of whether they are reusing the id value and will apply the style to all elements that match that id. The following is an example of the HTML that includes a link to the style.*
>
> ```
> I am not red text <span id='mainArticle'>but I am</span>.
> ```

Just as with the class selector, the id selector is case sensitive; you must have identical values in the ruleset and in the `id` attribute of the element in order for the browser to apply the style.

Universal Selector

All the selectors described so far are applied to a particular aspect of an HTML element. A type selector refers to the HTML element name; the class selector is a reference to a value in the `class` attribute; and the id selector is a reference to the value in the id attribute of the element. The universal selector, demonstrated in the following example, applies to every element in the page, regardless of type, class, or id:

```
* {
    color: red;
}
```

The universal selector is a simple asterisk: *. There is no required text for a universal selector because it applies to every element in the page.

OTHER SELECTORS

Many other selectors are available to use in your styling, including the attribute selector, which enables you to use other attributes in an HTML element as part of your selector. This approach also enables you to drill into the content of the attribute and create a selector that matches part of the value within the attribute. This topic is beyond the scope of this book, but be aware that a lot of other selectors are available as your need for additional control over the appearance of your content increases.

More on Grouping Selectors

This chapter previously discussed how you can group selectors for a ruleset using either a space or a comma. Using the comma acts as an OR, so any elements that match any of the selectors will have the style applied. Using the space means that the element has to match all of the selectors that are included. This section takes a closer look at how this works, and how it can affect selection.

Examine the following rule:

```
p .special {
    color: blue;
    font-size: 50px;
}
```

Here, the lack of a comma separating the two selectors means that an element would have to both be within a `<p>` element and be contained within an element that has a class attribute set to `special`. However, this approach is managed through inheritance, rather than through an element of type `<p>` that also has a class of `special`. Because the space implies inheritance, the following code will not be interpreted the same:

```
<p class="special">Hey, I am not styled.</p>
<p>But, <span class="special">I am</span> because I am inherited.</p>
```

Instead, when the `p .special` rule is applied, it looks like Figure 3-7.

As you can see, the presence of the space indicates inheritance. At this point you may be wondering if you can create a selector that will find the first case in that last code snippet:

FIGURE 3-7: Inheritance in CSS

`<p class="special">`, such that the selector will understand that the appropriate element to be styled is an element of type `<p>` that also has a class of `"special"`. It will probably not surprise you to know that there is a way to do that.

What happens when you omit the space? If multiple selectors are displayed together without a space, the browsers will look for elements that match both of the conditions within the same element without inheritance being considered. Thus, to style the .special `<p>` element, you would need to use a rule with a selector as follows:

```
p.special {
    color: purple;
    font-size: 45px;
}
```

This rule would be applied to every element of type `<p>` that also has a class of `"special"`. You can link multiple selectors together as needed, as long as you have no more than one of each type of selector. That means a selector such as `p.special.extraspecial` should not be used, as it implies that the element will have multiple classes assigned to it. A rule with a selector of `p.special#extraspecial` makes more sense because it finds all HTML elements that are of type `<p>`, have a class of `"special"` and have the `id` attribute set to `extraspecial`.

Properties

You have already seen how the ruleset is able to select the elements to which it should be applied, so this section describes in more detail what you can do with the styling information itself. Table 3-1 describes the CSS properties.

TABLE 3-1: CSS Properties

PROPERTY	DESCRIPTION
background	This property sets the background information for the element. Because this is a parent property, you can put all the different values for the background in the same line. For example: `background: black url("smiley.gif") no-repeat fixed center;`
background-color	This sets only the background color. Other parts of the background can be set individually, including image, position, repeating pattern, origin, and size. For example: `background-color: rgb(255,0,255);`
border	Creates a border around the element. Like background, border is a parent property that enables you to set many different subproperties in a single command. For example: `Border: 5px solid red;`
border-bottom	The "-bottom" indicates this is a subproperty that sets the bottom part of the border. Other options include left, right, and top; you can even set different colors for each side with bottom-color. An example of setting the border-bottom: `border-bottom: thick dotted #ff0000;`
display	Defines the type of box used for an HTML element. Multiple values are available for display, the most common of which are as follows: Block: Displays the element as a block element, like the `<p>` element Inline: Default value, displays the element as an inline element; like the default behavior for `<span>` Inline-block: The inside of the block is formatted as a block-level box, while the entire element itself is formatted as an inline-level box None: The element will not be displayed at all. There is no effect on layout; and no space is reserved.
font	Sets the font that will be applied to the element content. For example: `font: italic bold 12px/30px Georgia, serif;`
height	Defines the height that is given to the element's content. It sets the height of the area inside the padding, border, and margin of the element. For example: `height: 100px;`
left	When an element is absolutely positioned (more on this later), the `left` property sets the left edge of an element to the right side of the left edge of the containing element. Otherwise, the `left` property sets the left edge of an element to the left of its normal position. For example: `left: 5px;`

PROPERTY	DESCRIPTION
margin	Sets the margin around the element. More on this below.
padding	Sets the padding around the element. More on this below.
position	Specifies the type of positioning method used for an element:
	static: Default value; elements render in order, as they appear in the document flow
	absolute: Element is positioned relative to its first positioned (not static) ancestor element
	fixed: Element is positioned relative to the browser window
	relative: Element is positioned relative to its normal position. For example, `left: 25px` would move the element 25 pixels to the left of its normal position.
text-align	Specifies the horizontal alignment of text in an element. For example: `text-align: center;`
text-decoration	none: Defines that the element is normal text. This is the default.
	underline: Defines text that has a line below the text
	overline: Defines a line above the text
	line-through: Defines text with the line through it
visibility	Determines whether an element can be seen; if invisible, the browser reserves space for it

Several items in the preceding table need to be examined together. These are the padding, border, and margin properties, which all interact together to manage the placement of content within the element.

Figure 3-8 shows how all the pieces work together. The dark section is the element, while each layer around it demonstrates the other items. Padding is the area immediately surrounding the element. If an item has both padding and a border, the padding defines the distance between the outer edge of the element and the border. If you add a margin, you are defining the distance between the border and the surrounding elements. In other words, padding extends the outer limit of the element, while margin defines the space between the outer limit of the element and the adjacent element.

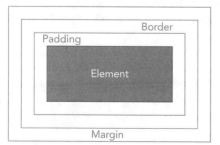

FIGURE 3-8: Padding, border, and margin

To understand how this plays out in HTML, consider the following snippet that has some style code and HTML:

```
<style type="text/css">
    .innerelement {
        border: 5px solid black;
        background-color: yellow;
        width: 200px;
        padding: 50px;
        margin: 100px;
    }
    .outerelement {
        border: 5px solid red;
        background-color: green;
        width: 200px;
    }
</style>
<div class="outerelement">
    <div class="innerelement">
        content
    </div>
</div>
```

This snippet will display in the browser as shown in Figure 3-9, but keep in mind the black and white images don't truly demonstrate what you should see on screen, which will appear in color.

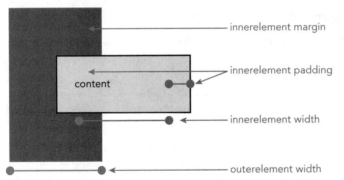

FIGURE 3-9: Rendered HTML with padding, margin, and width

Figure 3-9 illustrates some interesting points about styling. The space immediately between "content" and the first line is the padding. The space between that first line and the left, top, and bottom sections, as shown by the darker box on the left, is the margin. Note how the margin and padding affect the width of the element.

Both elements, innerelement and outerelement, have the same width. However, the inner element is obviously wider. That's because of the padding property. The use of padding extends the width of the element past the content. Margin, conversely, extends outside the element. This is why the leftmost box is spread outside the inner box—the margin pushes it out from the element.

Figure 3-9 also shows another interesting aspect of styling — the absolute nature of some of the properties. Even though the inner element is contained within the outer element, the outer element's width is still rendered at 200px, regardless of the overall width of the containing element. The overall width of the inner element is 510 pixels wide, and is calculated by combining the 200px of width, the left padding of 50px, the right padding of 50px, the left border of 5px, the right border of 5px, the left margin of 100px, and the right margin of 100px.

Precedence in Styles

You have seen some examples illustrating how styles can affect each other. This is an important concept, because the styles of nested and adjacent elements all interact with each other and may affect the display of other elements. This means that when an element does not look as expected, it may be due to the styling of an adjacent, containing, or contained element. Therefore, a base understanding of precedence may prevent some styling frustration.

The typical precedence takes multiple things into account. One of the things that it takes into account is something that you haven't really talked about, the origin of the style. Styles have three primary origins:

➤ **Author:** A style provided by the site's author, such as the styles that you have been creating

➤ **User:** A style created by the user, whereas the default style is the one built into the browser

➤ **Default:** A style that is built into the browser and acts as the style when no others have been added. This may be different depending upon the browser.

CREATING USER STYLE SHEETS

You may not realize it, but as a user you have control over the styles that are displayed in your browser. Microsoft's Internet Explorer, for example, allows you to create and apply your own style sheet to every page that you visit. You can do this by selecting Internet Options and then choosing the Accessibility button. This will bring up the dialog shown in Figure 3-10, from which you can change font settings and even add a custom-made user style sheet.

continues

continued

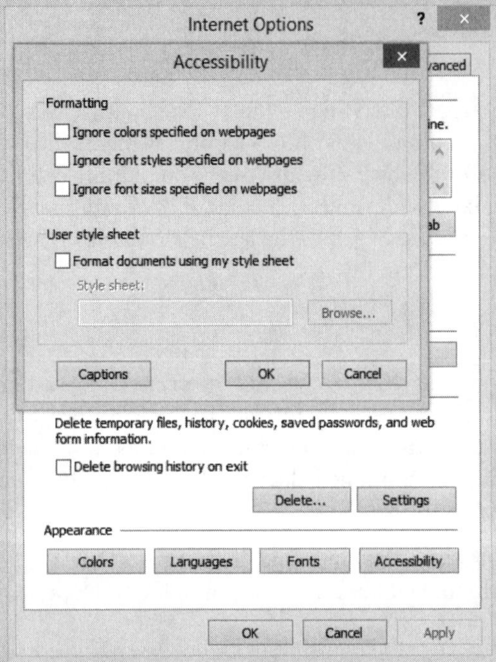

FIGURE 3-10: Adding a user style sheet to your browser

Each of the other major browsers have their own way to add user style sheets. You will learn more about what makes up a style sheet later in this chapter.

When the browser is determining how to render content, the initial specificity is calculated with the following rules:

1. Find all of the style assignments that apply to both the element and the property being parsed for display.

2. Sort by origin and weight. Origin was discussed previously, and weight refers to the importance of the declaration. Weight is calculated in the same order (author, then user, and then default) but it takes into account some special tags that can be added to the style.

3. The browser then calculates the specificity.

4. If any two rules are equal for all of the above, the one that declared last takes precedence. This means that CSS embedded in HTML always follows any page declared styles (as shown so far with styles contained in the `<head>` element), which comes after external style sheets (what you will be doing later in this chapter).

Step 3, calculating specificity, is more complex than it may seem. At the simplest level, an id is more specific than a class, which in turn is more specific than an element. However, it is not as clear as that. Examine the following code snippets:

```
div p.special {color: red;}
#superspecial p {color: purple}

<div id="superspecial">
 <p class="special">Content</p>
</div>
```

What color do you think the content will be? When you look at the first style, you see that it is for paragraph elements with a class of "special" that are contained within a <div> element. This pretty well describes the HTML code, doesn't it? The second style also seems to match the HTML code, as it selects paragraph elements that are contained within an element that has an id of "superspecial". Will the content be red or purple? You may be surprised by the answer: The content will be purple.

That may seem counterintuitive because the first styles just combine element matching and class matching, and the nesting within the element of the proper type seems very straightforward. However, because the second style is matched based on the parent element's id, it trumps the first style.

If you remove the "p" from the second line, what do you think happens? Does the specificity of the id in the containing element still override the first style? In this case, you will find that the content will display in red. This happens because the identification of the exact element in the first style offers more specificity than the second style after the paragraph reference has been removed. If the first style were completely removed, however, the content would again be displayed in purple because of the inheritance from the hosting element.

Understanding precedence will come with practice. The easiest way to understand the precedence calculation is by looking at the output. Visual Studio enables you to look at both the design and the output at the same time; don't hesitate to take advantage of this to see the full interaction of your styles with your HTML.

THE STYLE SHEET

You have done your first work with styles, but this is not the way that you will be styling the application as you move forward. While this approach is much more efficient than using HTML styling, in that you can put all the styles in one place on the page and enable them to be used everywhere on that page, it also means that if you want different pages to be styled the same, then you have to copy the styles to each of those pages. Thus, if you want to change these styles, you have to go through each page and update them. While this is definitely better than having to retouch every element on the page, it still is error prone.

This is where the "sheet" part of Cascading Style Sheets comes into play. You can put all your styles into a single page and then link that style-containing page to each page that will be using it. That means all pages in your site (if they have been set up correctly) will be able to use the same set of styles. With this capability, changing styles throughout your site becomes very easy, as you have only one file to work with, rather than one area on each page.

Adding CSS to Your Pages

You have learned about adding CSS styles to your page using the `<style>` element, and how that element defines the content within the element as being a style definition. The next thing to learn is how to add a separate file containing styles and then get your content pages to use those styles for display.

Linking your page to the CSS style sheet is simple. Assuming that you have a style sheet named `"styles.css"` you would add the following line to the `<head>` section of your HTML page:

```
<link href="styles.css" rel="Stylesheet" type="text/css" media="screen" />
```

The `<link>` element tells the browser that the information identified in the attributes should be linked to the page. The `href` attribute tells the browser what external file should be linked in, which is critical because the use of the `<link>` element implies attaching an external reference. The `rel` attribute gives the file context by defining its relationship. In this case, the external file is a style sheet. Other values for this attribute include `help`, `icon`, `author`, `license`, and many more relationships.

The `type` attribute is used to define the type of content that the file contains. The last attribute that you need is `media`. This attribute defines the type of media on which the document will be viewed. Other media types include `mobile` and `print`.

CONTENT TYPE

The content type enables you to provide additional information about the content of the file. It used to be known as a MIME type, but has evolved to include information about any kind of other content. This information is necessary because there is really no other way for the browser to understand what the external file is and how the page it is rendering and that external file need to interact. Other content types that you may work with as you build the sample application include the following:

➤ **text/html:** Tells the receiver that the content will be HTML

➤ **text/plain:** Tells the receiver that the content will be plain text

➤ **audio/mpeg:** Identifies the content as an audio file, such as an MP3

> ➤ **video/mpeg:** Used to label content as video
>
> ➤ **image/png:** Used to label image files. This is built into the `<img>` element.
>
> The next Try It Out demonstrates how the link element is used and how to create an external style sheet.

TRY IT OUT Converting In-Page Styling to Using an External Style Sheet

In this activity you'll convert the page and styles that you created earlier in this chapter to use the external style sheet.

1. Create the style sheet that you will use to hold the styles. Do this by right-clicking the Content directory in your Solution Explorer and selecting Add ➪ Item ➪ New Item. This brings up a dialog similar to the one shown in Figure 3-11.

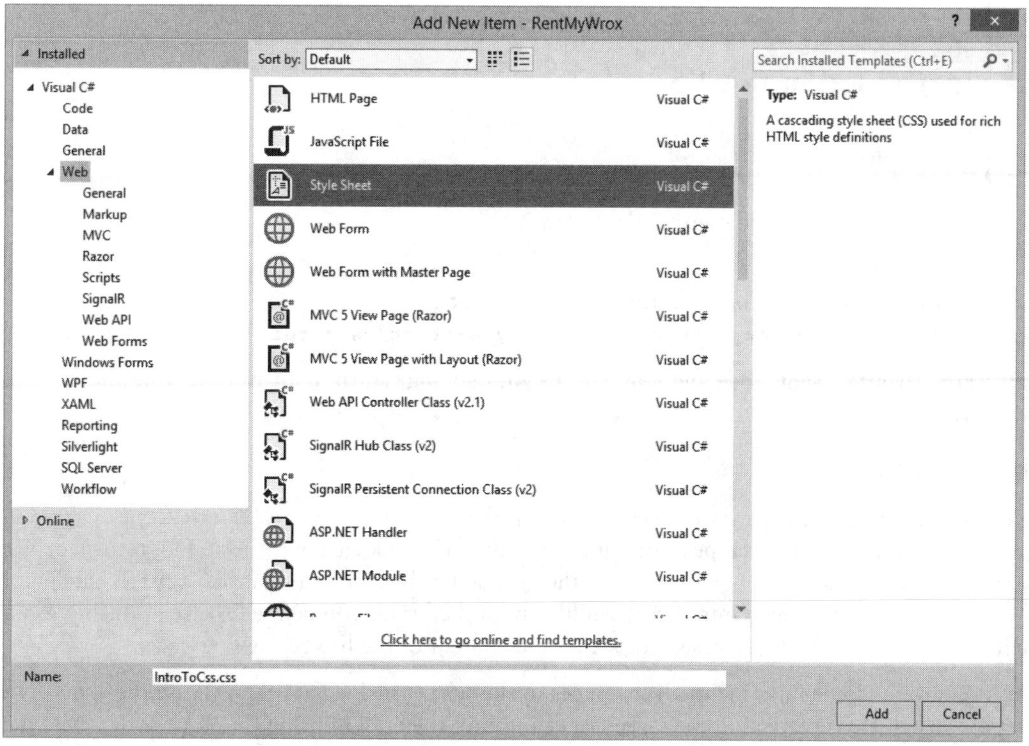

FIGURE 3-11: Adding a new style sheet

2. Select Style Sheet, name it **IntroToCss.css,** and click Add. This will add the file to the solution and open it in your Visual Studio working area.

3. Copy all the styles from the `IntroToCss.aspx` page and paste them into the style sheet that you just created. You do not have to bring the `<style>` elements over, just the style definitions. This is possible because you will be defining the content when you create the link tag. Once you have the styles in your style sheet, remove them from your `.aspx` page.

4. Ensure that you are in Split mode and refresh your Design mode to see what it looks like. It should look something like Figure 3-12, only styled with the default styles.

FIGURE 3-12: Page after removing style

5. Add the following text between the `<head>` elements:

    ```
    <link href="Content/IntroToCss.css" type="text/css" rel="stylesheet" />
    ```

6. Refresh your Design mode and you will see your styling return, but this time from the linked style sheet.

How It Works

In this activity, you created a style sheet and then linked it to your page. When the styles were removed from the page, the styling disappeared; but after adding the link element, the styling returned. When the styles were put into the `<head>` element, they needed to be contained in the `<style>` element. However, after you put them into their own file and linked it in, you defined the relationship as part of the link element so that the browser knew that the content of the linked file is styled.

You can add this same link line to all the pages in the site, ensuring that they all use the same style sheets. You can also create multiple style sheets and link them all in using the same code; there is no limit to the number of sheets that can be linked in.

In this example, all the styles were moved into a single sheet. Would you ever want to have separate style sheets? This approach would make sense when you have multiple websites for a company, and each site looks much like the others. The rules that are common to the sites could be put into one style sheet that is available to all of the sites, while the site-specific styles are put into another style sheet that is available only to the pages within that site.

When you were working with your Content directory you likely noticed that there were several files that were already in the directory. These were provided by the project scaffolding that created the default application. Each of these files is responsible for doing different work within the application. There is one group of files in particular that are interesting to consider; those that include the term "bootstrap."

Bootstrap is a set of JavaScript and CSS tools that manage the display of content in the web browser. These are special because they are part of a design approach known as "responsive," which is an approach to design that tries to build sites in such a way that they can support different sized view screens, from a user on a desktop machine with a large monitor, to a laptop user, to a tablet user, to a phone user.

The default site that is created by the Visual Studio project scaffolder uses Bootstrap by default. You can see Bootstrap in operation by running the application with the default page and then resizing the browser window. As the browser window shrinks you will see the UI change as well. For more information about Bootstrap you can visit their site at `http://www.bootstrap.org`.

Creating Embedded and Inline Style Sheets

There are three types of style sheets:

- ➤ External
- ➤ Embedded
- ➤ Inline

The first two you are already familiar with. You just finished converting an embedded style sheet (in which the styles were put into the `<head>` section of the page) into an external style sheet. The last type, not yet covered, is the inline style. An inline style is the closest style to the element being displayed, because it is actually part of the element itself.

All HTML elements that support content have a `style` attribute that enables you to add styles. Using this attribute you can add any of the CSS properties directly to the element. Here is an example:

```
<div style="color:blue;margin:30px;">This is an inline style.</div>
```

The assignation rules are the same as those for external or embedded styles; each has a property name and value separated by a colon, and a semicolon indicates the end of that property declaration. You can add as many CSS properties as you need to that single `style` attribute.

This approach is as difficult to maintain as the original HTML styling elements, but you might encounter scenarios in which a final override of an element and this will be the only way you can achieve that.

If you recall the precedence rules you learned earlier, the closer the style is to the element being rendered, the higher the precedence. That means anything in the element's `style` attribute will be automatically applied, overriding any of the properties set higher up the inheritance chain. The next precedence would be the embedded styles, those in the head of the HTML page. Last to be applied would be the styles defined in the external style sheet.

APPLYING STYLES

So far, you have created and applied styles by hand in order to gain an understanding of how they all work. However, Visual Studio was designed to help speed development, so several built-in tools are available to help you style your application. All of the work that you have done so far has been in the source window, after which you viewed the rendered output in the design window. You will now start to do more work in the design window as you learn how you can build styles by taking advantage of Visual Studio's support for working with CSS style sheets.

TRY IT OUT   Creating and Applying Styles in Visual Studio

In this Try It Out you will create some styles for text in the CSS test page using Visual Studio's built-in tools.

1. In Visual Studio, open the CSS test file, `IntroToCss.aspx`.

2. View the file in full Design mode, rather than Source or Split mode. This should give you a view like the one shown in Figure 3-13.

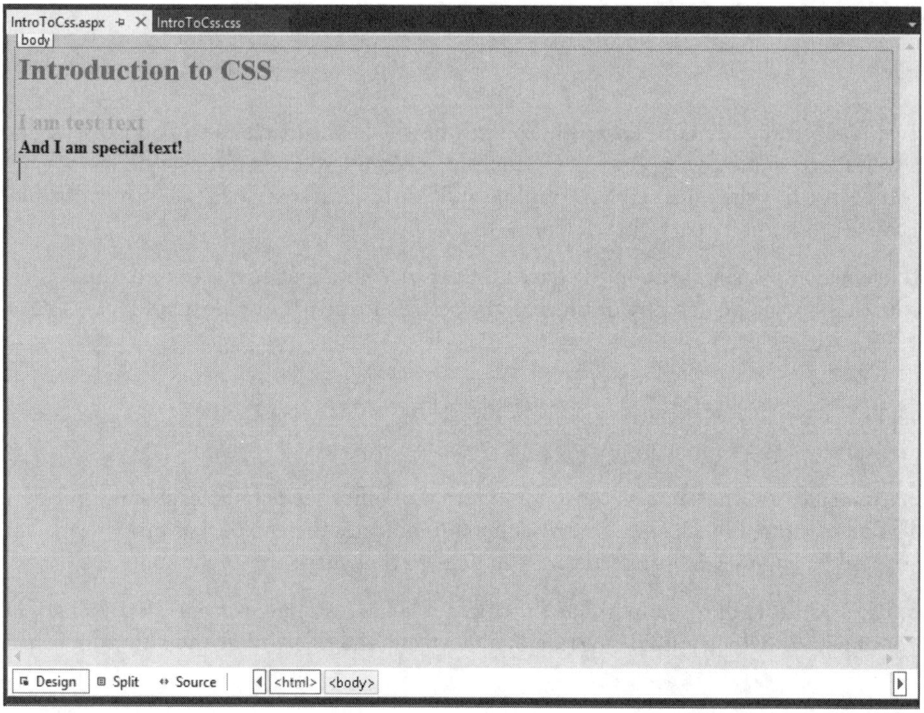

FIGURE 3-13: Viewing the file in Design mode

3. Now that you are in Design mode, a new toolbar is available in the Visual Studio toolbar area, the Formatting toolbar, shown in Figure 3-14.

FIGURE 3-14: Formatting toolbar

4. Click on various elements in your page and notice how the values change in the dropdown boxes of the Formatting toolbar. For example, select an item that is already styled (i.e., an element whose style appears in the dropdown), and note how the dropdown changes to the type of element that you selected.

5. Double-click anywhere on the word "Introduction." The entire word will be highlighted. In the Target Rule dropdown, select Apply New Style. This will bring up the New Style dialog shown in Figure 3-15.

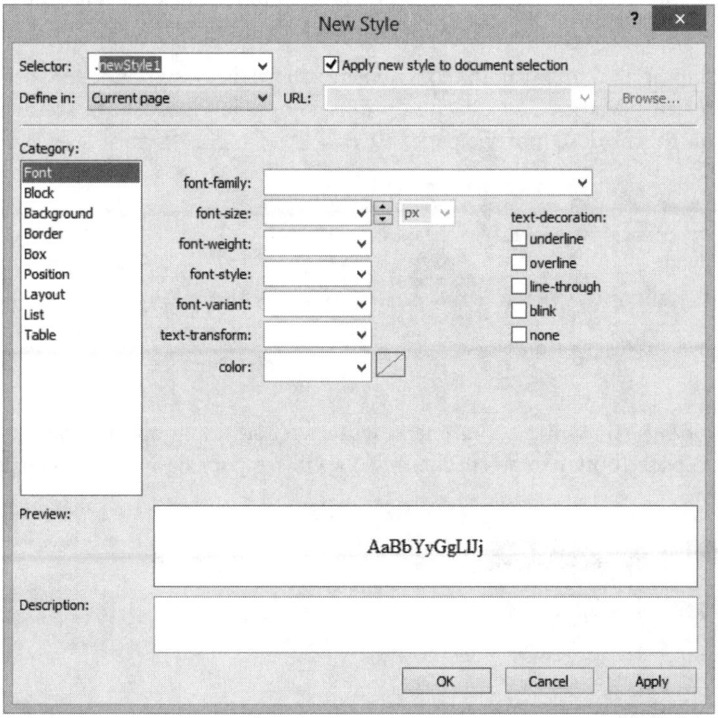

FIGURE 3-15: New Style dialog

6. In the top part of the dialog you can identify the selector to use, including naming a class selector. You can also choose where to save a new style, whether it is inline, embedded, or in a style sheet. Enter a new name into the selector: **.introduction**.

7. Select Define in Existing Style Sheet and click the Browse button to select the already existing `IntroToCss.css` file.

8. Select a font-family of "Arial, Helvetica, sans-serif," a font-size of "larger," and a color of #800000, and click OK.

9. Look at the `IntroToCss.aspx` source file to see how the page has changed. It should have a section that looks like the following: `<span class="introduction">Introduction </span>`

10. Examining the style sheet will show you that a new style was added. It should look something like the following (your choices may be different):

```
.introduction {
    font-family: Arial, Helvetica, sans-serif;
    font-size: large;
    color: #800000;
}
```

11. Now that you have gone over the creation and/or assignment of styles, the rest of this activity looks at the other help that Visual Studio offers when working in Design mode. Click the View menu item in the main menu.

12. There are three options at the top that are available only when you are in Design mode: Ruler and Grid, Visual Aids, and Formatting Marks. These menu options, shown in Figure 3-16, are designed to help you visualize and control the design of the page.

FIGURE 3-16: Menu options available in Design mode

13. Select the Ruler and Grid option. You will get a submenu with two additional options: Show Grid and Show Ruler. Select them both (both can be checked). You will see your design screen change as shown in Figure 3-17.

FIGURE 3-17: Screen changes after selecting both ruler and grid

14. The design view has changed to display a ruler and a grid in the background. The default unit for the grid is pixels, but you change both displays by selecting the View ⇨ Ruler and Grid ⇨ Configure option.

15. Figure 3-18 shows the result of enabling all of the options. When you click in the "And I am special text!" tab, you see the full selector that is responsible for the styling of this content. Note the small tab with the text.

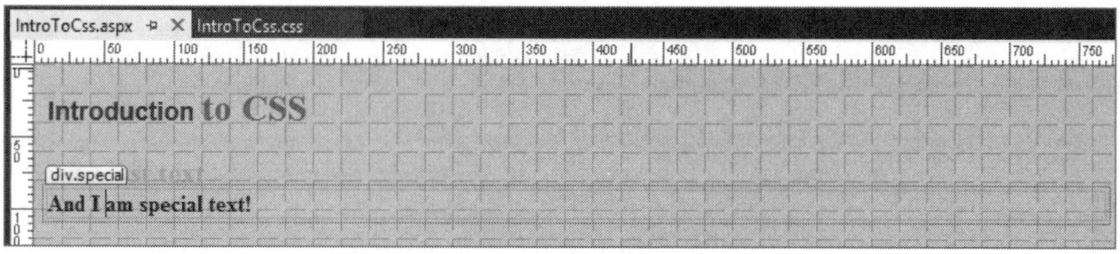

FIGURE 3-18: Design mode with all visual aids enabled

16. Click on the tab. You will see the Windows Move icon displayed. This enables you to drag the content around the page to position the element differently.

17. Ensure that the View ⇨ Visual Aids ⇨ Margins and Padding visual aids are enabled. You can set the margins and padding of the selected elements. This also helps you visualize how margin and padding manage interaction between various elements.

18. Ensure that the View ⇨ Formatting Marks ⇨ Show selection is checked. Also ensure that the Tag Marks item is selected. Once Tag Marks is selected, you should see tag information in Design mode, as shown in Figure 3-19.

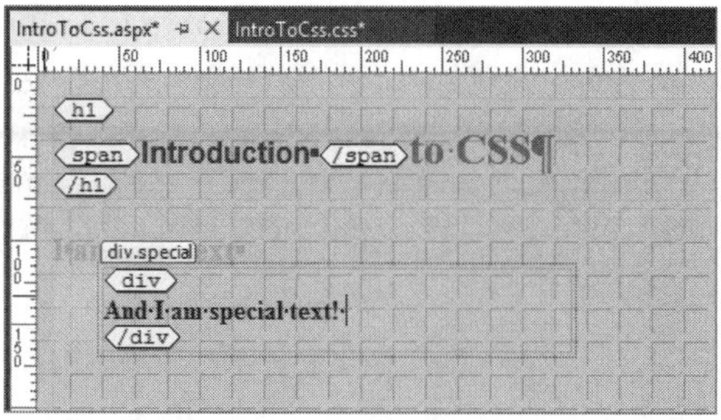

FIGURE 3-19: Displaying Tag Marks in Design mode

19. Go to the View menu item and select CSS Properties. A new window will open in your working area.

20. Highlight "And I am special text!" The CSS Properties window that you just opened should change to a display similar to that shown in Figure 3-20.

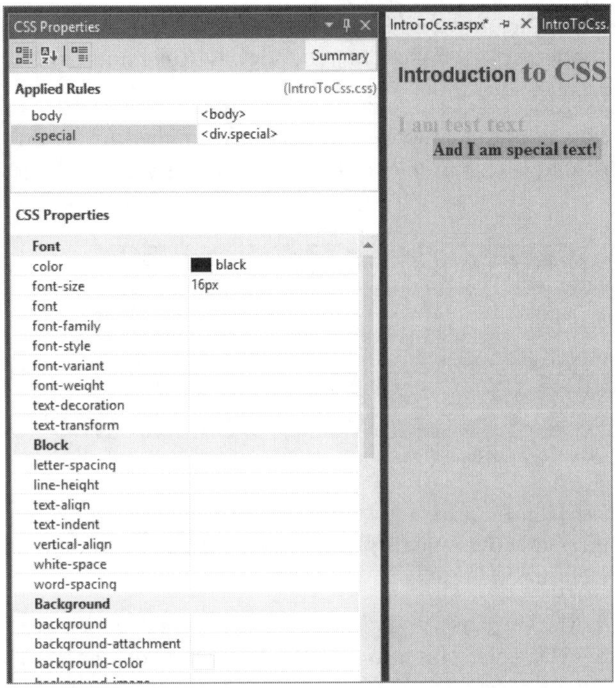

FIGURE 3-20: CSS Properties window

21. Examine the CSS Properties window. The top section, titled Applied Rules, provides information about all of the style properties that are being set. In this case, it indicates that a `"body"` style as well as a class style `".special"` is applied to the selected text. Change the color to purple and the font-size to xx-large. The visual display will change as you make the changes in the window.

22. Open the `IntroToCss.css` file to see the changes that are happening in the styles as you make your changes. Also notice that the CSS Properties window changes as you leave the Design mode window, because the content of the CSS Properties window is tied directly to the content selected in Design mode.

How It Works

Different people tend to have different preferences on how they do their work, especially when performing a creative endeavor such as styling and design work. This means that one person's favorite styling tool may be despised by the next person. This is why Microsoft took the approach of allowing you to toggle each different item on and off. This helps you set up the visual environment with which you are the most comfortable.

As you are considering your personal approach, you may also get an added benefit by having both the ruler and the grid enabled, as they give you a better idea of the effects that various settings have on the visual placement of the content. Another useful support tool is the Visual Aids menu options as they also help you get a visual understanding of the content in the design window. Available Visual Aid menu options are shown in Table 3-2.

TABLE 3-2: Visual Aids

MENU OPTION	DEFINITION
Block Selection	Block selection is displayed in two different ways. When you put your cursor in a block, a dotted rectangle will appear around the tag, and a tab displaying the name of the tag will appear. You can click the tab to select the tag. When you select a block, the margins and padding will be displayed and you can use the handles to resize the margins and padding.
Visible Borders	When this option is selected the IDE will show dotted borders around elements that have hidden borders. This enables you to visualize how properties such as `margin` and `padding` may affect the display of your content.
Empty Containers	This option ensures that all empty elements are surrounded by a dotted rectangle. An empty element is an HTML element, such as `<p></p>`, that does not have any content. Browsers, and the IDE, will generally completely collapse empty containers, so enabling this will affect the display, changing it. However, you will also get a visualization of those elements that can be safely removed.
Margins and Padding	Shows the margins and padding around all elements. When selected, margins will appear in red and padding will appear in blue. You cannot use this visual aid to change margins and padding; instead, enable the Block Selection visual aid and use the handles that appear as part of that aid.
CSS Display:none Elements	Shows those elements that are not displayed because they have a style that includes the CSS property `display:none`
CSS Visibility:hidden Elements	Shows those elements that would be selected by a style that includes `visibility:hidden`, and thus are hidden in the design window
ASP.NET Non-visual Controls	Shows a rectangle for ASP.NET controls that don't display anything. You will see more examples of these kinds of controls as you continue.
ASP.NET Control Errors	Shows an error message when an ASP.NET control encounters an error, such as not connecting to a data source
Template Region Labels	Shows a border around editable template regions, including a tab with the name of the region

Visual Studio provides a lot of different ways to manage the design of your pages. You can always build your HTML by hand as you did earlier in the chapter, but various tools are to help you visualize your design and manage your styles through different means. The Formatting toolbar enables you to apply existing styles to content, and helps you create new styles as necessary. Once you have the styles, the

CSS Properties window gives you access to the CSS properties that are being applied to the content, in addition to giving you the capability to change them through dropdowns.

Managing your styling through the CSS Properties window is especially powerful because when you have the design window and the CSS Properties window open side-by-side, you can make the style changes and watch how they affect the displayed selected content. This immediate feedback enables you to efficiently manage your design to meet your expectations.

MANAGING STYLES

You have gained a lot of information about creating and maintaining styles, but only a little about strategies for building styles that are reusable and take advantage of CSS capabilities such as inheritance. You shall learn about that now.

Before you start worrying about something as granular as a style, you need to consider the overall design of your website. First, determine the overall look and feel of the sample application. This gives you an understanding of how to build out your styles as you start to add your content.

The sample application is a lending library and it has a relatively simple set of requirements, which were discussed in Chapter 1. The following page views are required:

➤ A default view of all available items for checkout. You will make this your default home page, the first page that anyone sees when they come to the website.

➤ A special view for the administrator to add new items. This will need to include a list of items from which users can select an item to edit as well as add a new item.

➤ A registration page.

➤ A checkout page that displays the items that users have determined that they want to check out from the library.

Other requirements include implementation details that you need to manage as you build out the site and design. The first area of focus will be the home page. You know that there needs to be a list of items that are available for checkout. When you consider the needs of a home page as well as the requirements to support login and registration, you know that you have to include more than just a list of items on this page. These considerations could result in a simplified view of the home page that would look something like Figure 3-21.

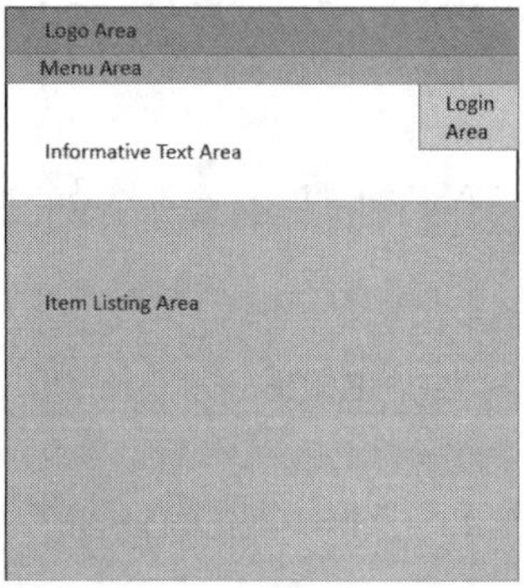

FIGURE 3-21: Simple design for sample application home page

You will build five different areas of this page.

➤ The logo area, where you will be doing your branding for the website

➤ The menu area, which enables visitors to go to different areas of the site.

➤ The login area, which is special because it contains the fields necessary to allow users to log in to the application—in this case, an e-mail address and a password.

➤ The informative text area. Because this page will be the default page for all site visitors, you need to give new users information about the services as well as instructions about how to proceed, whether it is through registration or through logging into the site.

➤ The product area, which is the only area that is directly part of the requirements: the listing of products that are available for lending. This listing will be made up of multiple pictures and text, so it warrants a bit more discussion. Figure 3-22 shows the simple design that you will use to display the items.

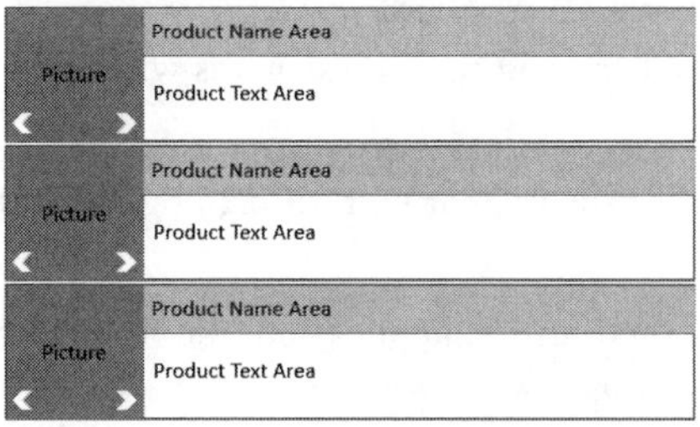

FIGURE 3-22: Simple design for the list of product items

Each item in the product area includes the following elements:

➤ Title

➤ Descriptive text

➤ One or more pictures of the item, and the capability for users to view each picture

You will now put these together and see what the potential impact would be when you create the style sheet. Figure 3-23 illustrates how these areas interact as you form your styling approach.

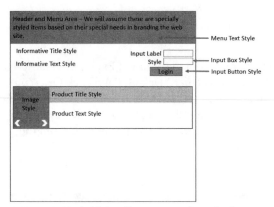

FIGURE 3-23: Initial styling approach to the home page

Each of the high-level items is now broken down a little bit more, with each initial style identified. The next thing to consider is whether there will be any reuse. For example, will you want to use the same visual text display for the informative text that you use for the product text? Will you want the input labels (where the user interface will have labels such as "e-mail address" and "password") to be the same as the product text, but different from the informative text? These are the considerations that you need to make as you work out your design.

For this design, the following typographical assumptions will be made:

1. The same font-face will be used for all titles, whether it is an informational title or a product title. The sizes will be different between the type of title, however.

2. The same font-face will be used for regular text, whether it is information or product text, but this font-face will differ from the title font-face. Both of these items will also have the same size of font.

3. The input label font-face will be different from the regular text, though the size remains the same.

With these rules in mind, you will create the initial shell for the application's home page in the following Try It Out.

TRY IT OUT Creating the Initial Styles for Your Home Page

In addition to creating the initial styles for the home page, you will also start removing some of the content that was added to the site through the project creation templates.

1. Within Visual Studio, ensure that you are not running the application, and delete the `site.css` file in the Content directory. To do so, highlight it and press the Delete key, or right-click the file in Solution Explorer and select the Delete menu item. This removes all of the previously created styles.

2. Do the same with the current `Default.aspx` file. This will be easier than trying to edit the content that was added during project creation.

3. Add a new CSS file. Right-click the Content directory in the Solution Explorer and select Add ⇨ Style Sheet. Name the file "**main**" and select OK.

4. Add a new `Default.aspx` page by right-clicking the project in the Solution Explorer window and selecting Add ⇨ Web Form. When the naming box appears enter "**Default**" and click OK. You can also add the file by going to the Project menu item, selecting Add New Item, and adding a Web Form from that dialog. It is quickest to do it from the Solution Explorer window, however. This new page should open in your working window. If not, open the file you just added. From the source window, the code should look like the following:

```
<%@ Page Language="C#" AutoEventWireup="true" CodeBehind="Default.aspx.cs"
Inherits="RentMyWrox.Default" %>

<!DOCTYPE html>
```

```
<html xmlns="http://www.w3.org/1999/xhtml">
<head runat="server">
    <title></title>
</head>
<body>
    <form id="form1" runat="server">
    <div>

    </div>
    </form>
</body>
</html>
```

5. Add some text to match the main items from Figure 3-23. This should give you something like the following:

```
<%@ Page Language="C#" AutoEventWireup="true" CodeBehind="Default.aspx.cs"
        Inherits="RentMyWrox.Default" %>
<!DOCTYPE html>
<html xmlns="http://www.w3.org/1999/xhtml">
<head runat="server">
    <title></title>
</head>
<body>
    I am Informative Text Title                          I am input text

    I am Informative Text

    I am Product Title

    I am Product Text

</body>
</html>
```

6. Now that you have the various items you need to style, you need to start defining their relationships in terms of HTML and styles. The first thing you should look at is the Informative Text Title. You know that is a title, so give it a header element, `<h1>`. Enclose that body of text with the `<h1>` elements.

7. You know that the Product Title area is also special, so you will make it an `<h2>` element, as it is a header, but at a lower level than the main header. Use "I am Product Title" as text content for the `<h2>` element.

8. At this point you have added some special elements, but the default look and feel is the same. Now you will add the first official style. From the previously outlined design approach, you know that the informational text and the product text will be the same font-face and the same size. You want to make this the default style. Go into Design mode. Your screen should look like what is shown in Figure 3-24.

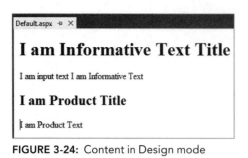

FIGURE 3-24: Content in Design mode

9. In the Formatting toolbar, select Apply New Style from the Target Rule dropdown. This will bring up the New Style dialog.

10. Set the options as follows: Selector to "body," Define in to "Existing Style Sheet," URL to Content/main.css, font-family to "Arial," and font-size to "medium." Your settings should match those in Figure 3-25.

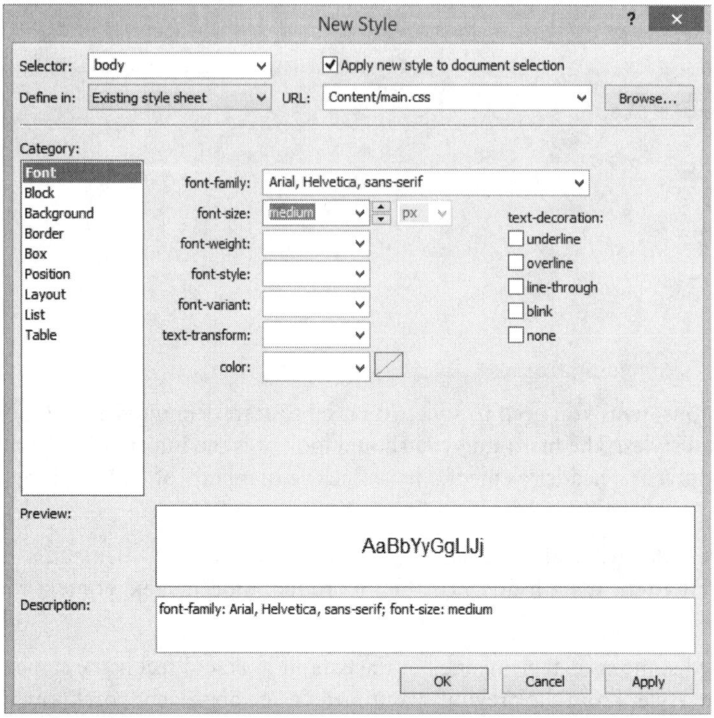

FIGURE 3-25: Setting body style

11. The item should update with this new style, but it hasn't because you haven't linked the new style sheet you created to the new page. To do that, return to Source mode and add the following code between the head opening and closing tags. Note how IntelliSense helps walk you through the process:

```
<link href="Content/main.css" type="text/css" rel="stylesheet" />
```

12. When you return to Design mode you will see that all the font faces have changed to Arial. That fulfills the second requirement, but you still need to add more styling because the title and regular text font-faces have to be different. To fix that, highlight the Informative Text Title, and use the Format toolbar to select Apply New Style. Set the options as follows: Selector to ".title," Define it to "Existing Style Sheet," URL to "Content/main.css," and Font-face to the "Cambria" list.

Click OK. Note that the highlighted text has changed to a different font-face from the rest.

13. The way that the wizard does this is not perfect. If you go into source view you will see that the wizard created a span element around your content. This is not ideal. Copy the `class="title"` from the span and put it into the `<h1>` element. Remove the span elements. While you are there, add this same class into the `<h2>` element for the Product Title. This should leave your source code looking something like this:

```
<body>
    <h1 class="title">I am Informative Text Title</h1>                I am input text
    I am Informative Text
    <h2  class="title">I am Product Title</h2>
    I am Product Text
</body>
```

14. Go back into Design mode and refresh if necessary. You will see that the titles have the same font-face, though they are different sizes, indicating that both the first and second requirements are met.

15. The last change to make is to style the input label text. Open the `main.css` file and add the following lines:

```
.label {
    font-family: Cambria, Cochin, Georgia, Times, "Times New Roman", serif;
}
```

16. Go back to the `Default.aspx` page and put the Input Text into a `<div>` tag with a class of "label." When you view it in Design mode, refreshing if necessary, you will see that the text font-face now differs from the regular text.

How It Works

This activity created the initial styles for the sample application. After determining the minimal criteria needed for the styles, you then created them in Visual Studio. You may have noticed one thing when you created the last style, label. The properties in that style are identical to those for the title style. However, the items being styled are very contextually different, as indicated by the names that you gave them. Sometimes you may have the same identical properties and values in styles, especially as you start the design. This is OK right now.

When you are done, there will be one more pass through the styles to see whether it would make sense to eliminate these redundantly valued styles. However, in this case you would likely keep these two as is, without renaming them, perhaps moving them to an approach such as the following:

```
.title, .label {
    font-family: Cambria, Cochin, Georgia, Times, "Times New Roman", serif;
}
```

That way, if there is ever a need in the future to select a different font-family for one of those styles it will be easy to separate them.

This brings up a critical point when designing your styles. You are aiming for abstraction, so always think of your styles contextually, as you did with "label" and "title." This enables you to understand the style's purpose, why it is different. This in turn helps you understand where this style will be used as you move forward.

SUMMARY

When HTML came upon the scene, managing the look and feel of a website was complicated because styling was provided by another HTML element. One of the main problems with this system was that any changes to the design needed to be propagated to each element. This made updates and changes difficult to manage. As more and more people accessed the Internet and started visiting websites, the user experience became more important. This led to the development of Cascading Style Sheets (CSS), a technique that enables separating design information from the content, thereby enabling the two to be maintained separately. It includes the concept of a selector, a way of designating a single ruleset that can be applied to multiple pieces of content based on well-understood relationships.

The key to CSS is a style, or a set of visual and interactive rules that are applied to an HTML element. Each HTML element in your page may have one or more styles applied to it; and the browser knows how to link a style to an HTML element based on the selector of the style, which defines to what elements it should be applied.

One of the more powerful features of CSS is the concept of cascading, which enables the styles of parent elements to filter down to contained elements, a feature referred to as inheritance. In addition, this inheritance happens at the property level. That means that setting a font-family at the body level will cascade down to every other element within the body unless an element has a style that specifically overrides it. Thus, when you build your styles, you want to put the most common items as "low down" in the stack as possible so that you only have to set them once and they will just work at every other level.

Visual Studio provides multiple different ways to help you build, apply, and manage styles, especially when you are working in Design mode, which gives you immediate feedback about changes in style and provides multiple options for visualizing the content. Each of these options gives the design additional context in terms of how it is displayed; and gives you, as the designer, different ways to manage and change styles that will be applied to your content.

EXERCISES

1. What are the differences between `.intro p`, `p.intro`, and `p, .intro`?

2. Margins and padding have different effects on an element. If you were going to stretch the "box" of an element, which would you use?

3. How do you provide your HTML elements on a page with access to styles from an external style sheet?

4. What are some of the various tools in Visual Studio that help developers manage styles for web pages?

▶ WHAT YOU LEARNED IN THIS CHAPTER

CSS	Cascading Style Sheets (CSS) is an approach to enhancing the look and feel of websites. It enables a designer to use selectors to identify a set of HTML elements that will have various properties applied to them as the browser parses the content.
Selectors	A section of a CSS ruleset that identifies the type of HTML element that will be styled. A selector can select HTML elements based on the type of element, the value of the `class` attribute, and the value of the `id` attribute.
Properties	Various items that can be managed using CSS. Examples of properties include `background`, `font-style`, `font-size`, and `color`.
Precedence in Styles	The approach that the web browser takes in determining which styles should be applied to an HTML element. The more specific the identification, the more precedence given that style. Precedence is applied at the property level, so different properties may end up with different precedents.
Embedded Styles	Styles that are defined within the HTML page header rather than through a linked-in style sheet
Inline Styles	Styles that are put directly onto the HTML element. No selector is needed with these styles, as they apply only to the type of element that matches the name in the selector.
Design Mode	A window in Visual Studio that displays the working page as if it were in a browser. It enables users to perform various design tasks, including creating and assigning styles and moving content.
Source Mode	A window in Visual Studio that shows the HTML code that makes up the page. It does not show any of the design, but rather enables the designer to work directly with the base code.
Split Mode	A mode in Visual Studio whereby both Design mode and Source mode are open at the same time. Changes made in one window are reflected in the other window.

4

Programming in C# and VB.NET

WHAT YOU WILL LEARN IN THIS CHAPTER:

➤ Understanding data types and variables

➤ How to use collections and arrays to process lists of information

➤ Code flow, branching, and looping

➤ How to separate code so it is easy to understand and maintain

➤ An introduction to object-oriented programming

CODE DOWNLOADS FOR THIS CHAPTER:

The wrox.com code downloads for this chapter are found at www.wrox.com/go/
beginningaspnetforvisualstudio on the Download Code tab. The code is in the
chapter 04 download and individually named according to the names throughout the chapter.

Now that you have spent some time on the designing part of your website, it's time to consider
how to handle the programming part, making your web application actually do something
other than change colors. There are many different aspects to programming a web application. This chapter gives you the foundation you need for when you start going deeper into
the different parts of ASP.NET as you build out the sample application. The constructs and
approaches covered in this chapter will be useful for every C# or VB application on which you
may ever work.

INTRODUCTION TO PROGRAMMING

Every application can be defined as a way to do things. Your application might play music,
handle customer registration for your company, help users pick a color to paint their house, or
anything else. When you consider all the potential things that an application can do, it might

seem a little overwhelming, but breaking the application down into its component parts helps you realize that all applications have things in common, regardless of the different purposes for which they will eventually be used.

Some of these commonalities are related to how the system interprets information and makes decisions. Because every application follows some kind of process, one or more of these decisions have to be made. Before your system can make a decision, however, it needs something on which to base it, something that holds information that can be used as criteria for your application's decision making. These things upon which you make decisions are called *data types* and *variables*.

Data Types and Variables

Data types provide a way to identify and group various kinds of information, or data, that your application needs to understand. .NET designers went through the exercise of defining these available base types because they determine the rules governing how the different types of data can be defined, how they interact, how they are stored in memory, and what can be done with them in an application. They are considered base types because they cannot be broken down further; they are the lowest denominator. A variable is a container for a value. Consider a value, such as a circle with a radius. You can consider the radius as a variable that you know will have a numeric value, or data type.

Defining a Variable

The importance of types in both C# and VB cannot be overstated; both are considered type-safe languages, which means the type of object has to be known at compile time (with a few exceptions) or the application won't compile, much less run. You tell the compiler the type of data it will be working with by declaring or defining your variable. Think of a variable as a container for your data. You want to give your variable a name that is meaningful in the context of your program, and use that name consistently throughout the program. In the following example, you declare a variable to hold a byte, a data type that defines the value as being a whole number between 0 and 255, and a string, a data type that holds text:

C#

```
// declare our variable that represents the in-stock quantity for a particular item
byte quantityInStock;

// declare our string that represents the name of the item
string itemName;
```

VB

```
' declare our variable that represents the in-stock quantity for a particular item
Dim quantityInStock As Byte

' declare our string that represents the name of the item
Dim itemName As String
```

This example shows the different approaches between the two languages for creating a variable and assigning its type. In C#, you declare a variable by stating its type and its name. In VB, you must start the declaration with the keyword Dim, followed by the variable name, then As, then the data type. Note that C# code requires you to indicate the end of the command by using the semicolon (;). VB does not have this requirement.

In addition, the names of the variables in the example give you an idea of what kind of information they contain in relationship to your application. You could just as easily give those variables nonsensical names such as "a" or "zz," but that would rob them of context; being able to glance at a variable and understand what it contains is important to keep your code maintainable and understandable.

The other lines in the example are comments. These lines in your code are not part of your application; instead, they enable developers to insert notes or other useful information. You will be going over comments in more detail later in the chapter.

You can take the preceding approach one step further, and actually assign a value to the variable. Thus, not only will you create a variable with a specific type, you will also give it a value, as shown in the following example:

C#

```
// declare our variable with the initial value
byte quantityInStock = 5;

// declare our string with the initial value
string itemName = "Electric Nail Gun";
```

VB

```
' declare our variable that represents the in-stock quantity for a particular item
Dim quantityInStock As Byte = 5

' declare our string that represents the name of the item
Dim itemName As String = "Electric Nail Gun"
```

While this example shows the declaration and assignment in the same line, it is not a requirement. They could be split into separate lines, as shown here:

C#

```
// declare our variable with the initial value
byte quantityInStock;

// declare our string with the initial value
string itemName;

// lots of work going on here as we figure out all the information

quantityInStock = 5;
itemName = "Electric Nail Gun";
```

VB

```
' declare our variable that represents the in-stock quantity for a particular item
Dim quantityInStock As Byte
```

```
' declare our string that represents the name of the item
Dim itemName As String

// lots of work going on here as we figure out all the information

quantityInStock = 5
itemName = "Electric Nail Gun"
```

Note how the name of the variable helps you understand what information it contains; this enables you to declare your variables apart from the actual assignment as needed. As you progress with the sample application, you will see how common this is.

Table 4-1 contains a brief list of the most common data types in .NET. This is only a tiny subset; there are literally thousands of data types available in the .NET Framework alone, without counting any custom types that you create.

TABLE 4-1: Common Data Types Available in C# and VB.NET

C# DATA TYPE	VB DATA TYPE	DESCRIPTION
byte	Byte	A byte is used to store small, positive whole numbers from 0 to 255. Defaults to 0 when no value is set.
short	Short	16-bit storage, holds whole numbers between −32,768 and 32,767. Defaults to 0.
int	Integer	32-bit storage, holds whole numbers between −2,147,483,648 and 2,147,483,647. Defaults to 0.
long	Long	64-bit storage, holds whole numbers between −9,223,372,036,854,808 and 9, 223,372,036,854,807. Defaults to 0.
float	Single	Stores large numbers between −3.4028235E+38 and 3.4028235E+38. These numbers may contain decimals, and float defaults to 0.0. When setting a float, you should use the indicator float x = 2.3f; otherwise the compiler will interpret the number as a double.
double	Double	A type that stores 64-bit floating-point values, it has an approximate range between ±5.0 × 10^324 and ±1.7 × 10^308, with a precision of 15–16 digits. Defaults to 0.

C# DATA TYPE	VB DATA TYPE	DESCRIPTION
decimal	Decimal	A decimal is a 128-bit data type. Compared to floating-point types, the decimal type has more precision (28–29 digits) and a smaller range, which makes it appropriate for financial and monetary calculations.
bool	Boolean	Used to hold a simple Boolean value; true or false (True or False in VB)
Datetime	Date	Holds date and time values. Defaults to 1/1/0001 12:00 a.m.
char	Char	Holds a single character, or a 16-bit Unicode representation. Unicode characters are used to represent most of the written languages throughout the world. Defaults to null (Nothing in VB).
string	String	Represents a sequence of zero or more Unicode characters. Strings are immutable—the contents of a string object cannot be changed after the object is created. Defaults to null (Nothing in VB).
object	Object	All types, predefined and user-defined, reference types and value types, inherit directly or indirectly from object (Object in VB). You can assign values of any type to variables of type object. Defaults to null (Nothing in VB).

The types in Table 4-1 represent some of the system types or types that are part of the .NET Framework. However, it's unlikely that everything that you need in your application can be put into the available types. You may need to create your own custom types. Custom types are covered later in this chapter, but for now you need to know that they provide the flexibility to create any kind of data container that may be needed to help solve the business problem.

Operators

Operators provide the capability to take action on an item—generally a variable. There are four main types of operators:

➤ Arithmetic

➤ Concatenation

➤ Comparison

➤ Logical

This section covers arithmetic and concatenation operators. You will learn about comparison and logical operators later in the chapter during the discussion of decision-making approaches.

Arithmetic Operators

Arithmetic operators are those operators that perform operations, or computations, on number types, such as addition, subtraction, multiplication and division. Table 4-2 describes these operators.

TABLE 4-2: Arithmetic Operators

C#	VB	DEFINITION
+	+	Adds one value to another
–	–	Subtracts one value from another
*	*	Multiplies two values
/	/	Divides one value into another
n/a	\	Divides one value into another, always returning a rounded integer
Math.Pow(x,y)	^	Raises one value to the power of another
%	Mod	Divides one value into another, returning the remainder

An example using these operators is shown here:

C#

```
int currentCount = 5;
int availableStock = currentCount + 1;    // availableStock = 6
int availableStock = currentCount - 2;    // availableStock = 4
double actualCost = availableStock * 3.5;    // actualCost = 14
double perItemCost = actualCost / 2;    // perItemCost = 7
double squaredValue = Math.Pow(perItemCost, 2);// squaredValue = 49
double remainder = actualCost % 2.5;    // remainder = 1.5
```

VB

```
Dim availableStock As Integer = currentCount + 1    ' availableStock = 6
Dim availableStock As Integer = currentCount - 2    ' availableStock = 4
Dim actualCost As Double = availableStock * 3.5    ' actualCost = 14
Dim perItemCost As Double = actualCost / 2    ' perItemCost = 7
Dim roundedDivision As Integer = actualCost \ 3    ' roundedDivision = 4
Dim squaredValue As Double = perItemCost ^ 2    ' squaredValue = 49
Dim remainder As Double = actualCost Mod 2.5    ' remainder = 1.5
```

Concatenation Operators

Whereas arithmetic operators are used for combining and working with numerical data, concatenation operators combine strings. These operators are different from arithmetic operators in that there is no concept of multiplication, division, or any other purely numeric operations. Instead, there is simply the combining of strings.

The two concatenation operators are + for C# and & for VB. They are used as shown in the following example:

C#

```
string itemName = "Electric Nail Gun";
string itemColor = "blue";

string sentence = "We have a " + itemColor + " " + itemName;
```

VB

```
Dim itemName As String = "Electric Nail Gun"
Dim itemColor as String = "blue"

Dim sentence as String = "We have a " & itemColor & " " & itemName
```

You create a more complete sentence by concatenating several variables together. Note that it is absolute—if you want a space between two values, you have to include that yourself; otherwise, the system directly appends the second string to the first string. In VB, the concatenation operator is different from the arithmetic operator, but in C# they are the same. However, if you use the concatenation operator with a non-string type, it automatically converts that non-string type to a string and uses that converted string during the concatenation operation.

Converting and Casting Data Types

There will be times when you need to convert one data type to another. One of the most common scenarios is converting a value to a string. This has to be done for display, as generally the only type that is ever displayed in a web page is a string. When you see a page that says "There are 5 Electric Nail Guns available" you know that the byte-typed variable you created in the preceding example was converted to a string for display.

Converting Data Types

Converting any type to a string is very simple—so simple, in fact, that if you append a .ToString() to all of your variables, you would see that it works, as it is a built-in capability of every type. That means the following will work:

C#

```
// declare our variable with the initial value
byte quantityInStock = 5;

// declare our string with the initial value
string itemName = "Electric Nail Gun";

// lots of work going on here as we figure out all the information

string sentence = "There are " + quantityInStock.ToString() + itemName;
```

VB

```
' declare our variable that represents the in-stock quantity for a particular item
Dim quantityInStock As Byte = 5

' declare our string that represents the name of the item
Dim itemName As String = "Electric Nail Gun"

// lots of work going on here as we figure out all the information

Dim sentence as String = "There are " & quantityInStock.ToString() & itemName
```

As mentioned earlier, there are also some built-in, automatic conversions. Both the "+" and "&" operators (in their respective language) act to combine, or add, different strings into a single string, so you can make your combined sentence. However, if you used the following approach, your effort would still be successful, because using these operators with mixed types is the same as converting all of the non-string types to string and combining them:

C#

```
...

string sentence = "There are " + quantityInStock + itemName;
```

VB

```
...

Dim sentence as String = "There are " & quantityInStock & itemName
```

Of course, because the concatenation is absolute, the string-converted version of `quantityInStock` and the `itemName` will be directly next to each other without a space separating them.

Doing a different type of conversion requires a different approach. This is where the `Convert` class becomes useful; it converts data in one type to data in another. It supports many different conversions and is simple to invoke, as shown here:

C#

```
DateTime orderDate = Convert.ToDateTime("01/14/2015");
```

VB

```
Dim orderDate as DateTime = Convert.ToDateTime("01/14/2015")
```

Many different conversions are supported by the `Convert` class. The preceding example shows a conversion from a string value to a DateTime, but there are many more. Table 4-3 describes all the options available when converting a type of double (Double in VB).

TABLE 4-3: Convert.ToDouble() Examples

CALL	DEFINITION
ToDouble(Boolean)	Converts the specified Boolean value to the equivalent double-precision floating-point number
ToDouble(Byte)	Converts the value of the specified 8-bit unsigned integer to the equivalent double-precision floating-point number
ToDouble(Char)	Calling this method always throws an `InvalidCastException`, which means the conversion will fail. You will learn more about exceptions in Chapter 17.
ToDouble(DateTime)	Calling this method always throws `InvalidCastException`.
ToDouble(Decimal)	Converts the value of the specified decimal number to an equivalent double-precision floating-point number
ToDouble(Double)	Returns the specified double-precision floating-point number; no actual conversion is performed
ToDouble(Int16)	Converts the value of the specified 16-bit signed integer to an equivalent double-precision floating-point number
ToDouble(Int32)	Converts the value of the specified 32-bit signed integer to an equivalent double-precision floating-point number
ToDouble(Int64)	Converts the value of the specified 64-bit signed integer to an equivalent double-precision floating-point number
ToDouble(Object)	Converts the value of the specified object to a double-precision floating-point number
ToDouble(SByte)	Converts the value of the specified 8-bit signed integer to the equivalent double-precision floating-point number
ToDouble(Single)	Converts the value of the specified single-precision floating-point number to an equivalent double-precision floating-point number
ToDouble(String)	Converts the specified string representation of a number to an equivalent double-precision floating-point number
ToDouble(UInt16)	Converts the value of the specified 16-bit unsigned integer to the equivalent double-precision floating-point number
ToDouble(UInt32)	Converts the value of the specified 32-bit unsigned integer to an equivalent double-precision floating-point number
ToDouble(UInt64)	Converts the value of the specified 64-bit signed integer to an equivalent double-precision floating-point number

As you can see, there are a lot of different types from which you can convert to a double; and only two of them will fail automatically. Some of the others may as well, such as from string or object, depending on the actual content of the data. Converting a string such as "165.32" converts successfully, while "I am not a number-like string" does not convert successfully.

The first approach to conversion discussed was ToString(), which converts any kind of type to a string. You can also try to convert a string to any other type with the Parse method. The following example shows how to use the Parse method.

C#

```
DateTime orderDate = DateTime.Parse("01/14/2015");
```

VB

```
Dim orderDate as DateTime = DateTime.Parse("01/14/2015")
```

The same rules for using the Convert method on a string apply when using the Parse method; the string value has to be a representative of the type to which the string is being parsed. Each type in .NET has a default Parse method that can be used to try to convert a string to the data type on which the Parse method is being called. An exception is thrown if the string value is not something that can be successfully parsed.

Casting Data Types

The last way to change one type to another is known as casting. Whereas the three methods just discussed involve converting one type to another, casting takes a different approach. It forces one type to become another. As you can imagine, this only happens for those types that are compatible with each other; you can cast an int to a double, for example, but you cannot cast a DateTime to a double. VB and C# both have different ways to cast items, as shown here:

C#
```
int baseCost = 100;

double pricePaid = (double)baseCost;
//OR
double pricePaid = baseCost as double;
```

VB

```
Dim baseCost As Int = 100

Dim pricePaid As Double = DirectCast(baseCost, Double)
'OR
Dim pricePaid As Double = CType(baseCost, Double)
```

When using C#, you have two approaches to casting. The first is to put the target type in parentheses before the variable to be cast. If the types are of incompatible types this could cause a runtime error. The second type of casting uses the as keyword, which is a little friendlier, in that if the types are incompatible no exception is thrown; instead, the variable being converted to is set to null.

There are also two different ways to cast in VB, CType and DirectCast. CType is more flexible than DirectCast because it allows you to cast between types that look similar, while DirectCast only allows you to cast between compatible types. As with the cast in C#, either of these approaches in VB causes an exception to be thrown when the types are not compatible.

Using Arrays and Collections

So far in this chapter you have learned that a type is a single unit, such as an integer or a string. However, groups of units are commonly used as you work through an application. There are two main approaches to grouping items: arrays and collections. An array is basically a stack of items with the same type. There is not much support to an array; items are identified by their index, or the number that shows their stack rank. A collection is a type that contains multiple objects, generally of the same type, with additional support built in to make them easier to use.

Using Arrays

All types can be easily converted into an array of types. You do this in C# by appending square brackets, [], after the type. In VB, parentheses, (), indicate an arrays after the type declaration. When you are building arrays you need to know how many items will be stored, because that information is part of the declaration. The following examples show how this is done:

C#

```
byte[] quantitiesInStock = new byte[2];

string[] itemNames = new string[2];
```

VB

```
Dim quantitiesInStock(1) As Byte

Dim itemNames(1) As String
```

These two approaches each create a list that can hold two items. As you can see, this means different things to C# than it does to VB. In C#, you set the array with the quantity of items that you are going to be storing in the array; in this case, two. VB is different in that you define the highest index that will be reached. Because arrays are zero-indexed lists, you use a "1" in your definition to indicate that the last value you use is 1, while the list actually contains two items, indexed at 0 and 1.

> **NOTE** An array is a zero-indexed list of units. When you hear zero-indexed, that means that the first item in the list is at space 0. Thus, the second item in the list is at space 1. This can lead to confusion, because getting the count of items in the list results in a value that is higher than your highest index.

When you work with arrays, you access the individual items in the list by their index, as shown here:

C#

```
string[] itemNames = new string[2];
itemNames[0] = "Electric Nail Gun";
itemNames[1] = "20 lb Sledge Hammer";
string secondName = itemNames[1];
```

VB

```
Dim itemNames(1) As String
itemNames(0) = "Electric Nail Gun"
itemNames(1) = "20 lb Sledge Hammer"
Dim secondName As String = itemNames(1)
```

Note you have to instantiate the array with a count or upper limit; so if you try to access the array outside of that count, an error is thrown. The following example throws an exception indicating that you are accessing the array outside of the index range:

C#

```
string[] itemNames = new string[2];
itemNames[0] = "Electric Nail Gun";
itemNames[1] = "20 lb Sledge Hammer";
itemNames[2] = "Does not matter what my name is, I am going to cause an exception";
```

VB

```
Dim itemNames(1) As String
itemNames(0) = "Electric Nail Gun"
itemNames(1) = "20 lb Sledge Hammer"
itemNames(2) = "Does not matter what my name is, I am going to cause an exception"
```

You have the opportunity to resize an array to prevent the throwing of the exception. C# has an `Array.Resize` method, whereas VB has the `ReDim` and `Preserve` keywords. `ReDim` tells the system to resize the array, while the `Preserve` keyword ensures that the original values are retained during the resizing process. Following are examples:

C#

```
string[] itemNames = new string[2];
itemNames[0] = "Electric Nail Gun";
itemNames[1] = "20 lb Sledge Hammer";
Array.Resize(ref itemNames, 3);
itemNames[2] = "I no longer cause an exception";
```

VB

```
Dim itemNames(1) As String
```

```
itemNames(0) = "Electric Nail Gun"
itemNames(1) = "20 lb Sledge Hammer"
ReDim Preserve itemNames(2)
itemNames(2) = "I no longer cause an exception"
```

Arrays are good to work with if all you want to do is load a known set of data and work with those items by index, because it's a fast way to manage a set of data as long as you know how large that data set will be. While both languages provide the capability to resize the array, it is an expensive process. The need to dimension the array limits their flexibility. Another side effect that enforces this limitation is that when an array is instantiated with an upper limit, the system automatically uses the allocated amount of storage for that array. This means, for example, that declaring an array with an upper bound of 1,000 would be counterproductive and impair performance if there will be considerably less than 1,000 members in the list.

Using Collections

Collections can be considered super-arrays. They enable you to better manage the information within the list than would an array. You can work with them as if they were arrays by accessing items by their index; but rather than having to limit your collection to a particular size, you instead just instantiate your collection and then add items to it, from one item to one billion items. As with arrays, collections are zero indexed; the first item in the collection will be in position 0.

Collections are a bit more complex than arrays in that they introduce the concept of a generic. A generic is a .NET construct that enables the creation of a special type that works with other types. It is generic because this special type works with any other type. Here is an example:

C#

```
List<string> itemNames = new List<string>();

List<byte> quantitiesInStock = new List<byte>();
```

VB

```
Dim itemNames As New List(Of String)

Dim quantitiesInStock As New List(Of Byte)
```

Here a new type is introduced, the List. It is a generic list in that the same type can be used to hold any other type. The preceding example sets itemNames equal to a List that contains strings, and quantitiesInStock to a List that contains bytes. This provides flexibility because the list accepts any type while still providing type-safety, in that when you instantiate the type, you define the type that is contained in the list.

Defining the type is important when using generic methods in order to ensure type-safety. That's why the type to be stored is part of the definition—List<string> in C# and List(of String) in VB, so that the compiler understands the type that needs to be enforced.

GENERICS

This discussion has barely scratched the surface of the power that generics brings to .NET. Microsoft has a good MSDN article on generics if you are interested in learning more about how they work and how you can incorporate them into your application. See `https://msdn.microsoft.com/en-us/library/ms172192(v=vs.110).aspx`.

Once you have the `List` defined, working with it is standard, regardless of the type that it contains. Table 4-4 shows some of the standard ways of working with items in a list.

TABLE 4-4: Using a List

METHOD NAME	DESCRIPTION

Add	Adds an item of the correct type to the list:
	
	`C# - itemNames.Add("Electric Nail Gun")`
	
	`VB - itemNames.Add("Electric Nail Gun")`

AddRange	Adds a list of items to another list of items; both lists have to contain items of the same type:
	
	`C# - itemNames.AddRange(anotherListOfStrings)`
	
	`VB - itemNames.AddRange(anotherListOfStrings)`

Clear	Removes all items from the list, basically emptying the list:
	
	`C# - itemNames.Clear()`
	
	`VB - itemNames.Clear()`

Contains	Determines if the list already contains the same value. The method returns a Boolean indicating whether the value is in the list:
	
	`C# - bool isItemInList = itemNames.Contains("Electric Nail`
	`      Gun")`
	
	`VB - Dim isItemInList As Boolean =`
	`      itemNames.Contains("Electric Nail Gun")`

Insert	Adds an item to a list at a particular place in the list. The value that is passed into the method is the zero-based index:
	
	`C# - itemNames.Insert(2, "Electric Nail Gun")`
	
	`VB - itemNames.Insert(2, "Electric Nail Gun")`

METHOD NAME	DESCRIPTION

InsertRange	Allows you to add another list of items at a specific location in the list:
	`C# - itemNames.InsertRange(3, anotherListOfStrings)`
	`VB - itemNames.InsertRange(3, anotherListOfStrings)`

Remove	Removes a particular value in the list:
	`C# - itemNames.Remove("Electric Nail Gun")`
	`VB - itemNames.Remove("Electric Nail Gun")`

RemoveAt	Removes the value at a particular index:
	`C# - itemNames.Remove(3)`
	`VB - itemNames.Remove(3)`

RemoveRange	Removes a range of values. It is like a RemoveAt except that you also pass in an integer defining how many items to remove. The following examples remove two items from the list, starting at index = 3:
	`C# - itemNames.Remove(3, 2)`
	`VB - itemNames.Remove(3, 2)`

There are many other functions that you can perform with lists that you cannot do with arrays, but they are out of the scope of this chapter. Others are introduced as you work through the sample application. As you move forward in your development career, you will find generic lists to be one of the most functional components of .NET. Working with collections is one of the most common tasks that developers do, and the .NET Framework includes in a lot of support for it.

Decision-Making Operations

A typical application is a series of actions and decisions: The system does some work and then looks at something to determine what step to next take. These determinations, or decisions, are critical in a modern system because virtually every step your application makes is based on the outcome of some previous action. This section walks through a scenario that is included in the sample application.

Our application holds a list of items, one or more of which may be available for lending. You know how many are available because there is a count of `AvailableItems`; thus, if the value in that property is greater than 0, you know that at least one item is available for lending. This determination of availability, based on whether the count is greater than 0, is a decision.

There are two primary decision-making statements, `if`, `then`, `else` and `switch\select case`. Both evaluate whether a certain condition exists. Typically, you would check whether a value has a relationship to another value and then return a Boolean (true/false) value that indicates whether that relationship exists. Creating and properly evaluating this relationship requires one of the operators that mentioned earlier in the chapter, the comparison operator.

Comparison Operators

Comparison operators are designed to evaluate the relationship between two different items and determine whether the relationship between those two items is what is expected. If the relationship between the two items matches the operator's expectation, then the operator returns True, else it returns False. The standard comparison operators are described in Table 4-5.

TABLE 4-5: Comparison Operators

C#	VB	DESCRIPTION
==	=	Evaluates whether two values are equal to each other. Note how C# has the double equals sign; this ensures that the compiler understands the difference between assigning a value and determining whether they are equal.
!=	<>	Evaluates whether two values are not equal to each other
>	>	Evaluates whether the first value is greater than the second value
<	<	Evaluates whether the first value is less than the second value
>=	>=	Evaluates whether the first value is greater than or equal to the second value
<=	<=	Evaluates whether the first value is less than or equal to the second value
is	Is	C#: Determines whether an object is a specific type VB: Determines whether two objects are the same

Comparison operators are the key to making decisions. The following examples show what they can do:

C#

```
int smallNumber = 3;
int largeNumber = 4;

smallNumber == largeNumber // returns false - 3 is not equal to 4
smallNumber != largeNumber // returns true - 3 is not equal to 4
smallNumber > largeNumber // returns false - 3 is not greater than 4
smallNumber < largeNumber // returns true - 3 is less that 4
smallNumber >= largeNumber // returns false - 3 is not greater than or equal to 4
smallNumber <= largeNumber // returns true - 3 is less than 4
smallNumber is double // returns false - smallNumber is an int, not a double
```

VB

```
Dim smallNumber As Integer = 3
Dim largeNumber As Integer = 4
```

```
smallNumber = largeNumber ' returns false - 3 is not equal to 4
smallNumber <> largeNumber ' returns true - 3 is not equal to 4
smallNumber > largeNumber ' returns false - 3 is not greater than 4
smallNumber < largeNumber ' returns true - 3 is less that 4
smallNumber >= largeNumber ' returns false - 3 is not greater than or equal to 4
smallNumber <= largeNumber ' returns true - 3 is less than 4
TypeOf smallNumber is Double ' returns false - item is an Integer, not a Double
```

Because the result of each of these operators is a Boolean value, you can use this result to evaluate whether the information fits a defined criterion.

Logical Operators

Comparison operators are important in helping your code make decisions. Generally, however, it is not as simple as a single condition check. Sometimes you may need to make multiple checks at the same time. This is where logical operators come in—they enable you to link multiple comparisons together using words such as AND as well as OR. This greatly expands your ability to analyze the condition of your data so that your code makes the appropriate the decisions. The logical operators are described in Table 4-6.

TABLE 4-6: Logical Operators

C#	VB	DESCRIPTION
And	&	Returns true only when all comparisons return true
Or	|	Returns true when at least one of the comparisons returns true
Not	!	Reverses the outcome, turning a true into false or vice versa
AndAlso	&&	Checks each condition from left to right (subject to precedence) and returns false as soon as one of the comparisons fails
OrElse	||	Checks each condition from left to right, and returns true as soon as one of the conditions returns true

These operators are demonstrated in the following examples:

C#

```
int smallNumber = 3;
int largeNumber = 4;

smallNumber == largeNumber || smallNumber != largeNumber
            // returns true - the 2nd condition is true
smallNumber != largeNumber && smallNumber > largeNumber
        // returns false - the 2nd condition is false
smallNumber == largeNumber | smallNumber != largeNumber
            // returns true - the 2nd condition is true
smallNumber != largeNumber & smallNumber > largeNumber
        // returns false - the 2nd condition is false
```

VB

```
Dim smallNumber As Integer = 3
Dim largeNumber As Integer = 4

smallNumber == largeNumber OrAlso smallNumber != largeNumber
              ' returns true - the 2nd condition is true
smallNumber != largeNumber AndAlso smallNumber > largeNumber
         ' returns false - the 2nd condition is false
smallNumber == largeNumber Or smallNumber != largeNumber
              ' returns true - the 2nd condition is true
smallNumber != largeNumber And smallNumber > largeNumber
         ' returns false - the 2nd condition is false
```

The differences between the || and |, Or and OrElse in VB is important. These differences, also seen with the && operator, cause the processor to move from the left to the right, evaluating the comparisons in order. If the system finds something that determines the answer to the question, the solution returns immediately, rather than proceeding through the entire list of conditions. Consider the following snippet:

C#

```
string name;
name != null & name.Length > 10
```

VB

```
Dim name As String = Nothing
name <> Nothing And name.Length > 10
```

The way that it is coded now, if the string is set to null (Nothing in VB), then the framework will react poorly as you try to find out about some information on the null object, as this causes a NullReferenceException. Replacing the & with a && and the And with AndElse prevents this from happening; the comparison will fail as soon as it evaluates the null.

If Statement

The first decision-making approach that uses the comparison and logical operators is the if, then, else statement, which evaluates a condition and then takes a particular action based on that decision. The following code snippet shows what this looks like:

C#

```
int availableItems = 1;

if (availableItems > 0) // evaluates whether there are available items
{
    // do some work here
}
else
{
```

```
        } // display a message that there are no available items to lend
```

VB

```
Dim availableItems As Integer = 1

If availableItems > 0 Then 'evaluates whether there are available items
    ' do some work here
Else
    ' display a message that there are no available items to lend
End If
```

As you can see, the structure of this statement is different for each language. C# uses the curly braces, {}, to define the code block that will run based on the results of the evaluation. In VB, the code block that is run is based on the code between the If - Else - and End If keywords. Another difference between the two languages is that C# expects the comparison to be contained within parentheses, whereas VB evaluates the statements between the If and Then keywords. All of the comparison operators listed in Table 4-5 are used when evaluating these conditions.

The example makes only one evaluation; you basically have two choices for the flow. However, you can add additional branches to the process:

C#

```
int availableItems = 1;

if (availableItems > 1) // evaluates whether there are available items
{
    // do some work here
}
else if (availableItems == 1)
{
    // do some special work when there is only one item left
}
else
{
    // display a message that there are no available items to lend
}
```

VB

```
Dim availableItems As Integer = 1

If availableItems > 1 Then 'evaluates whether there are available items
    ' do some work here
ElseIf availableItems = 1 Then
    ' do some special work when there is only one item left
Else
    ' display a message that there are no available items to lend
End If
```

Using the additional condition adds flexibility to the if statement. However, there is another statement that is designed to handle multiple evaluations. In C#, this is the switch statement; in VB it is called the Select Case.

Switch/Select Case Statement

The switch / Select Case statement is used to evaluate a value against a set of known values. It is different from the If statement in that there is no set of operators that are used; all the various options are assumed to be "equals." Here is an example:

C#

```
switch (availableItems)
{
    case 1:
        // do some special work when there is only one item left
        break;
    case 0:
        // display a message that there are no available items to lend
        break;
    default:
        // do some work here
        break;
}
```

VB

```
Select Case availableItems
    Case 1
        ' do some special work when there is only one item left
    Case 0
        ' display a message that there are no available items to lend
    Case Else
        ' do some work here
End Select
```

As mentioned previously, it is expected that one of the cases will match the item being evaluated. If no item matches the case, the statement selects the default case if there is one. This default case is identified with the keyword default in C# or by the phrase Case Else in VB. If the statement does not have this choice, then processing continues on the next statement after the closing curly brace (C#) or the End Select (VB).

Loops

One of the most common things that a developer does with a list of information is to go through the list and take the same action on each item. The process of repeating a set of code multiple times in a row is called *looping*, because the code flow loops from the beginning through the end of a code block and back to the beginning of the code block as many times as needed.

There are three main types of loops: for, for each, and do. Each represents a different way to satisfy the same need of enabling a set of code to be run multiple times.

For Loop

A for loop requires that you understand exactly how many times you are going to be running through the loop before you start the processing. This approach to looping looks like the following:

C#

```csharp
for(int loopCounter = 0; loopCounter < 5; loopCounter++)
{
    // do some work here 5 times
}
```

VB

```vb
For loopCounter As Integer = 1 To 5
    ' do some work here 5 times
Next
```

These constructs are quite different in terms of how they work with the information. In C#, the construction of the `for` has three sections separated by a semicolon. This semicolon is C#'s indication that the code has reached the end of processing for that section. The three sections in order are as follows:

➤ `int LoopCounter = 0` : This is the start condition. It sets the variable that will be used to trace the amount of times that the loop executes.

➤ `loopCounter < 5` : As long as this condition is true, the looping continues, so in this case the loop will continue until `loopCounter >= 5`.

➤ `loopCounter++` : This defines the step that will be taken at the end of each loop. In this case, the variable `loopCounter` is incremented by one each time the code block is processed.

INCREMENT AND DECREMENT OPERATORS AND ASSIGNMENT SHORTCUTS

Two common operators that you have yet to work with are the increment (++) and decrement (--) operators. These operators are only available in C# but you will find them very useful in loops and other processes that require a running count. These operators can go before the variable being incremented, such as "++variable", or after the variable, like "variable++". However, they have different results, as the order of precedence goes from left to right. Thus, in the preceding example with the `for` loop, the `loopCounter` is evaluated and then incremented. If the code were written with a `++loopCounter`, then the item would be incremented before evaluation; thus, the code would only be processed four times rather than the expected five times.

This does not mean that there is no easy way to do this short-cut approach of incrementing or decrementing a variable in VB, however. Both languages offer the capability to shortcut the assignment operator and an arithmetic operator. This allows `loopCounter += 1` to be equivalent to the ++ operators; the += is interpreted the same as `loopCounter = loopCounter + 1`.

Creating the `For` statement in VB is more obvious. The `For` keyword defines the starting point, and the assignment specifies the range for the loop: in the preceding example, `1 To 5`. The code within the `For` and `Next` keywords is the code block to be processed.

This is a simple application of the `For` loop. You can also use this construct to access every item in a collection. As you can imagine, this is an extremely useful implementation. Creating a `For` loop that iterates through each item in a collection is shown here:

C#

```
List<string> collection = new List<string>();

// do some work to put a lot of items into the list

for(int loopCounter = 0; loopCounter < collection.Count; loopCounter++)
{
    collection[loopCounter] += " processed";
    // do some work here as many times as there is items in the list
}
```

VB

```
Dim collection As New List(Of String)

' do some work to put a lot of items into the list

For loopCounter As Integer = 0 To collection.Count - 1
    Collection(loopCounter) += " processed"
    ' do some work here as many times as there is items in the list
Next
```

When you review the code, keep in mind that collections, like arrays, are zero-indexed. This is why the loop initialization starts with a 0. Also, because the count of the number of items in the collection is not zero-indexed, you have to ensure that you don't try to get an item at an index that is the same as the count of the collection. Doing so would result in being one item past the end and thus result in a runtime exception.

The `For` loop has some complexity in setup, and when working with collections it allows for the possibility that you might call an item outside the allowed range. Fortunately, another loop structure was created purely to work with collections, and it is very easy to set up: the `foreach` or `For Each`.

Foreach/For Each Loops

This approach to looping is designed specifically to work with collections, as it easily identifies each item in the list. The following example shows how these work:

C#

```
List<string> collection = new List<string>();

// do some work to put a lot of items into the list

foreach(string item in collection)
{
    item += " processed";
    // do some work here as many times as there is items in the list
}
```

VB

```
Dim collection As New List(Of String)

' do some work to put a lot of items into the list

For Each item As String In collection.Count
    item += " processed"
    ' do some work here as many times as there is items in the list
Next
```

The primary thing to notice here is that the foreach/For Each structure takes each one of the items in the collection, names it (item in the example), and then works with that named variable while within the loop. These variables are not available outside the loop, but any changes that are made to each item in the loop will persist with the item in the list after the loop is completed.

Both the for and for each loops have a safety factor; they have a built-in end. The for ends when the condition is completed, while the foreach ends when the list is completed. The last type of loop, the while loop, does not have the same protection built into it.

While Loop

The while loop processes until a condition is met. An example of code creating a while loop is shown here:

C#

```
bool isDone = false;
int total = 0;

while (!isDone)
{
    if (total > 100)
    {
        isDone = true;
    }
}
```

VB

```
Dim isDone As Boolean = False
Dim total as Integer = 0

While Not isDone
    If total > 100 Then
        isDone = True
    End If
End While
```

You have to be careful with While loops because they lack a built-in terminator.

Exiting Loops

There are a few keywords that you can use to exit the loop from within it. These keywords, `break` for C# and `Exit For` in VB, immediately stop the code flow within the loop.

C#

```
List<string> collection = new List<string>();

// do some work to put a lot of items into the list

for(int loopCounter = 0; loopCounter < collection.Count; loopCounter++)
{
    if (loopCounter > 100)
    {
        break;
    }
}
```

VB

```
Dim collection As New List(Of String)

' do some work to put a lot of items into the list

For loopCounter As Integer = 0 To collection.Count - 1
    If loopCounter > 100 Then
        Exit For
    End If
Next
```

ORGANIZING CODE

One of the most useful features in ASP.NET is the capability to extract code used in different places and put it in a central place from which all the other pieces of code that may need to run it can call it. This eliminates the need to copy and paste code all over your application, and it's quite useful when a defect needs to be resolved: Fixing it in one area of your code fixes any other pages that use that code.

Suppose, for example, your application will display recent news headlines in every page of your site. Rather than copy the code multiple times to achieve that, you can put the necessary code in a common place from which every page that needs it can call it. Write it once, call it often.

This is where code organization becomes important. Now that you know that this code should be located where numerous pages can call it, the next challenge is determining how to organize the code such that it makes sense and is easy to find and call from the rest of your application.

Methods: Functions and Subroutines

Functions and subroutines are ways to create blocks of code that can be called from other code. As covered later in this chapter in the discussion of object-oriented design, both of these approaches are also known as methods. There are two types of methods—one returns a type to the caller and the other doesn't return a type. In C# you use the same kind of approach when building either type of method; however, it is different in VB. Functions and subroutines are VB keywords; a `Function` returns a type, while a `Sub` does not. The following example shows how you call these two types of methods:

C#

```
string thirdWord = GetThirdWord(); // call a method called GetThirdWord

DoSomeWork();  // call a method called DoSomeWork
```

VB

```
Dim thirdWord As String = GetThirdWord()   'call a method called GetThirdWord

DoSomeWork()        'call a method called DoSomeWork
```

As you may have noticed, there are two main differences between a method and a variable. First, when calling a method you do not have to define the type. Second, the method is called with parentheses. These parentheses are important, because you can pass information into a method as well as get a type returned. This could look like the following:

C#

```
string completeSentence = "I am a much longer sentence";

// call a method called GetThirdWord, passing in another string
string thirdWord = GetThirdWord(completeSentence);
```

VB

```
Dim completeSentence As String= "I am a much longer sentence"

' call a method called GetThirdWord, passing in another string
Dim thirdWord As String = GetThirdWord(completeSentence)
```

Calling a method is straightforward. Defining and creating methods are more complicated. The following snippet shows a simple method that takes a string, uses the `Split` method to break the parameter into an array, and then returns the third value in the array (remember it is zero-indexed):

C#

```
public string GetThirdWord(string sentenceToParse)
{
    string[] words = sentenceToParse.Split(' ');
    return words[2];
}
```

VB

```
Public Function GetThirdWord(sentenceToParse As String) As String
```

```
      Dim words As String() = Split(sentenceToParse, " ")
      Return words(2)
   End Function
```

It was mentioned earlier that there is a type of method that doesn't return anything; instead, it does a unit of work and then ends. The following code snippet shows how this type of method is created:

C#

```
public void DoSomeWork()
{
    // code doing some work here
}
```

VB

```
Public Sub DoSomeWork()
    ' code doing some work here
End Function
```

The key is the return type. In C# there is no return type; instead, the method is labeled as void to indicate the lack of return. VB is different in that rather than a `Function`, which includes a return type, it is instead a `Sub` (short for subroutine).

Writing Comments and Documentation

Most of the code snippets in this chapter include some text that explains what the code is doing. This approach is useful not only for instructional books such as this, but also for any kind of coding. In an ideal world, you would write perfect code that would be perfectly suited to any future purpose. Were that even possible, however, it will almost certainly be worked on by someone who has never seen it before and who may have minimal contextual background. Or, because it was written so long ago, you yourself may not remember what decisions you made or why you made them. For these reasons, adding comments is useful, especially in areas of your code that may be complex or implement specific business rules.

Inline comments are those within the body of your code. These are usually used to provide additional details about that section of your code as shown in the following snippets. They may also be used to remove some lines of code when you are doing a refactoring; you don't want the code to be run but nor do you want to completely remove it until you are confident that the new code works as expected.

C#

```
// comment on its own line
int Id = 3; // comment on the same line as code

/*
* C# has a special comment type for doing multiple lines
```

```
* at the start you put the slash - asterisk and the end is asterisk and slash
* everything in between is commented out.  There is no comparable
* facility in VB
*/
```

VB

```
' comment on its own line
Dim Id as Integer = 3  ' comment on same line as code
```

You can enter the comments manually, or you can highlight the lines you want to comment, such as when commenting out existing code, and click the Add Comment button on the toolbar.

You can also add comments to methods. You may have noticed how IntelliSense provides information about the items that you may be selecting. You can have your methods provide the same kind of support through a different kind of comment, XML comments. XML comments enable you to add extra details to your methods, basically adding comments that apply to the entire method. The following snippets show you how to do this:

C#

```
/// <summary>Does some work on the parameter</summary>
/// <param name="thingToDoWorkOn">The thing that will have work done on it.</param>
/// <returns>This method returns true if the work was done successfully.</returns>
public bool DoSomeWork(string thingToDoWorkOn)
{
    // code doing some work here
    return true;
}
```

VB

```
''' <summary>Does some work on the parameter</summary>
''' <param name="thingToDoWorkOn">The thing that will have work done on it.</param>
''' <returns>This method returns true if the work was done successfully.</returns>
Public Function DoSomeWork(thingToDoWorkOn As String) As Boolean
    ' code doing some work here
    Return True
End Function
```

Several tags are available, each of which plays a different part in the documentation. The content in the summary element is displayed in IntelliSense, so it needs to give potential users enough information about the method that they can determine whether it is the method they need. Because the code is separated out to enable use in multiple areas, any additional support you provide based on the XML comments will be useful. The param element contains a description of the parameter that is being passed in, while the returns element provides a description of what is returned and what it means in the context of the method. Figure 4-1 shows how the XML comments help provide information in IntelliSense.

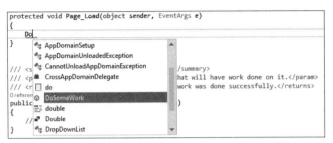

FIGURE 4-1: Demonstration of XML comments in IntelliSense

Comments become more important as methods and the work that they do gets further away from the code that may be requesting the work. Recall that earlier it was noted that moving the code into a shared area increases reuse. This software development approach, based on determining the best way to understand and organize code, is known as *object-oriented programming*.

OBJECT-ORIENTED PROGRAMMING BASICS

Object-oriented programming (OOP) is an approach to programming whereby everything that is part of your application can be defined as an object, or something that has properties and can take actions. This is fundamental to .NET, as everything is, at the base, an object. You can see this demonstrated with the following code snippets:

C#
```
int iAmAnInteger = 6;

object nowIAmAnObject = (object)iAmAnInteger;
```

VB
```
Dim iAmAnInteger as Integer = 6

Dim nowIAmAnObject as Object = DirectCast(iAmAnInteger, Object)
```

Everything in .NET can be successfully cast, or converted, into an object. Why should you care about this? It's important because it illustrates that an application can be viewed as a series of interactions between different objects.

When you review the requirements for the sample application you can see different kinds of constructs that would be useful. The following list describes these constructs, or ways to define parts of the program:

➤ **Item:** The material that is loaned

➤ **User:** The person who checks out the item

➤ **Order:** Represents the list of items that were checked out by the person

A preliminary review of the requirements resulted in three different objects that you need to define in the application. As you start getting into the implementation, you will discover more useful objects, but this provides a good starting point for the discussion.

IMPORTANT OO TERMINOLOGY

The preliminary list of objects that were just defined for the sample application are your starting blocks. In this section you'll look at how you build these out to be useful within the ASP.NET application.

Classes

An object is defined by the key word "class." The following snippet demonstrates creating a class that represents an Item—the thing that will be loaned out from the library:

C#
```
public class Item
{
}
```

VB
```
Public Class Item

End Class
```

The use of brackets (for C#) and the End keyword (for VB) indicate the expectation that a class contains other items.

A class, or object, can be considered a container for other information. The first type of information that it contains is called a descriptor. When you consider the item that will be loaned, there is a minimal set of information that can be used to describe that object. This minimal set of information is as follows:

- Name
- Description
- Cost
- ItemNumber
- Picture
- Person who has it checked out
- Date it was checked out
- Date it is due back in
- Date it was acquired
- Whether it is currently available

There are two different approaches to including this information about the class, fields and properties.

Fields

Fields are a way to store information within a class. Typically, a field is used to store information that isn't accessed by anything outside of the class, but that is not a requirement.

ACCESS MODIFIERS

You have seen the keyword `public` in some of the examples. This is an access modifier; it determines what can access the item to which it is applied. `Public`, the modifier used until now, means that any block of code can access that item. Another access modifier is `private`. Using this keyword indicates that the item being modified is not accessible outside of its defining class.

Classes, methods, fields, and properties can all have access modifiers as part of their definitions. You cannot make an internal item more accessible than the containing item; that is, a private class cannot have a public property.

A field is defined within a class as follows:

C#

```
public class Item
{
    private double temporaryValue;
}
```

VB

```
Public Class Item

    Private temporaryValue as Double

End Class
```

Setting the field is simple, and nothing happens when a field is set, other than the value changing. This is also familiar because it is how you were defining and setting variables up until now. The other approach to creating information holders in a class is more powerful in that it allows work to happen when a value is set or when its value is "gotten" or used. This other approach uses a property.

Properties

A property is different from a field in that the property is intended to define the characteristics of the object, whereas the field is intended to serve as a way to make types accessible within the class. The list created earlier includes all properties of an `Item`. Properties are defined differently than fields as well, as shown in the following code snippet, which shows the creation of properties:

C#

```
public class Item
{
    public string Name { get; set; }
}
```

VB

```
Public Class Item

    Public Property Name() as String

End Class
```

In C#, the difference between a field and a property is the addition of the `{ get; set; }`, whereas VB has a different keyword to demonstrate that the item being referred to is a property rather than a field. Also note that the property name has parentheses following it, just like the methods covered earlier.

The preceding snippet shows the easiest way to create a simple property. However, if you look at a more complete implementation, you start to see some of the power that is available. The following snippets show a different approach to creating a property:

C#

```
public class Item
{
    public string Name { get; set; }

    public string ShortName
    {
        get
        {
            if (Name.Length > 10)
            {
                return Name.Substring(0, 10);
            }
            else
            {
                return Name;
            }
        }
    }
}
```

VB

```
Public Class Item

    Public Property Name() as String

    Public Property ShortName() as String
        Get
            If Name.Length > 10 Then
                Return Name
            Else
                Return Name.Substring(0, 10)
            End If
        End Get
    End Property


End Class
```

Note several differences in this code snippet. While the Name property remains the same, a ShortName property has been added. Also added is some logic under the get keyword that determines whether the Name property is longer than 10 characters. If so, it returns the first 10 characters; when the Name is less than 10 characters, the value of the Name property is returned.

This shows you the power of properties as opposed to fields; they can perform business logic when they are gotten or set. When a property is accessed with the intention of getting its value, it is gotten, so it runs through the get code group. If the property is accessed so that it can be given, or assigned, a value, this access happens through the set code group.

Another aspect of a property displayed in the preceding code snippet is that the ShortName does not have a set code section. That means that trying to set the value will fail; in this case it "sets itself" by calculating its own value based on the value of another property.

The last aspect of a property to note is that you need to manage the actual value of the item if you are going to be doing some logic. You saw the shortcut way to create a property in the preceding example. It's called a shortcut because the work it does behind the scenes is equivalent to the following code snippet:

C#

```
private string _name;

public string Name
{
    get { return _name; }
    set { _name = value; }
}
```

VB

```
Private _firstName As String
```

```
Public Property FirstName() As String
    Get
        Return _firstName
    End Get
    Set(value As String)
        _firstName = value
    End Set
End Property
```

This concept of a backing field is important when working with properties because as soon as you start to do business logic, you lose the capability to use that property as an actual container. The preceding ShortName example didn't need to actually hold a value; it just performed a calculation on another property and returned the results from that action. Consider a different example. Suppose there is a business requirement that an item needs to have an AcquiredDate, the day that the item was acquired by the library. When an item doesn't have a date already assigned, the AcquiredDate should be set to the first day the library was in operation, January 5, 2014. The following code snippet shows how you can do that:

C#

```csharp
private DateTime _acquiredDate;

public DateTime AcquiredDate
{
    get
    {
        if (_acquiredDate == DateTime.MinValue)
//you use MinValue because that is what DateTime is created with
        {
            _acquiredDate = new DateTime(2014, 1, 5);
        }
        return _acquiredDate;
    }
    set { _acquiredDate = value; }
}
```
VB
```vb
Private _acquiredDate As DateTime

Public Property AcquiredDate () As DateTime
    Get
        If acquiredDate = DateTime.MinValue Then
            _acquiredDate = new DateTime(2014, 1, 5)
        End If
        Return acquiredDate
    End Get
    Set(value As DateTime)
        _ acquiredDate = value
    End Set
End Property
```

Here, the getter first checks whether the private value has been set to the `DateTime.MinValue`, the default value when a `DateTime` object is created. If it has that value, then it means that no "real" date was set; therefore, the rule kicks in and sets the date to the appropriate value. In addition, because not only is the value returned but the backing field is set, so the next time the getter is called the value is returned automatically without having to be reset. Also, if an outside action wants to set the value, it is able to do so without any problem; and if the value is set before the get is requested, then it will have the proper data. You will see how this works in more detail when you start working with databases in Chapter 9.

Methods

You have already spent some time looking at methods and how they are created. However, these become important when you consider objects, because objects can contain more than just properties and fields; they can contain methods as well. When a method is part of an object, the expectation is that the method performs an action on that object. This kind of approach provides abstraction, meaning that consumers of the object do not have to know everything about the object to make it work. The following code snippet shows a method on an `Item` that handles the process of a person checking out that item:

C#

```
public void CheckoutItem(Person personWhoCheckedOutItem, DateTime dateDue)
{
    CheckedOutBy = personWhoCheckedOutItem;
    DateOut = DateTime.Now;
    DateExpectedIn = dateDue;
    // lots of other work happening here
}
```

VB

```
Public Sub CheckoutItem(personWhoCheckedOutItem As Person, dateDue as DateTime)
    CheckedOutBy = personWhoCheckedOutItem
    DateOut = DateTime.Now
    DateExpectedIn = dateDue
    ' lots of other work happening here
End Function
```

This enables the calling code to perform its work without understanding exactly what is happening beneath the covers; the code just calls the method with the assumption that it is taking care of everything that the `Item` may need to do to be checked out. Methods are not the only way that you can perform actions on objects. Objects can also do work on themselves during their construction.

Constructors

Constructors are OO-based ways to manage the creation or instantiation of an item. In an earlier example you had a getter check a value and change the value as needed. Another solution would be to create the object with the default value being the desired value, rather than having the value check it each time it is called. The following code snippet demonstrates how this could be done through the use of a constructor:

C#

```csharp
public class Item
{
    public Item()
    {
        AcquiredDate = new DateTime(2014, 1, 5);
    }

    public DateTime AcquiredDate { get; set; }
}
```

VB

```vb
Public Class Item

    Public Sub New()
        AcquiredDate = New DateTime(2014, 1, 5)
    End Sub

    Public Property AcquiredDate As DateTime

End Class
```

The constructor in C# does not have a return type, and the name of the code block is identical to the class name. VB does it differently in that the constructor is a subroutine (Sub), with the name being the keyword New.

Because the constructor is really a special method that is called during instantiation of the object, it can have parameters as well. You can see how that would work by looking at the work you are doing in the constructor; the DateTime object is being instantiated using parameters for the constructor, the year, the month, and the day.

Inheritance

That anything in .NET can be cast as an object indicates one more key feature of object-oriented programming: inheritance. Inheritance enables you to build a type based upon another type, so the new type has all the properties and methods of the inherited type. Although inheritance is not part of the example application's requirements, this section takes a look at how the application could use it if needed, as you will almost certainly make use of inheritance in subsequent development work you do.

You have looked at the Item object and the role that it plays as the thing to be checked out. Imagine that you need to store a lot more information that may be specific to the type of item. For example, suppose you want to track the following properties in addition to all the properties that you defined for an Item object:

➤ Gas-powered item

    ➤ Type of fuel

    ➤ Size of gas tank

    ➤ Duration of use with full tank

➤ Oil required

➤ Electric-powered item

➤ Volts required

➤ Length of cord

➤ Needs ground plug

You could take three approaches to this. One, you could put all of these properties onto the item and just use those that you want, knowing that many properties may be unused. Two, you could copy all the properties from the item onto the two new types, GasItem and ElectricItem. Three, you could use inheritance such that both GasItem and ElectricItem inherit from Item so that all the properties and methods of Item become available to GasItem and ElectricItem. The following example shows how to do that, followed by an explanation:

C#

```
public class Item
{
    public DateTime AcquiredDate { get; set; }
    public string Name { get; set; }
}

public class ElectricItem : Item
{
    public double VoltsRequired { get; set; }
    public double LengthOfCord { get; set; }
}
```

VB

```
Public Class Item

    Public Property AcquiredDate As DateTime
    Public Property Name As String

End Class

Public Class ElectricItem Inherits Item

    Public Property VoltsRequired As Double
    Public Property LengthOfCord As Double

End Class
```

The preceding snippet has created two classes, Item and ElectricItem, and created ElectricItem in such a way that it inherits from Item. In C# this is done by appending the colon (:) and the name of the class to inherit after the inheriting class's definition. In VB, the keyword Inherits is used to define the relationship. Because ElectricCar inherits from Item, the properties on the Item, such as `AcquiredDate` and `Name`, are also available on the `ElectricItem`. This means that IntelliSense would display what is shown in Figure 4-2 when you look at the definition of an `ElectricItem`.

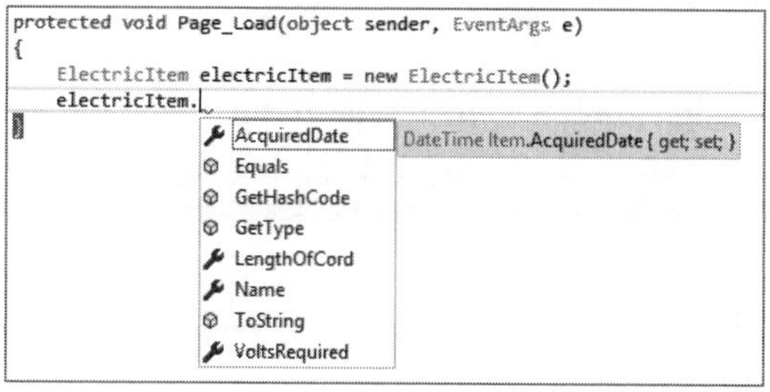

```
protected void Page_Load(object sender, EventArgs e)
{
    ElectricItem electricItem = new ElectricItem();
    electricItem.
```

🔧 AcquiredDate	DateTime Item.AcquiredDate { get; set; }
⚙ Equals	
⚙ GetHashCode	
⚙ GetType	
🔧 LengthOfCord	
🔧 Name	
⚙ ToString	
🔧 VoltsRequired	

FIGURE 4-2: Inheritance displayed in IntelliSense

Note also in Figure 4-2 that there are methods for `ToString`, `Equals`, and `GetHashCode`. Although you did not define these methods, these indicate that all custom types, such as your classes, inherit objects, and these methods are included in the object definition; thus, they are available through inheritance to all other custom objects.

Inheritance will be used several times throughout the application, used in both Web Forms and MVC to create functionality that is shared in multiple places, such as base classes for Web Form pages and MVC controllers.

Events

This chapter has described how an OO approach enables you to take code and put it in a central place where other code can use it. This enables you to create an object and then communicate with that object by changing properties and running methods. So far, however, there has not been a way for that object to communicate to the code that was using it outside of the value returned from the method. The .NET Framework provides that capability through events.

Events have been covered in a different context, as part of the flow of a Web Form submitting itself back to the server, during which the server breaks the processing into different stages, with each stage calling events when it is starting and stopping. Web Forms can also provide events when actions such as clicking a button or changing the value of a dropdown list are taken.

Any kind of action can fire an event, regardless of whether the object firing the event is a .NET object or a custom object. Because the purpose of an event is to communicate outside of the class, one of the keys to using events is having a clear understanding of what information may need to be communicated outside the class.

Another key to using events is that the code that is expecting the communication must have an instantiated version of that class. Finally, the class expecting the communication (the class that needs to know when an event has been triggered) must have an event handler, a special method that both registers for and receives the event as it is fired. This event handler must be assigned to the event as well as have the same message signature defined by the event.

This book doesn't cover creating events themselves. They are generally rare in web application development aside from the ASP.NET Web Forms built-in page life-cycle events. You do, however, need to learn about creating event handlers, because they are used frequently when developing within Web Forms.

An *event handler* is a method that has a prescribed signature, or return type and parameter list. The most common event handler, shown here, is created on a Web Form page by default:

C#

```
protected void Page_Load(object sender, EventArgs e)
{
}
```

VB

```
Protected Sub Page_Load(ByVal sender As Object, ByVal e As EventArgs)
Handles Me.Load

End Sub
```

As you can see, there are two parameters for this method, the object that fired the event and the arguments passed by the event. These EventArgs, or event arguments, pass the information that is needed by the method doing the listening.

The same approach is used when you are wiring event handlers to an event being fired from an item in a Web Form. The following snippet shows the ASP.NET control that was created in the page as well as the event handler for that event:

C#

```
<asp:Button runat="server" OnClick="Button_Click" />

protected void Button_Click(object sender, EventArgs e)
{
}
```

VB

```
<asp:Button runat="server" OnClick="Button_Click" />

Protected Sub Button_Click(ByVal sender As Object,
          ByVal e As EventArgs) Handles Me.Load

End Sub
```

If you are working within this method, you can cast the object named sender as a Button. This demonstrates that the sender is the object firing the event. The EventArgs holds information that may be relevant to the event being thrown, and the object that fires the event defines the type of information within that class. As you continue to build the sample application, you will see instances that use both of these parameters in the code.

SUMMARY

This short chapter covered the basics of programming used in almost all languages, especially object-oriented programming languages. Operators, loops, and decision-making structures are used everywhere, while most of the high-level programming languages, even other ones you may have heard of such as C++, C, and Java, also contain defined data types and classes.

The first part of this chapter provided background about the ways to define variables, use data types, and assign values to variables. It also described how to use collections of information, especially in arrays and lists. At this point, you should also have an understanding of looping, or how to execute the same block of code multiple times, sometimes doing the same operation on every item in a collection.

The chapter also covered making decisions—in particular, how using `If` or `Switch` statements enables the application to evaluate an object in order to determine what step to take next. This ability to make appropriate decisions is critical in any application.

The last half of the chapter provided a brief introduction to the complex topic of object-oriented programming. Entire books have been written about this topic, so curious readers are encouraged to explore those. This chapter touched on all of the pieces that you need going forward to build the sample application, so when you get to them in subsequent chapters, you will understand the terms and recognize the approaches.

This is also the last time that you will be seeing VB within the code samples. Going forward, you will only see C# code samples. However, the downloads available for this book have both versions, and the filenames and class names are the same to make it easy to find the appropriate area for reference if you plan to work with VB.

EXERCISES

1. What would the following code have as the final value for `resultsAsAString`?

    C#
    ```
    int oneNumber = 1;
    int twoNumber = 2;

    string resultsAsAString = "What is my result? " + oneNumber + twoNumber;
    ```
    VB
    ```
    Dim oneNumber as Integer = 1
    Dim twoNumber as Integer = 2

    Dim resultsAsAString as String = "What is my result? " & oneNumber & twoNumber
    ```

2. What is wrong with the following code?

C#

```
List<string> collection = new List<string>();

// do some work to put a lot of items into the list

string valueToWrite;

for(int loopCounter = 0; loopCounter <= collection.Count; loopCounter++)
{
    valueToWrite += collection[loop];
    // do some more work
}
```

VB

```
Dim collection As New List(Of String)

' do some work to put a lot of items into the list

Dim valueToWrite as String

For loopCounter As Integer = 0 To collection.Count
    valueToWrite += collection(loop)
    ' do some more work
Next
```

3. Which would be the better choice for iterating through an entire collection: `For Each` or `Do`?

▶ WHAT YOU LEARNED IN THIS CHAPTER

Array	A simple collection of items that are accessed by their index number. The array has to be dimensioned upon creation; that is, you must know the number of items that will be stored in the array.
Class	A class is how an object is defined; it is the base type of virtually everything in an object-oriented language.
Collection	A collection is a generic word describing any kind of type that is able to contain multiple other items.
Constructor	A special method that is called every time a class is instantiated
DataType	A classification that helps define the type of an object. It is generally used for base types such as integers, bools, doubles, etc.
Field	A value that is part of a class. A field is simply a container of data; it cannot do any processing when you get or set the value.
Inheritance	Describes a hierarchy whereby one class becomes a child of another; all the properties and methods of the parent class are accessible to the child class.
Instantiation	The process of creating a new version of an object. The constructor is called during instantiation of a class.
List	An object that will hold a generic list of pre-defined types. It differs from an array in that it provides a lot more functionality, including adding, removing, and adding multiple items. You can also check whether an item has already been added. You do not have to know the size of the list before you instantiate it.
Method	A method is a way to do work. It defines a code block, giving it a name, a set of parameters, and a return type if desired.
Object Orientation	A school of development that defines everything in the application domain as being an object. Each object has a set of properties and can take a set of actions (methods).
Properties	Properties contain the values that describe a class. They can also perform logic when the property is being set or requested.
void	A special return type for a method in C# that indicates there is no return from this method. It is equivalent to a VB subroutine.

5

ASP.NET Web Form Server Controls

WHAT YOU WILL LEARN IN THIS CHAPTER:

➤   Fundamentals of ASP.NET Web Form Server controls and how you can use them in an application

➤   The different kinds of available server controls

➤   How the server controls work

➤   How to configure the controls

CODE DOWNLOADS FOR THIS CHAPTER:

The wrox.com code downloads for this chapter are found at www.wrox.com/go/beginningaspnetforvisualstudio on the Download Code tab. The code is in the chapter 05 download and individually named according to the names throughout the chapter.

Earlier chapters listed the advantages of using the ASP.NET Web Form approach for building a web application. One of these advantages is the number of built-in controls available out of the box, as well as the large number of third-party controls that are available. These controls are all server controls, and in this chapter you will see how advantageous it is to have these kinds of server controls available to help support your development efforts. By the end of the chapter, you will be able to compare this approach with the approach taken in ASP.NET MVC in order to better understand which approach would best support your future projects.

INTRODUCTION TO SERVER CONTROLS

Server controls are add-ins to the markup section of your application, the area where you add the HTML. The ASP.NET server control is an element that is added to an .aspx file and exposes properties, methods and events that can be accessed by the code-behind file (the `aspx.cs` or `aspx.vb` file). The simple goal of a server control is to provide access to elements of the UI from code. However, many controls go far beyond that and provide built-in functionality that developers can take advantage of, enabling portions of the application to basically write themselves simply by wiring in the appropriate server controls. The controls themselves live and are run on the server, which takes the control's work and outputs HTML into the page sent back to the browser. Their purpose is to automate the creation of HTML as well as to help handle the information when it comes back to the server.

There are many different types of server controls that are either included with ASP.NET or are available from third party vendors. Some server controls act as wrappers around traditional HTML elements. Other controls provide access to and help manage the display of data. There is a third subset of controls that performs validation on other controls, ensuring that they fit a specific set of criteria. A fourth category of server controls handles navigation, or the moving from one page to another in your web application. The last major type of control that is covered is login controls, which were created to provide registration and authentication support. One additional subset of server controls is covered in this chapter, the HTML controls. These are not the same type of controls as your basic server controls in that they are traditional HTML elements that are "reachable" from code.

DEFINING CONTROLS IN YOUR PAGES

Because server controls are designed to provide support for the user interface, they are generally called in the HTML, or markup, section of the page—the same area where you were going over styling. There are two ways that you can add a server control to your page: through the combination of manual entering and IntelliSense or through the Visual Studio Toolbox. If you are unable to view the Toolbox window in Visual Studio, you can access it through the View menu option by selecting Toolbox. The Toolbox is shown in Figure 5-1.

You can also enter controls manually, with IntelliSense support, as shown in Figure 5-2.

Figure 5-2 gives you some idea of how server controls are created within the markup section. One important thing to realize is that regardless of the language being used in the code (C# or VB), the creation of server controls in the UI is the same. It is not language agnostic so much as it is in a different language altogether, feeling more like the HTML code with which it interacts.

Because it is HTML-like, the format of the control should come as no surprise:

```
<asp:ServerControlName runat="server" />
```

As you can see, it takes the same open bracket, attributes, and closing brackets that HTML does. The main difference that applies to all server controls is that the element name is always prefaced by `asp:`, and you need a `runat` attribute that is set to `server`. The `asp:` is the namespace of the controls, but this prefix also acts to group all server controls together in IntelliSense. The `runat` attribute, when set to `server`, enables the control to be accessed in the code-behind. Without this attribute set, it is not possible to interact with the control on the server, basically making it useless as a server control.

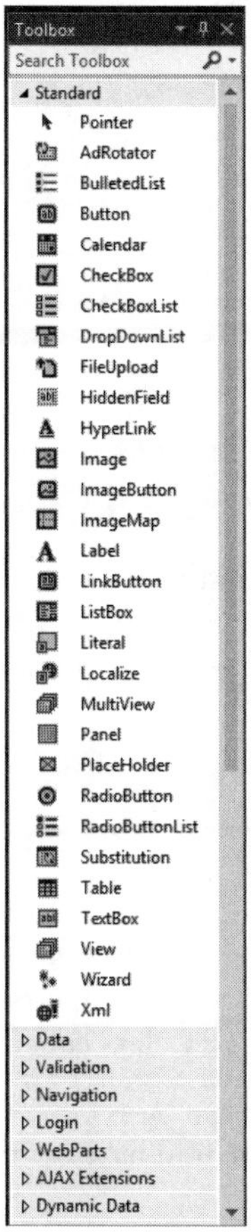

FIGURE 5-1: Toolbox menu in Visual Studio

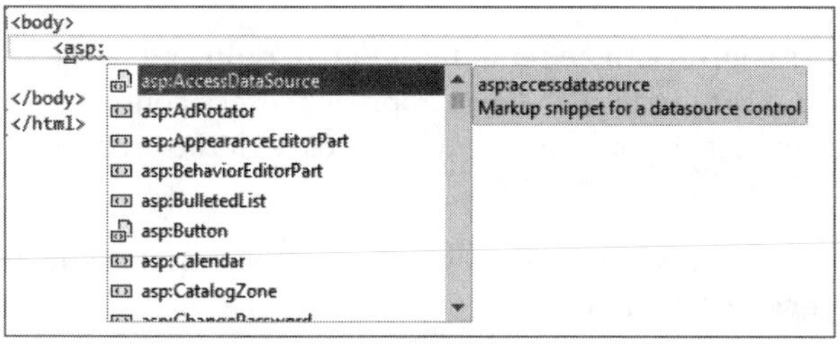

FIGURE 5-2: IntelliSense support for manually entering server controls

Consider what this would look like from both the UI side and the code side:

UI

```
<asp:TextBox runat="server" ID="mainTextBox" />
```

CODE-BEHIND

```
protected void Page_Load(object sender, EventArgs e)
{
    mainTextBox.Text = "I am text for the textbox";
}
```

The combination of these two, the server control in the .aspx page and the code in the aspx.cs page, create the following HTML:

```
<input name="mainTextBox" type="text" value="I am text for the textbox"
       id="mainTextBox" />
```

The preceding HTML is then rendered into the browser as shown in Figure 5-3.

FIGURE 5-3

You likely noticed how the `TextBox` control was given an ID of `mainTextBox`, and that was the name of the object referenced in the code-behind when you assigned a value to the `Text` property. Relating this back to the OO discussion in the previous chapter, there is an ASP.NET class called `TextBox` that contains a string property called `Text`.

Each control has its own set of attributes that are translated into properties. You could have set the `Text` property in the server control markup as well:

```
<asp:TextBox runat="server" ID="mainTextBox" Text="I am preset text" />
```

Each of the properties available on the server control can be set in both the markup and in the code-behind. This should give you an idea of the power of the Web Form approach; every control on your page is available as a pre-instantiated object whereby you can simply interact with the properties as needed.

Before going deeper into the various types of controls, the following activity demonstrates how to create a textbox in which the user can enter some text and a label that displays that text when a button is clicked.

TRY IT OUT Your First Interactive Control

In this activity, you clean up previous demo files by moving them into a new folder, create a new file in Visual Studio, add a few server controls to this new page, and then watch how it all interacts.

1. Open the RentMyWrox project in Visual Studio. At this point you have a set of files in your main solution folder, including the `IntroToCss.aspx` file that you were working with earlier. Right-click on the project name, and select Add ➪ New Folder. Name this new folder "**Demonstrations.**"

2. Click on the `IntroToCss.aspx` file, and while still holding down the left mouse button, drag the file into the newly created folder. You will see the file move into the folder.

3. Add a new file. Click the folder named Demonstrations and then right-click, select Add, and choose Web Form from the list. When the Name box appears enter **ServerControls**. A new file will appear in the directory with the appropriate name. This same file should also open in your editor.

4. Ensure that you are in the Source window; locate the form element. It should look like the following:

```
<form id="form1" runat="server">
```

5. Ensure that you are between the form elements and add a TextBox element. You can do this by either typing in the characters "**<asp:TextBox**" or by dragging and dropping a TextBox from the Toolbox into the appropriate place on your source code window. If you choose to select the control from the drop-down list and you select the wrong control you will have to delete your entire entry before you can get another drop-down list while typing. Give the textbox an ID of "**demoToolBox.**" It should look like the following when you are finished:

```
<asp:TextBox ID="demoToolBox" runat="server"></asp:TextBox>
```

6. Add a Label control right below the TextBox you just created. Give it the ID of "**displayLabel.**" You should now have the following:

```
<asp:TextBox ID="demoToolBox" runat="server"></asp:TextBox>
<asp:Label ID="displayLabel" runat="server"></asp:Label>
```

7. Add a Button control right below the Label control. Give this control the ID of "**submitButton.**" However, once you have created the ID and the runat attributes, there is one more attribute you have to create, and that is to assign an event handler in your code to the `OnClick` event. To do this, type in "**OnClick.**" You will see IntelliSense help narrow the list of available options, as shown in Figure 5-4.

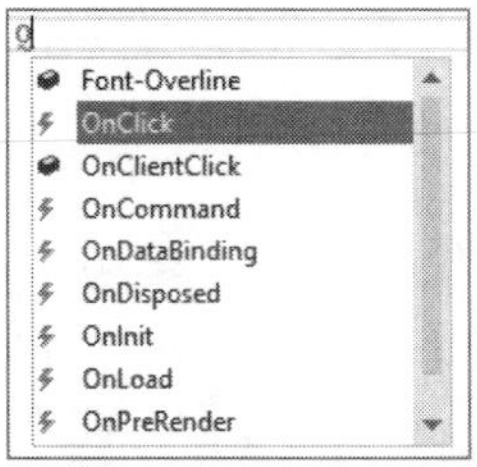

FIGURE 5-4: IntelliSense for help selecting the OnClick Event

8. Notice the lightning bolt next to the `OnClick` selection. This icon is used to indicate an event. Once you enter the equal sign, you should get the IntelliSense menu shown in Figure 5-5, which creates a new event handler for you. When you see the option, select it. It should fill out the value for you.

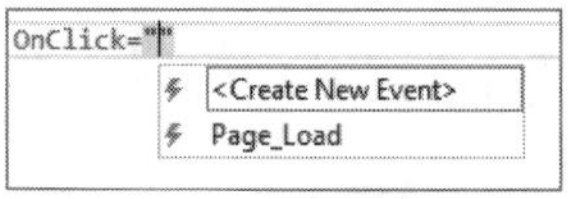

FIGURE 5-5: IntelliSense help for creating an event handler

9. Now you need to add the text that will display on your button. Use the Text attribute and set it to "**Display Text.**" Close the Button element. You should have the following:

```
<form id="form1" runat="server">
    <div>
        <asp:TextBox ID="demoToolBox" runat="server"></asp:TextBox>
        <asp:Label ID="displayLabel" runat="server"></asp:Label>
        <asp:Button ID="submitButton" runat="server" OnClick="submitButton_Click"
            Text="Display Text" />
    </div>
</form>
```

10. Open the code-behind, ServerControls.aspx.cs (or .vb), from the Solution Explorer window. If you don't see it in the Demonstrations folder, you should be able to click the arrow next to the ServerControls.aspx page, causing it to expand and show several hidden files. Double-click ServerControls.aspx.cs to open it in the working window. If you are working in VB.NET, you may need to right-click on the file and select View Code.

11. Take a moment to look at the contents of this page. Note first that there is a partial class whose name matches the name of the page. That indicates that this code-behind is assigned to that page. This class inherits the System.Web.Ui.Page. You will learn more about this base class as you move through the application. Notice also the two protected methods in the page, Page_Load and submitButton_Click. They both have the same signature (object sender, EventArgs e), so you know that they are both event handlers.

```
using System;
using System.Collections.Generic;
using System.Linq;
using System.Web;
using System.Web.UI;
using System.Web.UI.WebControls;

namespace csDCLapp.Demonstrations
{
    public partial class ServerControls : System.Web.UI.Page
    {
        protected void Page_Load(object sender, EventArgs e)
        {

        }
        protected void submitButton_Click(object sender, EventArgs e)
```

```
    {
        displayLabel.Text = demoToolBox.Text;  // set the text of the label to the
        //text from the text box
        demoToolBox.Text = string.Empty; // empty the text box
    }

  }
}
```

12. Type the following lines into the submitButton_Click method body:

```
protected void submitButton_Click(object sender, EventArgs e)
{
    displayLabel.Text = demoToolBox.Text;  // set the text of the label to the
                                           //text from the text box
    demoToolBox.Text = string.Empty; // empty the text box
}
```

13. Click the green arrow, or push the F5 key, to run the current web page. Your application should compile, and when your browser opens it should look similar to Figure 5-6.

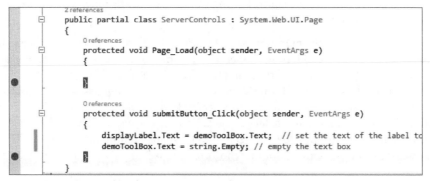

FIGURE 5-6: Initial display of HTML

14. Type some text in the textbox and then click the button. After clicking the button, the page is sent to the server, which copies the content you entered in the box to the label so that it is displayed between the textbox and the button while the textbox is emptied.

15. You now need to go to the code-behind page and put a breakpoint in the Page_Load method and the submitButton_Click button. To do so, click in the gray border to the left of the code page as shown in Figure 5-7. You cannot click in a spot where there is no code, so the only place you can click is the closing brackets within the Page_Load method.

```
        2 references
        public partial class ServerControls : System.Web.UI.Page
        {
            0 references
            protected void Page_Load(object sender, EventArgs e)
            {

            }

            0 references
            protected void submitButton_Click(object sender, EventArgs e)
            {
                displayLabel.Text = demoToolBox.Text;  // set the text of the label to
                demoToolBox.Text = string.Empty; // empty the text box
            }
        }
```

FIGURE 5-7: Setting breakpoints in your code

DEBUGGING YOUR WEB APPLICATION

One of the most powerful features of Visual Studio is the capability it provides developers to step through the code while it is running. This gives you the opportunity to trace the flow, validate variables, and see what is going on within your application at every step.

To debug an application you need to start in Debug mode. This is the default mode of the green arrow in the toolbar as well as the F5 function key. Typically, you would then insert a breakpoint in those places where you want to examine the work that is going on. When the code hits a breakpoint, it stops processing and takes you to that line of code. You can then mouse over variables and see their value. You can also use the F11 key to continue through your code one line at a time. To continue running the code when you are done, you can either click the green button again or click the F5 key.

The rest of this book uses the Debug feature extensively to show the state of various parts of the code and to confirm that your application is working as expected even before anything is rendered to the screen.

16. Run the code again. Note that the code processing stops in the `Page_Load` method during the initial running. If you continue, you will see that your breakpoint in `submitButton_Click` is not reached.

17. Enter some text and click the Display Text button. The `Page_Load` method, covered later, is called again. Continue with the debugging. The code next stops in the `submitButton_Click` method.

18. Mouse over the different items and note how you have access into their values. Click Continue to see your page come up with the text you entered displayed within the Label.

How It Works

You should have a conceptual grasp of how the code in the `submitButton_Click` method works; you assigned the value of the Text property in one control to the value of the Text property in the second control. But what does that mean in terms of the process?

Up until the point at which you clicked the button it was a traditional web page. However, once you clicked the button, the browser made a callback to the server with the content within the `<form>` element. The form element is important because of the ASP.NET Web Forms requirement that all server controls be placed within form elements. Web Forms depend upon the form submission protocol to ensure that all necessary information is sent from the browser back to the client. All the appropriate HTML elements within the form elements are included in a large post whenever there is any interaction with the server. When you look at it in the browser it seems to be simple, but if you look at the HTML source, shown in Figure 5-8, you can see that a lot more information is being passed around than just the text that was entered.

```
File  Edit  Format
 1 |
 2
 3 <!DOCTYPE html>
 4
 5 <html xmlns="http://www.w3.org/1999/xhtml">
 6 <head><title>
 7
 8 </title></head>
 9 <body>
10    <form method="post" action="ServerControls" id="form1">
11 <div class="aspNetHidden">
12 <input type="hidden" name="__VIEWSTATE" id="__VIEWSTATE" value="/K8FRh62QS0Inzswe8t+cDO62vCBpYx0V0N4h9EY1+ZmrVf0Y2duB5MzmnG+mbIraD7aF7Tzln0dGI1ZpN9UMP7IUANfJuD4t7xgAj0fGdU=" />
13 </div>
14
15    <div>
16       <input name="demoToolBox" type="text" id="demoToolBox" />
17       <span id="displayLabel"></span>
18       <input type="submit" name="submitButton" value="Display Text" id="submitButton" />
19    </div>
20
21 <div class="aspNetHidden">
22
23    <input type="hidden" name="__VIEWSTATEGENERATOR" id="__VIEWSTATEGENERATOR" value="E3695DD8" />
24    <input type="hidden" name="__EVENTVALIDATION" id="__EVENTVALIDATION"
25 value="M5KdWRNWIB6nMNC+JQyOY65xpu0ycZWSX0Fm9tgGMPZPFQRjfDXUZ2zhlF85aJfV0fEkJxsoAn4cRDrV702bVObj756jN9jE2rWK+VBfcGFyhpgNwLyLJ2bofd7maRcZJyT7L3ZYq45qAU3h6+AXnQ==" />
26 </div></form>
27 <!-- Visual Studio Browser Link -->
28 <script type="application/json" id="__browserLink_initializationData">
29     {"appName":"Internet Explorer","requestId":"43ae709785064832aaa405432e7d2695"}
30 </script>
31 <script type="text/javascript" src="http://localhost:1286/ea463069218748d8a0917a64097dca12/browserLink" async="async"></script>
32 <!-- End Browser Link -->
33
34 </body>
35 </html>
```

FIGURE 5-8: HTML created when using server controls

The ViewState was mentioned earlier. You can see a simple ViewState in Figure 5-7 on line 12. There are also other items that are sent back and forth between the server and the browser, including the _VIEWSTATEGENERATOR and the _EVENTVALIDATION hidden inputs. These items are created automatically by the server when processing ASP.NET Web Form pages.

Once all of this information is received by the server it is parsed and examined. The server is able to determine that the button was clicked; thus, because of the relationship between the button and a method in the code-behind that was set when you created the control, the server knows that as part of its process it needs to call the submitButton_Click method. However, it doesn't call that method right away. There is an order to the events, as described in Table 1-4: Lifecycle Events for ASP.NET Pages.

This process of calling the server back is known as a postback. You will spend more time learning about postbacks later in this chapter and as you build the sample application.

TYPES OF CONTROLS

Each of the different types of control discussed here fills a special need; together they provide developers with a set of functionality. These controls are:

➤ Standard controls

➤ Html controls

➤ Data controls

➤ Validation controls

➤ Navigation controls

➤ Login controls

➤ AJAX extensions

Some of these controls stand on their own, others interact with other controls; some controls are very complicated to work with, while others may be very simple. You have already seen some of the simpler controls, the `TextBox` and the `Label`. Both of these controls are representative of a standard control.

Standard Controls

A standard control is a built-in ASP.NET control that helps display information to the user or helps capture information from the user. These controls are shown in Figure 5-9.

FIGURE 5-9: Standard controls list from the Toolbox

Some of these controls serve almost as simple wrappers for HTML elements, such as the `TextBox` and `Label` controls that you worked with in the last example. Others are much more intricate, such as the `Calendar` control. Table 5-1 describes the most common standard controls.

TABLE 5-1: Common Standard Server Controls

CONTROL	DESCRIPTION
BulletedList	A bulleted list that can be data bound; this means that items can be put into the list in code rather than having to be added in the UI. Corresponds to an unnumbered list in HTML and consists of a list of ListItems.
Button	Creates an input element of type button. It contains events that can be called in the code-behind as well as events that can call JavaScript methods in the browser.
Calendar	Creates a UI for displaying a calendar, enabling users to select one or more dates as needed. It handles both the rendering of the calendar as well as the capturing of date-related user-entered information.
CheckBox	Creates an input element of type checkbox. You can evaluate whether the item has been checked in the code-behind.
CheckBoxList	Provides a list of checkboxes that can be data bound. Each of the items can be checked and then the code-behind can examine the list of items to determine whether the item has been checked. It also contains a list of ListItems.
FileUpload	Provides the capability to upload a file from the local file system to the server
HiddenField	Creates a hidden field on the page. By default, these items hold but do not display items to the user. They can hold data between server requests and are sometimes used to hold business information that may be needed on multiple pages.
HyperLink	Enables you to create an HTML hyperlink that takes users to a different page
Image	Used to place and size an image
Label	A server control that displays text. It does not accept any information to return back to the server.
LinkButton	A combination between a Button and a Hyperlink; it acts like a button but looks much more like a HyperlInk than a button.
ListBox	This control can be data bound and gives you the capability to display multiple items together. A ListBox is made up of a list of ListItem and one or more items can be selected at a time.
Panel	A container for controls. You can put a series of controls within a Panel and then control the visibility of those controls via the Panel rather than through individual controls.
RadioButton	Represents the HTML radio button. It enables users to select one and only one item within a group. The group is a property on the RadioButton.
RadioButtonList	Represents a list of RadioButtons. Only one can be picked from this list.
TextBox	As displayed previously, the Textbox control enables users to enter one or more lines of information into an application.

Most of the controls that are listed can be worked with much like you did with the TextBox, Label, and Button controls in the last example. The exceptions are those controls that support collections. You can recognize them in Table 5-1 because they have "List" as part of their name, such as CheckboxList, ListBox, and RadioButtonList. These require a different approach both when working in the markup section and when working in the code. The following snippet demonstrates how you need to load information into these controls:

UI

```
<asp:CheckBoxList ID="availableColors" runat="server">
    <asp:ListItem Text="Red" Value="red" />
    <asp:ListItem Text="Green" Value="green" />
    <asp:ListItem Text="Blue" Value="blue" />
</asp:CheckBoxList>
```

CODE-BEHIND

```
List<ListItem> colorsList = new List<ListItem>();
colorsList.Add(new ListItem { Text = "Red", Value = "red" });
colorsList.Add(new ListItem { Text = "Green", Value = "green" });
colorsList.Add(new ListItem { Text = "Blue", Value = "blue" });
availableColors.DataSource = colorsList;
availableColors.DataBind();
```

There are other approaches to loading the list controls from code. You will look at some of these in later chapters as you build the sample application. Using the values that were selected from the UI is different from how you got the information in the last example as well. The following snippet shows how you can determine what items in the CheckBoxList have been selected:

CODE-BEHIND

```
List<string> selectedColors = new List<string>();
foreach(ListItem item in availableColors.Items)
{
    if (item.Selected)
    {
        selectedColors.Add(item.Value);
    }
}
```

You should be able to recognize everything in the snippet based on the last chapter, so you know that you are going through each item in the list and evaluating whether it has been selected. If so, then you are adding it to the list of selected colors. You take this approach because this list was rendered as a list of individual checkboxes, each of which could be selected.

There is a set of common properties for standard controls that can be set in both markup and in code-behind. Some of these attributes are listed in Table 5-2.

TABLE 5-2: Common Standard Control General Attributes

ATTRIBUTE NAME	DESCRIPTION
AccessKey	Describes the control's shortcut key. This property specifies a single letter or number that the user can press while pressing ALT. For example, specify "K" if you want the user to press ALT+K to access the control.
Attributes	The collection of additional HTML attributes that are not covered by a standard property. This could cover standard HTML attributes or special custom attributes. You cannot set these in markup, but rather need to add them in code.
CssClass	The cascading style sheets (CSS) class to assign to the control
Style	A collection of attributes that are used in styling the control
Enabled	Makes the control functional when this property is set to true. When set to false, the control becomes grayed out rather than invisible.
EnableViewState	Enables view state persistence for the control
Font	Sets the font information for the control
ForeColor	Sets the foreground color of the control
Height	The height of the control
TabIndex	The control's position in the tab order. If this property is not set, the control's position index is 0. This enables users to use the Tab key to move between the various controls.
ToolTip	Text that appears when the user positions the mouse over the control
Width	The fixed width of the control. There are many different potential units, including pixel, inch, or percentage.

Some of the properties in Table 5-1 may seem contradictory; CssClass and ForeColor both affect the styling of the control. Each of the items that concern styling are placed on the control's outer element; these are all inline styles so they always override any of the other applicable styles. However, remember from Chapter 3 that while you have this ability, inline styles lead to a design that is difficult to maintain.

Although all controls have these standard attributes, some controls have specific attributes that provide special information that they need. These controls and some of their special attributes are listed in Table 5-3.

TABLE 5-3: Standard Server Control Special Attributes

CONTROL	SPECIAL PROPERTIES
BulletedList	`BulletImageUrl` — Path to an image to display for each bullet in a `BulletedList` control `BulletStyle` — Manages the style of the bullet `DataTextField` — The field of the data source that provides the text that is displayed `DataValueField` — The field of the data source that provides the value of the items being selected
Button LinkButton	`OnClick` — Event on the control that can be hooked up to an event handler in the code-behind `Command` — A special type of event that can be hooked up to anevent handler in the code-behind that is different than the event handler that supports the click event `CommandArgument` — An optional parameter that can be included as part of a command `CommandName` — The command name that is passed along with the command `OnClientClick` — Client-side JavaScript that executes when the button is clicked
Calendar	`FirstDayOfWeek` — The day of the week to display in the first day column of the `Calendar` control `NextMonthText` — The text displayed for the next month navigation control `PrevMonthText` — The text displayed for the previous month navigation control `SelectedDate` — The selected date `SelectedDates` — A collection of dates that were selected through the UI `ShowGridLines` — Displays gridlines within the control
FileUpload	`FileBytes` — An array of the bytes in a file that is specified from the control `FileContent` — Gets a `Stream` object that points to a file to upload `FileName` — Name of a file on a client to upload `HasFile` — Determines whether the control contains a file `HasFiles` — Determines whether the control contains multiple files `OpenFile` — Gets a stream used to open the file
HyperLink	`ImageHeight` — Sets the height of the image if using an image for the link `ImageUrl` — Sets the URL to the image if using an image for the link `ImageWidth` — Sets the width of the image if using an image for the link `NavigateUrl` — The URL that is linked to when clicked

CONTROL	SPECIAL PROPERTIES
Image	AlternateText — Sets the alternative text that is displayed as an image is downloading GenerateEmptyAlternateText — Indicates whether the control generates an alternate text attribute for an empty string text ImageUrl — The URL that provides the path to an image to display in the control
TextBox	MaxLength — Maximum amount of characters allowed in the box TextMode — Behavior mode for the control, such as multi-line, password, etc. Affects how the control is created and how it is displayed in the page. TextChanged — Event that is fired when the content changes between visits to the server

Each of the different controls provides different functionality and may therefore have different properties. The list in Table 5-3 is not complete by any means; it just describes the most commonly used other properties for those controls.

HTML Controls

Many of the standard controls act as wrappers around HTML elements. They give the developer access to the content as well as many of the attributes of the base HTML element. They also include many events that may be thrown, such as when values have changed or when something has been clicked. However, you may not always need all of that support; you might only want to set the content of an element that you want to style in the .aspx markup page.

You can convert a standard HTML element to a server control by adding the runat="server" attribute. You are then able to access that item in your code-behind, assuming that you have given it an Id, just as you would a standard control. The properties of an HTML control are different from the standard controls; for example, the content of an HTML element is accessed by the Value property rather than the Text property, as shown in the following snippet:

UI
```
<input type="text" runat="server" id="htmlText" />
```

CODE-BEHIND
```
htmlText.Value = "test this";
```

You cannot do all of the same work that you would with a standard control. Adding items to a list, for example, cannot be handled like it is with the various list controls. However, many of the attributes are available for setting as necessary.

Because many of their features are similar, you may be wondering when you would use a standard control versus an HTML control. There is some overhead with using a standard control; and if you do not need any of that extra functionality, such as event handling, then it may make sense to use HTML controls instead. If the HTML you are rendering is critical, you have more control over the HTML that is output from the server with HTML controls than you do with the standard controls.

However, if none of those points are critical for your application, you should use the standard controls. Not all of the standard controls are wrappers around HTML controls, so using standard controls for everything makes the usage more consistent, and the performance impact is so minimal that it would only be noticeable in a page with a considerable number of controls.

Data Controls

Data controls are those controls designed to help enter, access, and display data on a web page. Figure 5-10 shows the different data controls that are available.

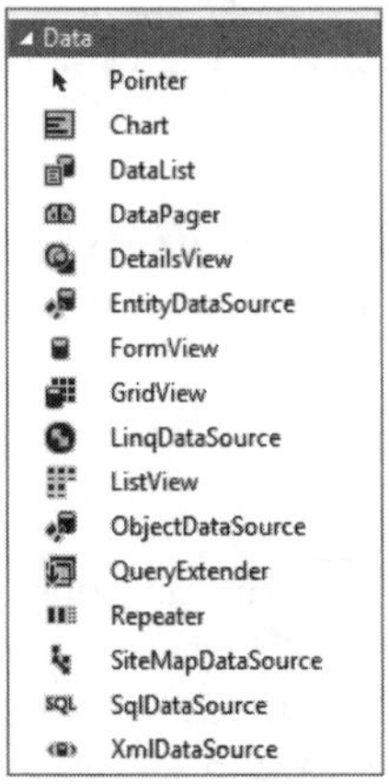

FIGURE 5-10: Data controls list from the Toolbox

An examination of the controls listed in the figure indicates that there are three major types of controls. The first type of controls are data source controls that all contain "DataSource" in their names and help you get data from various providers, including SQL server, and XML files. The next set of controls are data display controls, such as charts, grids, and lists that are identifiable because they tend to include "View" and "List" in their name while the last set of controls are data entry form management controls, which are another way to use those controls that include "View" in their name. Chapters 13 and 14 go into more detail about the various data controls that are available in ASP.NET Web Forms as you use them to display information from the database; they are not covered here.

Validation Controls

When you are developing a website that requests user information, you need to ensure that this information is actually what you are expecting. For example, if you are asking for an e-mail address, you want to ensure that it is a valid one. Similarly, if you need an integer to be used as an order quantity, you want to ensure it is actually an integer before you try to do anything with that

value. This is where the validation controls come into play. They enable you
to check the values of other controls to ensure that their content matches the
expected format of data. Figure 5-11 shows a list of the validation controls.

As you can see from the list, there are controls that validate that a field has
been entered if required, whether the value entered within a control fits
within a specified range, or whether the value in one control has the same
value as another, as well as several others. One of the neat things about these
controls is that the validation happens on both the client side and the server
side. If there is a problem, the user is notified before the information is even sent to the server.

FIGURE 5-11

You will be working through some validator examples in Chapter 10, so this chapter doesn't spend
any time on those controls.

Navigation Controls

As you look through websites, you can notice many common features. One of these is a
menu system that takes you to different areas of the site. Typical names for these different
areas include "About Us," "Support," and "Home." These are generally clickable words,
or links, across the top or down the side of the page. Many sites may also have a
Site Map, a page that provides a visual representation of the entire website, enabling
the user to drill down into the content.

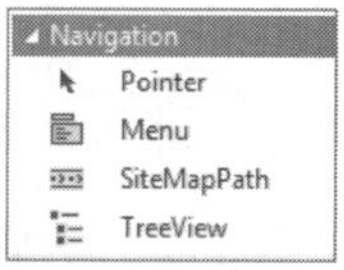

Many of these features are supported by the navigation controls. These controls,
shown in Figure 5-12, are designed to provide support as you build the navigational
structure of your site.

FIGURE 5-12

Chapter 8, "Navigation," covers these controls in more depth.

Login Controls

Security is a critical aspect of the Internet, so any site that conducts business online, especially
those that capture private information such as name, phone number, and e-mail address, or those
sites that accept credit cards or other forms of online payment, must ensure that they are as secure
as possible. While there is no way to ensure that a site is completely secure, following best practices
helps you build sites that are as secure as possible. Using the ASP.NET Web
Forms login controls helps you follow these best practices.

Login controls are a type of control that supports registration and authentication of users, as well as enabling you to display special content based on
whether or not the current user has logged in. Figure 5-13 shows the list of these
controls.

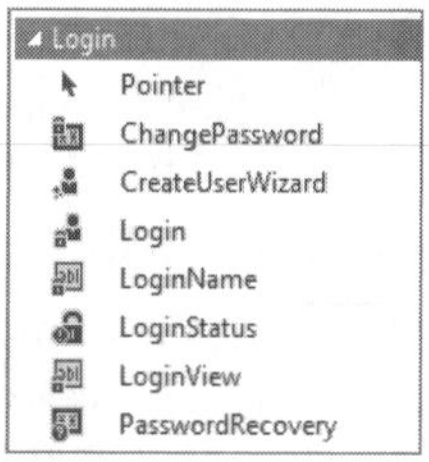

Chapters 15 and 16 cover security and personalization in detail.

FIGURE 5-13

AJAX Extensions

AJAX, or Asynchronous JavaScript and XML, is an architectural approach whereby web applications can send data to and retrieve data from a server without interfering with the display and behavior of the existing page. These calls happen in the background and therefore do not prevent the user from doing any work in the browser, unlike a traditional Web Form submission. AJAX can be used to update parts of a web page or the entire web page, as necessary, and these extensions help support the use of AJAX in ASP.NET Web Form pages. These controls are shown in Figure 5-14.

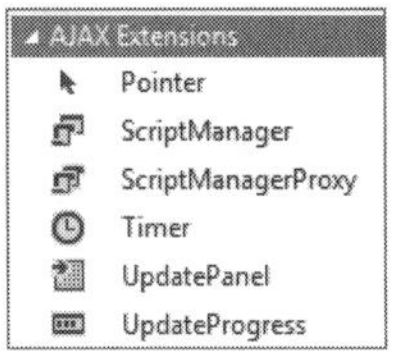

FIGURE 5-14: AJAX extensions

> **NOTE** AJAX is becoming very prevalent in modern web applications, though coincidentally most sites no longer use XML, instead using JSON (JavaScript Object Notation) because it compacts into smaller payloads for transmission across the network. However, no one seemed interested in renaming the approach to AJAJ. AJAX is covered in depth in Chapter 11.

Other Control Sets

There are other sets of controls listed in the Toolbox that are not covered any further in this book. These sets of controls are Dynamic Data, Reporting, and Web Parts, and are shown in Figure 5-15.

The Dynamic Data set of controls serve as scaffolding that helps you quickly build data-driven websites that work against a database and optionally enables you to do this work without having to build any pages manually. You do not use Dynamic Data controls in the sample application.

The reporting control is a report viewer. It displays reports, another type of file within an ASP.NET website, which can provide tabular, summary, and graphical data analysis. Creating a report control is shown in Figure 5-16.

Although you won't work with reports, and thus the report control, as part of the sample application, you should be aware that it is a powerful technology included with ASP.NET Web Forms. The report is created as a separate entity and then the reporting control is used to display the results of the report within a web page.

The last set of controls that is available are ASP.NET Web Parts. Web Parts enable end users to modify the content, appearance, and behavior of web pages directly from a browser. When users modify pages and controls, the settings can be saved to retain a user's personal preferences across future browser sessions. This enables the developer to create a site that is completely customizable by the user, who can can rearrange parts of the site, and add or remove content sections.

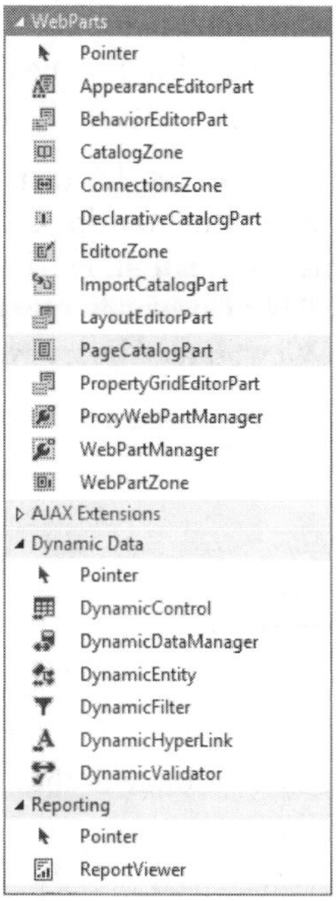

FIGURE 5-15: Other ASP.NET controls

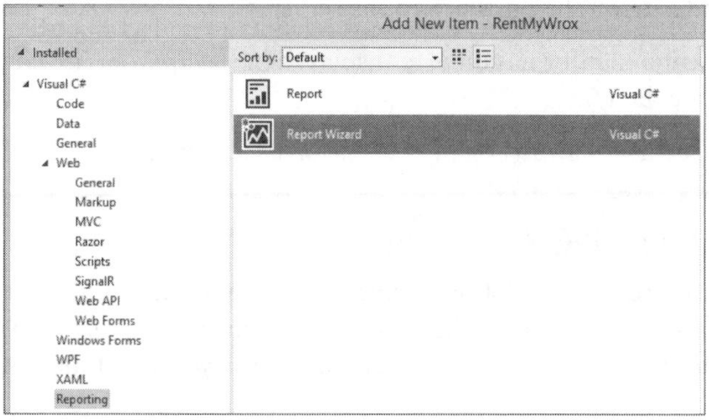

FIGURE 5-16: Create a report UI.

THE ASP.NET STATE ENGINE

Recall how ASP.NET helps a developer to maintain state in an application. State is important because it enables you to determine, on the server side, differences between posts to a page. Consider the situation in which you have a data entry page including some labels, textboxes, and a submit button. There are two times you use this page: when you want to create a new item and when you want to edit an existing item. The new item is simple to manage; it simply needs to be validated and persisted into the database. However, when an object is being edited you may have different concerns based on what was changed, so the system needs to understand when that field has changed.

There are two ways to determine whether that field is changed: Call the database to get the item back out to check it against the fields that were submitted, or have some kind of state to help you make this determination. Remember, the server cannot just "remember" this information; HTTP is a stateless protocol so by definition it does not have this ability. Instead, ASP.NET provides a way to get around this restriction by including the state information as part of the ViewState. Almost every server control is capable of having its state maintained.

HOW THE STATE ENGINE WORKS

In a nutshell, the state engine performs the following actions:

➤ Stores values per control by key name. This would look something like
  `ViewState["controlname"] = controlvalue`.

➤ Tracks changes to a ViewState value's initial state by comparing the current value to the stored value

➤ Serializes and deserializes (converting an object to and from a string) saved data into a hidden form field on the client. This allows non-string items (such as custom types/objects) to be managed as well.

➤ Automatically restores ViewState data on the postback to the server

➤ Automatically ensures that user-entered information is re-displayed in the appropriate controls, not necessarily the ViewState data

The following activity demonstrates what this all means by providing some examples for context.

TRY IT OUT Work through State Management

In this section you are going to create two different ASP.NET Web Form pages, take various actions on both, and compare the outcome. This enables you to get a handle on what happens during each phase of the control's lifecycle and how it plays into the various strategies that you use as you build the sample application.

1. Open Visual Studio and ensure that the RentMyWrox solution is open.

2. Create two new Web Form pages in the Demonstrations folder by right-clicking on the folder and selecting Add New Item. When the Dialogue opens, select Web from the left menu and select Web Form. Call these pages **Page1.aspx** and **Page2.aspx**.

3. In Page1, add a textbox and a button between the `<div>` tags:

```
<div>
    <asp:TextBox runat="server" ID="mainText" Text="123" />
```

```
            <asp:Button runat="server" Text="Submit" />
        </div>
```

4. In Page2, add a textbox and a button between the `<div>` tags. You want to add the same textbox and button, but ensure that the text value in the textbox is considerably longer:

    ```
    <div>
        <asp:TextBox runat="server" ID="mainText"
                    Text="1234567890ABCDEFGHIJKLMNOPQRSTUVWX" />
        <asp:Button runat="server" Text="Submit" />
    </div>
    ```

5. Save your changes and run your application while open on Page1. Do a view source on the page so you can see the HTML that was sent to the browser. Find the element called __VIEWSTATE and copy out the value. It should look something like this:

    ```
    jE0/S0v5pFKVYV8C96qDYkirKpK5UhMi0AVvi3IjErsWkAjnZj3pJtDnhiIpwfkqHbT
    HsmsskFKM1VT2FReFdG/143PG2lzq4131Bjvh38Q=
    ```

6. Do the same with Page2. If you put the two values together you can see that they are the same size—regardless of the size of the values that were set. If you think about this for a minute, however, it makes sense. There is no need for this to be put into ViewState because it is something that you have already put into code and the value has not been changed.

7. Run Page1 again. This time change the text; copy and paste the value from Page2 into the box and click the Submit button. Your results should look like what is shown in Figure 5-17, with the textbox repopulated with the content that you sent.

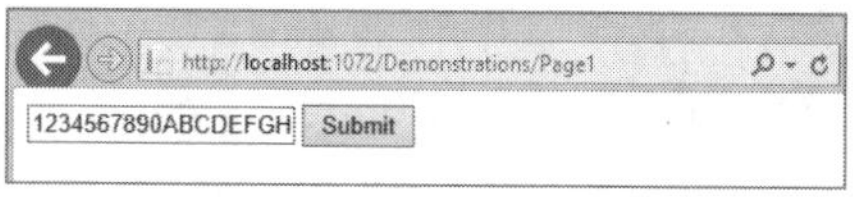

FIGURE 5-17: Changed textbox value is returned.

8. In Page1, remove the Text value from the markup declaration of the Textbox. That should leave it looking like this:

    ```
    <asp:TextBox runat="server" ID="mainText" />
    ```

9. In the code-behind for Page2, change the Page_Load method so that it looks like this:

    ```
    protected void Page_Load(object sender, EventArgs e)
    {
        if (!Page.IsPostBack)
        {
            mainText.Text = "set in code";
        }
    }
    ```

ISPOSTBACK

The `Page.IsPostBack` property provides the capability to quickly and easily determine whether the page is handling a postback call. This enables you to set defaults for controls and do other work such as creating and binding controls from databases only when it is the first visit to the page, before any posting of information back to the page. `ViewState` will continue to ensure that the information is available the next time it comes through the posting process. Also, if you do not do a check here, you will end up overwriting all the values that may have been set by the user with the values set in this method, as the code always runs through the `Page_Load` method.

10. Run the application while on Page2.aspx. Notice how the textbox displays the content that was set in the code-behind file. Click the Submit button. The page will flicker as it sends information to and receives information from the server, but the same text is displayed. Thus, no matter how the text is set, whether through markup, code-behind, or user entry, the state engine ensures that the same value is displayed when the textbox is redisplayed.

11. Stop the debugging session by closing the browser. In Page2, replace the textbox with a `Calendar` control as shown here:

```
<div>
    <asp:Calendar runat="server" ID="calendar" />
    <asp:Button runat="server" Text="Submit" />
</div>
```

You will also need to remove the changes from the Page2.aspx.cs that you added in step 9 above.

12. Run the app while on Page2. You should see a calendar above the button. If you select a date and click the Submit button, you will see a flicker as the new page is returned from the server, but the date is still selected. A look at the ViewState shows a value similar to the following:

```
8RRSe7RKwASfhd6hxWhIx+S9y59NbQbtW5fXe9xm66s0rIBS1wnHSsQOdk9+/qD1SI5mD+N6LOR6JdwEsexDVa
ITkTn6NogHq1I2jdXdbI7EGvJNeJEIhrY6pKUb/fto9wJQMKNGf4COb73znpC6Aw==
```

Notice that it is a longer value than you got from the textbox ViewState. Now, stop running the application and add the following to the calendar's markup: `EnableViewState="false"`. The final markup should look like this:

```
<asp:Calendar runat="server" ID="calendar" EnableViewState="false" />
```

13. Run the application again. Select a date and click the Submit button. Note that the date you had selected prior to the submission is now unselected. A look at the ViewState on the page shows something like the following:

```
x1P2ya4Xls0YdlMlpzQKGaora+5lKtjwZHnKeENAJN89iU2Gi81uvCaLauuz54T4CAsqSGCsoD1/
zcyxClbhvL4SpxojhTok1d10PHxxQWc=
```

Comparing this ViewState to the previous version shows that the ViewState is smaller; it is now the same size as the initial view states for a textbox. This demonstrates how ViewState is necessary for retaining data for some of the controls.

14. Go back to Page1, the page with the textbox. If you look in the code-behind for this page you should just have an empty `Page_Load` method and a regular textbox without any preset text. Add the `EnableViewState="false"` attribute to the textbox. The last time you made this change the value that was entered by the user in the `Calendar` control was not retained when the page was redisplayed. What do you think will happen when you run the app, enter a value, and click the button?

If you guessed that the entered value would be displayed then you are correct. You read earlier that the textbox, radio button, and checkbox controls differ from other controls; they always display the same values that they were submitted with, regardless of where, or how, those values were set.

How It Works

The ASP.NET state engine is an integral part of the page lifecycle. There are two main lifecycle events that interact with ViewState:

➤ **Load ViewState:** This stage follows the initialization stage of the ASP.NET page lifecycle. During the Load ViewState stage, ViewState information that was saved in the previous postback is loaded into controls. This is run only when the page is a postback. Initial runs of the page, i.e., when the user arrives there from a different page, do not go through this stage because there is no previous information to review.

➤ **Save ViewState:** This stage precedes the render stage of the page. During this stage, the current state, or value, of the controls is serialized into a 64-bit encoded string and then set as the value in the hidden field `__VIEWSTATE`. This happens after they may have been manipulated in code but before the rendering stage so the values are understood and can be written onto the page in the appropriate field.

These two events make it seem pretty simple; load all the data from ViewState after the controls are initialized and then save the data back into ViewState right before sending the page back to the client.

Let's go over the decisions that had to be made by the server. It gets a post to a page. When it creates the response, the server normally sets the content of the textbox to the value that was given as part of its instantiation—in this case, "123." However, the state machine instead ensures that the server fills the textbox with the value that was inserted at the client.

If you would look at the ViewState in the source code now, you may be surprised to see that the size of the value is the same, even though the value itself is different. This must mean that there is something special about the textbox control, and there is. The textbox, checkbox, and radio-button controls all retain values that were given them while in the browser unless deliberately changed.

However, there is some intricate work going on throughout this process. First, only those values that differ between ViewState and the initialized value are updated; not every property. This is a subtle point, but important. This is a very simple form, so the ViewState is simple as well. Imagine instead that you have several hundred controls on the page—a truly serious data entry form with labels, textboxes, calendars, dropdown lists, etc. That would be a complicated ViewState. If the system were designed to set every item, it would have to go through every item in ViewState, find the applicable control, and set the value.

Instead, because the system has both the ViewState data and the submitted data that holds the current version returned by the client browser, it can quickly analyze which fields were changed. It then only has to do the more expensive "find the control and set some properties" on a much smaller subset of the overall control set—those that have changed.

The key thing to realize is that ViewState is the key to managing all of this work. The next chapter works in MVC, which is completely different. There is no built-in state management, so you need to take different approaches when you want to do this type of work.

You just worked through an activity to help you understand how view state works. The following Try It Out helps you build one of the screens needed for the sample application.

TRY IT OUT Building the Web Page to Add Items to the Inventory

The sample application is based around the idea that you will provide a service enabling members to check out items. However, for this to happen you have to include the capability to create an item; otherwise, there is nothing for the members to check out.

The last chapter covered what you would need to capture for the object. The list of properties included the following:

➤ Name

➤ Description

➤ Cost

➤ ItemNumber

➤ Picture

➤ Date it was acquired

You will now build a data entry screen to create or edit this information. Obviously you will not be saving this into the database as part of this exercise; you will hook that up in Chapter 13. You will also revisit this page to add validation and user authentication when you get to those chapters.

1. Open the RentMyWrox solution in Visual Studio.

2. Create a new folder in the RentMyWrox project. This folder is used to hold all of the administrative pages that you need in order to manage the site, so call the folder "**Admin.**"

3. In the new folder, create a new Web Form named "**ManageItem.aspx**" by right-clicking the Admin folder, selecting "Add New Item" and ensuring that you select the Web Form with Master Page option, as shown in Figure 5-18.

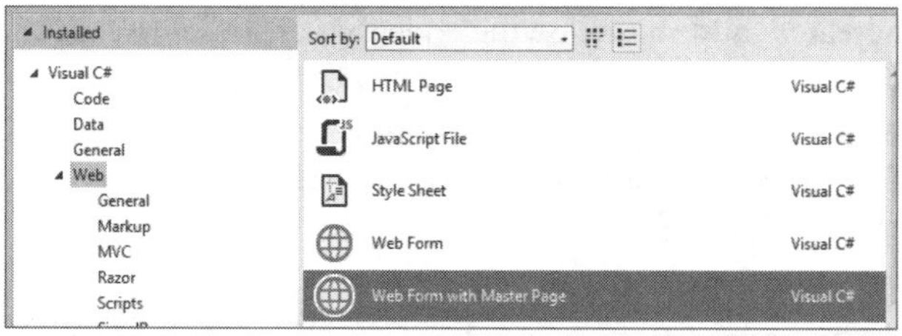

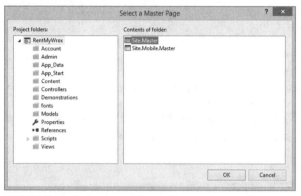

FIGURE 5-18: Web Form with Master Page

4. The dialog shown in Figure 5-19 will appear. Select Site.Master from the available options.

FIGURE 5-19: Selecting a Master Page

> **NOTE** *Master pages enable you to provide a common styling and design across multiple pages. A master page is a template that contains a set of sections for which other pages in the site provide content. Typically a Master page contains common menus and serves as a central point for CSS and JavaScript files that can then be available to all pages. A page that inherits a master page does not contain the <HTML> elements, and will very likely not contain the <Head> and <Body> elements. ASP.NET Web Forms master pages are covered in much more detail in Chapter 7.*

5. Looking at the new markup page you created demonstrates the differences between regular pages and pages created with a master page—there are only a couple lines of code. You have to do all of the entry between the content elements. Create an initial `<div>` set as shown next. This moves all the other items that you are going to create down onto the page 100 pixels, providing some separation:

```
<div style="margin-top:100px;" > </div>
```

6. Between the `<div>` tags that you just created, add the following code that creates a related textbox and label that are wrapped in a `<div>` tag:

```
<div class="dataentry">
    <asp:Label runat="server" Text="Name" AssociatedControlID="tbName" />
    <asp:TextBox runat="server" ID="tbName" />
</div>
```

7. Run your website by selecting F5. You should get a screen that looks similar to Figure 5-20.

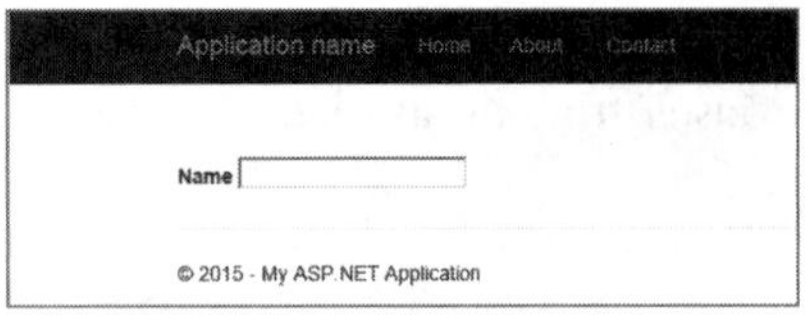

FIGURE 5-20: Newly created form fields

8. Add a couple more fields as shown next. Note the difference in the Description textbox. It has two additional attributes, `TextMode` and `Rows`. Because you know that the description can be a longer set of textual information, you are creating a box that enables users to enter multiple rows of data. When this HTML is created, that control renders into a `<textarea>` element rather than an `<input>` element.

```
<div class="dataentry">
    <asp:Label runat="server" Text="Description"
            AssociatedControlID="tbDescription" />
    <asp:TextBox runat="server" ID="tbDescription"
            TextMode="MultiLine" Rows="5" />
</div>
<div class="dataentry">
    <asp:Label runat="server" Text="Cost"
            AssociatedControlID="tbCost" />
    <asp:TextBox runat="server" ID="tbCost" />
</div>
```

9. Run the app. You should see a screen similar to Figure 5-21. Notice how the description is a different size compared to the other textboxes. Unfortunately, you can also see how poorly aligned everything is.

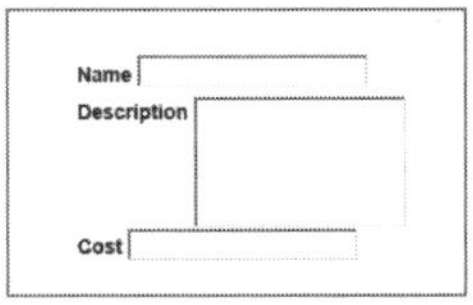

FIGURE 5-21: Poorly formatted form

You'll want to fix that. Add the styles listed next. You might remember doing this from Chapter 3; you are identifying each of the different types of elements within the `<div class="dataentry">`

elements. Also, for now you will simply put them at the top of the already added elements, rather than in a separate .css file. You will move this when you work more with master pages.

```
<style>
    .dataentry input{
        width: 250px;
        margin-left: 20px;
        margin-top: 15px;
    }

    .dataentry textarea{
        width: 250px;
        margin-left: 20px;
        margin-top: 15px;
    }

    .dataentry label{
        width: 75px;
        margin-left: 20px;
        margin-top: 15px;
    }
</style>
```

Run the app and note how much better the form looks.

10. Add the remaining fields and the button that you need to submit the form:

```
<div class="dataentry">
    <asp:Label runat="server" Text="Item Number"
            AssociatedControlID="tbItemNumber"  />
    <asp:TextBox runat="server" ID="tbItemNumber" />
</div>
<div class="dataentry">
    <asp:Label runat="server" Text="Picture" AssociatedControlID="fuPicture"  />
    <asp:FileUpload ID="fuPicture" ClientIDMode="Static" runat="server" />
</div>
<div class="dataentry">
    <asp:Label runat="server" Text="Acquired Date"
            AssociatedControlID="tbAcquiredDate"  />
    <asp:TextBox runat="server" ID="tbAcquiredDate" />
</div>
<asp:Button Text="Save Item" runat="server" OnClick="SaveItem_Clicked" />
```

11. Open the code-behind page. As you may have noticed, the button that you added in step 10 has an OnClick event that is registered to an event handler. You need to add that event handler. This handler needs to be within the brackets around the ManageItem class definition:

```
protected void SaveItem_Clicked(object sender, EventArgs e)
{

}
```

12. Run the page by clicking F5. Notice that the file upload section is not properly placed. The file upload control has an independent streak; it has its own bizarre sets of rules for appearance, so add the following to the styles that you created earlier so that you can style the control based on its id (as shown by using the "#" in the selector).:

```
#fuPicture {
        margin-top: -20px;
        margin-left: 120px;
    }
```

13. Now that you have the data entry form looking consistent, you'll add some code to the code-behind to demonstrate how you can use the content returned from the form. In the `SaveItem_Clicked` method created earlier, add the following lines of code:

```
string name = tbName.Text;
string description = tbDescription.Text;
string itemNumber = tbItemNumber.Text;
double cost = double.Parse(tbCost.Text);
DateTime acquiredDate = DateTime.Parse(tbAcquiredDate.Text);
byte[] uploadedFileContent = fuPicture.FileBytes;
```

This code that you are adding now will be changed in future chapters, but it gives you an idea of how to work with the values that are returned. As you can tell, there is some risk with this code because it relies on `tbCost` and `tbAcquiredDate` having the text input in the right format. You fix this as well through the use of validators. Lastly, the information that you are getting from the file upload control is simply the byte array that makes up the image. You will store this in the database, so this format makes it easier. You could also store the uploaded file on the server's file system if desired rather than just storing the content of the file as an array of bytes.

14. Put a breakpoint by the closing bracket of the method and run the application by clicking the green arrow or the F5 key. Mousing over the various values shows that you have captured the values from the form. Figure 5-22 shows the content of the byte array.

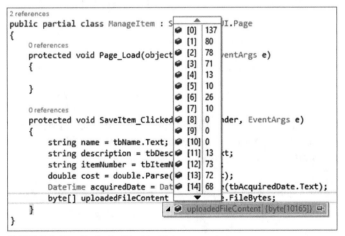

FIGURE 5-22: Code-behind in Debug mode

How It Works

You have created an initial data entry screen that is capable of persisting items into the database (which you will learn how to do later). You added several different types of controls, including labels, text-boxes, and file upload. You also created some code to capture information that has been submitted to the server through the form.

These two parts, the markup and the code-behind, work together to create multiple complete request/response sets. The first set covers when the client does the first request for a page and the server responds. At this point the communication is not a postback. When the client receives this first response, the form entry page is rendered in the browser. When the user completes filling out the form and submits it, the second request/response set starts.

When this second request gets to the server, the processor can recognize that it is a postback and is able to handle anything that may be implied by that difference, including accessing view state and running through specific areas of the code. At this point any event handlers may be called as necessary; the form has been delivered, filled out, and returned to the server.

You have not completed every data entry form, nor have you used every control, but you should have an idea of how the controls are added in the markup page and then accessed in the code-behind.

Creating and working with ASP.NET server controls is quick and simple. You can easily add a series of controls to a page, wire them up in the code-behind, and validate that they work correctly in a matter of minutes.

SUMMARY

ASP.NET Web Form server controls provide a robust set of functional support for web developers. These controls provide full control over many common pieces of a web-based user interface, ranging from simple blocks of text to textboxes that are used to capture data from within a Web Form. Other controls can provide calendars for date selection, file upload capability, and dropdown list selection, among other things; each fulfills a need that you may have during the construction of a website.

There are two parts to using server controls: putting them in the markup so they are written out to the client as part of the returned and rendered HTML, and working with the results in the code-behind after the filled out controls are returned to the server. Working with the results in the code-behind requires that you first access the control by Id, and then the property that you are trying to access.

Not only can you access the values in the control, you can have the server perform an analysis of the data that is coming in, comparing it against the previous version. This is all controlled by the state management engine. The state management system uses ViewState to maintain the previous values of controls—basically, an old copy of the data that can be compared against the newly submitted version in order to understand what changed.

EXERCISES

1. Can every property be set in the code-behind, or must some always be set in the markup?

2. What do you have to do differently in order to understand the selected items in a `CheckBoxList` versus what you do to understand the text in a `TextBox`?

3. Does adding a `runat="server"` attribute to an HTML element change anything?

4. What is view state?

► **WHAT YOU LEARNED IN THIS CHAPTER**

CssClass	A property on standard controls. When used, the value that is entered into this property will be put into the class attribute of the outermost HTML element.
Debugging	Debugging is a feature of Visual Studio that enables you to trace code as it runs. You can set breakpoints that tell the program where to stop while running, as well as look into the values of properties and other items while running through code.
EnableViewState	A standard control property that determines whether the control's content is stored in ViewState while running. Those items that do not enable view state may end up losing data or missing event calls.
HTML Controls	These controls are created by adding a runat="server" attribute to the HTML element in the markup. This enables you to access various values and attributes in code-behind.
Markup	A term that describes the .aspx page where the HTML is written
OnClick	An event on a button. To take advantage of the event in your code you have to wire it up to an event handler. This event handler must have a method signature of object and EventArgs.
Postback	Describes when a page is posted back to itself. This is one of the most common Web Forms approaches, because a file is downloaded to the client where the user can make changes and then that file is sent back to the server for processing. This sending back is the postback. The Page object in the code-behind has an IsPostback property that can be used to determine when the data is coming in through a postback.
Standard Controls	The most common type of controls. This set of controls includes textboxes, radio buttons, checkboxes, and labels—most of the items you need to make an interactive website.
ViewState	Enables ASP.NET to manage state. It is a hidden field in the HTML form containing hashed versions of all the information where ViewState is enabled that is sent to the client. This copy of the information is sent on the round-trip so that the server can understand both the current version of the data, as filled out by the user, and the previous version of the data.

6

ASP.NET MVC Helpers and Extensions

WHAT YOU WILL LEARN IN THIS CHAPTER:

> ➤ How to display dynamic information

> ➤ What Razor syntax is and how you use it in the view

> ➤ How routing works

> ➤ Creating actions on the controller

> ➤ Getting your controllers and views to work together

CODE DOWNLOADS FOR THIS CHAPTER:

The wrox.com code downloads for this chapter are found at www.wrox.com/go/ beginningaspnetforvisualstudio on the Download Code tab. The code is in the chapter 06 download and individually named according to the names throughout the chapter.

You have learned about how ASP.NET Web Forms take one type of approach, server controls, to do work whose outcome is rendered into HTML for consumption by the browser on the client machine. For example, a developer can add a server control to the markup and know that a textbox will be displayed in the browser. However, the complete structure of the HTML that is output is not within the developers' control unless they are using HTML controls, with their ancillary limited functionality.

The process is different in ASP.NET MVC. There is no such thing as a server control in the MVC world. There is, instead, a way of writing code "in the UI" that enables the developer to have complete control over the output that is sent to the client. As you can guess, however, "more control" means that you may have to do more writing of code. In some cases you may have scaffolding, or automatically created code (much like the project you started with), that can provide create, edit, view, and list functionality simply by clicking a few buttons. In other cases, you will have to perform the coding yourself.

One of the ways in which MVC provides support is by supporting various language structures in the part of the application that was called markup in ASP.NET Web Forms but in MVC is simply referred to as the view. This chapter introduces this new language structure, Razor, and describes the various approaches you can use for creating your own UIs in lieu of having them created through server controls. This chapter also covers how information from the UI is returned to the server and processed there to perform the work. This entire process provides an overview of the MVC approach to building websites, and by the end of the chapter you should begin to understand some of the fundamental differences between these approaches.

WHY MVC HAS FEWER CONTROLS THAN WEB FORMS

It has already been mentioned several times that MVC does not have as many controls as Web Forms. For example, there is no concept of an `<asp:TextBox />` in the world of ASP.NET MVC. The main reason is because of the different approaches of these two different ASP.NET technologies. In Web Forms, the markup and the code-behind are intertwined; they are always together. Their names are even together—for example, `SomePage.aspx` and `SomePage.aspx.cs` (or .vb)—and the Solution Explorer shows them together. This closeness is indicated by how the `Id` property from a server control is available in the code-behind, as the server control is an instantiated object with all properties available for examination or use. They are a single, bound instance.

It is not that way in ASP.NET MVC. Each piece is independent of the others. A view, whereby the HTML is created, is completely separate from the controllers and knows nothing about them. This separation explains the lack of server controls. Server controls were designed to help both the creation of the HTML and the management of content returned from the client. In MVC, that approach violates the concept of a separation of concerns. A view is concerned only with creating a user interface. A controller is concerned only with receiving information from, and providing information to, a view, and models are concerned only with performing the business logic. ASP.NET MVC separates all those responsibilities by default, whereas ASP.NET Web Forms only partially separates them.

That being said, there are still approaches that make building an ASP.NET MVC site more rapid and provide some help to both developers and designers. These approaches are just completely different from what you have worked with up until this chapter.

A DIFFERENT APPROACH

Whereas ASP.NET Web Forms makes content available between both markup and the code-behind, ASP.NET MVC takes a different approach. Rather than use a control to manage the passing of information, it instead uses the concept of a model. A model represents the underlying logical structure of the data. It is also important to understand that the model has no knowledge of either controller or the view. This model is populated in the controller and then fed into the view. The view then does the work of assigning these property values to the appropriate user interface items that are part of the HTML returned to the client. Figure 6-1 demonstrates this flow.

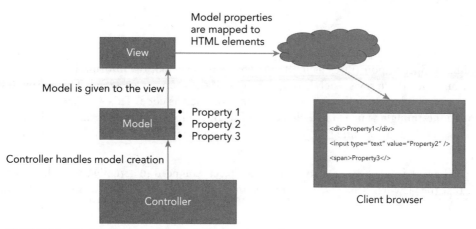

FIGURE 6-1: Workflow for a model being passed to a view

To examine what this looks like in code, first look at how the pieces fit together (later you will actually put them together):

MODEL

```
public class DemoModel
{
    public string Property1 { get; set; }
    public string Property2 { get; set; }
    public string Property3 { get; set; }
}
```

This first code snippet defines the model that you are displaying. This model is creatively named DemoModel and had three properties: Property1, Property2, and Property3. Each of these properties is a string. Now that you have defined the model you are going to display, take a look at how to display it:

VIEW

```
@model RentMyWrox.Models.DemoModel
<html>
<body>
    <div>
        <h4>Demo Model</h4>
        <div>
            @Html.DisplayFor(model => model.Property1)
        </div>
        <div>
            @Html.DisplayFor(model => model.Property2)
        </div>
```

```
            <div>
                    @Html.DisplayFor(model => model.Property3)
            </div>
        </div>
    </body>
</html>
```

The preceding snippet demonstrates using Razor syntax to write out the information. There is a small title and then three rows, each listing the value of the property specified. The @ provides a signal to the server that the following item is to be processed as code. This approach, Razor, enables you to intermingle your HTML elements with code snippets that perform some kind of work, likely using the model while still in the view. You will learn about the different aspects of this in a little bit.

Now that you have the code necessary to display the object, you need to actually create the object and ensure that the view has been given the information that is needed. This is demonstrated in the following snippet:

CONTROLLER

```
// GET: DemoModel/Details/5
public ActionResult Details(int id)
{
    DemoModel dm = new DemoModel {
        Property1 = id.ToString(),
        Property2 = string.Format("Property2 {0}", id),
        Property3 = string.Format("Property3 {0}", id)
    };
    return View("DemoModelView", dm);
}
```

The preceding controller action creates a new DemoModel object, gives it some values, and then returns the instantiated view with the filled-out value. Figure 6-2 shows what this looks like in a browser.

FIGURE 6-2: Simple model displayed in your MVC view

The last thing to examine in this process is the HTML that is generated for display:

```
<!DOCTYPE html>
<html>
<body>
    <div>
        <h4>Demo Model</h4>
        <div>
```

```
            5
        </div>
        <div>
            Property2 5
        </div>
        <div>
            Property3 5
        </div>
    </div>
</body>
</html>
```

As you can see, this code is considerably cleaner than the HTML that was created as part of the ASP.NET Web Form process. When you asked the system to display a property, that is all the system did. No additional HTML elements are created; it simply writes out the value.

VISUAL STUDIO BROWSER LINK

You may see additional information in your source code file that looks something like the following:

```
<!-- Visual Studio Browser Link -->
<script type="application/json"
            id="__browserLink_initializationData">
    {"appName":"Internet Explorer",
            "requestId":"f8988d1d98254450a17a5a2eb8cb978b"}
</script>
<script type="text/javascript" src="http://localhost:1560/7b3228a4
        51c34edcba6ff58fe23c0968/browserLink" async="async"></
script>
<!-- End Browser Link -->
```

This is added only when you are working with the application in Visual Studio. Browser Link creates a communication channel between Visual Studio and the browser. When Browser Link is enabled, it injects special <script> references into every page request from the server. These references use a technology called SignalR. SignalR allows you to add real-time web functionality to your applications, or the ability to have your server-side code push content to the connected clients as it happens, in real time, that enables Visual Studio to communicate with your open browser. This in turn enables you to make changes in Visual Studio, click a refresh button, and the browser refreshes with the changes you have made. You won't be using this functionality when you work through the sample application, but you may see this code when you view source—even though it isn't displayed in the browser when you view the created HTML. This code only is added when you are running in Debug mode from within Visual Studio.

This is a big difference from the ASP.NET Web Forms approach. You will now walk through the various parts of this triad. First is the model. In this case it is a simple class with three properties;

there's nothing special at all about it. In a real-world scenario this model is much more complex, but the process is the same.

Next is the view. The view is mostly HTML, very similar to the HTML source that was sent to the client and rendered in the browser, other than two types of lines of code. The first of these lines was:

```
@model RentMyWrox.Models.DemoModel
```

This is the very first line in the page, and it serves to define the model with which the view will be working. In this case, the model is in the `RentMyWrox.Models` namespace and is an object of type `DemoModel`. The @ sign indicates that the parsing will be done through Razor. The second type of line is shown next.

```
@Html.DisplayFor(model => model.Property1)
```

The preceding line tells the Razor view engine to display the property `Property1` from the model on the page.

Razor

Razor syntax is a simple programming syntax for embedding server-based code in a web page. In a web page that uses the Razor syntax, there are two kinds of content: client content and server code. Client content is the stuff you're used to in web pages: HTML markup (elements), style information such as CSS, maybe some client script such as JavaScript, and plain text.

Razor syntax is a syntactical approach to adding decision making, looping, and other code approaches in the view. It harkens back to the original Active Server Pages (ASP) approach that was around before the advent of the .NET Framework. Classic ASP had a mix of code and UI in a single page that would be run on the server to create the HTML that was sent to the client's browser. Razor supports the same approach—enabling UI logic to make some decisions based on the data with which the view is working.

The code that is written to take advantage of the Razor support is based on C# (or VB). Whereas Web Form server controls look more like HTML, using Razor in a view is like writing C# (or VB) code in the UI, so you only need to write in your language of choice, rather than also need to know the special server control attributes.

Be aware of the following when using the Razor language:

➤ **Code is added to a page using the @ character.** Using this special character tells the parser that the next set of commands should be looked at as if they were processing code rather than HTML elements. You saw these used twice in the example, first when you declared the type of the model and then when you told the parser to write out the value of a particular property.

➤ **You can enclose code blocks in braces.** Not all code can be written on a single line, so you can use braces to contain code blocks. This would look like one of the following two approaches:

```
@{var someValue = model.Property1;}
```

```
@{
    var someOtherValue = model.Property2;
    someOtherValue += " " + model.Property2;
}
```

➤ **Inside a block, you end each code statement with a semicolon.** Just as if you were writing the application code in C#, you must end each line of code with the semicolon to indicate the end of that particular instructional line.

➤ **You can use variables to store values.** Razor enables you to create and use variables in the view code itself. These variables are instantiated, accessed, and used just as they would be in traditional code.

➤ **You enclose literal string values in double quotation marks.** Another demonstration of the similarity between writing Razor syntax and regular C# code is that strings need to be declared in the view just as they would be when working within the code.

➤ **You can write code that makes decisions.** All of your decisions do not have to be made elsewhere; you can instead perform an analysis to determine some information from within your view using the same structure you would use in a Web Forms code-behind.

➤ You can intermingle code and HTML code. The parser is able to understand the difference between the two because the code is prefaced with a @ code and braces while HTML code is defined by the element braces "<>".

All of the preceding points should be familiar; they pretty much say that all the rules you have when working with your C# (or VB) code are also applicable when working with the Razor syntax; the sole exception is use of the @ character to identify the next command as being code-based rather than HTML markup.

Take a look now at another example of using C# code in Razor. In this case, you write out a list of numbers from 0 to 5:

```
<!DOCTYPE html>
<html>
<body>
    @{
        for(int i=0; i <= 5; i++)
        {
            <div>@i</div>
            <div>i</div>
        }
    }
</body>
</html>
```

This code snippet demonstrates how you can intermingle code and markup, and the Razor engine is smart enough to figure out which is which and ensure that the proper HTML is created and sent to the client.

In this example, the loop is contained within a code block that is marked with the @ character. This lets the Razor view engine know that processing happens within the block, which is why the line of code containing the `for` loop itself does not have to be marked. However, once the context was changed by adding the HTML elements, then the @ character had to be used, which is why the variable *i* is so prefaced. When the variable *i* is used without the @ character, the Razor view engine does not identify it as being the variable value and renders it as displayed in Figure 6-3.

FIGURE 6-3: Output when including the @ character

As you can likely imagine, you can also handle lists of objects as the model that is being passed into the view. That approach could look something like this:

```
@model List<RentMyWrox.Models.DemoModel>
<!DOCTYPE html>
<html>
<body>
    <table class="table">
    @foreach (var item in Model) {
        <tr>
            <td>
                @Html.DisplayFor(modelItem => item.Property1)
            </td>
            <td>
                @Html.DisplayFor(modelItem => item.Property2)
            </td>
            <td>
                @Html.DisplayFor(modelItem => item.Property3)
            </td>
        </tr>
    }
    </table>
</body>
</html>
```

Thus, if the model were a list of six DemoModel objects you would get the output shown in Figure 6-4.

FIGURE 6-4: Output of a @foreach loop writing the display

Razor is a powerful tool because it enables you to combine processing power with HTML markup. Although this chapter has talked about the fact that you can include code with the HTML elements, it hasn't yet covered the various special commands, such as those you have seen several times with the `@Html.DisplayFor()` method. Table 6-1 provides some information about each of the `Display` extension methods.

TABLE 6-1: Display Extension Methods

METHOD	DESCRIPTION AND EXAMPLE
Display()	This extension method is used when you do not know the model type that may be passed in. This could happen when a view is used for several different types of items that have similarly named properties, or perhaps when OO inheritance is involved. When using the `Display` method you pass in the property name as a string value. Example: `Html.Display("PropertyNameFromModel")`
DisplayFor()	This extension method enables you to create an expression that describes which value on the model is displayed. This expression is a lambda expression and gives direction the view engine. Example: `Html.DisplayFor(x => x.Property1)`
DisplayForModel()	This extension method enables you to use templates to display information, if you have built a custom template that manages the display. This is useful when you want to reuse the same display of an object in different views. Templates are covered in more detail in Chapter 9. Example: `Html.DisplayForModel("templateName")`

LAMBDA EXPRESSIONS

In its simplest form, a lambda expression is a reusable expression. In the `DisplayFor()` example in Table 6-1, the following lambda expression is used:

```
x => x.Property1
```

This can be translated to "for every given x (the variable name for the object), return the value of the property Property1." The variable name to the left of the equals sign names the object you are working with, and the block to the right of the => provides the work that is performed—in this case, returning the value of the property. You can do anything in the code block, such as the following examples:

```
x => RunSomeMethod(x)
y => y.SomeMethod()
```

continues

continued

In the first case, you are running a method, passing in the given variable; in the second, you are running a method on the object.

A special feature of lambda expressions is the capability to create a usable, in-line function out of them:

```
Func<DemoModel, string> myFunction = x => x.Property1 + " " +
x.Property2;
```

With the preceding function you can do the following work:

```
var newModel = new DemoModel
{
    Property1 = "blahblah",
    Property2 = "Property2",
    Property3 = "Property3"
};
string concatenatedProperties = myFunction(newModel);
```

While you won't be using lambda expressions as a standalone function, you will be using them frequently throughout the rest of the sample application, in particular when you interact with the database.

As you can see, some powerful features are part of the view definition. They enable you to build your UI using a combination of HTML elements and C# (or VB) code. It is important to keep in mind that although this part is called a view, all of this processing is still happening on the server; that is, all of this processing is completed before the page is sent to the client. This code that you run in the view is based on the information passed to it, generally a model. In the next section, you'll look at the part of the framework responsible for creating the model and handing it to the view: the controller.

Controller

The controller in an MVC framework is appropriately named, as it is in charge of managing which views are called and with what information, or model. The controller acts to connect the model to the view, and it is able to determine which model and view because it is also the functionality that handles the HTTP request.

You may remember from the earlier discussion about HTTP how communications between client and server are based on a request-response model whereby the client requests a specific URL with a specific verb (GET, PUT, POST, or DELETE). The server receives the request, perhaps doing some work, and then responds with the expected information. In an ASP.NET MVC application, the controller is what receives the request and determines what information is displayed.

Many different controllers participate in a web application, with each controller potentially having multiple methods, or actions. A controller is responsible for handling the functionality for a unique combination of URL and HTTP verb, especially the four major verbs just listed. This means there would be one controller method, or action, that handles a GET request, another that handles a

PUT request, one for POST requests, and another for DELETE requests in those cases where you may need to use all verbs. Listing 6-1 shows what this would look like for the DemoModel object created earlier.

LISTING 6-1: Controller methods that manage access to DemoModel

```
0.  public class DemoModelController : Controller {
1.  // GET: DemoModel
2.  public ActionResult Index()
3.  {
4.      List<DemoModel> list = new List<DemoModel>();
5.      for (int i = 0; i <= 5; i++)
6.      {
7.          list.Add(new DemoModel
8.          {
9.              Property1 = i.ToString(),
10.             Property2 = string.Format("Property2 {0}", i),
11.             Property3 = string.Format("Property3 {0}", i)
12.         });
13.     }
14.     return View("DemoModelList", list);
15. }
16.
17. // GET: DemoModel/Details/5
18. public ActionResult Details(int id)
19. {
20.     DemoModel dm = new DemoModel {
21.         Property1 = id.ToString(),
22.         Property2 = string.Format("Property2 {0}", id),
23.         Property3 = string.Format("Property3 {0}", id)
24.     };
25.     return View("DemoModelView", dm);
26. }
27.
28. // GET: DemoModel/Create
29. public ActionResult Create()
30. {
31.     return View(); // this view will be the form that needs to be filled
        out
32. }
33.
34. // POST: DemoModel/Create
35. [HttpPost]
36. public ActionResult Create(DemoModel model)
37. {
38.     // Do some work to create
39.     return View(); // view to confirm that a new item was created
40. }
41.
42. // GET: DemoModel/Edit/5
43. public ActionResult Edit(int id)
44. {
```

continues

LISTING 6-1 *(continued)*

```
45.     return View(); // this view will be the form that needs to be filled
        out
46. }
47.
48. // POST: DemoModel/Edit/5
49. [HttpPost]
50. public ActionResult Edit(int id, DemoModel model)
51. {
52.     // do some work here to save edits
39.     return View(); // view to confirm that the item was edited
54. }
55. }
```

This listing contains all the methods within a single controller, `DemoModelController`. There is a comment above each of the methods that describes the verb that it works with, as well as the URL to which it responds. Thus, the `Index` method on line 2 responds to a GET to http://websitedomain/ DemoModel, and the `Details` method on line 5 responds to a GET request to http://websitedomain/ DemoModel/Details/Id, where Id is an integer.

Routing

Examining the contents of Listing 6-1 may raise some questions, such as how does this controller know to respond to the URLs that are part of the path as demonstrated by http://websitedomain/ DemoModel; and how does the server know to call that method on that particular controller? The server is able to determine what action to take based on the routing configuration, as shown in Figure 6-5.

FIGURE 6-5: The RouteConfig.cs file in the App_Start directory

The App_Start folder that was created as part of the project template contains several files. The one that you are concerned with here is the `RouteConfig.cs` file. This file creates the maps that the server uses to determine which method in which controller to call based on the URL that was requested. It can create very specific routes or it can use templates, as shown in the figure.

Further examination of the route is in order. The following snippet shows the route describing the class and method that need to be called:

```
routes.MapRoute(
    name: "Default",
```

```
      url: "{controller}/{action}/{id}",
      defaults: new { action = "Index", id = UrlParameter.Optional }
);
```

The key to understanding what is happening is the line containing the `url:`. This sets the route template to be `Controller/Action/Id`. Thus, when a URL is requested that contains *DemoModel* as part of the path, the system looks for the controller that supports this object. It understands this through the convention of combining the string value of the request, "DemoModel" and the word "Controller," so any incoming request that includes *DemoModel* as part of the path is expected to be handled by a class called `DemoModelController`.

The action part of the route is the method on that controller that will be called. Thus, `http://websitedomain/DemoModel/Details/` calls the `Details` method in the `DemoModelController`. The `defaults:` line of the preceding snippet shows how to handle missing values. A default is set for the action: Index. This tells the system that if no action is included in the URL, the value given should be substituted—in this case, Index. This is demonstrated by lines 1 and 2 in Listing 6-1, where a method named `Index` is shown to respond to `http://websitedomain/DemoModel`, in this case with a list of DemoModels.

The last part of the route is the Id. The default section makes this optional, so it may or may not be included in the request URL. This item becomes the parameter of the method, so `http://websitedomain/DemoModel/Details/5` is the same as calling the `Details` method and passing in 5 as the parameter, as shown on line 18 of Listing 6-1.

Looking at the route you are working with, what do you think would happen to a request for `http://websitedomain/DemoModel/Details`? You would expect it to call the `Details` method on the `DemoModelController`; but the only such method also expects an integer parameter, and you are not providing one. What do you think will happen? If you guess that the system will explode, sending smoke everywhere, then you are pretty close, as shown in Figure 6-6.

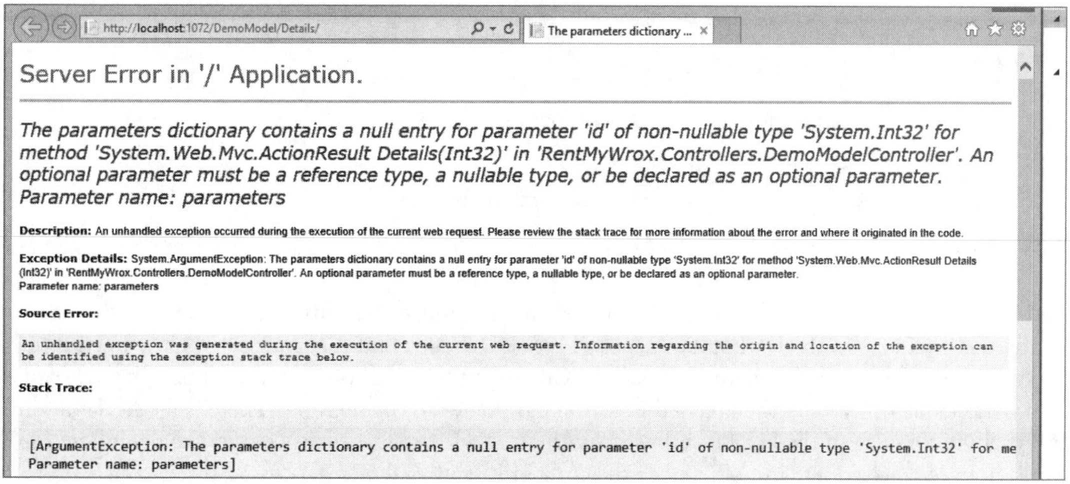

FIGURE 6-6: Error when Id is not included in the URL

In this case, you get an error because the system is trying to provide a null value as the parameter to the `Details` method, and integers cannot be null. If you think there's a chance that this URL will be called without a value, and you want to handle it, you can change the route to the following:

```
routes.MapRoute(
    name: "Default",
    url: "{controller}/{action}/{id}",
    defaults: new { action = "Index", id = 0 }
);
```

With the preceding change, the system now calls the `Details` method; and if no *Id* is provided as part of the URL, it calls the `Details` method with the default of `0`.

When you are working with the parameter it is critical that the variable name in the `url:` match the variable name of the parameter. If they are completely different, such as when `Route` was defined with `url: "{controller}/{action}/{itemId}"`, then the defaults will not be set and the error shown earlier in Figure 6-6 repeats. It is always best to ensure that the variable name you use when mapping the route is the name that you use when defining your method signature; that way it's easier to look at the route configuration and see an identifier that would be easily linked to the parameter being passed into the various actions.

HTTP Verbs and Attributes

You have learned that the server can determine what to do when a URL is requested; but what about an example such as the following, where there is an overload of the `Create` method, with the overload (when a method has the same name and return type but accepts a different set of parameters) expecting an object rather than a simple integer?

```
28. // GET: DemoModel/Create
29. public ActionResult Create()
30. {
31.     return View(); // this view is the form that needs to be filled out
32. }
33.
34. // POST: DemoModel/Create
35. [HttpPost]
36. public ActionResult Create(DemoModel model)
37. {
38.     // Do some work to create
39.     return View(); // view to confirm that a new item was created
40. }
41.
```

The item `[HttpPost]` on line 35 demonstrates the difference. This attribute tells the system that if there is a request to the URL `http://websitedomain/DemoModel/Create` using the HTTP verb POST, then the attributed method should be called and that the form content should be mapped to a `DemoModel` object and then passed in as the parameter to the method. There is a corresponding attribute for each of the HTTP verbs, including GET. However, because GET is the default action you do not see the attribute used in any of the code in Listing 6-1.

Another reason why you do not see the `HttpGet` attribute used is that the attribute also acts to limit the verbs on which the action method can work; therefore, the method with the `[HttpPost]` attribute responds only to those requests with the verb POST, while the other `Create` method is able to respond to any of the HTTP verbs. Giving it an `[HttpGet]` attribute would mean that it could not respond to other requests that contain other verbs such as a DELETE call to `http://websitedomain/DemoModel/Create`. If that method were so attributed, the DELETE call would cause an error, rather than simply being treated as a GET.

FORM-BUILDING HELPERS

This chapter has briefly covered models, views, and controllers, and how the URL of the request points to a specific method on the controller. The view that was covered shows how to display information on the page. Not yet discussed is building a form, and how that would work such that when a POST is sent to the server, the server knows how to understand the data and create the appropriate model from the form values. In this section you will learn all about that.

Form Extensions

The previous section showed some examples of how you could display data in your view. This is a pretty straightforward need. Creating the form entry fields is a little more involved, mostly because you want the system to be able to understand the information in the form fields that are sent back to the server so that it can build the appropriate model that you can easily work with in the controller.

You can help the server understand the relationship between an input element on the form and the model through the use of a tightly bound, type-safe approach of linking an HTML element to a specific property in the model. This is done by using the `#Html.InputType` (a Lambda expression showing which property to bind). Table 6-2 provides a list of these different input types as well as an example demonstrating how they are used and the HTML that is generated from the command.

TABLE 6-2: Type-Safe Extensions

EXTENSION	DESCRIPTION AND EXAMPLE
TextArea	Creates a text area control that holds multiple rows of text Razor: `@Html.TextAreaFor(m=>m.Address , 5, 15, new{}))` HTML: `<textarea cols="15" id="Address" name=" Address " rows="5">Addressvalue</textarea>`
TextBox	Creates a traditional textbox Razor: `@Html.TextBoxFor(m=>m.Name)` HTML: `<input id="Name" name="Name" type="text" value="NameValue" />`

continues

TABLE 6-2 *(continued)*

EXTENSION	DESCRIPTION AND EXAMPLE
CheckBox	Creates a checkbox Razor: `@Html.CheckBoxFor(m=>m.IsEnabled)` HTML: `<input id="IsEnabled" name="IsEnabled"` `type="checkbox" value="true" />`

Dropdown List	Used to create a dropdown box from which the user can select only one value
	
	Razor: `@Html.DropDownListFor(m => m.Gender,`
	    `new SelectList(new [] {"Male", "Female"}))`
	
	HTML: `<select id="Gender" name="Gender">`
	    `<option>Male</option>`
	    `<option>Female</option>`
	  `</select>`

HiddenField	Used to create a field that holds data but is not visible through the UI Razor: `@Html.HiddenFor(m=>m.UserId)` HTML: `<input id="UserId" name="UserId" type="hidden"` `value="UserIdValue" />`
Password	Creates a password field whereby the content typed in by the user is obscured and not visible on screen Razor: `@Html.PasswordFor(m=>m.Password)` HTML: `<input id="Password" name="Password" type="password"/>`
RadioButton	Creates a single radio button Razor: `@Html.RadioButtonFor(m=>m.IsApproved, "Value")` HTML: `<input checked="checked" id="IsApproved"` `name="IsApproved" type="radio" value="Value" />`

Multiple-select	Creates a list of items from which multiple values can be selected
	
	Razor: `Html.ListBoxFor(m => m.Pets,`
	    `new MultiSelectList(new [] {"Cat", "Dog"}))`
	
	HTML: `<select id="Pets" multiple="multiple" name="Pets">`
	    `<option>Cat</option>`
	    `<option>Dog</option>`
	  `</select>`

The differences between this approach and the server controls for Web Forms may seem negligible; you are still letting the system write the HTML. However, the main thing that is missing is the ability to reference a control in code, as the controller does not know about that particular HTML element. In the Web Forms example, the code-behind knew all about the control; it has access to its name, could change the style, or do all sorts of work on it. To be honest, the power of ASP.NET Web Forms is that it does have all this knowledge, which makes sharing information easy. In ASP .NET MVC, the controller knows nothing about the item that is actually created for the user; it has no idea how that information was created. All it knows is that information was submitted.

There are alternative ways to create input HTML elements that allow for data capture. Where the approaches listed in Table 6-2 are bound to a model field through the use of the lambda expression, you can always create the item with a string, rather than an expression; with that override, the element is named with whatever you input as the string. As long as the input name and the model's property name are the same, you will still have the luxury of the bound model as part of the submission.

Editor and EditorFor

You have learned that developers can choose the type of HTML element they will use to capture the data. You can also allow the Razor engine to determine how to render the input element. There is a special set of `HtmlHelpers` objects that do this work. These helpers, `Editor` and `EditorFor`, check the data type of the property to determine what kind of input element should be created:

```
@Html.EditorFor(model => model.Property1);
```

Because the system looks at the property's data type to determine what to display, it generally creates either a textbox or a checkbox, as anything can be entered into a traditional textbox—and nothing represents a Boolean value better than a checkbox. With what you have learned so far, using `EditorFor` might seem like a step back from having control over the HTML that is created and sent to the client, but there are additional benefits to using `EditorFor` as the default way of creating form fields.

One of the key features of `EditorFor` is its ability to work with attributes on the model properties. This book hasn't covered attributes on class properties yet, but you'll learn about their benefits when you start building out your models as part of your interaction with the database. At that point, you will look at various available attributes, one of which enables you to define, on the class property itself, what type of element should be created.

Having this attribute on the property enables you to change how the element is displayed across every representation of an editor for that property, rather than having to manually change the element type on every page. Adding this attribute is simple:

```
[DataType(DataType.MultilineText)]
public string Property2 { get; set; }
```

This changes the display from a traditional textbox to a `textarea` element with multiple rows. This approach would make sense if you were asking for a larger quantity of data, such as a product description or a customer review.

Model Binding

If you have ever looked at information received from an HTML form, you realize that this information is not provided in a nicely structured complex type. Instead, the whole thing is a set of key-value pairs, where the Id of the control is the key, and the value(s) that were entered or selected for that particular control are the values in the key-value pair. You can always work with the information that way as well; for example, the following snippet is perfectly valid:

```
[HttpPost]
public ActionResult ActionWithFormCollection(FormCollection formCollection)
{
    var property1 = formCollection["Property1"];
    var property2 = formCollection["Property2"];
    return View();
}
```

This approach could be useful when using a model doesn't make sense, such as when the action is receiving information from a third party. Creating a model to use just to support this method may be overkill when you can get the information you need from the key-value list in the form. Using models makes the most sense when that model is an object in your domain that you may be using elsewhere or it makes some business sense.

As you will see when building the sample application, when the system is doing the binding for you, it tries to map the object's properties in the following order:

1. Form fields

2. The property values in the JSON (JavaScript Object Notation) request body, but only when the request is an AJAX request

3. Route data

4. Query string parameters

5. Posted files

This order means that the first place it looks for information to bind a property on the model is in the form fields. Therefore, if the property is found in that set of values, then the parser evaluates type, and if the types can be converted correctly (remember that all fields are received by the server as a string), then it converts and assigns that value.

If the parser is unable to find the value in the form fields, it then goes through the JSON request body if the request is an AJAX request. You will learn more about this in the chapter on AJAX requests, Chapter 13. If it can't find the value there, it then snoops through the route data to see if that contains what it's looking for. It then goes through the query string values to see if it finds the information there. If not, it takes a quick look at uploaded files to see if they may match. If it doesn't find the property, the parser shrugs, gives the property its default value, and goes on to the next property.

QUERY STRING

A query string is part of the requested URL that does not fit into the typical HTTP address structure. With the URL of `http://someaddress/DemoObject?field1=value1&field2=value2`, everything after the `?` character defines the query string and the `&` character acts as the separator between each set of key\value pairs. Thus, when the value gets to the server it is a set of key-value pairs, just like the form values. Typically these values are used to qualify the request that is being called. In the example URL just given, the call to DemoObject returns a list of objects. Imagine the case where this list is paginated and sorted; each call to the DemoObject could also include the following query string:

```
?Sort=Property1&SortType=A&Page=2&ItemsPerPage=50
```

This would give additional information to the server to tell it to "sort all the DemoObjects by Property1 ascending and then return items 51–100." If the query string were empty, the request would still work, but the criteria added by the query string make it more specific.

You could also put these values into the URL itself as part of the route, but that would get complicated. There may be times when some of these values are not sent, so the routing can become complicated. Rather than make the routing engine figure out complicated paths, using a query string is suggested.

You can access the query string values in a pretty cool way. If you wanted to allow the following four key-value pairs to be used, you could change the method signature from the empty list of parameters that it has now as follows:

```
public ActionResult Index(string Sort, string SortType, int Page,
    int ItemsPerPage)
```

If you don't want to take that approach, perhaps because there are a lot of values and you don't want to add to the parameter list, you can also access the values as shown here:

```
NameValueCollection coll = Request.QueryString;
string sort = coll["Sort"];
```

The Request object that contains the Querystring property gives you access to the parsed HTTP request that is received by the server. This means that not only do you have the capability to let the various parsers and binders do some work for you, but you always have access to the base request itself if you need it.

The model binding is very straightforward for an object like DemoModel that has a set of simple types. You may be wondering how this would work with complex types, for which a property is not an integer or some other simple type but rather a different object. Consider the following structure

```
public class ComplexModel
{
    public int MyId { get; set; }
    public DemoModel DemoModel { get; set; }
}

public class DemoModel
{
    public string Property1 { get; set; }
```

```
        public string Property2 { get; set; }
        public string Property3 { get; set; }
}
```

where the new object `ComplexModel` contains a property that is a `DemoModel` object. In this case, your input names have to be set up differently. If you consider the parsing engine, when it is trying to find values that can be assigned to `DemoModel`, how do you think it will do it? It looks for input fields with a name of `DemoModel`. However, how can you create a textbox that takes in all the properties of the `DemoModel`? The answer is you can't, nor do you need to.

Although the parsing engine does not recognize that an input field named `Property1` needs to be assigned to the `DemoModel` property's `Property1` property, it does understand that an input field named `DemoModel.Property1` will, because it recognizes the `DemoModel` name and the dot notation indicates that the item to the right of the dot is a property of that particular object.

This dot notation relationship can go as deeply as needed. It is very common to have object graphs that are four to five layers deep; and the parsing engine is able to track the values down and assign them correctly as long as the dot notation is correct. This is also the way that you would access these properties in code, so it makes sense.

Collections work in much the same way in that you can work with them the same way that you can access them in code. Change the object definition as shown here to see what that means:

```
public class ComplexModel
{
    public int MyId { get; set; }
    public List<DemoModel> DemoModels { get; set; }
}
```

As you can see, the `DemoModel` was changed to a list of `DemoModel` objects. However, the dot notation works here as well if you consider that a list can be accessed as an array, through the [index] notation. That means that an input with a name of `DemoModel[0].Property1` is mapped to the first item in the collection's property `Property1`. An input named `DemoModel[1].Property1` is mapped to the second item in the list's `Property1` property, and so forth—again, just as if you were working through the items in code.

You have already seen how the model binder works but, to be frank, as long as you use the various approaches covered earlier to create the HTML elements with which users interact, you should not have to worry about this at all, as the binder is just able to work.

Now that you have learned how it all functions, you will create a data entry form. In the last chapter you created an ASP.NET Web Form data entry form to manage the administrative task of creating an item that is available in the lending library. The rest of the administrative functions for the Web Form already work, so in the following Try It Out you will create a form that captures demographic information about the user.

TRY IT OUT   Creating a User Demographic Information Capture Form

For many sites, it is useful, if not imperative, to know something about the people who have registered. What kind of information might you be interested in knowing about a person? Considering that in the future you may want to do directed marketing, in this activity you gather some demographic information that may be useful:

➤ Birth date

➤ Gender

➤ Marital status

➤ When they moved into the area

➤ Whether they own or rent a home

➤ Number of people living in the household

➤ Hobbies (multiple choices from a known list)

This should give you enough to build on for now. As before, when you were doing the initial Web Forms form, you won't be able to save it, but you will come back and update this as part of the database section in Chapters 8 and 9.

1. Ensure that you have Visual Studio running, your RentMyWrox solution is open and that the Solution Explorer window is available. Right-click the Models directory and select Add ⇨ New Item. When the Add New Item dialog appears, be sure you select the Code option in the left window, and then select Class. Name the file **UserDemographics.cs** (or.vb) as shown in Figure 6-7, and then click the Add button.

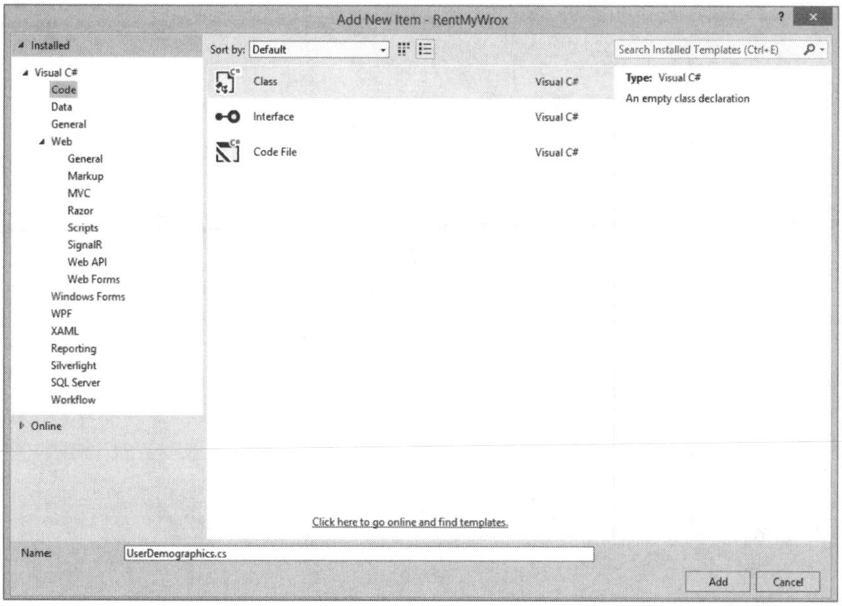

FIGURE 6-7: Creating the Model class

2. Add the following properties to this new class to get a structure like this:

```
public class UserDemographics
{
    public UserDemographics()
```

```
    {
        Hobbies = new List<string>();
    }
    public DateTime Birthdate { get; set; }

    public string Gender { get; set; }

    public string MaritalStatus { get; set; }

    public DateTime DateMovedIntoArea { get; set; }

    public bool OwnHome { get; set; }

    public int TotalPeopleInHome { get; set; }

    public List<string> Hobbies { get; set; }
}
```

3. Save your new model after adding all the properties by selecting File ⇨ Save.

4. Now add the controller that handles all the server work. Select the Controllers directory and right-click to get the context menu. Select Add Controller. The Add Item dialog shown in Figure 6-8 should appear. Select the MVC 5 Controller with read/write actions choice.

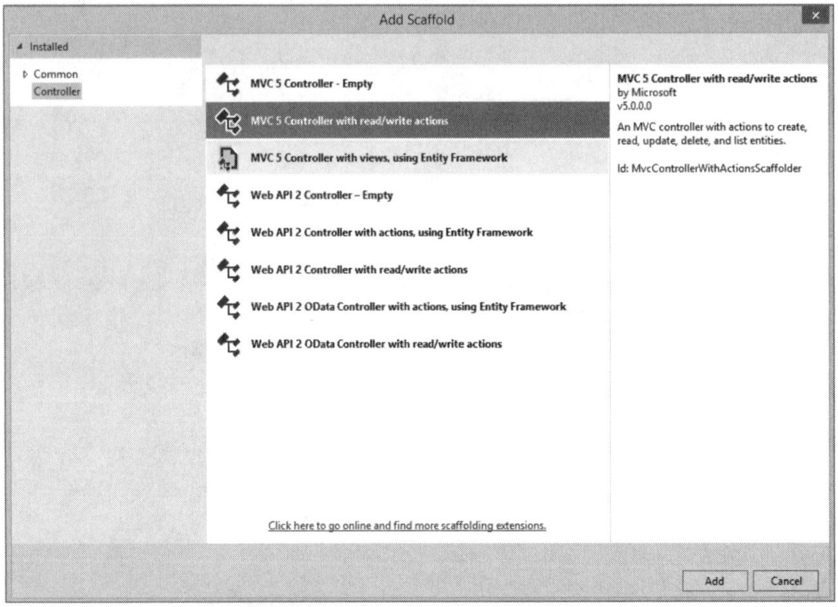

FIGURE 6-8: Creating the Controller class

5. Select the MVC 5 Controller with read/write actions option and click the Add button. When the dialog shown in Figure 6-9 appears, notice how it is already filled out with the "Default" area of the name highlighted. Because you want this controller to manage the `UserDemographics` class that you added earlier, name this file **UserDemographicsController** and then save.

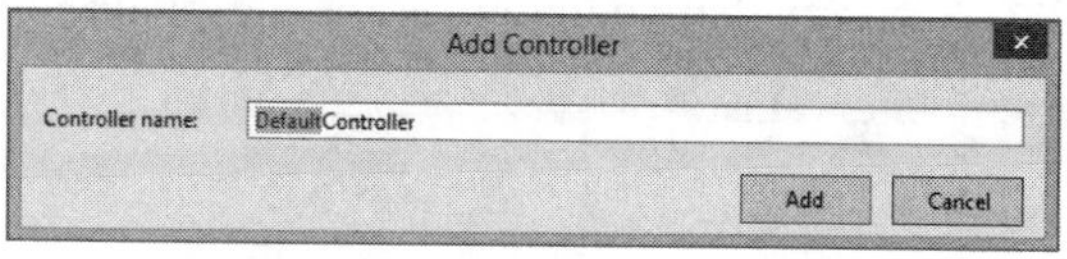

Add Controller

Controller name: DefaultController

Add   Cancel

FIGURE 6-9: Naming the Controller class

6. Ensure that the Views directory is expanded in the Solution Explorer. If you didn't notice, the process of adding a controller also added a folder under the Views directory, as shown in Figure 6-10. Ensure that there is a folder named UserDemographics. This is the folder where you add your views.

FIGURE 6-10: Views folder created when adding the controller

7. Select and right-click the UserDemographics folder to get the context menu. Select Add ➪ View to get the dialog shown in Figure 6-11

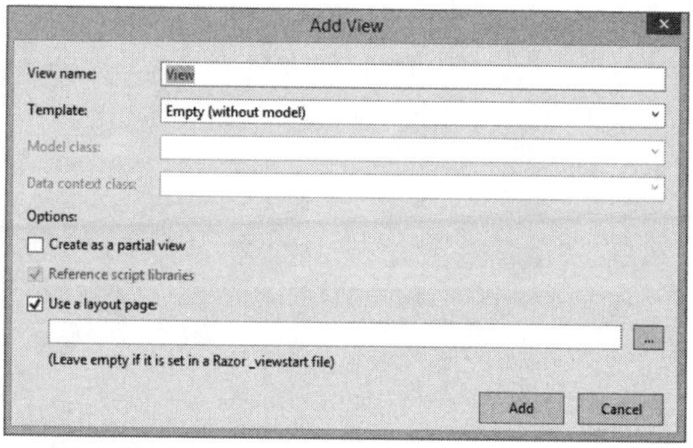

Add View

View name: View

Template: Empty (without model)

Model class:

Data context class:

Options:

☐ Create as a partial view

☑ Reference script libraries

☑ Use a layout page:

(Leave empty if it is set in a Razor _viewstart file)

Add   Cancel

FIGURE 6-11: Dialog to add a view

8. This dialog enables you to create a view that is responsible for doing a set of work. The first field to enter is the name of the view you are creating. The standard convention is to use the same name as the action that responds to the client with that view. Thus, the first view would be the Index view that responds to a request with a list of items. Follow these steps to make this view:

a. Change the view name to Index. You should ensure that you use the proper capitalization.

  i. In the Template area, change the template to List.

  ii. Select UserDemographics as the Model Class.

  iii. Leave DataContext class empty.

  iv. Check "Reference script libraries."

  v. Check Use a layout page.

b. Click Add.

9. Note that there is now a file named `Index.cshtml` (or `Index.vbhtml`) available in the UserDemographics folder. This file should also open in your code window. With that file as the active file in your IDE, select the green arrow or click F5 to run the application.

10. Your application should crash, giving you an error message that includes the phrase "NullReferenceException." Select the Continue button to close the dialog window or Stop debugging the application to recover from the error. This exception was caused because the default Index controller action expects a model, but because you never did any work on the controller action, a null model is sent, which is causing problems. You need to update the view code to prevent this from happening.

Locate the following line of code

```
@foreach (var item in Model) {
```

and change it to read as follows:

```
@if (Model != null)
{
    foreach (var item in Model)
    {
...
```

You also need to find the closing curly bracket (}) at the bottom of the page and add another one, so that there are two closing braces in a row. The change that you just made checks to see whether there is a non-null model before it tries to do any work with the model. Stop the application if it is still running, then run the application again; you should not get an error, but rather the screen shown in Figure 6-12. You have successfully created the view to display a list of UserDemographic objects.

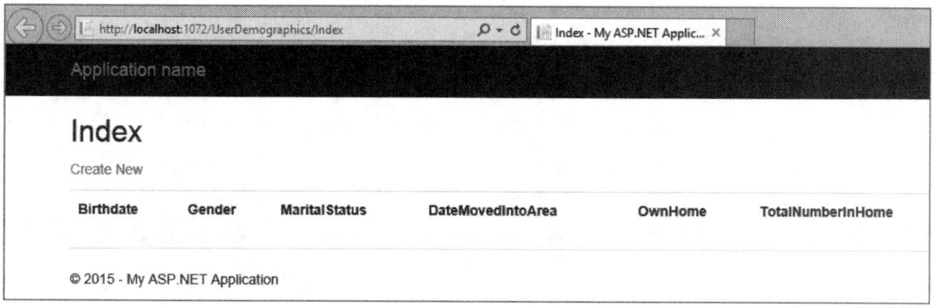

FIGURE 6-12: Browser display of the Index field

How It Works

You have created an initial data-entry form using the ASP.NET MVC framework that transfers information edited by the user to the server. You began by creating the model—the definition of the data to be transferred back and forth between the client and the server. You did this first because everything you do going forward involves management of the creation, editing, and viewing of that model.

Next, you used scaffolding to create a controller for that model. The model name for which you are building the controller is important because the name that you give the controller becomes part of the URL; therefore, if you left the "Default" value, the actions on this controller would be accessed through http://someurl/Default/. Because MVC routing uses RESTful standards, this controller is responsible for handling calls to a URL containing the object name—in this case, `UserDemographics`.

In addition, MVC manages relationships using a convention such that it expects to find the handler for an object in a controller that is named `ObjectNameController`, where the `Controller` part of the name is the standard. The scaffolding creates a set of actions that give the developer a head start on building the typical Read, Create, Update, and Delete processes that are usually needed when working with database items. You can see this if you look into the file and see how the scaffolding created actions, or methods, called Index, Details, Create, Edit, and Delete. Each of these relate to one of the actions we may want to take with UserDemographics as shown in Table 6-3

TABLE 6-3: Scaffold-Created Actions in a New Controller

METHOD SIGNATURE	DEFINITION
`Index()`	The default method that handles when a user goes to a URL of http://websiteUrl/UserDemographics. A typical response could be a list of the objects that are available. We will leave this action alone for now, but we will come back and revisit it after we have added authentication.
`Details(int id)`	The method that handles when a user goes to the URL of http://websiteUrl/UserDemographics/Details/5 and the expectation is that it will return a read-only display of the UserDemographic object.

continues

TABLE 6-3 *(continued)*

METHOD SIGNATURE	DEFINITION
`Create()`	Handles a GET to the URL of http://websiteUrl/ UserDemographics/Create. The view will contain the form fields required to create a new user demographics. This action does not handle the creation, only providing the HTML form to capture the information.
`Create(FormCollection collection)`	Handles a POST to the URL of http://websiteUrl/ UserDemographics/Create. The intent is that this will handle the processing of the form. When we add in the database we will be revisiting this action to handle the saving of the information.
`Edit(int id)`	Handles a GET to the URL of http://websiteUrl/ UserDemographics/Edit/6 and returns a form to change the values of a particular item. Typically the form would have some fields filled out with the current values of those properties as appropriate.
`Edit(int id, FormCollection collection)`	Handles a POST to the URL of http://websiteUrl/ UserDemographics/Edit/6 and handles the update of the object that was submitted.
`Delete(int id)`	Handles a GET to the URL of http://websiteUrl/ UserDemographics/Delete/6, and generally returns some information on the item to be deleted and asks for a confirmation.
`Delete(int id, FormCollection collection)`	Handles a POST to the URL of http://websiteUrl/ UserDemographics/Delete/6 and will handle the actual deleting of the item.

Notice how all of the items that handle the POST actions have a FormCollection as one of the parameters. The FormCollection is a key-value pair collection of items returned as part of the request's body. The Model Binder can instead turn this into the appropriate model. You will keep the FormCollection for the Edit method, but once you get to the Create handler, you change the signature to contain an object as opposed to this FormCollection.

You have created the model and controller that will manage the data and the processing of the request as well as the original view that interacts with that model and controller. Your next step in the following Try it Out is to create the additional views that will provide the UI that the user can interact with.

TRY IT OUT Creating a Simple Data Entry Form

In the last exercise you created a model and a controller as well as a simple view to allow the application to run. In this exercise you will be creating the simple data entry form that will allow the user to fill out and return all of their relevant user demographic information.

1. Ensure that you have Visual Studio running, your RentMyWrox solution is open. Ensure that the Views\UserDemographics folder is selected, and right-click, and select Add ⇨ View. Configure it as follows:

   a. Change the view name to Create. You should ensure that you use the proper capitalization.

   b. In the Template area, change the template to Create.

   c. Select UserDemographics as the Model Class.

   d. Leave DataContext class empty.

   e. Check "Reference script libraries."

   f. Check Use a layout page.

   g. Click Add.

   This adds a Create view to the directory and opens the file in your IDE.

2. Save the application and run the application on this page. The scaffolding builds you a data-entry form like the one shown in Figure 6-13.

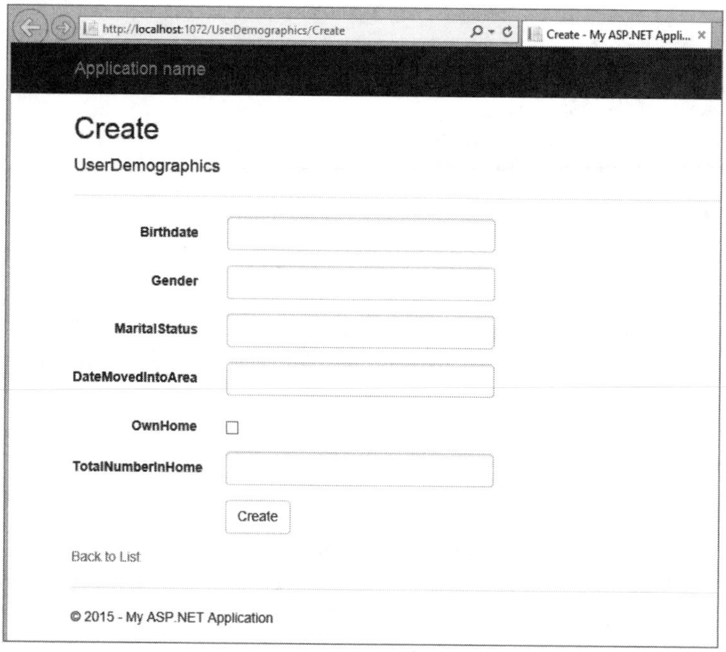

FIGURE 6-13: Initial data-entry form

3.   While this initial form is pretty close to what you need, you should make some changes to get it to the point where it's exactly what you want (just in the form part, you'll deal with styling later). Stop Debugging and locate the line that creates the Gender value. Rather than display a textbox, you want to change this to a dropdown so that you have control over the information being entered. Currently, this line of code looks like the following:

```
@Html.EditorFor(model => model.Gender, new { htmlAttributes = new { @class = "form-
control" } })
```

Change it to the following:

```
@Html.DropDownListFor(model => model.Gender,
        new SelectList(new[] { "Male", "Female", "Other" }),
        new { htmlAttributes = new { @class = "form-control" } })
```

Now you have replaced the textbox with a dropdown that has three different options. This ensures acceptable answers, so you don't have to worry about free-form responses such as "boy" or "F."

4.   Now make the same sort of change for marital status. The current code that you should change is as follows:

```
@Html.EditorFor(model => model.MaritalStatus,
        new { htmlAttributes = new { @class = "form-control" } })
```

Change it to this:

```
@Html.DropDownListFor(model => model. MaritalStatus,
        new SelectList(new[] { "Single", "Married", "Divorced", "Widow(er)", "Other" }),
        new { htmlAttributes = new { @class = "form-control" } })
```

After these edits, running the application will present a form that should look like the one shown in Figure 6-14.

5.   One thing that you may have noticed is missing from the form is the capability to add hobbies. You need to also add this. Go to the top of the Create form and find the section containing the following:

```
@{
    ViewBag.Title = "Create";
}
```

Make the following edit to create a list of potential hobbies:

```
@{
    ViewBag.Title = "Create";
    var hobbyList = new List<string>
        { "Gardening", "Reading", "Games", "Dining Out", "Sports", "Other" };
}
```

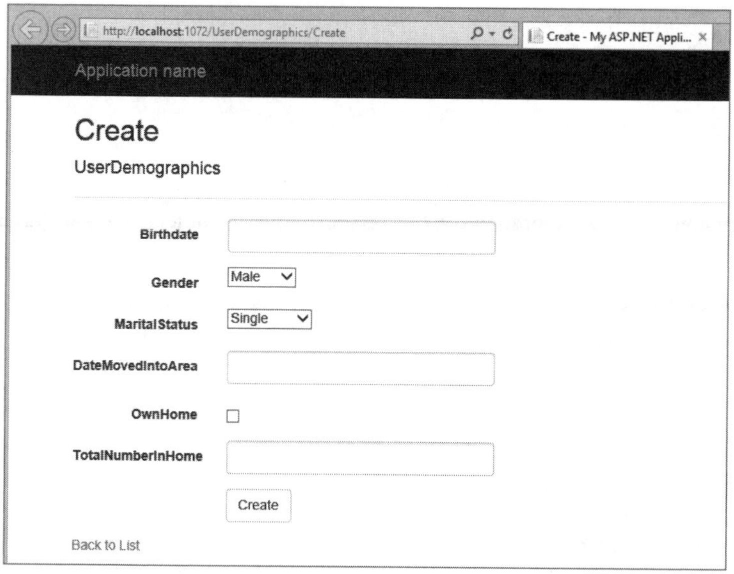

FIGURE 6-14: Edited data-entry form

6. Now you need to add a set of checkboxes, one for each hobby. To do this, locate the section right before the following:

```
<div class="form-group">
    <div class="col-md-offset-2 col-md-10">
        <input type="submit" value="Create" class="btn btn-default" />
    </div>
</div>
```

Add the following code before the previous section:

```
<div class="form-group">
    @Html.LabelFor(model => model.Hobbies,
            htmlAttributes: new { @class = "control-label col-md-2" })
    <div class="col-md-10">
        @foreach (string hobby in hobbyList)
        {
        <span>
            <input name="hobbies" value="@hobby" type="checkbox" />
            @hobby
        </span>
        }
    </div>
</div>
```

7. Now that you have changed the data-entry form, you need to make some changes to the controller action, or method, that handles the submission. In the UserDemographicsController file, find the following line of code:

```
public ActionResult Create(FormCollection collection)
```

To change the object coming in, update the method signature to the following:

```
public ActionResult Create(UserDemographics obj)
```

You also need to add a `using` statement to the top of the page:

```
using RentMyWrox.Models;
```

Adding the `using` enables you to easily reference the `UserDemographics` object without having to use the complete namespace.

8. To handle the hobbies you added, put a breakpoint in the method as shown in Figure 6-15 by clicking in the gray border to the left of the code. You need to ensure that the breakpoint is on the same line as code that can be run.

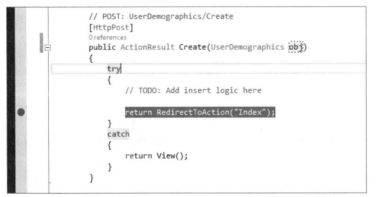

```
// POST: UserDemographics/Create
[HttpPost]
0 references
public ActionResult Create(UserDemographics obj)
{
    try
    {
        // TODO: Add insert logic here

        return RedirectToAction("Index");
    }
    catch
    {
        return View();
    }
}
```

FIGURE 6-15: Create a breakpoint in a method

9. Switch back to have the Create view as the active file and run the application in Debug mode. If you do not see the data entry screen, change the URL in the browser toolbar to the appropriate one: `/UserDemographics/Create`. Fill out the form with data in the correct format, such as ensuring you use a date for those fields asking for a date. Submit the form.

10. The processing runs and then stops at the breakpoint you created. If you hover over the item in the parameter list and then click the arrow, you can see the contents of the item. Note that all the information you entered into the form is available as a property on the object. Stop the application when you are completed.

11. At this point you need to decide how you want to handle an edit. You can either create a new view or reuse the Create view. If you create an Edit view, you will see that it looks exactly like the Create view you already created, so you will instead make some changes to reuse the Create view.

    However, using the Create view to also edit an object could be confusing going forward, so you'll first change the name of the view that you just created. Locate the view UserDemographics\
    Create.cshtml in the Solution Explorer, right-click, and select Rename. Change the name from Create to "**Manage**." Ensure that this file is your active file and debug the application. The URL in your browser bar should be UserDemographics/Manage, but you get a 404 error, or resource not found error page, as shown in Figure 6-16.

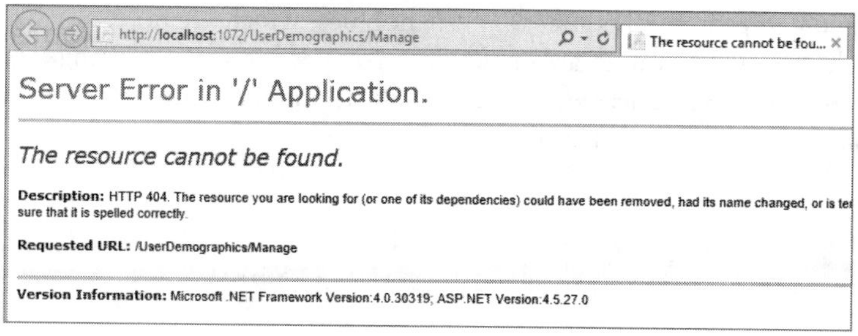

FIGURE 6-16: 404 error when running the Manage view

This error is expected because the system is looking for a Manage method but you don't have one.

12. Changing the URL from Manage to Create, which was how you were able to access it before, also causes errors. That's because the `Create` method, as it stands now, is looking for a view named "Create" but isn't finding it. You have to tell it to send the Manage view instead. To do this, go into the Controller file and change the basic `Create` method to the following:

```
public ActionResult Create()
{
    return View("Manage");
}
```

You have told the View method to look for a view named Manage rather than the default Create view—defaulting because the name of the view matches the name of the action. Run the application in debug mode now and go to UserDemographics/Create, the page should render.

13. You also need to make a change to the Edit method. In this case you will make a bit more changes because the Edit is expected to return a model. Find the Edit method (with a single parameter) and change it to the following:

```
public ActionResult Edit(int id)
{
    var model = new UserDemographics
    {
        Gender = "Male",
        Birthdate = new DateTime(2000, id, id),
        MaritalStatus = "Married",
        OwnHome = true,
        TotalPeopleInHome = id,
        Hobbies = new List<string> { "Gardening", "Other" }
    };
    return View("Manage", model);
}
```

You added a mocked-up model so that you can see what happens when you call the Edit method. Note how both the `BirthDate` and `TotalNumberInHome` properties are currently set to the Id passed into the method. That demonstrates that you have actually received the information and passed it back to the view. Run the application and go to UserDemographics/Edit/5 by adding those values after the "localhost" and port number in the URL address bar. You should get a screen that looks like Figure 6-17.

14. Everything seems to be displaying appropriately other than the hobbies, which are not being checked even though the Model has hobby values assigned. Now you need to make a change in the view to handle when those items have been selected. Stop the application and ensure that you are in the view and locate the code block you created earlier:

```
<div class="form-group">
    @Html.LabelFor(model => model.Hobbies,
            htmlAttributes: new { @class = "control-label col-md-2" })
    <div class="col-md-10">
        @foreach (string hobby in hobbyList)
        {
        <span>
            <input name="hobbies" value="@hobby" type="checkbox" />
            @hobby
        </span>
        }
    </div>
</div>
```

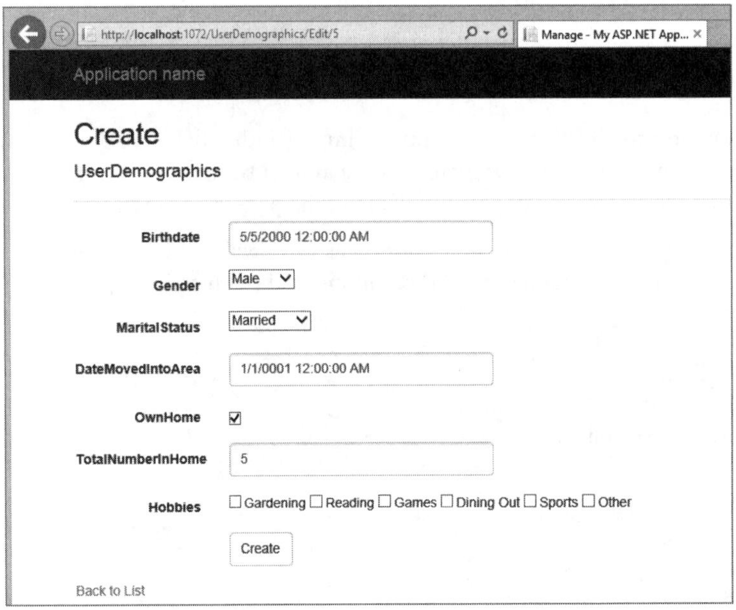

FIGURE 6-17: Displaying the Edit screen

The change you want to make now checks the checkbox if the model already contains the hobby. You tell a checkbox that it is checked by adding a `"checked"` attribute, so the code you are going to add evaluates each hobby in the loop to determine whether the hobby being added is part of the list of hobbies in the model. If it is, it adds "checked" to the input. If not, it adds an empty string. Update your code to look like the following. Changes are highlighted.

```
<div class="form-group">
    @Html.LabelFor(model => model.Hobbies,
```

```
            htmlAttributes: new { @class = "control-label col-md-2" })
    <div class="col-md-10">
        @foreach (string hobby in hobbyList)
        {
            string checkedText = Model.Hobbies.Contains(hobby)
                ? "checked"
                : string.Empty;
        <span>
            <input name="hobbies" value="@hobby" type="checkbox" @checkedText />
            @hobby
        </span>
        }
    </div>
</div>
```

If you run the application again and go to UserDemographics/Edit/5, you can see that the hobby checkboxes have been checked as desired.

15. The last task is to consider the deletion. In this case, it doesn't make sense to delete the UserDemographic, so rather than create anything to manage this functionality, you want to instead remove, or delete from the controller, all the methods that refer to "Delete." This means that the application will no longer respond to a URL containing UserDemographic/Delete.

How It Works

You created a new data entry form. One of the code snippets that you added is shown again below:

```
<div class="form-group">
    @Html.LabelFor(model => model.Hobbies,
            htmlAttributes: new { @class = "control-label col-md-2" })
    <div class="col-md-10">
        @foreach (string hobby in hobbyList)
        {
        <span>
            <input name="hobbies" value="@hobby" type="checkbox" />
            @hobby
        </span>
        }
    </div>
</div>
```

This section does two things: It adds a label for the hobbies, just as the other properties have, and includes a loop that creates a checkbox and outputs the hobby name. What's interesting here is that you are not using any of the HTML helpers, but are instead creating the input element manually. Also, you're using a combination of the hard-coded name "hobby" and the value of the hobby as it goes through the loop.

You want to take this approach because of the interesting way in which HTML checkboxes are handled when submitted. As you saw, each of the items ends up having the same name, but values for a checkbox are included only when the item is checked. If the user does not select any of the hobbies, then nothing is submitted. In addition, because all the inputs have the same name, when more than one item is selected the values are appended together with a comma between them, so the value ends up looking something like "Gardening, Other."

The especially nice thing about this approach is that because you used the name "Hobbies" for the element, the model binder can determine what's going on and fills the Hobbies collection with the list of items that were checked; you don't need to do any additional work in the controller. Thus, this approach for adding the list of checkboxes helped you fill your model.

You would have the same benefit if you had used a multi-select dropdown as well, because it would send the information to the server in the same format, as long as you named the select box with the correct name. However, checkboxes provide a friendlier user experience.

Once you had a controller and a model object, the views could be built. Because you had the model already defined, the scaffolding system was able to go through the various properties and build out the appropriate page, whether it was a list of items, a data-entry form, or a read-only display of the information. While each of the pages needed some tweaks to help it capture and/or display all the information, most of the work was done through the scaffolding process. On the data-entry pages, the scaffolding creates two actions: one to take the GET request and return a form and the other to take the POST request to process the form fields.

This difference between verbs is important to remember in ASP.NET MVC, which tends to use the verbs as designated in the HTTP definition. Also, the nature of HTTP means that you cannot access a form body when handling a GET, as the entire purpose of the GET is to provide read-only work. The changing of data explicitly goes against the expectations of using a GET verb.

As you advance through the chapters, you will revisit this work to add the information you are working with into the database, as well as adding security, because only authenticated users should be able to do anything with the demographics, and users should also be limited to working with only their own information.

SUMMARY

This chapter introduced using ASP.NET MVC to communicate information between the client and the server. You have learned how to create a view and display dynamic information through the use of HTML helpers, especially the HTML.DisplayFor. These HTML helpers also support the creation of HTML elements that create elements on the client side for capturing information to return to the server.

Two different types of HTML helpers create data-entry elements: generic and specific. The generic Html.EditorFor looks at the property it is displaying and determines the best way to capture the information. It is also capable of looking at attributes and influencing the design through attributes on the model. Those attributes were briefly covered, but you will learn more about them as you start adding attributes to the models for database management. The other type of HTML helper that can be used to create HTML input elements are the element-specific helpers, such as Html.TextboxFor or Html.CheckboxFor, which create an HTML element with the name of the property.

One of the most powerful aspects of the view is how it supports running code within the view itself through its support for Razor. Razor allows you to intermix code and HTML markup so that you can write code to do things like iterating through a list and writing the content, or performing calculations. Razor is also what makes the HTML helpers work. Having the property name match the element name is important, as it helps the model binding process. When a form is submitted, the server examines the information that is being submitted; and if the matching method (matching the URL due to the routing rules) contains an object as an input parameter, it tries to map the various incoming data points to the properties on the object. This enables the developer to use a type-safe object in the controller, rather than having to parse through a series of key-value pairs and work from those.

Although you did not do much work in the controller yet, the coordination between object, controller, controller action, or method, and view should make more sense now. A lot of ASP.NET MVC is convention driven, and this coordination is part of that convention, as the object name from the URL is matched to a controller that has a name using the object's name with "Controller" appended to it, such as `ObjectNameController`. The action name is also typically part of the URL string, so the system is able to determine what action, or method, on which controller needs to be run to handle the request.

EXERCISES

1. What is the difference between using `@Html.TextboxFor` and `@Html.Textbox`?

2. How does the Razor view engine understand the difference between code that it is supposed to run and text that should not be changed or affected, simply passed through?

3. Convention plays an important role in ASP.NET MVC. Must the view name always match the action name?

4. How does the model binder know how to bind the properties of nested types, or objects that are properties on other objects?

▶ **WHAT YOU LEARNED IN THIS CHAPTER**

Controller Action	A method on a controller that responds to a specific URL. The URL format is typically something like `ObjectName/Action`, where `ObjectName` gives direction to the controller that is going to be used and `Action` provides the name of the method, or action, that is called on that controller.
Display/DisplayFor	HTML helpers that bind the content of a model value to an HTML element on the web page. These elements are not input elements, but are used to display model information.
Editor/EditorFor	These helpers enable the system to create the appropriate HTML input element based on the object and property being bound. `EditorFor` also has the capability to look at various attributes on the model in order to determine how the display may be controlled.
Lambda Expressions	Inline functions that basically take the approach of identifying a property. Thus, `x => x.Property1` is defined as "for every given x (the variable name for the object), return the value of the property Property1."
Model Binding	The process whereby various values submitted to the server are parsed to identify which values match the property names of the object that was named in the parameter list of the `Action` method.
Razor	The name of the view engine that handles the capability to run C# (or VB) code within the view. The entire .NET stack is available for use within the view as necessary. The Razor view engine can understand the difference between code it should run and text it should ignore through the use of the @ character, which identifies code that should be run.
Routing	The process of determining from the URL which controller and action are responsible for handling the request. The `RouteConfig` file contains the routing definitions, with the traditional, default route likely being the only one needed for the sample application.
Type-Safe Extensions	These HTML helpers use lambda expressions to define the relationship between the model and a particular element.
Verb Attributes	These are used on a controller action to limit the type of verbs that can be used to access that controller. An action that does not have an attribute can be accessed through any verb. An action that has one of these attributes, such as `[HttpPost]`, only accepts requests with that specific verb.

7

Creating Consistent-Looking Websites

WHAT YOU WILL LEARN IN THIS CHAPTER:

➤ How to create and use an ASP.NET master page for your Web Forms pages

➤ How to create and use an ASP.NET MVC layout page

➤ How to create and use Razor sections in ASP.NET MVC

➤ How to create and integrate Web Forms content pages

➤ How to create and integrate MVC content pages

➤ How to create a base page

CODE DOWNLOADS FOR THIS CHAPTER:

The wrox.com code downloads for this chapter are found at www.wrox.com/go/ beginningaspnetforvisualstudio on the Download Code tab. The code is in the chapter 07 download and individually named according to the names throughout the chapter.

You have been doing bits and pieces of work for the sample application, plugging in some information here, some there. In this chapter, you start pulling this all together and unifying the look and feel of the website. You do this by creating a simple, single look and feel that you then ensure all pages will follow. This look and feel includes consistent styling, menus, footers, and the consistent display of information—all of which users expect in a website.

In future chapters you will be plugging in more functionality. In this chapter, you are building the shell of the application, the foundation on which all the rest of the items going forward will be built. You will also get an introduction on how to separate much of the design of the page from the functionality of the page by allowing the common areas to be managed independently of the actual page content.

CONSISTENT PAGE LAYOUT WITH MASTER PAGES

When you look at most websites on the Internet, such as http://www.wrox.com, you can see that they tend to have a consistent look and feel. For example, each page may have a menu at the top, a left menu, and even a footer menu at the bottom; and all of these areas look the same on every page.

You could easily repeat all the code to effect this on each page, but that isn't the best way to handle it. Changes would become a management nightmare because you would have to replicate changes across every page in the site. Clearly, it would be better to have some way to store all these shared design elements in the same place, so you would only have to make a change in one location in order to replicate it to the entire site. Luckily, ASP.NET provides a single place to maintain all this information: the master page in Web Forms and the layout page in MVC.

In a nutshell, a master page is a special type of ASP.NET Web Forms page that defines the markup common to all content pages as well as regions that are customizable on a content page–by–content page basis. Whereas a master page is the template, a content page is an ASP.NET page that is bound to the master page, as it uses the template as its primary design template. Whenever a master page's layout or formatting is changed, all of its content pages' output is likewise immediately updated, which makes applying site-wide appearance changes as easy as updating and deploying a single file, the master page.

The layout provides the same functionality in ASP.NET MVC as the master page does in ASP.NET Web Forms: keeping the UI elements and theme consistent throughout the application. Recall from Chapter 6 that the Razor layout introduced two new concepts:

➤ **Web body**—Used to render the content of the referencing view in a specific place

➤ **Web page sections**—Used to declare multiple sections in a layout, which are then defined by the referencing views

Both approaches are supported when creating a new file through the various scaffolding frameworks. The scaffolding framework is responsible for creating a file, or set of files, based on a template. When you are adding a file (or project for that matter) you are really selecting a scaffold template. The content that is added is the result of the scaffolding framework creating the content based on that template. They can each be retrofitted into existing pages as well. You will learn both approaches: creating new pages that use the templates as well as converting existing content to use the centralized template approach.

These two approaches, while different in implementation, both provide the same set of functionality. Take a look at Figure 7-1.

The light area in Figure 7-1 is the area that would typically come from the template page, while the dark area is from the content page. Both Web Forms and MVC support this approach. The next section describes how this works.

Creating and Using Master Pages in ASP.NET Web Forms

When ASP.NET version 1.0 launched in early 2002, it didn't have any support for the concept of a master page. Some of this functionality was handled by server-side includes, whereby the web server, when writing out an HTML page to the response stream, would come across a marker indicating that content from another file should be inserted at that point. This worked fine, as long as you didn't need the inserted pages to be dynamic as well. These inserted pages could not be dynamic because they did not go through the same processing pipeline as did the standard request so any code in the included file would not be run. Typically the server only allowed files with extensions such as .html or .txt to be included. In addition, because this was all handled post rendering, it was impossible to work with the final page as a complete entity; the "added in" sections would not be visible in the IDE, so it became an exercise in "let's run it and see what it looks like."

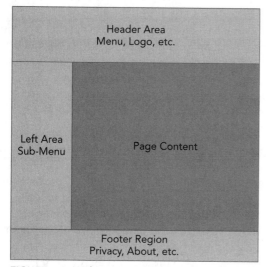

FIGURE 7-1: Web page within a template

ASP.NET 2.0 changed this with the addition of master pages. These separate template pages can contain code and can be executed just like the content pages. Master pages are a different page type; you may have seen them available as an option when you were creating some of your other new pages. They typically have a .master extension. A master page looks very much like the other HTML pages you have looked at before, but they have a few new sections. Listing 7-1 shows the HTML that is part of a new master page.

LISTING 7-1: A simple ASP.NET Web Forms master page

```
<%@ Master Language="C#" AutoEventWireup="true" CodeBehind="DemoMaster.master.cs"
        Inherits="RentMyWrox.Demonstrations.DemoMaster" %>
<!DOCTYPE html>
<html xmlns="http://www.w3.org/1999/xhtml">
<head runat="server">
    <title></title>
    <asp:ContentPlaceHolder ID="head" runat="server">
    </asp:ContentPlaceHolder>
</head>
<body>
```

continues

LISTING 7-1 *(continued)*

```
    <form id="form1" runat="server">
    <div>
        <asp:ContentPlaceHolder ID="ContentPlaceHolder1" runat="server">
        </asp:ContentPlaceHolder>
    </div>
    </form>
</body>
</html>
```

If you looked at this page in a browser it would be a completely blank page. The empty master page looks like any other HTML page, with two additions: the ContentPlaceHolder server controls. You can tell that these are server controls because they follow the traditional asp:control naming convention and contain the runat="server" attribute. This control is different from the others, however, in that it does not fully control everything that goes on as part of the control. It instead acts as the link between the content and the master page; with the area inside the control being filled by the content page.

Note that there are two areas in this default page: one in the HTML head and the other in the body, within the form. The content section in the body is pretty straightforward, because that is where the visible content goes, but the reason why there is a content section in the header may be less obvious. However, when you consider the kind of information contained in the header section, it becomes clearer. You could put links to JavaScript files or stylesheets that are only used on this particular content page; or provide any other page meta information that you feel is important. You might use this section only on some pages, but having it available for use provides a lot of functional support. Typically there may only be two sections, but you can include as many sections as you need for your design. Figure 7-2 shows an example of how this might look.

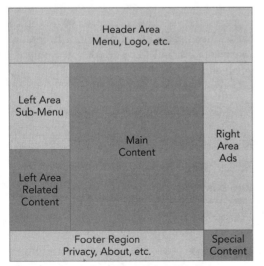

FIGURE 7-2: Master page with multiple content sections

In this case, there would be a content section in the header, a content section that defines the "Left Area Related Content" that could hold links to other content similar to the content in the page, a content section for the main content, and another content section for the right-most area of the footer. This kind of approach looks like Listing 7-2. Note the HTML comments that show where real content would be inserted.

LISTING 7-2: A complex ASP.NET Web Forms master page

```
<%@ Master Language="C#" AutoEventWireup="true" CodeBehind="Site1.master.cs"
     Inherits="RentMyWrox.Demonstrations.Site1" %>
<!DOCTYPE html>
<html xmlns="http://www.w3.org/1999/xhtml">
<head runat="server">
    <title></title>
     <link href="~\content\styles.css" rel="stylesheet" type="text/css" />
    <asp:ContentPlaceHolder ID="head" runat="server">
    </asp:ContentPlaceHolder>
</head>
<body>
    <form id="form1" runat="server">
    <header>
        <!-- Header content here, logos, menu, etc. -->
    </header>
    <div id="leftpane">
        <div class="leftmenu">
            <!-- Regular menu stuff here -->
        </div>
        <asp:ContentPlaceHolder ID="LeftContent" runat="server">
        </asp:ContentPlaceHolder>
    </div>
    <div>
        <asp:ContentPlaceHolder ID="MainContent" runat="server">
        </asp:ContentPlaceHolder>
    </div>
    <footer>
        <!-- footer content here -->
        <asp:ContentPlaceHolder ID="FooterContent" runat="server">
        </asp:ContentPlaceHolder>
    </footer>
    </form>
</body>
</html>
```

Each of these `asp:ContentPlaceHolder` controls prefers that the content page provide content that can be inserted into that area. This content may well be empty, but the system expects a content page to have corresponding areas for each of the placeholders. When creating a new content page that is attached to a master page during creation, as you do in the next Try It Out, the scaffolding creates a content section for each placeholder in the master page. However, removing those content sections from the content page doesn't result in an error; there just won't be any content put into those placeholder areas.

Another powerful feature of master pages is the capability to nest them. Consider the sample application's site design. There are two major, different areas of the site: one for the regular user to view and check out items and the other for an administrator to manage the items available for checkout. Each of those areas is likely to have a different menu structure because the user and administrator have different goals, but you still want most of the other structure and look and feel to remain the same. One way to do this is to put the determination of which menu to display in the master page, i.e., an approach along the lines of the pseudocode shown here:

```
if user is administrator
      show administrator menu
else
      show regular menu
```

PSEUDOCODE

Pseudocode is a term that is used to refer to a merging of regular language and a programming language. Nearly all languages have the same capabilities, such as if/then/else or loops; it is their implementation that differs. Pseudocode enables you to break down a set of requirements with a technical approach that still uses regular language which can be translated by a developer—regardless of the language that is used to implement the business requirements. We will be using pseudocode throughout the rest of the book as the business requirements are reviewed, with the implementation being language specific.

The other approach is to instead abstract out the decision by creating a primary master page that contains the areas you want repeated on every page, and then another set of master pages that contain the various menus you want to display. This separation is displayed in Figure 7-3.

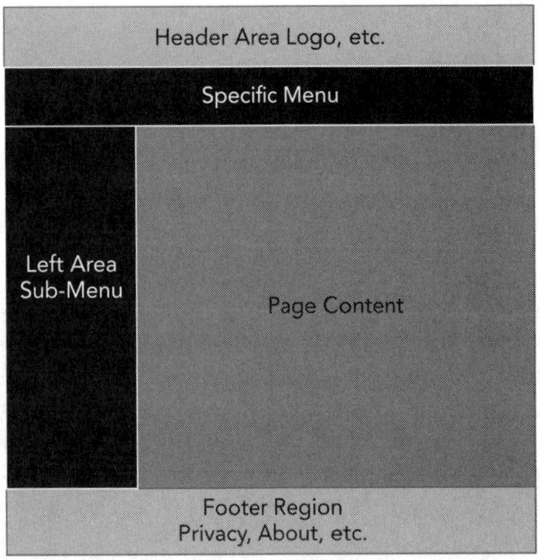

FIGURE 7-3: Nested master pages

The dark areas of Figure 7-3 show the content that would be managed in the nested content page. The code to make this work is shown here:

PARENT MASTER PAGE

```
<%@ Master Language="C#" AutoEventWireup="true" CodeBehind="DemoMaster.master.cs"
        Inherits="RentMyWrox.Demonstrations.DemoMaster" %>
<!DOCTYPE html>
<html xmlns="http://www.w3.org/1999/xhtml">
<head runat="server">
    <title></title>
    <asp:ContentPlaceHolder ID="head" runat="server">
    </asp:ContentPlaceHolder>
</head>
<body>
    <form id="form1" runat="server">
    <header>
        <!-- Header Area, logos, etc. -->
        <asp:ContentPlaceHolder ID="Header" runat="server">
        </asp:ContentPlaceHolder>
    </header>
    <div id="leftpane">
        <asp:ContentPlaceHolder ID="LeftContent" runat="server">
        </asp:ContentPlaceHolder>
    </div>
    <div>
        <asp:ContentPlaceHolder ID="MainContent" runat="server">
        </asp:ContentPlaceHolder>
    </div>
    <footer>
        <!-- footer content here -->
    </footer>
    </form>
</body>
</html>
```

NESTED MASTER PAGE

```
<%@ Master Language="C#" MasterPageFile="DemoMaster.master"
        AutoEventWireup="true" CodeFile="NestedMaster.master.cs"
        Inherits="RentMyWrox.Demonstrations.NestedMaster" %>
<asp:Content ID="Content0" ContentPlaceHolderID="head" Runat="Server">
    <asp:ContentPlaceHolder ID="HeadContent" runat="server">
    </asp:ContentPlaceHolder>
</asp:Content>
<asp:Content ID="Content1" ContentPlaceHolderID=" Header " Runat="Server">
    <!-- specific menu here -->
</asp:Content>
<asp:Content ID="Content2" ContentPlaceHolderID="LeftContent" Runat="Server">
    <!-- left-area sub-menu here -->
</asp:Content>
<asp:Content ID="Content3" ContentPlaceHolderID="MainContent" Runat="Server">
    <asp:ContentPlaceHolder ID="PrimaryContent" runat="server">
    </asp:ContentPlaceHolder>
</asp:Content>
```

There is nothing different in the main master page; it knows nothing about what will be filling its content sections, so it just makes the necessary content placeholders available. The nested master page is where it becomes interesting. Note the difference in the declaration section. The nested master page has an additional attribute, `MasterPageFile`, which establishes the connection between the current page and the master page with which it will be linked. You use this same approach later in this chapter when creating the content pages.

You are also introduced to a new server control here, the `<asp:Content />`. This tag, as you likely suspect, links content on this page to the template areas that will display that information. The content sections later in this chapter describe this relationship in detail, so we won't spend any more time on it here other than to note that this is how content is related to an `<asp:ContentPlaceHolder />` server control. Figure 7-4 demonstrates the complete relationship.

FIGURE 7-4: Nested master pages

Just as you can have multiple placeholders in a master page, you can have multiple layers of master pages. The only consideration is that a content page can only refer to the placeholder in its referenced master page, it cannot reference a placeholder in a master page higher up the stack. It does not work like object-oriented inheritance; it is instead more like a one-to-one relationship between the content and template pages.

TRY IT OUT Creating an ASP.NET Web Forms Master Page

The scaffolding that created your initial project files also included a master page called `Site.Master`. Rather than try to edit that file, you will instead create a new one that enables you to start from scratch. Keep in mind as you go through this exercise that there are a few unusual things in the application, in that you are building a system that integrates both ASP.NET Web Forms and MVC.

You are going to keep two parts specific to Web Forms: the administrative section and the authentication/authorization system. You are keeping the authentication and authorization section in Web Forms because those pages were already created for you when the project was created. These two different areas highlight the interesting conundrum discussed earlier about supporting two potentially different looks and feels, one for the administrative section and one for the non-admin section. This topic is revisited later in the chapter when you work on the content pages.

1. Start Visual Studio and ensure that the RentMyWrox project is open. Right-click on the project in Solution Explorer and select Add ➪ Web Forms Master Page, as shown in Figure 7-5. When the name box appears, name it **WebForms** and click OK. If you do not have the same option in your right-click menu, instead select Add ➪ New Item and then selecting Web Forms Master Page from the Web section of the resulting dialog.

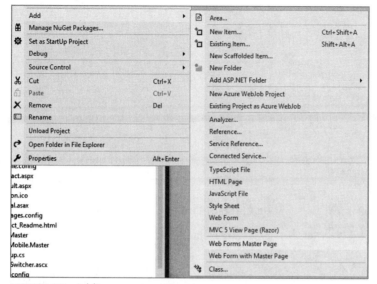

FIGURE 7-5: Adding a new master page

This should provide a very empty-looking master page:

```
<%@ Master Language="C#" AutoEventWireup="true" CodeBehind="WebForms.Master.cs"
        Inherits="RentMyWrox.WebForms" %>
<!DOCTYPE html>
<html xmlns="http://www.w3.org/1999/xhtml">
<head runat="server">
    <title></title>
    <asp:ContentPlaceHolder ID="head" runat="server">
    </asp:ContentPlaceHolder>
</head>
<body>
    <form id="form1" runat="server">
    <div>
        <asp:ContentPlaceHolder ID="ContentPlaceHolder1" runat="server">
        </asp:ContentPlaceHolder>
    </div>
    </form>
</body>
</html>
```

2. Add the initial design for the master page as shown in the highlighted sections of the code below. When you are done, you should have the following:

```
<%@ Master Language="C#" AutoEventWireup="true" CodeBehind="WebForms.Master.cs"
Inherits="WebApplication2.WebForms" %>
```

```
<!DOCTYPE html>
<html xmlns="http://www.w3.org/1999/xhtml">
<head runat="server">
    <title></title>
    <asp:ContentPlaceHolder ID="head" runat="server">
    </asp:ContentPlaceHolder>
</head>
<body>
    <form id="form1" runat="server">
    <div id="header">
    </div>
    <div id="nav">
        Navigation content here
    </div>
    <div id="section">
        <asp:ContentPlaceHolder ID="ContentPlaceHolder1" runat="server">
        </asp:ContentPlaceHolder>
    </div>
    <div id="footer">
        footer content here
    </div>
    </form>
</body>
</html>
```

3. Save your master page.

4. Because you don't yet have a style sheet created for your sample application, you need to create a new one. Right-click on the Content directory in Solution Explorer and select Add ⇨ Style Sheet. Name this style sheet **RentMyWrox** and click OK.

5. Add the following content to the style sheet and then save it.

```
body {
    font-family: verdana;
}
#header {
    background-color:#C40D42;
    color:white;
    text-align:center;
    padding:5px;
}
#nav {
    line-height:30px;
    background-color:#eeeeee;
    height:300px;
    width:100px;
    float:left;
    padding:5px;
}
#section {
    width:750px;
    float:left;
    padding:10px;
```

```
}
#footer {
    background-color:#C40D42;
    color:white;
    clear:both;
    text-align:center;
    padding:5px;
}
```

6. Return to your master page and go into Design mode. You should see something like what is shown in Figure 7-6.

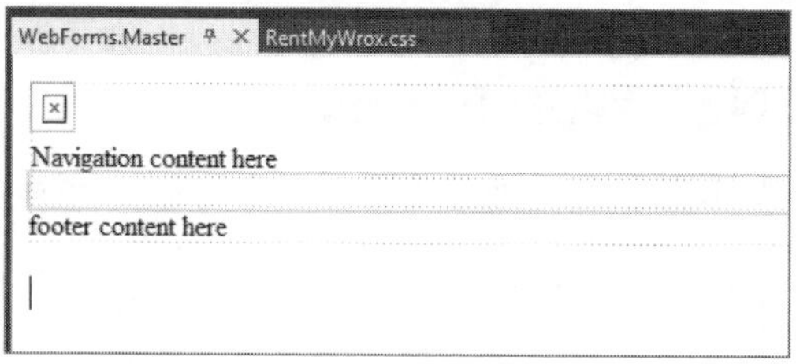

FIGURE 7-6: Unstyled master page in Design mode

7. Click the style sheet you just created in Solution Explorer. Drag it into the master page and drop it. The styling should change to resemble what is shown in Figure 7-7.

FIGURE 7-7: Styled master page in Design mode

8. Go back to Source mode on the master page, where you will see that the link to the style sheet was added to the header of the master page. Your head section should look like the following (though the style sheet may be in a different area within the `head` element):

```
<head runat="server">
    <title></title>
    <asp:ContentPlaceHolder ID="head" runat="server">
```

```
        </asp:ContentPlaceHolder>
        <link href="Content/RentMyWrox.css" rel="stylesheet" type="text/css" />
    </head>
```

How It Works

You used the ASP.NET Web Forms scaffolding to create a new type of page, a master page, and then added some content to it. The navigation structure was stubbed in rather than completed because you will be using navigation controls later in the book to fill out this area.

Now that the master page is created, it will be available for selection on content pages. The next section covers content pages and the next Try It Out will link a new content page to this master page that you just added.

Creating a Content Page in ASP.NET Web Forms

Now that you know how master pages are created, this section describes how you get your content to display in conjunction with the master page. Your initial look at master pages, in Listing 7-1, had two `<asp:ContentPlaceHolder />` controls. Listing 7-3 contains a content page that uses that same master page.

LISTING 7-3: An ASP.NET Web Forms content page

```
<%@ Page Title="" Language="C#" MasterPageFile="~/WebForms.Master"
AutoEventWireup="true" CodeBehind="ContentPage.aspx.cs"
Inherits="RentMyWrox.ContentPage" %>
<asp:Content ID="Content1" ContentPlaceHolderID="head" runat="server">
    <!-- content for the head goes here -->
</asp:Content>
<asp:Content ID="Content2" ContentPlaceHolderID="ContentPlaceHolder1"
    runat="server">
    <!-- content for the body goes here -->
</asp:Content>
```

There are two new parts to this page that need to be understood. The first is the `MasterPageFile` reference in the definition of the page. This establishes the link between this particular content page and the master page. With this link, the system is able to determine where each control's content will be placed. Every page that is going to use a master page must have this attribute, and it will need to be populated with the appropriate page, including path.

USING THE TILDE (~) CHARACTER IN ASP.NET URLS

You will see the tilde character used in various areas of your ASP.NET application. When you are working with ASP.NET Web Forms, the tilde character refers to the application root directory. The tilde will be translated correctly in server control properties such as `NavigateUrl`, `MasterPageFile`, `CodeBehind`, or other areas that expect either a URL-based path or a relative path to the running page. In the code that is part of Listing 7-3, the tilde means that in `MasterPageFile="~/DemoMaster.Master"` the `DemoMaster.Master` file is stored in the application root, or at the first level of the project. This is demonstrated in Figure 7-8.

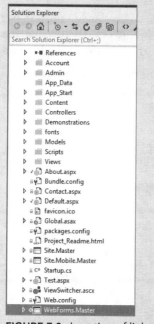

FIGURE 7-8: Location of linked master page in the project

Note also that there is no content outside of the two content controls; the only thing that will be displayed within the master page content is the content within the content controls. As a matter of fact, anything, including extraneous text, outside of the content controls causes an error. Figure 7-9 shows the error caused by adding a line of text outside of the last content control.

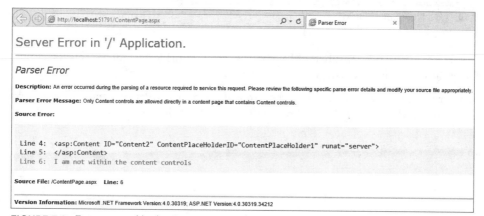

FIGURE 7-9: Error caused by having text outside content control

Although the system throws an error if anything is outside the content controls, as mentioned earlier there would be no error if not all of the placeholder controls have a matching content control. The server simply replaces those content controls with an empty value.

TRY IT OUT Adding a New Content Page and Linking to a Master Page

In this exercise, you create a new page and link it to the master page you created in the last exercise. In a previous chapter, you created a page that is going to be used by administrators to manage the items available. This exercise also increases the administrative sections of the application by providing administrators with the capability to view a list of orders.

You will not be putting any content into this file in this chapter; you will simply be creating it. Content will start to get added in Chapter 8.

1. Open Visual Studio and ensure that your RentMyWrox solution is open. Locate the Admin directory, click on it to select it, and then right-click on the directory to open the context menu. Select Add ⇨ New Item. This should present the dialog shown in Figure 7-10.

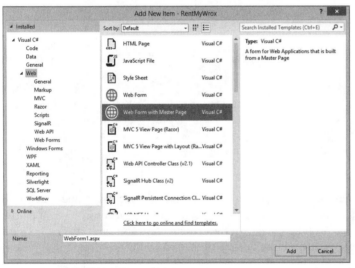

FIGURE 7-10: Add New Item dialog

2. If you see something different, ensure that "Web" is selected in the left window. This filters the file types to only those files that are part of web applications.

3. Select Web Form with Master Page, change the name of the file to **OrderList**, and click the Next button. The Select a Master Page dialog shown in Figure 7-11 will appear.

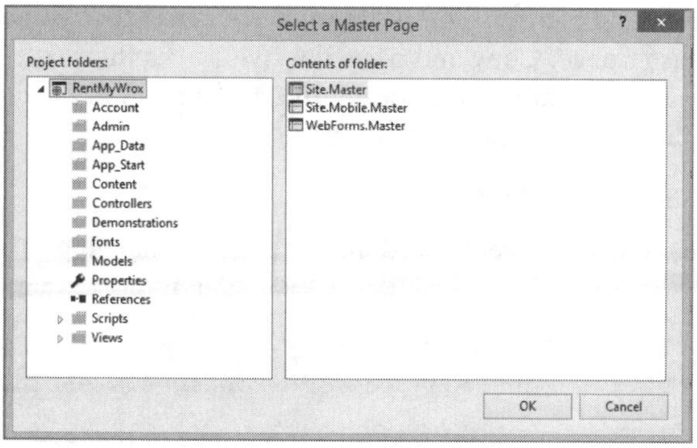

FIGURE 7-11: Selecting the master page

4. Select the `WebForms.Master` file that you created in the last exercise and click OK. This will save the file. If you examine the file in the editor, you will see that it is not a typical initial file, but instead a file with two different content sections that match the sections in your master page.

How It Works

You used the ASP.NET Web Forms scaffolding to create a new Web Form page that uses a master page to provide a templated display of content. Because you selected the master page to use, Visual Studio was able to parse that master page and determine the content sections that are available for use. The system then stubbed in those content sections so they would be available. By default, all content sections available in the selected master page will be available in the created Web Form.

Sometimes a project is started without a master page or a Web Form page is created by accident, such that there is no link between the content page and the master page. In those cases, you will need to convert your non-templated page into a page that uses the master page's content placeholders by adding the `MasterPage` reference in the definition and adding the `Content` control(s). You may also have to change the master page that a file has assigned as shown in the next activity.

TRY IT OUT Changing Master Pages in a Web Form

Often in the course of a project you may have to convert a Web Form that does not use a master page into a content page that is based on a master page. This activity walks you through this process to convert a page created earlier in the book, the `Admin/ManageItem.aspx` page, so that it uses the master page you created earlier in this chapter.

1. Open Visual Studio and ensure that your RentMyWrox solution is open. Open the `ManageItem.aspx` file that is in the Admin folder.

2. Open the `RentMyWrox.css` file in the Content directory. This is the same stylesheet that you cre-ated earlier when you created the new master page. Copy and paste the styles from the header of the `ManageItem` file into the stylesheet, ensuring that you do not put the content within the curly braces of one of the other styles already in the file. Do *not* copy the style tags.

3. Delete the style tags (and styles if still present) from the `ManageItem` file.

4. In the page definition section, change the name of the referenced master page by changing `MasterPageFile="~/Site.Master"` to `MasterPageFile="~/WebForms.Master"`.

5. In the content control, change the name of the linked content section by changing `ContentPlaceHolderId="MainContent"` to `ContentPlaceHolderId="ContentPlaceHolder1"`.

6. Remove the hard-coded style (`style="margin-top:100px;"`) in the top `<div>` of the `ManageItem.aspx` file.

7. In the `ManageItem` file, click the Run button. You should see an updated look, as shown in Figure 7-12.

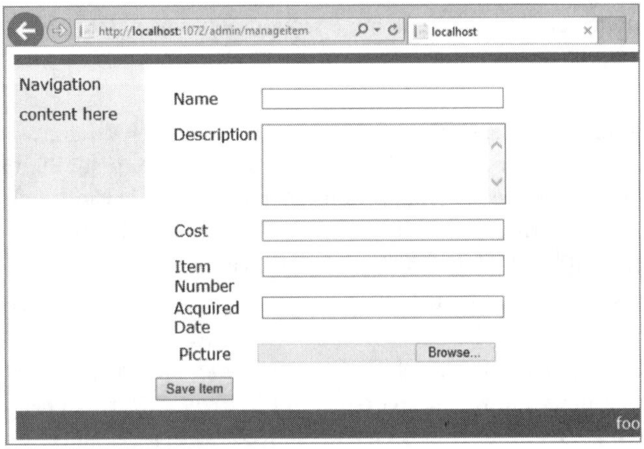

FIGURE 7-12: Form in the new master page

How It Works

As you just saw, it is generally a simple process to convert a content page to use a different master page. You merely change the referenced master page and then ensure that the content controls are linked to a valid `ContentPlaceholder`.

Creating Layouts in ASP.NET MVC

ASP.NET Web Forms master pages enable you to create a template that affects any page linked to that master page, giving you the capability to plug content into each of the areas made available from the master page. Layouts in ASP.NET MVC are a little different, because whereas master pages rely on server controls to indicate both content placement and content identification, MVC does not have server controls. The relationship is built between pages and then matched, one content placeholder control to one content control.

ASP.NET MVC takes a different approach. One difference is that any kind of view can be a layout; you do not necessarily have to use a special kind of file. What makes a layout file a layout file is the fact that another file has designated it as such, and the layout file defines where content should be displayed. Listing 7-4 shows what this empty layout file could look like.

LISTING 7-4: An ASP.NET MVC layout page

```
<!DOCTYPE html>
<html>
<head>
    <title>@ViewBag.Title</title>
</head>
<body>
    <div>
        @RenderBody()
    </div>
</body>
</html>
```

As you can see, nothing in this layout page distinguishes it as a layout page, other than a Razor syntax command that hasn't been shown yet: the RenderBody command. The ASP.NET MVC RenderBody command means much the same as a content placeholder in an ASP.NET Web Form master page, in that it specifies where content from another file should be rendered.

There is a difference between a default layout file and a default master page, in that a master page tends to be created with two different placeholder sections, one in the HTML head and another in the body; conversely, the layout page is generated with just the one @RenderBody command. However, you can add additional areas where content can be inserted by using a @RenderSection command. This enables you to create a master page with a section that is separate from the main body, as shown in Listing 7-5.

LISTING 7-5: An ASP.NET MVC layout page with a section

```
<!DOCTYPE html>
<html>
<head>
    <title>@ViewBag.Title</title>
</head>
<body>
    <div>
        @RenderSection("Navigation", required: false)
    </div>
    <div>
        @RenderBody()
    </div>
</body>
</html>
```

You can add as many of these different sections as needed, just as you were able to do with the content placeholder controls in Web Forms. In the following Try It Out, you create an MVC layout page.

TRY IT OUT   Creating an ASP.NET MVC Layout Page

This page will have a body area and a section on the right for special information. You will also add the same default styling that you added for the Web Forms master page. However, like the master page, you will later add the menu structure and other items as you progress through the appropriate chapters.

1. Ensure that the RentMyWrox solution is open in Visual Studio. Right-click on the Shared folder that is within the Views folder, and select Add ➪ MVC 5 Layout Page (Razor), name it **_MVCLayout**, and click OK. This creates a file in that directory and opens it in the editor with the following content:

```
<!DOCTYPE html>
<html>
<head>
    <meta name="viewport" content="width=device-width" />
    <title>@ViewBag.Title</title>
</head>
<body>
    <div>
        @RenderBody()
    </div>
</body>
</html>
```

2. Update the content of the file as follows:

```
<!DOCTYPE html>
<html>
<head>
    <meta name="viewport" content="width=device-width" />
    <title>@ViewBag.Title</title>
    <link href="~/Content/RentMyWrox.css" rel="stylesheet" type="text/css" />
</head>
<body>
    <div id="header">
    </div>
    <div id="nav">
        Navigation content here
    </div>
    <div id="section">
        @RenderBody()
    </div>
     <div id="specialnotes">
        @RenderSection("SpecialNotes", false)
    </div>
    <div id="footer">
        footer content here
    </div>
</body>
</html>
```

How It Works

You started by using the Visual Studio scaffolding to create a new page. You then added content, including the styling. This was all easier to do this time compared to when you did the Web Forms master page because all the ancillary items were completed, such as building the style sheet.

Of key importance here is the location of the layout file that you created. The convention is to start the filename with an underscore (_) and place it within the Shared directory. That's not required here because you will be using the name and path of the layout file when you make the assignment, so you can name the file as desired and put it anywhere. However, placing the file in the Shared directory and using the underscore signifies that it is a view available to other views.

The other difference between this layout and the Web Forms master page you created earlier is that you created a special section called "Special Notes" that is optional; pages that use this layout do not have to provide the section in order for the page to work.

Creating a Content View in ASP.NET MVC

Having a layout page is only part of the process; also needed is a content page that references it before the layout page can be seen. ASP.NET MVC content pages are still views; in fact the only real difference between a view that uses a content page and one that does not is generally the presence of containing HTML elements such as <head> or <body>, as these elements are typically assumed to be part of the layout page. This means that whereas ASP.NET Web Form content pages have links to the content placeholder in the master page, that isn't always necessary in ASP.NET MVC. The default behavior in MVC is for the entire content of the view to be written out by the RenderBody command, as shown in Figure 7-13.

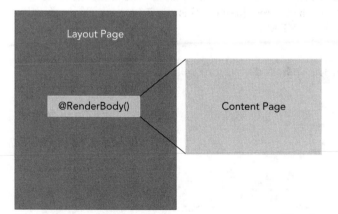

FIGURE 7-13: Relationship between content page and Render command

Linking of the content page to the layout page is pretty simple as well, and there are two approaches: Assign every page to a single layout page, or assign a content page to a specific layout page.

For the first approach, which links every page, recall the Web Forms approach, whereby you have the capability during content page creation to select a master page to which it will be assigned. You have much the same capability when creating an MVC view. In Figure 7-14, which shows the Add View dialog, note the bottom section.

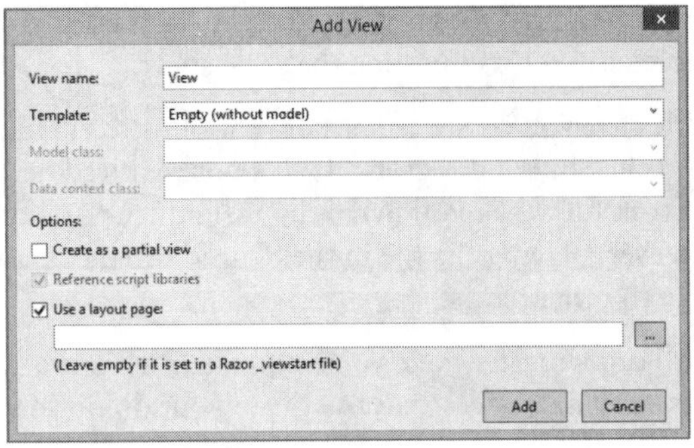

FIGURE 7-14: Add View dialog

The "Use a layout page" option is generally checked by default, and you can open a file selector and choose a layout page. However, it is the line below that's of interest (Leave empty if it is set in Razor _viewstart file). The _viewstart file is a file that will be read by any full view parsed in MVC. If you look in Solution Explorer in your project, you will see that a default _ViewStart.cshtml file was created in the Views directory. Every view that is served out of this directory, and its subdirectories, will go through this file. Generally, the content of the ViewStart file is relatively simple:

```
@{
    Layout = "~/Views/Shared/_SomeLayoutFile.cshtml";
}
```

This line indicates that for all files for which it is not already designated within the file itself, the view should use the _SomeLayoutFile in the Shared directory. Listing 7-6 shows the three different base outputs when creating a view in ASP.NET MVC.

LISTING 7-6: Different content provided based on layout selection

NO LAYOUT

```
@{
    Layout = null;
}
<!DOCTYPE html>
<html>
<head>
    <meta name="viewport" content="width=device-width" />
    <title>PageWithoutLayout</title>
</head>
<body>
    <div>
    </div>
</body>
</html>
```

LAYOUT USING DEFAULT

```
@{
    ViewBag.Title = "PageWithDefaultLayout";
}
<h2>PageWithDefaultLayout</h2>
```

LAYOUT USING NAMED FILE

```
@{
    Layout = "../Shared/_MVCLayout.cshtml";
    ViewBag.Title = "PageWithNamedLayout";
}
<h2> PageWithNamedLayout </h2>
```

As you can see, the primary differences between having a layout and not having a layout are the HTML tags that are generated and how the layout itself is referenced. If the layout is null, then you know that the page is not a content page so that it will need to have all of the HTML elements, including `<html>`, `<title>` and `<body>`; if the layout is missing altogether, then you know the page being used for the layout is the page set in the `ViewStart` file, which will already contain the `<html>`, `<title>` and `<body>` elements. Otherwise, you know that the layout page being used is the one defined in the file itself.

Once the connection is made between the content page and the layout page, the entire content of the content page is rendered into the layout page at the position of the `RenderBody` command. However, you may be asking yourself about the `RenderSection` command, and how that content is populated.

Providing content to a `RenderSection` command is similar to the approach used in ASP.NET Web Forms, whereby you have to identify the content that will be added to the section command, but rather than use server controls you use a special Razor-syntax approach, as shown here:

```
@section SpecialNotes {
    <div class="primary">
        There are special notes here.
    </div>
}
```

To create the content section, use the Razor @ key character followed by the keyword `section`. Then, provide the name of the section and the curly brackets that indicate the extent of the code block. Everything within these curly brackets replaces the `@RenderSection` command. Because the brackets make it a completely standalone set of code, it can be put anywhere within the content page. However, you typically see it at either the very top or the very bottom of the page because it provides less visual interference with the rest of the page when it's at either end of the main content. You can have as many sections as you need; just be sure to provide all the required sections.

Also, keep in mind that there may be many different layout pages. Consider how your sample site has a master page for the files in the Admin directory and another template for the MVC files and how the content is different. If the site was entirely MVC or Web Forms, you would still need multiple layout files because of the difference in the information being displayed based on the area of the application.

The following Try It Out walks you through the process of converting ASP.NET MVC content pages from one layout page to another.

TRY IT OUT Converting an ASP.NET MVC Content Page from One Layout Page to Another

Though you will not be doing this often in a production site, this activity describes two different ways to perform the conversion so that you can practice both ways to control the layout of an MVC view.

1. Ensure that the RentMyWrox project is open in Visual Studio. Find and double-click the `Index` `.cshtml` file in the Views/UserDemographics directory while in the Solution Explorer window. The opened page should display the following:

```
@{
    Layout = "../Shared/_Layout.cshtml";
    ViewBag.Title = "Index";
}
```

2. Replace _Layout.cshtml with the name of the file you created earlier in this chapter, **_MVCLayout.cshtml**. This should leave you with the following:

```
@{
    Layout = "../Shared/_ MVCLayout.cshtml";
    ViewBag.Title = "Index";
}
```

3. Open the `Manage.cshtml` file in the Views/UserDemographics directory. If you look at the top of this file, you will see that it does not have any line for assigning the layout. This tells you that it uses the `ViewStart` file for its template management, so there is nothing to do here.

4. Open the `ViewStart.cshtl` file in the Views/UserDemographics directory. Change the layout assignment to the following:

```
Layout = "~/ViewsShared/_MVCLayout.cshtml";
```

How It Works

Linking an ASP.NET MVC content page to an MVC layout page is simple; you do it either explicitly by setting the `Layout` property to the page or by setting the `Layout` property to null to specify that no layout is assigned. Leaving the layout unassigned tells the system to use the default layout defined in the `ViewStart` file. This is a big difference from Web Forms, for which you have to make an effort to use master pages; they are assumed to be part of the regular design standards in MVC, as shown in

Figure 7-15, where the use of a layout page is already checked automatically. It is assumed that you will be using default _viewstart at a minimum.

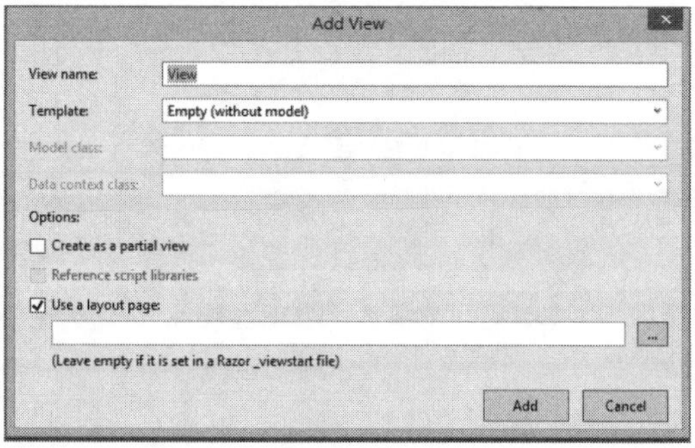

FIGURE 7-15: Initial dialog when creating a brand-new view

USING A CENTRALIZED BASE PAGE

When you were working with the code-behind in your ASP.NET Web Form pages, you likely noticed something without giving it much thought:

```
public partial class ManageItem : System.Web.UI.Page
```

You might recall from Chapter 4 that the preceding snippet tells you that the ManageItem class inherits the System.Web.UI.Page class, so all public properties and methods from the System.Web.UI.Page class are available in the ManageItem class. The use of inheritance here enables you to easily access all the Web Form custom logic and event handlers.

You can also do the same thing with your ASP.NET MVC controllers, as you might have noticed that the controllers are defined in much the same way, except they inherit from Controller as opposed to System.Web.UI.Page:

```
public class UserDemographicsController : Controller
```

You can take advantage of this inheritance and abstract it out one more layer. This enables you to create a different page containing code that will be available automatically across multiple pages. Typical examples of where this could be useful include database configuration and access management, logging, internationalization (the capability to display the application in multiple languages and cultures), or other scenarios in which you may need the same code on each page. Figure 7-16 gives you an idea of what this would look like. There are two sections, one without a base class and another to which a base class was added.

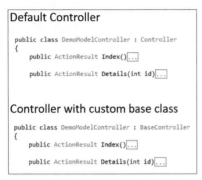

FIGURE 7-16: Addition of a base class

You will be creating a base class for your ASP.NET Web Form pages. This base class will help with the setting of meta tags in the rendered HTML page. You may think this is redundant because we have a content placeholder in the HTML head section, but you will see how much easier it will be to work with them using the base class.

META TAGS

Metadata is data about data. It gives context to the data to which it is applied. HTML has the `<meta>` tag, which provides metadata about the HTML document. Metadata is not displayed on the page, but it is machine understandable. Typically, meta tags on an HTML document are used to specify a page description, keywords, the document's author, when it was last modified, and other details about the content.

The most common use of this metadata is to provide search engines with additional details about information on the page. An example of meta information is displayed here:

```
<head>
<meta charset="UTF-8">
<meta name="description" content="Tool lending library for the local
area.  We have...">
<meta name="keywords" content="Tools, Library, Checkout Tools">
</head>
```

Each page in your site can contain a different set of meta information, as each page is displaying different items.

If you were not going to use a base page, you would have to ensure that you include the header `ContentControl` and then build the meta tags using HTML`<meta>` elements. The following Try It Out shows you a quicker and simpler process.

TRY IT OUT Creating a Base Page for Your ASP.NET Web Form Pages

In this exercise, you create a new base page, add some code that creates the meta information for you, and then convert your current Web Form pages to use this new base page.

1. Open Visual Studio and ensure that the RentMyWrox solution is open. Right-click on the RentMyWrox project and select Add ➪ New Item. When the Add New Item dialog appears, ensure that Code is selected in the pane on the left, select Class, and name it **WebFormsBaseClass.cs** as shown in Figure 7-17. This adds the new file and opens it in your editor.

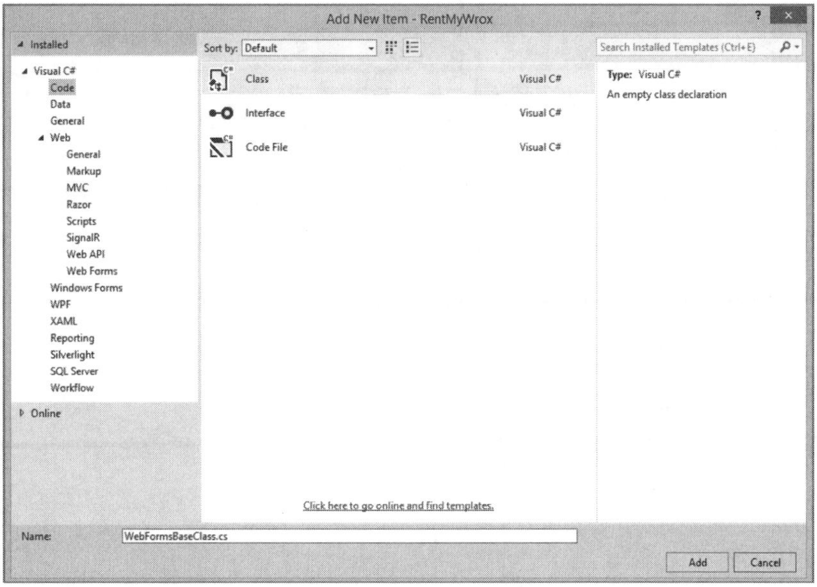

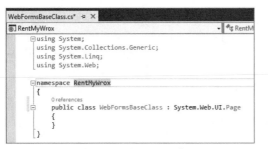

FIGURE 7-17: Creating a new base class

2. Ensure that this new class inherits the Page class (see Figure 7-18).

```
WebFormsBaseClass.cs* ✦ ×
RentMyWrox                                              ✦ RentM
    using System;
    using System.Collections.Generic;
    using System.Linq;
    using System.Web;

    namespace RentMyWrox
    {
        0 references
        public class WebFormsBaseClass : System.Web.UI.Page
        {
        }
    }
```

FIGURE 7-18: Inheriting the Page class

3.   Add the following two properties to this class:

```
public string MetaTagKeywords { get; set; }
public string MetaTagDescription { get; set; }
```

4.   Add an `OnLoad` method with the content shown in Figure 7-19. Ensure that you also add the last using statement; without this using statement you won't have access to the `HtmlMeta` class.

FIGURE 7-19: Overriding the OnLoad method

5.   Open the `Admin/ManageItem.aspx.cs` code behind page and replace the `System.Web.UI.Page` with `WebFormsBaseClass`. You must also add a using statement to ensure that your pages can find this class:

```
using RentMyWrox;
```

Repeat these same steps with `Admin/OrderList.aspx.cs`.

6. Run the application while on either one of the pages that you converted. You will see that the application runs successfully. If you look into the source of the page you will see the following:

```
<head>
<title>
</title>
<link href="../Content/RentMyWrox.css" rel="stylesheet" type="text/css" />
</head>
```

7. Stop the application. Open `ManageItem.aspx` and add the content shown in Figure 7-20 to the page definition.

```
<%@ Page Title="" Language="C#" MasterPageFile="~/WebForms.Master" AutoEventWireup="true" CodeBehind="ManageItem.aspx.cs" Inherits="RentMyWrox.Admin.ManageItem"
    MetaTagDescription="Manage the items that are available to be checked out from the library"
    MetaTagKeywords="Tools, Lending Library, Manage Items, actual useful keywords here" %>
```

FIGURE 7-20: Adding values to the page definition

8. Run the application while still on the `ManageItem` page. If you look into the source of the page now, you will see that this content has been added to the header:

```
<head>
<title>
</title>
<link href="../Content/RentMyWrox.css" rel="stylesheet" type="text/css" />
<meta name="keywords" content="Tools, Lending Library, Manage Items,
        actual useful keywords here" />
<meta name="description" content="Manage the items that are available to be
        checked out from the library" />
</head>
```

9. Go back into the new base page and add the lines shown in Figure 7-21.

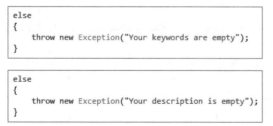

```
else
{
    throw new Exception("Your keywords are empty");
}
```

```
else
{
    throw new Exception("Your description is empty");
}
```

FIGURE 7-21: Adding validation that keywords and description are set

10. Ensure that `ManageItem` is active in your editor window and run the application. Everything should work just as before. Change to the `OrderList` page from the `ManageItem` page in the address bar and press Return. Rather than render successfully, it should instead return the error screen shown in Figure 7-22.

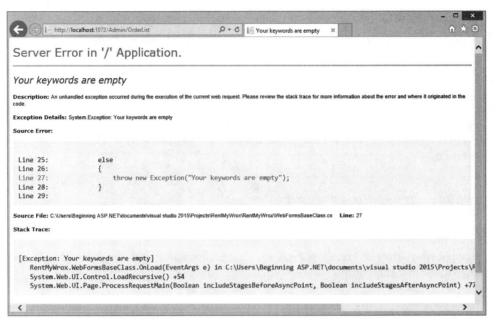

FIGURE 7-22: Error thrown when keywords and description are not set

11. Open the `OrderList` markup page and add the keywords and the description. If you run the application now the server error is no longer returned.

How It Works

You did several things during this exercise. First, you took advantage of the object-oriented feature of inheritance to create a class that contains common logic you're using in multiple places. This is a feature that ASP.NET was already taking advantage of because, as you saw, the pages that you changed were already inheriting from another page; all you did was add a page in between.

One of the important things that your base page did was to also inherit from the `System.Web.UI.Page` class. If you didn't take that step and instead had the web page inherit from a non-extended base class, you would get an error similar to that shown in Figure 7-23, which explains that the page you are trying to access does not extend class `System.Web.UI.Page`—a pretty obvious error at this point.

Looking at the base class you created demonstrates several new features. The first is where you overrode the `OnLoad` method. The keyword that you used there, `override`, means that there is a method in the inherited class with the same name and method signature (the parameter list) and that you want to extend that method. Because of this preexisting method, you would have had to use either the `override` keyword to extend the base method or the `new` keyword, which tells the compiler to replace the method in the base class.

It was necessary to override this method because it's part of the default ASP.NET Web Forms event processing stack. Using this approach ensures that the method will be called every time the page is processed—you didn't have to do anything else to tie it in.

The finished code in the method does two different things for each one of your sets of metadata. First, it creates the tag that will be written to the output HTML. This is done through the use of the `HtmlMeta` class, where you set the `Name` and `Content` properties and then added the class to the header collection of controls. Just like the other server controls that you looked at earlier, this item ended up creating the HTML meta tags that you wanted.

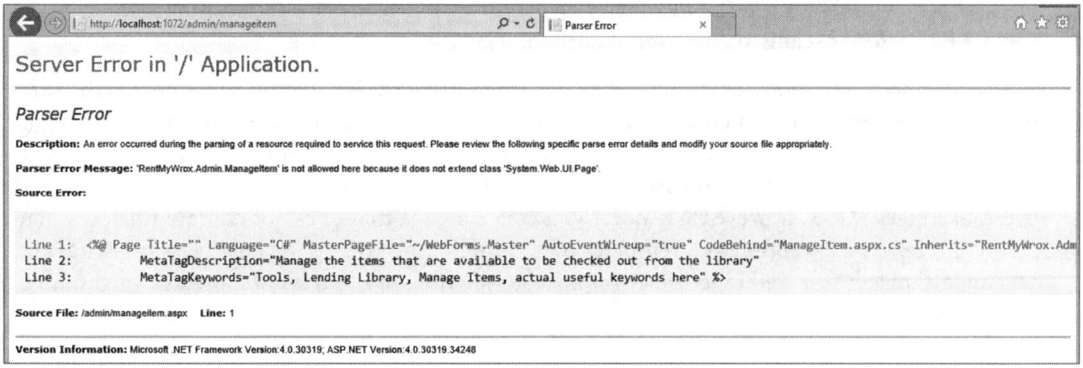

FIGURE 7-23: Error thrown when the page does not extend System.Web.UI.Page

The second thing that you did in the `OnLoad` method was to add a check to determine whether the property value was set. If the method discovered that the values were not set, it would throw an exception rather than continue through the process. This means that any page that didn't provide the necessary information would not be functional, and missing keywords and description would become readily apparent. This is why the application returned an exception the first time it was run without the keywords, yet was able to run successfully once the keywords were added.

After the new base class was created, you had to change the already existing pages to use the new class. This was straightforward because you only needed to replace the default inheritance with the new inheritance.

SUMMARY

Keeping a consistent look and feel is an important part of website branding, and ASP.NET provides support to help fulfill this need. In ASP.NET Web Forms this support is master pages, while in MVC it is called a layout. They both fulfill very similar needs; however, their implementation is different because of the difference in the specific framework.

In the master page, sections of the page that will be filled with content from elsewhere are defined through the use of a `ContentPlaceholder` server control. For each placeholder control in the master page there may be a linked content control in the content page. For example, if the master page had three placeholder controls, then the content page could have up to three content controls, with each linked to a particular placeholder in the master page. With this approach, all of the content enclosed between the content elements in the content page basically replace the placeholder controls.

MVC has a different approach. The content page becomes a complete replacement to the @RenderBody command in the layout page, rather than just the content of one control replacing a designated area of content within the template. The only exception to this is the @RenderSection method, which takes a subset of the content page for its replacement—the section of the page enclosed within a specially defined set of curly brackets.

While the implementation of templates within each framework is different, their goal is the same: to give the web application a consistent look and feel. ASP.NET Web Forms, in particular, offer you the opportunity to do more to ensure consistency in your application. You created a base class that will help you ensure that you are easily configuring the metadata on all your pages, an easily overlooked task. Now, however, whenever you create a page that does not contain this information, you will receive an exception as a reminder to add that data. Adding the base class takes advantage of standard object-oriented inheritance to provide functionality that will be used throughout your application.

EXERCISES

1. Why is it not as straightforward to use base classes on views as it is to use base classes on either a Web Form web page or an MVC controller?

2. What is the advantage of using the Layout command in the ViewStart page?

▶ WHAT YOU LEARNED IN THIS CHAPTER

Base Class	A class containing shared functionality that may be useful in multiple pages. ASP.NET Web Form pages can have base classes, or classes that are inserted into the inheritance tree. ASP.NET MVC controller pages can have them as well.
@RenderBody	A Razor syntax command that the view engine uses to determine where content needs to be written. This command is placed in the layout page and, when used, all the output from the content page is used to replace this command.
@RenderSection	Another command in Razor. Whereas RenderBody drops the entire set of output into the areas as a replacement, the RenderSection only finds any named sections in the content page and uses that delimited output. It is part of the layout page.
@Section	The Razor keyword that defines a named area of content displayed in a @RenderSection command. The section is part of the content page.
Content Control	The asp:Content control is used in an ASP.NET Web Forms content page. It defines the content that will be displayed in the ContentPlaceHolder control in the master page. The Content control is referenced to the placeholder control through the presence of a ContentPlaceHolderId on the Content control.
ContentPlaceHolder Control	The asp:ContentPlaceHolder control is used on a master page to indicate where content provided from the content page will be placed. It has no knowledge of the content that will be retrieved, only that there may be some. No error occurs if the content is not provided by the content page.
Template	Both ASP.NET Web Form master pages and ASP.NET MVC layout pages provide the capability to template the appearance of the website, enabling much of the design to be located in one page so that a change made in one place can affect all pages.

8

Navigation

WHAT YOU WILL LEARN IN THIS CHAPTER:

➤ How to create navigational schemas in ASP.NET Web Forms and MVC

➤ Incorporating absolute and relative URLS into your flow

➤ A closer look at how ASP.NET MVC routing works

➤ How to programmatically send users to a different page

CODE DOWNLOADS FOR THIS CHAPTER:

The wrox.com code downloads for this chapter are found at www.wrox.com/go/ beginningaspnetforvisualstudio on the Download Code tab. The code is in the chapter 08 download and individually named according to the names throughout the chapter.

Helping your site visitors find what they are looking for is critical to the success of your web application. You must have a logical and intuitive navigation structure. If users can't find what they are looking for, they will lose interest in being your customer, and your work to create the site in the first place would all be for naught. This presence of an intuitive navigation structure is a key factor to the overall site User Experience (UX), or how well the user can understand and work within your site design and structure.

The last chapter covered master and layout pages that are used to provide a consistent look and feel to a web application. In this chapter, you build these pages out even further, because the navigation structure is among the most commonly shared parts of an application. You will once again see the different approaches between Web Forms and MVC applications as you build each type, as ASP.NET Web Forms uses server controls and MVC uses various other, non–server control approaches.

You not only learn about the use of menus and navigation structures in the chapter, but you also take a more detailed look at routing in ASP.NET MVC. In ASP.NET Web Forms the understanding of what page should serve which request is straightforward. There is an .aspx page for each of the valid page requests. You have seen how that differs from MVC; and you will learn many of the more advanced aspects of routing and how you can manage which action on a controller will be selected based on the URL of the request.

DIFFERENT WAYS TO MOVE AROUND YOUR SITE

The goal of the navigation structure is to enable users to move easily and intuitively from one page to another. When you look at the menu structure of a standard website, you are really seeing nothing more than a way to move to a particular part of that site. Other parts could be anything from a static "About Us" page to an e-commerce product page that enables users to purchase a car. Each of those pages represents a single resource—one specific request from the client browser whereby the web server receives the request, performs some analysis on it, and then determines how to respond in such a way that a specific resource fulfills the request.

The primary way to move from one location to another is through the HTML anchor tag, `<a href="Login.aspx">Login to the Site</a>`. This causes an HTTP request to be sent to the URL in the `href` attribute. Virtually every form of a navigational structure that you encounter is based on this single HTML element.

As you likely guessed, because there is an HTML element to do this work, there is also an ASP.NET Web Forms–based set of functionality to help you build an anchor tag through the use of a server control. In this case, that is the `asp:HyperLink` server control. Although there may be a unique server control, the output is a standard HTML anchor tag.

Understanding Absolute and Relative URLs

The HTML anchor element does a lot of the work in sending users to a different page of your website. However, there are several different ways that you can define the address for this resource. It is important to remember that an HTTP request is made to a specific resource address. This address is known as the URL, or uniform resource locator.

URLS AND URIS

In this book, you might also see a value called a URI, or uniform resource identifier, used alongside URLs. These are not quite the same thing, though in many cases they may look the same. The main difference is the last character, the locator versus the identifier. A URI identifies an object, the URL locates the object. This is more than a semantic difference. A URL does not necessarily identify the resource that it is getting, it just gets it. A URI identifies the resource, with one of the characteristics being the address of the resource, or the URL. Thus, all fully identified resources have a locator (URL), but not all URLs are part of a URI.

There are two different types of URLs: absolute and relative. An absolute URL contains the complete address to a resource, meaning no knowledge about the site that contains the navigation structure is needed in order to find the resource. The following example is an absolute URL. Note how it includes the protocol and full server address:

```
<a href="http://www.rentmywrox.com/account/login">Login</a>
```

There is no doubt as to where the resource is located. However, using an absolute URL can be problematic. In your sample application, for example, using this approach means you cannot link to any of the pages in the working solution, because the links would instead be associated with the deployed site, not your local working site. While using an absolute URL is not always ideal for linking to pages within your current application, it is required for linking to pages with different domains, such as external sites.

The relative URL, on the other hand, defines the locator using an approach that is more like directions for getting to the needed page. These directions are based on the page that displays the link. The following code is an example of a relative URL:

```
<a href="../Admin/ManageItem">Login</a>
```

As you can see, there is no server name in the address, instead there are some periods and slashes. Each of the double periods represents moving up one level in the directory structure; they serve as the directions for getting to the resource that you want. Because this a set of directions, the URL in the preceding example tells the browser to first go up one level in the file structure and then go into the admin directory and look for the page named ManageItem. In Figure 8-1, this URL would be appropriate for the highlighted ManageItem page in the Admin directory.

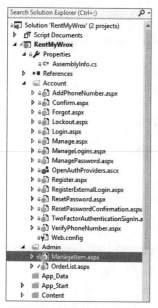

FIGURE 8-1: Relative URLs

As mentioned in an earlier chapter, you can also build a URL using the tilde character (~). Taking this approach would change the preceding example to the following:

```
<a href="~/account/login" runat="server">Login</a>
```

This is an important difference, because with the "dot" approach the link has to be updated whenever either page is moved—the page containing the link as well as the page with which it is being linked. Using the tilde approach tells the system to go to the root directory for the application and start from there, so any change in the location of the page holding the link does not affect the system's ability to determine where to find the resource. However, you may have noticed that you also have to include the runat attribute to ensure that the server processes the HTML control. This is because using the tilde character requires server-side processing; the value of the root directory replaces the tilde, so you wind up with a more flexible approach.

Although the tilde requires server participation, there is still another approach that enables the system to ask for a server root-based URL. This approach looks like the following code:

```
<a href="/account/login">Login</a>
```

The difference is subtle, but by prefacing the URL with the forward slash character (/), you are telling the system to start from the server root and work its way down the directory tree.

VIRTUAL APPLICATIONS

IIS 7 and above formalize the concepts of sites, applications, and virtual directories. Virtual directories and applications are now separate objects that are maintained within a hierarchical relationship as part of the configuration within IIS. In general, a single website contains one or more applications. An application may contain one or more virtual directories, with each virtual directory mapped to a physical directory on a computer.

What does that really mean to you? The most important part is the concept that a website may have more than one application. There will always be one application, the default application, but there may be others. Each of these applications is hosted within its own directory; if your sample application is running as a secondary application on the web server, then your base URL won't be what you expect — it will end up using "http://server.domain.com/hostingdirectoryname/" as the root directory, as opposed to the http://server.domain.com that it would use without the virtual application. Figure 8-2 shows what this would look like in the IIS management console if RentMyWrox were a virtual application that is part of the default website.

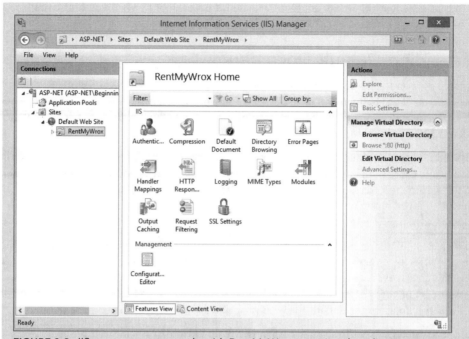

FIGURE 8-2: IIS management console with RentMyWrox as a virtual application

The concept of the virtual application is why the tilde is an important construct. If you know that your application will be in a production environment where it's deployed as a virtual application, then using the tilde is important because it will correctly include the relative directory in the URL that is being linked. This is different from using the prefaced slash because that takes you to the root directory, which is actually one level above the directory that actually contains your code.

You might not notice this when you are working in Visual Studio because by default, IIS Express, the local application that serves the content you are creating, always starts in the application root. Therefore, you would not see any problems during debug using either solution, as there is no default application. However, when deployed to a server as a virtual application, those links that use the slash approach don't work because they don't take the virtual application directory into account.

Prefacing the URL with the slash character (/) should be done only when you know that the application you're working on will never be deployed as a virtual application.

Understanding Default Documents

Have you ever wondered how typing in a simple URL such as `http://www.wrox.com` takes you to a page of content? That happens because the server has been assigned a specific file in a direction that handles calls to a directory (including the root directory), which is to say that page's content has been defined as a default document.

The designation of default documents is part of IIS configuration and is specific to ASP.NET Web Forms because there is an expectation that a file will be assigned to handle those calls that do not contain a document to retrieve. Traditionally, several documents are defined as potential default documents, but the most common file is `Default.aspx`. When a request is made to `http://server.domain.com/`, the `Default.aspx` file in the root directory is returned.

The server uses default documents whenever there is a request for a directory as opposed to content within that directory; therefore, a `Default.aspx` file in a subdirectory from the root handles default calls to that directory. Because of this built-in capability, it is recommended that you not declare the default part of the URL when trying to link to it; instead, reference the directory name only and allow the server to serve the default file as appropriate.

You can also set default documents for ASP.NET Web Form directories in the web.config configuration file. The code to do this is shown here:

```
<system.webServer>
  <defaultDocument>
    <files>
      <clear />
      <add value="Default.aspx" />
    </files>
  </defaultDocument>
</system.webServer>
```

The preceding code snippet also sets the default document to Default.aspx, or whatever other file you designate. The `defaultDocument` element is defined as part of the `system.WebServer` element. While the example lists one default, you can add multiple add elements that are contained within the `files` element. The server will try to return the page listed first and if that file does not exist will go to the next file name and attempt to return that file. It will continue through the list until if finds a matching a file to return.

Note the `clear` element. This is necessary to remove any other default documents that may have been set, such as in IIS for that web site. You are not required to add the `clear` element; however, by doing so you ensure that the only default documents being set are from your web.config file.

Friendly URLs

When you create an ASP.NET project, it includes a default set of configurations, including a default route. This default information is part of the `App_Start\RouteConfig.cs` file (see Figure 8-3).

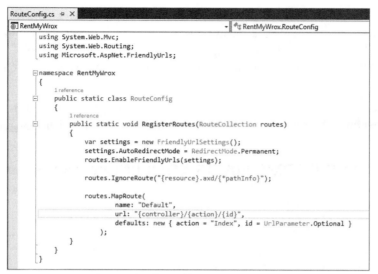

FIGURE 8-3: Initial RouteConfig.cs file

At this point you are concerned with only one of this file's sections, the first part that includes `FriendlyUrlSettings`. Adding the `FriendlyUrlSettings` allows you to call ASP.NET Web Forms without having to use the .aspx extension. That means you can create a link that accesses a file called `ManageItem.aspx` by calling `ManageItem`, without needing to include the extension in the URL.

Not only does `FriendlyUrlSettings` allow the use of a filename without the extension, it also allows other information to be added to the URL. This is another feature of friendly URLs, the ability to parse the complete URL value and break the information down for use within the code-behind of the page. Thus, `ManageItem\36` is understandable to the system and allows access to the value in the URL. This doesn't occur automatically, however; you have to do a little work to access this information. For example, suppose you want the user to access the URL `http://www.servername.com/SomePage/2/20/2015`, where the work will be handled by a page called `SomePage.aspx`. If the values appended to the URL represent a date, you would be able to access them as shown here:

```
protected void Page_Load(object sender, EventArgs e)
{
    List<string> segments = Request.GetFriendlyUrlSegments();

    int month = int.Parse(segments[0]);
    int day = int.Parse(segments[1]);
    int year = int.Parse(segments[2]);
}
```

Using `FriendlyUrls` enables you to build a consistent user experience, in terms of URLs, for both the ASP.NET MVC and Web Forms approaches. Before the introduction of `FriendlyUrls`, you would have had to take a more traditional query string approach such as

```
http://www.servername.com/SomePage.aspx?SearchDate=2-20-2015
```

Looking at the difference between the two URLs, you can see how it would be easier for something like a web search engine crawler to understand a specific resource that includes the data as part of the address, rather than a URL to a resource that simply includes some extraneous information stuck onto the end of the URL, as is the case with a query string.

There are additional ways to manage the URL segments that are the results of parsing a friendly URL, but they are included within other server controls that you work with in future chapters.

USING THE ASP.NET WEB FORMS NAVIGATION CONTROLS

ASP.NET Web Forms provides more than the anchor tag to build out navigation features in your website. There are three different server controls that help you: the TreeView, Menu, and SiteMapPath controls. Each of these provides a different way to manage your links and the navigation within your web application. The TreeView and Menu controls create a list of links that are available for the user to click, while the SiteMapPath control provides a "breadcrumb" approach to viewing one's location in the context of the site. Figure 8-4 shows how the two link-management controls are rendered by default.

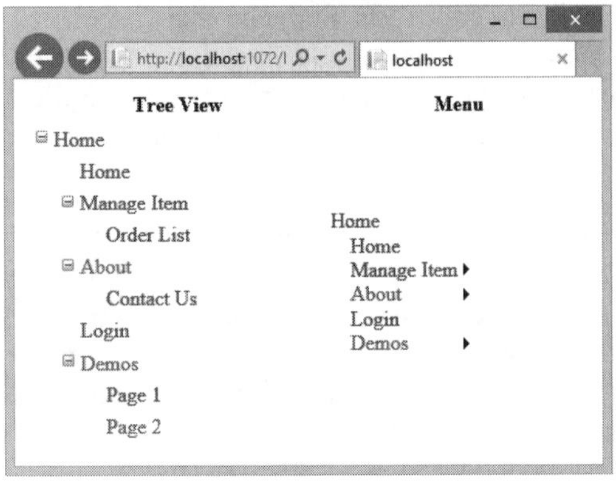

FIGURE 8-4: Default display of TreeView and Menu controls

These two controls have a slightly different way of rendering the same content. The TreeView uses an expander that opens or closes any contained submenu content, whereas the Menu control uses a "grow-out" approach that provides an area to mouse over that causes a submenu to expand and become visible.

As you may have noticed, both controls write out the same navigation structure. This structure is defined in a special type of file, a sitemap. In ASP.NET Web Forms, a sitemap is a special XML file containing the definition of the structure that the application uses. Listing 8-1 shows the content of the Web.sitemap file used to create the items displayed in Figure 8-4.

LISTING 8-1: Example of a Web.sitemap file

```xml
<?xml version="1.0" encoding="utf-8" ?>
<siteMap xmlns="http://schemas.microsoft.com/AspNet/SiteMap-File-1.0">
  <siteMapNode url="~/" title="Home" description="Home">
    <siteMapNode url="~/Default" title="Home" description="Home"/>
    <siteMapNode url="~/Admin/ManageItem" title="Manage Item" >
      <siteMapNode url="~/Admin/OrderList" title="Order List" />
    </siteMapNode>
    <siteMapNode url="~/About" title="About" >
      <siteMapNode url="~/Contact" title="Contact Us" />
    </siteMapNode>
    <siteMapNode url="~/Account/Login" title="Login" />
    <siteMapNode url="~/Demonstrations" title="Demos">
      <siteMapNode url="~/Demonstrations/Page1" title="Page 1" />
      <siteMapNode url="~/Demonstrations/Page2" title="Page 2" />
    </siteMapNode>
  </siteMapNode>
</siteMap>
```

Each of the nodes in the file is a `siteMapNode` and may or may not contain other `siteMapNodes`. When one node contains others it creates a parent-child relationship that the control is able to interpret. The `Menu` control uses the right-facing arrow by default, while the `TreeView` control uses the +/– convention to enable access to child nodes.

Three attributes are part of a `siteMapNode`: the `url`, the `title`, and the `description`. The `url` is the page that you want to open, the `title` is the text that will be displayed as the clickable part of the link, and the `description` becomes the tooltip that appears when you hover the mouse over the link.

Getting the `web.sitemap` linked to the `Menu` and `TreeView` controls is not very complicated. Listing 8-2 shows the entire markup for the page shown earlier.

LISTING 8-2: Markup that adds Menu and TreeView controls as well as links in SiteMapDataSource

```csharp
<%@ Page Language="C#" AutoEventWireup="true" CodeBehind="Page1.aspx.cs"
        Inherits="RentMyWrox.Demonstrations.Page1" %>
<!DOCTYPE html>
<html xmlns="http://www.w3.org/1999/xhtml">
<head runat="server">
    <title></title>
</head>
<body>
    <form id="form1" runat="server">
```

continues

LISTING 8-2 *(continued)*

```
<div>
    <table width="100%">
        <tr>
            <th>Tree View</th>
            <th>Menu</th>
        </tr>
        <tr>
            <td><asp:TreeView DataSourceId="ds" runat="server" /></td>
            <td><asp:Menu StaticDisplayLevels="2" DataSourceID="ds"
                    runat="server" /></td>
        </tr>
    </table>
    <asp:SiteMapDataSource ID="ds" runat="server" />
</div>
</form>
</body>
</html>
```

The new control that hasn't been discussed yet is a `SiteMapDataSource`. This is a server control that acts as a data source: a control that provides information to other controls. You may notice that it is not pointing to any specific sitemap file. That's because the default file it is looking for is the `Web.sitemap` file in the root directory of your application. If you want to use multiple sitemaps, or a nontraditionally named file, you need to do some extra work, making both configuration and code-behind changes. In the following Try It Out you aren't taking that route, instead creating a single `Web.sitemap`.

TRY IT OUT Creating a Web.sitemap file

In this activity you create a `Web.sitemap` file that you use to create the menu structure for the administrative portion of the sample application.

1. Ensure that your sample application is open in Visual Studio.

2. While in Solution Explorer, right-click the project and select Add ➪ New Item. Using the appropriate language (C# or VB), go to the Web/General section and select sitemap, as shown in Figure 8-5. The default name is `Web.sitemap`, which is what you want it to be called.

3. Replace the content in the file with the following and save the file:

```
<?xml version="1.0" encoding="utf-8" ?>
<siteMap xmlns="http://schemas.microsoft.com/AspNet/SiteMap-File-1.0" >
  <siteMapNode url="~/Admin/" title="Admin Home"
            description="Home page for the admin section">
    <siteMapNode url="~/Admin/Default" title="Admin Home"
            description="Home page for the admin section" />
    <siteMapNode url="~/Admin/ItemList" title="Items List"
```

```
                    description="List of available items" />
        <siteMapNode url="~/Admin/OrderList" title="Order List"
                    description="List of orders" />
        <siteMapNode url="~/Admin/UserList" title="User List"
                    description="List of users" />
    </siteMapNode>
</siteMap>
```

You are done with the `Web.sitemap` file.

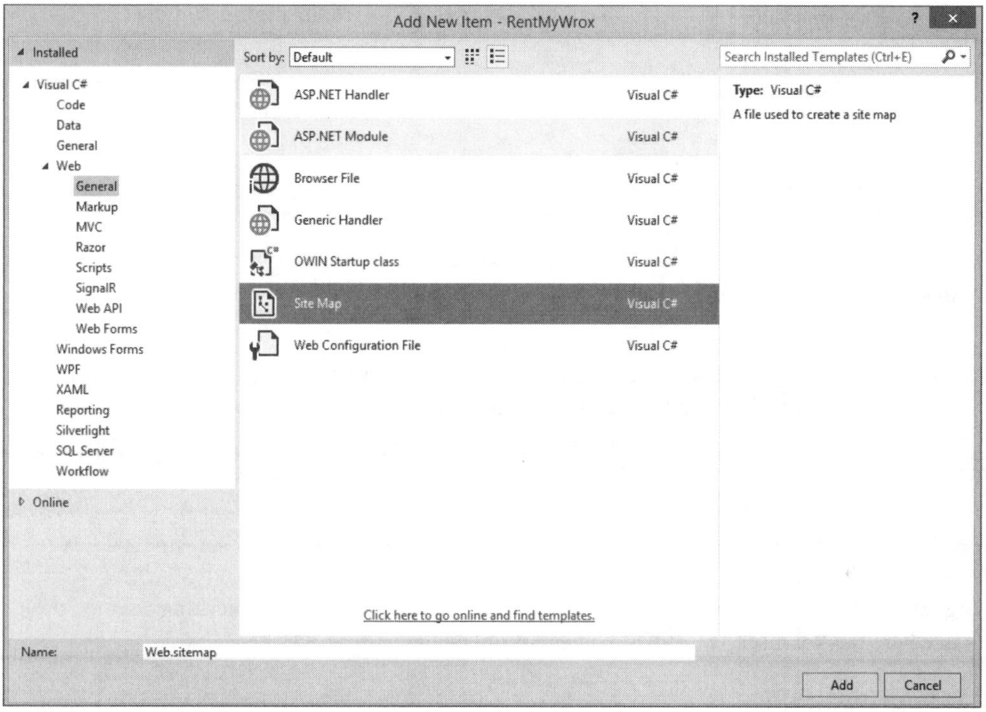

FIGURE 8-5: Creating the Web.sitemap file

How It Works

Note first that the code you entered calls out only four different pages, three of which have not even been added to the sample application yet: `Default.aspx`, `ItemList.aspx`, and `UserList.aspx`. Therefore, don't be concerned that they are not contained in your local solution.

Because the sitemap is an XML file, a couple of standard rules apply. First, there is a `sitemap` element. This base node defines all of the content contained within it as sitemap content. The next item in the page is a `siteMapNode` element. You may notice that all the rest of the siteMapNodes are contained within this first node. This is required; if you try to add more than one siteMapNode within the `siteMap` element, you will get a server exception, as shown in Figure 8-6.

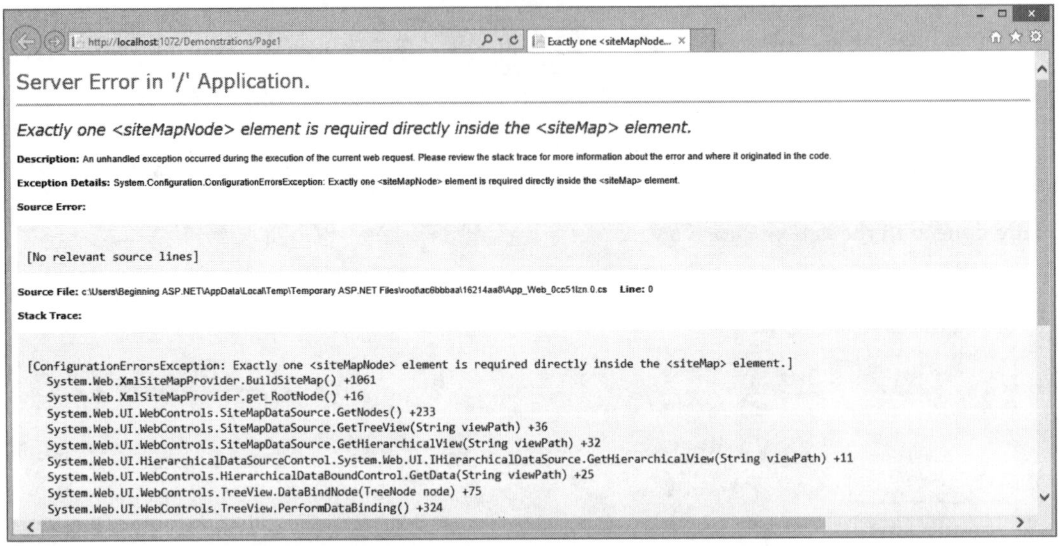

FIGURE 8-6: Error displayed when multiple siteMapNodes appear within the sitemap element

One last thing to note about the `Web.sitemap` is that you cannot have the same URL in more than one element, likely because the ASP.NET development team thought it unlikely that you would ever need two separate menu links going to the exact same page The data you added was able to work around this limitation because the first two elements take advantage of the concept of default pages, as one of the URLs points to the directory while the other points directly to the `Defaut.aspx` file.

Now that the data for the menu is configured, the next task is adding something that uses the data. This is where the `Menu` server control comes into play.

Using the Menu Control

The ASP.NET Web Form `Menu` control takes the sitemap file and parses it into a series of HTML anchor elements that enable users to navigate through your application. As a typical server control, you can manage the various attributes of it, as shown in Table 8-1.

TABLE 8-1: Attributes of a Menu Control

PROPERTY	DESCRIPTION
CssClass	Assigns a class name to the HTML elements that are written out during processing of the server control
DataSourceId	Manages the relationship between the `Menu` control and the `SiteMapDataSource` control that manages the connection to the sitemap file

PROPERTY	DESCRIPTION
DisappearAfter	Controls the amount of time a dynamic submenu is visible after the mouse is moved away. This value is in milliseconds, with a default value of 500, or .5 of a second.
IncludeStyleBlock	Specifies whether ASP.NET should render a block of cascading style sheet (CSS) definitions for the styles used in the menu. You can get a copy of the default CSS block that the Menu control generates by setting the property to true, running the page, and viewing the page in a browser. You can then view the page source in the browser and copy and paste the CSS block into the page markup or a separate file.
MaximumDynamicDisplayLevels	Specifies the number of dynamic submenu levels that the client is provided. A 3, for example, means that only those values nested three or fewer levels deep will be rendered. Any items that are more than three levels deep are not displayed as part of this menu.
Orientation	Provides the direction in which the menu will be written, horizontal or vertical
RenderingMode	Specifies whether the Menu control renders HTML table elements and inline styles, or list item elements and Cascading Style Sheet (CSS) styles
StaticDisplayLevels	Defines the number of non-dynamic levels that will be written out by the Menu control
Target	Specifies the target window where the requested page will be opened

The next step is to take advantage of this information and add a menu control to the sample application, as demonstrated in the following Try It Out.

TRY IT OUT   Adding a Menu Control

Now that you have created your sitemap, the next step is to create a menu that displays its contents. In this Try it Out, you create a Menu control in the master page that has been configured for the administrative area of your sample application.

1.   Ensure that Visual Studio is running and you have the RentMyWrox application open. Open the WebForms.Master file from the root directory into the markup window. Find the page's placeholder text, **Navigation content here**, and delete it.

2.   Open the Toolbox: expand the Navigation section, and click the Menu option. The ToolBox will generally be a vertical tab in the upper left quadrant of your IDE. If you do not see it there you can

also select View ⇨ Toolbox. Drag the item and drop it into the same area where you just deleted the placeholder text. After doing so, it should look something like the following:

```
<div id="nav">
    <asp:Menu ID="Menu1" runat="server"></asp:Menu>
</div>
```

3. Switch to Design mode. Click the Menu control to invoke the expander arrow. Click the arrow to view the configuration dialog shown in Figure 8-7.

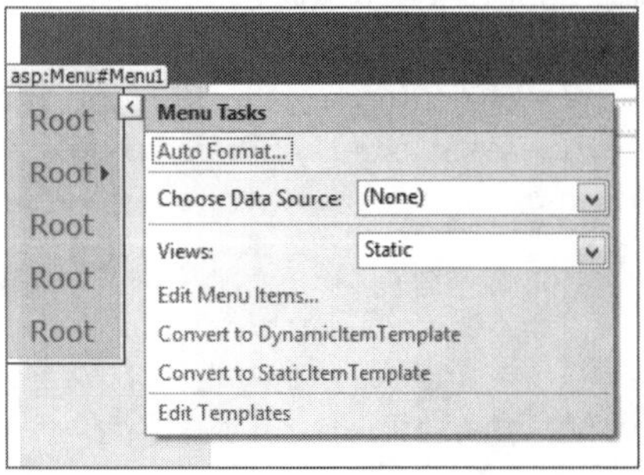

FIGURE 8-7: Configuring the Menu control in Design mode

4. In the Choose Data Source dropdown, select <New data source…>. This opens the dialog shown in Figure 8-8.

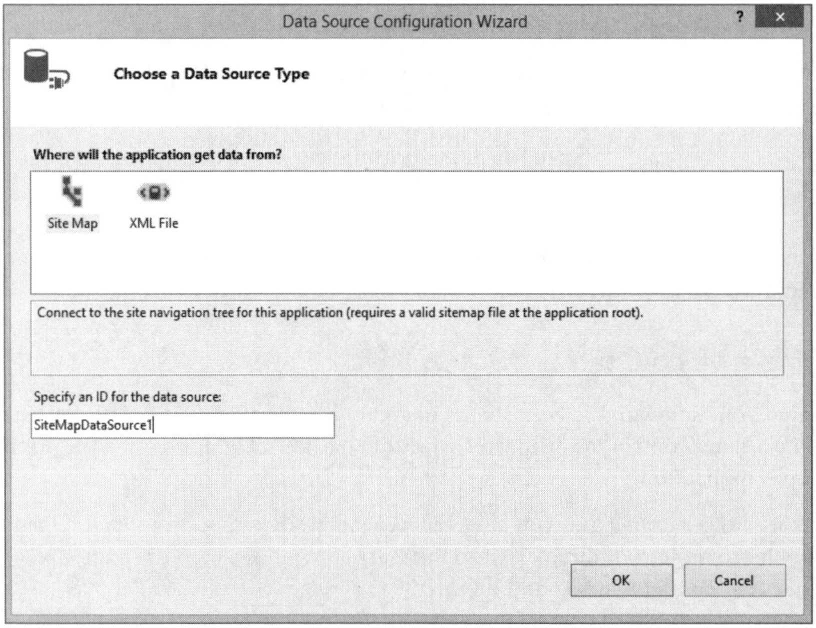

FIGURE 8-8: Selecting data source for the Menu control

5. Select Site Map and click OK. This should return you to the design screen where you can see that the first item in your sitemap is now displayed in the Menu control.

6. Click once on SiteMapDataSource and then press the F4 key to open the Properties window. This window may open in the area where Solution Explorer is generally displayed. Find the property named ShowStartingNode and change its value to false. As soon as you take this action, the Menu control will change to display all the items contained within the parent node, rather than just the parent node, as shown in Figure 8-9.

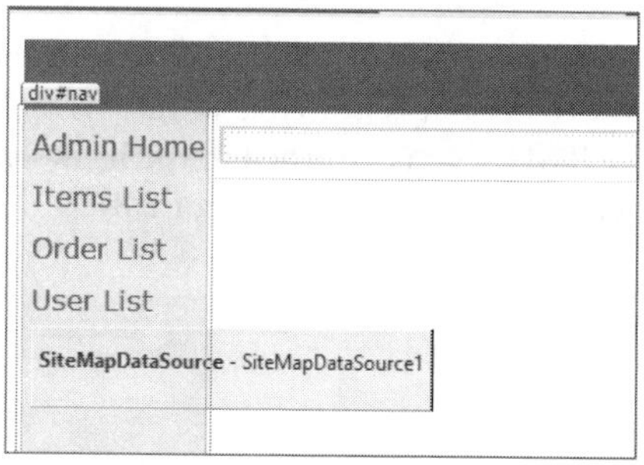

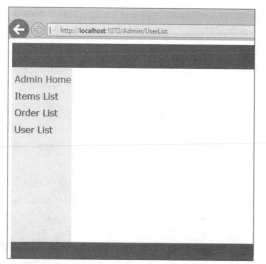

FIGURE 8-9: Menu display after turning off the starting node

7. Return to Solution Explorer, right-click the Admin directory, and create the following three new Web Form with Master Page pages: Default.aspx, ItemList.aspx, and UserList.aspx, selecting WebForms.Master as the master page.

8. Run in Debug mode while on any page within the Admin directory. You should see the menu render correctly and be able to click all of its pages. The only change you would see at this point is the URL in the address bar—and it should look something like what is shown in Figure 8-10.

FIGURE 8-10: Rendered example of the menu

9.   Stop debugging. Return to the `WebForms.Master` page and go back into Source mode. You will see the `Menu` control and the `SiteMapDataSource` control that were added during the process.

How It Works

Once you have created the sitemap, displaying it in the `Menu` control is as simple as configuring it correctly. You used the Toolbox to drag a `Menu` control onto the page, but you could just as easily have typed the commands directly into the markup window, for both the `Menu` control and the `SiteMapDataSource`.

The `SiteMapDataSource` is important because it is the control that understands how to find the information that is contained within the sitemap. Once this information is found it is available for use in the `Menu` control. The `Menu` control will then go through and create the HTML that is returned to the browser. This HTML is interesting in that there is a lot of information created by this control. Figure 8-11 shows the HTML source that is created.

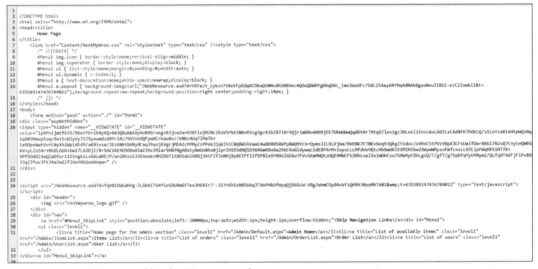

FIGURE 8-11: HTML created by the Menu control

Two major areas are written out by the `Menu` control. The first is in the HTML head section, which contains some local styles. These are created by the `Menu` control so that you can easily style them; by copying these styles into your style sheet and disabling the writing out of the style sheet by setting the `IncludeStyleBlock` attribute to `false`, you can take advantage of fully styled menus.

The second area written out by the `Menu` control is the content within the `<div id="nav">` tags, where the actual control can be seen when looking at the HTML code. Note that the first line includes `SkipLink`; this is an anchor tag that is completely invisible in the browser. This link is added for screen readers and other programs that provide differently abled users with access to the screen content. In this case, the `SkipLink` anchor takes them to another anchor immediately after the list of navigation items. This enables programs to travel from the link before the menu structure to the link immediately after the menu structure, basically eliminating the need for the screen reader to read out the same navigation links on every page if the screen reader is so configured.

One last item is written out that does not currently affect the way that you use the menu in the sample application—a JavaScript reference, on line 24, as shown in Figure 8-11. If you were using dynamic menus, whereby submenus fly out from parent menus when hovered over, the JavaScript accessed through this link would be critical because that's what controls the opening and closing of the submenu area.

The content in Figure 8-11 includes an interesting item that you will take advantage of when adding styling to the Menu control. There are two major approaches to styling user controls, and the Menu control enables both of them. The first is the "old-school" approach whereby you add styling directly to the control. That is why you see attributes such as BackColor and BorderColor available in the Menu control; these give you complete control, at the control level, over the look and feel of the rendered control.

The second approach, and the one that you have used so far, is through the use of CSS. In the following Try It Out, you add some styling to your menu structure.

TRY IT OUT Styling Your Menu Control

Now that you have added the Menu control to the master page, you can see the menu on each of the pages. However, you likely noticed that it appears to use the default styling that you added earlier—and you are right. In this exercise, you add some styling to the menu to make it look more like part of the sample application.

1. Ensure that Visual Studio is running and you have the RentMyWrox application open. Open the WebForms.master page in the Markup window. If you didn't make any changes in the previous walkthrough, your Menu control likely still has the default ID, Menu1. Change the name of the control to **LeftNavigation** and save.

2. Open the RentMyWrox.css file in the Content directory and add the following lines at the bottom of the file:

```
#LeftNavigation ul
{
    list-style:none;
    margin:0;
    padding:0;
    width:auto;
}

#LeftNavigation a
{
    color: #C40D42;
    text-decoration: none;
    white-space: nowrap;
    display: block;
}
```

```
ul.level1 .selected
{
    /* Defines the appearance of active menu items. */
    background-color: white;
    color: #C40D42;
    padding-right: 15px;
    padding-left: 8px;
}

a.level1
{
    /* Adds some white space to the left of the main menu item text.
    !important is used to overrule the in-line CSS that the menu generates */
    padding-left: 5px !important;
    padding-right: 15px;
}

a.level1:hover
{
    /* Defines the hover style for the main and sub items. */
    background-color: #509EE7;
}
```

3. Go back to the `WebForms.master` page and ensure that the `Menu` control has the following
    attribute set: `IncludeStyleBlock="false"`. The menu control should appear as:

    ```
    <asp:Menu ID="LeftNavigation" runat="server" DataSourceID="SiteMapDataSource1"
            IncludeStyleBlock="false"></asp:Menu>
    ```

4. Save the file and run the application. Go to one of the pages in the Admin folder, and you should
    see that the navigation area is styled as shown in Figure 8-12.

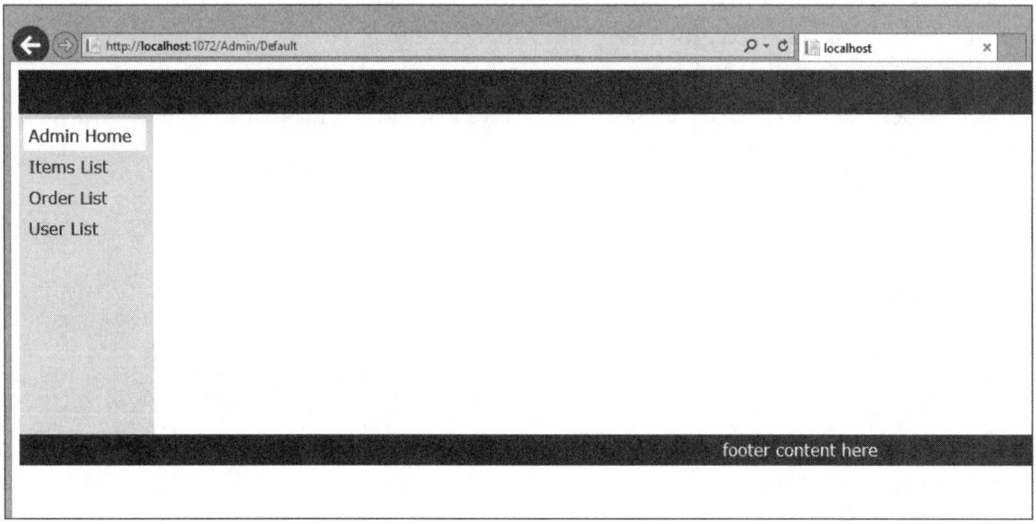

FIGURE 8-12: Page with styled menu

How It Works

Before going into the details of the styles you added, take a look at the HTML that was created from the Menu control. The SkipLink references were removed, leaving the following rendered HTML:

```
<div id="nav">
    <div id="LeftNavigation">
        <ul class="level1">
            <li><a title="Home page for the admin section" class="level1 selected"
                    href="/Admin/Default">Admin Home</a></li>
            <li><a title="List of available items" class="level1"
                    href="/Admin/ItemList">Items List</a></li>
            <li><a title="List of orders" class="level1"
                    href="/Admin/OrderList">Order List</a></li>
            <li><a title="List of users" class="level1" href="/Admin/UserList">
                User List</a></li>
        </ul>
    </div>
</div>
```

Notice how the first anchor tag has a class of "level1 selected". The selected value was added by the Menu control because the page from which this text was taken is the page that is referenced in that "selected" section of the Menu control; therefore, you can specially style the page that you are on. You can see this with the selector you added for ul.level1 .selected.

Two other special areas are created by the Menu control. One is the <div> tag with the id of LeftNavigation. You may remember that you changed the name of the Menu control to LeftNavigation; this is the effect of that. The other is the unordered list <ul> with the class of level1. The level1 value is assigned because the menu items being displayed are from the first level. If you had nested menu items, then they would be styled with a level2 or level3 depending upon how deep the nesting went.

Navigation in ASP.NET Web Forms is supported by the traditional Web Forms approach of a server control, in this case a Menu control. The Menu control reads in an XML file and then renders the appropriate HTML out to the page. You may be asking yourself why you would want to take this approach rather than just build out the menu yourself manually. One of the main benefits that this approach offers is the capability to change your menu structure on the fly. Because the file is read every time the menu is created, you can change the complete navigation schema of your site without having to make any code changes. This can be especially useful as you get feedback on your site from your users. This flexibility allows you to continually monitor the user's experience and change your site without having to maintain any source code.

You do not have the same capability when using the ASP.NET MVC approach to building a navigation structure, as it requires building those menu links manually. You look at this next.

NAVIGATING IN ASP.NET MVC

Navigation in an ASP.NET Web Forms application is pretty easy to understand: a URL is requested, and if there is a corresponding separate, physical page that has the same name, then that page is called, the processing occurs, and the output from the processing is returned to the client. Interpreting the request is straightforward. However, ASP.NET MVC is different because determining what code should be called involves a completely different process. There is no physical page that responds to the request. Instead, a simple method is called—once the system has figured out which method to call.

Doing this work of determining which method to call is known as ASP.NET MVC *routing*. Routing is a pattern-matching system that is responsible for mapping incoming browser requests to specified MVC controller actions (methods). When the ASP.NET MVC application launches, the application registers one or more URL patterns within the framework's route table. These patterns tell the routing engine what to do with requests that match those patterns. When the routing engine receives a request at runtime, it attempts to match that request's URL against the URL patterns registered with it and returns the response according to a pattern match, as shown in Figure 8-13.

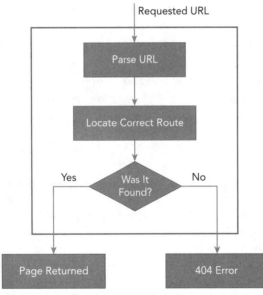

FIGURE 8-13: Routing process

Routing

ASP.NET MVC routes are responsible for determining which controller method is executed for a given URL. A route is a URL pattern that is mapped to a handler, an action on a controller. The route consists of the following properties:

➤ **Route name:** A route name is used as a specific reference to a given route. Each route must have a unique name. Generally this name is only necessary when defining the route, but it also provides the capability to access a specific route in code if needed.

➤ **URL pattern:** A URL pattern contains both literal values, such as a known string value, and variable placeholders (referred to as URL parameters). These literals and placeholders are segments of the URL that are delimited by the slash (/) character.

➤ **Defaults:** Whenever you define a route with a variable placeholder, you have the opportunity to assign a default value to that parameter. You can assign defaults to every placeholder or not at all—whatever makes sense for the approach you are going to take in building your routes.

➤ **Constraints:** A set of constraints are rules that are applied to a URL pattern to more narrowly define the URLs to which it may be matched.

Each different approach to building out a URL structure needs to have a corresponding route definition. An ASP.NET application built through Visual Studio scaffolding also includes a default route.

Default Configuration and Route

When you create an ASP.NET MVC project it includes a set of routing configurations, including a default route. This default information is part of the `App_Start\RouteConfig.cs` file, shown in Figure 8-14.

FIGURE 8-14: The initial RouteConfig.cs file

As shown, the default ASP.NET MVC project templates add a generic route that uses the following URL convention to define the URL pattern for a given request into three named segments:

```
url: "{controller}/{action}/{id}"
```

With the preceding template, a URL of `http://www.servername.com/DemoModel/Details/57` would result in the application trying to find a controller named "DemoModelController" that has an action (method) named "Details" that accepts a parameter that is either a string or an integer.

MVC has a very convention-based approach whereby controller files need to have the phrase "Controller" as part of the filename so that the ASP.NET MVC routing engine can find the appropriate class to call.

Once the routing engine finds the correct controller, the next thing it tries to do is find an action that matches the name that is part of the URL. When the engine finds the action(s) that fit the name, it then analyzes the parameter list to determine whether there's a match between the information within the URL and the parameters required for those action(s). However, you have to be careful about how you set this up. Consider the following code:

```
public ActionResult Details(int id)
{
    return View();
}

public ActionResult Details(string id)
{
    return View();
}
```

This seems pretty straightforward in that one might expect `http://www.servername.com/DemoModel/Details/57` to go to the first method while `http://www.servername.com/DemoModel/Details/Orange` would go to the second method. However, you will instead get the error shown in Figure 8-15.

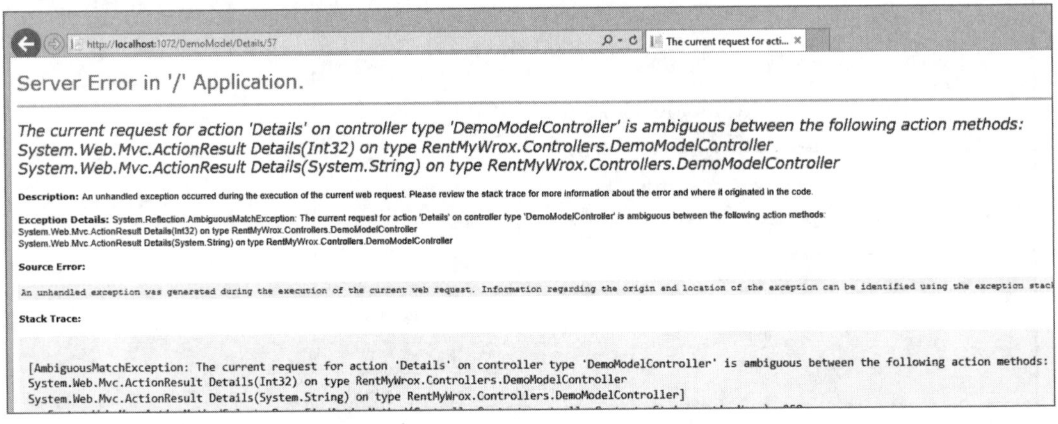

FIGURE 8-15: Ambiguous action exception

This error indicates that the route parsing is not as obvious as it may seem. The expectation is that the URL can be parsed into a single action on a specific controller. This means you have to ensure that you avoid the type of method overloading that you can do in traditional C# development. Therefore, if you want to be able to pass either an integer or a string into a method, then you have to make some changes to your approach by either creating a new action to handle one of the approaches, such as a `DetailsByName(string name)` action, or making a single method and doing work within the method, as demonstrated in the following example:

```
public ActionResult Details(string id)
{
    int idInt;
    if (int.TryParse(id, out idInt)
    {
        // do work if id is an integer that can pull product from database by Id
    }
    else
    {
        // do the work when id is NOT an integer, such as getting product by name
    }
    return View();
}
```

In this case, the best approach is to always create a new action that specifically handles the different case. Having a set of actions as shown in the following example is easier for both developers and the system in order to successfully understand what the expectation is when looking at the route parsing:

```
public ActionResult Details(int id)
{
    // do work to pull product from database by Id
    return View();
}

public ActionResult DetailsByName(string id)
{
    // do work to pull product from database by Name
    return View();
}
```

The first method would be called by `http://www.servername.com/DemoModel/Details/57`, while the second would be called by `http://www.servername.com/DemoModel/DetailsByName/Orange`. Both of these approaches would then be covered by the default route, so no additional routing configuration would be required.

The default route does not necessarily serve every need, however. Imagine the case in which you may want users to have the capability to get more specific details than with a single parameter value—such as looking at the DemoModel and wanting details about an orange one. The URL that you would want to use is `http://www.servername.com/DemoModel/SomeAction/8/orange`. The default route doesn't match this; in fact, if you add this to any of the links that are already working, you will see that the system tries to parse the URL, but it won't find a successful match and you'll get a 404 - File Not Found Error.

What you need to do instead is create a new route in the `RouteConfig.cs` file and then add the new action to the controller, as shown in the following code snippet. This ensures that the URL of `http://www.servername.com/DemoModel/SomeAction/8/orange` is able to find the appropriate action and the parameters are set successfully.

```
routes.MapRoute(
        name: "twoParam",
        url: "{controller}/{action}/{id}/{name}",
        defaults: new { action = "Index"},
        constraints: new { id = @"\d+" }
    );

public ActionResult DetailsWithName(int id, string name)
{
    return View();
}
```

There are two different approaches to building routes and actions. In the first, routes are configured in such a way that the same method can be called through multiple different URLs. In the second, there is less concern with reuse, so more actions are created to handle each of the various cases. It is recommended that you always take the second approach; it may require you to create more actions, but each action will be more specific to the given criteria. This results in an application that is easier to understand because it is easier to predict which action serves each request.

Understanding the relationship between the URL and the actions that respond to the request is rather important when you are attempting to build a navigational schema in ASP.NET MVC. Now that you have a deeper understanding of how routing works, the next section explains how to create navigational structures without ASP.NET Web Forms server controls.

Creating a Navigational Structure

As you saw earlier, the main component of a navigational structure is the `<a>` HTML anchor tag. This is all that was created from the ASP.NET Web Forms `Menu` control, so that is all that you have to create when working with an ASP.NET MVC application. Because there is no concept of a server control to help with this, you have to create all of the structure by hand, albeit with support from HTML helpers.

Fortunately, however, you already have an understanding of what the output needs to look like because you already created the HTML as part of the Admin section. This means that you only have to create the same structure to achieve a user interface that is identical to the look and feel of the Web Forms area of the site.

As you start to do this, you will find that some helpers are available:

➤ The `@Html.ActionLink` method writes out a complete anchor tag.

➤ The `@Url.Action` method creates a URL, rather than a complete anchor tag.

An example of each follows:

```
@Html.ActionLink("textLink", "actionName", "controllerName")

<a href="@Url.Action("actionName","controllerName")">textLink</a>
```

These are both rendered to the same HTML:

```
<a href="/controllerName/actionName">textLink</a>
```

This means that when you create an ASP.NET MVC navigation structure, you create the links yourself, rather than having a server control do it. However, you do not have to write them all by hand because you can use the helpers, as demonstrated in the next Try It Out.

TRY IT OUT Creating an ASP.NET MVC Navigation Structure

You have already created a navigational structure for ASP.NET Web Forms using the Menu control. Here, you have to forgo the support of a server control and write the code for the menu yourself.

1. Ensure that Visual Studio is running and you have the RentMyWrox application open. Open the Views\Shared_MVCLayout.cshtml file and find the section that looks like the following snippet:

```
<div id="nav">
    Navigation content here
</div>
```

2. Delete the "Navigation content here" text, and replace it with the following:

```
<div id="LeftNavigation">
  <ul class="level1">
    <li><a href="~" class="level1">Home</a></li>
    <li>@Html.ActionLink("Items", "", "Items", new { @class = "level1" })</li>
    <li>@Html.ActionLink("Contact Us", "ContactUs", "Home",
          new { @class = "level1" })</li>
    <li>@Html.ActionLink("About Us", "About", "Home",
          new { @class = "level1" })</li>
  </ul>
</div>
```

3. Now that the menu has been created, you need to create the controller and views that serve the last two of these links. Right-click the Controllers directory in Solution Explorer and select Add ➤ Controller. When the Add Scaffolding dialog appears, choose "MVC 5 Controller - Empty" and click the Add button. When the Controller name box appears, replace the highlighted section with "Home" so that the name is HomeController.

4. When you created the controller you may have noticed that the scaffolding added a new folder, named "Home," into your Views folder as well. Right-click this Home folder and Select Add ➤ View. This brings up the dialog as shown in Figure 8-16.

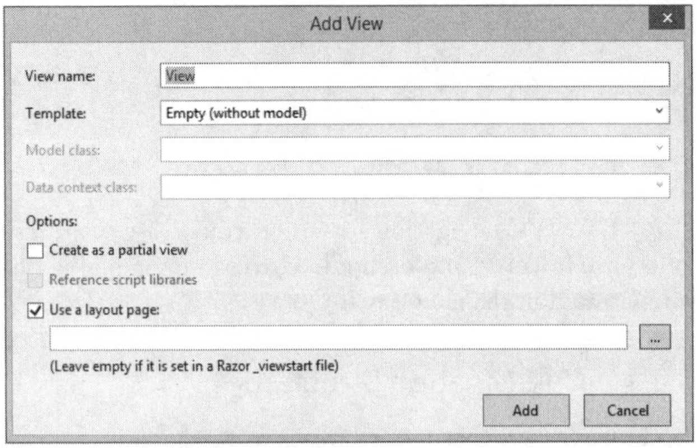

FIGURE 8-16: Add View dialog

5. Change the name to "**ContactUs**" and click Add. Perform the same steps again to add a view named "**About**."

6. Open the `HomeController` file. Highlight the default action that was created, the code that looks like this:

```
public ActionResult Index()
{
    return View();
}
```

7. Replace the highlighted code with the following:

```
public ActionResult ContactUs()
{
    return View();
}

public ActionResult About()
{
    return View();
}
```

8. Run the application and go to /Home/ContactUs. You will see your newly created menu, along with the default header that was created when you created the view. You should be able to go to the About Us menu selection as well.

How It Works

You just finished manually creating a simple menu structure. As you saw, it was relatively straightforward. You added four styled links to the default layout page using the `ActionLink` HTMLHelper. These helpers create HTML that matches the HTML created by the `Menu` control.

One of the code snippets that you added is repeated below.

```
@Html.ActionLink("About Us", "About", "Home", new { @class = "level1" })
```

This code builds a link to a controller named "Home" and calls an action named "About," both of which you already created; and the text displayed in the link is specified as "About Us." The last section of the `ActionLink` is setting HTML attributes, in this case setting the `class` attribute to the value `"level1"`.

Programmatic Redirection

Programmatic redirection is a very useful and common action in ASP.NET web applications. One of the most common uses is when a form is submitted to create some kind of new item in the database. When using ASP.NET Web Forms, the page containing the form that was filled out posts back to itself, where the information is validated and persisted. A traditional scenario would then send the user to a list page where they are able to see the item that they just added to the list.

ASP.NET Web Forms support two different approaches to redirecting users to a different page programmatically: client-side and server-side. When using client-side redirection, the server sends a special response to the client that the browser interprets as a request to fetch a new page. With server-side redirection, the server accepts the request at one resource and then programmatically uses another resource to process it.

Programmatically Redirecting the Client to a Different Page

You can use two different commands to manage redirection that happens within the browser on the client side: `Response.Redirect` and `Response.RedirectPermanent`. They each do slightly different things: The `Redirect` returns a 302 status code to the browser, while the `RedirectPermanent` command sends a 301 code to the browser. The 302 code means the requested resource has temporarily moved to another location, while the 301 code tells the browser that the resource has permanently moved to a different location.

Neither the user nor the browser notices a difference between the two codes. However, both are important for search engine optimization (SEO). If a search engine robot crawling the website encounters the temporary redirect, it knows to continue going. However, when the search engine robot encounters the permanent redirect it knows that it should not index the old location and instead ensure that the new location is indexed in its place.

Using either of these two commands is relatively straightforward:

```
Response.Redirect("~/SomeFile.aspx");

Response.RedirectPermanent("~/SomeFile")
```

As soon as the system comes to a `Redirect` or `RedirectPermanent` command, it immediately returns the status code to the client browser. This means that any code after this command is not called. This flow is shown in Figure 8-17.

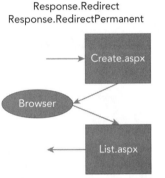

FIGURE 8-17: Client-side redirection flow

These client-side redirects are generally used only in ASP.NET Web Forms, not MVC. The technology is supported in MVC, but the ability to return any view from the controller generally means that there is no need to take this step. You will learn more about this in the section "Server-Side Redirects."

In this next activity you will add a new page that will redirect the user to a different page.

TRY IT OUT User Redirection

To get a better understanding of how this works, imagine a scenario in which you want to offer a product that has special pricing. This product changes every week, but you want your site visitors to be able to bookmark a single page showing this item, `http://www.rentmywrox.com/weeklyspecial`. You will use the temporary redirect to create a page that forwards the user to the standard item detail page for the item on special for that week.

1. Ensure that you have the RentMyWrox solution open in Visual Studio. Right-click the project name and select Add ⇨ New Item. Select the option to add a Web Form named WeeklySpecial, as shown in Figure 8-18. Click the Add button and save the file.

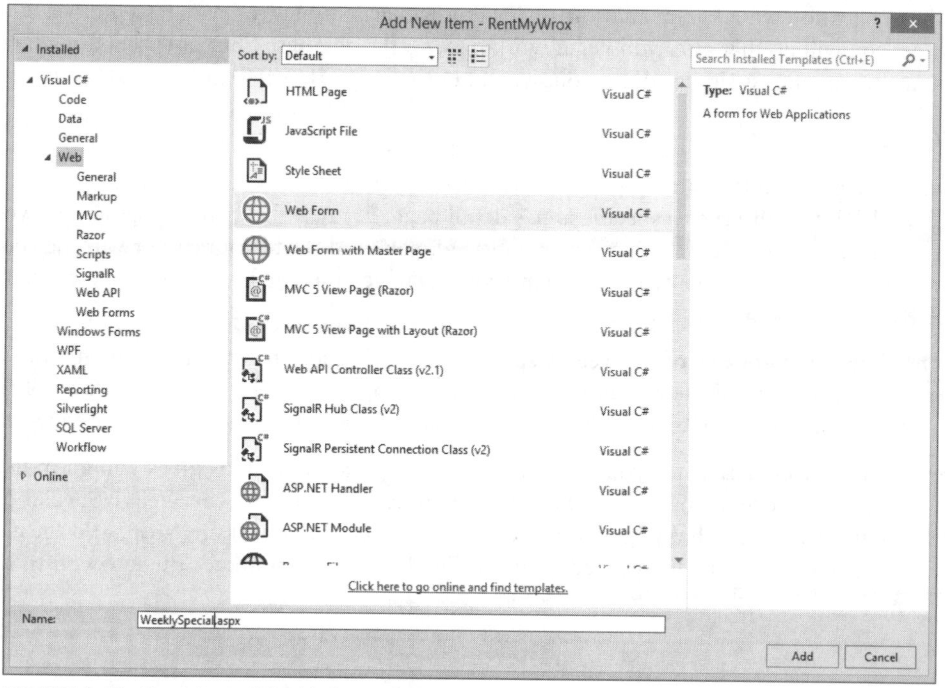

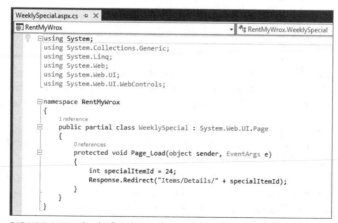

FIGURE 8-18: Creating a WeeklySpecial page

2. You don't need to do anything with the markup page. Instead, open the markup page and add the code so that it looks like what is shown in Figure 8-19.

```
WeeklySpecial.aspx.cs    ⊣ ✕
RentMyWrox                                    RentMyWrox.WeeklySpecial
using System;
using System.Collections.Generic;
using System.Linq;
using System.Web;
using System.Web.UI;
using System.Web.UI.WebControls;

namespace RentMyWrox
{
    1 reference
    public partial class WeeklySpecial : System.Web.UI.Page
    {
        0 references
        protected void Page_Load(object sender, EventArgs e)
        {
            int specialItemId = 24;
            Response.Redirect("Items/Details/" + specialItemId);
        }
    }
}
```

FIGURE 8-19: Code for the redirect of the WeeklySpecial

3. Run the application while on the markup page. You will get a 404 error (you have not yet added this page; you will do that after you begin working with the database), but note that the address bar points to an address similar to the following: `http://localhost/Items/Details/24`.

How It Works

In this activity you created a forwarding page that enables the `http://servername.com/weeklyspecial` URL to redirect to a specific item's detail page. Because this item changes every week, you did not use the permanent forwarding scheme; instead, you used the temporary forwarding command that sends a 302 status response to the client browser, which then makes the re-request call to the forwarded URL.

You had to hard-code the id value of the weekly special item and send it to an items page that does not yet exist. You will be adding this items controller and supporting view in the database section of this book, and at that point you come back to this page and make the id reflect the correct item on special.

Did you notice the address bar when you were running the application? This gives you an indication of how the redirection process works. If you start the application while on the WeeklySpecial page, you see that it starts to run on that page. However, you then see the processing stop, and the content of the address bar changes to the forwarded address. The browser then makes the new call to the forwarded page.

Client-side redirects enable the developer to tell the client to request a different resource from a different address. This means that there is an extra request-response when the client gets the redirection request. As a result, there is a performance cost because of the second call. ASP.NET Web Forms also support server-side redirects. In addition, ASP.NET MVC supports server-side work that enables the developer to return various views as needed, basically eliminating the need for any client-side redirection at all.

Server-Side Redirects

Server-side redirects, or transfers, are different from client-side redirects in that the request is made for a specific resource. Rather than respond with that resource, the server runs the redirection command and instead responds with the content from that alternate resource as specified in the transfer.

There are two different ways to perform this transfer: `Server.Transfer` and `Server.TransferRequest`. The `Transfer` method terminates execution of the current page and starts execution of a new page by using the specified URL path of the page. The `TransferRequest` method differs in that it performs an asynchronous execution of the specified URL using the specified HTTP method and headers. This means that using the `Transfer` method requires a physical page that can be called (a Web Form), whereas the `TransferRequest` does not. Instead, the `TransferRequest` makes a complete call so that it can also transfer control to an MVC page.

When using `Server.Transfer` there are two possible parameters:

➤   The first is the URL of the resource that will be used to handle the request.

➤   The second, optional, parameter specifies whether the form body should be transferred with the new call.

The code looks like this:

```
Server.Transfer("/Admin/ItemList", true);
```

This line of code tells the server to stop processing the current request and instead process the page at "Admin/ItemList". The second parameter tells the system to include any of the form content that was submitted to the initial resource. In many cases you don't need to send the information along, but there may be situations when it would be useful. Because all the work is handled by the server, no additional time is spent moving the information around; therefore, it depends on whether you need that information. If you don't need it, don't include it. The second parameter is optional. If you don't include it, then the default behavior is to transfer the query string and form information during the transfer.

The second approach, `TransferRequest`, looks much the same, except it can have many more parameters:

```
public void TransferRequest(
    string path,
    bool preserveForm,
    string method,
    NameValueCollection headers
)

Server.TransferRequest("/DemoModel/Details/3", true, "GET", null);
```

You can transfer with just the first parameter, or with the first and second parameters if necessary, just as you can with the `Transfer` method. However, in many cases you may want to designate the HTTP verb to be used with the request, which requires that you also send along a set of request headers. In the preceding example, `null` is used because you didn't need to add any additional headers.

In this next Try It Out, you work with both of the transfer approaches to become familiar with what each one does as part of the request processing.

TRY IT OUT Server-Side Redirection

In this activity you work with both approaches to setting up server-side redirection in ASP.NET MVC, the `Transfer` and the `TransferRequest`.

1. Ensure that you have your RentMyWrox solution open in Visual Studio. Open the code-behind for the file you used in last activity, `WeeklySpecial.aspx.cs`.

2. Change the `Response.Redirect` to `Server.Transfer` so that you have the following line of code:

```
Server.Transfer("Items/Details/" + specialItemId);
```

3. Save the file and run the application while on that page. You should get an exception, as shown in Figure 8-20.

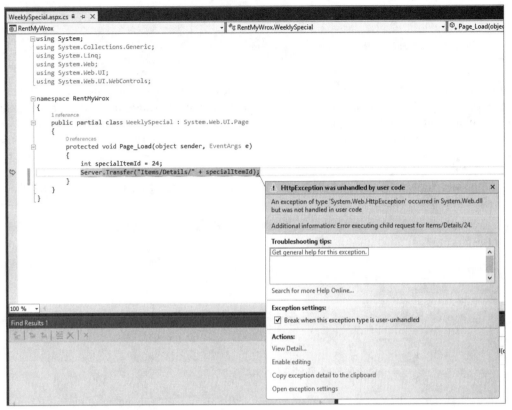

FIGURE 8-20: Exception using Server.Transfer

4. This exception was caused because there is no physical page to which to transfer the request. Stop the application and change the transfer as shown here:

```
Server.Transfer("/Admin/UserList.aspx");
```

5. Run the application. You should get a screen similar to that shown in Figure 8-21. Note that the address bar still shows WeeklySpecial, yet it is rendering the response created by the UserList page.

6. Stop the application. Change the `Server.Transfer` line of code so that it reads as follows:

```
Server.TransferRequest("Items/Details/" + specialItemId);
```

7. When using the `Server.Transfer` this approach failed. Now see what it does when using the `Server.TransferRequest`. Run the application while on this page. You won't get an exception, you instead get a 404 error that contains the following text: `Requested URL: /Items/Details/24`. This indicates that the forwarding was successful—or at least it *will be* successful once you actually add that page to the application.

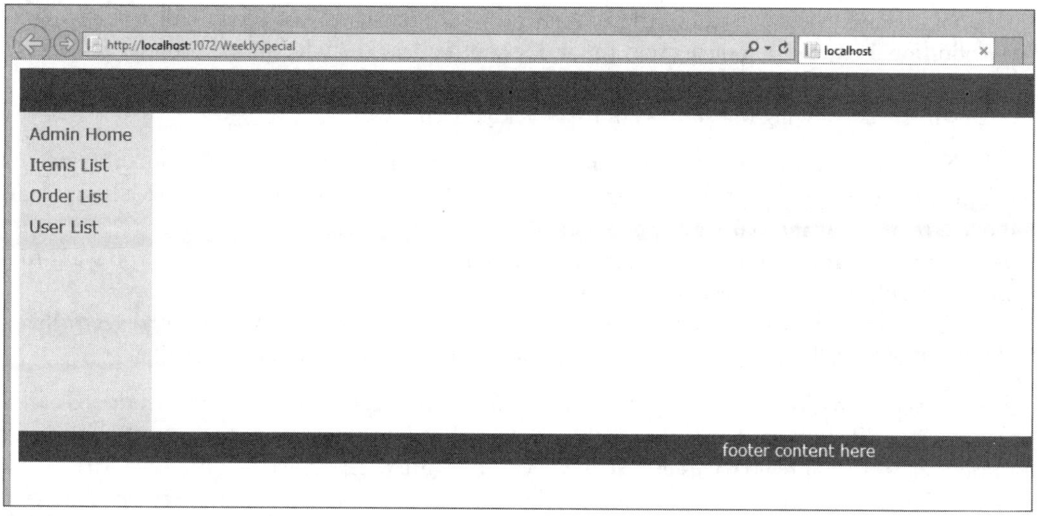

FIGURE 8-21: Server.Transfer to .aspx page

How It Works

In the last activity you took advantage of the `Redirect` functionality to have the client redirect the request to a different page. In this activity you eliminated the response to the client that told them to request a different page, and instead returned the content of a different resource as if it were the originally requested resource.

There are two different approaches to doing the server transfer. The `Server.Transfer` method has been around for a long time, and forwards the request to a physical page. Note that you even had to include the extension on the server transfer; if you had tried it without the extension, it would have thrown an exception. All of this work happens after the friendly URL parsing is done by the server. That is also why you were not able to get it to successfully transfer to an MVC route; the server transfer happens after the routing engine does its work, so the transfer is incapable of parsing the URL to determine what controller and action need to be called.

However, it all worked correctly when you used the `Server.TransferRequest` method, as this method actually "restarts" the request, only using the URL that was set in the method. This means that friendly URLs and routing are able to run on the URL so that it can handle MVC routes as well as Web Form pages using friendly URLs. You will generally find it safer to use the `TransferRequest` approach because you don't have to worry about how the request is being managed (Web Forms page vs. MVC route)—you only have to ensure that you send it to the correct page.

While both server and client transfers enable you to provide a different resource to manage processing of the request, they take a different approach. The client-side approach causes a redirection request to be sent to the browser. This means an additional client request-response cycle, as well as showing the user the new URL in the address bar of the browser. The server-side transfer eliminates the additional request-response cycle and it does not replace the URL in the browser's address bar. The last activity demonstrated how this enabled you to display the item detail created by another page while still showing the address of the WeeklySpecial.

Which approach you want to take depends upon your requirements. Generally, it comes down to whether or not you want to publicize the transfer. If you do, such as when a page has actually moved, then you want to use a `Response.Redirect`, perhaps even the `Response.RedirectPermanent` so that the replaced page can eventually be removed. If all you want to do is something like what the WeeklySpecial does in the sample application, then the `Server.TransferRequest` is a more appropriate way to manage the redirection. As with every other choice, it ultimately depends on what you want the end user's experience to be like.

The last type of redirection is the concept of server-side redirection in MVC. As mentioned earlier, this is a very different concept, because the idea of redirecting from one page to another is just not the same because there are no pages in ASP.NET MVC. Figure 8-22 shows the difference between the two approaches if you were using a process whereby when an item is created, the UI returns the user to a list page.

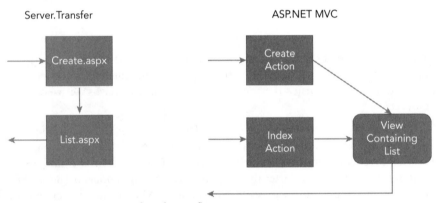

FIGURE 8-22: Server transfer of page flow

The key difference between redirection in ASP.NET Web Forms and MVC is that the MVC controller simply determines what view will be returned, so there is no concept of transfer; the controller just returns the appropriate view.

PRACTICAL TIPS ON NAVIGATION

Navigation is simultaneously one of the easiest parts of a website to build and one of the hardest parts of a site to design because it requires that you anticipate the reasons that all of your users will need and ensure a pleasant user experience for each of those reasons—especially for a site that will continue to grow. Keep in mind the following tips as you build out your navigational structure:

➤ Categorization is critical. As the information and functionality offered by your web application grows, it will become increasingly important for you to keep it organized in a way that makes sense to your users. Remember: It has to be something that your users can understand.

➤ Keep menu depth limited. Multiple submenus leads to confusion and difficulty in understanding the appropriate choice. When you legitimately have a deep set of relationships, don't make them all available at once. Instead, categorize them and expose additional levels as the user selects a certain path.

➤ The typical approach to building a set of MVC functionality is to have a controller for each individual model that you may want to work with. That isn't always necessary. Instead, your controllers should be aligned with the navigation path that your users will travel, rather than your data model. Sometimes they are strongly related, but don't assume that they always have to be that way.

➤ You know your business. Most likely your users do not. Don't build your navigation structure to emulate your business divisions unless these differences are obvious to your visitors. Instead, build your structure to emulate the reasons why your users are visiting your site, and categorize your menu options to reflect those reasons.

SUMMARY

Creating a clear, intuitive navigation schema for your website is critical because it helps users access the site's different areas. The key to a navigational structure is the HTML anchor tag, <a>. This tag is the primary way to move from one page to another, so whenever you consider navigation you are actually considering how you are going to build your anchor tags.

An important part of the anchor tag is the address, or URL, of the resource being requested. There are two different types of these URLs, relative and absolute. An absolute URL points to the desired resource by using a complete Internet address. A relative URL, conversely, points to resources that are contained within your own application. Typically, absolute URLs are used when referencing URLs that are outside of your website or those URLs that remain the same regardless of where the application is running.

There are three primary menu-support controls in ASP.NET Web Forms, the Menu control and the TreeView control, both of which create complete navigational structures, while the SiteMapPath control displays a breadcrumb. This chapter covered the Menu Control, but using the TreeView control is very similar. When you are working in MVC, you do not have the luxury of being able to use server controls, so you have to build the navigational structure yourself, but you do have several helpers: one that creates an anchor tag for you, and another that builds a URL based on various parameters.

The navigational structure enables users to move around your application. You also have the capability to move around your site programmatically. There are two primary ways. With the first, your application sends a code to the client and the client requests the new resource, the

`Response.Redirect`. With the second, the server handles the transfers; a request is made for one resource, and the server transfers the request to a different resource that creates the response, a `Server.Transfer` and `Server.TransferRequest`.

Both of the programmatic approaches are ASP.NET Web Forms–based, MVC does not use the same kind of page-to-page transfer approach. Rather, the controller handles the request and determines which view to return to the user. There is no transfer, simply a selection of views, because, unlike in Web Forms, the URL references a piece of code rather than a physical page in the file system.

EXERCISES

1. Your user is on a page at `http://www.servername.com/admin/list.aspx` and you have the following link: `<a href="~/default.aspx">Home</a>`. Where would they end up if they clicked the link?

2. If you were a new developer on a project for which a bug report is received regarding a page found at `http://www.servername.com/results/`, where would you look for the code that caused that specific defect?

3. Why were friendly URLs implemented and what advantages do they bring to ASP.NET Web Forms development?

▶ WHAT YOU LEARNED IN THIS CHAPTER

Absolute URL	A URL that contains the full description of the resource being requested. This means that not only does it reference the location within the site, it also references the location on the Web through the use of domain and server names.
Client-Side Redirection	Redirection in which the server sends a redirect message to the client. These messages have a status of either 302 or 301, with the latter indicating a permanent move, and the former indicating a temporary move.
Default Document	An ASP.NET Web Forms concept whereby a server administrator can assign a specific page that handles requests to a directory when a specific page is not requested. This is how the system knows, for example, to respond to a request to `http://servername.com` with the code in the `Default.aspx` page; it is the default document. The default document can be assigned across the site or be set up for each directory within the site.
Friendly URLs	Firendly URLs are an enhancement to ASP.NET Web Forms that enables the system to understand requests to `.aspx` pages that do not contain the file extension. It is also provides the built-in capability to parse information from the URL for access within the code-behind. This enables replacing querystring variables with URL variables.
HTML.ActionLink	An HTML helper for ASP.NET MVC that accepts a set of parameters (such as controller and action) to build out a complete anchor tag.
Menu Control	ASP.NET Web Forms server control that builds out a complete menu. It has built-in dynamic menuing that creates fly-out submenus from parent menu items. It takes an XML file as the reference source; this file contains all the menu information needed to create the visual element.
Relative URL	Provides direction to the requested resource by working with everything after the server and domain names. This means that it can only point to items within the same server application.
Routing	A concept whereby ASP.NET MVC applications can build out interpretation schemes for incoming URLS. This enables the system to determine, from the requested URL, what controller needs to be called and which action in that controller will be used to create the response object, generally a view.
Server-Side Redirection	The capability to respond to a specific request by running a different set of code. Typically, a request is received by a resource that handles the creation of the response. However, in a server transfer, the request is received by a resource that then forwards that request to a different resource which provides the response.

TreeView Control	An ASP.NET Web Forms server control that builds out a complete menu. It has built-in dynamic menuing that enables opening and closing submenus. It takes an XML file as the reference source; this file contains all the menu information needed to create the visual element.
URI	Uniform Resource Identifier, a complete description of a URL. A URI contains a URL that adds extra metadata that may be useful programmatically.
URL.Action	An ASP.NET helper that assists in building a URL. Typically, the helper is used to build the `href` content of an `anchor` element, but it is also used to create visible URLs. It takes a series of parameters, generally including at least the controller and the action, to build the complete URL.
Virtual Application	Concept whereby an IIS website can run many different applications in subdirectories. There is always a default application, but there can be as many different virtual applications as necessary. They are generally referenced through a URL such as `http://www.servername.com/virtualapplicationname/*`.

9

Displaying and Updating Data

WHAT YOU WILL LEARN IN THIS CHAPTER:

➤ How to install Microsoft SQL Server Express

➤ Using SQL Server Express Manager

➤ Viewing and managing data in Visual Studio SQL Server Explorer

➤ Working with various ASP.NET Web Forms data controls

➤ Managing data in ASP.NET MVC applications

➤ Handling sorting and pagination in a web application

CODE DOWNLOADS FOR THIS CHAPTER:

The wrox.com code downloads for this chapter are found at `www.wrox.com/go/ beginningaspnetforvisualstudio` on the Download Code tab. The code is in the chapter 09 download and individually named according to the names throughout the chapter.

There are very few websites that need the dynamic capabilities provided by ASP.NET that don't also need a way to store data either about the visit or about actions taken during the visit. This data could be as simple as persisting the pages that were clicked by visitors as they went through the site, to as complex as a multi-million-dollar order for thousands of various widgets.

There are various ways that you can persist this data.

➤ You can store it on the local file system as a specially delimited file.

➤ Another, and the most common, way to store information is in a database system. A database system is an application whose primary reason for existence is to manage the creation, editing, deletion, and fetching of data. There are many different types of database systems, from very simple to extremely complex. This chapter introduces the free version of Microsoft's flagship data management application, Microsoft SQL Server.

After installing this product as part of the introduction, you learn about several parts of the application, although you won't spend a lot of time on the database itself. Our approach will be to abstract out the database as much as possible, so after the installation and introduction you will have little need to return to the database system.

The bulk of the chapter is dedicated to communicating with the database. After a brief introduction to the Entity Framework, Microsoft's way of converting objects to database tables, you plunge straight into the use of data that you can now persist. In addition to working with data-specific server controls, you will see how MVC uses various approaches to make up for its lack of controls.

WORKING WITH SQL SERVER EXPRESS

Microsoft's SQL Server product is one of the most popular database systems in the world. SQL Server is a Relational Database Management System (RDBMS), which means that it breaks information down into related entities, or tables. In a way that is very similar to the object modeling discussed in Chapter 4, each of these tables contains different pieces of information about that entity and stores it as a type in a column. Each item in the table, or row, typically has some kind of column, or property, which uniquely identifies that row. Because of this unique identifier, it is possible for an entity in one table to be related to an entity in another table. This is the relationship aspect of the name, and it is one of the primary characteristics of an RDBMS.

Another primary characteristic of an RDBMS is how the data is accessed from external systems—through the use of a customized language, Structured Query Language (SQL). There is an ANSII definition of SQL, but all the major RDBMS vendors have their own interpretation of the language, generally because they offer special competitive features. Microsoft's own version of SQL is known as Transact-SQL (T-SQL), and it offers various additions such as string processing, date processing, and mathematics—all features that are not part of the standard SQL definition.

NOSQL DATABASES

RDBMS systems, by definition, are very structured. There is a well-known set of properties for an item represented by a table, and this definition rarely changes. While this approach enables you to easily understand, parse, and interpret the data, it limits the information that you can store because you have to understand its relationship with the other entities in your system. It is this rigorous definition and the resulting understanding of each field and its relationship to the other entities in the system that directly accounts for the RDBMS's inflexibility. For example, if your database allows only three lines for an address but some users need four lines to accurately describe their address, then you have a problem.

A newer type of database was created to solve the flexibility problem, but at the cost of understanding each entity in the system. These database systems are typically referred to as NOSQL databases, short for "not only SQL." It is called that because these databases differ in terms of how data is accessed and managed, as they do not support the concept of a relationship. Many instead concentrate on storing the object as a whole item, rather than a list of specified fields. This enables the values being stored to be different for each item, thus storing that third address line becomes a very simple exercise.

Throughout the rest of this book you will be working with SQL Server Express, a free version of SQL Server. The Express version is not feature-limited in any way that affects your usage here; it is instead limited in terms of maximum memory usage, database size, and CPU cores that it can use.

Installation

A database server is not a typical piece of software. By design it has to be ready to respond to calls from multiple applications, both on the same machine and from over the network. It also has to be reliable, performant, and able to handle large amounts of data quickly. All of these requirements mean that installing a database is not as simple as installing other applications, such as Visual Studio.

There are many more steps to installing SQL Server Express, and the current condition of your machine may impact how your installation proceeds. If you have a brand-new machine with all the latest patches and settings, then you may be able to install without any issues. If you do not, then you may have to do some extra steps throughout the process. The installation program does a good job of explaining what you have to do to solve any problems, and the following Try it Out instructions include running the system verification step before the install so that your installation can run successfully once you get there.

TRY IT OUT Installing Microsoft SQL Server Express

Before you go any further into working with databases, you should install one so that you have something to refer to. As mentioned earlier, you will be installing Microsoft SQL Server Express. If your machine is running Visual Studio comfortably, then it should also be able to run SQL Server Express as long as you have the hard drive space available.

1. Open a browser and go to `http://www.microsoft.com/SqlServerExpress`. This should bring you to a page from which you can download SQL Server Express. If you do not have the ability to download from this screen you may need to go into the different editions of SQL Server and find SQL Server Express from there. Click the download link to access a page where you can select the version of SQL Server Express that you would like to install. Choose SQL Server 2014 Express with Tools. It is available in two versions, 32 bit or 64 bit. Ensure that you choose the correct version for your processor type. Download the file. You will likely be asked to log in to your Microsoft Live account. Note that the download is over 800MB, so it may take a while.

2. Once you have the file downloaded, run the installer. If the User Account Control dialog appears, as shown in Figure 9-1, select Yes.

FIGURE 9-1: User Account Control dialog

3. In the Choose Directory for Extracted Files dialog, shown in Figure 9-2, you can either use the default or choose a different folder. Once the installation process is completed you will be able to delete the folder. After selecting a directory, click the OK button.

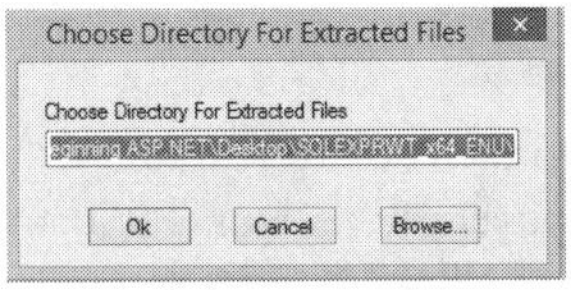

FIGURE 9-2: Selecting extract directory

4. The extract process may take some time. Once it is completed, the SQL Server Installation Center dialog shown in Figure 9-3 will open.

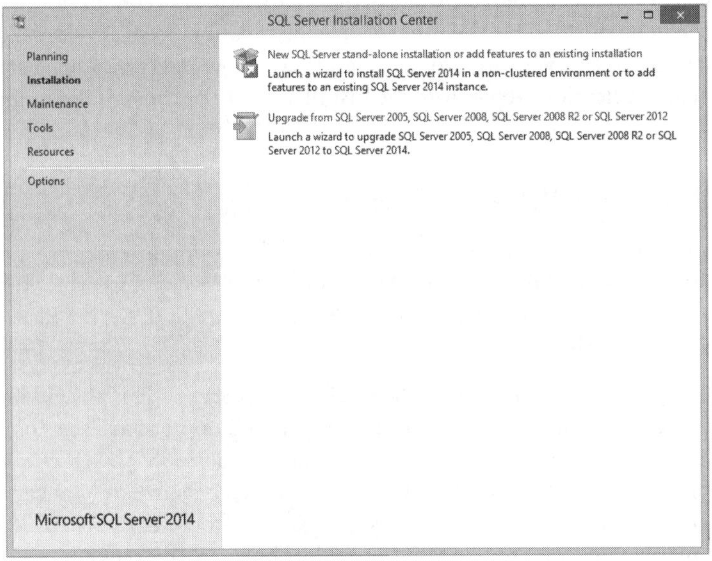

FIGURE 9-3: SQL Server Installation Center

5. Select Tools from the menu on the left. This should bring up a screen similar to the one shown in Figure 9-4.

6. Select the top option, System Configuration Checker. After the scan, whose progress you can follow, the results dialog shown in Figure 9-5 will appear.

7. In Figure 9-5 all but the last option passed. You may have other ones that did not pass, especially the ".NET 2.0 and .NET 3.5 Service Pack 1 update." If you have any that fail you can click the Failed link on the right side of the line that failed and a dialog will open that walks you through the process required to support SQL Server Express on your system. Go through all the items that failed and correct them according to the popups. You may have to restart your computer several times during the process. If so, return to the installer after each fix and keep going through the configuration check until everything passes.

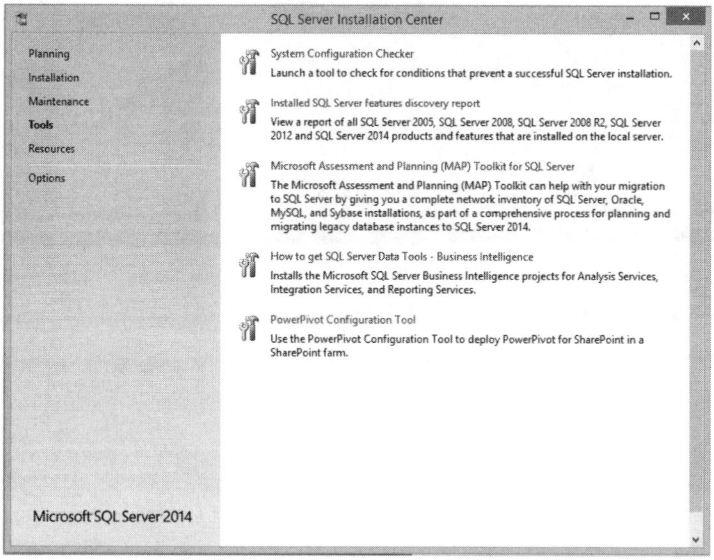

FIGURE 9-4: SQL Server Installation Center - Tools

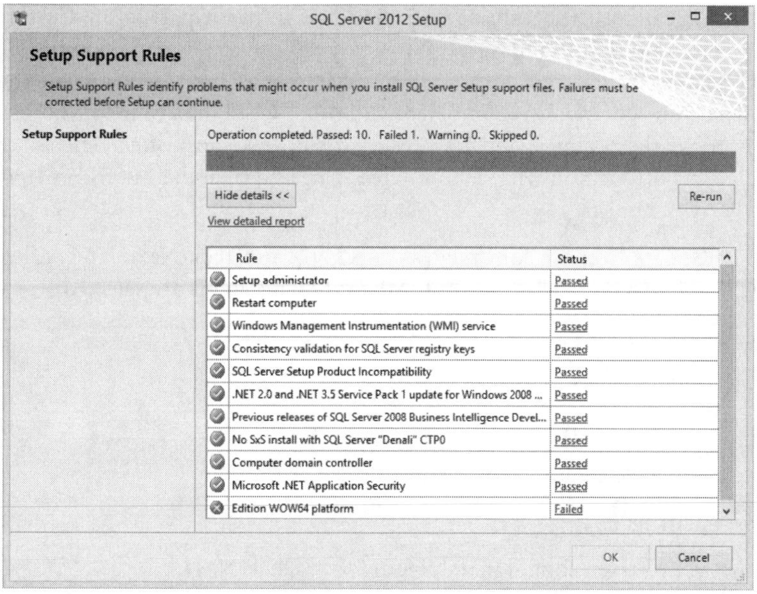

FIGURE 9-5: Setup Support Rules

8. When all the items have been updated and your system passes, select Installation from the left menu of the Installation Center.

9. Select the top option, "New SQL Server stand-alone installation or add features to an existing installation." It may take a few minutes before anything happens, but you should eventually get the License Terms dialog shown in Figure 9-6.

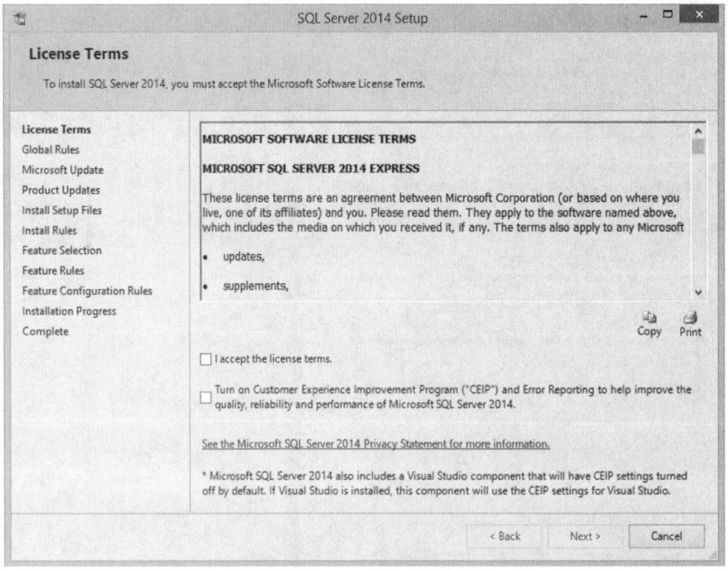

FIGURE 9-6: License Terms dialog

10. Accept the license terms. You can also select the second checkbox to participate in the Customer Experience Improvement Program (CIEP) if desired. When you choose to participate in the CEIP, your computer or device automatically sends information to Microsoft about how you use certain products. Information from your computer is combined with other CEIP data to help Microsoft solve problems and to improve the products and features customers use most often. This is an optional step. Click the Next button. You will see a progress bar, and then the Microsoft Update dialog shown in Figure 9-7 will appear.

11. Check the "Use Microsoft Update to check for updates" checkbox and click Next. You will get the Feature Selection dialog. Ensure that the checkboxes for the following items are selected:

    a. Database Engine Services

    b. Client Tools Connectivity

    c. Management Tools - Basic

    d. SQL Client Connectivity SDK should be unchanged.

    e. LocalDB should be unchanged.

    When you are done, your screen should match Figure 9-8. Click Next.

12. The Feature Rules will run next. You should not have any problems with this since you already ran this in Step 6. Click Next to continue.

13. Once the Rules run is complete, you will get the Instance Configuration dialog shown in Figure 9-9.

14. Accept all the default settings and click Next. The dialog shown in Figure 9-10 will appear.

15. Accept all the default settings and select Next. This brings you to the Database Engine Configuration dialog shown in Figure 9-11.

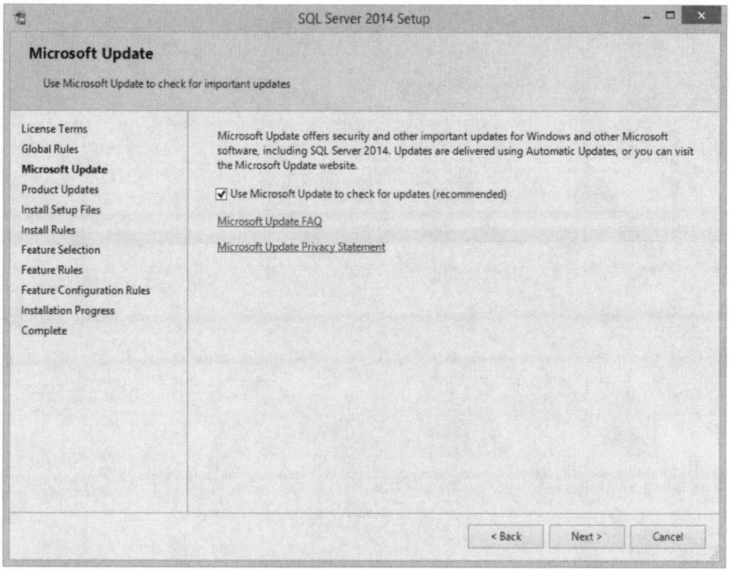

FIGURE 9-7: Microsoft Update dialog

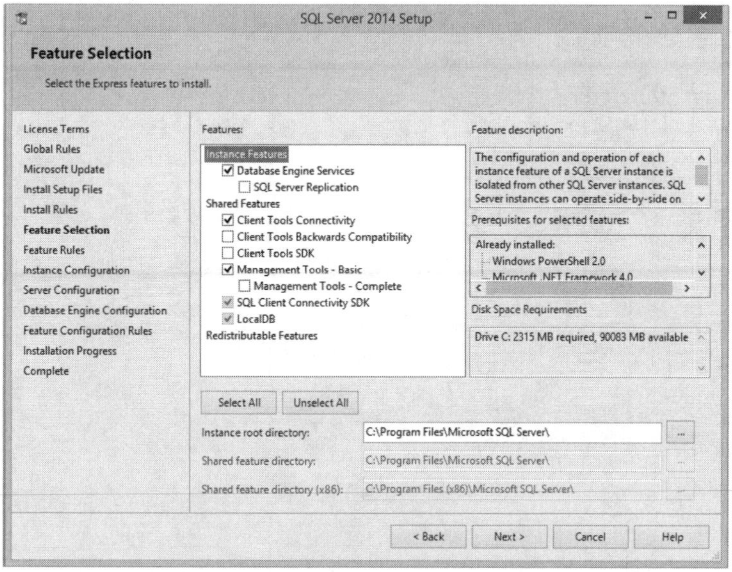

FIGURE 9-8: Feature Selection dialog

16. Accept all the default settings by selecting Next. The installation process will start. It can take some time, but you can follow its progress in the Installation Progress dialog. When the process is finished you should see a Complete dialog, indicating the installation was successful.

17. Click the Close button. This returns you to the Installation Center dialog.

18. Click the close icon on the top right of the window. This completes installation of SQL Server.

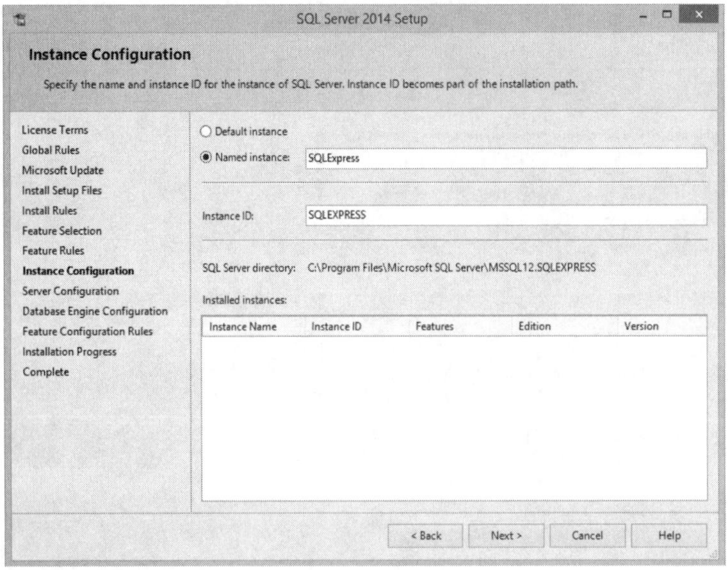

FIGURE 9-9: Instance Configuration dialog

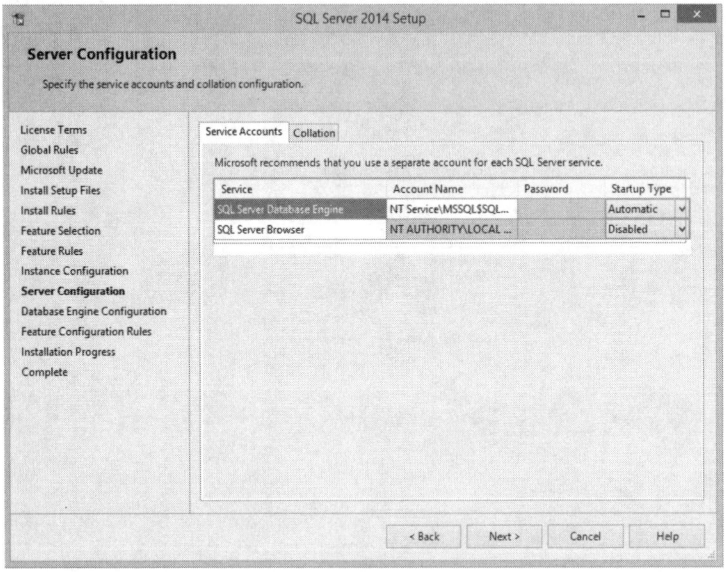

FIGURE 9-10: Server Configuration dialog

How It Works

Typically, installing a Windows application is pretty simple. However, as you see, SQL Server is not a typical application. There is a complex set of different applications and services, applications that run without any user interaction, that make up SQL Server. Figure 9-12 shows the Windows services that were installed as part of the SQL Server installation.

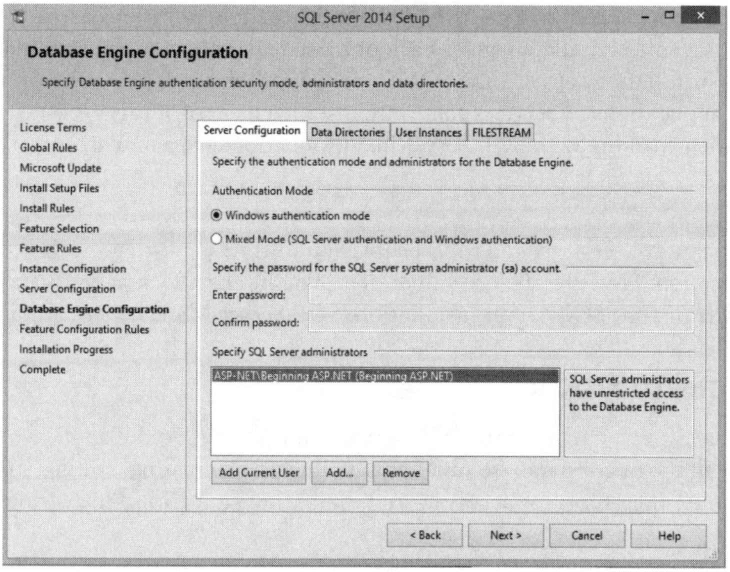

FIGURE 9-11: Database Engine Configuration dialog

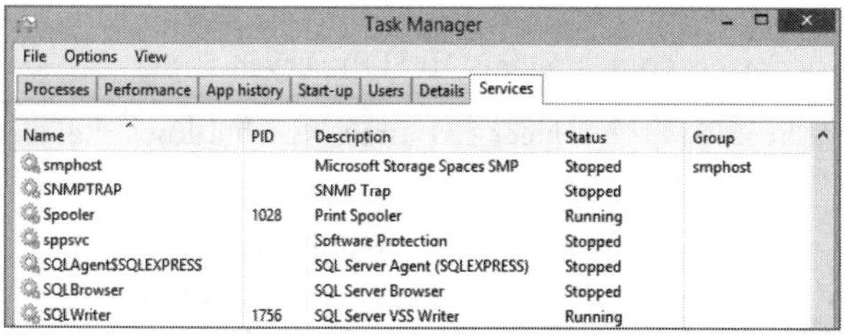

FIGURE 9-12: Windows Services installed as part of SQL Server

As well as installing various different services, there are some expectations around the system that will be running SQL Server as well as some limitations. These are all shown in Table 9-1.

TABLE 9-1: Minimum and Maximum System Settings

ITEM	SETTING
.NET 2.0 and 3.5 Service Pack 1	Installed
Registry check	All required registry keys are available
Windows Management Instrumentation (WMI) service	Installed
Compute capacity used by a single instance	Limited to lesser of 1 socket or 4 cores
Maximum memory utilized	1 GB
Maximum relational database size	10 GB

Along with the various services that were shown in Figure 9-12, multiple client applications are installed as well, including wizards, centers, and managers. Each of these plays a part in the running and maintenance of a SQL Server installation. Other than SQL Server Management Studio, you won't spend any time on the remaining applications or services that were installed as part of this process; however, they are all necessary when working with SQL Server in a production environment.

Installing the SQL Server applications, services, and tools enable you to start persisting the data from your RentMyWrox application. However, before you do that, you'll take a look at the main application tool installed as part of your SQL Server installation, SQL Server Management Studio.

SQL Server Management Studio

After installation you should have an icon to start the SQL Server Management Studio application, which provides access to all the major database functionality, including creating, editing, and deleting database items. It also provides tools for accessing and evaluating data within the various databases.

In order to work with SQL Server Management Studio, you first need to connect to a SQL Server. This is because SQL Server is a service application that's generally running the entire time that the operating system is running, unless otherwise configured, but it lacks its own user interface; the only way to know that SQL Server is running on your machine is to check the list of active services. This is why Management Studio is so important; it acts as your interface to SQL Server.

A central feature of SQL Server Management Studio is the Object Explorer, which allows the user to browse, select, and act upon any of the objects within the server.

In the following Try It Out you use SQL Server Management Studio to create a database and some tables, and then manage some data within those tables. This process enables you to see how all the concepts fit together, why SQL Server is called a relational database, and the advantages this can bring.

TRY IT OUT Running Microsoft SQL Server Management Studio

In this activity you connect to a SQL Server, create a database, and then manipulate the content within that database by creating tables and data.

1. Find the icon to open SQL Server Management Studio. If you are running Windows 8.0 or newer you will find a section in your Apps area that looks like Figure 9-13. The icon within the box is SQL Server Management Studio. Going forward, you may want to pin this icon to your Start menu or to your desktop for easy access.

2. Double-click the SQL Server Management Studio icon to start the application. The Connect to Server dialog will open, as shown in Figure 9-14.

FIGURE 9-13: SQL Server shortcut

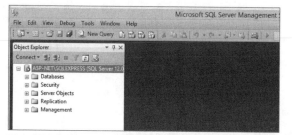

FIGURE 9-14: Connect to Server dialog in SQL Server Management Studio

3. Ensure that the server name represents both your computer name and the default name that was added in the last activity. Click the Connect button. This opens the Object Explorer window shown in Figure 9-15.

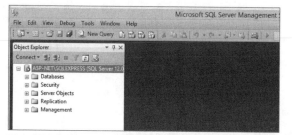

FIGURE 9-15: Object Explorer, showing connected server

a. If you were not able to connect, ensure that your settings match those shown in Figure 9-14 (with the exception that you use the correct machine name to replace "ASP-NET").

4. Right-click on the Databases folder. Select New Database from the context menu. This brings up the New Database dialog, shown in Figure 9-16.

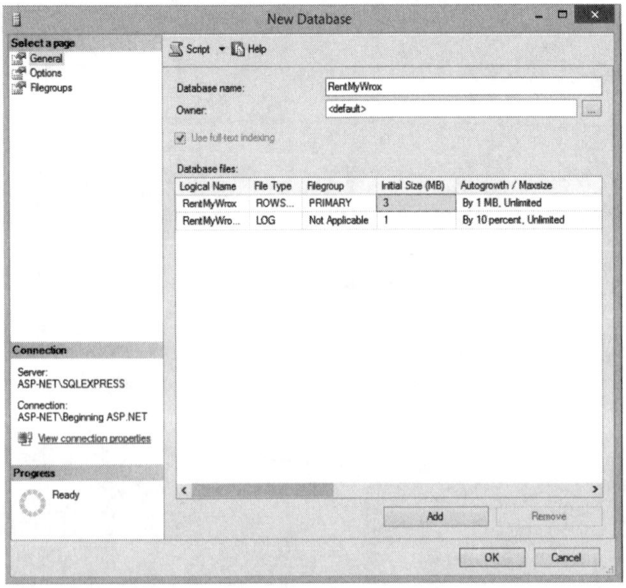

FIGURE 9-16: New Database dialog

5. Name the Database "**RentMyWrox**" and leave the rest of the settings at their default value. Click OK. You should now see a cylindrical icon named RentMyWrox under the Databases folder.

6. Expand RentMyWrox by clicking the plus sign to the left of the icon. Your window should look like Figure 9-17.

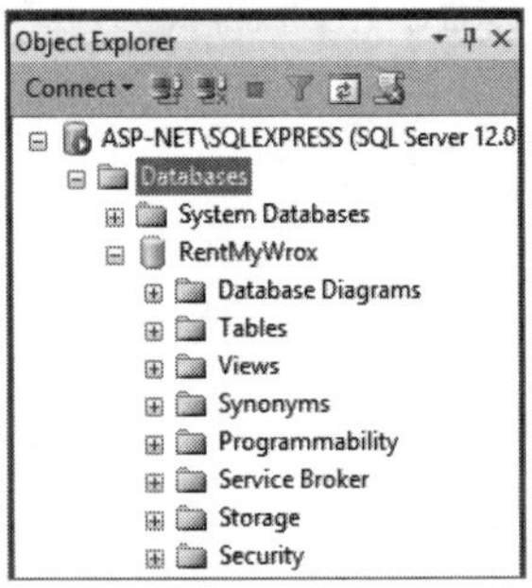

FIGURE 9-17: Expanded database

7. Right-click on Tables and select Table. This opens a table creation window, as shown in Figure 9-18.

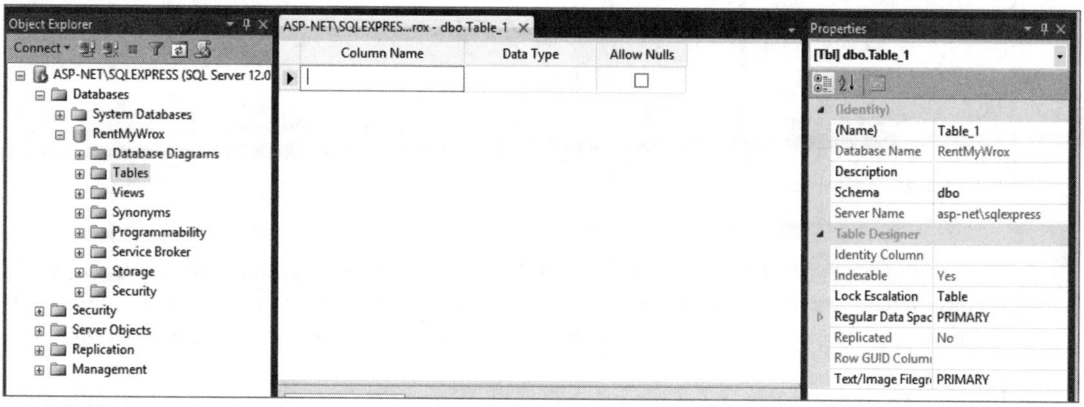

FIGURE 9-18: Window for creating a table

8. Enter "Id" for Column Name, change DataType to int, and uncheck the Allow Nulls checkbox. In the Properties pane on the right, change (Name) from Table_1 to "TestingTable." Also on the right, change the Identity Column to "Id" in the dropdown box.

9. Click the Row below where you entered Id, and enter "Name" for the Column Name. Select varchar(50) for the DataType. Add one more column Named "Description" with a DataType of varchar(MAX). Your screen should look like Figure 9-19.

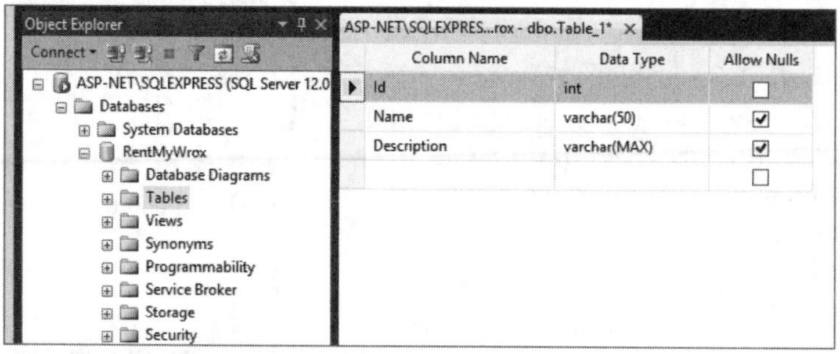

FIGURE 9-19: Filled-out table information

10. Click the disk icon in the toolbar to Save. Expand the Tables directory. If you don't see the item that you just created, select the refresh icon in Object Explorer to refresh the list of items.

11. Right-click on the table and select Edit Top 200 Rows. This opens an editing window that looks like Figure 9-20.

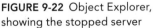

FIGURE 9-20: Editable window

12. Type a value, such as "Test" into the field under the Name column header and another value into the field under Description and click Enter. A value will appear in the Id column of the row that you were on, and another set of entry boxes appears under the row you were working on.

How It Works

The first step in doing any work with SQL Server is to connect to the database. There are two different approaches to managing security in a SQL Server database: using Windows or having SQL Server manage the authentication protocol. You had that choice during the installation of the software, choosing to use Windows Authentication Mode. Since you chose Windows Authentication you are able to log in to your database automatically because you have already logged in to your computer. If you had selected SQL Server authentication you would have to enter a username and password each time you wanted to connect with Management Studio.

This connection between Sql Server Management Studio and SQL Server is important because you have to ensure that you follow the same process every time you want to connect to the database, whether through Management Studio or through your ASP.NET application.

FIGURE 9-21 Object Explorer, showing the active server

When you log in through Management Studio you can see whether SQL Server is running by looking at the small symbol next to the name of your server. The green arrow, as shown within the dark box in Figure 9-21, indicates that the server is running.

If the server is not running, which is indicated by a red box, as shown within the dark box in Figure 9-22, you can right-click the server and select Start. You can also take the same approach to stop the server: right-click on the server name and then select Stop from the context menu. You will see several User Account Control and confirmation dialogs, but the server will start or stop as directed.

FIGURE 9-22 Object Explorer, showing the stopped server

Once you have connected to the server, you will see multiple folders listed under it. These folders are described in Table 9-2.

TABLE 9-2: SQL Server Management Studio Folders

FOLDER	DESCRIPTION
Databases	Contains all the databases available on the server. This list includes not only the user-created databases but also the system databases that are used by the server itself to manage all the relationships within and without the user databases.
Security	As the folder name suggests, this folder maintains security information. In SQL Server the primary security concepts are logins that provide authentication, and roles that support authorization. Access to a database is determined by assigning a login a role in that database. This role could be anything from read-only to full administrative control.
Server Objects	Contains various different support items, such as backup devices for configuring backups for your databases or other servers with whom this server has open communications.
Replication	Replication is a group of technologies that support information distribution and mirroring between different databases. SQL replication enables not only copying data between databases, but also copying any database objects. These databases can be on the same server or any other server that has connectivity, even across the Internet.
Management	Items within this folder support management of the server itself, and contains items such as logs and events.

As a developer, you will spend virtually all of your time working within the Databases folder, because this is where you can work with the databases that support your application. A database is a collection of tables with typed columns. SQL Server supports different data types, including primary types such as `Integer`, `Float`, `Decimal`, `Char` (including character strings), `Varchar` (variable length character strings), `binary` (for unstructured blobs of data), and `Text` (for textual data), among others. Thankfully, the approach that you take here to work with the database will hide the database types from you, enabling you to work with .NET types instead.

Now that you have been able to create a database and table using SQL Server Management Studio, the next section moves maintenance and access to your data into Visual Studio so that you will be able to evaluate your application's interaction with the database within your primary development tool. Going forward, you can use SQL Server Management Studio to access your database. Although you will generally be doing this in Visual Studio, you will see that there are multiple ways to access your data even while working in Visual Studio.

Connecting in Visual Studio

While you have already worked with multiple windows in Visual Studio, there is one to which you have yet to be introduced, the SQL Server Object Explorer window. This window is different from the Object Explorer window that you worked with in SQL Server Management Studio. From here you can connect to your SQL Server and access your databases and tables just as if you were using Management Studio. In this activity, you connect Visual Studio to the database that you just created.

Connect to the Database from within Visual Studio

In this activity you will connect to the SQL Server instance that you just installed and manipulate the various server objects and data just as you did in SQL Server Management Studio. However, you will be doing all of this in Visual Studio.

1. Ensure that Visual Studio is running and you have the RentMyWrox application open. From the View menu option select SQL Server Object Explorer. This will open the window shown in Figure 9-23. It may open in one of many different areas, including in the same area as your Solution Explorer. If so, drag it into your main working pane.

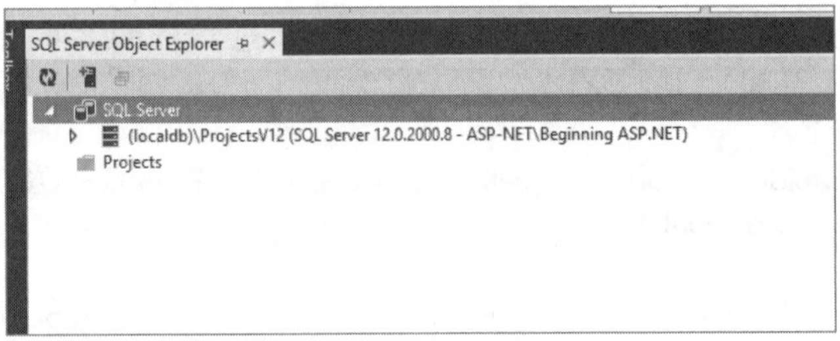

FIGURE 9-23: SQL Server Object Explorer

2. In the Object Explorer window, right-click on SQL Server and select Add SQL Server. This brings up the Connect to Server dialog, shown in Figure 9-24.

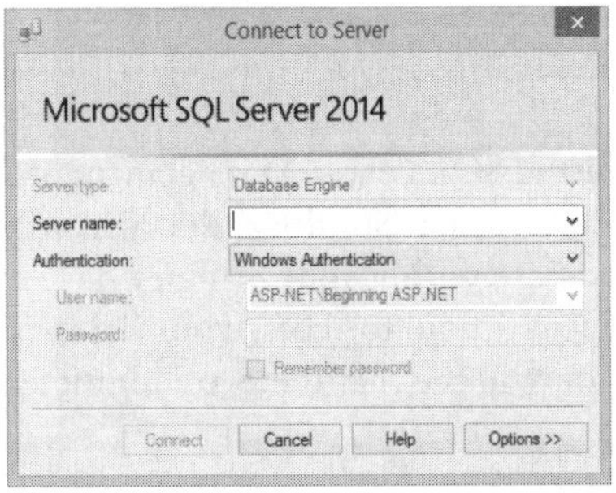

FIGURE 9-24: SQL Server Object Explorer Connect to Server dialog

3. From the Server Name dropdown select Browse for More. This opens the Browse for Servers dialog shown in Figure 9-25, including the name of the server that you created when installing SQL Server Express.

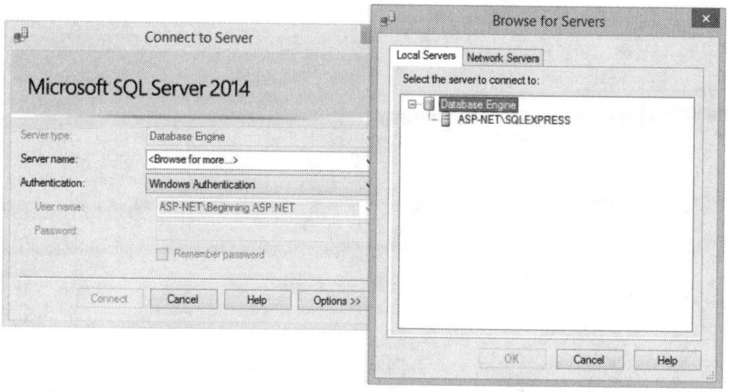

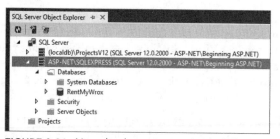

FIGURE 9-25: SQL Server Object Explorer Browse for Servers dialog

4. Select your SQL server and click OK. This returns you to the Connect to Server dialog. Click the Connect button. This adds your SQL Server to the list of connections under Sql Server as shown in Figure 9-26.

FIGURE 9-26: New database connection in SQL Server Object Explorer

5. Expand the RentMyWrox database by clicking the arrow. If the Tables folder is not expanded you can open the folder by clicking the arrow.

6. Right-click on dbo.TestingTable and select View Data. This opens a data window similar to the one shown in Figure 9-27.

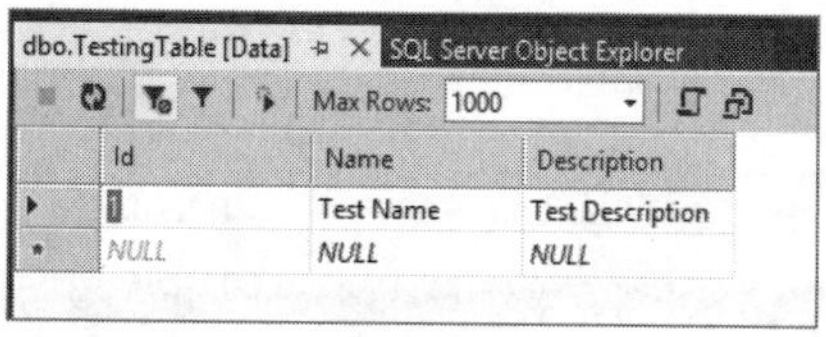

FIGURE 9-27: Working with the data in SQL Server Object Explorer

7. Close the data window and right-click once again on the dbo.TestingTable table. Select Delete from the context menu. This brings up the Preview Database Updates dialog, shown in Figure 9-28.

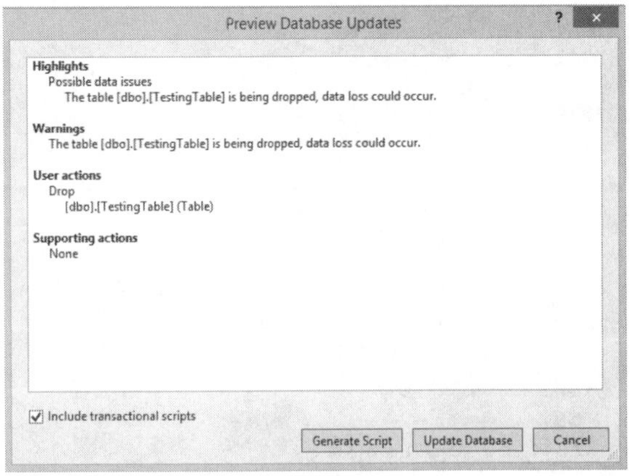

FIGURE 9-28: Preview Database Updates in SQL Server Object Explorer

8. Click the Update Database button. Note that the table was deleted.

How It Works

Visual Studio is a complete development environment in that it also enables you to access databases and evaluate data. The steps that you just took to connect Visual Studio to the database so that you can access that database's objects are the same as those you performed when connecting SQL Server Management Studio to the server. These steps include identifying the server to which you are going to connect and then authenticating to the server, in this case using the Windows authentication schema.

While Visual Studio Object Explorer does not have the same set of functionality that is offered through SQL Server Management Studio, it does enable you to easily and quickly evaluate whether or not your connection to the database is working correctly and whether all the fields are being stored in the right columns. The main thing to remember as you evaluate whether information was persisted correctly is that you need to refresh before you can see any new table or rows of data that may have been added since the last refresh. Table 9-3 lists some different database management functionality items and whether that item is available in Management Studio and/or Visual Studio SQL Server Object Explorer.

TABLE 9-3: Database Management Feature Availability

FEATURE	MANAGEMENT STUDIO	VISUAL STUDIO
Add / Edit / Delete database	X	X
Add / Edit / Delete table	X	X

FEATURE	MANAGEMENT STUDIO	VISUAL STUDIO
Add / Edit / Delete data within table	X	X
Run SQL scripts	X	X
Run data analysis	X	
Manage backups and replication	X	

Now that you have SQL Server installed and can connect to the server in several different ways outside of your application, the next step is enabling your application to communicate with the database.

ENTITY FRAMEWORK APPROACH TO DATA ACCESS

ASP.NET uses the Entity Framework to access the database. The Entity Framework is a set of technologies that support the development of data-oriented software applications. Developers have typically struggled with the need to achieve two very different objectives: modeling the entities, relationships, and logic of the business problems they are solving, and working with the data engines used to store and retrieve the data. This data may span multiple storage systems, each with its own protocols; even those applications that work with a single storage system, such as SQL Server, must balance the requirements of the storage system against the requirements of writing efficient and maintainable application code.

The key feature of the Entity Framework is that it enables developers to work with the data as they need it for their application, rather than having to worry about the database tables, columns, and data types. Because the Entity Framework can manage all of this, it frees developers to work at a higher level of abstraction when they deal with data, and enables them to create and maintain data-oriented applications with less code than other database access approaches.

When the Entity Framework first became available it was simply a way to convert your database into a set of objects that were available in your code. It has evolved since then to support multiple approaches to accessing your database. The two primary approaches are *data first* and *code first*, which refers to what is handled first, the database design or the code design.

Data First

In a data first approach, the code is created based on the tables in a database. This approach is especially common when converting a preexisting system, as the database is already created. Using this approach, you create class files from the database tables that have already been created by pointing a tool at the database and letting it run against the tables and other server objects that you select.

The larger the preexisting set of tables and relationships, the more time you can save using a data first approach. However, when doing new application development for which you don't have a set of already created databases with which you will be interacting, you can use the code first approach.

Code First

In a code- first approach, you create your business models as you need them for your application and then the Entity Framework creates the database tables from them. Because you are building a completely new application, you will take this approach, in particular because it enables you to concentrate on the ASP.NET part of the system, rather than spend much more effort walking through the database.

Just as with connecting SQL Server Manager, the first step is ensuring that you can reach the new server and authenticate. This allows your application to connect to the server. However, after this is configured the process will proceed differently from what you are used to in that you certainly do not want the application displaying login screens every time you want to access the database. Instead, you have to take your login information, such as server name, user, password, and perhaps the default database, and put it into a format that the server will be able to understand; and then put this information in a location where the application will be able to understand it. This format is called a *connection string*, and you will be storing this connection string in the configuration file, web.config.

The connection string is a set format that contains all the information necessary to connect to the database. The following snippet shows a typical connection string:

```
data source=ASP-NET\SQLEXPRESS;initial catalog=RentMyWrox;integrated security=True;
MultipleActiveResultSets=True;App=EntityFramework
```

You may have recognized some of these values from the last activity. Table 9-4 describes the most common parts of a connection string.

TABLE 9-4: Parts of a Connection String

SECTION	DESCRIPTION
Data source	Name of the server to which the application will be connecting
Initial catalog	Name of the database to which you will be connecting
Integrated security	A Boolean value that determines whether the authentication is going to use a Windows authentication approach. If so, as in your case, then this should be true.
MultipleActiveResultSets	A Boolean field that defines whether multiple queries can be running at the same time
App	Specifies which framework is going to be managing the connection. In the preceding case this is the Entity Framework.

SECTION	DESCRIPTION
uid	When you are not using Windows authentication (integrated security=False), you need to include a username when creating any authentication requests.
Password	When you are not using Windows authentication (integrated security=False), you need to include a password along with the username when creating any authentication requests.

Looking at the connection string displayed earlier, you can see that the database server name is ASP-NET\SQLEXPRESS, that the database connected to by default is RentMyWrox, that Windows authentication is used, that multiple result sets are wanted, and that the Entity Framework is used to manage access.

The application accesses this connection string because it has access to it through the configuration file. This configuration file, called Web.Config when working with an ASP.NET application, contains many different items, one of which is the group of connection strings that will be used to enable the application to get dynamic data.

Historically, creation of the connection string was a manual task, and it was easy to get something wrong during the process, leading to unexpected results that could be difficult to debug. The new scaffolds that are available when working with Entity Framework items now do much of the work in building those strings for you—you just need to update the data source and the initial catalog.

The last remaining task in connecting your application to the database is building the database context. The connection string enables the application to understand what it is connecting to, while the context handles all of the actual communication.

The context is the part of the application that uses the connection string, so it is also the part of the framework that manages the rest of the interaction with the database. The context basically defines the relations between models in your application and the objects, such as tables, within your database. In the next activity you add the context class to your project.

TRY IT OUT Adding a Database Context to Your Application to Allow Database Access

Using the following steps, begin the process of linking your application to the database.

1. Ensure that Visual Studio is running and you have the RentMyWrox application open. Right-click on the Models directory and select Add New Item. When the Add New Item dialog appears, ensure that you are in the Data directory under your appropriate language and select ADO.NET Data Entity Model. Name it **RentMyWroxContext**, as shown in Figure 9-29.

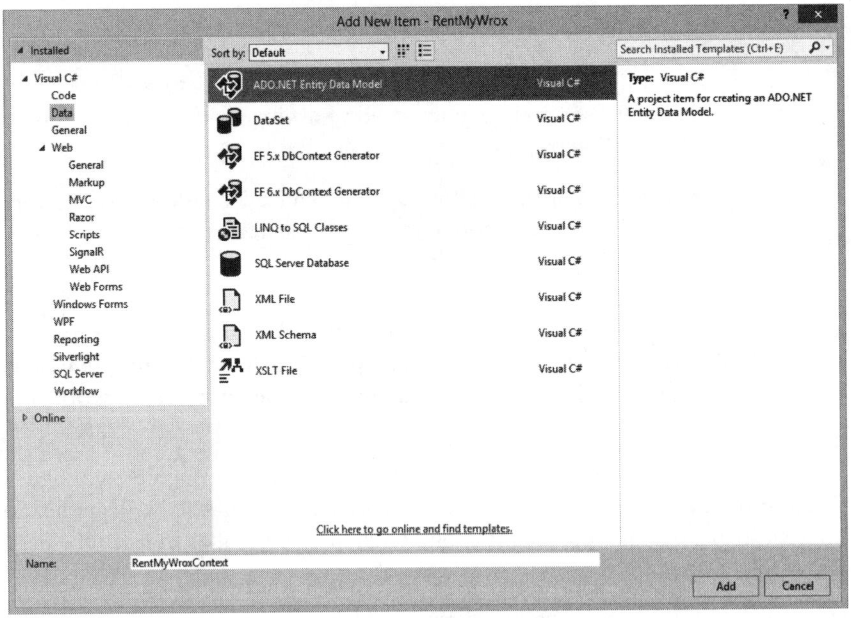

FIGURE 9-29: Adding the database context file

2. Click the Add button. This will bring up the Entity Data Model Wizard shown in Figure 9-30.

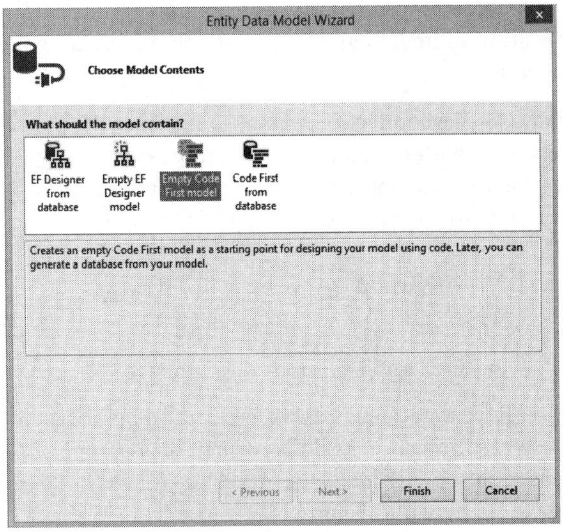

FIGURE 9-30: Entity Data Model Wizard

3. Select Empty Code First Model and click Finish. This creates the file and opens it in your main working window. It should look similar to Figure 9-31.

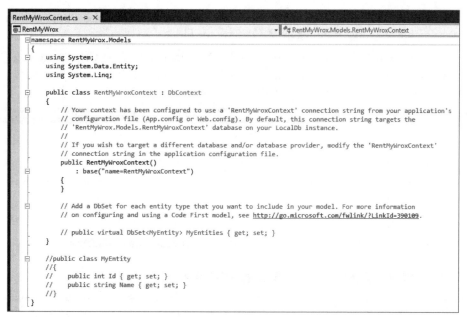

FIGURE 9-31: Basic DbContext file

4. Open SQL Server Object Explorer. Note the name of your server, the section that is highlighted in Figure 9-32.

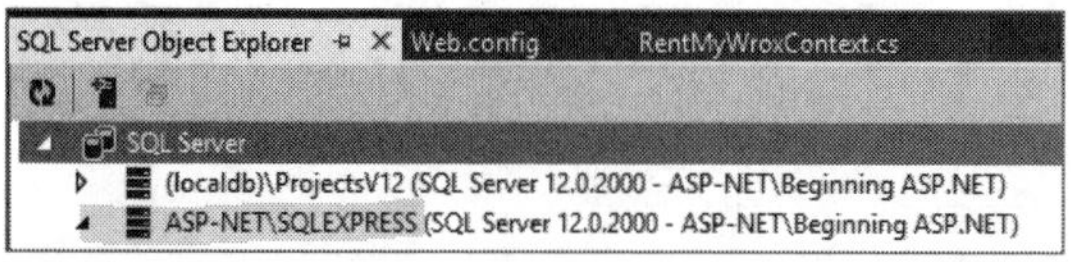

FIGURE 9-32: SQL Server Object Explorer with server name

5. Open your `Web.Config` file. It is in the root directory of your web project. Scroll down until you find a section that says `connectionStrings` (see Figure 9-33).

FIGURE 9-33: Web.Config file connection strings

5. Find the node that has `name="RentMyWroxContext"`. Change the current value of `"initial catalog=xxx"` to `"initial catalog=RentMyWrox"`.

6. In that same node, change `"data source=xxx"` to `"data source= the name of your server"` (found in the highlighted area from Figure 9-32). Save the file.

7. Right-click on the Models directory and select Add ⇨ New Item ⇨ Code ⇨ Class. Name the class "**Hobby**" and when the file opens in Visual Studio add the `using System.ComponentModel .DataAnnotations;` using statement at the top of the file.

8. Add the following properties and save your work. When complete, your file should look like Figure 9-34.

```
[Key]
public int Id { get; set; }

public string Name { get; set; }

public bool IsActive { get; set; }

public virtual ICollection<UserDemographics> UserDemographics { get; set; }
```

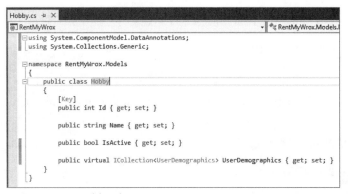

FIGURE 9-34: Hobby class

9. Open the model that you created in Chapter 6, `UserDemographics.cs`. It's located in the Models directory. Locate the `Id` property and add an attribute so that it looks like the following:

```
[Key]
public int Id { get; set; }
```

10. Change two other lines as well by replacing the "string" in the `List<string>` with `Hobby`. You need to change the Property as well as the line in the constructor. When you are changing the property, also add the keyword `virtual`. When completed, it should look like Figure 9-35. Save the file.

11. If the Models\RentMyWroxContext that you created in Step 1 is not open, open it again. You should see a commented version of a similar line. Add the following lines to the file. These lines can go in place of the commented line as illustrated in Figure 9-36, which shows just the `RentMyWrox` class section of the file.

```
public virtual DbSet<UserDemographics> UserDemographics { get; set; }

public virtual DbSet<Hobby> Hobbies { get; set; }
```

```
public class UserDemographics
{
    public UserDemographics()
    {
        Hobbies = new List<Hobby>();
    }

    [Key]
    public int Id { get; set; }

    public DateTime Birthdate { get; set; }

    public string Gender { get; set; }

    public string MaritalStatus { get; set; }

    public DateTime DateMovedIntoArea { get; set; }

    public bool OwnHome { get; set; }

    public int TotalNumberInHome { get; set; }

    public virtual List<Hobby> Hobbies { get; set; }
}
```

FIGURE 9-35: UserDemographics class

```
public class RentMyWroxContext : DbContext
{
    // Your context has been configured to use a 'RentMyWroxContext' connection string from your application's
    // configuration file (App.config or Web.config). By default, this connection string targets the
    // 'RentMyWrox.Models.RentMyWroxContext' database on your LocalDb instance.
    //
    // If you wish to target a different database and/or database provider, modify the 'RentMyWroxContext'
    // connection string in the application configuration file.
    public RentMyWroxContext()
        : base("name=RentMyWroxContext")
    {
    }

    // Add a DbSet for each entity type that you want to include in your model. For more information
    // on configuring and using a Code First model, see http://go.microsoft.com/fwlink/?LinkId=390109.

    public virtual DbSet<UserDemographics> UserDemographics { get; set; }

    public virtual DbSet<Hobby> Hobbies { get; set; }
}
```

FIGURE 9-36: Updated data context class

12. Expand your Controllers directory and open the `UserDemographicsController` file. Find the Edit action. Note that there is a section where a new UserDemographic was created. Replace that code with a simple new statement for now. That action should look like the following snippet when finished:

```
public ActionResult Edit(int id)
{
    var model = new UserDemographics();
    return View("Manage", model);
}
```

13. In that same class, find the Index action and change it to the following:

```
public ActionResult Index()
{
    using (RentMyWroxContext context = new RentMyWroxContext())
    {
```

```
            var list = context.UserDemographics.OrderBy(x => x.Birthdate).ToList();
            return View(list);
        }
    }
```

14. Run the application and navigate to \UserDemographics. This initial run may take a little bit longer than normal.

15. Open SQL Server Object Explorer, and expand the RentMyWrox database. Go into the Tables folder. If you do not see anything, click the Refresh button. You should see four tables listed, as shown in Figure 9-37.

FIGURE 9-37: Newly created database tables

How It Works

In this activity you created the context file that you will be using to access the database. Figure 9-31 shows a simple context file. The first thing to examine is the class definition, shown in the following snippet:

```
    public class RentMyWroxContext : DbContext
```

When the class was generated it was created so that it inherits DbContext. As mentioned earlier, DbContext handles all interaction with the database, so the choices that you had during the creation process were all related to how Visual Studio would build out the DbContext, and had nothing to do with whether or not there would be a DbContext. When in the dialog to add a new context file, each of the four options you had during the creation process simply build the DbContext file differently, generally with more information than what occurs with the Empty Model approach that you chose.

As you created this file you came across a dialog with four options:

➤   EF Designer from Database

➤   Empty EF Designer Model

➤   Empty Code First Model

➤   Code First from Database

There are two different sets of criteria: The first is whether or not the information is created from the database and the second is whether or not a visual designer is created. This chapter has already discussed building the models from a database, but there has not yet been any mention of using the visual designer.

The original approach to the Entity Framework was tied to a database, so much so that there was even a visual designer that looked like a database creation tool. Figure 9-38 shows what the visual approach would look like, using two different simple models.

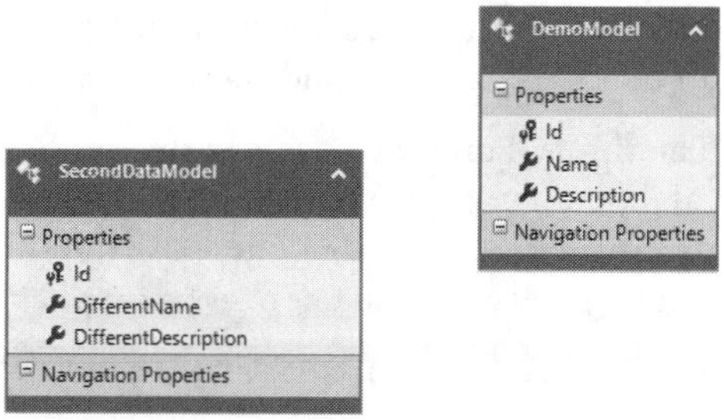

FIGURE 9-38: Visual Designer approach

Creating everything in the visual designer gives developers an experience very similar to the approach they would have taken before the Entity Framework supported code first. This means you do the configuration in one place (the visual tool), which is separate from the models. In the code first approach, any needed configuration is part of the model definition itself. The approach that you took to creating the tables in the database shows how different it is to use the code first approach. There is no concept of a designer, just a set of classes with which you build the relationships so that they make sense for your code.

However, this leads to some interesting effects. Look back at the changes that you made to the `UserDemographics` class, and especially the `Hobbies` property. You went from a `List<string>` to a `List<Hobby>`. Why couldn't this be left as the original type, a list of strings? The reason goes back to the Entity Framework having no awareness of how to store this information, mainly because it doesn't have an `Id` that is defined as a `Key`, which would enable it to manage getting information in and out of the database. Understanding that this is a key value is important because it acts as a unique identifier; there can never be two rows with the same value in this property.

As you go further into the Entity Framework, you will notice that there are some rules, a primary one of which is that there needs to be a `Key` attribute, or some way that the Entity Framework can specify an individual row. As you learn about getting information in and out of the database, you will see how important this is and how it helps support many of the built-in EF methods. Examining the database will demonstrate that the Id columns have been set as primary keys and are columns defined as Identity. The primary key constraint guarantees that one, and only one, value is allowed into the table. Trying to insert a new item using an already existing value will not work. The use of Identity means that the server will create the value, and create these values in order. This ties back into the key value that was discussed earlier; this is the database's interpretation of that attribute.

Because EF needs a key, it becomes clear why there had to be a Hobby model, as it contains the `Id` and the `Name` properties, with the name being the string that you used to have on the `UserDemographics`. The `IsActive` flag enables you to turn hobbies on and off in the UI without deleting the data, and is therefore straightforward, but why did you add a virtual `List<UserDemographics>` to the Hobby? Why would that be necessary?

The main reason that property was added is that the list of available hobbies is maintained independently. It is intended that the values in the Hobby table will be used to fill the checkboxes from which users can select. However, if the expectation is that the Hobby is an independent object, that means that this two-way relationship needs to be defined somewhere; otherwise, you will never be able to understand that John's hobby is gardening, because while John's demographic information is stored as a `UserDemographics`, and Gardening is stored as a `Hobby`, there is nothing connecting the two.

The Entity Framework solved this problem by creating the intermediate database table, `UserDemographicsHobbies`, which contains only two columns, `Hobby_Id` and `UserDemographics_Id`. These are important columns, however, because they establish the relationship between the `UserDemographics` and the `Hobby`, enabling the following two things:

➤   A `UserDemographic` can have more than one `Hobby`.

➤   A `Hobby` can be available to more than one `UserDemographic`.

Note that there is no corresponding C# class; the table is used behind the scenes to manage this many-to-many relationship. However, this table would not have been created without that property on the `Hobby` model.

Once the models were completed, there were still a few steps that had to be taken. The first was ensuring that the class that acts as the mediator between your application and the database, RentMyWroxContext, understands that there are `UserDemographics` and Hobbies that need to be maintained. You did this by adding them as properties onto the context. This enables the Entity Framework to understand that these classes are to be persisted, and defines the names that you will use when you access the information. Without this step, these tables would not be created.

Now that you have linked the tables to the data context, the next step is to use the data context somewhere. The first implementation of this class is in the Index action—the action that returns the complete list of items in the database. Take a closer look at this section of code; the important part is listed here:

```
using (RentMyWroxContext context = new RentMyWroxContext())
{
    var list = context.UserDemographics.OrderBy(x => x.Birthdate).ToList();
    return View(list);
}
```

The first part is the line containing the using statement. This using is different from the keywords that you have used before at the top of a class file to link functionality from other namespaces to the current file. In this case, it's shorthand for "when you are done using the object that is being created, destroy that object." Destroying the object ensures that it is available for garbage collection and that the memory using that item is cleared. This is important because an application server can quickly run out of available memory if connections such as this (this is a connection to the database after all!) are not cleaned up when you are done with them. You should get in the habit of ensuring that you use the using statement to wrap your creation of the database context.

Once you have the context created, the next step the code takes is to access the data. When you added the items into the context file earlier you made them properties. One of these properties, `UserDemographics`, is the item that is being worked with. In this case you can consider it directly related to the table because the rest of the line is sorting every entry in the database by the BirthDate and then creating a List of the resulting items.

You had to add that code at this point because you need to instantiate, or create it, and access the context before it creates the tables in the database. You accessed the context when you changed the URL to go to UserDemographics; the reason it took longer than normal is because it was doing all the comparing and creation of the databases. This shows one of the advantages of the code first approach: Every time the context starts, it evaluates the models in the system and compares these models to the tables in the database. If it is the first time creating tables in this database, it simply creates them. If there are more tables than classes, it will simply ignore them. If the tables in the database do not match the models in your application, however, the system will throw an exception. This helps you ensure that you keep the models and the database in sync. Later in this chapter you will learn about modifying already existing tables due to changes in the model.

Creating the initial connection to the database, adding the context, and creating some initial models enabled you to see how the code first approach in the Entity Framework can hide a lot of the database work for you. It makes you look carefully at the relationships within your models, however; otherwise, you may not get the expected outcome. The many-to-many relationship was an excellent example. You will be seeing more of this as you continue to build out your models throughout this chapter.

Selecting Data from the Database

There was a new construct in the last activity, the OrderBy method that was used in the controller. Earlier, in Chapter 4, you were introduced to some of the dot operators that are used when working with collections, such as Add or AddRange. There are additional operators that support interacting with collections. Table 9-5 contains a list of some of the most commonly used operators when interacting with information contained within a collection.

TABLE 9-5: SELECTING AND SORTING DATA

OPERATOR	DESCRIPTION
Find	Takes a value that is of the type of the [Key] property. If the Entity Framework can find an item containing that Key, then that item is returned. An exception will be thrown if the item is not available in the table. This method never returns more than one item. List.Find(5);
First	Returns the first item that matches a set of criteria. If there is no item, then the operator throws an exception. The easiest way to use this method is through the use of a Lambda expression. This method never returns more than one item. List.First(x=>x.FirstName="Arnold");

continues

TABLE 9-5 *(continued)*

OPERATOR	DESCRIPTION
FirstOrDefault	Works like the First operator except the `FirstOrDefault` method returns a null if the value is not found, rather than throwing an exception. Therefore, it is recommended that you use `FirstOrDefault` in preference over `First`, and handle a potential null result instead of an exception being thrown by the application. `List.FirstOrDefault(x=>x.FirstName="Arnold");`
Where	Allows filters to be added to the list. It is configured like the `First` and `FirstOrDefault` methods with the use of Lambda expressions, but instead of selecting the first item that meets the criteria it instead returns all items that match the criteria. If no items meet the criteria, the method returns an instantiated list with no elements. By definition, you will always get a list back, regardless of the number of items that meet the criteria. `List.Where(x=>x.FirstName="Arnold");`
OrderBy	Sorts the result set in ascending order. It can be used before or after other methods and uses a Lambda expression as well. Because `OrderBy` chains with other methods, you can see how you might have different results based on the order in which items are chained together. Whereas the other methods support the concept of and and or, there is an implicit expectation that an `OrderBy` contains only one field, the primary field to be sorted on. `List.OrderBy(x=>x.FirstName);`
OrderByDescending	Acts like the `OrderBy` method except the sorting is done in descending order rather than ascending order by the field within the lambda expression
ThenBy	Enables you to chain multiple sorts together. It must be used immediately after an `OrderBy` and adds an additional ascending sort on the item identified in the Lambda expression. `List.OrderBy(x=>x.FirstName).ThenBy(x=>x.LastName);`
ThenByDescending	Similar to `ThenBy`, the `ThenByDescending` method adds an additional sort on an `OrderBy` or `OrderByAscending`. Just as with `ThenBy`, you can chain multiple statements together to add ordered sorting using other fields.
Take	Enables you to take a subset of items from a larger collection. The parameter for the method is an integer that defines how many items the method will take. The method never returns more than the parameter, but it may return less if the number of records is less than the parameter value. `List.Where(x=>x.FirstName="Arnold").Take(10);`

There is a lot of potential overlap in outcome when you are using the dot operators, because `List.First(x=>x.Id == 3)` will give you the exact same outcome as `List.Find(3)`, or `List.Where(x=>x.Id == 3).First()`. The order in which the methods are assigned can also be important; `List.OrderBy(x=>x.FirstName).Take(10)` will most likely not return the same set as `List.Take(10).OrderBy(x=>x.FirstName)` if there are more than 10 items in the list because the first approach will sort and then take 10 rows, whereas the second approach will take the first 10 rows (unsorted) and then sort the output.

A lot of new developers approach working with a database with a little trepidation. However, there is no reason to do so; while there is indeed a database behind the scenes, it doesn't affect what you are doing when you work with the data because there is absolutely no difference between working with the database and working with a collection that you manually created. The context hides all of that from you; just work with the data lists and let the context take care of doing all the actual interaction with the system.

DATA CONTROLS IN WEB FORMS

Now that you have created the database context and set up the first models, the next step is to start integrating the database and working through different approaches of creating, editing, displaying, and deleting data, as there are many different ways to manage this. Some of these ways can involve the use of a server control specifically designed to interact with live data, while others can involve a manual approach to designing the form and handling all the interaction. In this section you will learn about several of the Web Form server controls that manage database interaction.

Details View

The `DetailsView` is a server control that is meant to eliminate a lot of the manual work of creating a data entry form. In Chapter 5 you built a data entry form for an item using labels and textboxes. In this chapter you are going to look at using model binding in server controls designed specifically to support interaction with the database.

Model binding allows you to map and bind HTTP request data to a model that you have defined. Model binding makes it easy for you to work with form data because the request data (POST/GET) is automatically transferred into a data model you specify. ASP.NET does this work behind the scenes for you.

Some properties are common between various data controls. The first is defining what will be displayed, generally as either a column or a field. This definition gives you some control over the properties that will be displayed, how these properties will be labeled, and the order in which they will be displayed. Table 9-6 shows the major field definitions.

TABLE 9-6: Data Control Field Definitions

NAME	DESCRIPTION
BoundField	Displays the value of a property from the bound object or data source.
ButtonField	Displays a command button as defined. Generally used for Add or Remove buttons.
CheckBoxField	Displays a checkbox for the item from the bound object. This is generally used to display Boolean-typed properties.
CommandField	Displays predefined command buttons, such as for selecting, editing, or deleting actions.
HyperlinkField	Displays the value of a property as a hyperlink. This approach also allows you to bind a second field to the URL.
ImageField	Displays an image in the control.
TemplateField	Displays user-defined content for each bound item. This enables you to create custom columns and/or fields.

The second item common to various data controls is the binding of specific actions to different event handlers in the code-behind. This is necessary because although the server control is relatively smart about building different parts of the UI, it understands that it should leave some of the crucial parts to the developer; in this case, interacting with the database, mainly because it doesn't want to assume that the object it is working with in the UI is actually the same object persisted in the database. It may instead be a view model that holds different information from various models, rather than all fields for a single model. Table 9-7 shows these different methods.

TABLE 9-7: Data-Binding Methods

METHOD	DESCRIPTION
SelectMethod	Allows the control to access a method where it can pass in a key value and get back one instance of the object with which it is working
InsertMethod	Allows the control to bind to a particular method that will handle creating a new item in the database
DeleteMethod	Allows the control to bind to a specific method that will handle deleting an item from the database
UpdateMethod	Allows the control to bind to a method that is used when the control is updating an item in the database

Between these two different sets of properties you can define where properties from your model are going to be displayed, as well as how to handle database interaction. In the following activity, all the concepts are used together to manage a control that will be used to input data into your database.

TRY IT OUT Create a Data Entry Form That Will Save Information to the Database

In this activity you continue to build the functionality of the sample application by creating a page that supports the data entry of the Hobby model you created earlier in the chapter.

1. Ensure that Visual Studio is running and that you have opened your RentMyWrox solution. Right-click the Admin directory in the RentMyWrox project and select to Add a New Item. Add a new Web Form with Master Page. Be sure to select the `WebForms.Master` master page and name the file **ManageHobby**.

2. Ensure that you are in the Source view of the ManageHobby markup page. Add the following content to the second content control. When you are done, the page should look like what is shown in Figure 9-39.

```
<asp:DetailsView ID="DetailsView1" AutoGenerateRows="false" runat="server"
      DataKeyNames="Id" DefaultMode="Insert">
   <Fields>
      <asp:BoundField DataField="Name" HeaderText="Name" />
      <asp:CheckBoxField DataField="IsActive" HeaderText="Active ?" />
      <asp:CommandField ShowInsertButton="True" ShowCancelButton="false" />
   </Fields>
</asp:DetailsView>
```

```
ManageHobby.aspx
<%@ Page Title="" Language="C#" MasterPageFile="~/WebForms.Master" AutoEventWireup="true" CodeBehind="ManageHobby.aspx.cs" Inherits="RentMyWrox.Admin.ManageHobby" %>
<asp:Content ID="Content1" ContentPlaceHolderID="head" runat="server">
</asp:Content>
<asp:Content ID="Content2" ContentPlaceHolderID="ContentPlaceHolder1" runat="server" >
<asp:DetailsView ID="DetailsView1" AutoGenerateRows="false" runat="server" DefaultMode="Insert" >
    <Fields>
        <asp:BoundField DataField="Name" HeaderText="Name" />
        <asp:CheckBoxField DataField="IsActive" HeaderText="Active ?" />
        <asp:CommandField ShowInsertButton="True" ShowCancelButton="false" />
    </Fields>
</asp:DetailsView>
</asp:Content>
```

FIGURE 9-39: New DetailsView control

3. Click in the end of the opening tag, between `"Insert"` and the closing `>` tag. Add a space and then start to type "Insert." IntelliSense will display a dropdown of potential attributes. Highlight InsertMethod and click Enter.

4. Type in =. This will bring up a dropdown that says "`<Create New Method>`." Select this option. Repeat with `"Select"` to add a SelectMethod. You should have a screen similar to what is shown in Figure 9-40.

```
ManageHobby.aspx
<%@ Page Title="" Language="C#" MasterPageFile="~/WebForms.Master" AutoEventWireup="true" CodeBehind="ManageHobby.aspx.cs" Inherits="RentMyWrox.Admin.ManageHobby" %>
<asp:Content ID="Content1" ContentPlaceHolderID="head" runat="server">
</asp:Content>
<asp:Content ID="Content2" ContentPlaceHolderID="ContentPlaceHolder1" runat="server">
<asp:DetailsView ID="DetailsView1" AutoGenerateRows="false" runat="server" DefaultMode="Insert"
      InsertMethod="DetailsView1_InsertItem" SelectMethod="DetailsView1_GetItem">
    <Fields>
        <asp:BoundField DataField="Name" HeaderText="Name" />
        <asp:CheckBoxField DataField="IsActive" HeaderText="Active ?" />
        <asp:CommandField ShowInsertButton="True" ShowCancelButton="false" />
    </Fields>
</asp:DetailsView>
</asp:Content>
```

FIGURE 9-40: DetailsView control with methods assigned

5.   Open the code-behind file for the ManageHobby Web Form. You should see two empty methods that were created when you selected the Create New Method option. Fill them out as follows:

```
public void DetailsView1_InsertItem()
{
    Hobby hobby = new Hobby();
    TryUpdateModel(hobby);
    if (ModelState.IsValid)
    {
        using (RentMyWroxContext context = new RentMyWroxContext())
        {
            context.Hobbies.Add(hobby);
            context.SaveChanges();
        }
    }
}

public object DetailsView1_GetItem(int id)
{
    using (RentMyWroxContext context = new RentMyWroxContext())
    {
        return context.Hobbies.Find(id);
    }
}
```

6.   Run the application. This will bring you to a screen similar to the one shown in Figure 9-41.

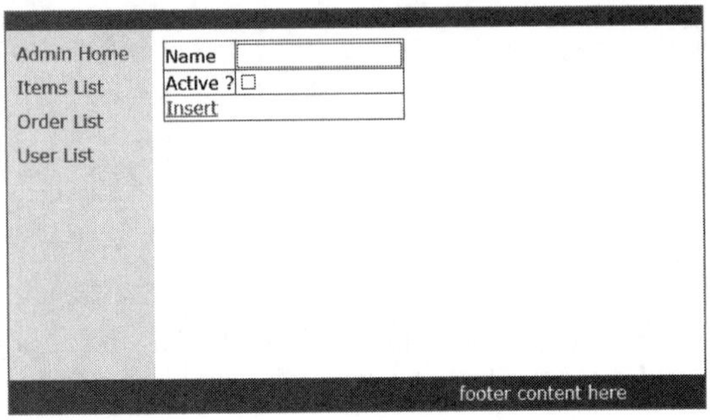

FIGURE 9-41: DetailsView rendered in the browser

7.   Enter some information and select Insert. The page will refresh, and the box will be returned empty.

8.   Open SQL Server Object Explorer and drill down into the RentMyWrox database. Go into the Tables folder, right-click on dbo.Hobbies, and select ViewData. You should see the values you just entered in the database.

How It Works

In this activity you added a new page with a DetailsView server control. A few key attributes on this control made it work as needed. First you set `AutoGenerateRows` to `false`. If you didn't set that attribute, the page would have thrown an exception because it was being loaded without any object already bound to the control and it would have tried to bind the integer Id to a column, failing because the field does not exist. The second important attribute is `DefaultMode`, set to `Insert`. If you didn't take that action you would have had the same exception thrown, again because there was no item to display.

The other attributes that you added, the methods that linked to event handlers in the code-behind, all provided the actual business functionality needed to persist the data. The HTML created by the control is made up of standard input elements, so when you clicked the Insert link it returned all the form field values to the code-behind in a postback.

The last part of the control definition in the markup page is the Fields list. This is where you bound the various properties of the model into a UI element. Each of the items listed in the Fields set was displayed in the UI when the page was rendered. You did this by providing the DataField, which bound that particular control to a property on the model. As you will see when you look at the code-behind, this binding is important for both display and processing.

Take a moment to review the `InsertItem` method in the code-behind. The first three lines of this method are shown here:

```
Hobby hobby = new Hobby();
TryUpdateModel(hobby);
if (ModelState.IsValid)
```

The first line is pretty standard—you constructed a new Hobby. The next line is interesting, however, in that it actually performs some work. The `TryUpdateModel` method takes the new object that was just created and tries to map the data that came across in the request to the appropriate properties, matching them up by name. This is an important concept in that it enables the developer to focus on the model rather than manually map the request fields to a model property.

When the process is completed, the `ModelState.IsValid` property is checked. This property evaluates the model that was just filled (in the `TryUpdateModel` method) to confirm it's valid, such as all required fields have been filled out. Because you have yet to define any of these requirements, this model should always pass, even if no information was provided in any of the forms. The functionality of the `TryUpdateModel` method adds a lot of capability to Web Forms as it enables developers to avoid time repeatedly writing trivial code.

Once you have a valid model, it's a simple step to add it to the Hobbies table by using the `Add` method, just as you would if adding the item to a list; that's really what you are doing in this case. The only new part is the `SaveChanges` method, but this is a very important item. The `SaveChanges` method actually does the work of saving the information to the database.

The separation between adding the item to the collection and calling the `SaveChanges` method is important. Consider a situation in which you may be working with multiple objects and you add each one to a different database collections set. None of the items that you add to the list will actually be persisted until after you call the `SaveChanges` method.

This can cause some interesting behavior with related types, especially when you are doing a fresh add rather than a change. This is because when you are using the `Key` attribute (that relates directly to the

Identity column-type whereby the database creates the Key value for you), you do not actually have the value until after the framework has ran the SaveChanges method. Figure 9-42 shows the debug values of an item running through the code. You can tell the location of the running process by the arrow indicator on the left side of the code line. Note that the code flow was stopped after the Add method was called but before the calling of the SaveChanges method, and how the Id value is shown as 0.

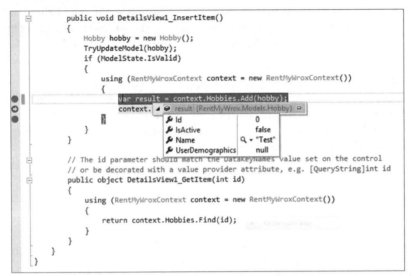

FIGURE 9-42: Debug values before running the SaveChanges method

Figure 9-43 shows the debug value after the SaveChanges method is called. Note how the Id value has been changed.

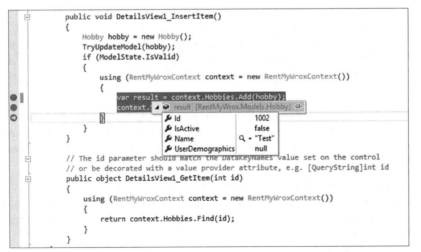

FIGURE 9-43: Debug values after running the SaveChanges method

This change is due to the item actually interacting with the database. However, you should also be able to understand how interacting with some of the database-created values could be problematic. If you had set a variable equal to the Id value before running the SaveChanges method, then you would not have the correct value.

The SaveChanges method needs to be run before any changes are persisted to the database—either adds, as you just performed, or updates, whereby information is changed but not added. As mentioned earlier, you do not have to have a one-to-one relationship between acting on items in the database and calling the SaveChanges method, as the SaveChanges method operates on any items run on the context since the last time it ran. This enables you to chain multiple changes into one call to the database.

The DetailsView provided a demonstration of how some of the ASP.NET server controls can work on one item in a list at a time. There are other controls that help ASP.NET Web Form developers when working with sets of data. One of these controls is the GridView, covered next.

Web Form GridView

A GridView is used to display the values of a series of data in a table format. Each column represents a field, while each row represents a record, much like working with a spreadsheet application. Some of the built-in functionality of a GridView includes the following:

➤ Sorting

➤ Updating and deleting

➤ Paging

➤ Row selection

The GridView supports the various column options that are available with the DetailsView, as was shown in Table 9-5, and you create the definition much like you did with the DetailsView. In the following activity, you add a GridView to the sample application to help manage the items that you will be making available for rent.

TRY IT OUT Add A GridView Control

In this activity you are adding a GridView server control to your site in order to manage database access to the items available for rent.

1. Ensure that Visual Studio is running and that you have opened your RentMyWrox solution. Right-click on the Models directory and add a new class named **Item**.

2. Add the properties as defined here:

```
[Key]
public int Id { get; set; }

public string Name { get; set; }
```

```
public string Description { get; set; }

public string ItemNumber { get; set; }

public string Picture { get; set; }

public double Cost { get; set; }

public DateTime? CheckedOut { get; set; }

public DateTime? DueBack { get; set; }

public DateTime DateAcquired { get; set; }

public bool IsAvailable { get; set; }
```

3. Open the `RentMyWroxContext.cs` file from the Models directory.

4. Add the new DbSet for Item to ensure that the tables are created in the database. The line of code to add this DbSet is as follows:

```
public virtual DbSet<Item> Items { get; set; }
```

5. Run the application in Debug mode and navigate to \UserDemographics. You should get an error, as shown in Figure 9-44.

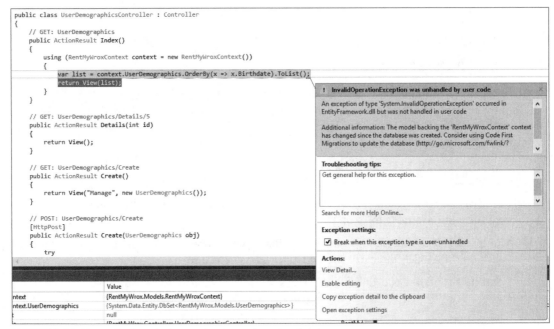

FIGURE 9-44: Error displayed when trying to update the database

6. Go to Tools ⇨ NuGet Package Manager ⇨ Package Manager Console. This will open a new pane within Visual Studio (see Figure 9-45).

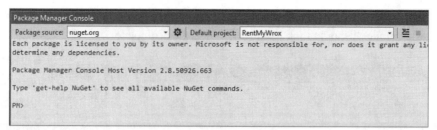

FIGURE 9-45: Package Manager Console

7. Click to the right of PM>, type in the following command, and press Enter:

```
enable-migrations  -ContextTypeName RentMyWrox.Models.RentMyWroxContext
```

8. When the processing is complete, type in the following command and press Enter:

```
Add-Migration "Adding Items"
```

9. When the processing is complete, type in the following command and press Enter:

```
Update-Database
```

10. Expand the Admin folder, open the ItemList.aspx page created previously, and go into Design mode. Also, open the Server Explorer window by selecting View ➪ Server Explorer.

11. In the Data Connections section, expand your database, and then open the Tables folder. You should see a new table, Items. Your arrangement should look something like Figure 9-46 after some screen rearrangement.

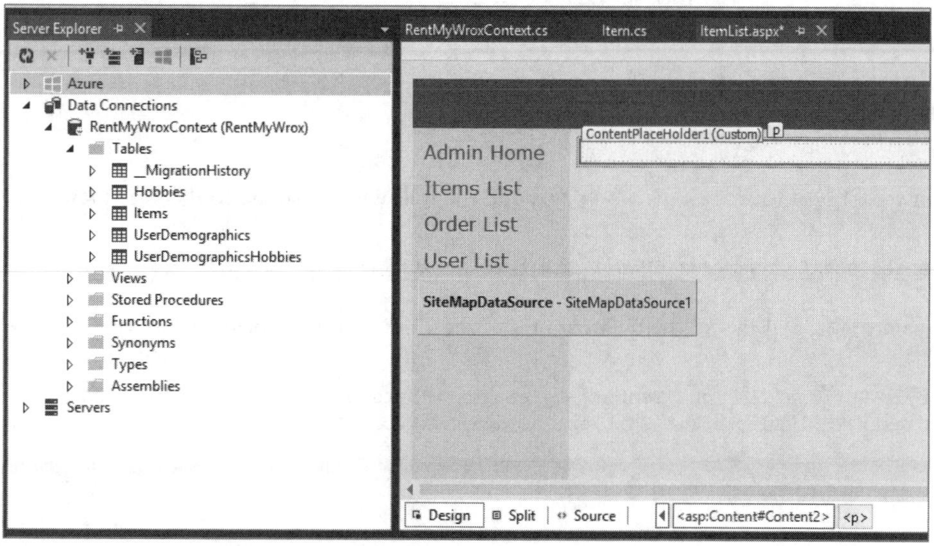

FIGURE 9-46: Server Manager and Design mode

12. Click the new table in the Server Explorer window and drag it into the ContentPlaceHolder1 box in the page's Design mode. It should look like Figure 9-47 when complete.

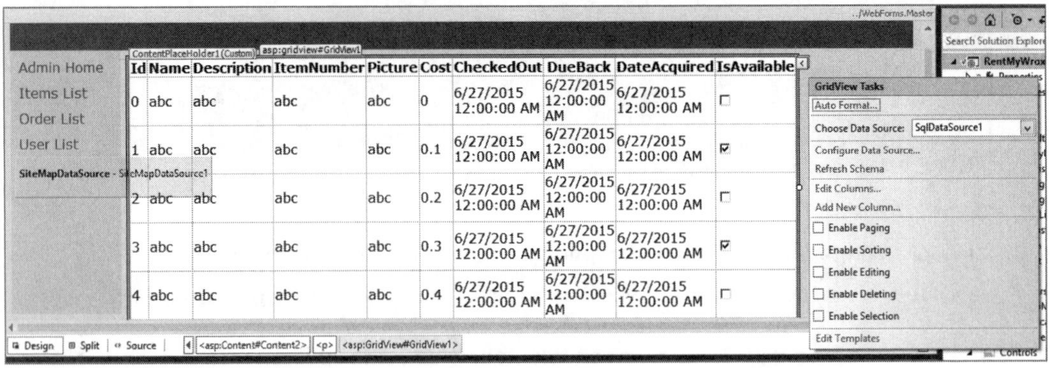

FIGURE 9-47: Screen after dropping table into page design

13. Check all the boxes in the GridView Tasks window. In the Server Explorer window, right-click on the Items table and select Show Table Data. This will open a window in which you can enter data.

14. Seed the database by entering some information. You do not have to enter data in the CheckedOut or DueBack columns.

15. Run the application. Ensure that you are on Admin\ItemList. You should see the information that you added in Step 10, and it should look similar to Figure 9-48.

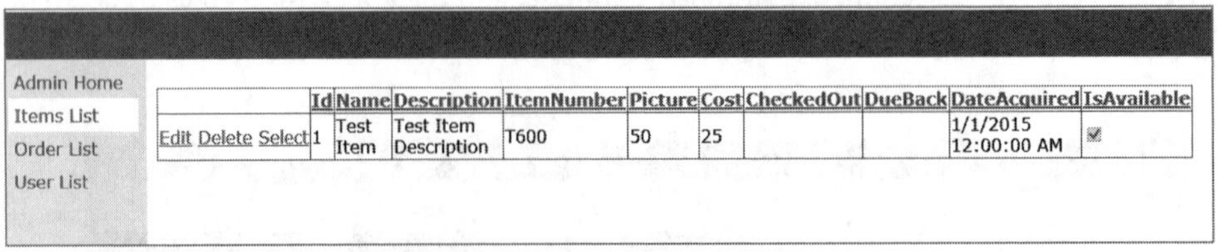

FIGURE 9-48: Displaying the GridView

16. Back in your `ItemList.aspx` markup page, add the following attribute to the GridView element:

```
OnSelectedIndexChanged="GridView1_SelectedIndexChanged"
```

17. In the same page, add the following attributes to the CommandField element:

```
ItemStyle-HorizontalAlign="Center" DeleteText="Delete<br/>"
SelectText="Full_Edit<br/>" EditText="Quick_Edit<br/>"
```

18. In the rest of the columns, take some time to update the HeaderText attribute by adding spaces as necessary.

19. In the code-behind (`ItemList.aspx.cs`), add a new method:

```
protected void GridView1_SelectedIndexChanged(object sender, EventArgs e)
{
    GridViewRow row = GridView1.SelectedRow;
    string id = row.Cells[1].Text;
    Response.Redirect(@"ManageItem\" + id);
}
```

How It Works

Several new concepts were introduced as part of this activity, mainly code first database migration, the Server Explorer window, and the GridView server control and SQLDataSource. Creating the Item model class and adding it to the database context were straightforward affairs, no different than the steps that you took earlier in this chapter. However, once that was completed you had to do some extra work to manage the movement from the code first class file to the database.

This is where the database migration process comes into the foreground. Once the initial database is created, by default every change to the structure of the models requires creating a migration. This is necessary because the Entity Framework and Visual Studio have no real understanding of where you are in the development lifecycle. Understanding whether you are creating a completely new application or whether you are updating a long-running production application is unknown.

Because the framework doesn't know what effect each database change has on the underlying system, it falls to the developer to make that determination. By default, the system is set to always expect migration scripts, but you have the capability to configure the system to automatically update the database upon changes. However, you won't take that approach in this process because it is bad practice to lose that control. By default, the system drops and recreates the tables; and even in this environment it would be better if that didn't happen.

When working with code first and the Entity Framework, a migration is the process of updating the database based on changes in the applicable model file. A change could be as simple as altering a field in a table, or it could affect multiple tables; each set of changes can be thought of as a migration, with the end of the process being when the migration itself is run.

As you saw in the walk-through, once you made the change to the system by adding the new class, you were unable to successfully run the application. That's because the Entity Framework did an evaluation of the models, comparing them to the defined and managed database. When it determined that there was a difference it threw an exception. After you got the error, the next step you had to take was to turn on the migration process. While you may not have noticed the change, enabling migrations added items to your project.

Among the items that were added to the project is a new directory named Migrations. If you look in this directory you will see that it currently contains three different files. One of these files is

Configuration.cs, while the other two start with the current date. One of them includes "InitialCreate" in the name, while the other includes "Adding_Items," a representation of the information that you used in Step 6. That directory should be similar to the one shown in Figure 9-49.

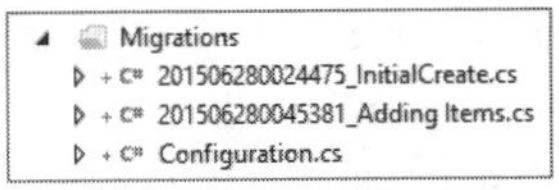

FIGURE 9-49: Migrations directory after enabling and running code first migrations

Each of these files acts as a script that updates the system. The first one, InitialCreate, was created when you enabled migration. That file is a snapshot of the initial database—the version of the database that was created the first time the database context was run. The second script was created when you ran the add-migration command. That command instructs the Entity Framework to create a new script that contains the differences between the current version of the database and the current version of the models. If you look into that file you will see the following method:

```
public override void Up()
{
    CreateTable(
        "dbo.Items",
        c => new
            {
                Id = c.Int(nullable: false, identity: true),
                Name = c.String(),
                Description = c.String(),
                ItemNumber = c.String(),
                Picture = c.String(),
                Cost = c.Double(nullable: false),
                CheckedOut = c.DateTime(nullable: true),
                DueBack = c.DateTime(nullable: true),
                DateAcquired = c.DateTime(nullable: false),
                IsAvailable = c.Boolean(nullable: false),
            })
        .PrimaryKey(t => t.Id);
}
```

As you can probably decipher, the action taking place during this migration is the creation of a single table. If there were more changes, then there would have been more tables being managed.

After creating the migration script, the next step is to run the update command. If there have been additional changes in the model after the add-migration command was run but before the update command, you can always bring the current migration script up to date by running the same command again.

Each migration name should be unique; otherwise, the framework will try to update an already existing script. This may seem confusing because the name under which the script is actually saved includes the full date-time on which it ran, but the framework parses these values to determine whether there is a script that needs to be updated.

All these migration scripts anticipate that you are running against a single database server. When you deploy your code against a new database, perhaps in a different environment, the framework evaluates the state of the database assuming that one already exists. If the database in the new environment is empty, then the framework simply creates the complete set of tables as necessary by running through all the applicable scripts.

Conversely, if the new database already contains a version of the model, the framework evaluates this new database to determine where it needs to start running the applicable database scripts. It does this by looking into the __MigrationHistory table in the database. This table contains a history of all the Entity Framework upgrades that have been run against the server. The framework is able to determine which migration scripts are missing and run them in the correct order; this order is understood because each of the script names also contains a timestamp indicating when they were created.

After running the update database command, you were able to see the new table in the Server Manager window. This is another Visual Studio window that enables you to interact with SQL Server, including the capability to see, create, edit, and delete data. You used the Server Manager window because it supports the drag-and-drop approach that you took when dropping the GridView onto the markup page; the SQL Server Object Explorer window that you used earlier does not support this action.

Once you dropped the GridView onto the page another control was created as well, the SQLDataSource. The SQLDataSource enabled you to define the relationship between the GridView control and the database. This was done through three sets of parameters, Insert, Update, and Delete. Each of these defined the various sets of information that were managed through each call, with Insert and Update containing a complete list of all the object properties, while the Delete contains just the Id.

These various items were all added because that is the default set of functionality with a GridView. It enables you to view items in the list, as well as update and delete information. If you had clicked on the Update link, you would have seen that all the read-only text fields on that row suddenly converted to textboxes that allowed you to enter the information. The Delete link would delete that item from the database upon clicking. All of this functionality is included when using the GridView.

Looking in the attributes of the data source definition reveals several of interest, including InsertCommand, UpdateCommand, and DeleteCommand. As you can imagine, each of these is related to a set of parameters. The following code sample shows this relationship for one of the attribute sets:

```
UpdateCommand="UPDATE [Items] SET [Name] = @Name, [Description] = @Description,
    [ItemNumber] = @ItemNumber, [Picture] = @Picture, [Cost] = @Cost,
    [CheckedOut] = @CheckedOut, [DueBack] = @DueBack, [DateAcquired] = @DateAcquired,
    [IsAvailable] = @IsAvailable WHERE [Id] = @Id"

<UpdateParameters>
    <asp:Parameter Name="Name" Type="String" />
    <asp:Parameter Name="Description" Type="String" />
    <asp:Parameter Name="ItemNumber" Type="String" />
    <asp:Parameter Name="Picture" Type="String" />
    <asp:Parameter Name="Cost" Type="Double" />
    <asp:Parameter Name="CheckedOut" Type="DateTime" />
    <asp:Parameter Name="DueBack" Type="DateTime" />
    <asp:Parameter Name="DateAcquired" Type="DateTime" />
    <asp:Parameter Name="IsAvailable" Type="Boolean" />
    <asp:Parameter Name="Id" Type="Int32" />
</UpdateParameters>
```

The command text is pure SQL, with the items prefaced by the @ symbol being the values that will be replaced by the content in edit fields. If you look carefully through the command text, you will see that each item with the @ symbol has a corresponding entry as an asp:Parameter. This means, however, that a GridView goes completely around the intermediary offered by the Entity Framework and instead communicates directly with the database using the queries displayed in the various Command attributes. This becomes especially clear if you open and look at your web.config file. You will find a new connection string added to the file by the act of dragging and dropping the table onto the page.

You might expect that there would be a more Entity Framework–like approach to doing this work; but with the changes in the most recent versions of both ASP.NET and the Entity Framework, you will find that the other approaches do not work together as well as one would hope. Therefore, you need to decide whether or not the risk of accessing the same table in two different ways (direct vs. Entity Framework) is greater than the benefits of using the simple data source. In this case, you will accept the additional risk of dual access, as the table definition is firm at this point, so the pain of having to maintain changes in multiple places is minimal.

The last item added was a method that would respond to the clicking of the Select link (that you renamed to Full Edit). This code is shown again here:

```
protected void GridView1_SelectedIndexChanged(object sender, EventArgs e)
{
    GridViewRow row = GridView1.SelectedRow;
    string id = row.Cells[1].Text;
    Response.Redirect(@"ManageItem\" + id);
}
```

This method responds to the SelectedIndexChanged event from the GridView that is thrown when the user clicks the Select link. In this method you are finding the row where the link was clicked, GridView1.SelectedRow, and then finding the content in the second cell (remember, zero-based index), which happens to be the Id of the Item. You are then using a Response.Redirect command to forward the user to the previously created ManageItem page with the Id as part of the URL.

As you have just seen, getting a GridView into your application and configured to enable you to present, edit, and delete information is relatively painless as long as you are willing to make some compromises regarding data access and the control's output. In our case, this is an administrative page, so you will worry less about presentation and concentrate on functionality.

The same concerns are not present when working with ASP.NET MVC, however, as there are no server controls to help you build the application. In the following section, you'll take a look at how these approaches differ.

DATA DISPLAY IN MVC

The approaches to managing data display in ASP.NET MVC are different from the approaches used in Web Forms. Rather than providing you with a server control with which you can do a lot of different work, you instead can use scaffolding to get you part of the way to a finished page. Then you can rearrange the content to exactly how you want it to display in the finished form—the approach that you will take now.

List Display in MVC

Listing items in MVC takes a different approach by relying on a combination of HTML and your programming language of choice (C# or VB) to give you the ability to manage your content. This enables you to craft the look that you want for each row, without any potential limitations caused by the use of a control to do the management, and simply use code to repeat the writing of the row. In this next activity you create the list of items that your visitors will be able to rent.

TRY IT OUT Create a List of Items in ASP.NET MVC

In this activity you create the new home page for your RentMyWrox application. This page contains a short list of items that visitors can check out. If they want the full list, they will be able to go to a page of items.

Handling this requires a new controller and several new views: the controller to manage the interaction with the item, the default view for the site, and the view to display the full product list to the user.

1. Ensure that Visual Studio is running and you have the RentMyWrox application open. Open the App_Start\RouteConfig.cs file and add the following line above any MapRoute statements:

   ```
   routes.MapMvcAttributeRoutes();
   ```

2. Right-click on the Controller directory and add a new Empty MVC 5 controller, naming it "**ItemController.**"

3. Add the following using statement:

   ```
   using RentMyWrox.Models;
   ```

4. Change the content of the Index method as shown here and save the file:

   ```
   [Route("")]
   public ActionResult Index()
   {
       using (RentMyWroxContext context = new RentMyWroxContext())
       {
           List<Item> itemList = context.Items.Where(x => x.IsAvailable).Take(5).ToList();
           return View(itemList);
       }
   }
   ```

5. When you added the new controller file, Visual Studio added a new directory named Item. Right-click on that directory and add a new view. Ensure that the name of the file is **Index**, that it uses an "Empty" template, and that no Model class is selected (see Figure 9-50).

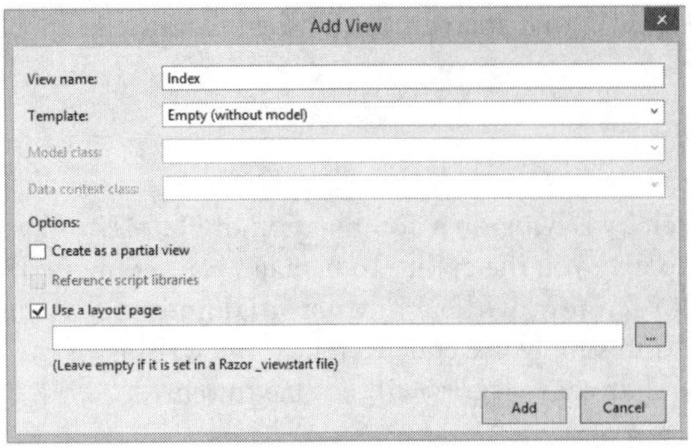

FIGURE 9-50: Adding the view file

6.   Add the following content to this new view file:

```
@model IEnumerable<RentMyWrox.Models.Item>

@{
    ViewBag.Title = "Index";
}

@foreach(var item in Model)
{
<div>
    <div class="listtitle">
        <span class="productname">@item.Name</span>
        <span class="listprice">@item.Cost.ToString("C")</span>
    </div>
    <p>
        @item.Description.Substring(0, 250)
        @if (item.Description.Length > 250)
        { <span>...</span> }
        @Html.ActionLink("Full details", "Details", new { @item.Id },
                new { @class = "inlinelink" })
        <a class="inlinelink" href="">Add to Cart</a>
    </p>
</div>
}
```

7.   Open the `Content\RentMyWrox.css` file and add the following at the bottom:

```
.productname
{
    color: #C40D42;
    font-size: x-large;
}
.inlinelink
{
    margin-left:25px;
    color: #C40D42;
}
.listprice
```

```
{
    float:right;
    color: #C40D42;
    font-size: x-large;
    text-align:right;
}
.listtitle
{
    background-color: #F8B6C9;
    padding:5px;
    width:750px;
}
```

8. Enter some additional information in your Item database table so that you have at least two items available for viewing.

9. Run the application and go to the home page of the site. Your page should look much like the one shown in Figure 9-51.

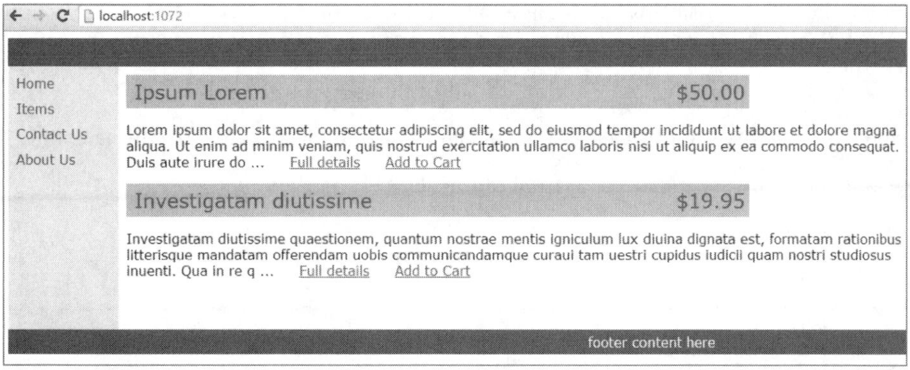

FIGURE 9-51: List of items on front page

How It Works

In this activity you were introduced to quite a few new concepts. The first was a new way to create routes that was introduced as part of MVC version 5. All of your routing up to this point was created using the MapRoute template approach. However, in MVC 5 a new way to create routes was introduced, *attribute routing.* The first thing you did in this activity was enable the capability to use attribute routing by adding a line to the RouteConfig.cs file, routes.MapMvcAttributeRoutes(). This method ensures that upon startup the framework will go through all the available actions and evaluate whether they have Route attributes. If the action has attributes, the framework then creates the applicable mapped route. You will typically want to set your attribute routes before you do your template-based mapped routes.

When you created the controller action you took advantage of attribute routing by assigning the Index method the route of "", which means the default home page. You can assign any string value at this point and it will define the actual route necessary to reach that action. You can also use optional variables and constraints, just as you can with the templates. You'll learn more about this usage in the next activity when you create the detail views.

The action method that you created will pass five items to the applicable view as the model. You can see this on the view that you created because it defined the model as `IEnumerable<RentMyWrox.Models .Item>`. In the view you simply added a loop that goes through each item in the result set and displays several fields to the user—mainly the title, price, and description. The description was capped at displaying 250 characters, adding ellipses (...) to the description if the value is truncated so that users are informed that additional information is available. Two links are added to each item as well—one is a link to see the full details page, and the other enables adding the item to the shopping cart. You will build the full details page in the next activity. The "add to cart" functionality is covered in Chapter 13, which covers AJAX.

The `ActionLink` that you used to build the link to the details, `Html.ActionLink ("Full details", "Details", new { @item.Id }, new { @class = "inlinelink" })`, uses the method signature that accepts the following:

➤ The text to display

➤ The action method to call—in this case, it assumes the same controller as the view that contains the call

➤ Additional URL objects—in this case, adding the Id of the item to the URL

➤ Additional element items—in this case, adding a class attribute, with value, to the element

The following code is the entire element as written out in the HTML page:

```
<a class="inlinelink" href="/Item/Details/3">Full details</a>
```

In the preceding activity, you created a list that displayed a custom view of your information, and it was certainly more development effort than using the Web Forms `GridView` server control. However, you also had full control over the information and how it is displayed because of the capability to run code in your view. Therefore, while it may indeed be more work, it is also much more customizable.

Details Views

Now that you know how to create lists in MVC, this section briefly covers how to manage details views, as you have already created an MVC form in Chapter 6. At this point, however, you will be linking the form that you created to the database.

If you recall from Chapter 6, you created an edit view for the UserDemographics model by using the default scaffolding, selecting the template and model to use. Those various template scaffold approaches are all available when working in ASP.NET MVC; however experienced developers tend to avoid these templates because they would usually delete most of the content and recreate it manually anyway. In the following activity, you build out the single product page that fully describes the product.

TRY IT OUT Create a Details Page

In this activity you create a product page to display the full set of information about a particular product.

1. Ensure that Visual Studio is running and that you have opened your RentMyWrox solution. Open your `ItemController` and add the following action:

```
public ActionResult Details(int id)
{
    using (RentMyWroxContext context = new RentMyWroxContext())
    {
        Item item = context.Items.FirstOrDefault(x => x.Id == id);
        return View(item);
    }
}
```

2. Right-click on your Views\Item directory and add a new view. Name it "**Details**" and ensure that it is an empty view.

3. Delete the content of this new view and add the following to the page:

```
@model RentMyWrox.Models.Item

@if (Model == null)
{
    <p>That is not a valid item.</p>
}
else
{
    ViewBag.Title = Model.Name;

    <div>
        <div class="detailtitle">
            <span class="productname">@Model.Name</span>
            <span class="listprice">@Model.Cost.ToString("C")</span>
        </div>
        <div>
            @if (!string.IsNullOrWhiteSpace(Model.Picture))
            {
                <img src="@Model.Picture" class="textwrap" runat="server" height="150" />
            }
            <p>
                @Model.Description
            </p>
        </div>

        @if (Model.IsAvailable)
        {
            <a class="inlinelink" href="">Add to Cart</a>
        }
        else
        {
```

```
        <span class="checkedout">
            This article was checked out on @Model.CheckedOut.Value.ToString("d")
            and is due back on @Model.DueBack.Value.ToString("d").
        </span>
        }
    </div>
}
```

4. Add the following to `RentMyWrox.css`:

```
.detailtitle
{
    background-color: #F8B6C9;
    padding:5px;
    width: 950px;
}
.textwrap
{
    float: right;
    margin: 10px;
}
.checkedout
{
    font-weight:bold;
    color: #C40D42;
}
```

5. Run the application. Ensure that you are on the home page. Click one of the Full Details links. You should get a page similar to the one shown in Figure 9-52.

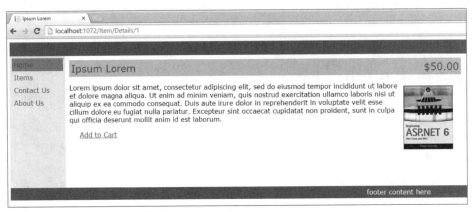

FIGURE 9-52: Details page for an item

How It Works

In this activity you added a new, simple action to the `ItemController` that will retrieve the specified item from the database and provide it to the view. Because you used the `FirstOrDefault` method when you retrieved the item, no exception is thrown, which would have been the case if you used the

`Find` or `First` methods, because both of those methods expect that the item you are requesting exists. However, this does mean that there is a chance your view will be provided a null model.

This possibility is why the first thing that happens in the view (after defining the type of the model) is a check to determine whether the item is null. If the value passed in does not exist within the database, then a simple page notifies the user about this issue, as shown in Figure 9-53.

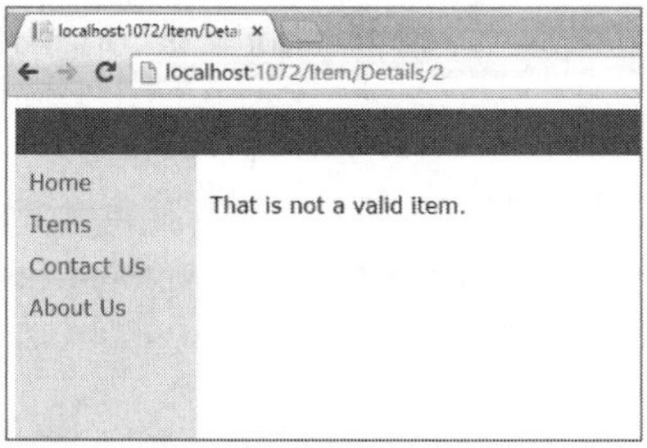

FIGURE 9-53: Details page when an item does not exist

Once you know that you are working with a valid model, you then set the tab display to the name of the item and create the rest of the display.

There are only a few more pieces of logic in this view code. The first is determining whether an image was assigned to the item by checking the `Picture` property to confirm that it is not null or whitespace. The second check determines whether the item is available. If it is, the Add to Cart link is displayed; if the item is not available, a line of text is displayed indicating when the item will be available. Figure 9-54 shows what the page would look like if there were no image for the item and it were not available.

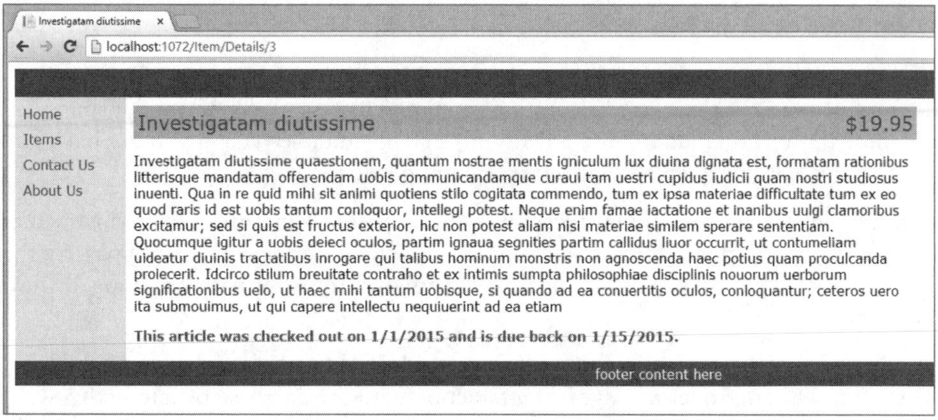

FIGURE 9-54: Details page when an item is not available

While creating a details page in ASP.NET MVC may take more work, it makes up for that by using Razor syntax that allows the mixture of code and markup. This enables you to put view logic into the system to easily make decisions and show content as desired.

SUMMARY

A lot of new information was introduced in this chapter, including new software applications, new Visual Studio windows, new Web Forms server controls, and new .NET concepts. As part of this, you started to wire different parts of your application together, and you now have the ability to persist information in a database.

The use of databases in a web application is important, and for this web application it is critical. You installed Microsoft SQL Server Express, a free and functional version of Microsoft's flagship database system SQL Server, to act as your local database during the development process.

You accessed the database in three different ways: SQL Server Management Studio, an external program, and two new Visual Studio windows, SQL Server Object Explorer and Server Explorer. Each of these tools enables you to view information in the database and ensure that the information you expect to be present is being persisted and displayed successfully.

Although there are various tools the developer can use to access the information in the database, this project is taking an Entity Framework code first approach, which enables you to write the various class files needed by the application. This communication is managed through the DbContext file by adding virtual DbSets of each model class that you want persisted. Those DbSets then become available on the context file to be accessed as if they were typical lists, using all the same operators and Lambda expressions.

When running the context for the first time it will create all the tables to support the models that have been added to the context. Each change to a model after that period, however, requires that you run a database migration. These migrations, run in the NuGet Package Manager Console, require the developer to name the migration and then run the update. This enables each set of incremental changes to be applied to a database based on its current state, which is tracked in a database table that was created when the first set of tables were created.

DetailsView and GridView are data-specific server controls that are available in ASP.NET Web Forms. The DetailsView enables you to determine what information to display, and it supports the capability to show this information in both a read-only and an editable version without having to do a lot of coding support; it pretty much supports it straight out of the box.

The GridView does much the same thing, except it displays a list of items and allows you to edit or delete them one at a time. The GridView communicates directly with the database, bypassing the Entity Framework, but it gives you almost complete control over the information contained within that database table.

ASP.NET MVC supports the interaction between pages and database differently from the way that Web Forms do. The controller manages all interaction with the database by interacting with the DbContext. It can select multiple items or a single item as needed, and then gives this information to the view as the model. The view can then use a combination of code and markup to build out the final HTML that's be returned to the user. When working with the MVC approach, rather than worry about ensuring that controls are configured correctly, you can instead focus on ensuring that the display is what you wanted. The capability to interact with the model's properties enables a lot of decision-making to happen in the view in order to support this customization of the view's output.

You'll see a lot more interaction with the database going forward in the other chapters; this was just an introduction to the possibilities for managing this interaction. There are slightly different ways to manage this, as demonstrated in the rest of the chapters, but all of it is based on what was covered in this chapter.

EXERCISES

1. From what you know about code first migration (in the Entity Framework), what kind of information do you think is contained within the __MigrationHistory table?

2. What does attribute routing enable you to do that the template approach does not?

3. Why do the code examples that are interacting with the database have the following line? What benefit does it offer?

```
using (RentMyWroxContext context = new RentMyWroxContext())
```

▶ **WHAT YOU LEARNED IN THIS CHAPTER**

add-migration	The add-migration command runs in the NuGet Package Console and has the Entity Framework create a new migration package—basically a new script added to the Migrations folder that manages changes to the database based on model changes in the code. When you run the add-migration command you have to pass in the name of migration package. This should be as unique as possible to ensure that there is no confusion with historical migrations.
Code First	Code first is an Entity Framework approach whereby the developer writes code rather than interacts with the database. The Entity Framework then builds out the database tables based on the relationships built within the code classes.
Connection String	The connection string is stored in the web.config file and contains all of the necessary information describing how to log in to the database so that the application can successfully interact with the data.
Data First	Data first is an Entity Framework approach whereby the developer creates the database structure first and then relies on the Entity Framework to create the models that will be used in the application.
DbContext	The DbContext is the brains behind the communication between the application and the database. An application creates a context class that inherits from the DbContext class and then adds all the items that need to be retained in that inheriting class. Once the items have been added to the context with the appropriate type, DbSet, the context enables the developer to interact with these properties as if they were the database tables, allowing collection operations that go directly to the database.
DetailsView	An ASP.NET Web Forms server control that is designed to view and maintain a single item
Entity Framework	A .NET set of functionality that abstracts communication with a database. It acts as an object-to-relational database mapping system and handles a lot of the mapping of a database field to an object property behind the scenes. It also supports many other aspects of database interaction, including database migration and validation.
GridView	The GridView is an ASP.NET Web Forms server control that manages the display of a list of information in a grid, much like the presentation of a spreadsheet. It provides more than that, however, by providing built-in support for updating and deleting information directly from the database in conjunction with the SQLDataSource.

RDBMS	RDBMS stands for relational database management system and refers to a persistence approach whereby like entities are grouped together into a single table. Any connections these entities have with other entities are defined through relationships.
Server Explorer	A Visual Studio window that enables the developer to access different items, including Windows Server and SQL Servers. It supports a lot of drag-and-drop functionality when working with Web Form markup pages.
SQL	SQL, which stands for Structured Query Language, is used to communicate directly with a database. The Entity Framework abstracts out the developer's need to interact with SQL, but using the GridView and the SQLDataSource exposes some simple SQL to the developer because it is used to define the relationship between the control and the database.
`SQLDataSource`	An ASP.NET Web Forms server control that acts as the intermediary between a data control and the database. It enables you to define the fields that are affected by using parameters that are mapped to placeholders in the SQL statements.
SQL Server Express	A free version of Microsoft SQL Server for use in development and learning environments. It is the RDBMS that handles all the persistence from both the Entity Framework and SQLDataSources.
SQL Server Management Studio	A user interface to SQL Server. It enables you to visually create, modify, and delete database objects, including databases, as well as any specific data stored within the database itself.
SQL Server Object Explorer	A Visual Studio window that is designed to help you interact directly with a SQL Server instance.
`update-database`	This command, when run in the NuGet Package Manager Console window, compares the version of the database to the version of the code. If there are any differences, it then runs the necessary migration scripts from the Migrations directory.

Working with Data—Advanced Topics

WHAT YOU WILL LEARN IN THIS CHAPTER:

- ➤ Integrating pagination and sorting into an application
- ➤ Different approaches to inserting and updating data
- ➤ Non-Entity-Framework approaches to database access
- ➤ Caching in a web application
- ➤ Practical advice about using databases in web applications

CODE DOWNLOADS FOR THIS CHAPTER:

The wrox.com code downloads for this chapter are found at www.wrox.com/go/
beginningaspnetforvisualstudio on the Download Code tab. The code is in the chapter
10 download and individually named according to the names throughout the chapter.

You learned a lot of information about databases in the last chapter, including how to set them
up and interact with them. This chapter takes a deeper dive into the process of interacting
with the database, including connecting the pages that you created in earlier chapters.

Two of the more important usability items when looking at a list of information are sorting and
pagination. Sorting enables users to see items in their preferred order rather than in a database-
defined order, while pagination is the capability to break long lists of information into sets of
defined size, or items on a page as pagination is the breaking of a data list into small pages of
data. Using pagination enables the user to work with smaller sets of information at one time,
providing both a reprieve from the intimidation of an extremely long list as well as faster performance resulting from transferring and rendering smaller sets of information.

The last chapter served as an introduction to working with Entity Framework code first and
hiding the actual database behind the code. In this chapter, you will have the opportunity to

peek through the curtain a bit more and work a little closer to the database so that you can take better advantage of some of the powerful features provided by the database server.

Just as knowing how to interact with the database is a useful skill, so is knowing when not to interact with the database. Caching provides an opportunity to make decisions about what information should be delivered to a user straight from the database or from a cache where the data was already retrieved once and then stored in memory for a certain period. This means that cache hits are more performant because there is no need to make a call to the web server and/or a database unless a certain amount of time has passed.

SORTING AND PAGINATION

Whenever you are working with a list that contains more than a dozen or so items, you should always consider a few things. The first is sorting, putting the items in the list in a particular order. This is important to all lists containing more than a few items because it provides immediate context to the information being displayed, enabling users to readily understand it. Consider the list of items that you created in the last chapter. Because it wasn't sorted, users have no way to quickly identify what they want. This means they will be forced to examine every item to see if it is what they are looking for. Alphabetizing the list, however, enables users to skip through it to find what they want; if, for example, the user is looking for a rake, it is a simple matter of jumping to items that start with an "R." Clearly, finding an item is much more difficult without any obvious sorting.

Not only should you have a pre-defined sorting on each list, you should consider whether it makes sense to offer users the capability to control how they want items sorted. One of the most common areas where users have control is over the capability to sort in descending order, or reverse-alphabetical order. Using the same example, if users are searching for a rake, it would be useful to provide a clickable button that enables the user to have to scroll through only the eight or so letters that precede R (if going in reverse order) before they get to the one item they care about, saving them time and making their user experience more positive.

The same rules can apply to pagination. An 80-item list can be intimidating to work with, but four 20-item lists are much less daunting. It also enables each database call to return less information, so less information needs to be passed over the network, and less information has to be interpreted by the browser on the client side. If users have the capability to sort based on their needs, then adding paging can help them find their information even faster.

Handling pagination and sorting is different between Web Form server controls and MVC approaches. Many Web Form controls allow sorting and pagination to be performed directly in the control.

Sorting and Pagination in Web Form Server Controls

This section first examines sorting in a `GridView`. When you dragged the control into the markup there was really nothing that you had to do after that before it was simply working. Setting up pagination is almost as easy, as there are attributes in the control that handle the management of this functionality for you. Table 10-1 lists and describes these attributes.

TABLE 10-1: GridView Pagination and Sorting Attributes

ATTRIBUTE	DESCRIPTION
`AllowCustomPaging`	Normally, every row in the data source is read every time the `GridView` control moves to a different page. This can consume a lot of resources when the total number of items in the data source is very large. Custom paging enables you to read just the items you need for a single page from the data source. Using `AllowCustomPaging` means you need to handle the `PageIndexChanging` event. Handling the `PageIndexChanging` event will give you the information on the current page and the expected page count where you can limit the amount of data brought in from the database rather than going through every item.
`AllowPaging`	This is a Boolean value that tells the control to turn paging on. When paging is enabled, all of the other paging properties become available.
`AllowSorting`	This is a Boolean value that lets the control know that sorting is available. When sorting is enabled, all columns become sortable unless otherwise turned off in the column. When used in combination with pagination, this approach ensures that sorting is maintained across postbacks so that when you are performing sorting you are sorting each page correctly.
`EnableSortingAndPagingCallbacks`	When this property is set to true, a service is called on the client to perform sorting and paging operations, which eliminates the need to post back to the server.
`PagerSettings-FirstPageText`	When the `Mode` property is set to the `NextPreviousFirstLast` or `NumericFirstLast` value, use the `FirstPageText` property to specify the text to display for the first-page button.
`PagerSettings-LastPageText`	When the `Mode` property is set to the `NextPreviousFirstLast` or `NumericFirstLast` value, use the `LastPageText` property to specify the text to display for the last-page button.

continues

TABLE 10-1 *(continued)*

ATTRIBUTE	DESCRIPTION
PagerSettings-Mode	Four different modes are built into the GridView pagination, each of which sets up a different display for the pagination structure: **NextPrevious:** Previous-page and next-page buttons **NextPreviousFirstLast:** Previous-page, next-page, first-page, and last-page buttons **Numeric:** Numbered link buttons to access pages directly **NumericFirstLast:** Numbered and first-link and last-link buttons
PagerSettings-PageButtonCount	Manages the number of page buttons to display in the pager when the Mode property is set to the Numeric or NumericFirstLast value. The default value is 10.
PagerSettings-Position	Determines where the pagination should be located. There are three options: Top, Bottom, and TopAndBottom. TopAndBottom duplicates the pagination both above and below the visible list.
PagerSettings-Visible	Specifies whether or not the pagination links are visible and available for use
PageSize	Specifies the number of items that will be displayed on each page

Looking through the items in Table 10-1 shows a discrepancy between the amount of configuration needed for sorting versus pagination. That is because the standard behavior for sorting within a GridView is very straightforward. With sorting enabled, the column header becomes a clickable link that will sort based on that column. The first click sorts in ascending order, while clicking it again sorts the data results by that column in descending order.

One important consideration is that sorting occurs not only across the items displayed on the screen, but across the entire result set, returning you to the first page of the list with each sort. In addition, if you simply turn sorting on in the GridView, then every visible column becomes sortable. That might be overkill for your application, so you also have the capability when you bind the column/field to disable sorting for that particular column. There is no property such as "EnableSorting" on the bound field, but there is an attribute SortExpression.

Typically, SortExpression is set like

```
<asp:BoundField DataField="Name" HeaderText="Name" SortExpression="Name" />
```

where the SortExpression defines the field name in the data source on which the GridView will be sorted. By completely removing that attribute, you remove that column from the list of sortable columns.

In the following activity, you add pagination and sorting to the administrative list of items that you created in the last chapter.

TRY IT OUT Styling

In this activity you will be enhancing the usability and readability of the list of rentable items that are presented within the administrative section of the demo application. This list will hold all the items that you have available for rent, so in a real-world scenario that would hopefully be a list with thousands of different objects.

1. Ensure that Visual Studio is running and that you have opened your RentMyWrox solution. Open the Admin\ItemList.aspx page.

2. Change the GridView control configuration to the following (new or changed items are highlighted):

```
<asp:GridView ID="GridView1" OnSelectedIndexChanged="GridView1_SelectedIndexChanged"
        runat="server" AutoGenerateColumns="False" DataKeyNames="Id"
        DataSourceID="SqlDataSource1"
    AllowPaging="True" AllowSorting="True" PageSize="5"
    PagerSettings-Mode="NumericFirstLast" PagerSettings-Visible="true"
    PagerSettings-Position="TopAndBottom" PagerSettings-PageButtonCount="3"
    EmptyDataText="There are no data records to display.">
    <Columns>
        <asp:CommandField ShowDeleteButton="True" ShowEditButton="True"
            ShowSelectButton="True" ItemStyle-HorizontalAlign="Center"
            DeleteText="Delete<br/>"  SelectText="Full_Edit<br/>"
            EditText="Quick_Edit<br/>" />
        <asp:BoundField DataField="Id" HeaderText="Id" ReadOnly="True"
            SortExpression="Id" />
        <asp:BoundField DataField="Name" HeaderText="Name" SortExpression="Name" />
        <asp:BoundField DataField="Description" HeaderText="Description" />
        <asp:BoundField DataField="ItemNumber" HeaderText="Item Number"
            SortExpression="ItemNumber" />
        <asp:BoundField DataField="Picture" HeaderText="Picture" />
        <asp:BoundField DataField="Cost" HeaderText="Cost" SortExpression="Cost" />
        <asp:BoundField DataField="CheckedOut" HeaderText="Checked Out"
            SortExpression="CheckedOut" />
        <asp:BoundField DataField="DueBack" HeaderText="Due Back"
            SortExpression="DueBack" />
        <asp:BoundField DataField="DateAcquired" HeaderText="Date Acquired"
            SortExpression="DateAcquired" />
        <asp:CheckBoxField DataField="IsAvailable" HeaderText="Is Available"
            SortExpression="IsAvailable" />
    </Columns>
</asp:GridView>
```

3. Run the application. You should see a screen similar to what is shown in Figure 10-1.

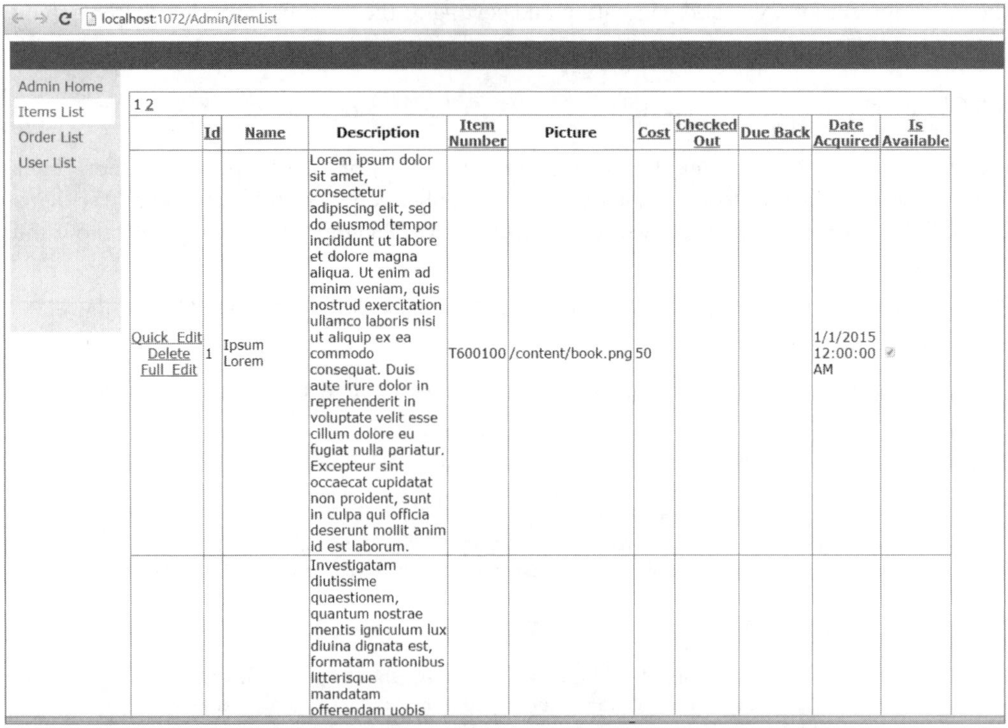

FIGURE 10-1: GridView with pagination and sorting

4. Click several column headers such as "Name" and "Description" and notice the sorting change. Do the same by clicking to other pages.

How It Works

ASP.NET Web Form server controls were designed to help developers write more efficient code, and adding pagination and sorting to a control demonstrates how this relatively complex behavior can be simply implemented. The only work you had to do was add some sorting and pagination-specific configuration attributes and then remove some SortExpression attributes anywhere you didn't need the capability to sort, such as the Picture URL column.

The change that you just made added five new attributes to the GridView:

```
PagerSettings-Visible="true"
PagerSettings-Position="TopAndBottom"
PageSize="5"
PagerSettings-Mode="NumericFirstLast"
PagerSettings-PageButtonCount="3"
```

The first attribute, PagerSettings-Visible, made all the pagination management links visible so that you could move between pages. Removing this attribute, or setting it to false, would remove all the pagination links, as shown in Figure 10-2.

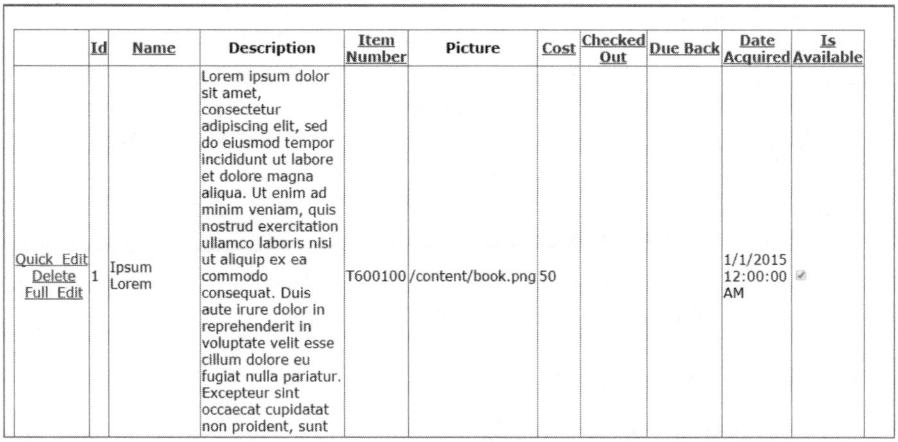

	Id	Name	Description	Item Number	Picture	Cost	Checked Out	Due Back	Date Acquired	Is Available
Quick Edit Delete Full Edit	1	Ipsum Lorem	Lorem ipsum dolor sit amet, consectetur adipiscing elit, sed do eiusmod tempor incididunt ut labore et dolore magna aliqua. Ut enim ad minim veniam, quis nostrud exercitation ullamco laboris nisi ut aliquip ex ea commodo consequat. Duis aute irure dolor in reprehenderit in voluptate velit esse cillum dolore eu fugiat nulla pariatur. Excepteur sint occaecat cupidatat non proident, sunt	T600100	/content/book.png	50			1/1/2015 12:00:00 AM	☑

FIGURE 10-2: GridView with pagination turned off

The next attribute of interest is PagerSettings-Position. This attribute enables you to specify whether pagination is visible at the top of the grid, below the grid, or both. When you are looking at a page that has any scrolling, it typically makes sense to have the links both above and below so that users don't have to scroll up or down as far. Next is the PageSize attribute, which specifies the number of items to be displayed in each page, in this case five. This means, for example, that if there were six items in the list, there would be two pages, the first with five items and the second with one item.

As described in Table 10-1, the PagerSettings-Mode attribute determines how the menu will be displayed. In the case of this selected attribute, NumericFirstLast, the GridView displays a First and Last link (usually as << or >>), as well as a list of page numbers from which users can select to go to a specific page. The number of page numbers displayed is defined by the next attribute, PagerSettings-PageButtonCount, which specifies how many numbers are displayed. Table 10-2 shows how the links would be built in a 30-item list using the preceding settings.

TABLE 10-2: Displaying Links by Page

PAGE #	DISPLAY	EXPLANATION
1	1 2 3 ... >>	The ... takes you to Page 4, while the >> takes you to Page 6
2	1 2 3 ... >>	The ... takes you to Page 4, while the >> takes you to Page 6
3	1 2 3 ... >>	The ... takes you to Page 4, while the >> takes you to Page 6
4	<< ... 4 5 6	The ... takes you to Page 3, while the << takes you to Page 1
5	<< ... 4 5 6	The ... takes you to Page 3, while the << takes you to Page 1
6	<< ... 4 5 6	The ... takes you to Page 3, while the << takes you to Page 1

Once pagination configuration was complete, you then did some customization of sorting. When the control was created, the SortExpression for each column was set to the same column to which the field was bound. You removed this attribute from several of the columns, thus rendering those columns unsortable. The `SortExpression` can also be used when creating and working with custom sorting methods, but in this simple scenario they instead refer to the column used during the default sorting scenario. While all of these columns refer to themselves in the `SortExpression`, if the `SortExpression` exists, they could also refer to a different column if desired. This would mean that the user clicks on one column header but the results are instead sorted by another column value.

Now that you have introduced sorting and pagination into an ASP.NET Web Forms `GridView` control, you need to add sorting and pagination to a list in an MVC view.

Sorting and Pagination in MVC Lists

Whereas ASP.NET Web Form server controls handle a lot of sorting and pagination for you, in ASP .NET you generally have to manage all that work yourself. Typically you have to provide information to the view upon rendering so it knows how to build the pagination links and then provides that same information back to the controller upon submission so that the controller then knows how to build the next page.

The items that you generally need on the client side include the following:

- ➤ Current page number
- ➤ Count of items per page
- ➤ Total number of items in a list
- ➤ Sorting method, if any

Items that you generally need on the server are as follows:

- ➤ Desired page number
- ➤ Count of items per page
- ➤ Sorting method, if any

With each of those items you will be able to display information to users about where they are in reference to the complete list. This communication is one of the things handled by an ASP.NET server control. Also handled by the control is processing of the information that you have to handle manually. The next Try It Out demonstrates the processing that you need to add on both the client side and the server side to manage pagination and sorting.

TRY IT OUT Add Pagination and Sorting to MVC

In this activity, you update the home page of your demo application to support both pagination and sorting. It requires changes to the controller and the view, as well as the addition of several more simple styles.

1. Ensure that Visual Studio is running and that you have opened your RentMyWrox solution. Open the `Controller\ItemController.cs` file.

2. Add the following to the method signature of the `Index` method. When completed it should look like what is shown in Figure10-3.

```
int pageNumber = 1, int pageQty = 5, string sortExp = "name_asc"
```

```
[Route("")]
public ActionResult Index(int pageNumber = 1, int pageQty = 5, string sortExp = "name_asc")
{
```

FIGURE 10-3: New Index method signature

3. Update the contents of this method to the following code. It should look like Figure 10-4 when completed.

```
using (RentMyWroxContext context = new RentMyWroxContext())
{
    // set most of the items needed on the client-side
    ViewBag.PageSize = pageQty;
    ViewBag.PageNumber = pageNumber;
    ViewBag.SortExpression = sortExp;

    var items = from i in context.Items
                    where i.IsAvailable
                    select i;

    // setting this here to get the count of the filtered list
    ViewBag.ItemCount = items.Count();

    switch(sortExp)
    {
        case "name_asc":
            items = items.OrderBy(i => i.Name);
            break;
        case "name_desc":
            items = items.OrderByDescending(i => i.Name);
            break;
        case "cost_asc":
            items = items.OrderBy(i => i.Cost);
            break;
        case "cost_desc":
            items = items.OrderByDescending(i => i.Cost);
            break;
    }

    items = items.Skip((pageNumber - 1) * pageQty).Take(pageQty);
    return View(items.ToList());
}
```

```
[Route("")]
public ActionResult Index(int pageNumber = 1, int pageQty = 5, string sortExp = "name_asc")
{
    using (RentMyWroxContext context = new RentMyWroxContext())
    {
        // set most of the items needed on the client-side
        ViewBag.PageSize = pageQty;
        ViewBag.PageNumber = pageNumber;
        ViewBag.SortExpression = sortExp;

        var items = from i in context.Items
                        where i.IsAvailable
                        select i;

        // setting this here to get the count of the filtered list
        ViewBag.ItemCount = items.Count();

        switch(sortExp)
        {
            case "name_asc":
                items = items.OrderBy(i => i.Name);
                break;
            case "name_desc":
                items = items.OrderByDescending(i => i.Name);
                break;
            case "cost_asc":
                items = items.OrderBy(i => i.Cost);
                break;
            case "cost_desc":
                items = items.OrderByDescending(i => i.Cost);
                break;
        }

        items = items.Skip((pageNumber - 1) * pageQty).Take(pageQty);
        return View(items.ToList());
    }
}
```

FIGURE 10-4: New Index method

4. Open the `Views\Item\Index.cshtml` file. Update the initial bracketed code section to the following. It should look like Figure 10-5 when completed.

```
@{
    const string selectedText = "selected";
    ViewBag.Title = "Index";
    int itemCount = ViewBag.ItemCount;
    int pageSize = ViewBag.PageSize;
    int pageNumber = ViewBag.PageNumber;
    int fullPageCount = (itemCount + pageSize - 1) / pageSize;
    string sortExp = ViewBag.SortExpression;
}
```

```
@model IEnumerable<RentMyWrox.Models.Item>

@{
    const string selectedText = "selected";
    ViewBag.Title = "Index";
    int itemCount = ViewBag.ItemCount;
    int pageSize = ViewBag.PageSize;
    int pageNumber = ViewBag.PageNumber;
    int fullPageCount = (itemCount + pageSize - 1) / pageSize;
    string sortExp = ViewBag.SortExpression;
}
```

FIGURE 10-5: New view code

5. In this same file, add the following code below the bracketed section and above the loop. It should look like Figure 10-6.

```
<form>
    <div>
        <div class="paginationline">
            <span class="leftside">
                Sort by:
                <select name="sortExp"
                    onchange='if(this.value !="@sortExp"){ this.form.submit(); }'>
                    <option value="name_asc"
                            @if (sortExp == "name_asc") { @selectedText }>
                     Name
                    </option>
                    <option value="name_desc"
                            @if (sortExp == "name_desc") { @selectedText }>
                        Name (Z to A)
                    </option>
                    <option value="cost_asc"
                            @if (sortExp == "cost_asc") { @selectedText }>
                        Price
                    </option>
                    <option value="cost_desc"
                            @if (sortExp == "cost_desc") { @selectedText }>
                        Price (high to low)
                    </option>
                </select>
            </span>
            <span class="rightside">
                @if (pageNumber > 1) // means there are additional pages backwards
                {
                    <a href="?pageNumber=@(pageNumber - 1)&pageQty=@pageSize
                            &sortExp=@sortExp">
                        Previous Page
                    </a>
                }

                You are currently on Page @pageNumber of @fullPageCount

                @if (fullPageCount > pageNumber) //means that there are pages forward
                {
                    <a href="?pageNumber=@(pageNumber + 1)&pageQty=@pageSize
                            &sortExp=@sortExp">
                        Next Page
                    </a>
                }
            </span>
        </div>
    </div>
</form>
<br />
```

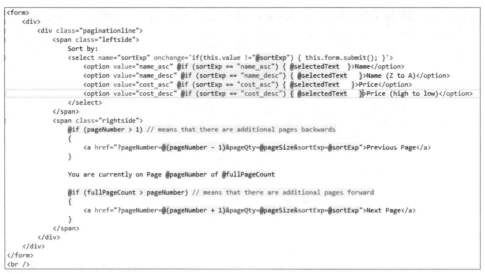

```
<form>
    <div>
        <div class="paginationline">
            <span class="leftside">
                Sort by:
                <select name="sortExp" onchange='if(this.value !="@sortExp") { this.form.submit(); }'>
                    <option value="name_asc" @if (sortExp == "name_asc") { @selectedText }>Name</option>
                    <option value="name_desc" @if (sortExp == "name_desc") { @selectedText }>Name (Z to A)</option>
                    <option value="cost_asc" @if (sortExp == "cost_asc") { @selectedText }>Price</option>
                    <option value="cost_desc" @if (sortExp == "cost_desc") { @selectedText }>Price (high to low)</option>
                </select>
            </span>
            <span class="rightside">
                @if (pageNumber > 1) // means that there are additional pages backwards
                {
                    <a href="?pageNumber=@(pageNumber - 1)&pageQty=@pageSize&sortExp=@sortExp">Previous Page</a>
                }

                You are currently on Page @pageNumber of @fullPageCount

                @if (fullPageCount > pageNumber) // means that there are additional pages forward
                {
                    <a href="?pageNumber=@(pageNumber + 1)&pageQty=@pageSize&sortExp=@sortExp">Next Page</a>
                }
            </span>
        </div>
    </div>
</form>
<br />
```

FIGURE 10-6: New view pagination code

6. Open `Content\RentMyWrox.css` and add the following selectors at the end of the file:

```
.paginationline
{
    font-size:medium;
}

.leftside
{
    text-align:left;
}

.rightside
{
    margin-left: 100px;
    text-align:right;
}
```

7. Before going any further, ensure that you have at least 6 items loaded into your application.

8. Run the application. You should get a screen similar to the one shown in Figure 10-7. Change the dropdown to see the sort working. Click through the pages if you have enough information in your system to have multiple pages.

How It Works

Converting an MVC list to support pagination and sorting is more complicated than doing the same with an ASP.NET Web Forms server control, but you were able to take advantage of some built-in features to make the conversion process easier. The first of these is the capability to have the system parse items that are submitted in the form's request values into the parameters of the action method.

FIGURE 10-7: Running the paginated list

In the first step you added three new parameters to the method. Because of this mapping capability, both `http://localhost:port/?sortExp=name_asc` and a request in which a form key/value pair was "sortExp=name_asc" would each have its value mapped to the action method parameter named "sortExp". As long as the variable names are the same, the system understands and maps the appropriate values. When there is a conflict (such as the same variable in both the query string and the request form values), the item in the query string will win.

This concept is important because of how the view was changed to send pagination and sorting information back to the controller. Before going into more detail in the controller, consider how the UI was changed to take advantage of this capacity. There are two different approaches to informing the server that a change in page or sort order was requested: a dropdown list of possible sorting options, and hyperlinks to the page being requested. First, look closer at the dropdown list, whose code has been copied here:

```
<select name="sortExp" onchange='if(this.value !="@sortExp"){ this.form.submit(); }'>
    <option value="name_asc" @if (sortExp == "name_asc") { @selectedText }>
        Name
    </option>
```

```
        <option value="name_desc" @if (sortExp == "name_desc") { @selectedText }>
            Name (Z to A)
        </option>
        <option value="cost_asc" @if (sortExp == "cost_asc") { @selectedText }>
            Price
        </option>
        <option value="cost_desc" @if (sortExp == "cost_desc") { @selectedText }>
            Price (high to low)
        </option>
    </select>
```

Note a few things when considering the `<select>` definition itself. First, the name attribute is `sortExp`. This is important because there is a method parameter named `sortExp` as well, so the value selected in this dropdown will be the value that is mapped to that particular parameter in the action. It is important that these two names are the same so that the value can be properly mapped.

The next item to consider is the `onchange` event. Although you haven't yet covered JavaScript, the line of code within the `onchange` single quotes causes the browser to check the value of the selected item and if it is not the same as the value returned from the controller to the view, the system knows that the user has requested a change in sorting and the browser will immediately submit the form. However, when the form is submitted the only value returned to the controller is the `sortExp` value in the Request's form value collection. Because the new action parameters all were assigned a default value when defined in the method signature, if the value is not passed into the method then the default value is substituted.

The dropdown list is coded to automatically submit the form whenever the selected value is changed to a new value, so the next thing to analyze is the information that will be sent back to the controller. Within the definition of each `option` element is the `value` attribute, which defines the value that is sent back to the server. In the case of the first item, this value is `"name_asc"`, which means that the sort should be by the `Name` property in ascending alphabetical order.

The `@if (sortExp == "name_asc") { @selectedText }` part of the element definition determines whether the current option's value is the same as what was returned from the controller in the `ViewBag.SortExpression` field. If so, then a constant value named `selectedText` that was defined earlier in the page is written out. Each of the options has this same logic, its value compared to the value sent back from the controller, and a successful comparison results in "selected" written out during processing. The user's browser would then cause that item to be selected in the dropdown list. This means that as the sorting expression is changed by the user, the dropdown list continues to display the correct sorting type—the one that represents the result set that the user is viewing. The `select` element is rendered into the following HTML code:

```
    <select name="sortExp"
            onchange='if(this.value !="name_asc") { this.form.submit(); }'>
        <option value="name_asc" selected>Name</option>
        <option value="name_desc" >Name (Z to A)</option>
        <option value="cost_asc" >Price</option>
        <option value="cost_desc" >Price (high to low)</option>
    </select>
```

Notice how the default sorting value is the one that has "selected" as part of the option element definition.

You may have noticed that there is nothing within the form that you entered in Step 4 that sets the other values that were added to the parameter list of the Index action. That is OK, because the expected behavior is for the user to always be brought back to the first page of the result set whenever the sorting changes, so the default values set during parameter creation are the correct values. You go back to the first page because once you change the sort, you no longer have any context about the data that was on the page where you changed the sorting. They could easily be scattered across every page in the list; it just becomes more consistent and clear to send the user back to the first page based on their new sort order.

The other new functionality in the view is related to pagination. There are three UI items in the approach taken in this screen: going to the previous page, going to the next page, and displaying where the user is in the entire list. The code section that does this work is displayed here:

```
<span class="rightside">
    @if (pageNumber > 1) // means that there are additional pages backwards
    {
        <a href="?pageNumber=@(pageNumber - 1)&pageQty=@pageSize&sortExp=@sortExp">
            Previous Page
        </a>
    }

    You are currently on Page @pageNumber of @fullPageCount

    @if (fullPageCount > pageNumber) // means there are additional pages forward
    {
        <a href="?pageNumber=@(pageNumber + 1)&pageQty=@pageSize&sortExp=@sortExp">
            Next Page
        </a>
    }
</span>
```

The first thing to notice is that the links to go to the previous or next page are only displayed when a page fits that criteria: The Previous Page link is displayed only when the user is on the second or greater page. Similarly, the Next Page link is displayed only when the user is not yet on the last page of the list. The full page count was calculated using the following formula:

```
int fullPageCount = (itemCount + pageSize - 1) / pageSize;
```

This formula ensures that the proper number of pages is calculated because it always accounts for the remainder, whether it is 0 or pageSize - 1. It is important to recognize the calculation that is going on with the pageNumber in the link, as the previous link does not pass the current page that the user is on, but rather passes the current page number – 1; or the actual page that would be displayed. The same type of calculation is used for the next page link by asking for the current page number + 1.

The last part of this code reflects where the user is in the list by displaying a string that indicates both the current page and the total number of pages.

The controller and action were updated to handle all this additional information being returned by adding the appropriate parameters that will be set as needed. Getting the information from the user is handled by the parameters; but if you recall from the material about the UI, it is expecting some information from the controller as well. The section of code is shown here:

```
ViewBag.PageSize = pageQty;
ViewBag.PageNumber = pageNumber;
ViewBag.SortExpression = sortExp;
```

In this snippet you are adding some values to the `ViewBag`. You might recall that the `ViewBag` can act as a data transfer mechanism between the controller and the view to hold and pass information that may not make sense as part of the model but is still needed to give the user a full experience.

Now that much of the applicable information has been sent to the user, the action gets ready to take advantage of this same information to determine which items need to be returned to the user in the model. However, before it does this you see it making the communication with the database and retrieving the set of items after applying a filter. The approach that was taken here though was different from any other list work that you have used so far in this book. The code is shown here:

```
var items = from i in context.Items
                where i.IsAvailable
                select i;
```

Logically this code snippet is the same as using the dot notation filter that you are already familiar with: `context.Items.Where(x => x.IsAvailable)`. The preceding approach is in Language Integrated Query (LINQ), a language designed to work with sets of objects just as SQL works with tables in a database. LINQ is a very powerful feature that you will use more of as we progress through the rest of the book. The main advantage that it has over dot notation is that it is easier to read, especially with complicated queries that may span multiple different sources. This example uses only one collection, but LINQ easily supports joining multiple sets of objects in an intuitive fashion. The dot notation approach also offers this capability but it is handled in a much less readable fashion.

Three LINQ sets of keywords are being used: `from \ in`, `where`, and `select`. The `from` keyword defines the instance and the collection that provides the source data for the query. In this case it specifies that the query is against the Items collection in the `DbContext` and that each instance is accessible by using "i." You can think of the value after the `from` keyword as being equivalent to the value before the `=>` indicator in a Lambda statement.

The `where` keyword acts as a filter, just as when using dot notation. If you want to have multiple criteria, then you can use the standard and as well as or notations (& as well as |). The `select` keyword is slightly different from the dot notation approach in that it is always required when using LINQ. You can return either the complete object, as shown in the example, or parts of the object. When returning parts of an object, LINQ has the capability to create anonymous types, or read-only undefined types.

If you changed those lines of code to

```
var items2 = (from i in context.Items
                 where i.IsAvailable
                 select new
                     {
                         Id = i.Id,
                         Name = i.Name
                     }).ToList();
```

you would no longer get a collection of `Item` objects, but instead a list of anonymously typed objects that have two properties, `Id` and `Name`. Unfortunately, it is more complicated to pass anonymous types to a view so you won't generally see this approach as a way to communicate with the UI; instead, you may see it in code where the results are not sent to the UI. Anonymous types are not used anywhere in our sample application but they provide a very flexible piece of functionality when working with collections.

Looking back at the controller code, after the initial filtered dataset is pulled from the database the last piece of miscellaneous information for the UI is captured: the count of items in the filtered list. It is important to ensure that you use the filtered list because these are the actual items that would be provided to the user—using the count of the database table would provide an inaccurate number.

The only work left to do in the action is to perform the sorting and get the page worth of content. There is always sorting that will happen—either the default name sorting or sorting as specified by the user. The appropriate sorting is selected through a switch statement that evaluates the selected search expression and performs the search.

The last step is getting the page worth of data. The code performing this work is shown here:

```
items = items.Skip((pageNumber - 1) * pageQty).Take(pageQty);
```

Two key steps are taken in this line. The first is the `Skip` method, which ignores items that are on pages prior to the requested page that will be displayed. The `-1` needs to be included to ensure that when users are on the first page the system won't skip any items. This means that when users are on the second page, the `Skip` method requires the application to go past "2 – 1"—or one page of items.

After the application has gone past, or skipped, the previous pages' worth of information, the `Take` method runs in order to add a specific number of records to the list: the number of items on a page. After this subset is narrowed down it is passed to view and used there as the model that fills the UI.

Although more coding is required when adding pagination and sorting to ASP.NET MVC lists than with ASP.NET Web Forms list server controls, it is not typically a complex requirement. You tend to have much more control over the output and how paging and sorting all interact.

UPDATING AND/OR INSERTING DATA

Now that you have a much stronger understanding of how to work with lists through your practice with pagination and sorting, it is time to spend some more time on updating and inserting data when using the Entity Framework. Chapter 9 touched briefly on persisting data in the database. In this section you learn more about that and updating other parts of the application that have not yet been updated.

Saving new data when using the Entity Framework is as simple as adding the new item to the `DbContext` collection and running the `DbContext.SaveChanges` method; and as long as all the necessary properties are set in the object being saved, the attempt to save will be successful.

However, editing an item does not necessarily work the same way. You will not be able to add it to the collection, as it is already in the database; instead, you need to edit the existing item. In the old days that would have required you to manually map all the fields from the request, both query string and form body, to the applicable property in the model. It is no longer the dark days of programming, and ASP.NET has a wonderful method that was touched on in the last chapter named `TryUpdateModel`.

`TryUpdateModel` and its close sibling `UpdateModel` both map incoming values to properties with the same names. The general approach to using these is to instantiate an object of the type that you need (such as an `Item` or `UserDemographics`) and then pass that object into the method. The system will then go through all the properties on the object and try to find matching values in the data that was attached to the request. If there is a match, then the system tries to set the property. The difference between `UpdateModel` and `TryUpdateModel` is that the `UpdateModel` method throws an exception if it encounters a binding error, such as trying to set "red" to a decimal-typed price, whereas the `TryUpdateModel` method simply skips that binding, leaving that property value at its initial value.

In ASP.NET Web Forms there is a bit of a problem in using the `TryUpdateModel` approach across the board. That's because `TryUpdateModel` is designed to be used within data-bound server controls. If you are working on the supporting methods for a server control, then you will be able to perform the work without a problem. If not, such as in the instance where you created a data entry form by hand, then you have to do the mapping yourself, old-school style.

This means that when you are working in ASP.NET MVC, you have two different approaches to managing the values that are returned from the browser:

➤ The `TryUpdateModel` approach

➤ The straight model-binding approach that you used in Chapter 6 whereby you include a parameter of a specific type in the action method's signature and the system attempts to populate that parameter; basically running a `TryUpdateModel` on a just constructed object. You do not have this same capability to use model binding when using ASP.NET Web Forms.

Other than the capability to perform model binding in MVC, there are no differences between working with the model in either MVC or Web Forms. In this next Try It Out, you update some previously created items, both Web Forms and MVC, to persist the items that were created from the form.

TRY IT OUT   Connecting Pages to the Database

In this activity you finish up some of the forms that were left unfinished. These forms, the saving of the `UserDemographics` and the `Item` classes, were created in earlier chapters, but they were never connected to the database to save the newly created object.

1. Ensure that Visual Studio is running and that you have opened your RentMyWrox solution. Open the `UserDemographicsController` file.

2. Delete the method that is defined as `public ActionResult Details(int id)`.

3. Change your non-attributed `Create` method as shown here:

```
public ActionResult Create()
{
    using (RentMyWroxContext context = new RentMyWroxContext())
```

```
    {
        ViewBag.Hobbies = context.Hobbies.Where(x => x.IsActive)
                .OrderBy(x => x.Name).ToList();
    }
    return View("Manage", new UserDemographics());
}
```

4. Change your attributed Create method to the following:

```
[HttpPost]
public ActionResult Create(UserDemographics obj)
{
    try
    {
        using (RentMyWroxContext context = new RentMyWroxContext())
        {
            var ids = Request.Form.GetValues("HobbyIds");
            obj.Hobbies = context.Hobbies
                    .Where(x => ids.Contains(x.Id.ToString())).ToList();
            context.UserDemographics.Add(obj);
            context.SaveChanges();
            return RedirectToAction("Index");
        }
    }
    catch
    {
        return View();
    }
}
```

5. Change your non-attributed Edit method as follows:

```
public ActionResult Edit(int id)
{
    UserDemographics result = null;
    using (RentMyWroxContext context = new RentMyWroxContext())
    {
        ViewBag.Hobbies = context.Hobbies.Where(x => x.IsActive)
                .OrderBy(x => x.Name).ToList();
        result = context.UserDemographics.FirstOrDefault(x => x.Id == id);
    }
    return View("Manage", result);
}
```

6. Change your attributed Edit method to the following:

```
[HttpPost]
public ActionResult Edit(int id, FormCollection collection)
{
    try
    {
        using (RentMyWroxContext context = new RentMyWroxContext())
        {
            var item = context.UserDemographics.FirstOrDefault(x => x.Id == id);
            TryUpdateModel(item);
```

```
            context.SaveChanges();
            return RedirectToAction("Index");
            }
        }
        catch
        {
            return View();
        }
    }
}
```

7. Open the Manage view for UserDemographics. In the initial code section, change the definition of `hobbyList` to the following. It should look like Figure 10-8 when you are done.

```
List<RentMyWrox.Models.Hobby> hobbyList = ViewBag.Hobbies;
```

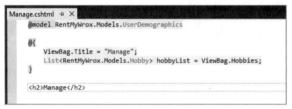

FIGURE 10-8: Initial change to the Manage view

8. While still in the Manage view, replace the current section that is managing the Hobbies with the following code. When completed it should look like Figure 10-9.

```
<div class="form-group">
    @Html.LabelFor(model => model.Hobbies,
        htmlAttributes: new { @class = "control-label col-md-2" })
    <div class="col-md-10">
        @foreach (var hobby in hobbyList)
        {
            string checkedText = Model.Hobbies.Any(x=>x.Id == hobby.Id)
            ? "checked" : string.Empty;
            <span>
                <input name="HobbyIds" value="@hobby.Id" type="checkbox" @checkedText />
                @hobby.Name
            </span>
        }
    </div>
</div>
```

8. Run the application and go to UserDemographics. You should see the list with any items that you entered into the database. Click the Create link.

9. Add a new UserDemographic and save. You should be sent back to the list screen, where you can see the data that you just entered.

10. Open your `Admin\ManageItem.aspx.cs` file. Add a new using statement, using `System.IO;`, to the list at the top of the page.

```
<div class="form-group">
    @Html.LabelFor(model => model.TotalNumberInHome, htmlAttributes: new { @class = "control-label col-md-2" })
    <div class="col-md-10">
        @Html.EditorFor(model => model.TotalNumberInHome, new { htmlAttributes = new { @class = "form-control" } })
        @Html.ValidationMessageFor(model => model.TotalNumberInHome, "", new { @class = "text-danger" })
    </div>
</div>
<div class="form-group">
    @Html.LabelFor(model => model.Hobbies, htmlAttributes: new { @class = "control-label col-md-2" })
    <div class="col-md-10">
        @foreach (var hobby in hobbyList)
        {
            string checkedText = Model.Hobbies.Any(x=>x.Id == hobby.Id) ? "checked" : string.Empty;
            <span>
                <input name="HobbyIds" value="@hobby.Id" type="checkbox" @checkedText />
                @hobby.Name
            </span>
        }
    </div>
</div>
```

FIGURE 10-9: Redoing the Manage view

11. Add a new property inside the partial class: `private int itemId;`. It should look like Figure 10-10 when completed.

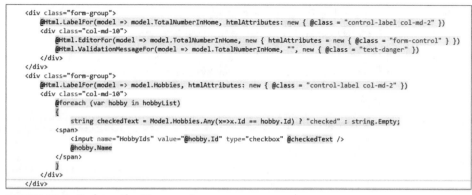

```
namespace RentMyWrox.Admin
{
    public partial class ManageItem : WebFormsBaseClass
    {
        private int itemId;

        protected void Page_Load(object sender, EventArgs e)
        {
```

FIGURE 10-10: New property in the code-behind

12. Update the `Page_Load` method as follows:

```
protected void Page_Load(object sender, EventArgs e)
{
    IList<string> segments = Request.GetFriendlyUrlSegments();
    itemId = 0;
    if (segments != null && segments.Count > 0)
    {
        int.TryParse(segments[0], out itemId);
    }

    if (!IsPostBack && itemId != 0)
    {
        using (RentMyWroxContext context = new RentMyWroxContext())
        {
            var item = context.Items.FirstOrDefault(x => x.Id == itemId);
            tbAcquiredDate.Text = item.DateAcquired.ToShortDateString();
            tbCost.Text = item.Cost.ToString();
            tbDescription.Text = item.Description;
            tbItemNumber.Text = item.ItemNumber;
            tbName.Text = item.Name;
        }
    }
}
```

13. Update the `SaveItem_Clicked` method as shown here:

```
protected void SaveItem_Clicked(object sender, EventArgs e)
{
    Item item;
    using (RentMyWroxContext context = new RentMyWroxContext())
    {
        if (itemId == 0)
        {
            item = new Item();
            UpdateItem(item);
            context.Items.Add(item);
        }
        else
        {
            item = context.Items.FirstOrDefault(x => x.Id == itemId);
            UpdateItem(item);
        }
        context.SaveChanges();
    }
    Response.Redirect("~/admin/ItemList");
}
```

14. Add the following new method to the file:

```
private void UpdateItem(Item item)
{
    double cost;
    double.TryParse(tbCost.Text, out cost);
    item.Cost = cost;

    DateTime acqDate = DateTime.Now;
    DateTime.TryParse(tbAcquiredDate.Text, out acqDate);
    item.DateAcquired = acqDate;

    item.Description = tbDescription.Text;
    item.Name = tbName.Text;
    item.ItemNumber = tbItemNumber.Text;
    item.IsAvailable = true;

    if (fuPicture.PostedFile != null && fuPicture.HasFile)
    {
        Guid newPrefix = Guid.NewGuid();
        string localDir = Path.Combine("ItemImages",
                newPrefix + "_" + fuPicture.FileName);
        string fullPath = Path.Combine(
                    HttpContext.Current.Request.PhysicalApplicationPath,
                    localDir);
        fuPicture.SaveAs(fullPath);
        item.Picture = "/" + localDir.Replace("\\", "/");
    }
}
```

15. Open your `Admin\ItemList.aspx` file and add the following lines just above the `GridView`. It should look like Figure 10-11 when completed.

```
<asp:HyperLink runat="server" Text="Add New Item" NavigateUrl="~/Admin/ManageItem" />
<br /><br />
```

FIGURE 10-11: Add New Item link in the Item List page

16. Add a new directory to your project and name it ItemImages.

17. Run your application.

18. Go to \Admin\ManageItem and add a new item.

19. Got to the item list, select and edit an existing item.

How It Works

When working with the first set of screens in MVC you had to modify several different parts. The first part was how the application works with the list of hobbies that a UserDemographic may contain. When the screen was originally built, this list of hobbies was a list of strings. However, that had to be changed in the last chapter, so you needed to update both the UI and the actions to ensure that the correct information was being passed to the views.

The first change was adding the hobbyList to the ViewBag. This enabled the hobbies to be available in the view. You took advantage of that in the view by setting a local field to this list and then later iterating through the list and assigning the hobby.Name property as the label for a checkbox. This was not as straightforward of a process as the rest of the binding, as shown in the following code snippet:

```
<div class="col-md-10">
    @foreach (var hobby in hobbyList)
    {
        string checkedText = Model.Hobbies.Any(x=>x.Id == hobby.Id)
            ? "checked" : string.Empty;
        <span>
            <input name="HobbyIds" value="@hobby.Id" type="checkbox" @checkedText />
            @hobby.Name
        </span>
    }
</div>
```

The preceding code iterates through the list of hobbies and adds a new checkbox to the UI for each one. Note how the name of the checkbox is "HobbyIds"; and that because this is in a loop, each checkbox that will be created ends up with the same name. The value assigned is the Id of the hobby. Figure 10-12 shows the HTML that was created from the preceding code.

```
<span>
    <input name="HobbyIds" value="9" type="checkbox"  />
    Camping
</span>
<span>
    <input name="HobbyIds" value="2" type="checkbox"  />
    Cooking
</span>
<span>
    <input name="HobbyIds" value="8" type="checkbox"  />
    Dancing
</span>
```

FIGURE 10-12: HTML created to support the hobby selection

Because all the different checkboxes have the same name, the resulting form value sent by the browser to the server will be a comma-delimited list of Ids that were selected, with the key/value defined as HobbyIds="3,6,7,8" so that when it is accessed in the action after posting it will be a single list.

The next code snippet shows how saving a new item is handled in the action method. The object is passed to the action as a bound model, so there is no need for a TryUpdateModel method to be called.

```
[HttpPost]
public ActionResult Create(UserDemographics obj)
{
    try
    {
        using (RentMyWroxContext context = new RentMyWroxContext())
        {
            var ids = Request.Form.GetValues("HobbyIds");
            obj.Hobbies = context.Hobbies
                .Where(x => ids.Contains(x.Id.ToString())).ToList();
            context.UserDemographics.Add(obj);
            context.SaveChanges();
            return RedirectToAction("Index");
        }
    }
    catch
    {
        return View();
    }
}
```

In the preceding method, also note how the application is accessing the Request.Form.Values and getting the HobbyIds values. In particular, notice that the GetValues method returns an array, so when there are multiple values (such as when a user selected multiple hobbies) it will be returned as an array of strings that does not need to be further broken down.

Once the values have been retrieved from the form, the Hobby list on the object is filled by pulling out the hobbies with the matching Ids. You can put a breakpoint after that line to see the results of the call. When that updating is completed, the last thing that happens is adding the item to the context and saving the changes.

When working with the Web Forms, you had to take a different approach. Because you were not able to use any of the built-in methods to manage the mapping, you had to do the mapping yourself. Most of that mapping was straightforward and is patterned after how work is done with the built-in UpdateModel method. The system assigns the appropriate values from the controls to the appropriate property on the item that was passed into the mapping method. In several places you used the `TryParse` method when converting the string value from the request to the item of the appropriate type.

The most unusual part of this mapping method is managing the uploaded picture file, as shown here:

```
if (fuPicture.PostedFile != null && fuPicture.HasFile)
{
    Guid newPrefix = Guid.NewGuid();
    string localDir = Path.Combine("ItemImages",
            newPrefix + "_" + fuPicture.FileName);
    string fullPath =
            Path.Combine(HttpContext.Current.Request.PhysicalApplicationPath,
            localDir);
    fuPicture.SaveAs(fullPath);
    item.Picture = "/" + localDir.Replace("\\", "/");
}
```

This file is passed to the server as an attached item in the body of the request. If the server control has content, the code first creates a new Globally Unique Id, or GUID, the intent being that this unique value will become part of the filename that's saved locally. This is necessary because you cannot otherwise guarantee that the saved files will have unique names.

You then use the `Path.Combine` method. This method takes at least two strings and merges them using the appropriate character (in this case a "\"). The first combination creates the \ItemImages\FileName link, while the second links the physical path of the application to the first combination that you just created. This provides a complete directory structure using the local drive rather than the website, which enables saving the file onto the server itself, so it can be referenced from the website.

The last part of the code is morphing the information used to save the file to a version that is necessary for accessing the uploaded file. In this case you are prepending a directory symbol "/" to the local directory. However, because the path is differentiated differently (web vs. local I/O), you had to replace the folder separators. Once you had the directory in the appropriate format you were able to save the item.

Once you had the code completed, you tied it all together by putting the "Add New Item" link on to the page. This allows you to actually use the functionality that you just finished.

A NON-CODE FIRST APPROACH TO DATABASE ACCESS

One of the Entity Framework's primary strengths is that it eliminates the developer's hassle of dealing with the database. However, there will still likely be some times when the work that you are trying to do cannot be efficiently handled by it. Reporting, for example, may be an instance of a requirement for which the Entity Framework is not the best solution. Another common task for which the Entity Framework is not useful is when you are working with multiple applications that access the same database and you want to ensure that they all use the same approach, especially if business rules are involved.

The Entity Framework can be considered an abstraction layer over ADO.NET. ADO.NET is a set of classes that expose data access services for .NET developers. ADO.NET provides a rich set of components for creating distributed, data-sharing applications. It is an integral part of the .NET Framework.

Because Entity Framework lies over ADO.NET, all of the functionality that is part of ADO.NET is available in any application that is already using the Entity Framework. This enables you to take a "non-code first" approach to getting information in and out of the database, yet still stay within the confines of the Entity Framework, taking advantage of all the power and ease of use that it offers.

Virtually all of the discussion about the EF so far has been related to using the `DbSet` properties that were added to the context file. However, there is another property that you will be using in this section, `Database`. The `Database` property can be thought of as a direct line to the database itself, as it enables you to use various flexible approaches to getting information into and out of the database. Some of the more common methods are shown in Table 10-3.

TABLE 10-3: Methods Available on DbContext.Database

METHOD	DESCRIPTION
CompatibleWithModel	Determines whether the database is compatible with the current code-first model. It's not something that you would use very often, but this is the same method used when the context first starts.
Create	Creates a new database on the database server
Delete	Deletes the database from the database server
ExecuteSqlCommand	Executes the given command against the database. There is no expectation that items are returned from the execution. It is important to parameterize any user input to protect against a SQL injection attack. You can include parameter placeholders in the SQL query string and then supply parameter values as additional arguments.
Exists	Determines whether the database exists on the server
SqlQuery	Creates a SQL query that returns elements of the given type. The returned type can be any type with properties that match the names of the columns returned from the query, or it can be a simple primitive type such as `int` or `string`, as the type does not have to be an entity type. The results of this query are never tracked by the context even if the type of object returned is an entity type. It is important to parameterize any user input to protect against a SQL injection attack. You can include parameter placeholders in the SQL query string and then supply parameter values as additional arguments.

The key to interacting with the database through the `DbContext.Database` property is knowing whether you expect to get data back through the interaction. If you are not expecting anything other than a success/failure notification, then you should use the `ExecuteSqlCommand` method. Conversely, when you want data returned, you must use the `ExecuteSql` method.

SQL INJECTION ATTACK

SQL injection is a technique whereby users can inject SQL commands into a SQL statement, generally through some kind of user-directed input such as a web page. These injected SQL commands may have a variety of effects on your database, from deleting tables to changing data. The purpose of a SQL injection attack is to convince the application to run SQL code that was not intended.

Suppose you had the following simple query that was built using string concatenation:

```
string sql = "SELECT username,password FROM sometable WHERE
email='";
sql += emailAddress
sql += "'"
```

The expectation here is for users to enter their e-mail address into a data entry field, and for the query that would be built to end up looking something like the following:

```
SELECT username,password FROM sometable WHERE email='name@
server.com'
```

However, with a SQL injection attack, the nefarious user would not enter an e-mail address but instead something more like this:

```
x'; DROP TABLE sometable;--.
```

This would result in the following final SQL statement:

```
SELECT username,password FROM sometable WHERE email=' x'; DROP
TABLE sometable;--'.
```

This would be bad, because when the whole statement is run it will first try to find the information using "x" as the e-mail, and once that statement has been completed it will run the next statement, which in this case happens to be a drop table command that will remove that table from your database.

The most common and powerful way to stop SQL injection is through the use of parameters. Parameters enable the database server to look at the entire value being passed in as a single item, rather than as a chain of commands. Using parameters would have created the following SQL:

```
string sql = "SELECT username,password FROM sometable WHERE email=@
email";
```

The process would be called by passing in a parameter with the name of `email`. This means that when the select is performed, it would be looking for the `x'; DROP TABLE sometable;--` as the actual value in the column, and more than likely not finding anything.

Regardless of whether you are using the `ExecuteSqlCommand` or `ExecuteSql` approach, you need to ensure that you are using parameters. Both of these methods have a method signature that includes a string for the SQL command to be run and an array for the parameters. Using one of these methods would look like

```
var results = context.Database.ExecuteSql("select * from table where name=@name",
                        new SqlParameter("@name", nameToLookFor));
```

where the value that you are searching for has been parameterized. When you don't need to pass in any values, then you do not need to use the parameters; however, you should get into the habit of parameterizing any information that will be going directly into or against the database, even information that the user did not enter. Better safe than sorry!

Using SQL Queries and Stored Procedures

When you are using the `ExecuteSql` or `ExecuteSqlCommand` you can run either some designated SQL or a stored procedure. A stored procedure can be thought of as a set of SQL that is stored on the server rather than being passed into the server each time a query is requested. Stored procedures may be slightly more performant than SQL that was generated in your code. In addition, keeping the query as a stored procedure enables you to change the stored procedure independently from your application, giving you the capability for different behavior without having to redeploy your application.

> **NOTE** *The next few activities include a lot of SQL code, some of which contain commands not covered in the chapter. These activities demonstrate why you might choose to take a stored procedure approach, but they may be slightly confusing if you do not have any SQL experience. For more information about how to program directly with the database, get yourself a copy of* Beginning Microsoft SQL Server 2012 Programming, *by Paul Atkinson and Robert Vieira (Wrox, 2012). It provides a deep dive into SQL, stored procedures, database functions, and other powerful features when working with SQL Server.*

The process, and most of the language, when running either a SQL query or a stored procedure is the same; the only difference is the text that you provide the method. In the next activity you work with both a SQL query and a stored procedure.

TRY IT OUT Building Reports in Your Sample Application

In this activity you build out several interesting reports that your users can use to get an understanding of their fellow members. The first report provides information about the hobbies selected by your users. It includes the following information:

➤ Age Range <20, 20-40, 40-60, 60+

➤ Hobby

➤ Count of the people in that age range who chose that hobby

The second report provides this information:

➤ Age Range <20, 20-40, 40-60, 60+

➤ Count of the people in that age range

➤ Average length of time in the area

1. Ensure that Visual Studio is running and that you have opened your RentMyWrox solution. Right-click on the Model directory and add a new class file named **HobbyReportItem**.

2. Add the following properties to this new class file:

```
public string Name { get; set; }

public string BirthRange { get; set; }

public int Total { get; set; }
```

3. Open your UserDemographicsController and add the following code. When complete it should look like Figure 10-13.

```
public ActionResult HobbyReport()
{
    string query = @"select
                    h.Name,
                    brud.BirthRange,
                    Count(*) as Total
                from UserDemographicsHobbies udh
                inner join Hobbies h on h.Id=udh.Hobby_Id
                inner join UserDemographics ud on ud.Id=udh.UserDemographics_Id
                inner join (select Id,
                        case
                        when Birthdate between  DATEADD(YEAR, -20, getdate()) and
                            GetDate() then ' < 20 '
                        when birthdate between DATEADD(YEAR, -40, getdate()) and
                            DATEADD(YEAR, -20, getdate()) then '20-40'
                        when birthdate between DATEADD(YEAR, -60, getdate()) and
                            DATEADD(YEAR, -40, getdate()) then '40-60'
                        else ' >60 '
                        end as BirthRange
                        from UserDemographics) brud on brud.Id = udh.UserDemographics_Id
                group by brud.BirthRange, h.Name";
    using (RentMyWroxContext context = new RentMyWroxContext())
    {
        var list = context.Database.SqlQuery<HobbyReportItem>(query).ToList();
        return View(list);
    }
}
```

```
public ActionResult HobbyReport()
{
    string query = @"select
                    h.Name,
                    brud.BirthRange,
                    Count(*) as Total
            from UserDemographicsHobbies udh
            inner join Hobbies h on h.Id=udh.Hobby_Id
            inner join UserDemographics ud on ud.Id=udh.UserDemographics_Id
            inner join (select Id,
                    case
                    when Birthdate between  DATEADD(YEAR, -20, getdate()) and GetDate() then ' < 20 '
                    when birthdate between DATEADD(YEAR, -40, getdate()) and DATEADD(YEAR, -20, getdate()) then '20-40'
                    when birthdate between DATEADD(YEAR, -60, getdate()) and DATEADD(YEAR, -40, getdate()) then '40-60'
                    else ' >60 '
                end as BirthRange
                from UserDemographics) brud on brud.Id = udh.UserDemographics_Id
            group by brud.BirthRange, h.Name";
    using (RentMyWroxContext context = new RentMyWroxContext())
    {
        var list = context.Database.SqlQuery<HobbyReportItem>(query).ToList();
        return View(list);
    }
}
```

FIGURE 10-13: New method in UserDemographicsController

4. Right-click on the Views\UserDemographics folder. Select the option to add a new view. Name it "**HobbyReport**" and use an Empty model as shown in Figure 10-14.

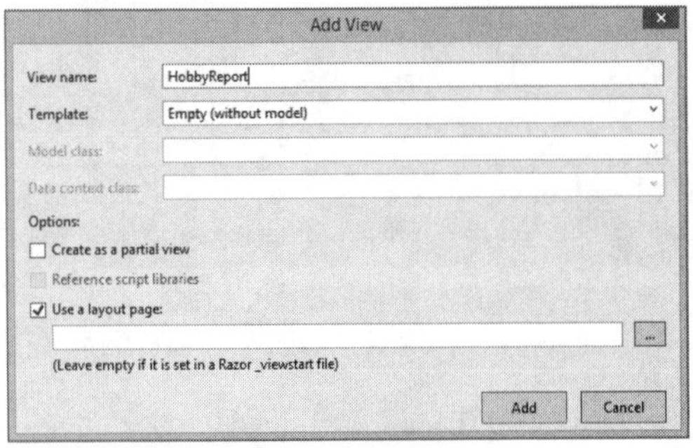

FIGURE 10-14: Add View dialog

5. Replace the content of the new view file with the following code. When complete it should look like Figure 10-15.

```
@model IEnumerable<RentMyWrox.Models.HobbyReportItem>
@{
    ViewBag.Title = "Hobby Report";
}
<h2>HobbyReport</h2>
<table class="table">
    <tr>
        <th>
            @Html.DisplayNameFor(model => model.Name)
```

```
            </th>
            <th>
                @Html.DisplayNameFor(model => model.BirthRange)
            </th>
            <th>
                @Html.DisplayNameFor(model => model.Total)
            </th>
        </tr>
    @foreach (var item in Model) {
        <tr>
            <td>
                @Html.DisplayFor(modelItem => item.Name)
            </td>
            <td>
                @Html.DisplayFor(modelItem => item.BirthRange)
            </td>
            <td>
                @Html.DisplayFor(modelItem => item.Total)
            </td>
        </tr>
    }
    </table>
```

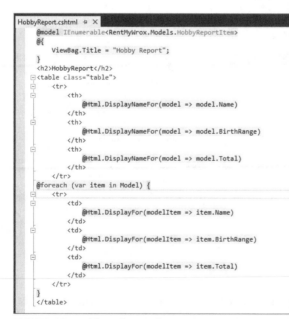

FIGURE 10-15: New view code

6. Run the application and navigate to UserDemographics ⇨ HobbyReport. You should see a screen similar to Figure 10-16. If you need more data, use the UserDemographics ⇨ Edit screen that you created in the previous example.

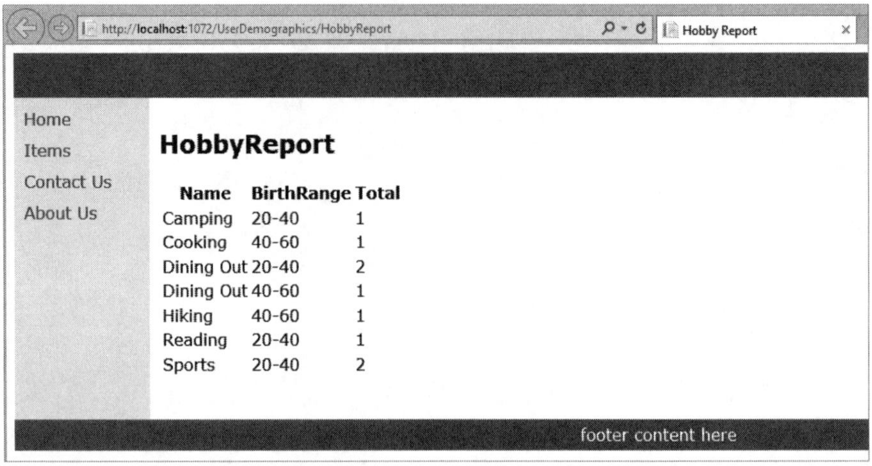

FIGURE 10-16: Running HobbyReport

7. While in Server Explorer and still under the RentMyWrox database, right-click on Stored Procedures and select Add New Stored Procedure.

8. When the window appears, delete all the content, replacing it with the following code. When completed it should look like Figure 10-17.

```
CREATE PROCEDURE [dbo].[UserDemographicsTimeInArea]
AS
    select BirthRange, count(*) as Total, AVG(MonthsInArea) as AverageMonths
from
    (select
    case
        when Birthdate between  DATEADD(YEAR, -20, getdate()) and GetDate()
then ' < 20 '
        when birthdate between DATEADD(YEAR, -40, getdate())
                and DATEADD(YEAR, -20, getdate()) then '20-40'
        when birthdate between DATEADD(YEAR, -60, getdate())
            and DATEADD(YEAR, -40, getdate()) then '40-60'
        else ' >60 '
    end as BirthRange,
    DATEDIFF(month, DateMovedIntoArea, getdate()) as MonthsInArea
    from UserDemographics) details
group by BirthRange
```

9. Right-click on the window into which you just entered the code and select Execute. You should get a message that tells you "Command(s) completed successfully."

10. Close the window (no need to save) and expand the Stored Procedures folder. You should see the new stored procedure.

11. Create a new model named **ResidencyReportItem** with the following properties:

```
public string BirthRange { get; set; }
```

```
public int Total { get; set; }

public int AverageMonths { get; set; }
```

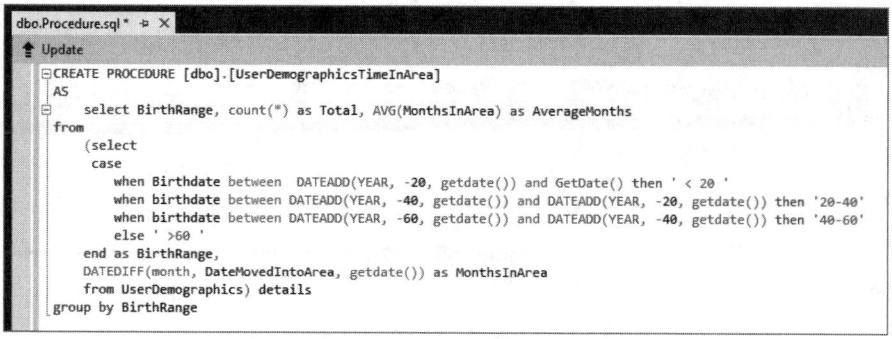

```
dbo.Procedure.sql *  ⊀  ×
⬆ Update
 ⊟CREATE PROCEDURE [dbo].[UserDemographicsTimeInArea]
  │ AS
 ⊟     select BirthRange, count(*) as Total, AVG(MonthsInArea) as AverageMonths
  │from
  │      (select
  │       case
  │         when Birthdate between  DATEADD(YEAR, -20, getdate()) and GetDate() then ' < 20 '
  │         when birthdate between DATEADD(YEAR, -40, getdate()) and DATEADD(YEAR, -20, getdate()) then '20-40'
  │         when birthdate between DATEADD(YEAR, -60, getdate()) and DATEADD(YEAR, -40, getdate()) then '40-60'
  │         else ' >60 '
  │       end as BirthRange,
  │       DATEDIFF(month, DateMovedIntoArea, getdate()) as MonthsInArea
  │      from UserDemographics) details
  │group by BirthRange
```

FIGURE 10-17: Setting up the new stored procedure

12. Go back into the `UserDemographicsController` and add the following new action:

```
public ActionResult ResidencyReport()
{
    using (RentMyWroxContext context = new RentMyWroxContext())
    {
        var list = context.Database.SqlQuery<ResidencyReportItem>(
                "exec UserDemographicsTimeInArea").ToList();
        return View(list);
    }
}
```

13. Add a new view under the UserDemographics folder named **ResidencyReport**. Add the following content:

```
@model IEnumerable<RentMyWrox.Models.ResidencyReportItem>
@{
    ViewBag.Title = "Residency Report";
}
<h2>Residency Report</h2>
<table class="table">
    <tr>
        <th>
            @Html.DisplayNameFor(model => model.BirthRange)
        </th>
        <th>
            @Html.DisplayNameFor(model => model.Total)
        </th>
        <th>
            @Html.DisplayNameFor(model => model.AverageMonths)
        </th>
    </tr>
@foreach (var item in Model) {
    <tr>
```

```
        <td>
            @Html.DisplayFor(modelItem => item.BirthRange)
        </td>
        <td>
            @Html.DisplayFor(modelItem => item.Total)
        </td>
        <td>
            @Html.DisplayFor(modelItem => item.AverageMonths)
        </td>
    </tr>
}
</table>
```

14. Run the application and navigate to UserDemographics ➪ ResidencyReport. You should see something similar to what is shown in Figure 10-18.

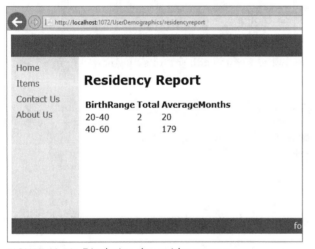

FIGURE 10-18: Displaying the residency report

How It Works

The preceding activity added two new pages to your site that will help your users get an understanding of the community that they have joined. Unfortunately, getting the information necessary to make these reports using the model-first Entity Framework approach and the dot notation that you have used so far would be complex and likely poorly performing.

Instead of using the table abstraction provided by the Entity Framework, you instead ran SQL directly against the database. You used two different approaches—straight SQL and executing a stored procedure—but they were handled similarly. The key piece of functionality that you were able to use was the SqlQuery command, with the following:

```
context.Database.SqlQuery<ResidencyReportItem>("exec UserDemographicsTimeInArea")
    .ToList();
```

What makes this method so easy to use is the ability of the query to return a list of known items. When you run a `SqlQuery` and assign a class, the Entity Framework populates a list of items of the same type as the class that you assigned when defining the call. The framework then looks at the names of the columns in the result set returned from the database server and maps the values from the database to properties on the defined object that have the same type and name. This was how you were able to make a generic call to the database and get back a set of populated objects. If you had extra properties in either object or the query results, those values would not be mapped; only those that are in both property lists will be assigned. This mapping facility is a huge functionality booster because you can use defined types without having to worry about manually mapping the database values to properties on a newly created object.

The SQL that was used for either approach relies on two different features to get you the necessary information: subqueries and grouping. A subquery is a database query that you create as part of another database query. This subquery has a set of results that are used in the main query. Both of the queries that you used to create the reports contained a subquery that looked like the following code:

```
(select Id,
    case
            when Birthdate between  DATEADD(YEAR, -20, getdate()) and
              GetDate() then ' < 20 '
            when birthdate between DATEADD(YEAR, -40, getdate()) and
              DATEADD(YEAR, -20, getdate()) then '20-40'
            when birthdate between DATEADD(YEAR, -60, getdate()) and
              DATEADD(YEAR, -40, getdate()) then '40-60'
            else ' >60 '
        end as BirthRange
    from UserDemographics) brud
```

That listing is an example of a subquery. It is taking the Id of the table row and then creating a value called `BirthRange` by determining which date range the record falls between. The case\when statement is the SQL equivalent to the `switch` statement in .NET. This statement then wraps the results from this subquery and gives it a name (in this case "brud"), which enables this result set to be used as if it were a regular table—allowing joins and other table-like access to the results of this subquery.

The other important feature of these queries is grouping. Grouping gives SQL Server the ability to perform aggregate functions. There are several of these aggregate functions in these queries, mainly `count` and `avg`. The `count` function counts the number of items that were defined by the grouping fields, while `avg` calculates the average value of a field. The grouping fields are defined in the `group by` clause.

This `group by` clause is important, because the items listed in the `group by` clause, and there can be more than one, become the definitions of the items that are being calculated. The direct SQL code had two columns in the `group by` clause, meaning every calculation was based on every unique combination of those two fields. When more than one row has the same values in the `group by` fields, those rows are all available for inclusion in any aggregate functions.

Although accessing data in an efficient manner helps to ensure a well-performing application, imagine how much more performant your application might be if the system did not have to access the data as frequently. That's the subject of the next section.

CACHING

Caching is a development strategy that helps improve performance and reliability in your web application. Some of the ways in which it does this include the following:

- ➤ It reduces the amount of data being sent over the network.
- ➤ It decreases the number of calls to a database.
- ➤ It reduces the amount of code that needs to be run to return an item.

The main feature of caching is that once an item is retrieved, whether it is over the Internet or from a database, those results are "saved" somewhere local and then returned the next time the item is requested. This means that the action first taken to retrieve the information does not have to be run again.

Caching can add some complexity to your application, depending on where and how it is implemented. The most powerful caching approaches generally require the most complex configuration and support, but they provide your application with the most overall benefit in terms of responsiveness and reliability. Reliability is critical because any areas of your application that cache information from other areas of the application have to ensure that their ability to recover this information from their cache is at least as reliable as the method used to get the original copy of the information. It is an unacceptable trade-off to implement a caching system that can negatively impact the performance of your system—that would defeat the entire purpose of caching in the first place.

Different Ways to Cache Data in ASP.NET Applications

The first way to add caching to an ASP.NET application is through data caching. Data caching is when a new caching layer is added between your application and the data access layer. This new layer then becomes responsible for managing some data outside of the database when that data has been determined as being cacheable. The Entity Framework provides some support for caching in long-running applications, but in typical web applications there is no support for caching, and adding a data caching layer is beyond the scope of this project.

The next level of caching is storing page content at the user and browser level. In this case, the browser stores a local copy of the content with an expiration period set by the server. These expiration periods could be anything from seconds to minutes to days, and are generally based on the kind of data being cached. A user's shopping cart, for example, would be a poor piece of information to cache. Conversely, an "About Us" page might be a good candidate for caching, simply because the content does not frequently change.

The last level of caching is also within the browser. This approach to caching, called the Application Cache API (AppCache), is an HTML 5 specification that gives developers access to the local browser cache. It is different from output caching in that the AppCache is designed to store data that could be accessed multiple times. AppCache enables the developer to store this information locally on the client machine, rather than send it from the server to the client multiple times. It is not used for storing whole pages, but rather to store data for either the life of the connection or simply the lifetime of a single page. There is no further discussion of the AppCache in this project.

PROXY SERVERS

A proxy server is a computer that functions as an intermediate system between a web browser and the Internet. Proxy servers are designed to help improve web performance by storing a copy of frequently used web pages. When a browser requests a web page stored in the proxy server's cache, it is provided by the proxy server, which is faster than going through the web to the server. Proxy servers can also help improve security by filtering out some web content and malicious software. This is possible because every request between the client and the Internet has to pass through the proxy server.

Proxy servers are used mostly by networks in public organizations and private companies. Typically, people connecting to the Internet from home will not use a proxy server. Proxy servers are rarely under the developer's control, so a developer can never count on them being part of the request process. This means that the proxy server will determine, using its own rules, whether or not to send the request to the server or simply return the cached copy that is held on the server. This means that changes you make to the output may not be reflected when you look at the page. You can imagine how troublesome this could be when you are trying to determine why the page does not meet your expectations.

Web Forms and MVC handle configuration of caching differently, just as they handle everything else differently. When using Web Forms you define the output configuration at the page level by adding a new configuration item below the page definition:

```
<%@ OutputCache Duration="1200" Location="ServerAndClient" %>
```

In this example the page is going to be cached for 1,200 seconds, or 20 minutes. The second attribute specifies the location where caching can happen. Table 10-4 defines the various locations where you can configure caching.

TABLE 10-4: Caching Locations

LOCATION	DESCRIPTION
Any	The output cache can be located on the browser client (where the request originated), on a proxy server (or any other server) participating in the request, or on the server where the request was processed.
Client	The output cache is located on the browser client where the request originated.
Downstream	The output cache can be stored in any HTTP 1.1 cache-capable devices other than the origin server. This includes proxy servers and the client that made the request.
None	The output cache is disabled for the requested page.

continues

TABLE 10-4 *(continued)*

LOCATION	DESCRIPTION
Server	The output cache is located on the web server where the request was processed.
ServerAndClient	The output cache can be stored only at the origin server or at the requesting client. Proxy servers are not allowed to cache the response.

You can take a similar approach when working with ASP.NET MVC output caching. However, rather than being at the page level as you just saw with Web Forms, the output from an action is cached for a predefined period. Configuring caching on an action uses attribution on that method, as shown here:

```
[OutputCache(Duration = 1200, Location = OutputCacheLocation.ServerAndClient)]
public ActionResult Details(int id)
```

The preceding attribute sets caching to the same 20 minutes, with the item being cached using the `ServerAndClient` setting. With this setting, checking the Internet Explorer browser cache will indicate a 20-minute caching period, as shown on the highlighted item in Figure 10-19.

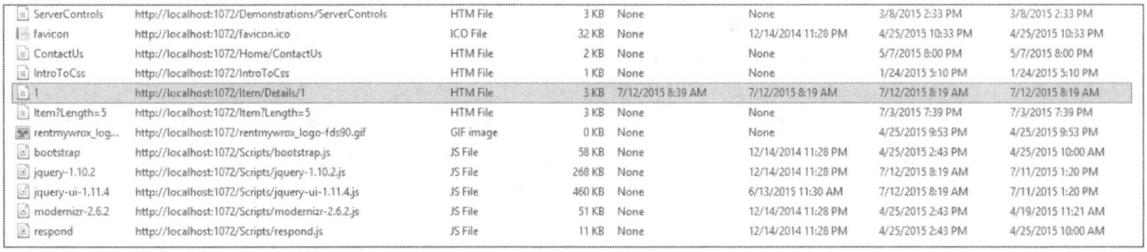

ServerControls	http://localhost:1072/Demonstrations/ServerControls	HTM File	3 KB	None	None	3/8/2015 2:33 PM	3/8/2015 2:33 PM
favicon	http://localhost:1072/favicon.ico	ICO File	32 KB	None	12/14/2014 11:28 PM	4/25/2015 10:33 PM	4/25/2015 10:33 PM
ContactUs	http://localhost:1072/Home/ContactUs	HTM File	2 KB	None	None	5/7/2015 8:00 PM	5/7/2015 8:00 PM
IntroToCss	http://localhost:1072/IntroToCss	HTM File	1 KB	None	None	1/24/2015 5:10 PM	1/24/2015 5:10 PM
1	http://localhost:1072/Item/Details/1	HTM File	3 KB	7/12/2015 8:39 AM	7/12/2015 8:19 AM	7/12/2015 8:19 AM	7/12/2015 8:19 AM
Item?Length=5	http://localhost:1072/Item?Length=5	HTM File	3 KB	None	None	7/3/2015 7:39 PM	7/3/2015 7:39 PM
rentmywrox_log...	http://localhost:1072/rentmywrox_logo-fds90.gif	GIF image	0 KB	None	None	4/25/2015 9:53 PM	4/25/2015 9:53 PM
bootstrap	http://localhost:1072/Scripts/bootstrap.js	JS File	58 KB	None	12/14/2014 11:28 PM	4/25/2015 2:43 PM	4/25/2015 10:00 AM
jquery-1.10.2	http://localhost:1072/Scripts/jquery-1.10.2.js	JS File	268 KB	None	12/14/2014 11:28 PM	7/12/2015 8:19 AM	7/11/2015 1:20 PM
jquery-ui-1.11.4	http://localhost:1072/Scripts/jquery-ui-1.11.4.js	JS File	460 KB	None	6/13/2015 11:30 AM	7/12/2015 8:19 AM	7/11/2015 1:20 PM
modernizr-2.6.2	http://localhost:1072/Scripts/modernizr-2.6.2.js	JS File	51 KB	None	12/14/2014 11:28 PM	4/25/2015 2:43 PM	4/19/2015 11:21 AM
respond	http://localhost:1072/Scripts/respond.js	JS File	11 KB	None	12/14/2014 11:28 PM	4/25/2015 2:43 PM	4/25/2015 10:00 AM

FIGURE 10-19: Directory of cached items

As shown in the figure, any request for that particular page before the expiration period will not require a server call, as the page will instead be returned from the local cache.

In the next activity you implement some caching in several areas of the application and then validate that the caching is actually working.

TRY IT OUT Add Caching to Your Sample Application

In this activity you implement caching in your sample application. The purpose of this caching is to increase response time for the user and limit the amount of work that has to be done on the server. The steps that you will take during this activity are unusual in that there will be a lot of breakpoint setting in order to track program flow.

1. Ensure that Visual Studio is running and that your RentMyWrox solution is open.
2. Open the `Controller\ItemController` file. Add the following attribute above the Details action. When completed it should look like Figure 10-20.

```
[OutputCache(Duration = 1200, Location = OutputCacheLocation.ServerAndClient)]
```

```
[OutputCache(Duration = 1200, Location = OutputCacheLocation.ServerAndClient)]
public ActionResult Details(int id)
{
    using (RentMyWroxContext context = new RentMyWroxContext())
    {
        Item item = context.Items.FirstOrDefault(x => x.Id == id);
        return View(item);
    }
}
```

FIGURE 10-20: Output caching on the Details action

3. Insert a breakpoint on the return line inside the action.

4. Run the application and go to the home page.

5. Click one of the Full Details links. This should take you to your breakpoint, as shown in Figure 10-21.

```
[OutputCache(Duration = 1200, Location = OutputCacheLocation.ServerAndClient)]
public ActionResult Details(int id)
{
    using (RentMyWroxContext context = new RentMyWroxContext())
    {
        Item item = context.Items.FirstOrDefault(x => x.Id == id);
        return View(item);
    }
}
```

FIGURE 10-21: Breakpoint in the Details action

6. Click the Continue button to keep running.

7. After the page has rendered, click the Home link on the left menu.

8. Click the Full Details link on the same product that you just clicked. You will see the content render but your breakpoint will not be hit.

9. Go back to the home page and click a different product. Your breakpoint will be hit.

10. Open your `Admin\ItemList.aspx` page. Add the following code immediately below the `Page` declaration:

```
<%@ OutputCache Duration="1200" Location="ServerAndClient" VaryByParam="*" %>
```

How It Works

Output caching is the capability to configure caching duration for a page, whether that page is an ASP.NET Web Form page or the output from an ASP.NET MVC controller action. Many of the characteristics are the same for both MVC and Web Forms in that you set a duration, in seconds, specifying how long the page will be cached and what areas can support caching the content.

All of this information is stored within the response headers, the metadata that is returned to the client from the server. Using the settings that were used in the activity, the response headers will include the following:

```
HTTP/1.1 200 OK
Cache-Control: private, max-age=1200
Content-Type: text/html; charset=utf-8
```

```
Expires: Sun, 12 Jul 2015 16:57:11 GMT
Last-Modified: Sun, 12 Jul 2015 16:37:11 GMT
```

There are two lines that directly relate to caching and the configuration that you used: `Cache-Control` and `Expires`. The `Cache-Control` line includes the keyword `private`. In this case, `private` means that the content can be cached only on the client and the server, but not any systems in between, such as a proxy server. A value of `public`, conversely, allows the request to be cached anywhere in between the server and client that caching may take place. A third value can be used here as well, `no-cache`, which means there is no caching anywhere past the server.

The other value that is part of the `Cache-Control` is the `max-age`. This is the same value that you set in the configuration, and the value that is used by the browser when determining cache expiration. This value overrides the `Expires` line in the header when it is present. If, however, there is no `max-age` value, then the value from the `Expires` line is used. ASP.NET sets both expiration items appropriately.

You discovered a new attribute as part of the Web Forms configuration, `VaryByParams`. This is one of the many additional values that you can use to fine-tune the caching definition. The `VaryByParams` property expects a semicolon-delimited list of query string or form `POST` parameters that the output cache uses to vary the cache entry. The setting that you used, `*`, means that whenever there is any difference in the parameters, a new request should be sent to the server rather than being retrieved from cache.

This brings up an interesting point about the difference between using MVC and Web Forms. Generally, a call to a Web Form page is going to be differentiated by query string values because it does not generally use the same URL approach used by default in MVC. Each URL for a details page in MVC, for example, is different, whereas in Web Forms the URL may be the same but the parameter string is different. You may not have noticed, but `VaryByParams` was a required field when configuring the `.aspx` page because of these differences.

In those cases where you would like the same experience in Web Forms that you have with MVC, rather than use the `*` as the value in the `VaryByParams` property, you would instead use `Id` to indicate that you want the page to be cached using the Id. This ensures that the only time there is a call to the server is when the Id is different. This would give the exact same experience as the MVC caching experience that is caused by the difference in URL.

On the face of it, it might seem like you would want to configure caching on everything you do in your site. However, this may not always be the best decision. You have seen a lot of the benefits of caching, but there are also some complications and issues that may make caching problematic in some situations

Common Pitfalls with Caching Data

If caching solved every performance problem that a site might have, then it would have been highlighted in Chapter 1. Although it can help enhance the perception of speed, it does this at some risk of getting old, incorrect data. It should be clear that the longer the expiration time, the fewer the calls made to the server. However, you can probably guess what this might mean on a page whose content often changes: Changes will not be picked up until the caches expires, rather than when the page changes. This results in what is known as stale data.

The most common problem when using caching is ensuring both that the cache period is long enough to make a difference yet short enough that incorrect information is not displayed to the user. There is no firm number for this; it is instead completely dependent upon the content of that particular page. For example, consider the sample application and what a typical user would see.

The first page that users would likely visit is the default, the home page. Reviewing the content on this page reveals that the list of available products may frequently change, conceivably with every checkout or return of products, and there is no way to foresee when this happens.

What would stale data mean in this case? There are two potential problems if the data is stale. One, available items are not listed; and two, listed items may no longer be available. Neither of those options is desirable, as missing items mean someone else cannot check them out, affecting revenue. If an item is no longer available yet still listed, any user selecting that item will have a negative experience when they try to add the item to their shopping cart but then find out it isn't truly available.

One last point to consider with caching is that the cache settings you define on the server output are not obligatory; they should instead be considered strong recommendations. Users can always set their local client to follow caching rules that they determine, which may be different from what you are expecting. The same is true for systems that may be between the server and client, such as proxy servers. While you may make a recommendation for caching, the intermediate system may make its own caching decision. This means that you cannot always guarantee the behavior regarding when and what items are cached. While there is not really anything you can do about these cases, typically they only apply to those items where caching is turned on. Disabling caching for a page will generally turn off all caching anywhere.

When would specifically turning cache off be a good choice? If you consider a typical e-commerce application, it is unlikely that you would ever want caching performed on the shopping cart page, because hopefully every time users visit that page, the information has been updated to accurately reflect items added, removed, or purchased.

SUMMARY

Saving data when working with ASP.NET and the Entity Framework is a straightforward process because the Entity Framework does so much of the work for you. What complicates the process is the HTTP protocol and how information is transferred from the client to the server, because getting this information into a format that can be linked to the Entity Framework can be complicated.

Several approaches are available for linking request information to an Entity Framework model for persistence. The first is through the use of the `UpdateModel` methods, which help map bound UI controls to the appropriate model property. MVC gives you the option to simplify this even more through the use of model binders that populate a model defined in the method signature, bypassing the need to call the `TryUpdateModel` method in your code.

The second option is a more manual approach whereby the developer manually links the incoming value from the request to a property in the Entity Framework object. This is especially common when dealing with older approaches or third-party integrations for which you don't have control over the form itself, instead just needing to link the values coming in to your own object.

While working with database tables through the Entity Framework has been simplified as much as possible, there are still times when you need to interact with the database outside of an EF table object. This is still provided as part of the EF, however, as you can run custom SQL code, stored procedures, or take any other actions that you need with the database. When you are selecting data from the database, you even have the option to bind the results to a custom type (class) that maps to a model you created, thus enabling you to still work directly with code that you defined, and avoiding the need to work with any database-specific types.

This chapter also described various approaches to adding caching to your project. Caching enables you to control the frequency of calls made to the server for a page versus being called from the local browser cache. When a page is retrieved from the local cache it provides a quicker response to the user, and reduces the amount of load on your servers, a virtual double win. However, too long of a cache period can result in presenting stale data, not the correct data, to the client, so care needs to be taken regarding what information is cached and how long it is cached.

EXERCISES

1. With the setup you currently have after the Try it Out activities, what do you think the default behavior of the screen would be after caching was added to the ItemList page? What would happen when you add an item?

2. What other options do you have for passing the list of hobbies to the view if you did not use the `ViewBag` or any of the `ViewBag`-type approaches (i.e., `ViewData`, etc.)?

3. What would be some reasons to use a more direct route to the database, such as `ExecuteQuery` rather than using the traditional EF approach?

▶ WHAT YOU LEARNED IN THIS CHAPTER

Caching	Storing the results of a query or request. Subsequent requests for this information would retrieve the stored results, rather than fetching the results from the source. Caching is most common between the client and the server by having page results cached on the client device.
`ExecuteSqlCommand`	Executing SQL directly upon the database. When using `ExecuteSqlCommand`, the assumption is that you are not requesting data, as there is no result set from this method.
Pagination	Breaking down a large list of data into smaller pages and then providing users with the capability to move between these different pages.
Database parameters	A form of passing information into direct-to-database calls. They enable the system to avoid SQL injection attacks and ensure type compatibility.
Query string to parameter mapping	Query string to parameter mapping is a feature of ASP.NET MVC whereby query string values are mapped to values in the action method signature if the variables names are identical between the text used in the query string and the variable defined in the method signature.
Sorting	Putting the results of a list in a particular order. Users typically have some control over how sorting is managed by selecting either the field to sort on, the order of sorting (ascending or descending), or both the field and the order. This order is retained across pages if pagination is also in play.
SQL injection	SQL injection is a form of attack whereby the user tries to maliciously affect either the structure of your database or its data by filling out web entry forms in such a way as to allow access to the database if the incoming strings are not properly handled. The most common way of handling these incoming values is through the use of database parameters. The Entity Framework does a lot of this protection for you, so this risk is highest when you are building your SQL yourself.
`SqlQuery`	A direct call to the database that may return some data. An override to `SqlQuery` allows you to provide a model that the EF will try to fill with the results from the query. If the database call returns a field name that matches the property name, the mapping will be successful.
Stale data	Data that results from too long of a cache expiration period, which returns incorrect data to the user.
`TryUpdateModel`	A method used when you are using model binding that will automatically populate the values of the object from the various request sources, including form values, query string values, and attached files. If there is a type mismatch, this approach will simply not set that particular property.
`UpdateModel`	A method like `TryUpdateModel`, but rather than simply ignoring presented data that cannot be converted to the required type, this method will throw an exception.

11

User Controls and Partial Views

WHAT YOU WILL LEARN IN THIS CHAPTER:

➤ What an ASP.NET Web Forms user control is, and how to use it in a website

➤ Creating user controls that provide common functionality to multiple pages

➤ Creating an ASP.NET MVC partial view and using it in your web application

➤ Working with controllers that return partial views

➤ How user controls and partial views differ

➤ Creating ASP.NET MVC templates

CODE DOWNLOADS FOR THIS CHAPTER:

The wrox.com code downloads for this chapter are found at www.wrox.com/go/beginningaspnetforvisualstudio on the Download Code tab. The code is in the chapter 11 download and individually named according to the names throughout the chapter.

There was a lot of discussion in Chapter 4, "Programming in C# and VB.NET," about reusing the same code in multiple areas as opposed to rewriting the code multiple times. This is a useful concept not only when approaching your code design, but also when approaching your page design. You have seen how reuse is provided through the use of master pages and layout pages; now you will learn other ways to provide reusable sections in a web application.

A typical example of this could be something like a login window. While you may want the same functionality on every page, you might prefer that functionality to appear in different places on the page, based on the visitor's current location. Because they may be on different parts of the page, it's not possible to put this functionality into the master or layout page because that approach assumes that the functionality is in the same place on every page. Instead, you create either an ASP.NET Web Forms user control or an ASP.NET MVC partial view, and place that new item wherever you need it.

The user control or partial view acts as a common container for functionality. It combines UI and processing just as a complete page does, but it is rendered as a set of HTML elements that can be placed anywhere in your page. You have seen built-in server controls that provide this functionality. In this chapter you will learn how you can provide the same set of support for both the Web Forms and the MVC approaches by creating your own user controls and partial views.

INTRODUCTION TO USER CONTROLS

You already know that server controls are the means through which ASP.NET Web Forms bundle sets of functionality into easy-to-use sets of code. This bundled functionality includes both UI elements that become rendered HTML, and processing code. The availability of these server controls is a tremendous efficiency enhancer, because they enable developers to perform some complicated tasks through configuration and simple code, rather than having to do the work themselves.

However, server controls don't provide every set of functionality that you might need to support your web application, especially when you want to use specific business rules. This is where user controls come into play. These are developer-created controls that can be used within your application just like a standard server control. The only real difference is that you develop the control rather than having the control provided by the framework or a third party; it is specific to your application.

A user control offers you the same functionality, or support, as a regular Web Form page. This means that when you develop a user control you can do the following:

➤   Create HTML markup.

➤   Use code-behind and the complete page life cycle.

➤   Consume traditional ASP.NET server controls as well as other user controls.

One of the primary differences is that whereas an ASP.NET Web Forms page has an .aspx extension, the ASP.NET user control has an .ascx extension. In addition, the file is defined differently. The page is defined as

```
<%@ Page Title="" Language="C#"
    CodeBehind="Default.aspx.cs"
    AutoEventWireup="true"
    Inherits="RentMyWrox.Admin.Default" %>
```

while the control is defined as

```
<%@ Control Language="C#"
    CodeBehind="NewsControl.ascx.cs"
    AutoEventWireup="true"
    Inherits="RentMyWrox.Admin.NewsControl" %>
```

The last difference, and probably the most important, is that a user control cannot be called directly from a client as a requested resource. The user control exists only when it has been created in an .aspx page or in another user control that is created in an .aspx page.

Creating User Controls

Creating a user control is much like creating anything else in an ASP.NET application in that it uses the Add New Item dialog. In the next activity, you create a user control that provides special notifications to users.

TRY IT OUT Creating a User Control That Provides Special Notifications

In this activity you create a user control that you can add to Web Form pages. This user control pulls the most recent notification from the database and displays it on the page.

1. Ensure that Visual Studio is running and that you have your RentMyWrox solution open.

2. Create a new folder under your project directory named **Controls**.

3. Right-click on the new Controls directory and select Add ⇨ New Item. Choose Web Forms User Control as shown in Figure 11-1 and name the file **NotificationsControl**.

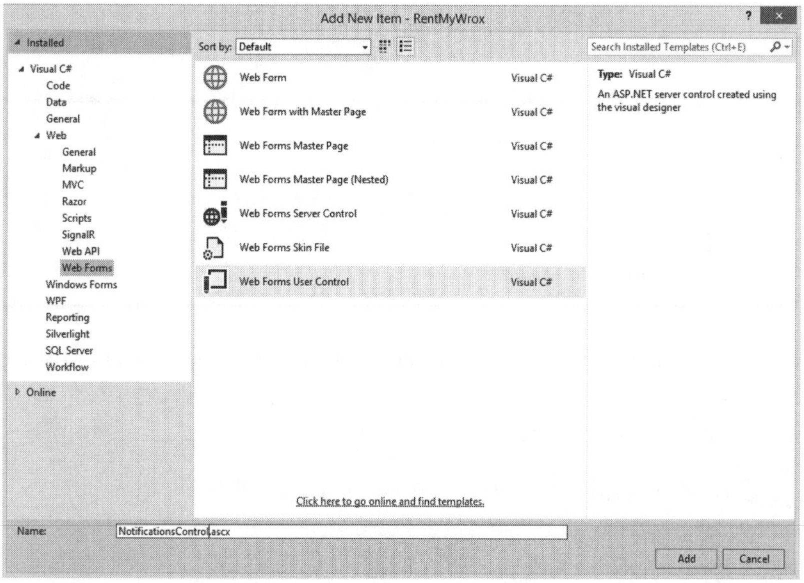

FIGURE 11-1: Creating a Web Forms user control

4. Add the following content to the NotificationsControl.ascx page. When completed it should look like Figure 11-2.

```
<asp:Label runat="server" ID="NotificationTitle" CssClass="NotificationTitle" />
<asp:Label runat="server" ID="NotificationDetail" CssClass="NotificationDetail" />
```

FIGURE 11-2: Editing the markup of your control

5. Right-click the Models directory and select Add New Item. Select Code, and then Class, as shown in Figure 11-3, and name it **Notification.cs.**

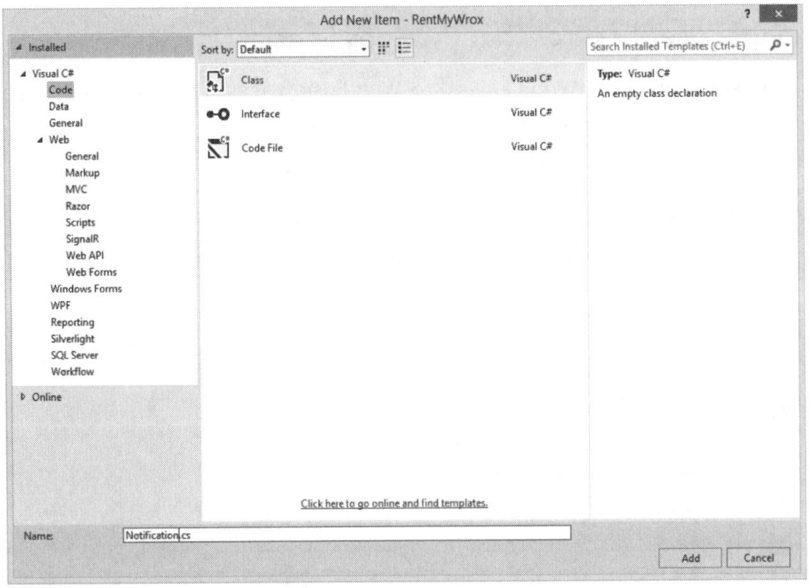

FIGURE 11-3: Adding the Notification model

6. Ensure that the `Notification.cs` class is open. Add the following `using` statement at the top of the file:

```
using System.ComponentModel.DataAnnotations;
```

7. Add the following properties and attributes to the `Notification.cs` class:

```
[Key]
public int Id { get; set; }

[MaxLength(50)]
public string Title { get; set; }

[MaxLength(750)]
public string Details { get; set; }

public bool IsAdminOnly { get; set; }

public DateTime DisplayStartDate { get; set; }
```

```
public DateTime DisplayEndDate { get; set; }

public DateTime CreateDate { get; set; }
```

8. Open the `RentMyWroxContext.cs` file from within the Model directory. Add the following code to the list of tables within the `RentMyWroxContext` class:

```
public virtual DbSet<Notification> Notifications { get; set; }
```

9. Open the code-behind page of the control, `NotificationsControl.ascx.cs`. Add a new using statement at the top of the page:

```
using RentMyWrox.Models;
```

10. Add the following code to the `Page_Load` method. It should look like Figure 11-4 when you are done.

```
using (RentMyWroxContext context = new RentMyWroxContext())
{
    Notification note = context.Notifications
        .Where(x => x.IsAdminOnly
            && x.DisplayStartDate <= DateTime.Now
            && x.DisplayEndDate >= DateTime.Now)
        .OrderByDescending(y => y.CreateDate)
        .FirstOrDefault();

    if (note != null)
    {
        NotificationTitle.Text = note.Title;
        NotificationDetail.Text = note.Details;
    }
}
```

```
NotificationsControl.ascx.cs ⇆ X
RentMyWrox                                              RentMyWrox.Controls.NotificationsContr
    1  using System;
    2  using System.Collections.Generic;
    3  using System.Linq;
    4  using System.Web;
    5  using System.Web.UI;
    6  using System.Web.UI.WebControls;
    7  using RentMyWrox.Models;
    8
    9  namespace RentMyWrox.Controls
   10  {
   11      public partial class NotificationsControl : System.Web.UI.UserControl
   12      {
   13          protected void Page_Load(object sender, EventArgs e)
   14          {
   15              using (RentMyWroxContext context = new RentMyWroxContext())
   16              {
   17                  Notification note = context.Notifications
   18                      .Where(x => x.IsAdminOnly
   19                          && x.DisplayStartDate <= DateTime.Now
   20                          && x.DisplayEndDate >= DateTime.Now)
   21                      .OrderByDescending(y => y.CreateDate)
   22                      .FirstOrDefault();
   23
   24                  if (note != null)
   25                  {
   26                      NotificationTitle.Text = note.Title;
   27                      NotificationDetail.Text = note.Details;
   28                  }
   29              }
   30          }
   31      }
   32  }
```

FIGURE 11-4: Editing the code-behind of your control

11. Build the solution to ensure that all the code seems correct. You won't be able to see the control on any page until it has been added to a page.

How It Works

Just as with a traditional ASP.NET Web Forms page, a user control has two different sections: the markup where you add the HTML and server controls, and the code-behind where you perform all the business logic.

The markup page for a user control typically lacks any of the traditional HTML tags such as `<head>` or `<body>` because a user control is generally used to add output snippets that are shown within the `<body>` tag, just like a traditional server control. In your markup page, you added two simple server controls, labels that are used to display the notification's title and detail properties. Some styling components and other defining HTML elements were also added to make the controls look better.

Because you did not yet have a `Notification` class, you next had to create the class definition for the item that you are going to be displaying. As discussed in Chapter 9, you need an integer Id field in order to uniquely identify the notification that will be displayed. The other fields are all specific parts of the model, and are described in Table 11-1.

TABLE 11-1: Notification Properties

PROPERTY	TYPE	DBTYPE	DESCRIPTION
Title	string	nvarchar(50)	The title of the notification and a brief description of the content
Details	string	nvar-char(750)	The notification details, the full content of the notification that is displayed to the user
IsAdminOnly	bool	Bit	Defines whether the notification is for regular users or only administrators
DisplayStartDate	DateTime	Datetime	The date when a notification becomes available for display. This enables you to enter multiple notifications and set them to display for a day, such as on a holiday, or forever, by choosing a start date in the past.
DisplayEndDate	DateTime	Datetime	The date when a notification is no longer eligible to be displayed. This enables you to enter multiple notifications and set them to display for a day, such as on a holiday, or forever, by choosing an end date in the future.
CreateDate	DateTime	Datetime	The day when the item was created. When displaying a list of notifications they will be typically ordered by this property.

Once the class was added, you then added it to the context file. By doing this, you ensure that the table will be added, if it is not already there, when the code is run. Once created, the table will look like what is shown in Figure 11-5.

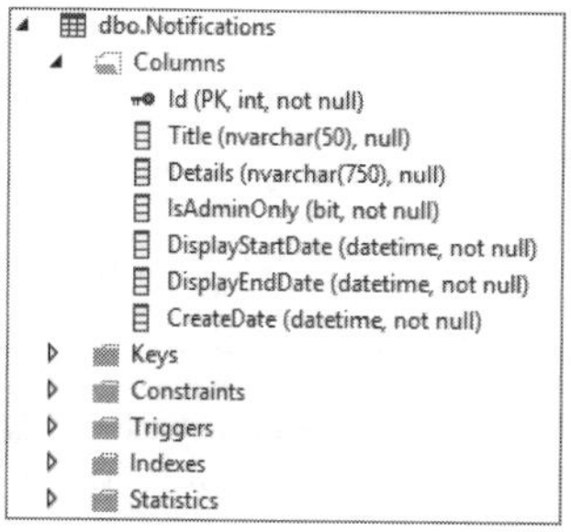

The code-behind contains the initial logic required to get the notification that will be displayed. Using the database context you were able to add a LINQ query that will evaluate the properties of items in the database table to determine which items are as follows:

➤ For administrative use only (IsAdminOnly is true)

➤ DisplayStartDate is in the past

➤ DisplayEndDate is in the future

FIGURE 11-5: Database view of the Notifications table created by the application

The resulting list of items is then sorted in descending order by the created date, and the first item is selected. It is sorted such that the most recently created notification that meets the date criteria is selected. Once this item is selected, the Title and Details are added to the Text properties of the label controls you added to the markup page, which ensures that they will be displayed as part of the rendered page.

Adding User Controls

Once you have created your user control, the next step is to add it to your site pages. As with any default server control, you can add your user control to either master pages or content pages as necessary.

WHY WOULD YOU PUT A USER CONTROL IN A MASTER PAGE?

You always need to decide where to manage the UI and code when a certain set of consistent behavior is going to be added to a master page. Should that functionality just be built into the master page or should you create a separate user control?

When you are asking yourself this question, remember that an ideal software design should have all of the logic for a set of functionality together, in one place, and created in such a way that no other logic needs to know about how that functionality works. This approach is known as *encapsulation,* so adhering to it also suggests that you create a separate user control to handle the work.

This approach also enables you to manage the control as a discrete entity, and enables your master pages to be more layout specific rather than functionality-driven, both of which are expected because the master page is a template determining where content should be placed and how it should look. It should not do a lot of processing itself.

There are two steps to adding a user control to a page. The first is registering the control with the page, and the second is placing the control into the page. In the registration step, you are building the link to the control that you are planning to use in your page. The registration looks like the following snippet and is generally added at the top of the markup page, under the `Page` definition:

```
<%@ Register Src="ControlName.ascx" TagName="ControlName" TagPrefix="rmw" %>
```

The element tag layout follows the `Page` definition in that it starts with the `<%@` character combination. The attributes, conversely, are different, and are defined in Table 11-2.

TABLE 11-2: Attributes for User Control Registration

ATTRIBUTE	DESCRIPTION
`Src`	The URL of the control you will be using in your page. Typically, you would use the tilde approach to defining the address, so it would generally look something like `Src="~/PathToControl/ControlName.ascx"`.
`TagName`	The value you want to use when you refer to the control in your markup. Much like when you defined `ContentPlaceholders` with an Id and then referred to that Id in your content page, the `TagName` defines the value that you will use to relate to your control. Generally, this value is the same as the control name, but it can be anything.
`TagPrefix`	A user-defined value that is used in the same way as the `asp:` prefix when defining a standard server control. The system will default to using "uc" followed by a counter for the number of controls that have been defined in the page. However, in the previous code snippet it was defined as `"rmw"`. If you are using multiple user controls on the same page, it would be easier to use the same TagPrefix so that all of the custom controls show up together in Intellisense.

Once you have the user control registered with the page, the next step is to implement the control on the page. The following code snippet shows how this is done:

```
<rmw:ControlName runat="server" />
```

As you see, the syntax for using a user control in your page is very similar to that of a server control.

As with almost everything in ASP.NET Web Forms, there is another way to register and use your user controls through the Design window in Visual Studio. The next activity demonstrates how to do this.

TRY IT OUT   Adding Your User Control to the Page

Creating the user control is only part of the battle; the rest is implementing your user control on the page(s) where you want the output from the controls to be displayed and used.

1.   Ensure that Visual Studio is running and that you have your RentMyWrox solution open. Open the `Default.aspx` file from your Admin directory and add the following code directly underneath the `Page` definition:

```
<%@ Register Src="~/Controls/NotificationsControl.ascx"
        TagName="Notifications" TagPrefix="rmw" %>
```

2. While still in the `Default.aspx.cs` page, locate the `Content` control with the ID of `Content2` and add the following line between the opening and closing tags. The page should look like Figure 11-6 when completed.

```
<rmw:Notifications runat="server" ID="BaseId"/>
```

```
Default.aspx
1  <%@ Page Title="" Language="C#"
2      MasterPageFile="~/WebForms.Master"
3      AutoEventWireup="true"
4      CodeBehind="Default.aspx.cs"
5      Inherits="RentMyWrox.Admin.Default" %>
6  <%@ Register Src="~/Controls/NotificationsControl.ascx" TagName="Notifications" TagPrefix="rmw" %>
7  <asp:Content ID="Content1" ContentPlaceHolderID="head" runat="server">
8  </asp:Content>
9  <asp:Content ID="Content2" ContentPlaceHolderID="ContentPlaceHolder1" runat="server">
10     <rmw:Notifications runat="server" ID="BaseId"/>
11 </asp:Content>
12
```

FIGURE 11-6: Page after registering your user control

3. Run the application and go to \Admin\. The application will run but you won't see anything because there is no data in the database.

4. Open the SQL Server Object Explorer window. Expand the RentMyWrox database and right-click on the dbo.Notifications table, and select View Data. This opens the Data screen in the main window. It should look similar to Figure 11-7.

```
dbo.Notifications [Data]
Max Rows: 1000
  Id      Title     Details   IsAdminOnly  DisplayStartDate  DisplayEndDate  CreateDate
* NULL    NULL      NULL      NULL         NULL              NULL            NULL
```

FIGURE 11-7: Empty Notifications table

5. Enter a row of data in the window, as shown in Figure 11-8. Do not enter a value in the Id column. You should also ensure that you enter several sentences of data into the Details column. Finally, ensure that the current date is between the values you enter for `DisplayStartDate` and `DisplayEndDate`. When you are done, press the Enter key.

```
dbo.Notifications [Data]
Max Rows: 1000
  Id      Title          Details           IsAdminOnly  DisplayStartDate   DisplayEndDate    CreateDate
  2       Initial Title  This is the very  True         1/1/2015 12:00:...  12/31/2017 12:0... 5/1/2015 12:00:...
► NULL    NULL           NULL              NULL         NULL               NULL              NULL
```

FIGURE 11-8: Entering data into the Notifications table

6. Run the application and go to \Admin\. You should get a result similar to what is shown in Figure 11-9 but containing the data that you entered into the database.

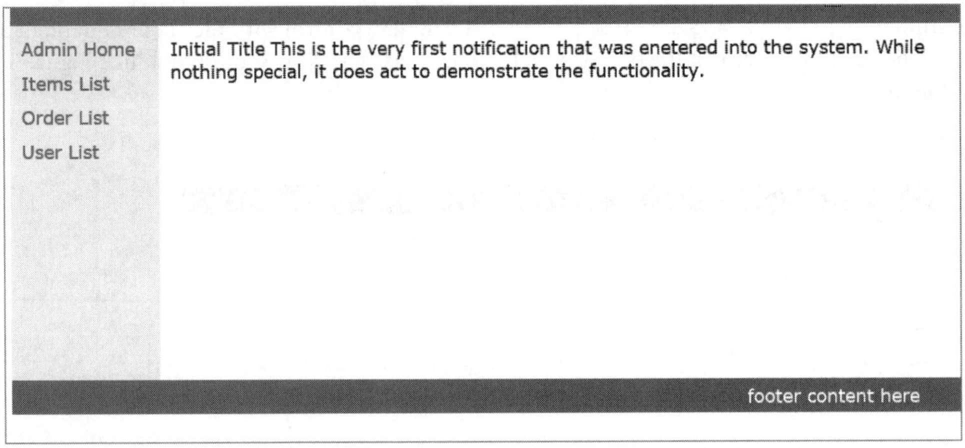

FIGURE 11-9: Default page showing the user control

How It Works

The first step in this exercise was registering the control into the page. This creates the link between the page and the control, and defines how the control will be called during instantiation. This was done through the `TagPrefix` and `TagName` attributes in the `Register` element, both of which are required by the system.

After defining the registration, you were able to determine where you would instantiate the control. After the registration step, you use the control in the same way that you would use a traditional server control. Nothing else needs to be done to manage the display of the items.

When you ran the application and went to the page that includes your user control, it didn't seem to work because there was no visible information. That's because although the database table was correctly created without requiring you to take any actions other than adding the item into your database context, the system wasn't able to add any data for you. After you added the data to these new database tables, the data became visible in your control.

You have just successfully added a user control to a content page. If you look at the page that you changed, you will see that adding the same control to multiple pages creates a large set of repetitive code because you add the `Register` command to every page that will be using the control. This means the same code has been written multiple times. Typically, good developers try to avoid that as much as possible. You will see how you can do that in the next section.

Sitewide Registration of a User Control

Replicating code is generally not a good idea, so rather than register your user control in every page it will be used, ASP.NET gives you the capability to instead register it once in the `Web.config` file. A default `Web.config` file is shown in Figure 11-10.

FIGURE 11-10: Default Web.Config file

Adding sitewide registration for a control requires the addition of a new node in the `Controls` node of the `Pages` element, as shown in line 36 of Figure 11-10. The node that you would add is very similar to the register command, as shown here:

```
<add tagPrefix="RMW" tagName="Banner" src="~/Controls/Banner.ascx" />
```

As you can see, all the attributes are the same as those for the `Register` command. The next activity guides you through the process of implementing these changes.

TRY IT OUT Implementing Sitewide User Control Registration

In the last activity you registered and added the same user control to several pages. In this activity, you will register the control so that it is available to every page in your site, without having to register it on each page.

1. Ensure that Visual Studio is running and that your RentMyWrox solution is open.

2. Open your `Web.config` file and find the `<system.web>` element.

3. Locate the `<pages>` element and find the `<controls>` sub-element. Within the `<controls>` element, add the following code and save your work. Once added, that section of your configuration file should be similar to Figure 11-11.

```
<add tagPrefix="RMW" tagName="NotificationsControl"
     src="~/Admin/NotificationsControl.ascx" />
```

```
<system.web>
  <authentication mode="None" />
  <compilation debug="true" targetFramework="4.5" />
  <httpRuntime targetFramework="4.5" />
  <pages>
    <namespaces>
      <add namespace="System.Web.Helpers" />
      <add namespace="System.Web.Mvc" />
      <add namespace="System.Web.Mvc.Ajax" />
      <add namespace="System.Web.Mvc.Html" />
      <add namespace="System.Web.Optimization" />
      <add namespace="System.Web.Routing" />
      <add namespace="System.Web.WebPages" />
      <add namespace="Microsoft.AspNet.Identity" />
    </namespaces>
    <controls>
      <add assembly="Microsoft.AspNet.Web.Optimization.WebForms" namespace="Microsoft.AspNet.Web.Optimization.WebForms" tagPrefix="webopt" />
      <add tagPrefix="RMW" tagName="NotificationsControl" src="~/Admin/NotificationsControl.ascx" />
    </controls>
  </pages>
```

FIGURE 11-11: Web.config after registering your user control

4. Open the `ManageItem.aspx` file in your Admin directory. Immediately below the `Content` control with the ID of `Content1`, start typing **RMW**. IntelliSense should highlight the control as shown in Figure 11-12.

FIGURE 11-12: Adding the user control

5. Finish entering the line of code as shown here and save the file:

```
<RMW:NotificationsControl runat="server" />
```

6. Run the application and go to Admin/ManageItem. You should get a screen similar to that in Figure 11-13.

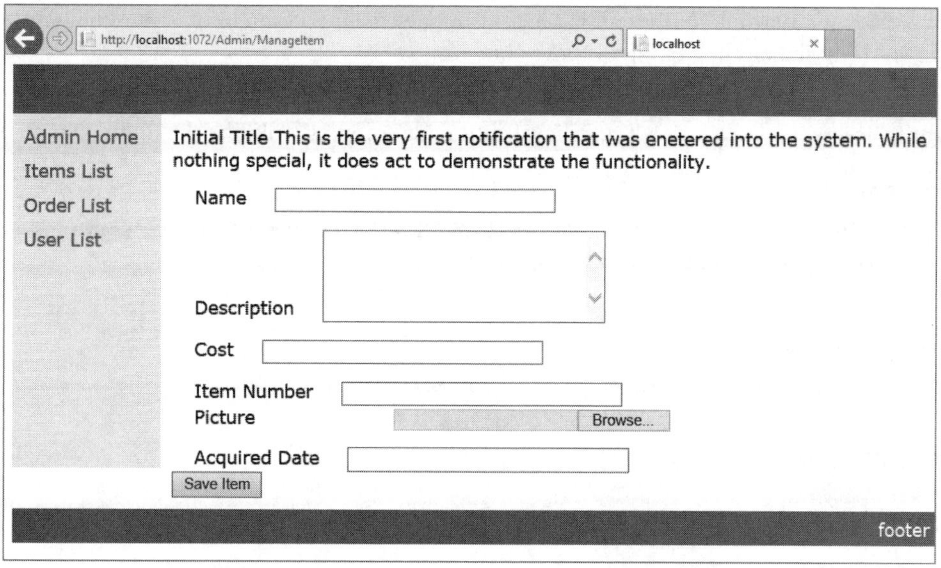

FIGURE 11-13: ManageItem page after the control is successfully added

How It Works

Just as it supports the capability to register a control on a page, ASP.NET supports the registering of a control sitewide. The sitewide registration does not happen in code, however, but through configuration. Once the configuration has been added, it is possible to add the control to a page just like a server control—without having to specially register it on a page.

One of the interesting peculiarities of user controls is how they affect the ID of various server controls contained within them.

Managing the IDs of Any Controls

When you work with server controls within your user control you will find that the ASP.NET runtime takes some liberties with the values that you set. Consider a traditional `Label` server control. The following code snippet shows both the code used to create the label in your content page and the created HTML:

MARKUP PAGE

```
<asp:Content ID="Content2" ContentPlaceHolderID="MainContent" runat="server">
    <asp:Label runat="server" ID="DefaultLabel" Text="I am a label" />
</asp:Content>

Rendered HTML

<span id="MainContent_DefaultLabel">I am a label</span>
```

As you can see, ASP.NET changes the id of your rendered HTML by using the entire nested chain of controls to create the ID, ensuring that each control's ID is referenced in the output HTML. Thus, the label with an ID of `DefaultLabel` that is contained in a `Content` control with an ID of `MainContent` would output an HTML `<span>` element with an id of "`MainContent_DefaultLabel`" based on the nesting of those controls.

Consider the following situation. Your user control contains a standard server control whose ID you may want to access, perhaps for styling. The various code snippets look like the following:

MARKUP PAGE

```
<asp:Content ID="Content2" ContentPlaceHolderID="MainContent" runat="server">
    <rmw:ServerControl ID="BaseId" runat="server"/>
</asp:Content>
```

CONTROL CONTENT

```
<asp:Label runat="server" ID="UserControl" Text="I am a control" />
```

RENDERED HTML

```
<span id="MainContent_BaseId_UserControl">I am a control</span>
```

As you can imagine, this approach makes it difficult to find an item on the client side, especially if it is nested within other controls, because its HTML id will be based on the relationships between all of the controls, so predicting the ID can be problematic. This became a big enough issue when using Web Forms that an attribute was added to all controls (both server and user) by default, `ClientIdMode`. `ClientIdMode` enables the developer to define how client-side Ids will be generated based on ASP.NET control IDs. The available values are described in Table 11-3.

TABLE 11-3: ClientIdMode Values

NAME	DESCRIPTION
`AutoId`	Creates a client-side id that is basically a concatenation of all ids from all controls in the hierarchy. The output of this approach would be the same as the preceding examples. This is also the value from all versions of ASP.NET prior to 3.5.
`Static`	Using this `ClientIdMode` means there will be no concatenation within the control's client id. Thus, any ID that you assign the control will be given to the rendered element. However, there is no validation that the ID is unique, even though this is a requirement of HTML. You have to manage this uniqueness yourself as you build out your markup.

NAME	DESCRIPTION
Predictable	This mode is generally used in databound controls for which you want every item in the set of output to have an Id that you can predict. This is useful in cases where you may have a user control that is displayed with each row in a list of items. Using `Predictable` and the `ClientIDRowSuffix` attribute enables you to define the Id of the output element to include some known value such as the Id of the item in the list. If you are not using this mode in an area where there are multiple instantiations, such as a list, the output will be the same as `AutoId`.
Inherit	This value sets the `ClientIdMode` of a control to the `ClientIdMode` of its hosting item—whether it is another control (either user control or server control) or a page. This is actually the default value of all controls, whereas `Predictable` is the default mode for all pages.

At this point, nothing needs the `ClientIdMode` in the sample application. You will later see how these different modes can be useful, both on the client side and on the server.

Adding Logic to Your User Controls

You have created a user control that performs a specific set of functionality. With this design, however, if you wanted the control to be able to do something slightly different you would have to create another control to perform that slightly different action. Instead of creating a new user control, wouldn't it be better to provide additional functionality in this same control? In this section you'll learn how you can do that.

You likely remember that the default Web Form server controls are capable of using attributes as part of control instantiation. You can add the same type of support to your user controls; that is, you can add properties (which become available as attributes during control creation) to your control and then make decisions within your code based on those additional values. This enables you to instantiate your control as follows:

```
<rmw:SomeKindOfListControl runat="server" SortOrder="Descending" ID="MyUserControl"
        MaxNumberDisplayed="3" />
```

This code not only instantiates the control, it sets some properties. The changes you have to make in your control are minimal. Supporting the preceding control just described would require an approach such as the following:

```
public enum Sortorder
{
    Ascending,
    Descending,
```

```
    None
}

public partial class SomeKindOfListControl : System.Web.UI.UserControl
{
    public int MaxNumberDisplayed { get; set; }

    public Sortorder SortOrder { get; set; }

    protected void Page_Load(object sender, EventArgs e)
    {

    }
}
```

As shown in the preceding snippet, there are two public properties whose names match the attributes in the previous example. During page creation and control instantiation, these values will be set by the attributes. Because this happens during control instantiation, the values are available during the `Page_Load` event handler.

An interesting part of this code sample is the use of the enum. As you may remember, an enum enables you to define a set of values that are available—in this case, three different sort orders. Using an enum in this instance enables the user control to have some control over the different kinds of values that are input, as shown in Figure 11-14.

```
 9  ⊟<asp:Content ID="Content2" ContentPlaceHolderID="ContentPlaceHolder1" runat="server">
10        <rmw:SomeKindOfListControl runat="server" SortOrder=" MaxNumberDisplayed="3"/>
11  └</asp:Content>                                    ⊟ Ascending
12                                                     ⊟ Descending
                                                       ⊟ None
```

FIGURE 11-14: Enum values shown in IntelliSense

Along with the capability to have IntelliSense understand enums, because you are working with a type-safe language, either C# or VB.NET, there is enforcement of type as well. The `MaxNumberDisplayed` expects an integer value. If you try to enter a different value, such as a string, you will get a validation warning, as shown in Figure 11-15.

```
 9  ⊟<asp:Content ID="Content2" ContentPlaceHolderID="ContentPlaceHolder1" runat="server">
10        <rmw:SomeKindOfListControl runat="server" SortOrder="Descending" MaxNumberDisplayed="three"/>
11  └</asp:Content>
12                          Validation (ASP.Net): The values permitted for this attribute do not include 'three'.
```

FIGURE 11-15: Validation when using an incorrect type

Trying to run the application with an incorrect type results in an error, as shown in Figure 11-16.

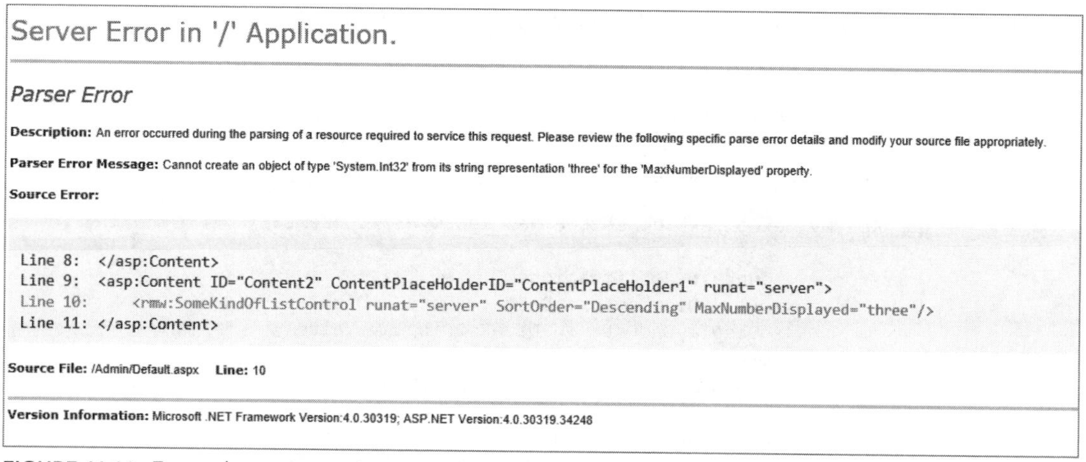

> Server Error in '/' Application.
>
> **Parser Error**
>
> **Description:** An error occurred during the parsing of a resource required to service this request. Please review the following specific parse error details and modify your source file appropriately.
>
> **Parser Error Message:** Cannot create an object of type 'System.Int32' from its string representation 'three' for the 'MaxNumberDisplayed' property.
>
> **Source Error:**
>
> ```
> Line 8:  </asp:Content>
> Line 9:  <asp:Content ID="Content2" ContentPlaceHolderID="ContentPlaceHolder1" runat="server">
> Line 10:    <rmw:SomeKindOfListControl runat="server" SortOrder="Descending" MaxNumberDisplayed="three"/>
> Line 11: </asp:Content>
> ```
>
> **Source File:** /Admin/Default.aspx   **Line:** 10
>
> **Version Information:** Microsoft .NET Framework Version:4.0.30319; ASP.NET Version:4.0.30319.34248

FIGURE 11-16: Error when using an incorrect type in a user control

By adding public properties to the user control, you can customize its output. However, you need to ensure that you code your application so that it can successfully run if it contains attributes that are not set, such as through the use of default values. The following Try It Out will give you hands-on experience with adding logic to your user controls, and it demonstrates several approaches to ensuring that your control can work regardless of the attribute that was entered in the calling page.

TRY IT OUT   Adding Logic to Your Controls

Our initial server control made some assumptions regarding how items will be managed. In this activity, you allow the calling page to manage some of those assumptions, making your control more flexible and manageable from the page. You do this by allowing two new fields, DisplayType and DateForDisplay, to be set as attributes in the control.

1.   Ensure that Visual Studio is running and that you have your RentMyWrox solution open. Open
     Controls\NotificationsControl.aspx.cs.

2.   Add the following code to the page, above the Page_Load method:

```
public enum DisplayType
{
    AdminOnly,
    NonAdminOnly,
    Both
}

public DisplayType Display { get; set; }

public DateTime? DateForDisplay { get; set; }
```

3. Change the `Page_Load` method to the following:

```
protected void Page_Load(object sender, EventArgs e)
{
    if (!DateForDisplay.HasValue)
    {
        DateForDisplay = DateTime.Now;
    }
    using (RentMyWroxContext context = new RentMyWroxContext())
    {
        var notes = context.Notifications
            .Where(x => x.DisplayStartDate <= DateForDisplay.Value
                && x.DisplayEndDate >= DateForDisplay.Value);

        if (Display != null && Display != DisplayType.Both)
        {
            notes = notes.Where(x => x.IsAdminOnly ==
                    (Display == DisplayType.AdminOnly));
        }

        Notification note = notes.OrderByDescending(x => x.CreateDate)
                .FirstOrDefault();

        if (note != null)
        {
            NotificationTitle.Text = note.Title;
            NotificationDetail.Text = note.Details;
        }
    }
}
```

4. Run the application and go to \Admin to confirm that everything still works.

5. Open `Admin\Default.aspx`. Go into the Notifications control that has already been added to the page and add the new attribute as shown here:

```
Display="AdminOnly"
```

6. Run the application and go to \Admin to confirm that everything still works.

How It Works

You made changes to the user control that enable it to support different needs. The original control that you created had no customization capability; it made some business decisions without input and then displayed the output. You just changed that, adding several new properties, as shown in Figure 11-17.

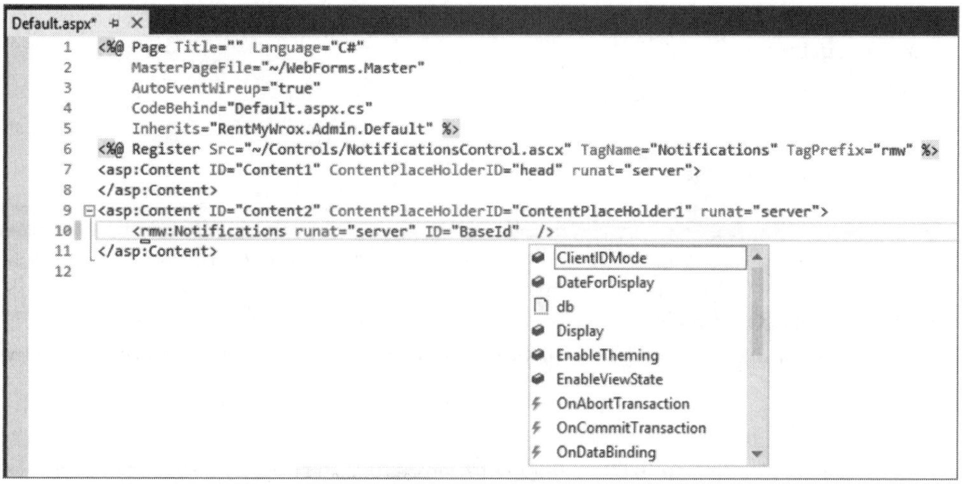

FIGURE 11-17: Adding in user control with additional properties

The first property you added is `DateForDisplay`, which enables the control to use a date other than the current date if needed. However, the type that you used, `DateTime?`, is a nullable type, which means that you don't have to set a value. Because this type is being used in the code, you added a few lines to set the default value to the current date if the property wasn't passed in. The application will use this default value because the changes you made to the instantiation of the control did not include this property.

The next property is `Display`, a property of type `DisplayType`. `DisplayType` is an enum that has three values: Admin, non-Admin, and Neither. This enables you to use the same control whether you want to display an admin-only item, a non-admin only item, or you don't care which one is displayed. Because there is no requirement that this property be set, you had to add a check to determine whether it had a value; the code `Display != null` checks to ensure that the property has been set.

Finally, you changed the database access language to use the values of the various properties. This was the biggest change because you could no longer use a single line of code, instead having to make a series of commands whereby you filtered down the list step by step.

Now that you have added some logic to your user control, consider a slightly different scenario. You added attributes to the markup code that set various values in the user control. You can also set these values programmatically in your code because a user control is as easily accessible in the code-behind as a standard server control. Suppose you have the following control set as shown:

```
<rmw:SomeKindOfListControl runat="server" SortOrder="Descending" ID="MyUserControl"
        MaxNumberDisplayed="3" />
```

You can access this control in your code-behind as shown here and change these values as necessary while in your code-behind:

```
protected void Page_Load(object sender, EventArgs e)
{
    MyUserControl.MaxNumberDisplayed = 5;
    MyUserControl.SortOrder = Sortorder.Ascending;
}
```

Because you have full control in your code-behind, there may be times when you don't want to set the values in the control definition at all but rather, for a particular page, always set them in code. This gives you flexibility based on logic that is happening within your page; for example, the attribute value you use might depend upon the type of information in the page or on actions taken by the user.

Not setting the properties in the control is straightforward but the implementation may affect the way your user control is designed. This may happen because of differences in how these properties are being set. When setting a property through the control's attribute, you are setting that value during the control's instantiation. That means the value is set at the very beginning of the ASP.NET page life cycle. Setting the values at a different time in the life cycle, such as during the `Page_Load` event manager as shown earlier, may mean that the values have not yet been set when the control does its processing.

The life cycle provides some protection for ensuring that property values are set because it always runs the hosting page's event handler before it runs the same event handler on the control. This means that the process will look like the diagram in Figure 11-18.

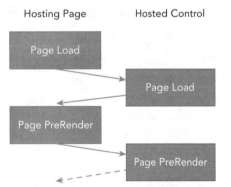

FIGURE 11-18: Page life cycle with page and hosted control

Thus, you would be able to set values in the `Page_Load` method of the hosting page and then access those values in the control's `Page_Load` method. However, if you ended up setting those values in the hosting page's `Page_PreRender` event handler (which comes after the `Page_Load` event handler), yet expected to be able to access those values in the control's `Page_Load` method, then you will get unexpected behavior because those properties were not set as required. This can be mitigated by not doing any work in your control until after `Page_Load` has been called.

Another potential problem is one that you ran into earlier in the discussion of server controls: values being set in code but maintained in `ViewState`. This may or may not be a problem, depending on your needs; but if retaining `ViewState` is necessary, it is possible and fairly simple to achieve. The following code shows the two different approaches, one in which the values are lost upon submission and the other in which the values are retained in `ViewState`:

VIEWSTATE NOT MAINTAINED

```
public int MaxNumberDisplayed { get; set; }
```

VIEWSTATE MAINTAINED

```
public int MaxNumberDisplayed
{
    get { return (int)ViewState["MaxNumberDisplayed"]; }
    set { ViewState["MaxNumberDisplayed"] = value; }
}
```

With the second approach, you are manually manipulating the information in the `ViewState` by actually using the `ViewState` as the backing fields for the variable's getter and setter. You can do this for all the properties in the control or just those properties for which remembering the values between posts is important.

Sharing functionality between pages in an ASP.NET Web Forms site can be managed by creating a user control to manage the requisite needs. When creating your user control, ensure that you keep it focused on doing one thing. Adding properties gives you some control over the work happening in the control, but don't go overboard and start trying to do too many unrelated things within a single control. It is better to have multiple well-defined controls than a single control that does multiple different actions. Once you need to start adding if/then statements to determine the work that the control will do, you should consider adding an additional control instead.

USING PARTIAL VIEWS

Whereas ASP.NET Web Forms support the reuse of functionality through user controls, ASP.NET MVC does not have the concept of a user control. It supports the same functionality through the use of partial views. Like a Web Forms user control, a partial view can contain just a view (perhaps with some Razor processing within the view), or the partial view can be called from within another view by calling the controller and action, thus taking advantage of business processing and the inherent separation of concerns.

A partial view is very similar to a regular view, except that it is expected to be placed on another page, so it looks more like a view that is designed to use a layout page because it will not have any code created by default unless you use the scaffolding to build it off a particular model. Because a partial view is intended to be a shared view, it follows some of the same rules as a layout file in that the view file belongs in the Shared folder under the Views directory, and the view is traditionally prefaced with an underscore, "_ViewName." The Shared folder is where the MVC system looks for referenced views by default; and while the underscore (_) is not required, it is the standard convention.

Creating a Partial View

You have already created a user control that enables you to create reusable content for use in an ASP .NET Web Forms page. In this Try It Out you do the same using ASP.NET MVC to create a partial view, content that is reusable across multiple pages in an ASP.NET MVC application.

1. Ensure that Visual Studio is running and that you have your RentMyWrox solution open.

2. Right-click on the Shared subdirectory under the Views folder and select Add ➪ View. Name it **_Notification**, use the Details template, select the Notification as the model to use, and ensure that you are using the RentMyWrox context. Also, ensure that "Create as a partial view" is checked. Your Add View dialog should match the one shown in Figure 11-19.

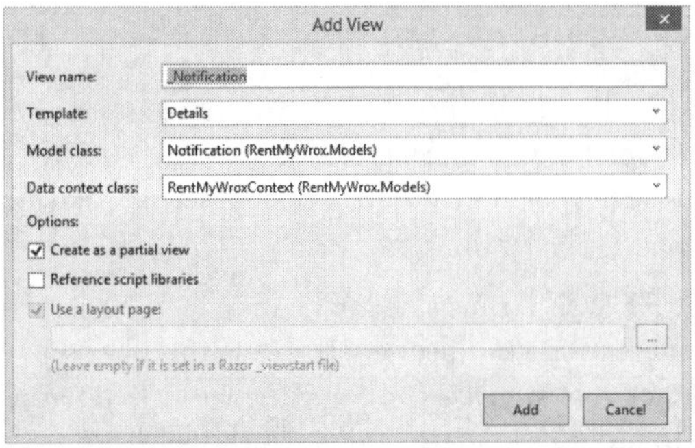

FIGURE 11-19: Adding a partial view

3. Click the Add button to save the view and open it in the main window. Delete all the information other than the first line. This will leave you a page that looks like the one shown in Figure 11-20.

```
_Notification.cshtml
1  @model RentMyWrox.Models.Notification
2
```

FIGURE 11-20: Removing scaffolded information

4. Add the following code and save the file. When completed, it should look like Figure 11-21.

```
@model RentMyWrox.Models.Notification
@if(Model != null)
{
```

```
    <span class="NotificationTitle">@Model.Title</span>
    <span class="NotificationDetail">@Model.Details</span>
}
```

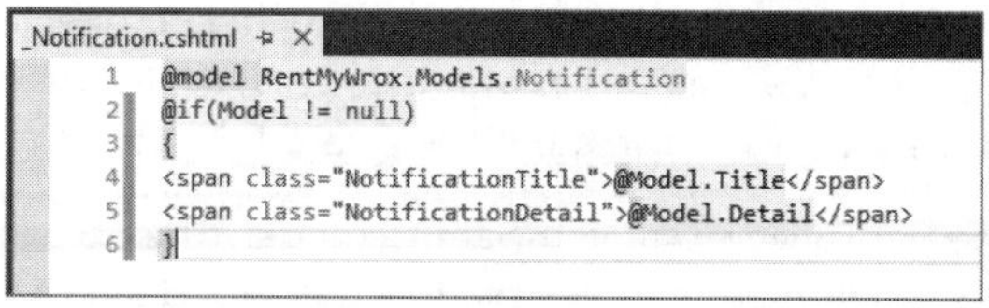

FIGURE 11-21: Finished partial view

How It Works

Comparing this example to the activity in which you created the ASP.NET Web Forms user control, you should see the difference right away between the concept of a partial view and a user control. In that case, when you were done creating the control, it was fully functional, it just wasn't shown in any pages so you didn't get a chance to see it. That's not the case with the partial view.

The separation of concerns offered by ASP.NET MVC is something that you have to remember whenever you approach the creation of reusable user interface code. All the view knows is that it expects a type of `RentMyWrox.Models.Notification` to be "given" to it so that it can display the appropriate fields. The beauty of this approach is that unlike the tightly bound Web Forms approach, it doesn't matter to the view how it gets the appropriate information—only that it gets it. You'll see this demonstrated in the next few examples.

Adding a Partial View

Once you have the partial view created, the next thing you need to do is add it to the hosting view. Here is the simplest way:

```
<div>
  @Html.Partial("_PartialViewName")
</div>
```

This approach uses an HTML helper that processes the partial view into a string and then inserts that string into the hosting view. You can also capture the string into a variable where you can work with it as necessary. Another approach instead parses it directly into the response stream as it is being created. This approach, using the `HTML.RenderPartial` extension method, does not allow you to manipulate the output of the partial view. Because the `RenderPartial` method does not write out a string it is more performant than the `Partial` method.

Four different sets of parameters are available to the `Partial` and `RenderPartial` methods, each of which enables you to pass in different sets of information to the partial view. Table 11-4 describes these different signatures.

TABLE 11-4: Method Signatures for Including Partial Views

SIGNATURE	DESCRIPTION
string	The string represents the partial view name. Note that no directory structure or anything else is added in with the name, as the system assumes that the partial view is in the Views\Shared directory.
string, object	The string is the partial view that you want to render. The object is the model passed into the partial view. If you do not define a specific model to be passed into the partial view, then the system passes in the same model that the hosting view was given.
string, ViewDataDictionary	The string is the partial view that you want to render. The ViewDataDictionary represents the viewData that you want the partial view to be able to access. You can access viewData by using constructs such as ViewData["SomeKeyName"].
string, object, ViewDataDictionary	The string is the partial view that you want to render. The object is the model that is passed into the partial view. The ViewDataDictionary represents the viewData that you want the partial view to be able to access.

When you are rendering a partial view, you have control of the information you pass in to the view. When you do not specify the model or viewData, then the hosting view's model and/or viewData will be provided to the partial view. When taking this approach, you have to remember that the hosting view has to provide all of the data to the partial view. That means there is no associated controller providing the information, so you have to do it from the calling view. The following Try It Out walks you through adding a partial view.

TRY IT OUT Adding a Partial View

You have already created a partial view that enables you to create reusable content for use in an ASP .NET MVC view. In this exercise you add this partial view to your MVC view.

1. Ensure that Visual Studio is running and that you have your RentMyWrox solution open. Open the main layout page, Shared_MVCLayout.cshtml. Locate the end of the menu on the left and insert the following code below the menu. The page should look like Figure 11-22.

```
<br />
@{
    var model = new Notification {
            Title = "This is a hardcoded title",
            Details = "this is hardcoded details" };
}
@Html.Partial("_Notification", model)
```

```
11 ⊟<body>
12 ⊟    <div id="header">
13              <img src="rentmywrox_logo.gif" />
14        </div>
15 ⊟    <div id="nav">
16 ⊟        <div id="LeftNavigation">
17 ⊟            <ul class="level1">
18                  <li><a href="~/" class="level1">Home</a></li>
19                  <li>@Html.ActionLink("Items", "", "Items", new { @class = "level1" })</li>
20                  <li>@Html.ActionLink("Contact Us", "ContactUs", "Home", new { @class = "level1" })</li>
21                  <li>@Html.ActionLink("About Us", "About", "Home", new { @class = "level1" })</li>
22              </ul>
23              <br />
24              @{
25                  var model = new Notification {
26                      Title = "This is a hardcoded title",
27                      Details = "this is hardcoded details" };
28              }
29              @Html.Partial("_Notification", model)
30          </div>
31      </div>
32 ⊟    <div id="section">
33          @RenderBody()
34      </div>
35 ⊟    <div id="specialnotes">
36          @RenderSection("SpecialNotes", false)
37      </div>
38 ⊟    <div id="footer">
39          footer content here
40      </div>
41      @Scripts.Render("~/bundles/jquery")
42      @Scripts.Render("~/bundles/bootstrap")
43 </body>
```

FIGURE 11-22: Finished partial view

2. Run the application and go to \UserDemographics. You should get a page similar to that shown in Figure 11-23.

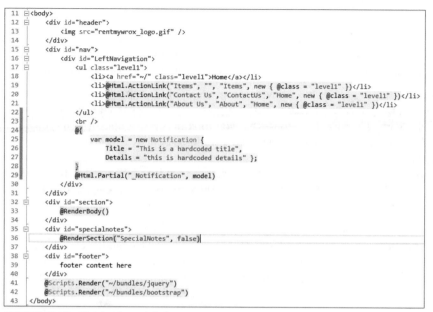

FIGURE 11-23: Partial view shown in the UI

How It Works

As mentioned in the last activity, the view does not care how it gets the model that it is going to display. In this case, you created a model using hardcoded strings and then sent this model to the partial view by passing the model as a parameter in the helper method that instantiated the partial view.

Obviously, this isn't an ideal way to do this. However, using the `Partial` method requires that the calling view already contain the information that needs to be passed into the partial view. There are several ways that this can work. The first is the route that you took in this example, which is creating the model manually and sending it into the partial view. This could be done when the values that you want to have displayed are already part of the model that was sent into the view. They could be other properties on your model that when combined make up the model that needs to be passed to the partial view, or your hosting view's model could have a property that is the same type as the partial view's model, so that particular property would simply be passed in as opposed to creating a new model object.

As this code now stands, there is no access to a model in your layout, because this is a layout page that will serve as a template for multiple pages, each of which may have its own model. However, by default, the layout has access to the model passed to the content page. Therefore, the page has access to the model, it just currently has problems being able to predict the type of model that will be passed, especially given the current approach whereby the model being presented to the view is tightly bound to the database.

This brings up the concept of a ViewModel, or a model that is specifically designed to be passed to a view. It represents information that is necessary for the view to display correctly, rather than information specific to a particular item. So far, every view that you have worked with expects a type that is directly related to a business entity—in this case one that is also directly related to a database table. That is not always the case, especially in enterprise applications which might have complex UIs that represent several different models, all of which are gathered together into a single ViewModel that acts as a container. Future chapters cover a couple of examples of this.

One other way to pass information around is through the `ViewBag` and `ViewData` objects. Both of these are sets of information that are available in both the controller and the view, and serve as a flexible way of passing information that does not necessarily need to be created as part of the model. A good example is the list of values that would be available in a dropdown. Most likely, the entire set of information will not be part of the business model because it will only retain information about the selected item, not all available items, in the dropdown. Getting this information into the view would require either a ViewModel that contains both the business model information as well as a list of values for the list box or a different way to pass data from the controller to the view. Also, because the context of the hosting page is passed into partial views by default (there are methods where you can pass in objects that overwrite the default content), the `ViewBag` and `ViewData` objects are available for consumption in the partial view as well.

The `ViewData` is a dictionary object to which you can add data; it's a derivative of the `ViewDataDictionary` class. This means you would access it using approaches like those demonstrated in the following code:

```
ViewData["NotificationModel"] = new Notification();

Notification notificationFromViewData = ViewData["NotificationModel"] as Notification;
```

The ViewBag object is different in that it is a wrapper around the ViewData object that enables you to create dynamic properties for the ViewBag. This in turn enables you to access them differently, as shown here:

```
ViewBag.NotificationModel = new Notification();

Notification notificationFromViewBag = ViewBag.NotificationModel;
```

Each of these approaches enables you to pass information from the controller to the hosting view, and from there to the partial view.

As this last activity shows, when using the HTML.Partial approach, you have to provide all the data to that view from the hosting view. However, there will be times when you don't want to add this computation to all of the controllers that will be returning views containing the partial view. Instead you will want the partial view to be able to do its own processing. Fortunately, you have that capability as well.

Managing the Controller for a Partial View

With an ASP.NET Web Forms user control, you have the same default functionality provided by a Web Forms page: the markup and the code-behind. In the last activity you saw how MVC offers you the capability to create a partial view and call the view directly. However, the implementation that you just went through does not allow the equivalent of the code-behind, or the capability to do business processing outside of the view itself—a capability that would be very useful.

Whereas the Partial and PartialRender commands directly add the partial view into an area within the page, there is another approach that calls a controller action which then returns the partial view for rendering. This approach enables you to use the complete processing power of a controller to create a specific model to provide to the partial view.

Using a controller to perform this work provides several significant advantages. The first is that you do not have to do any processing in the hosting view. If the partial view needs a specific model, the action responding to the original request does not have to worry about that—it can just ensure that the non-partial view information is available for consumption by the hosting view. This also means that you can eliminate the need for that code on each action that provides a view using that partial view.

By adding a controller to the flow, you are also helping enforce the MVC pattern by separating the different concerns into their appropriate places. This ensures that the various parts of the application remains extensible and reusable.

One more reason why using an action to create the partial view is useful is because of caching. By using a controller-based action, you can cache the output on the server so that different calls over a short period return the same content, without having to actually rerun the business logic. If the content changes infrequently, controller-based caching favorably impacts both performance and system utilization because the work is not redone on each call, only when the cache expires.

SERVER CACHING IN MVC

In its simplest form, caching provides a way to store frequently accessed data and reuse that data. Caching has some significant advantages:

➤ Reduce database server round-trips.

➤ Avoid time-consumption for regenerating reusable content.

➤ Improve performance.

Note the following points when considering the use of caching in your MVC application:

➤ Use caching for content that is accessed frequently.

➤ Avoid caching for content that is unique per user.

➤ Avoid caching for content that is accessed infrequently/rarely.

➤ For caching of dynamic content that changes frequently, define a short cache–expiration time, rather than disable caching.

As you can see, there are a lot of advantages to providing server caching in MVC. It is also easy to add because it is all attribute based, as shown here:

```
[OutputCache(Duration=300)]
public ActionResult Index()
{
    return View();
}
```

The preceding snippet will cache the output for 300 seconds, or 5 minutes. If you consider a call that may happen on every requested page, and you have 10 users calling one page per minute, over the five-minute caching period you will save 49 calls to the database. If you are working with data that changes only once a day, imagine the savings in performance and system utilization that you would have by extending the caching period to several hours. However, make sure that you do not set the caching period to several hours if the data changes every hour!

The differences between a traditional action that returns a view and an action that returns a partial view are very subtle, as shown in the following code:

ACTION THAT RETURNS A VIEW

```
public ActionResult Details(int id)
{
    return View();
}
```

ACTION THAT RETURNS A PARTIAL VIEW

```
public ActionResult Details(int id)
{
        return PartialView("_NewsList");
}
```

The only change here is that you are returning a `PartialView` rather than a `View`, and returning a named view. The named view is useful in this case because it makes it easier for the processor to find the correct partial view to use. The default is still to use a view with a name that matches the action name, but in this case that could be confusing because it would be easy to think of cases where you may have multiple "detail" partial views.

Calling the appropriate controller action to get a partial view is not too different from instantiating a partial view through the `Partial` and `RenderPartial` methods. Instead of calling those HTML extension methods, you instead call a different set of methods, `Action` and `RenderAction`, as shown here:

```
<div>
        @Html.Action("News","List")
</div>

<div>
        @Html.RenderAction("News","List")
</div>
```

The differences between the two methods are the same as those between the `Partial` methods; the `Action` method returns a string that you can capture into a variable if desired, while the `RenderAction` renders the output directly into the response stream. The parameters being passed into the method indicate the controller name and the action name that provides the partial view inserted into the hosting view.

It is important to correctly configure the controller and action to ensure that the action is returning a `PartialView` rather than a `View`. The system will error out as multiple different items try to control the response stream. Using the `PartialView` ensures that the action knows that it is going to be participating in a response stream that was created by another action, so that it does not try to directly interact with the response.

In the following Try It Out, you create a full controller-accessed partial view and then add it to several pages as necessary.

TRY IT OUT Creating and Calling a Partial View through an Action

You have already created a partial view that enables you to create reusable content for use in an ASP .NET MVC view. Now you add this partial view to your MVC view.

1. Ensure that Visual Studio is running and that you have your RentMyWrox solution open.

2. Right-click on the Controllers directory and select Add ⇨ Controller. When the Add Scaffold dialog appears, as shown in Figure 11-24, select the MVC 5 Controller - Empty template and click the Add button.

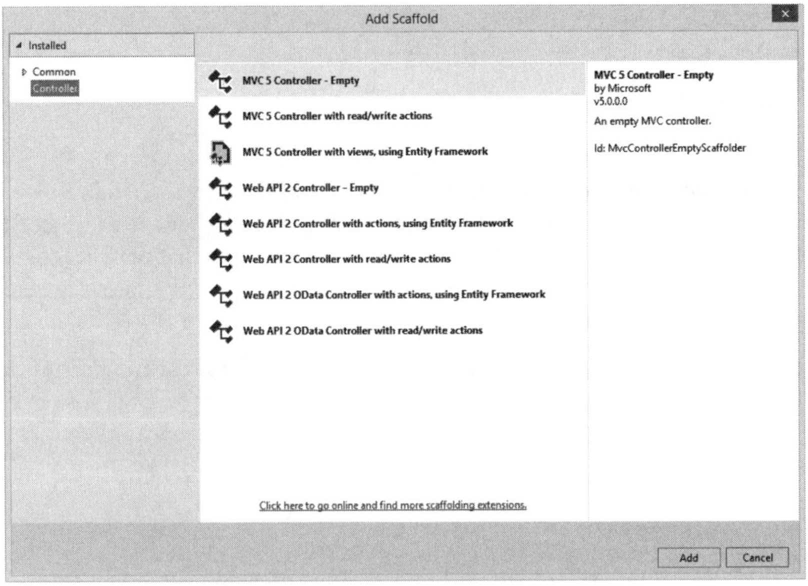

FIGURE 11-24: Scaffolding for adding a new controller

3. Name the controller **NotificationsController** and click the Add button. This creates the file and opens it in your main window. This file should look something like Figure 11-25.

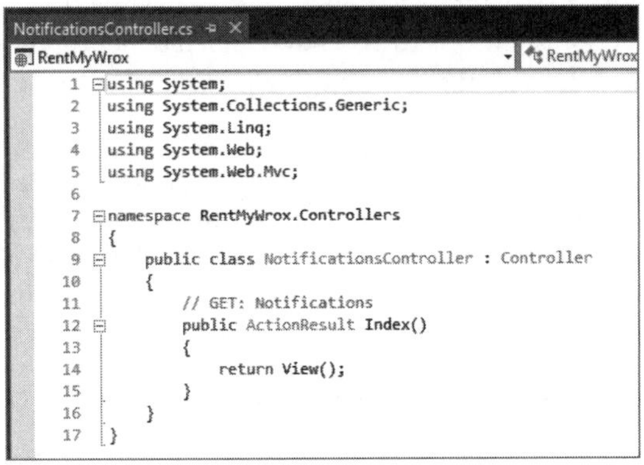

FIGURE 11-25: Empty controller

4. Add a new using statement at the top of the page so that you have access to the classes in the Models namespace:

```
using RentMyWrox.Models;
```

5. Delete the Index method. Add the following code in its place. When this is done you should have a page similar to the one shown in Figure 11-26.

```csharp
[OutputCache(Duration = 3600)]
public ActionResult AdminSnippet()
{
    using (RentMyWroxContext context = new RentMyWroxContext())
    {
        Notification note = context.Notifications
        .Where(x => x.DisplayStartDate <= DateTime.Now
            && x.DisplayEndDate >= DateTime.Now
            && x.IsAdminOnly)
        .OrderByDescending(x => x.CreateDate)
        .FirstOrDefault();
        return PartialView("_Notification", note);
    }
}


[OutputCache(Duration = 3600)]
public ActionResult NonAdminSnippet()
{
    using (RentMyWroxContext context = new RentMyWroxContext())
    {
        Notification note = context.Notifications
        .Where(x => x.DisplayStartDate <= DateTime.Now
            && x.DisplayEndDate >= DateTime.Now
            && !x.IsAdminOnly)
        .OrderByDescending(x => x.CreateDate)
        .FirstOrDefault();
        return PartialView("_Notification", note);
    }
}
```

```csharp
 8  namespace RentMyWrox.Controllers
 9  {
10      public class NotificationsController : Controller
11      {
12          [OutputCache(Duration = 3600)]
13          public ActionResult AdminSnippet()
14          {
15              using (RentMyWroxContext context = new RentMyWroxContext())
16              {
17                  Notification note = context.Notifications
18                  .Where(x => x.DisplayStartDate <= DateTime.Now
19                      && x.DisplayEndDate >= DateTime.Now
20                      && x.IsAdminOnly)
21                  .OrderByDescending(x => x.CreateDate)
22                  .FirstOrDefault();
23                  return PartialView("_Notification", note);
24              }
25          }
26
27          [OutputCache(Duration = 3600)]
28          public ActionResult NonAdminSnippet()
29          {
30              using (RentMyWroxContext context = new RentMyWroxContext())
31              {
32                  Notification note = context.Notifications
33                  .Where(x => x.DisplayStartDate <= DateTime.Now
34                      && x.DisplayEndDate >= DateTime.Now
35                      && !x.IsAdminOnly)
36                  .OrderByDescending(x => x.CreateDate)
37                  .FirstOrDefault();
38                  return PartialView("_Notification", note);
39              }
40          }
41      }
42  }
```

FIGURE 11-26: Notifications controller with actions

6. Open the layout file, Shared_MVCLayout.cshtml. Locate the code that you added earlier and replace it with the following code. When completed, the content will be as shown in Figure 11-27, following the change you just made on line 24.

```
@Html.Action("NonAdminSnippet", "Notifications")
```

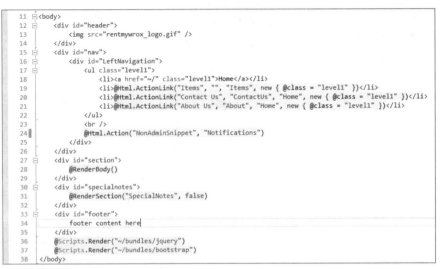

```
11  <body>
12      <div id="header">
13          <img src="rentmywrox_logo.gif" />
14      </div>
15      <div id="nav">
16          <div id="LeftNavigation">
17              <ul class="level1">
18                  <li><a href="~/" class="level1">Home</a></li>
19                  <li>@Html.ActionLink("Items", "", "Items", new { @class = "level1" })</li>
20                  <li>@Html.ActionLink("Contact Us", "ContactUs", "Home", new { @class = "level1" })</li>
21                  <li>@Html.ActionLink("About Us", "About", "Home", new { @class = "level1" })</li>
22              </ul>
23              <br />
24              @Html.Action("NonAdminSnippet", "Notifications")
25          </div>
26      </div>
27      <div id="section">
28          @RenderBody()
29      </div>
30      <div id="specialnotes">
31          @RenderSection("SpecialNotes", false)
32      </div>
33      <div id="footer">
34          footer content here
35      </div>
36      @Scripts.Render("~/bundles/jquery")
37      @Scripts.Render("~/bundles/bootstrap")
38  </body>
```

FIGURE 11-27: Updated layout view

7. Run the application and go to \UserDemographics. You should not be seeing the notification at this point, which is expected. Open your SQL Server Object Explorer, expand your database, go into your Tables, and right-click dbo.Notifications and select View Data. Add a new row to your table, ensuring that IsAdminOnly is set to False, that DisplayStartDate is before today, and that DisplayEndDate is in the future. The result should resemble what is shown in Figure 11-28.

Id	Title	Details	IsAdminOnly	DisplayStartDate	DisplayEndDate	CreateDate
2	Initial Title	This is the very ...	True	1/1/2015 12:00:...	12/31/2017 12:0...	5/1/2015 12:00:...
3	Non Admin Item	There are the d...	False	1/1/2015 12:00:...	12/31/2017 12:0...	5/23/2015 12:00...
NULL	NULL	NULL	NULL	NULL	NULL	NULL

FIGURE 11-28: SQL Table view after adding new item

8. Run the application and go to \UserDemographics. You should now see the information you just added to the database, as shown in Figure 11-29.

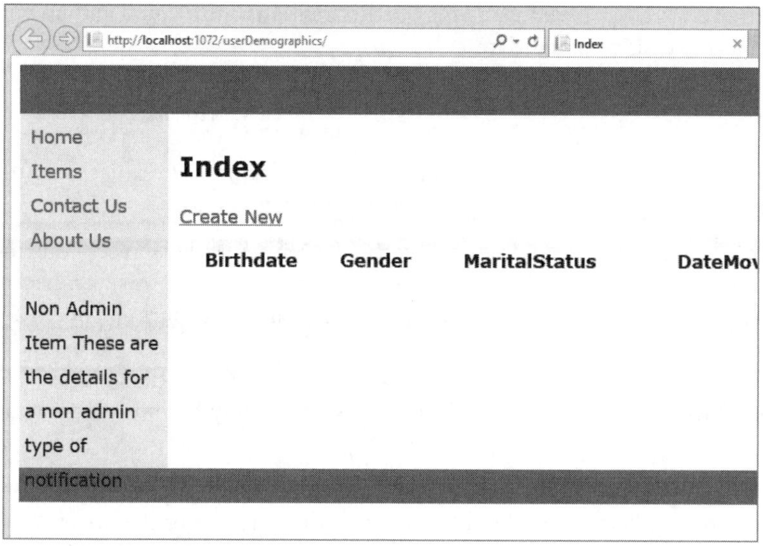

FIGURE 11-29: New notification displayed in the UI from a partial view

How It Works

In the previous example, you had to provide a model to the partial view by sending a model in from the hosting view. With this new approach, however, you changed the application so that the model was provided to the view by a controller; all the hosting view had to do was call a specific controller and action. This is a huge step, because the controller that creates the model used for populating the hosting view doesn't have to be concerned with performing any business logic for creating a notification, instead leaving it to an action that knows how to get the appropriate model. This enforces many of the rules of object-oriented programming regarding encapsulationand separation of concerns.

The process of building the controller is unchanged from creating controllers for a regular ASP.NET MVC page. The only difference is that the controller returns by calling a `PartialView` method rather than a `View` method. You created two different actions, one to return an Admin notification and the other to return a non-Admin notification. When you created the Web Forms user control you added a parameter to the control that allowed a single user control to perform the logic for both, yet here you created two different actions. Why do you think that is?

Consider what the instantiation would look like if you performed the work in a single method. Currently, instantiating each version requires the following lines:

```
@Html.Action("NonAdminSnippet", "Notifications")
@Html.Action("AdminSnippet", "Notifications")
```

If you changed it so that there were a URL-based value for the differentiator, you could end up with something like the following as the calls to instantiate:

```
@Html.Action("Snippet", "Notifications", new {DisplayType = "NonAdmin"})
@Html.Action("Snippet", "Notifications", new {DisplayType = "Admin"})
```

There would have to be logic in the controller similar to that in the code-behind of the user control to build out the query to get the correct type of notification to be displayed to the user.

Consider what would be needed to take the same approach with ASP.NET Web Form user controls. If you were not going to use parameters, you would have had to create two controls. However, because the UI is the same for each approach, you would have had to copy and paste the markup code from one control to the other, and then you would be able to do the simplified logic in the code-behind that would have been comparable to the code in each of our actions. However, because the view (Web Forms markup) and controller (Web Forms code-behind) in MVC is not tightly bound, you were able to get full reuse of the view.

The separate actions also provide a logical breakdown of responsibilities. They can be tested individually and you can change one knowing that you will not be affecting the outcome of the other. You cannot say the same thing with the single user control approach used in the previous Try It Out. Also, because the logical separation is obvious, instantiating the control is also simpler, because you do not have to worry about passing in parameter values. Web Forms user controls made it easy to pass in parameters, even supporting them in IntelliSense, but MVC does not have the same IDE support, nor does it really need it as much.

TEMPLATES

ASP.NET Web Form user controls and MVC partial views support a lot of the same requirements, including the capability to create sections of UI and business logic that are reusable and consumable from within a standard page or view (master pages and layout templates). MVC offers an additional approach to creating reusable code: templates. You worked with built-in templates in Chapter 6 when you used methods such as `EditorFor` or `DisplayFor`. These methods took the properties that you were using and provided the default template for that type. MVC provides you with the capability to create and define your own templates that enable you to use the same approach and render custom types based on a custom template.

Creating both editor and display templates for a custom type is very similar to what you have already done when creating partial views; in fact they are partial views that follow strictly defined location and naming conventions. The first part of the convention stipulates that custom templates must be stored within the appropriate folder in your MVC application: Templates that respond to `DisplayFor` need to be placed in the Views/Shared/DisplayTemplates directory, while those templates that respond to the `EditorFor` method need to be placed in the Views/Shared/EditorTemplates directory. The naming convention stipulates that the name of the file must match the name of the type for which the template will be used, such as `DateTime` or `Address`.

In the next Try It Out, you get a chance to see how these work and how they are instantiated differently than traditional partial views.

TRY IT OUT Creating and Using Custom Templates

In this activity, you create Editor and Display templates for a `DateTime` type. This allows for a standard implementation across all areas of the site that may display or edit a date.

1. Ensure that Visual Studio is running and that you have your RentMyWrox solution open. Start the application and navigate to UserDemographics\Create. You should get a screen similar to that shown in Figure 11-30.

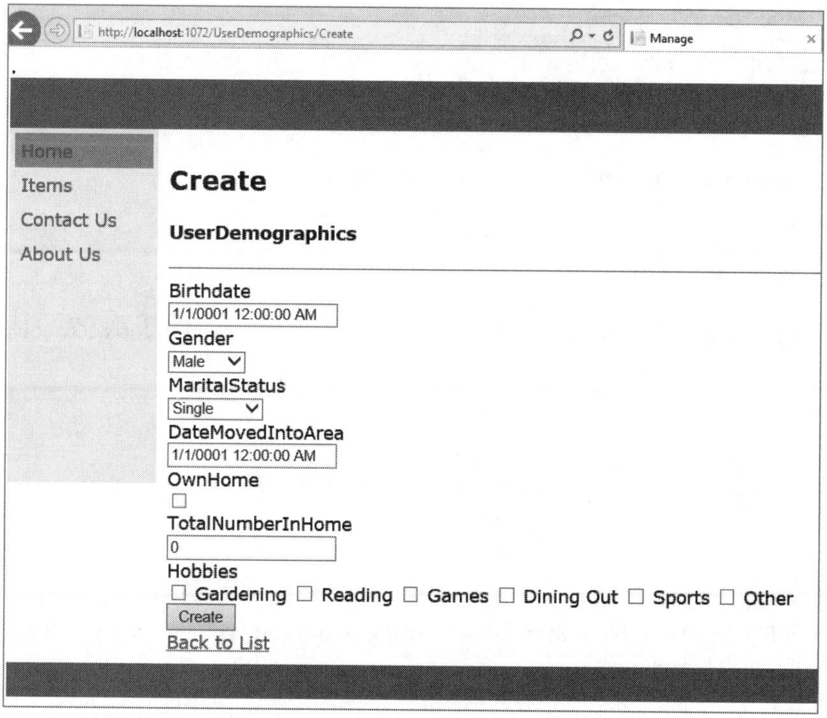

FIGURE 11-30: Initial screen showing default DateTime management

2. Create two new directories under the Views\Shared folder, **DisplayTemplates** and **EditorTemplates**. Your Views directory should look like Figure 11-31.

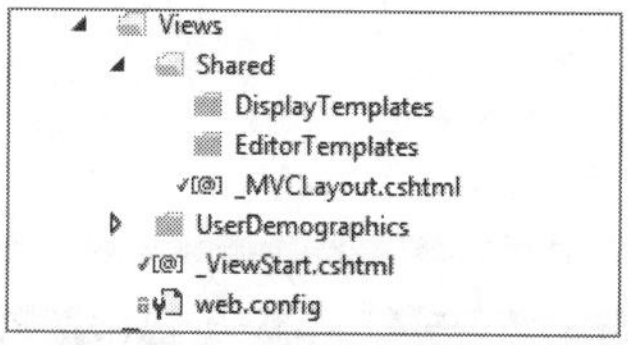

FIGURE 11-31: Views directory after Templates directories are added

3.   Right-click on the DisplayTemplates folder and select Add View. Name the view **DateTime** and ensure that the option to create as a partial view is checked, as shown in Figure 11-32.

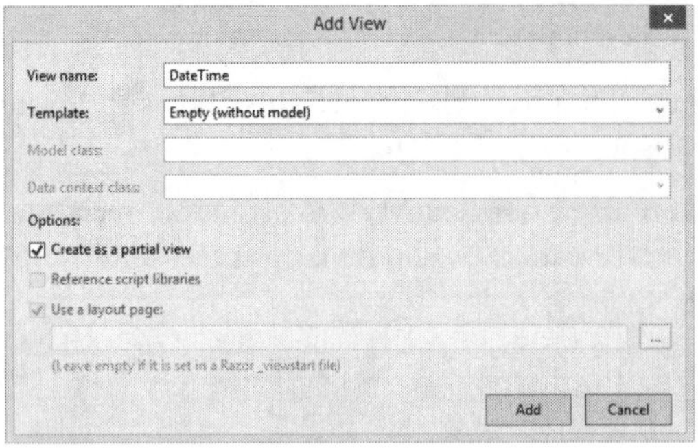

FIGURE 11-32: Adding DateTime Display template

4.   Add the following two lines to the new view you created and save:

```
@model DateTime

@Model.ToString("MMMM dd, yyyy")
```

5.   Open the `UserDemographicsController.cs` file. Change the Index method to look like the following code:

```
public ActionResult Index()
{
    List<UserDemographics> list = new List<UserDemographics>();
    list.Add(new UserDemographics { Birthdate = new DateTime(2000, 6, 8) });
    return View(list);
}
```

6.   Run the application and set the browser to go to UserDemographics. You should get a page similar to the one shown in Figure 11-33. Note that the formatting of the DateTime values match the format you set in the DisplayTemplate.

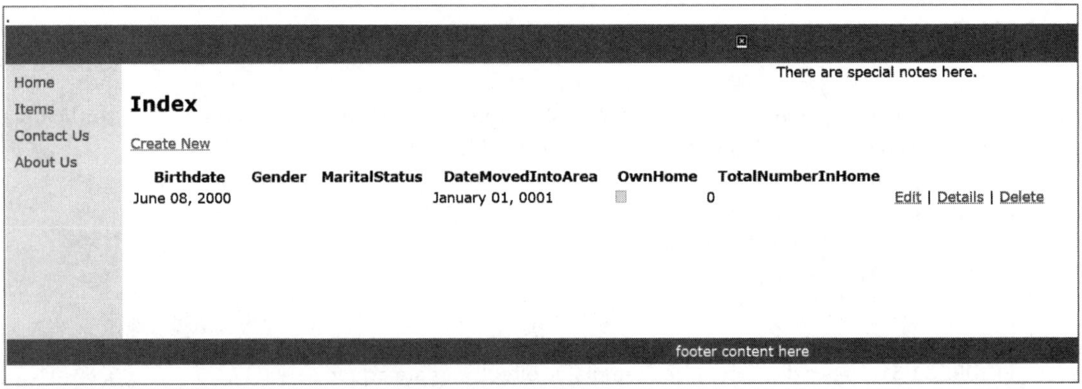

FIGURE 11-33: Viewing the DisplayFor template

7. Right-click on the EditorTemplates folder and select Add View. Name the view **DateTime** and ensure that the option to create as a partial view is checked (refer to Figure 11-32). This is just in a different directory.

8. Add the following code:

```
@model DateTime

@Html.TextBoxFor(model => model, new { @class = "editordatepicker" })
```

9. Open your Scripts folder and check whether you have any jquery-ui scripts in it, as shown in Figure 11-34. If you do, skip to Step 12.

FIGURE 11-34: Content of the project's Scripts directory

10. If you did not have the jquery-ui files, right click your RentMyWrox project and select Manage NuGet Packages. This will bring up the Manage NuGet Packages dialog, shown in Figure 11-35.

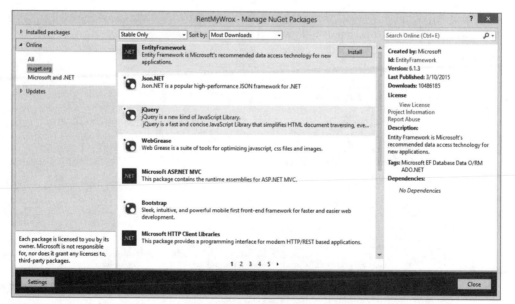

FIGURE 11-35: Selecting jQuery package in Package Manager

11. Select Online ⇨ nugget.org on the left side of the dialog, and in the search box at the upper right of the dialog enter "**jquery-ui**" and press Enter. This brings up a list of results. Find jQuery UI (Combined Library) as shown in Figure 11-36 and click the Install button. Once the install has been completed you should get a green check in place of the Install button.

FIGURE 11-36: Installing the jQuery UI package

12. Open your layout page, `Views\Shared\_MVCLayout.cshtml`. Add the following code to the `<head>` section so that it is similar to Figure 11-37:

```
<script language="javascript" type="text/javascript"
        src="~/Scripts/jquery-1.10.2.js"></script>
<script language="javascript" type="text/javascript"
        src="~/Scripts/jquery-ui-1.11.4.js"></script>
<link rel="stylesheet"
        href="//code.jquery.com/ui/1.11.4/themes/smoothness/jquery-ui.css">
<script type="text/javascript">
$(document).ready(function () {
    $(".editordatepicker").datepicker();
});
</script>
```

```
 5  <head>
 6      <meta name="viewport" content="width=device-width" />
 7      <title>@ViewBag.Title</title>
 8      <link href="~/Content/RentMyWrox.css" rel="stylesheet" type="text/css" />
 9      <script language="javascript" type="text/javascript" src="~/Scripts/jquery-1.10.2.js"></script>
10      <script language="javascript" type="text/javascript" src="~/Scripts/jquery-ui-1.11.4.js"></script>
11      <link rel="stylesheet" href="//code.jquery.com/ui/1.11.4/themes/smoothness/jquery-ui.css">
12      <script type="text/javascript">
13      $(document).ready(function () {
14          $(".editordatepicker").datepicker();
15      });
16      </script>
17      @RenderSection("scripts", required: false)
18  </head>
```

FIGURE 11-37: Updating the layout page

13. Run the application and go to UserDemographics/Create. You should see a screen similar to Figure 11-38. To get the jQuery calendar picker, click the textbox.

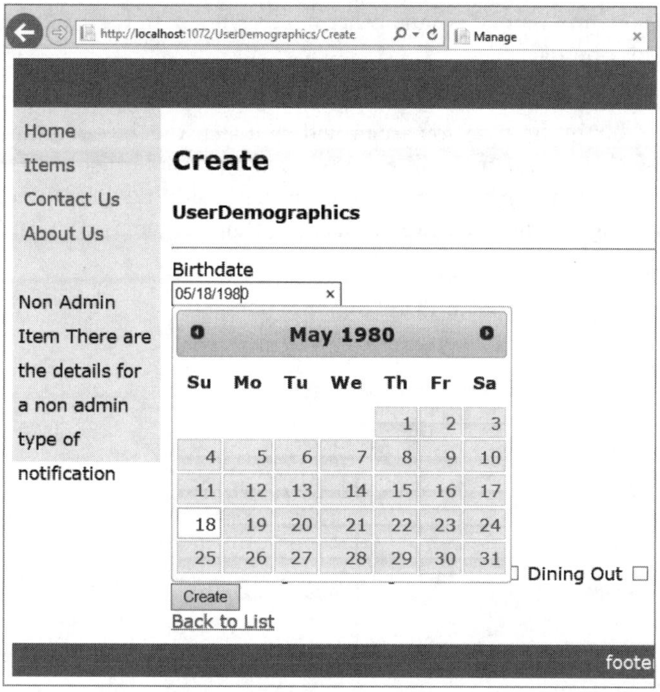

FIGURE 11-38: Finished Editor template

How It Works

Custom Display and Editor templates are very similar to partial views (without controllers) in how they are created and how they interact within the code. The main difference is that ASP.NET MVC uses a convention-based approach to understand the roles that these particular template views play because of their location in the directory structure. These same templates, put in a different directory, could not be used in an `EditorFor` or `DisplayFor` call.

Other than having the templates in special directories, the relationship is defined by the name of the file and the data type of the model that the view supports. The default is to give the file the same name as the type, but you also have the capability to create different versions that will support the same type. Perhaps you have a case where you want a DateTime displayed in one way, and a different case where you want it displayed in a second format. This is supported through the use of the `UIHint` attribute, which enables you to point that particular property to a different definition. The following code takes the property `SomeDate`, and when used with an `EditorFor` or `DisplayFor` call it will first look for a template named `"SpecialDateTime.cshtml"` rather than the default `DateTime.cshtml`:

```
[UIHint("SpecialDateTime")]
public DateTime SomeDate { get; set; }
```

As the framework parses through the code in the view, it is able to interpret these various template calls just like it would the `Html.Partial` and `Html.Action` methods. In this example, your display template is only managing the formatting of the date that is displayed; it could do the same thing for a full custom type whereby the view contains many different labels and other `DisplayFors`. In the same way, your editor template could take the same approach.

The custom `DisplayFor` that you used ensures that dates are displayed in a consistent format. You have seen the `ToString` method before, but in this case you are providing it a custom layout structure. `DateTime` is an interesting type because there are so many different ways that it can be displayed. While it is a pretty simple concept, displaying the type can be complicated. There are cultural and language differences as well as a size impact (spelling out the month versus using the integer representative, two-digit years vs. four-digit years, etc.).

Table 11-5 lists the most commonly used formatting identifiers for DateTimes.

TABLE 11-5: DateTime Formatting

FORMAT	DESCRIPTION	EXAMPLE
d	Day of the month 1–31	January 7, 2015 -> 1
dd	Day of the month, 01–31 (2-digit)	January 7, 2015 -> 01
ddd	Abbreviated day of the week	January 7, 2015 -> Wed
dddd	Compete day of the week	January 7, 2015 -> Wednesday
h	Hour, using 12-hour clock, 1–12	2:08 PM -> 2
hh	Hour, using 12-hour clock, 01–12 (2-digit)	2:08 PM -> 02
H	Hour, using a 24-hour clock, 0 to 23	2:08 PM -> 14
HH	Hour, using a 24-hour clock, 00 to 23 (2-digit)	2:08 PM -> 14
m	Minute, 0–59	2:08 PM -> 8
mm	Minute, 00–59 (2-digit)	2:08 PM -> 08
M	Month, 1–12	January 7, 2015 -> 1
MM	Month, 01–12 (2-digit)	January 7, 2015 -> 01
MMM	Abbreviated name of month	January 7, 2015 -> Jan
MMMM	Complete name of month	January 7, 2015 -> January0
t	First letter of AM/PM designator	2:08 PM -> P
tt	Complete AM/PM designator	2:08 PM -> PM
y	Year, 0–99	January 7, 2015 -> 15

FORMAT	DESCRIPTION	EXAMPLE
yy	Year, 00–99 (2-digit)	January 7, 2015 -> 15
yyy	Year, three digits	January 7, 2015 -> 015
yyyy	Year, four digits	January 7, 2015 -> 2015

The `DisplayFor` template that you created used the formatting string of (`"MMMM dd, yyyy"`). Looking at Table 11-5, you can determine that this will be displayed as the full month name, the two-digit day, and the four-digit year, or January 07, 2015.

Your `EditorFor` template was simple as well; you didn't really need to do anything in the template itself other than add an override so that the class attribute of the text box is set to `"editordate picker"`. This was the beginning of a series of changes you then made to do some special work with this specific class name. All of these changes were made so that you would be able to configure the jQuery UI `DatePicker` to be the default method for editing values of type `DateTime`.

jQuery UI is a set of user interface interactions, effects, widgets, and themes built on top of the jQuery JavaScript Library. To take advantage of one of these widgets, the `DatePicker`, you had to install the jQuery UI NuGet package.

NuGet is an open-source package management system that is built into Visual Studio. It enables developers to add sets of functionality, in this case the JavaScript files that are necessary to provide the client-side functionality. Using NuGet enables you to work with the various scripts and other files as a set, rather than having to worry about managing the scripts separately in a more manual fashion.

After adding the jQuery JavaScript files to your project, the last thing you did was ensure that your web pages would be able to use them. Adding the script links to the header of the layout file ensured that they would be available to every page that uses the layout. This is important because the `EditorFor` for the `DateTime` could be called anywhere. The only way to ensure that the necessary JavaScript code was available was to put it into either the layout page or the template itself. However, putting it into the template itself would lead to redundant calls because, as in the example, the `DateTime` might be used multiple times on a page. Therefore, this code would be downloaded as many times as there are `DateTimes`, which could lead to performance issues as well as make the JavaScript code more difficult to work with—what happens when the same method is loaded multiple times?

The jQuery function that was added to the layout page is shown here for easy reference:

```
$(document).ready(function () {
    $(".editordatepicker").datepicker();
});
```

There's a whole chapter (Chapter 14) on jQuery coming up, so you'll learn more details later, but at this point you should just understand what the function is doing. Once the document is loaded, clicking any HTML element with a class of `editordatepicker` will run the `datepicker` function. This `datepicker` function is what opens the UI element with the calendar and supports the movement of information between the calendar and the textbox.

You also added a link to a stylesheet file from the jQuery site. This file could just as easily be copied to your local application and referenced there; and if any styling changes were required, the stylesheet file would have to be copied locally so that it could be changed. However, the default behavior is acceptable at this time, so you took advantage of the jQuery site hosting the file and used their version.

SUMMARY

User controls and partial views enable you to build reusable components to manage interaction with the client. The purpose of both is to fulfill a specific subset of functionality and each control is responsible for gathering all the necessary information and displaying it to the user. This is especially true with ASP.NET Web Form user controls because they always have code-behind that supports the entire page life cycle, just like a traditional Web Form.

As shown in the example, the MVC partial view gives you a little more flexibility. It can be used to display an item that is passed into the view using the `Html.Partial` method from a view; or through the `Html.Action` method, which doesn't call a partial view but instead calls an action on a controller that returns the partial view. Because the controller is involved, you have the capability to do business logic behind the scenes to create the model given to the view. Thus, the same MVC partial view can be called from a view and passed in a model or it can be returned from an action with a model. Because of the decoupled nature between the two, it doesn't matter from where the view gets its model—only that it has it.

Before user controls can be used they need to be registered, which can be done at the page level or the application level. Once they have been registered, you can drop them onto the markup page just like any other server control. When you are using partial views, registering them is not necessary; simply determine how you want to reference the view (partial vs. action) and the system takes it from there.

You can take partial views a little further by designating them as templates. A template is simply a partial view that is put it into a special folder. By its presence in the `EditorTemplate` or `DisplayTemplate` directory of the Shared directory under Views, the system knows to use it for the appropriate model type.

MVC also allows you to use property attribution to define the relationship between a specific implementation of a type and a template. This enables you to create multiple templates and then determine according to the model property itself which template should be used as necessary.

User controls and partial views enable you to take specific parts of the page output and separate them into different objects that can be called from other pages. If a piece of functionality is only going to be used on one page, then it may not make sense to break it into user controls or partial views; but if the functionality is, or might be, replicated on other pages, then you should always pull it out into its own control or partial view. That way you can reuse it as much as desired.

EXERCISES

1. The ASP.NET MVC template displays a model in a certain format. Is it possible to do the same thing in an ASP.NET Web Forms application?

2. When you want to get a partial view that has been processed on the server, when do you *not* have to pass the controller into the `Html.Action` method?

3. When you are working with ASP.NET Web User Controls, what would happen if you have a property that is a string and you pass an integer into it though an attribute? What happens if the property is an integer and you pass a string into it?

▶ **WHAT YOU LEARNED IN THIS CHAPTER**

Action	An HTML extension method that runs an action on a controller. The output from the action should be a partial view. When you call the method, you typically pass in an action name, which assumes that the action is on the same controller that rendered the current view; otherwise, you need to pass in the controller name as well. Taking this approach results in a string value that can be written directly into the markup or assigned to a variable and further worked with.
AutoId	An approach that creates a client-side ID that is basically a concatenation of all ids from all controls in the hierarchy. The output of this approach is the same as the examples in this chapters examples. This is also the value from all versions of ASP.NET prior to 3.5.
Display Template	An MVC partial view that is used to display a specific type. In order for a partial view to act as a display template, it needs to be located in the DisplayTemplates directory under the Views\Shared directory.
Editor Template	An MVC partial view that is used to display a specific type. In order for a partial view to act as a display template, it needs to be located in the EditorTemplates directory under the Views\Shared directory.
Inherit ClientIdMode	This value sets the ClientIdMode of a control to the ClientIdMode of its hosting item, whether it is another control (either user control or server control) or a page. This is actually the default value of all controls, while Predictable is the default mode for all pages.
Partial	This extension method on HTML is used to reference a partial view that should be displayed. It is generally called with the name of the view and the model that is needed by the partial view. Taking this approach results in a string value that can either be written directly into the markup or assigned to a variable and further worked with.
Predictable ClientIdMode	This mode is generally used in databound controls for which you want every item in the set of output to have an ID that you can predict. This is useful in cases where you may have a user control that is displayed with each row in a list of items. Using `Predictable` and the `ClientIDRowSuffix` attribute enables you to define the Id of the output element to include some known value, such as the Id of the item in the list. If you are not using this mode in an area where there are multiple instantiations, such as a list, the output will be the same as `AutoId`.
Register	A command used to build the link to a Web Form user control. As part of the Register, you set both the `TagName` and `TagPrefix` that are used in the page to identify and instantiate the user control.

`RenderAction`	This is the same as the `Action` extension method, except that it does not return a string. Instead, it writes the output directly into the response stream. Take this action if you do not expect to use the output of the action call, because it increases performance by removing that overhead.
`RenderPartial`	This is the same as the `Partial` extension method, except that it does not return a string. Instead, it writes the output directly into the response stream. Take this action if you do not expect to use the output of the partial call, as it increases performance by removing that overhead.
Server Caching	Server caching is configurable on an action, whose output is retained on the server for a specific duration of time. This is especially useful for those actions that return output which rarely changes.
Sitewide Registration	Sitewide registration of a Web Forms user control replaces the page-by-page registration process using `Register` with a single registration using the Web.config file. As with the regular `Register`, sitewide registration requires that you identify the `TagName` and `TagPrefix` that are used to instantiate the control.
Static ClientIdMode	Using this means there will be no concatenation within the control's client ID. Thus, any ID that you assign the control will be given to the rendered element. However, there is no validation that the ID is unique even though this is a requirement of HTML. You have to manage this uniqueness yourself as you build out your markup.
`TagName`	This is set when you register an ASP.NET Web Forms user control. This value, along with the `TagPrefix`, is used to define the relationship between the control being referenced in the markup and the particular control that is being referenced. This has to be unique for each control being registered.
`TagPrefix`	This is set when you register your ASP.NET user control and is used to help define the relationship between the item placed on the page and the user control that is going to be used on the page.

Validating User Input

WHAT YOU WILL LEARN IN THIS CHAPTER:

➤ How client-side and server-side validation of input data differs

➤ Changing your model classes to help support validation

➤ Using validation controls to validate input in ASP.NET Web Form pages

➤ Enforcing validation in ASP.NET MVC views and controllers

➤ Working with controllers that return partial views

➤ Some tips for implementing validation

CODE DOWNLOADS FOR THIS CHAPTER:

The wrox.com code downloads for this chapter are found at www.wrox.com/go/beginningaspnetforvisualstudio on the Download Code tab. The code is in the chapter 12 download and individually named according to the names throughout the chapter.

There is an old saying, "garbage in, garbage out" (GIGO). The implication is clear: When you allow bad data (garbage) into your application, you will have problems from then on out because your application will give you garbage back. The best way to ensure that your application does not have garbage data is to validate as much of the incoming information as possible to ensure that it fits some known criteria, such as ensuring that a phone number includes all digits, that an e-mail address has the correct format, or a quantity is an integer; for all sorts of user-entered pieces of information, you can, and should, define some expectations regarding how that data should appear.

Both MVC and Web Forms provide support to help you keep your application as garbage-free as possible. In this chapter, you will examine some of the more common validation needs, and work with them in both MVC and Web Forms.

GATHERING DATA FROM THE USER

Gathering information from visitors to your site is key to your success. Because this information is so important to your business, you have to help ensure its validity and correctness. Obviously you can't always ensure the correctness of the input data; if George Smith enters his name as Janet Jones, there is no way to determine that. However, you can ensure that the user has entered a first name and a last name and that they are actual names—for example, such as not including numbers or symbols.

When you approach validation, you want to look for a couple of things on each piece of data received by the user:

> ➤ **Required fields:** There are some values that a user must provide in order for your system to work. Is this particular property one of them?

> ➤ **Data type:** Any data that is input must be of a particular type. A value entered in a quantity box needs to be numeric at least, most likely an integer.

> ➤ **Data size:** Just as you may need to have data fit a specific type, you may also need the data to fit some particular ranges of sizes. The most common of these is a maximum size, or length. This is necessary because each column in a relational database table was defined with a size in characters. Trying to insert a value larger than that value will either lose data or cause an exception.

> ➤ **Format validation:** A piece of data that represents, for example, an e-mail address, needs to follow some kind of standard template: name@server.domain. Phone numbers have their own rules, credit card numbers have their own rules, and so on.

> ➤ **Range validation:** Some data must fall between a realistic range. Entering a birth date of January 1, 1756, for example, should raise some red flags.

> ➤ **Comparison validation:** Sometimes an entry in one field implies a set of values in another field. For example, selecting a gender of female implies a title of Ms. but not Mr. Another example is comparing the two values in a date range to ensure that the "from value" is less than the "to value."

> ➤ **Others:** Custom validations may be necessary as well—those that fall outside the scope of the other validation approaches already listed. These will be completely dependent upon your application needs.

Ideally, all this validation would work on the client side, so if the user enters invalid data then the form cannot be submitted. This gives users a more immediate update when information is incomplete or incorrect. However, as a responsible developer, you cannot rely on the client to do all of your validation, as the user may have turned that functionality off. Thus, you have to ensure that the information that comes across the network to your server is correct as well, so server-side validation is also a requirement. In fact, if you had to choose between supporting only one of the validation approaches, client-side or server-side, you should always choose server-side because you want full control over the information being validated.

When you review all of the preceding considerations, the ideal form of validation is one that you could use on both server and client. Another useful function would be defining the requirements as close to the model as possible, ideally even on the model itself. This means when you look at the class file you would be able to understand, right there, the data expectations.

Keep all of this in mind as you take your journey through validation. As you have likely already surmised, MVC and Web Forms each manage the requirement of validation differently.

VALIDATING USER INPUT IN WEB FORMS

There is a special set of server controls designed to perform validation. Briefly mentioned earlier in the book, these are the aptly named validation server controls, and they are available in the Visual Studio Toolbox, as shown in Figure 12-1.

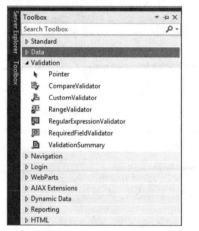

FIGURE 12-1: Validation controls in Visual Studio Toolbox

Each of these ASP.NET Web Form validation controls supports one or more of the necessary validations. Table 12-1 describes each one in detail.

TABLE 12-1: Validation Server Controls

CONTROL	DESCRIPTION
CompareValidator	Use the `CompareValidator` control to compare the value entered by the user in an input control, such as a `TextBox` control, with the value entered in another input control or a constant value. The `CompareValidator` control passes validation if the input control's value matches the criteria specified by the `Operator`, `ValueToCompare`, and/or `ControlToCompare` properties. You can also use the `CompareValidator` control to indicate whether the value entered in an input control can be converted to the data type specified by the `Type` property. When compared to the list of validation needs from the list in the previous section, this control fills both the "DataType" and "Compare" needs.
CustomValidator	The `CustomValidator` control applies a user-defined validation function against a control. When using this control, the developer first creates the JavaScript functionality to ensure that the values entered into the control are correct. This control enables you to perform any validation you need, as long as you can figure out how to write the JavaScript to support it. However, the JavaScript portion is only the client-side validation. You also need to write server-side logic to validate on the server. The combination of these two approaches ensures full validation. When compared to the list of validation needs, this control can fulfill any type, as it is completely customizable.
RangeValidator	The `RangeValidator` control tests whether the value of an input control is within a specified range. You supply a minimum value and a maximum value, and the type of the item being compared.
RegularExpressionValidator	The `RegularExpressionValidator` control checks whether the value of an input control matches a pattern defined by a regular expression. This type of validation enables you to check for predictable sequences of characters, such as those in e-mail addresses, telephone numbers, and postal codes. This control provides formatting validation and can also be used to provide minimum and maximum length validation.

CONTROL	DESCRIPTION
RequiredFieldValidator	Use this control to make an input control a required field. The input control fails validation if its value was not changed from the InitialValue property upon losing focus. This control supports the required field's validation, likely the most common scenario; it only validates that there is data rather than anything about that data.
ValidationSummary	The ValidationSummary control is used on a page to display all the validation errors that have occurred. Generally at the top of the form, it displays the validations as well as a link that takes the user to the field that failed validation.

Because each of the controls typically does a specific validation, you have the capability to link multiple validation controls to an input field, thus performing multiple different validations. For example, if Date of Birth were both required and expected to be between a set of values, you could hook up both a RequiredFieldValidator and a RangeValidator to the same input item, as shown here:

```
<div class="dataentry">
    <asp:Label runat="server" Text="Date of Birth" AssociatedControlID="tbDOB" />
    <asp:TextBox runat="server" ID="tbDOB" />
    <asp:RequiredFieldValidator ID="tbDOB_Req" ControlToValidate="tbDOB"
            runat="server" Display="Dynamic"
            ErrorMessage="Please enter a Date of Birth" />
    <asp:RangeValidator ID="tvDOB_Range" ControlToValidate="tbDOB" runat="server"
            Display="Dynamic" ErrorMessage="Please enter a valid Date of Birth"
            Type="Date" MinimumValue="1/1/1915" MaximumValue="12/31/2010" />
</div>
```

The preceding code snippet includes four different server controls:

➤   A Label control

➤   A TextBox control

➤   A RequiredFieldValidator

➤   A RangeValidator

All the controls are related in that the two validators and the label are all associated with the TextBox control. Neither the Label control nor the TextBox control are new, but this is the first time you have seen the validator in action.

Many validators share some common properties. Table 12-2 lists these common properties, as well as other attributes.

TABLE 12-2: Validator Properties

PROPERTY	DESCRIPTION
ControlToCompare	The input control to compare with the input control being validated. This property is valid only on the CompareValidator.
ControlToValidate	This property is available on every validation control. The ControlToValidate property defines the input control that is being validated. A validator that does not have this value set is not doing any validation.
Display	Another common property, the Display property defines how the message will be displayed. There are three options: Dynamic, None, and Static. When Display is set to Static, the area taken up by the error message being displayed is always blocked out, regardless of whether it is actually visible. In the preceding example, if the two Display properties were set to Static, there would be a space between the textbox and the second error message, assuming it were the RangeValidator that failed. Because they are dynamic, the space taken up by the first error message is not reserved and the error message from the second control can be displayed as if the first validation control is not there. Choosing None means the error message is never displayed inline, rather only in a ValidationSummary control. Static is the default value.
EnableClientScript	This property is available on all validation controls. Use the EnableClientScript property to specify whether client-side validation is enabled. Server-side validation is always enabled, but you can turn off client-side validation if desired. The default value is true.
ErrorMessage	Available on all validation controls, this property defines the message that's displayed in a ValidationSummary control when the validator determines that the content in the input box fails validation. It will also display inline if the Text property is not set.
MaximumValue	This property is available on the RangeValidator and is used to set the upper end of the range being used for the comparison.
MinimumValue	This property is available on the RangeValidator and is used to set the lower end of the range being used for the comparison.

PROPERTY	DESCRIPTION
Operator	Available on the `CompareValidator`, the `Operator` attribute defines the type of comparison to be done. The options are as follows: Equal: A comparison for equality between the values of the input control being validated and another control, or a constant value. NotEqual: A comparison for inequality between the values of the input control being validated and another control, or a constant value. This is the same as !=. GreaterThan: A comparison for greater than between the values of the input control being validated and another control, or a constant value. This is the same as >. GreaterThanEqual: A comparison for greater than or equal to between the values of the input control being validated and another control, or a constant value. This equates to !=. LessThan: A comparison for less than between the values of the input control being validated and another control, or a constant value. This is the same as <. LessThanEqual: A comparison for less than or equal to between the values of the input control being validated and another control, or a constant value. This is the same as <=. DataTypeCheck: A data type comparison of the value entered in the input control being validated and the data type specified by the Type property. Validation will fail if the value cannot be converted to the specified data type.
Text	A common property, the value assigned to `Text` will display inline when the validation fails.
Type	The data type to which the values being compared are converted to before the comparison is made. The options are String, Integer, Double, Date, and Currency. The Type property is available in the RangeValidator and the CompareValidator. The default value is String.
ValidationExpression	The regular expression that determines the pattern used to validate a field

continues

TABLE 12-2 *(continued)*

PROPERTY	DESCRIPTION
ValidationGroup	A special property that is available on all validators. What makes it special is that it is also available on other controls as well, such as Buttons and other controls that support posting to the server. The ValidationGroup enables you to group validators and various post-back mechanisms so that only a subset of validation is run when a post-back to the server happens. This enables you to have different sections of the page doing different actions without having to worry about an action taken in one area causing validation to occur in another area.

In this next Try It Out, you start to put various controls together to validate the input of a data entry form.

TRY IT OUT   Adding Web Forms validation

In this activity you update the ManageItem form that you created earlier in the book to ensure that the values input by the user meet a certain set of criteria.

1. Ensure that Visual Studio is running and your RentMyWrox solution is open. Open your Admin ⇨ ManageItem.aspx page.

2. Add the following code above the first line of the form. You can do this by either typing the information directly in or dragging and dropping the control from the Toolbox. It should look something like Figure 12-2.

    ```
    <div>
        <asp:ValidationSummary ID="ValidationSummary1" runat="server" ForeColor="Red" />
    </div>
    ```

FIGURE 12-2: Adding the ValidationSummary control

3. Add a RequiredFieldValidator to tbName. You can do this by either typing in the information directly, as shown below or dragging and dropping the control from the Toolbox and filling in the required properties:

    ```
    <asp:RequiredFieldValidator ID="rfName" ControlToValidate="tbName" runat="server"
            ErrorMessage="Name is Required" Text="*" Display="Dynamic"/>
    ```

4. Add another one to tbDescription:

```
<asp:RequiredFieldValidator ID="rfDescription" ControlToValidate="tbDescription"
        runat="server"
        ErrorMessage="Description is Required" Text="*" Display="Dynamic"/>
```

5. Add a CompareValidator and a RequiredFieldValidator to tbCost as shown below. When you are done, your markup should match what is shown in Figure 12-3.

```
<asp:RequiredFieldValidator ID="rfCost" ControlToValidate="tbCost" runat="server"
      ErrorMessage="Cost is Required" Text="*" Display="Dynamic"/>
<asp:CompareValidator ID="cCost" ControlToValidate="tbCost" runat="server"
      ErrorMessage="Cost does not appear to be the correct format" Text="*"
      Type="Currency" Operator="DataTypeCheck"/>
```

FIGURE 12-3: Adding some validation controls

6. Add a RequiredFieldValidator to the Item Number.

7. Add a RequiredFieldValidator and a CompareValidator to Acquired Date. When you are done, your markup should match what is shown in Figure 12-4.

```
<asp:RequiredFieldValidator ID="rfAcquiredDate" ControlToValidate="tbAcquiredDate"
      runat="server" ErrorMessage="Acquired Date is Required" Text="*"
Display="Dynamic"/>
<asp:CompareValidator ID="cAcquiredDate" ControlToValidate="tbAcquiredDate"
      runat="server"
      ErrorMessage="Acquired Date does not appear to be the correct format" Text="*"
      Type="Date" Operator="DataTypeCheck"/>
```

```
<div class="dataentry">
    <asp:Label runat="server" Text="Item Number" AssociatedControlID="tbItemNumber" />
    <asp:TextBox runat="server" ID="tbItemNumber" />
    <asp:RequiredFieldValidator ID="rfItemNumber" ControlToValidate="tbItemNumber" runat="server" ErrorMessage="Item Number is Required" Text="*"/>
</div>
<div class="dataentry">
    <asp:Label runat="server" Text="Acquired Date" AssociatedControlID="tbAcquiredDate" />
    <asp:TextBox runat="server" ID="tbAcquiredDate" />
    <asp:RequiredFieldValidator ID="rfAcquiredDate" ControlToValidate="tbAcquiredDate" runat="server" ErrorMessage="Acquired Date is Required" Text="*" Display="Dynamic"/>
    <asp:CompareValidator ID="cAcquiredDate" ControlToValidate="tbAcquiredDate" runat="server" ErrorMessage="Acquired Date does not appear to be the correct format" Text="*"
       Type="Date" Operator="DataTypeCheck"/>
</div>
```

FIGURE 12-4: Additional validation controls

8. Run the application and select Admin ⇨ ManageItem. Click the Submit button without entering any information. You should see a screen like Figure 12-5.

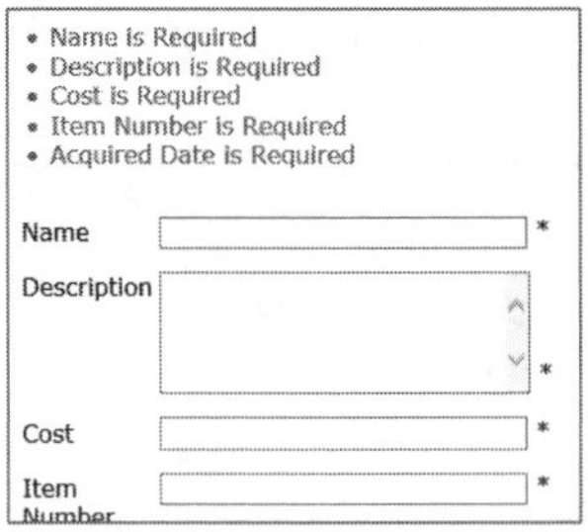

- Name is Required
- Description is Required
- Cost is Required
- Item Number is Required
- Acquired Date is Required

Name

Description

Cost

Item
Number

FIGURE 12-5: Validation displayed

9. Open the code-behind by selecting Admin ⇨ ManageItem.aspx.cs. Update the SaveItem_Clicked method by adding the code that is highlighted in the below snippet:

```
protected void SaveItem_Clicked(object sender, EventArgs e)
{
    if (IsValid)
    {
        Item item;
        using (RentMyWroxContext context = new RentMyWroxContext())
        {
            if (itemId == 0)
            {
                item = new Item();
                UpdateItem(item);
                context.Items.Add(item);
            }
            else
            {
                item = context.Items.FirstOrDefault(x => x.Id == itemId);
                UpdateItem(item);
            }
            context.SaveChanges();
        }
        Response.Redirect("~/admin/ItemList");
    }
}
```

How It Works

In this exercise you added two different types of validators, the RequiredFieldValidator and the CompareValidator, to the data entry form that you built earlier for the Item. Because every item in the form other than the picture is required, you had to add multiple RequiredFieldValidators. The code for one of them is displayed here:

```
<asp:RequiredFieldValidator ID="rfName" ControlToValidate="tbName" runat="server"
        ErrorMessage="Name is Required" Text="*" Display="Dynamic"/>
```

The attributes all help define the rules that define the control's behavior. The most important property is `ControlToValidate`, which defines the input control that this validator is going to evaluate. In this case, the control is evaluating a control with the ID of `"tbName"`. Both the `Text` and `ErrorMessage` properties are set. Because the `Text` property is the one that displays inline (where the control itself is located), you would expect to see an asterisk next to the input field where validation failed. The `ErrorMessage` is the text that displays in the `ValidationSummary` control. Reviewing Figure 12-5 shows how both of these are working. The `ErrorMessage` is displayed in the bulleted list at the top of the page that was created by the `ValidationSummary` control, while each of the text boxes has an asterisk next to it that was defined by the value in the `Text` property.

On two of the controls you also added a `CompareValidator`. Both of these validators are shown here:

```
<asp:CompareValidator ID="cCost" ControlToValidate="tbCost" runat="server"
    ErrorMessage="Cost does not appear to be the correct format" Text="*"
    Type="Currency" Operator="DataTypeCheck"/>
<asp:CompareValidator ID="cAcquiredDate" ControlToValidate="tbAcquiredDate"
    runat="server"
    ErrorMessage="Acquired Date does not appear to be the correct format" Text="*"
    Type="Date" Operator="DataTypeCheck"/>
```

These validators are not comparing the input value to another control, but are instead ensuring that the value being input can be converted to a specific type—in these cases a date and to a numeric value that represents a valid currency amount. You can have this control handle both because of the `Type` parameter, which defines the parsing that the control will try against the input value.

Refer back to Figure 12-5 and pay special attention to those controls that have two different validators applied to them. Note that only one message is being displayed in both the `ValidationSummary` and inline, and that is the validation for RequiredField. The reason why this occurs is because the default behavior for all non-`RequiredFieldValidators` is that they only work when the input value isn't null. Thus, leaving the value of the field blank ensures that those other validators don't. This is why they had to be combined with a `RequiredFieldValidator`. The `RequiredFieldValidator` ensures that a value is entered, and then the `CompareValidator` ensures that the value entered can be converted to the correct type.

This client-side validation is all handled by JavaScript because that is the only language that you can be confident that the browser supports. Fortunately, you didn't have to write any of that JavaScript yourself; it was all generated from the control. Viewing the source of the rendered HTML shows how this happens. Figure 12-6 illustrates a section of the created HTML.

FIGURE 12-6: Validation displayed

If you review the HTML that was created, you will see that there are script references that you did not put into the code—mainly those that reference a `WebResource.axd`. `WebResource.axd` is a handler that enables control and page developers to download resources that are embedded in a server-side assembly to the end user. The code that is visible in Figure 12-6 requests a certain set of JavaScript to be down-loaded to the client. If you went directly to that resource you would be able to download a file that is actually pure JavaScript—the JavaScript that is then used to perform the validation.

When the validation fails, the submission to the server is stopped and the error messages and error text are displayed as requested. Each time there is an attempt to post information to the server, the process repeats itself until all items pass validation. Only when that occurs is the submission to the server completed.

If you played with any of the fields that failed validation, you may have noticed one more interesting fact. Whenever you enter and then leave a field, the validation is again run against that input item. This means that if you make a change to a failing field, you will get an almost immediate update as to whether you pass that field's expected validation. This only affects the inline warning, however; the ValidationSummary only updates when the process attempts to post to the server, and you will not see the summary control change when you leave the individual field.

Whereas the changes that you had to make in the markup to provide validation support were relatively significant, the change you had to make in the code-behind was very simple. The Page class, from which all Web Form pages inherit, contains a property that is populated when the request is received at the server. Server-side validation happens automatically. You can choose to disregard it by not looking at the IsValid property, but it will always be populated correctly based on the configured rules and the data that was input in the Web Form.

As you can see, ASP.NET server controls have provided an easy and efficient way to get work done, this time by providing validation services on one or more input controls. As a bonus, this validation happens on both the client side, through the use of JavaScript, and on the server side during normal page processing. Although only two validation controls were demonstrated, most of the others work in much the same way.

Understanding Request Validation

Another type of validation occurring on ASP.NET Web Form pages that you probably have not even seen yet is request validation, and it is always enabled by default. Request validation is a feature in ASP.NET that examines an HTTP request to determine whether it contains potentially dangerous content. In this context, potentially dangerous content is any HTML markup or JavaScript code in the body, header, query string, or cookies of the request. ASP.NET performs this check because markup or code in the URL query string, cookies, or posted form values might have been added for malicious purposes.

For example, if your site has a form on which users enter comments, a malicious user could enter JavaScript code in a script element. When you display the comments page to other users, the browser executes the JavaScript code as if the code had been generated by your website. Request validation helps prevent this kind of attack. If ASP.NET detects any markup or code in a request, it throws a "potentially dangerous value was detected" error and stops page processing, as shown in Figure 12-7.

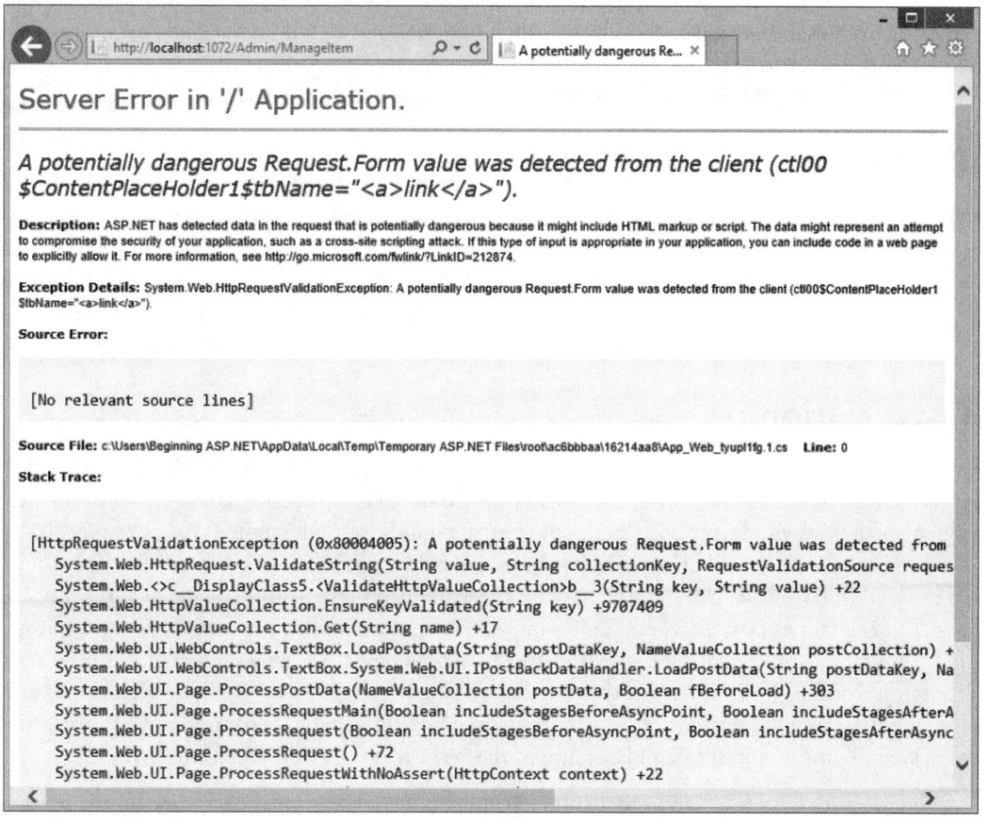

FIGURE 12-7: Error thrown during request validation

You can see this happen yourself by simply entering some HTML type elements into the form page that you were just working with.

As mentioned earlier, this validation is enabled by default but you can turn it off as needed, such as when users are expected to enter information that may contain HTML or JavaScript elements. You can control the settings by adding `ValidateRequest="False"` to the Page directive. This will turn off request validation for that page.

There may be times when you don't want to turn off request validation for a whole page, but instead perform the validation on only a set of the controls on the page. This would be common in those instances where capturing HTML is allowed, such as the screen where you can enter the description of the `Item` class. In this case, you can enable or disable the check on a control level through the use of the `ValidateRequestMode` property:

```
<asp:TextBox ValidateRequestMode="Enabled" runat="server" ID="tbDescription" />
```

With the preceding code, the content placed in the `tbDescription` will always go through request validation, even if it is turned off at the page level.

VALIDATING USER INPUT IN MVC

You may have noticed that your validation expectations are defined as part of the UI construction in ASP.NET Web Forms. This means that any pages that might be accepting the same type of information in the page have to implement this validation independently. Thus, changing a validation requirement requires you to make the changes in multiple pages. ASP.NET MVC takes a more centralized approach, putting control of the validation where it really belongs: on the model itself.

Model Attribution

Putting the validation on the model itself was a logical next step, as there is no place in the application that should better understand what values are valid or invalid. Putting these validation rules on the model also enables validation to become part of the database management process as well, by putting some of the model validation rules, such as the field's maximum length or whether a field is required at the database level too. Lastly, putting the validation at the model level ensures any data that doesn't fit the rule is not persisted. This same level of security isn't present when working with the ASP.NET Web Form validation controls—those only ensure that the values sent with the request are valid, but it does nothing to ensure that the data being persisted is valid. The validation controls are only for submission validation. However, you can also add attributes to models that are being used from Web Forms and still take advantage of the built-in validation functionality.

Adding validation to a model is done by using attribution. Provided with the Entity Framework is a large set of validation attributes that ASP.NET MVC can take advantage of when interpreting the validation requirements. Some of the available attributes are listed in Table 12-3.

TABLE 12-3: Data Attributes Used in Validation

ATTRIBUTE	DESCRIPTION
`CreditCard`	Ensures that the value of the property is compatible with well-known CreditCard number templates `[CreditCard(ErrorMessage = "{0} is not a valid credit card number")]`

ATTRIBUTE	DESCRIPTION
DataType	Use the `DataType` attribute to specify the type of data that is expected for the property beyond the data type of the property. Following are the values of the supported types: CreditCard: Represents a credit card number Currency: Represents a currency value Custom: Represents a custom data type Date: Represents a date value DateTime: Represents an instant in time, expressed as a date and time of day Duration: Represents a continuous time during which an object exists EmailAddress: Represents an e-mail address Html: Represents an HTML file ImageUrl: Represents a URL to an image MultilineText: Represents multi-line text Password: Represents a password value PhoneNumber: Represents a phone number value PostalCode: Represents a postal code Text: Represents text that is displayed Time: Represents a time value Upload: Represents file upload data type Url: Represents a URL value `[DataType(DataType.Date)]`
Display	The Display attribute is not really a validation attribute, but rather the value that is displayed in the UI whenever that property is referenced. This field will affect the `@Html.LabelFor` values used in the view and is also used in the `ErrorMessages` when the property name is being displayed. `[Display(Name="Marital status")]`
EMailAddress	Ensures that the value of the property is compatible with well-known phone number templates `[EmailAddress(ErrorMessage = "{0} is not a valid email address")]`
FileExtensions	Ensures that the value of the property ends with the appropriate values listed within the `Extensions` property. Note that you do not add the "."; the validation framework does that for you. You can display the string of filtered extensions as part of the `ErrorMessage`. `[FileExtensions(Extensions = "jpg,jpeg", ErrorMessage = "{0} is not a valid extension - {1}")]`

continues

TABLE 12-3 *(continued)*

ATTRIBUTE	DESCRIPTION
MaxLength	Ensures that the property's value does not exceed the number of characters defined in the attribute. This attribute becomes part of the database definition, as the column in the table is set with this same value as its width. The `ErrorMessage` enables you to add the value that you set as the maximum length. `[MinLength(5, ErrorMessage="{0} needs to be at least {1} character")]`
MinLength	Ensures that the property's value does not have fewer characters than the attribute defines. The `ErrorMessage` enables you to add the value that you set as the minimum length. `[MinLength(5, ErrorMessage="{0} needs to be at least {1} character")]`
Phone	Ensures that the value of the property is compatible with well-known phone number templates `[Phone(ErrorMessage = "{0} is not a valid phone number")]`
Range	Ensures that the value of the property is within a known range of values. When using this validator you first define the data type and then define the string version of the range from lowest to highest. When you create the `ErrorMessage` that will be displayed to the user (or thrown as part of an exception), it uses the `string.Format` notation: {0} = the display name of the field, {1} = the bottom of the range, and {2} = the top of the range. `[Range(typeof(DateTime), "1/1/1900", "12/31/2020", ErrorMessage = "{0} must be between {1} and {2}")]`
RegularExpression	Enables you to use a `RegularExpression` to validate the data that is being stored `RegularExpression(@"^[a-zA-Z''-'\s]{1,40}$", ErrorMessage = "Characters are not allowed.")]`
Required	Defines a field as mandatory. This means some value must be entered into the property. The Required attribute also interacts with the database when using the code first approach because it ensures that the table being constructed defines the mapped column as not being able to support a null value. `[Required(ErrorMessage = "Please tell us how many in your home")]`

ATTRIBUTE	DESCRIPTION

`StringLength`	This attribute can be used to set both the minimum and maximum length of a property that is a string. The main difference between StringLength and MinValue/MaxValue is that StringLength enables you to set both maximum and minimum values and it can only be used on properties that are of type string.
	
	`[StringLength(15, MinimumLength = 2, ErrorMessage = "{0}`
	`must be between {2} and {1} characters")]`

`Url`	Ensures that the value of the property is compatible with a URL format `[Url(ErrorMessage = "{0} is not a valid URL")]`

In this next activity you update a data model to use data attribution and validation.

TRY IT OUT   Adding Data Annotation

In this activity you will be updating the `UserDemographics` class to use data annotation. Because some of this annotation will affect the database table, you also have to update the database to support the changes.

1. Ensure that Visual Studio is running and your RentMyWrox solution is open.

2. Open your `UserDemograhics` model class. Add the following annotations to the `Birthdate` property. When completed, this property should look like Figure 12-8.

    ```
    [Required(ErrorMessage = "Please tell us your birth date")]
    [Range(typeof(DateTime), "1/1/1900", "12/31/2010",
            ErrorMessage = "{0} must be between {1} and {2}")]
    ```

    ```
    public UserDemographics()
    {
        Hobbies = new List<Hobby>();
    }

    [Key]
    public int Id { get; set; }

    [Required(ErrorMessage = "Please tell us your birth date")]
    [Range(typeof(DateTime), "1/1/1900", "12/31/2010", ErrorMessage = "{0} must be between {1} and {2}")]
    public DateTime Birthdate { get; set; }
    ```

    FIGURE 12-8: Attributed property

3. Add the following attributes to the `MaritalStatus` property:

    ```
    [Display(Name="Marital status")]
    [Required(ErrorMessage = "Please tell us your marital status")]
    [StringLength(15, MinimumLength = 2)]
    ```

4. Add the following attributes to the `DateMovedIntoArea` property:

    ```
    [Display(Name = "Date you moved into area")]
    [Required(ErrorMessage = "Please tell us when you moved into the area")]
    ```

```
[Range(typeof(DateTime), "1/1/1900", "12/31/2020",
        ErrorMessage = "Your response must be between {1} and {2}")]
```

5. Add the following attributes to the `TotalNumberInHome` property. When completed, your class should look like Figure 12-9.

```
[Display(Name = "How many people live in your house?")]
[Required(ErrorMessage = "Please tell us how many live in your home")]
[Range(typeof(int), "1", "99", ErrorMessage = "Total must be between {1} and {2}")]
```

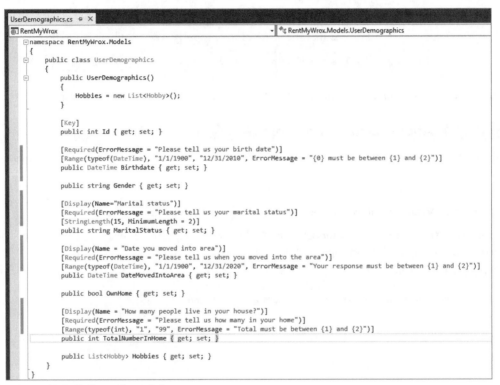

FIGURE 12-9: Fully attributed class

6. Save the file. On the Visual Studio menu, click Tools ⇨ NuGet Package Manager ⇨ Package Manager Console. This should open the Package Manager Console, likely in the bottom of your screen.

7. Ensure that you are in the Package Manager Console window and type in `add-migration "data annotations"`. It should look like Figure 12-10.

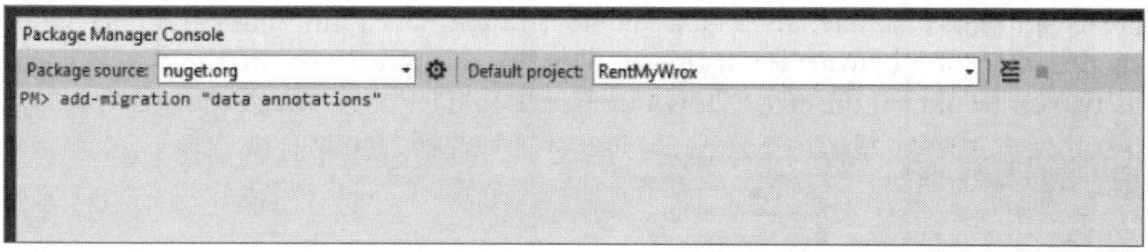

FIGURE 12-10: Package Manager Console

8. Ensure that the Migrations directory contains a new file that has today's date and "data annotations" as part of the filename.

9. In the Package Manager Console window, type in **update-database**. The system should process for a bit and display a message when completed.

How It Works

Four different types of attributes were added to the model: `DisplayAttribute`, `RequiredAttribute`, `RangeAttribute`, and `StringLengthAttribute`. Each created different expectations on the data property to which they were applied, and each of these expectations could be stacked such that a property might have to pass multiple types of validation before it could be considered "valid."

Of the various attributes that you added, the `DisplayAttribute` had the least to do with the data validation being performed with the model, but it had the greatest effect in terms of making any validation failures that might be received easier to understand. When you go back into the view you will also see how the values set here show up in the UI through the use of the `Html.LabelFor` method.

The `RequiredAttribute` is another relatively simple validation attribute. It notifies the validation framework that the property being attributed needs to be set, as opposed to being null. When applied to a type that is non-nullable, such as an integer whose default value is 0 rather than a null, the attribute is less useful. When you want to ensure that an integer is required, a `RangeAttribute` is generally used instead.

The `RangeAttribute` is a very flexible validation tool in that it can support multiple types. In this activity you used it in two different ways: to ensure that `DateTime` properties fell within a useful date range and that an integer fell within an expected range. An interesting aspect of the `RangeAttribute` is that it takes the minimum and maximum values as strings. It is able to understand these strings because it has both the data type of the property to which it is being applied as well as a type defined in the attribute itself. The framework uses this type to attempt to parse the values that are being passed in and then uses the built-in comparer to determine whether the property value falls between the starting and ending values. By passing in a type and the range values as strings, the attribute is flexible and able to work with multiple types; otherwise, you would need a different attribute for each data type.

The last attribute used in this example, `StringLengthAttribute`, sets a minimum and maximum length of a string property (or a byte array). If this attribute were applied to a different type, such as the integer `Id` property, you would get the error shown in Figure 12-11.

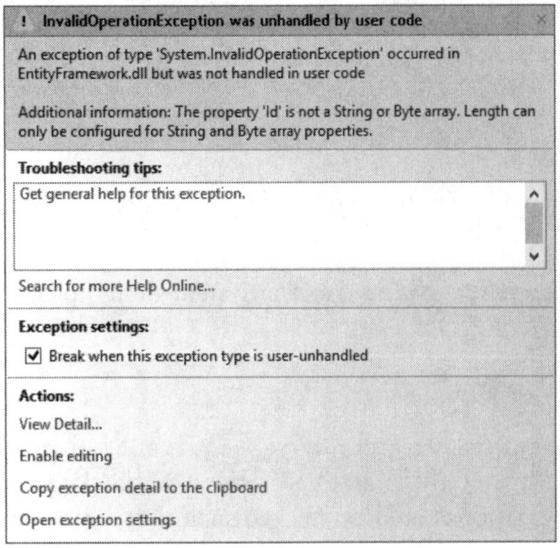

FIGURE 12-11: Error caused by StringLength on the integer property

The `StringLengthAttribute` caused one of the database changes. If you open the migration file that was just created in the Migrations directory you will see a line like the following:

```
AlterColumn("dbo.UserDemographics", "MaritalStatus",
        c => c.String(nullable: false, maxLength: 15));
```

This sets the maximum length to 15 characters. The outcome of this line can be seen in the Server Explorer, where the properties of the MaritalStatus column will show that the column has a length of 15, as shown in Figure 12-12.

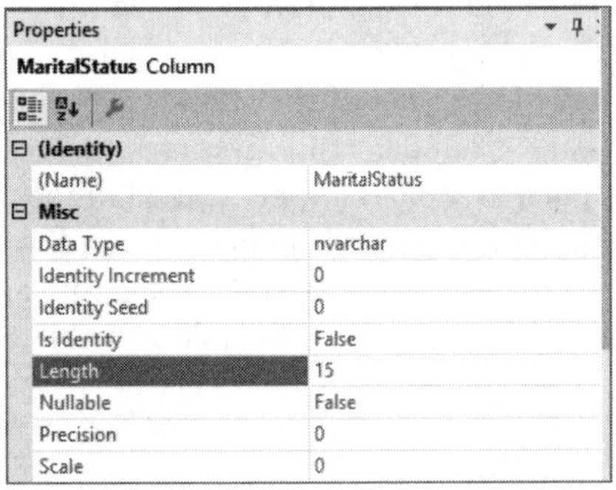

FIGURE 12-12: Properties showing 15-character column

It may strike you odd, however, that you don't see anything in the migration script for the other required fields that were set in this activity, such as `DateMovedIntoArea`, `TotalNumberInHome`, and

`BirthDate`. That is because all those items were set as being required in the database from the very beginning. The reason becomes clear when you think about what these types—DateTime and integer—mean in .NET as opposed to what they mean in the database. The database is OK having these fields as nullable, but that's not possible in .NET. Neither DateTime nor integer are allowed to be null; they will always be set with a default value whenever they are created through a model first class, so the framework sets the database up to support that need. Therefore, adding this particular attribute to those properties did not affect the database design, but it will affect the UI and how it handles client-side validation.

What do you think will happen when the following code is run from within a controller?

```
using (RentMyWroxContext context = new RentMyWroxContext())
{
    var item = new UserDemographics {
            DateMovedIntoArea = DateTime.Now,
            Birthdate = DateTime.Now,
            TotalNumberInHome = 0,
            MaritalStatus = "A" };
    context.UserDemographics.Add(item);
    context.SaveChanges();
}
```

It appears that the item would not pass validation because it contains several items that don't pass validation—and that is what happens, as shown in Figure 12-13.

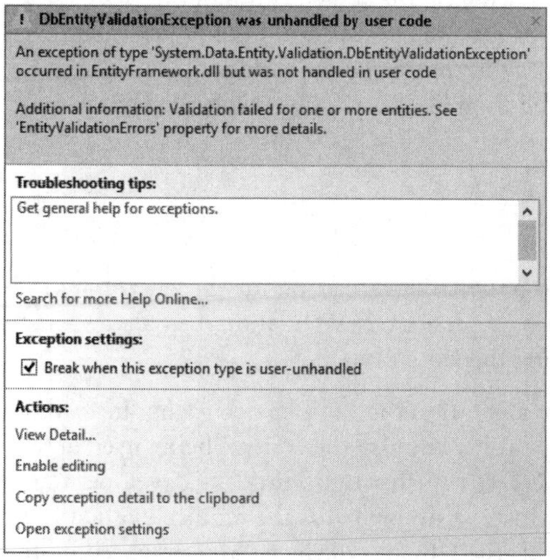

FIGURE 12-13: Error when trying to save invalid data in the controller

That the system always validates the information being persisted for that model is very important—using data annotations literally affects the values of data that can be stored in the database; this is the definition of server-side validation.

Once you have added data validation rules on the server side you need to hook these rules to the UI so that you can also support client-side validation.

Client-Side Validation

Server-side validation is a required part of any application that is persisting data and may have expectations about the validity of the data. However, as mentioned earlier in the chapter, having client-side validation as well provides a much better overall user experience because users can get much more timely feedback when their validation fails, as the round-trip to the server isn't necessary.

When you added client-side validation to the ASP.NET Web Form, all you did was set the rules for that field in the validation server control that was placed on that page, and that control handled both server and client-side validation. The control was easy to configure and using it was simple. Fortunately, the MVC framework provides a way to manage client-side validation that is almost as straightforward, once it has been properly configured and set up.

Just as with validation server controls, MVC views rely on JavaScript to manage the client-side validation of information being submitted through the web browser. However, whereas the Web Forms validation relies on JavaScript being provided by a `WebResource.axd` file behind the scenes, the validation used within MVC relies entirely on open-source JavaScript libraries—namely, the jQuery and jQuery validation libraries.

These libraries know how to interact with the information on the screen through the MVC `Html.ValidationMessageFor` helper. This helper takes a Lambda expression of the model field that is being validated. When the view goes through the rendering event, the validation rules are translated into a configuration supported by the validation libraries. The code for the `Html.ValidationMessageFor` is shown here:

```
@Html.ValidationMessageFor(model => model.Birthdate,
        "", new { @class = "text-danger" })
```

This code snippet tells the engine to create a class to handle the validation for the `BirthDate`. The empty string that is being passed in represents the UI override of the validation message, while the last parameter sets the class of the element containing the validation.

Notice that nothing in the helper defines the type of validation that will be occurring; instead, it just identifies the property being validated. This is possible because the control being used here relies on the validation that was defined at the model level. Rather than force the developer to create an entirely new implementation of validation, it instead simply reads the required validation of the model that was passed to the view and then builds the UI parts of the validation based on those characteristics.

In this next Try It Out activity, you explore this relationship further by adding validation to an MVC view.

TRY IT OUT Adding Validation to an MVC View

In this activity, you take advantage of the validation rules that you just added to the `UserDemographics` class by tying them to the view so that the same model attribute-based rules provide support for client-side data validation.

1. Ensure that Visual Studio is running and your RentMyWrox solution is open.

2. Open the NuGet Package Manager by right-clicking from within the Solution Explorer on the project name. Select Manage NuGet Packages. This will open a popup window.

3. Select Online ⇨ Microsoft and .NET on the left and search for "validation" as shown in Figure 12-14.

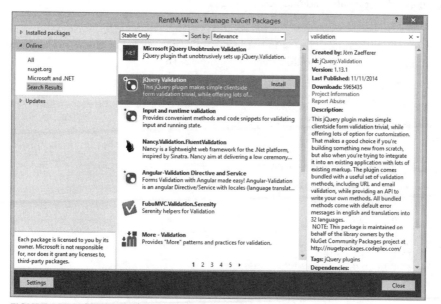

FIGURE 12-14: Nuget Package Manager Window

4. You should see multiple results. Find one called jQuery Validation and click the Install button. You may have to accept some licensing agreements. When the process completes, the item that you initially selected may have a green check mark on the selection tile.

5. In this same window, look for Microsoft jQuery Unobtrusive Validation and add this package as well.

6. Go to your Solution Explorer window and expand the Scripts directory. The files it contains should be similar to those shown in Figure 12-15.

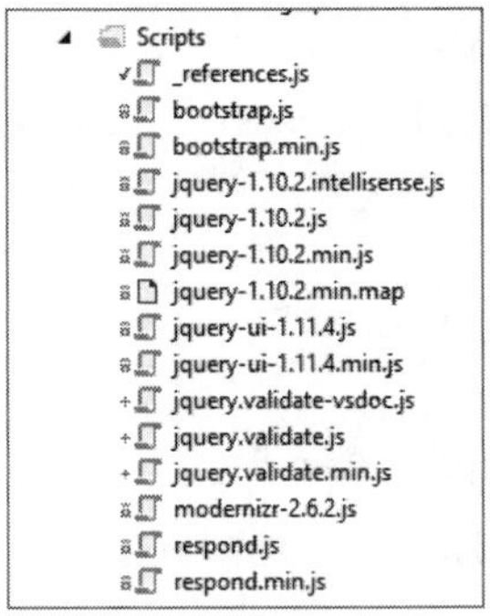

FIGURE 12-15: Scripts directory after adding new packages

7. Open your `App_Start\BundleConfig.cs` file. Add the following entries to the `RegisterBundles` method. When completed, this file should resemble Figure 12-16.

```
bundles.Add(new ScriptBundle("~/bundles/jquery")
    .Include("~/Scripts/jquery-{version}.js"));

bundles.Add(new ScriptBundle("~/bundles/jqueryval")
    .Include("~/Scripts/jquery.validate*"));
```

```
public static void RegisterBundles(BundleCollection bundles)
{
    bundles.Add(new ScriptBundle("~/bundles/WebFormsJs").Include(
            "~/Scripts/WebForms/WebForms.js",
            "~/Scripts/WebForms/WebUIValidation.js",
            "~/Scripts/WebForms/MenuStandards.js",
            "~/Scripts/WebForms/Focus.js",
            "~/Scripts/WebForms/GridView.js",
            "~/Scripts/WebForms/DetailsView.js",
            "~/Scripts/WebForms/TreeView.js",
            "~/Scripts/WebForms/WebParts.js"));

    // Order is very important for these files to work, they have explicit dependencies
    bundles.Add(new ScriptBundle("~/bundles/MsAjaxJs").Include(
            "~/Scripts/WebForms/MsAjax/MicrosoftAjax.js",
            "~/Scripts/WebForms/MsAjax/MicrosoftAjaxApplicationServices.js",
            "~/Scripts/WebForms/MsAjax/MicrosoftAjaxTimer.js",
            "~/Scripts/WebForms/MsAjax/MicrosoftAjaxWebForms.js"));

    // Use the Development version of Modernizr to develop with and learn from. Then, when you're
    // ready for production, use the build tool at http://modernizr.com to pick only the tests you need
    bundles.Add(new ScriptBundle("~/bundles/modernizr").Include(
            "~/Scripts/modernizr-*"));

    bundles.Add(new ScriptBundle("~/bundles/jquery").Include(
    "~/Scripts/jquery-{version}.js"));

    bundles.Add(new ScriptBundle("~/bundles/jqueryval").Include(
            "~/Scripts/jquery.validate*"));

    ScriptManager.ScriptResourceMapping.AddDefinition(
        "respond",
        new ScriptResourceDefinition
        {
            Path = "~/Scripts/respond.min.js",
            DebugPath = "~/Scripts/respond.js",
        });
}
```

FIGURE 12-16: Content of the BundleConfig file

8. Open your `View\Shared\_MVCLayout.cshtml` file. Find the following lines and delete them:

```
<script language="javascript" type="text/javascript" src="~/Scripts/jquery-
1.10.2.js"></script>
```

```
<script language="javascript" type="text/javascript"
        src="~/Scripts/jquery-ui-1.11.4.js"></script>
```

9. Add the following line to the same spot:

```
@Scripts.Render("~/bundles/modernizr")
```

10. In this same area of the page, find the following lines and move them closer to the bottom of the page, right below the @Scripts.Render lines:

```
<script type="text/javascript">
    $(document).ready(function () {
        $(".editordatepicker").datepicker();
    });
</script>
@RenderSection("scripts", required: false)
```

11. Open your Views\UserDemographics\Manage.cshtml file. Find the ValidationSummary. Change true to false. When completed, this section of the file should look like Figure 12-17.

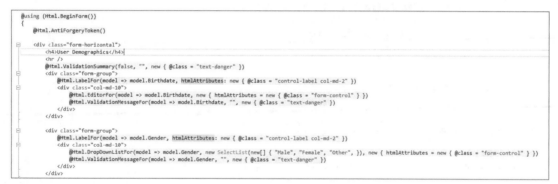

```
@using (Html.BeginForm())
{
    @Html.AntiForgeryToken()

    <div class="form-horizontal">
        <h4>User Demographics</h4>
        <hr />
        @Html.ValidationSummary(false, "", new { @class = "text-danger" })
        <div class="form-group">
            @Html.LabelFor(model => model.Birthdate, htmlAttributes: new { @class = "control-label col-md-2" })
            <div class="col-md-10">
                @Html.EditorFor(model => model.Birthdate, new { htmlAttributes = new { @class = "form-control" } })
                @Html.ValidationMessageFor(model => model.Birthdate, "", new { @class = "text-danger" })
            </div>
        </div>

        <div class="form-group">
            @Html.LabelFor(model => model.Gender, htmlAttributes: new { @class = "control-label col-md-2" })
            <div class="col-md-10">
                @Html.DropDownListFor(model => model.Gender, new SelectList(new[] { "Male", "Female", "Other", }), new { htmlAttributes = new { @class = "form-control" } })
                @Html.ValidationMessageFor(model => model.Gender, "", new { @class = "text-danger" })
            </div>
        </div>
```

FIGURE 12-17: New ValidationSummary configuration

12. Open your UserDemographicsController. Update your Post version of the Create method to the code shown here:

```
[HttpPost]
public ActionResult Create(UserDemographics obj)
{
    using (RentMyWroxContext context = new RentMyWroxContext())
    {
        var ids = Request.Form.GetValues("HobbyIds");
        if (ids != null)
        {
            obj.Hobbies = context.Hobbies.Where(x => ids.Contains(x.Id.ToString())).
            ToList();
        }
        context.UserDemographics.Add(obj);
        var validationErrors = context.GetValidationErrors();
```

```
        if (validationErrors.Count() == 0)
        {
            context.SaveChanges();
            return RedirectToAction("Index");
        }
        ViewBag.ServerValidationErrors =
        ConvertValidationErrorsToString(validationErrors);
        return View("Manage", obj);
    }
}
```

13. Add the following method to your controller:

```
private string ConvertValidationErrorsToString
        (IEnumerable<DbEntityValidationResult> list)
{
    StringBuilder results = new StringBuilder();
    results.Append("You had the following validation errors: ");
    foreach(var item in list)
    {
        foreach(var failure in item.ValidationErrors)
        {
            results.Append(failure.ErrorMessage);
            results.Append(" ");
        }
    }
    return results.ToString();
}
```

14. Update your Post Edit method to the following:

```
[HttpPost]
public ActionResult Edit(int id, FormCollection collection)
{
    using (RentMyWroxContext context = new RentMyWroxContext())
    {
        var item = context.UserDemographics.FirstOrDefault(x => x.Id == id);
        TryUpdateModel(item);
        var ids = Request.Form.GetValues("HobbyIds");
        item.Hobbies = context.Hobbies.Where(x => ids.Contains(x.Id.ToString()))
        .ToList();
        var validationErrors = context.GetValidationErrors();
        if (validationErrors.Count() == 0)
        {
            context.SaveChanges();
            return RedirectToAction("Index");
        }
        ViewBag.ServerValidationErrors = ConvertValidationErrorsToString(validationEr
rors);
        return View("Manage", item);
    }
}
```

15. Back in the `Manage.cshtml` file, add the following line to the top block of code. It should look like Figure 12-18 when completed.

```
string serverValidationProblems = ViewBag.ServerValidationErrors;
```

FIGURE 12-18: Updated code block

16. Add the following code immediately after the `ValidationSummary`. When finished it should look similar to Figure 12-19.

```
@if(!string.IsNullOrWhiteSpace(serverValidationProblems))
{
    <div class="alert">@serverValidationProblems</div>
}
```

```
Manage.cshtml ↗ ✕
    @model RentMyWrox.Models.UserDemographics

    @{
        ViewBag.Title = "Manage";
        List<RentMyWrox.Models.Hobby> hobbyList = ViewBag.Hobbies;
        string serverValidationProblems = ViewBag.ServerValidationErrors;
    }

    <h2>Manage</h2>

    @using (Html.BeginForm())
    {
        @Html.AntiForgeryToken()

        <div class="form-horizontal">
            <h4>User Demographics</h4>
            <hr />
            @Html.ValidationSummary(false, "", new { @class = "text-danger" })
            @if(!string.IsNullOrWhiteSpace(serverValidationProblems))
            {
                <div class="alert">@serverValidationProblems</div>
            }
            <div class="form-group">
                @Html.LabelFor(model => model.Birthdate, htmlAttributes: new { @class = "control-label col-md-2" })
                <div class="col-md-10">
                    @Html.EditorFor(model => model.Birthdate, new { htmlAttributes = new { @class = "form-control" } })
                    @Html.ValidationMessageFor(model => model.Birthdate, "", new { @class = "text-danger" })
                </div>
            </div>
```

FIGURE 12-19: Changed view page

17. Run your application and go to `\UserDemographics\Create`. Without filling out any information, click the Create button. You should get output similar to that shown in Figure 12-20.

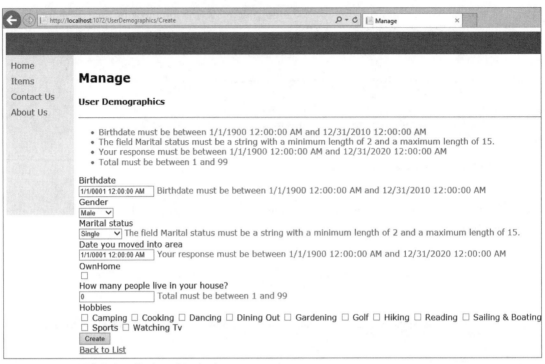

FIGURE 12-20: Validation displayed in the browser

18. Properly fill out the data in the screen and click Create. Note that you are returned to the list page and that the item you just added is in the list.

How It Works

Working with data validation in ASP.NET MVC views is similar to working with validation in Web Forms since the work required by the developer is mostly getting the validation onto the page. Once the proper control, whether it is a server control or an HTML helper, is on the page, the ASP.NET page creation process takes over and builds the appropriate output so that the client browser can understand the validation requirements.

An MVC view uses a jQuery-based approach to building validation. This means the code that actually performs the validation is part of the jQuery framework, so all the ASP.NET framework has to do is ensure that the output of the validation control is what is expected when working with the validation library.

The following code snippets show the data elements in the view, the model definition, and the HTML output from the page that includes the information created by the validation helper:

```
View content
<div class="form-group">
    @Html.LabelFor(model => model.DateMovedIntoArea,
            htmlAttributes: new { @class = "control-label col-md-2" })
    <div class="col-md-10">
        @Html.EditorFor(model => model.DateMovedIntoArea,
```

```
                    new { htmlAttributes = new { @class = "form-control" } })
            @Html.ValidationMessageFor(model => model.DateMovedIntoArea, "",
                    new { @class = "text-danger" })
        </div>
    </div>
```

Model Definition
```
[Display(Name = "Date you moved into area")]
[Required(ErrorMessage = "Please tell us when you moved into the area")]
[Range(typeof(DateTime), "1/1/1900", "12/31/2020",
        ErrorMessage = "Your response must be between {1} and {2}")]
public DateTime DateMovedIntoArea { get; set; }
```

HTML Output
```
<div class="form-group">
    <label class="control-label col-md-2" for="DateMovedIntoArea">
        Date you moved into area
    </label>
    <div class="col-md-10">
        <input class="editordatepicker"
            data-val="true"
            data-val-date="The field Date you moved into area must be a date."
            data-val-range="Your response must be between 1/1/1900 12:00:00 AM
                        and 12/31/2020 12:00:00 AM"
            data-val-range-max="12/31/2020 00:00:00"
            data-val-range-min="01/01/1900 00:00:00"
            data-val-required="Please tell us when you moved into the area"
            id="DateMovedIntoArea" name="DateMovedIntoArea" type="text"
            value="1/1/0001 12:00:00 AM" />
        <span class="field-validation-valid text-danger"
            data-valmsg-for="DateMovedIntoArea"
            data-valmsg-replace="true"></span>
    </div>
</div>
```

Looking at these three sections together shows how an element needs to be configured to work within the jQuery validation framework. The key to success when working within jQuery is the use of custom attributes on a common HTML element. These custom attributes are found in the input element and all start with "data-val" to indicate that they are data validation values.

With the inclusion of the jQuery files, a method was added that intercepts the form submission. As part of that interception, the method goes through all the elements that are part of the form submission, looking for a known set of element attributes. When the jQuery method finds these attributes it examines the values they contain to determine what kind of validation needs to happen.

The first attribute that it looks for is data-val. When that attribute is present and set to true, the jQuery validation framework then reviews the element to determine the type of validation to perform. In this case it finds three different validations that need to happen: datatype, range, and required. You can determine this because each of those validation types has a representative attribute. Range has additional elements because it needs to support a minimum value and a maximum value.

These attributes were added because the Razor view engine understood the relationship between the EditorFor and ValidationMessageFor items and was able to create the attributes based on the settings in the model. You can see this relationship because all the values used in the validation are the same values as those used in the attribution on the model's property.

You can create these attributes yourself, by hand, and take advantage of the validation framework that was provided when you added the appropriate NuGet packages. (Please note that multiple JavaScript and jQuery validation frameworks are available, each of which differs in implementation.) The Unobtrusive Native jQuery library that you added to the project enables the management of validation through the `data-val` approach.

The `data-val` approach takes advantage of HTML5, which allows custom attributes to be created and analyzed by the browser. These custom attributes are then available to be analyzed through jQuery just like the standard attributes on an element. There is a whole chapter, Chapter 14, on using jQuery coming up soon, so that's all on the subject for now.

You also made some changes in the controller. While not completely necessary, as you know that the Entity Framework will not allow bad data to be saved to the database, doing some work in the controller helps to create a better user experience, as a thrown exception can result in showing users the infamous ugly yellow exception screen.

The primary change that you made to ensure a positive user experience was adding a validation check in the controller before the `SaveChanges` method is called. You may wonder why you made this effort because you also put all the validation in the view. The answer goes back to the concept of always ensuring that you try to avoid throwing exceptions—understanding that an exception will be thrown if you actually make the call enables you to avoid having the framework throw an exception.

You can make this determination through the `GetValidationErrors` method on the context. Running this method causes the context to evaluate all the changed items against their validation rules. If there are any instances where the item fails validation, then that item is added to the list of failed validation items. One `DbEntityValidationResult` is returned for each item that fails validation. This is per object, not per property on the object that failed validation; the specific property that failed is listed in the `ValidationErrors` collection on the `DbEntityValidationResult`.

The `GetValidationErrors` method runs only on items that have been added to the context, so typically it would generally be run right before the `SaveChanges` method is processed. However, in larger applications in which the same data context may be passed from method to method, it is considered good form to run `GetValidationErrors` because the method that added the bad data is the best method to handle management of the invalid data.

When you run the `GetValidationErrors` method, you get a list of the validation issues. You added a method to the controller to translate this collection of validation errors to a string that you added to the `ViewBag` so that you could report back to the user any specific problems that were discovered.

As you can probably surmise, there are other routes to validating your data. The `Controller` class has a method, `ValidateModel`, that validates the information returned from the request to ensure that the incoming item passes validation. This approach is good because you can do it before actually instantiating the data context, thus saving processing on the server. Using this method in the controller could look like the following:

```
ValidateModel(obj);
if (ModelState.IsValid)
```

```
    {
        using (RentMyWroxContext context = new RentMyWroxContext())
        {
            context.UserDemographics.Add(obj);
            context.SaveChanges();
            return RedirectToAction("Index");
        }
    }
}
```

Accessing the failed items is a little more complicated using this approach, however, as you have to iterate through each of the values in the `ModelState`, with each value in the `ModelState` corresponding to a property on the model, and then evaluate the `Errors` collection that was attached to that `ModelState` value, something like the code snippet shown here:

```
foreach(var value in ModelState.Values)
{
    if (value.Errors.Count > 0)
    {
        // do something with the error
    }
}
```

Parsing through the properties of the model to find those with errors is more complex code, which is why the code was written using the `GetValidationErrors` method; it is easier to understand and maintain. However, just like virtually all work that needs to be done in ASP.NET, there are multiple ways of solving a problem, each having its own sets of strengths and weaknesses.

The information that is input by the user is validated against the rules that were defined for the model class. There is one more set of validation that is performed by the server when a controller handles a request.

Request Validation in ASP.NET MVC

Like ASP.NET Web Forms, MVC enables you to perform request validation. Request validation is a check whether a form field contains HTML elements or other potential scripting items when that field is submitted to an MVC application. As a matter of fact, request validation is occurring in every submittal unless you decide to turn it off because request validation is turned on by default.

In ASP.NET Web Forms, you control request validation for the entire page. Because MVC does not really have the concept of a page, you control the settings from an attribute that can be used on a controller or on an individual action, as shown here:

```
[ValidateInput(false)]
[HttpPost]
public ActionResult Create(UserDemographics obj)
```

In the preceding snippet you can see the attribute that determines whether or not the input is validated, `ValidateInput`. When you do not manually set the attribute, the system treats every request as if it were attributed with `ValidateInput(true)`. To turn off request validation, simply set the attribute to false.

When the attribute is set to false, the action will not validate any of the information coming to the server. In some cases this may be acceptable, but if you have a large form with multiple fields you may not be willing to have every field open to accept HTML (the default when validation is turned off for a controller).

The developers of ASP.NET MVC recognized this need and added a special type of attribute that you put on a model class, `System.Web.Mvc.AllowHtml`. When used on a typical model property it could look like the following code:

```
[AllowHtml]
[Display(Name="Description")]
[Required(ErrorMessage = "Please enter a Description")]
[StringLength(150, MinimumLength = 2)]
public string Description { get; set; }
```

By attributing only those properties where you expect HTML, you can keep input validation on—only allowing HTML to be used on specific properties and not across the entire request.

VALIDATION TIPS

The following list provides practical tips on validating data:

➤ Always validate all user input. Whenever you have a public website on the Internet, you lose the ability to control its users. To stop malicious users from entering bogus or malicious data into your system, always validate your users' input using the ASP.NET validation controls.

➤ All data being passed in from the client should go through some type of validation; it is easy to accidentally enter invalid data, such as using the capital "O" instead of the number 0, or a letter "l" instead of the number 1.

➤ Always provide useful error messages in your validation controls. Either assign the error message to the `ErrorMessage` property and leave the `Text` empty, or use a `ValidationSummary` control to show a list of error messages. The more details you can give users about a problem, the easier it will be for them to resolve the issue.

➤ Whenever possible, point to the problem data that the user is working with rather than trying to describe it through text. The most common approach is to put the validation message right next to the input that is being validated.

➤ If you have to make a choice between client-side validation or server-side validation, always choose server-side validation. Client-side validation can be voided by a malicious user.

SUMMARY

Validation is the process of ensuring that the information provided by a user fits a certain set of criteria. When validating data, approaches may vary depending on where you will be performing the validation and how you will be checking the data.

Where you will be performing the validation is pretty straightforward because you only have two options for this: the server and the client. You should never consider it optional to do validation on the server because only there can you be sure that the validation is applied to the information being persisted; client-side validation can be turned off or gone around. Client-side validation provides a better user experience and can eliminate unnecessary round-trips to the server, but server-side validation is responsible for checking data immediately before persistence.

When you consider validation, you need to ensure not only that your system is protected from bad data, but that you provide the appropriate feedback to users should they need to fix the data. This messaging back to users tends to work best with client-side validation because they can get immediate response to problems.

Because of this need for both client and server validation, ASP.NET Web Form controls provide both. They enable you to define validation rules that will be used to check the input values and then provide both JavaScript that the browser uses to validate information before submission as well as server-side code that can be checked to ensure that values are valid. Various validation controls are available, each of which supports a different approach to validating the data that is entered into the particular field with which it is linked.

Validation in MVC is different, but you can perform validation on both sides based on rules that are created on the model. The view has a helper that takes advantage of the rules from the model and configures the input element in such a way that a jQuery library automatically performs validation upon submission of the form. When the data gets back to the server, the same validation can be run against the request to ensure that it is valid before making use of the information.

Both Web Forms and MVC provide support to validate data on both the client and the server. They take different approaches but they both solve the same need, helping you ensure the best data possible is added to your system.

EXERCISES

1. What would be the expected behavior of the server when a user puts HTML code only into the Title field of a view that is linked with the following code? What happens if HTML code is put only in the Description field?

    ```
    [ValidateInput(true)]
    public class TestController : Controller
    {
        [HttpPost]
    ```

```
    public ActionResult Create(MyModel model)
    {
        return View();
    }

    public ActionResult Create()
    {
        return View();
    }
}

public class MyModel
{
    [Required]
    [StringLength(50)]
    public string Title { get; set; }

    [Required]
    [AllowHtml]
    [StringLength(5000)]
    public string Description { get; set; }
}
```

2. Imagine you are working with an ASP.NET Web Forms page and you place a `RangeValidator` above a `RequiredValidator` when they are both validating the same control. What would be the difference in behavior if you switched the order of the validation controls?

3. Is it possible to put validation on a model in such a way that a model can never be valid?

▶ WHAT YOU LEARNED IN THIS CHAPTER

Client-Side Validation	Client-side validation is the process of ensuring that information entered by a user fits a defined template. It is called client-side because all the checking happens within the browser, before the form is submitted to the server. If validation fails, then the form information is never submitted to the server; instead, a message displaying the validation errors is generally shown to the user.
Compare Validation	When you are doing a compare validation you are comparing the value in one field with another value. This other value could be another field, a constant value, or some sort of calculation. The primary consideration is that the value in an element is compared against another.
Data Length Validation	The process of determining whether the entered information is of the appropriate length, or amount of characters. This type of validation is generally performed only on strings. It consists of a minimum length, defaulting to 0, and a maximum length.
Data Type Validation	A determination made against the value in a submitted element as to whether that value can be cast or parsed into a defined type
`ModelState`	A construct that contains information regarding, surprisingly enough, the state of the model. After the `ValidateModel` method is run, the `IsValid` property provides information as to whether all validation rules passed successfully.
`Page.IsValid`	This is a code-behind check, in ASP.NET Web Forms, as to whether the content of the page successfully passes all the validation rules defined in the various validation controls. It is the server-side verification that the information is valid.
Range Validation	Determines whether the value of an element falls between a specific set of two values. Generally used for numeric types and dates, in range validation the first check is to confirm whether the value is parseable to the appropriate type, and the second check confirms whether it is between the minimum and maximum values set for the range.
Regular Expression Validation	Compares the value of an element against a regular expression. If the value fits the template established by the regular expression, then the validation is successful.

Request Validation	A process that determines whether the data being submitted by the client contains anything that is formatted in such a way that it poses some risk when displayed directly to another user (such as JavaScript to download viruses, etc.). Request validation is typically enabled by default, which means information containing HTML-looking tags will not be allowed to be processed on the server.
Required Field	Ensures that an element has a value. Having a value is typically defined as being set with a value other than the default, e.g., a string defaults to NULL, so any value, even an empty string, would be considered a value for this purpose.
Server-side Validation	This is the most important validation because it is the final check on the server that the data the system received from the user matches all necessary requirements.
Unobtrusive Validation	Unobtrusive validation is the jQuery approach to validation that is used with ASP.NET MVC. It enables the developer to use pre-defined (by the JavaScript library) custom attributes on an input element to provide validation information to the validation subsystem. The values in these attributes help the subsystem determine what rules need to be checked as well as provide feedback to the user about the state of the process.
`ValidateModel`	A method on the controller that validates the model against the data annotations in the model. Typically used with the ModelState that contains various sets of information about the model, including whether the validation was successful.

13

ASP.NET AJAX

WHAT YOU WILL LEARN IN THIS CHAPTER:

➤ How AJAX fits into the ASP.NET Framework

➤ Taking advantage of Web Forms controls to make AJAX calls

➤ Using a Web Forms control to show status to the user

➤ Creating REST web services to support AJAX

➤ Using jQuery to support AJAX in MVC

CODE DOWNLOADS FOR THIS CHAPTER:

The wrox.com code downloads for this chapter are found at www.wrox.com/go/
beginningaspnetforvisualstudio on the Download Code tab. The code is in the chapter 13
download and individually named according to the names throughout the chapter.

When you are talking about web development and you hear the term AJAX, it is very rarely
referring to the hero from Greek mythology. Instead, it refers to a web communications
approach that started to become popular in 2005 and 2006, Asynchronous JavaScript and
XML. The primary purpose of AJAX is to enable communications between the user's browser
and the server without having to do a full page refresh.

This communication is not outside the HTTP protocol, but instead uses HTTP to communicate smaller pieces of information within sections of the web page, rather than the default
"whole page" approach. This is becoming increasingly common, as it provides an experience
that seems more desktop-like because pieces of information on the page are refreshed based on
some condition (timing, user action, and so on) without having to go through the whole page
fetch that prevents users from being able to work in the browser while the request is managed.

AJAX has evolved considerably, but the main changes are related to how the JavaScript
calls are managed and how the information is formatted for transfer. You will be working

with these new changes throughout the next couple of chapters as you use jQuery to handle the JavaScript, and JavaScript Object Notation (JSON) to define the format for data transference, rather than XML. In other words, you won't be really doing AJAX; instead you will be doing something like JQJN (jQuery with JSON, but since that does not really roll off the tongue we will respect tradition and keep calling it AJAX.

INTRODUCING THE CONCEPT OF AJAX

The whole point of AJAX is to support asynchronous communication. The traditional web page approach that you have worked with to this point has been synchronous in that once the request to the server was sent, the browser tends to stop what it is doing and wait for the server to respond with the next set of content. With the synchronous approach, once you click the submit button you are sitting there waiting for a response.

The waiting for a response cannot be mitigated. The whole point of a web application is to communication between clients and servers that are physically separated—almost always on different networks and possibly even different continents. However, what can be controlled is the stoppage of other work while you are waiting for the server to respond. This is where asynchronous communication comes into play. Clearly, if a more asynchronous approach to communication is possible, then it's also possible for users to avoid waiting for the server to respond and can instead continue working on the client side while the communications with the server happen in the background. Admittedly, this provides a more complicated communications model, as shown in Figure 13-1, but it provides a more fluid and positive experience for the user.

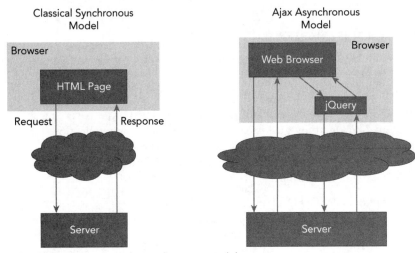

FIGURE 13-1: Classic and asynchronous models

Figure 13-1 demonstrates some of the differences between the two models. There are definitely some parts in common, such as page transitions in both approaches whereby the entire page is replaced with another page. However, some extra communication is going on from the web page, through jQuery, to the server, which then responds back to the jQuery call, with jQuery taking the response and updating the UI. This represents the asynchronous part of this communication—the request sent to the server that enables the user to continue working while the processing happens behind the scenes.

There are differences between the responses provided by the server. As you have seen, in some cases the response to a request is the HTML for an entire page. You have also worked with user controls and partial views that create and manage smaller sets of HTML that can be inserted into the over-all page. Calling such a section again—only this section and not the rest of the page—is one form of AJAX whereby the service returns an HTML snippet that replaces another set of HTML that is already present in the web page.

A third type of response, and a second AJAX approach, is returning a single object to the page, much like you pass a model to an MVC view, and then the JavaScript takes that model and parses it into the HTML elements that hold each value. This approach is common in functionality such as a stock ticker, whereby an object that contains all the information being displayed is downloaded as needed and the old values are simply replaced with the new values. The HTML elements are not replaced during the call; the JavaScript functionality instead replaces the values within the element.

SINGLE-PAGE APPLICATION

There is an approach to building a web application, called single-page application (SPA), whereby there is one full page refresh on the entire site, and that is when you first visit the site to download the original content. All subsequent processing is handled as AJAX, whereby resources, including HTML, data, CSS, and other items, are downloaded and displayed as necessary.

A single-page application provides the closest experience to a desktop application because there are no page transitions, so the period spent waiting for the request to complete is removed throughout the site. However, you pay for it by deploying a much larger set of information at the beginning, because not only do users have to download the traditional "first page," they also have to download the libraries to manage all the transitional work, in essence spending extra time at the beginning to eliminate the time wasted while working on the page.

One of the more complex factors when doing the development work for AJAX is debugging the process and ensuring that the information you are getting back from the server is correct. All of the debugging that you have been doing up to now has been in server-side code, or perhaps looking at the HTML source code that was returned by the server; however, asynchronous communications bring in a whole different set of complications because the snippets of information that are being returned by the server do not show up in any of these approaches. You will see some of these com-plications, and how they can be remediated, in more detail in the next few sections.

F12 Developer Tools

You may not be aware of this, but most of the available web browsers include a set of development tools that you can use to understand and debug the HTML that was sent to the browser. Google Chrome's Developer tools are shown in Figure 13-2.

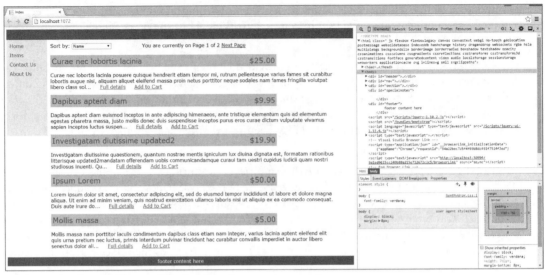

FIGURE 13-2: Google Chrome Developer tools

These tools with Google Chrome enable you to review the HTML elements, see how the styles are applied, and allow you to make temporary changes to see how they may affect your site's layout. They also provide the capability to obtain useful information, such as total download size, time for download, and many other pieces of information that gives you a better understanding of the HTML output from the website and how the browser will interpret that information.

Mozilla Firefox has its own version of developer tools, shown in Figure 13-3. The appearance is different, but much of the base information is the same, as the information that you are interested in about a web page is the same, regardless of the browser that you are using to parse and view the content.

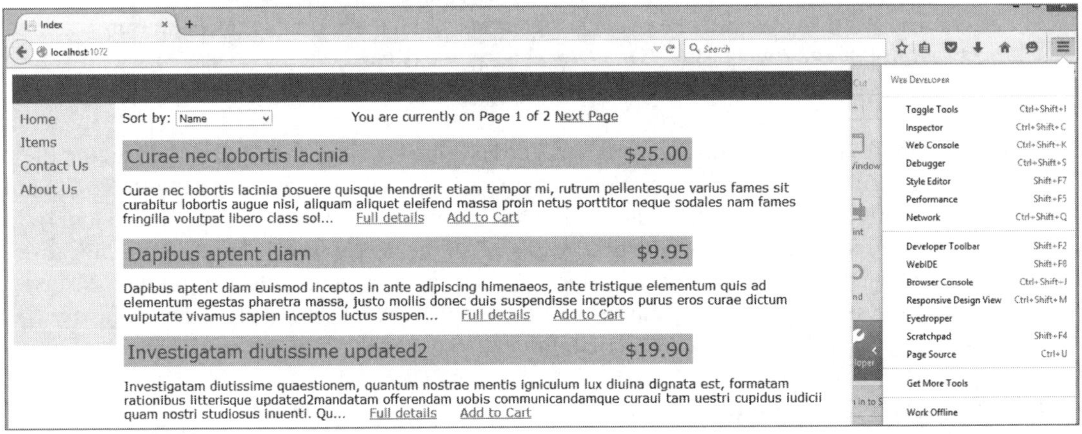

FIGURE 13-3: Mozilla Firefox Developer tools

As you work through the next few chapters you'll be taking advantage of a third set of development tools, Internet Explorer's F12 Developer Tools. They are cunningly called F12 Tools because you can use the F12 function key to access them. If you do not have function keys on your keyboard, you can use the Tools menu in Internet Explorer. These same tools are available in Microsoft's Windows 10 Edge browser, the Windows 10 replacement for Internet Explorer. This next Try It Out will walk you through using F12 tools using your sample application.

TRY IT OUT   Using F12 Development Tools

This Try It Out walks through some of the features of Internet Explorer's F12 Developer Tools that you will be using as you work through the various AJAX enhancements you add to your site.

1. Ensure that Visual Studio is running and your RentMyWrox solution is open at the home page. Start the application in Debug, ensuring that you are using Internet Explorer to view your application.

2. Use your F12 key to open the Developer Tools. You can also open the tool by selecting Tools ⇨ F12 Developer Tools, as shown in Figure 13-4.

FIGURE 13-4: Opening the F12 Developer Tools through the menu

3. Verify that you are on the DOM Explorer tab. Select the element that represents one of your products. You may have to expand areas on the left to find them; they will be in the `<div>` with an id of "section." It should look like Figure 13-5 when you have selected the item.

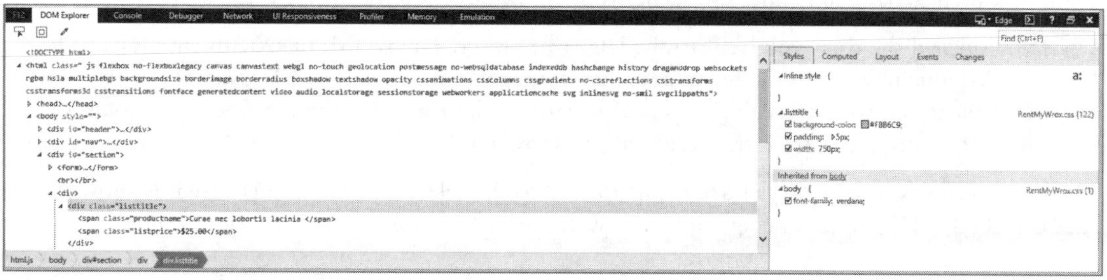

FIGURE 13-5: Dom Explorer and the Styles tab

4.   Click through the Styles, Computed, and Layout tabs in the pane on the right side of the tools and notice the information that is available in each tab.

5.   Select the Network tab from the right side of the Developer Tools. You should get the screen shown in Figure 13-6.

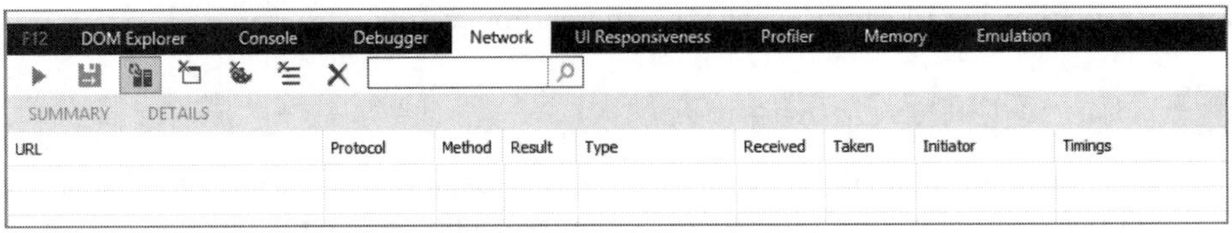

FIGURE 13-6: Network tab

6.   Click the green arrow in the tab, and then click the Full Details link of one of the items listed on the front page. The page should change similarly to what is shown in Figure 13-7.

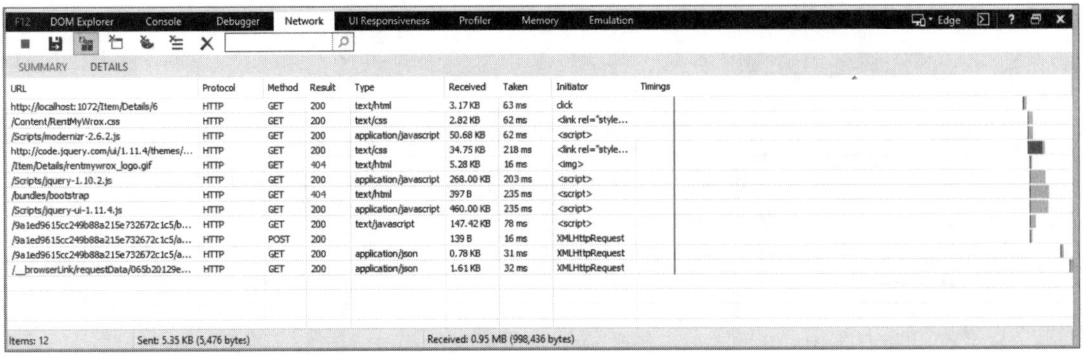

FIGURE 13-7: Network tab recording requests

How It Works

The F12 Developer tools provide a lot of information about your application and its interaction with the client's browser. Not only do you get information about how the browser is interpreting the HTML that it received, it also provides access to the communications between the client and the user; all the work that used to happen behind the scenes is now available for your review and study.

Once you opened the tools you went to the DOM Explorer. The DOM, or Document Object Model, is the HTML document that the browser is displaying. When in the DOM Explorer, you selected an HTML element and were then able to get information relevant to how that element is displayed. The first tab in the Dom Explorer is the Styles tab, as shown in Figure 13-8.

Figure 13-8 shows how the styles are being applied to the selected item. In this case it is showing that the "body" CSS style is being applied as well as the "listtitle" class. If you go to the next tab,

Computed, you will see all the styles that are cascading onto that particular element, as shown in Figure 13-9.

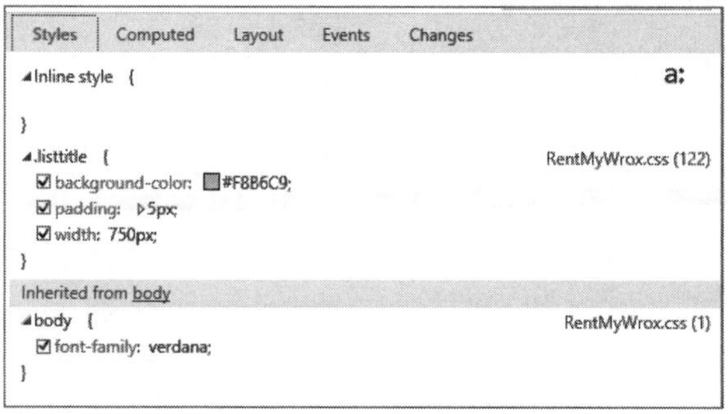

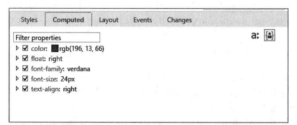

FIGURE 13-8: DOM Explorer tab showing Styles

FIGURE 13-9: DOM Explorer tab showing the Computed tab

An interesting feature of these two areas is how they support changing the values of the various CSS elements. In the Styles tab you can turn off the feature by removing the check from the checkbox to the left of the name. You can also change a value by clicking on its display and then typing in the new value.

The Computed tab displays the information differently in that it shows the entire list of CSS elements that the browser applies to the highlighted item. If you expand the item you can see from where the value that is currently being displayed came. You will be able to completely remove the style property through the checkbox next to the item; however, when you try to edit the value, you will find that you cannot do so from this default screen. Instead, expand each of the top-level items to see another box with the same value. This line represents the actual value that is available for editing and supports changing. When you change the value in the window, the display will immediately update the browser using the newly changed values.

Adding new values is almost as easy in the Styles tab. Clicking on the row with the opening brace will bring up a new property for which you can fill out the value as desired. You can then see how the display updates with the change, giving you immediate feedback to any changes that you want to propagate back to the application code.

Switching to the Layout tab gives you a look at the spacing for that element, as shown in Figure 13-10.

FIGURE 13-10: DOM Explorer tab showing the Layout tab

Here you can see how the Layout tab shows the pixel spacing that is being used by every factor of the element. The area in the center reflects the height and width of the element itself, in this case 750 pixels wide and 29.17 pixels high. The visualization in the tab then shows the current values for padding, border, and margin, all elements that you managed in the CSS. The last item displayed on this screen is the Offset. The Offset gives you the location of the element as it relates to the screen, based on all the other CSS that may have been set around the current element. All of this relates to the CSS box model that was discussed in Chapter 3.

The DOM layout information is very useful in debugging your layout. The other tab that you clicked through, the Network tab, will be important as you start working with AJAX calls because it tracks all the requests from the client and all the responses from the server. Clicking the green arrow in the F12 menu starts the monitoring process, and once the monitoring process has been started all outgoing requests will be captured. The information that is captured and available to review in this section includes the entire request and the entire response, including body content, headers, and status code. Figure 13-11 shows what this could look like.

F12	DOM Explorer	Console	Debugger	Network	UI Responsiveness	Profiler	Memory	Emulation

■ 💾 📇 📑 🐝 📈 ✕ | 🔍 |

SUMMARY   DETAILS   ◀ 16 / 54 ▶   http://localhost:1072/

Request headers	Request body	Response headers	Response body	Cookies	Initiator	Timings

Key	Value
Request	GET / HTTP/1.1
Accept	text/html, application/xhtml+xml, */*
Accept-Language	en-US
User-Agent	Mozilla/5.0 (Windows NT 6.3; WOW64; Trident/7.0; rv:11.0) like Gecko
Accept-Encoding	gzip, deflate
Host	localhost:1072
DNT	1
Connection	Keep-Alive
Cache-Control	no-cache

FIGURE 13-11: Network tab showing the Request headers

The lower set of tabs shown in Figure 13-11 are the various parts of the request/response that you now have visibility into: Request headers, Request body, Response headers, Response body, Cookies, Initiator, and Timings. The tabs that you will use most often during this process include Response Body, so that you can see the information returned by the server, and the Request Body and Headers, so that you can see what information the client asked for.

The other activities in this chapter spend some time in the F12 Developer tool, and these windows in particular, ensuring that the information you are expecting is what is actually returned.

Now that you will be able to evaluate the data that is being transferred back and forth between the client and server, you can get started adding AJAX into your application.

Using ASP.NET AJAX in Web Forms

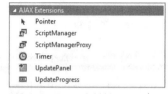

FIGURE 13-12: AJAX controls available in Visual Studio

The most obvious way to tell when a site and page are not using AJAX is by the flashing, or flickering, as a new page loads. AJAX enables you to avoid that by refreshing only a part of a page. Implementing AJAX within ASP.NET Web Forms requires some new server controls. The list of AJAX controls is shown in Figure 13-12.

The Initial AJAX Experience

The most important of these AJAX-specific controls is the `UpdatePanel`. The `UpdatePanel` is used to define the section of the page that will be updated through AJAX, with the items contained within the control being the refreshed area. While the `UpdatePanel` may be the most important control, it cannot work without access to a `ScriptManager` control on the page as well.

You can have any number of `UpdatePanel` controls in your page, each containing the area of the screen that you wish to make asynchronous. Typically there will be information to display and a way to update the content, such as a button or a dropdown list set to automatically post-back upon change. No matter how many `UpdatePanels` you have in the page, you only need one `ScriptManager` control because it is designed to hold the scripts for all the panels in that same page.

The only time you do not need a `ScriptManager` on the same page as the `UpdatePanel` is when you have a `ScriptManager` in the referenced master page. However, while in that case you do not have to ensure that you include a `ScriptManager` on that particular page, you do need a `ScriptManagerProxy` control so that the local `UpdatePanels` will be able to work up the line to the `ScriptManager` in the hosting page. Figure 13-13 shows the links between all of these controls.

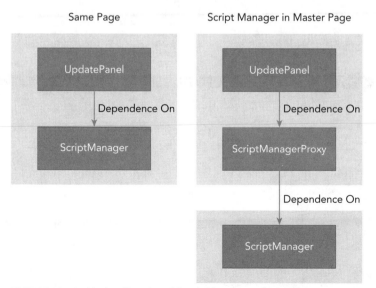

FIGURE 13-13: UpdatePanel and ScriptManager relationship

All of the discussion so far has been about having `UpdatePanels` on a page. You are not limited to putting them on pages, or in master pages; `UpdatePanels` can also be added to user controls. In the next Try It Out, you update the Notifications control that you built in Chapter 11 so that you can see other notifications in the same control, through paging, without having to postback the entire page.

TRY IT OUT Adding AJAX to Support Notification Display

In this exercise you add the capability to move between notifications that are visible within the application. To do that, you add the necessary AJAX controls to the User Control and change the code-behind to allow the display of the appropriate notification.

1. Ensure that Visual Studio is running and your RentMyWrox solution is open. Open the `Controls\NotificationsControl.ascx` markup page.

2. Add the following code above the first label:

```
<asp:ScriptManager Id="smNotifications" runat="server"></asp:ScriptManager>
<asp:UpdatePanel ID="upNotifications" runat="server">
    <ContentTemplate>
        <asp:HiddenField runat="server" ID="hfNumberToSkip" />
```

3. Add the following code after the second label. When completed, this markup page should look like Figure 13-14.

```
        <div class="paginationline">
            <span class="leftside">
                <asp:LinkButton ID="lbPrevious" Text="<<" runat="server"
                    ToolTip="Previous Item" OnClick="Previous_Click" />
            </span>
            <span class="rightside">
                <asp:LinkButton ID="lbNext" Text=">>" runat="server"
                    ToolTip="Next Item" OnClick="Next_Click" />
            </span>
        </div>
    </ContentTemplate>
</asp:UpdatePanel>
```

FIGURE 13-14: Updated notifications control markup page

4. Open the code-behind. Add the following method below the `Page_Load` method. Much of the `using` statement is cut and pasted from the `Page_Load` method, with several additions.

```
private void DisplayInformation()
{
    hfNumberToSkip.Value = numberToSkip.ToString();

    using (RentMyWroxContext context = new RentMyWroxContext())
    {
        var notes = context.Notifications
            .Where(x => x.DisplayStartDate <= DateForDisplay.Value
                && x.DisplayEndDate >= DateForDisplay.Value);

        if (Display != null && Display != DisplayType.Both)
        {
            notes = notes.Where(x => x.IsAdminOnly ==
                    (Display == DisplayType.AdminOnly));
        }

        lbPrevious.Visible = numberToSkip > 0;
        lbNext.Visible = numberToSkip != notes.Count() -1;

        Notification note = notes.OrderByDescending(x => x.CreateDate)
                            .Skip(numberToSkip).FirstOrDefault();

        if (note != null)
        {
            NotificationTitle.Text = note.Title;
            NotificationDetail.Text = note.Details;
        }
    }
}
```

5. Add a private field above the `Page_Load` method:

```
private int numberToSkip;
```

6. Update the `Page_Load` method to the following:

```
protected void Page_Load(object sender, EventArgs e)
{
    if (!DateForDisplay.HasValue)
    {
        DateForDisplay = DateTime.Now;
    }

    if (!IsPostBack)
    {
        numberToSkip = 0;
        DisplayInformation();
    }
```

```
        else
        {
            numberToSkip = int.Parse(hfNumberToSkip.Value);
        }
    }
}
```

7. Add a new event handler for the Previous button:

```
protected void Previous_Click(object sender, EventArgs e)
{
    numberToSkip--;
    DisplayInformation();
}
```

8. Add a new event handler for the Next button:

```
protected void Next_Click(object sender, EventArgs e)
{
    numberToSkip++;
    DisplayInformation();
}
```

9. Run the application and go to \Admin. You should see a screen similar to the one shown in Figure 13-15.

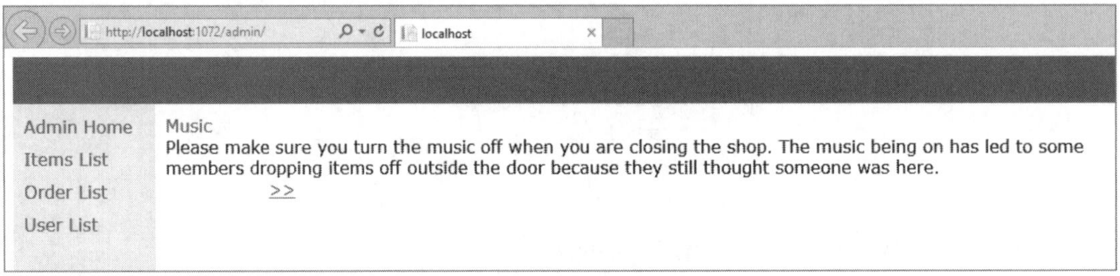

FIGURE 13-15: Rendered Notifications control

10. Click the Next link to see the content change without doing a full page refresh.

How It Works

You made two major changes in this activity. The first was setting up the Notifications control to support pagination, and the second was supporting that pagination without doing a full page reload. It was important to set up the pagination so that there would be some form of interaction that required a postback to the server; however, we don't spend much time going over either the markup or the code-behind to support the pagination, as these changes should be familiar from Chapter 10.

The other change that you added to the markup was the addition of the `ScriptManager` and the `UpdatePanel`. The combination of these two items led to some additional scripts that were linked into the file:

```
<script src="/ScriptResource.axd?d=zvkqIRNUspAvS1yKeFhMb7BiRxM-
        vLIWoR6Zh8gDvfSPqEd2iSYh_akklB94pGyizBj8bNHY0trAt37sX4L3rqFliPkS36-
        ER9N5HkxM1evYOoqe03rwnLG6EcJN891gORBhKWLDtdelfIsJ7Iqf4Q2&amp;t=ffff
        fffff2209473" type="text/javascript"></script>
<script src="../Scripts/WebForms/MsAJAX/MicrosoftAJAX.js"
        type="text/javascript"></script>
<script type="text/javascript">
//<![CDATA[
if (typeof(Sys) === 'undefined')
        throw new Error('ASP.NET AJAX client-side framework failed to load.');
//]]>
</script>

<script src="../Scripts/WebForms/MsAJAX/MicrosoftAJAXWebForms.js"
        type="text/javascript"></script>
```

As you can see, these scripts reference "AJAX" (rather than the ScriptResource link), so you can tell that they were added because of the inclusion of the AJAX server controls.

Additional code was also added at the point where the `ScriptManager` was added:

```
<script type="text/javascript">
//<![CDATA[
Sys.WebForms.PageRequestManager.
    _initialize('ct100$ContentPlaceHolder1$BaseId$smNotifications',
    'form1',
  ['tct100$ContentPlaceHolder1$BaseId$upNotifications',
  'ContentPlaceHolder1_BaseId_upNotifications'], [], [], 90, 'ct100');
//]]>
</script>
```

The code added here makes a little more contextual sense when you look at the HTML that was added by the `UpdatePanel` control. Because the `UpdatePanel` acts as a container, the output from the control is simply a div wrapper as shown here:

```
<div id="ContentPlaceHolder1_BaseId_upNotifications">
    ... content here ...
</div>
```

You can now see how the id of the `<div>` is referenced in the `_initialize` method contained within the `<script>` tag. This links the output from the `UpdatePanel` to the JavaScript method that makes just that area of the page updateable, rather than then requiring a full postback.

This new script changes the complete communications approach between the client and the server. If all the paginations were present but the `UpdatePanel` was not, the F12 Developer Tools would show a network summary like the one shown in Figure 13-16 when going between pages.

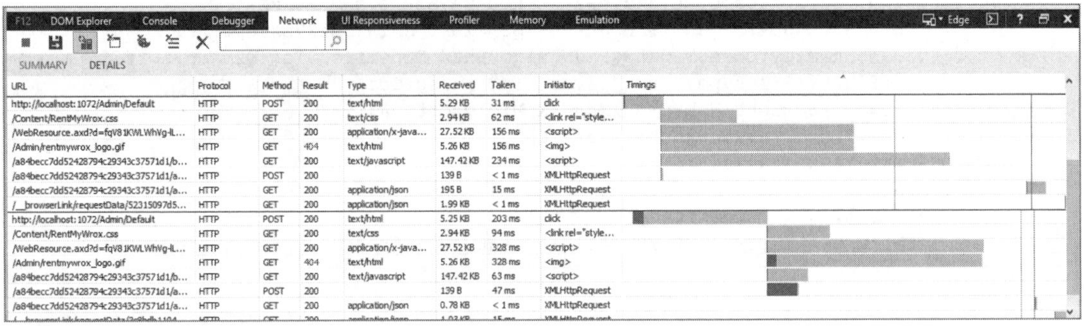

FIGURE 13-16: F12 Network tab without the UpdatePanel

As shown in Figure 13-16, each request (where the URL reads `http://localhost:1072/Admin/Default`) is also accompanied by seven other items, including the .css file, the logo file, and multiple script files. The response body shows the entire HTML page, as shown in Figure 13-17. This means that the entire page was returned with the request, just as you would expect from a full postback.

FIGURE 13-17: F12 Response body without the UpdatePanel

The F12 Network calling view is much different when the `UpdatePanel` has been added. Figure 13-18 shows what this looks over the course of the initial load and then viewing two additional notification items (two additional clicks on a page link).

The initial page load is represented by the top 11 lines in the list, which makes sense when you consider the additional scripts that were added by the `UpdatePanel` control. However, each click after that had only two different items downloaded, the POST content to the page and one script file. A bigger part of the story is shown when you go into the response body of one of the secondary POSTs, as shown in Figure 13-19.

Figure 13-19 shows the stark differences between each approach, as the only content in the response body is the content for that one panel.

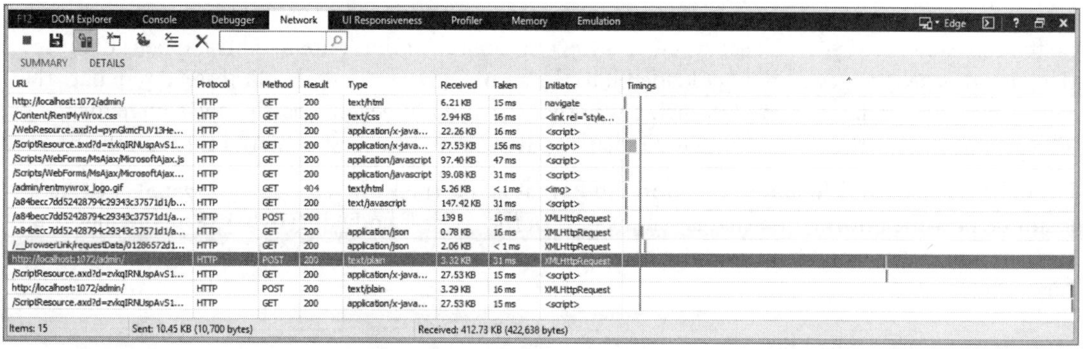

FIGURE 13-18: F12 Network tab with the UpdatePanel

FIGURE 13-19: F12 Response body with UpdatePanel

One thing to understand when working with UpdatePanels is how information is managed in the browser and why the F12 tools are so important. When you visit a new page and get the full download, the source of the page is set to the content that was downloaded. If you try to view the source in the browser, you will get the information that was downloaded. If you then change a section of the page using an UpdatePanel, however, you will run into a problem, as shown in Figure 13-20.

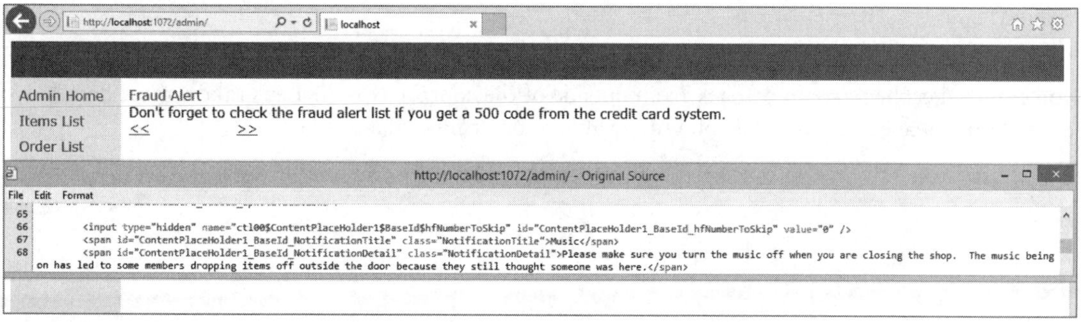

FIGURE 13-20: Difference between displayed item and view source output

This difference is apparent when the content that is actually being displayed in the browser does not match the values that you will see when you view the source of the content. This happens because the partial page changes do not get loaded into the actual downloaded file but instead populate the replaced content in memory and in such a way that they do *not* become part of the source for the page. This means getting the details on that particular partial request is best achieved through the F12 tools.

Now that we have talked about the information that is returned when using an UpdatePanel, let's examine how the information that is sent as part of the request body differs between a request that used an UpdatePanel and one that did not use an UpdatePanel. Figure 13-21 shows the request bodies for each approach.

Request Body when there is no UpdatePanel

__EVENTTARGET=ctl00%24ContentPlaceHolder1%24BaseId%24lbNext&__EVENTARGUMENT=&__VIEWSTATE=o58bG5dXUw4P7pHq9Nchw7NsSbO036ryT68jvwQ4dd%2FjNYMpll1rhWa6%2BrveCpPqydFe6jYfajqEljct0orM
Q3HYmldQ%2Fvtg3f60IrY1HbgAQIhoylq6De59I2qGfndxqSvT%2FZZYdH7P3VRW6tRvEqpMVNMUjwpdVxHjilDZTDZbQlj5db8X8vsBL7rS8vt2dRTAXncWdcXT6E7HzXjAx9KC%2Bz8yCsEYwhKXZf%2FWw8J%2BAzUFWE2E5ko%2F
ipUHAh%2BW%2FKpDvicnRU2E2LMVMN1JCm%2Fqk2vfTuxq8Z74GpeuZmpr3e0RCSD7gpYymHPcfBAYNER6y9Ts%2Fs504jXMK9iloDyr3YtFI%2FSFLUdXjzy3HmftmaicntQRIAXze89VjmRtrVziOnwftuTxAug8IbAkkpf87TIw9QY6
Lo4A8hfqu9xEzPll2gwo6uUbPb1hnHzEWeVCg03lwnh3AYHXvhLGelWnDQYvBN8Jgdvczbsj HfmWQDpy91CRM8ByZABJYmRS6ToHa7mQmWCCS3sCLVjsPL%2F6YxlqgTIL4ZzxhRjUd0XYVpCnmV3iqFO9hSpEuurOvN87E7I5dAXd
Ugo65JGxMdMbi%2B3ypzg5ttWVLB7HDRpQn700bM56WjC4zVrAzwMNE%2FPXtaMsB%2F%2Bvx7r4Gt4f0LiOWgaGW8BwSfvy5DeDmE0smkSixJr2LinP9%2B0udWyKIUG49RIIOuL3wGiz76clSyHSBkyuVxYy56H7isE%2B34arNa
KR19lXX0Rtr5Z%2BRjhq7jRma%2FbX6qyrPrxEgXfNK5dhQbzUkbHDQ%2FUMVPoNqD9lu7v3avSgWi%2B8Wq5w64GETLz9igihueQUZbQJ%2BdXAt1fUKr6L%2B2B%2BjmOnLgb%2BSURwkd8eGj0%2FVT9el0QeZ7n3Pfw5fBzBt8qacc
vLWVSPZidOC9s38d4qgNdqniHcoCRVUa47WOJke%2FqpqwVU0N9L915H%2F1Zn%2Fli1wUjqb744%2F7DIsPcxYhMFTqW2Bd0jfo58t55L1z%2BxPmDNMaTzMhMcNqhWKC2P2FyWEK%2BBskVWM3OfGuRk6Oz%2FH2KrzNM
CFvh7WqRgDgS%2FeOwSUnlcOVvs74bAcsQ5G2xdyhUEWAi1krtp7K3Q6AB5cPMrNzHnOqiMSzDoU1rrjXIX0Fg%2BbH%2BJMH%2F98up8p31hFb2sifBmo4AF8w%3D%3D&ctl00%24ContentPlaceHolder1%24BaseId%24
hfNumberToSkip=0&
__VIEWSTATEGENERATOR=CD4DC1CD&
__EVENTVALIDATION=3n8ZbmUJRvKL5rVqfvTlmpapE85xD71UM7MC7ixLbLNH4C7gJtMqM9VPE5Eh1eBk1OgUINdTEdHt2LpiLhgLuH4U5j%2BEd8bE1DIH432vu2p6OReF%2FURkZywbr7jjf9X2DslEuJBmLddQ9WP54viFxg%3D
%3D

Request Body when there is an UpdatePanel

ctl00%24ContentPlaceHolder1%24BaseId%24smNotifications=ctl00%24ContentPlaceHolder1%24BaseId%24upNotifications%7Cctl00%24ContentPlaceHolder1%24BaseId%24lbNext&__EVENTTARGET=ctl00%24ContentPl
aceHolder1%24BaseId%24lbNext&__EVENTARGUMENT=&__VIEWSTATE=s5%2Fuqv3r9LRIKy%2BMsyb0wqYy9qxcUVFLc5v99DBYoikmAvifJtBs7Y4nKxhFoGunHFpEixilubExVkEseXK%2BEDUkKeL%2BOB8mAHWfTtcig%2BeJl
BG8RxHhcBxZAMzbwu84ex53JfVnvjh1o%2B%2BB42CTxpoErPpYYXQbC6uV8hCDnV9WLaNgl051AjOi3agsc7QL1n%2BV88i1JgK%2BEizhUb28UJdi%2BcNuZB4EedzA5Rvp2zkNYcI6KXcbtMdIt41lpnzyr3eU8XgTkwG32p7nyDb
wxyVQXqyi%2FaiAiUlrlfre6YHGR7pNjzFQnbxUj8xSk%2B2l1PM9GWpdFa1FqkMmKIzUpIxMn2O76BVi1LpP9BFx7leurD92IHazNXZCFQgnGZZeh4Q39pX29blrGlzenfZDigUvE%2BkA%2Fje34FwIE6dx7xDe%2FuxLThq4C%2FGU9
OFDOTwXDBnGa5aUvwHKbQwwUZsArfqatp%2BSGhXgJkWwbiyAAua82Z8DRilPAXvpxk2b2htbFWrIeLxiwtEyt8fz1Zn3TpneK52JxZ55pgNJjkmKTOOxKRe8TxmVv9v5UVK7OhvF2kCAuLmB0PZp2hy7OrV3c1ZDujVY2q6H UUenB
b6YSKJV8PviTwWGpqiUggJ9D2%2FrxYHMxOoxvRhjvzO9cdnF7cTPglxklYq8%2BDi9XLO9KSdQH%2F7pAZ0gbSpUt2qOkpLPfpqyxSLIZnG4fOmcFiYIMQtyLVFmZVCrBYDKID3xNSwYdPTVuvrdV%2B2BTwBuz%2F2bycsHalvVMhmb5
4NwSbo%2FYUIIT4X%2BWG1a0%2B81CYsYioFq4ALr2hSO%2FrbglEET7BVTF1K1jj1LEjeW91v3BTZPz6Lv4R4dv65djlzZaKEU6YxIfT4VOx4zOhyeQnsaLjqLre64KbwmIKgfc0Ntfqv2B1gMYM8u%2BmcWcYI1zPP6XHNP4FSfa%2B5
635N%2FRlvWMu8EwHHfCS296BCgtK1nTAwqORdLDeVj4jUIFDCGutyY%2FzHjP1QGs4LF9D0yU3xUPko4Lzc7kZptb6GzHtUM9Sjwcg4NpI8AfiI52UC674SZILmad%2FyqpB%2BThF2VYgOkz3Opnm5JDyPtthZ%2FaaN2gHpKp
mopY%2FBizRkOkyn2rG%2BFtDOxxBhj%2FClrtaVVX54yH9muXp61kr0qeX2YTaRvHbtgU7fUq9SdJ%2BtWBvzZ7sgQBCQ%3D&ctl00%24ContentPlaceHolder1%24BaseId%24
hfNumberToSkip=0&
__VIEWSTATEGENERATOR=CD4DC1CD&
__EVENTVALIDATION=2YcgBhz7dCSsMDv29VqB8Z7ChMbjKY1Q6q2iesEhHhgEtDLXEEqqj9RAS2R2vgZbPJMrdhp%2FjkxAIQJbGNm8hPtb%2FFfvFxETGzTweg2%2FHqHO%2FQ1rerib3UPcalsX3GX5QnT0C6swd5j3%2BNbwQXB
8DmQ%3D%3D&__ASYNCPOST=true&

FIGURE 13-21: Request body differences

As Figure 13-21 shows, there is virtually no difference in the size of the request. This means that the complete content of the form is sent back with the request, rather than just the information within the UpdatePanel. This is confirmed when you notice that the ViewState values are included, as those values are definitely outside the content within the UpdatePanel. That means that you can take advantage of information from outside the UpdatePanel when you are calculating the content for the partial request.

Now that you know that you can take advantage of values outside the UpdatePanel, does that mean you can trigger the partial postback from outside of the control as well? Let's take a more detailed look at the UpdatePanel control and you will be able to determine that answer.

The most frequently used properties of the UpdatePanel are listed in Table 13-1.

TABLE 13-1: Common UpdatePanel Properties

PROPERTY	DESCRIPTION
ChildrenAsTriggers	Defines whether the panel will allow controls that are contained within the ContentTemplate to cause a refresh of the UpdatePanel. As you were able to tell from the example, the default for this is true. When this property is set to false, the system throws an exception if the UpdateMode is set to Always. If this property is set to false and UpdateMode is set to Conditional, then the POST request will call the server, but the area of the panel will not refresh with the updated content—the call happens but you will not be able to see the results.
ContentTemplate	The ContentPanel control is used as the container for all the elements that make up the panel. This property is the actual wrapper for the content that is updated.
Id	It may seem silly to call out the Id at this point, but you need to ensure that the Id is set to a unique value. If you think back to the lines that were added to the HTML content when you added the UpdatePanel, you may remember that there were references back to the <div> element that was created. Without the Id, this reference becomes problematic and in many cases results in a script error. The safest way to ensure that this does not happen is to provide a value for the Id.
RenderMode	This property enables you to determine the type of HTML element that the UpdatePanel will use to surround the content. The default property is Block, which causes the control to use a <div> control to contain the content. If you choose Inline, however, the panel will use a <span> element instead.
Triggers	This property is a collection of different triggers. There are two primary types of triggers, PostBackTrigger and AsyncPostBackTrigger. A PostBackTrigger is used to cause a full page refresh, whereas an AsyncPostBackTrigger is used to hook up the update of the UpdatePanel to a control that is outside of the body of the control.
UpdateMode	This property determines whether the control is going to be refreshed with every update. The default value is Always, which means that whenever there is a postback this section will be updated. The other possible value, Conditional, sets the panel so that the content is only updated under certain conditions, such as when an item that is attached as a trigger is fired.

As shown in the property list, it is indeed possible to cause an update of the panel from a control outside of the panel. If you wanted to do an asynchronous update, it would look something like the following:

```
<asp:ScriptManager Id="ScriptManager1"  runat="server"></asp:ScriptManager>
<asp:UpdatePanel ID="UpdatePanel1" runat="server" ChildrenAsTriggers="false"
           UpdateMode="Conditional">
    <ContentTemplate>
        ... some content ...
    </ContentTemplate>
    <Triggers>
        <asp:AsyncPostBackTrigger ControlID="bOutsideButton"  />
    </Triggers>
</asp:UpdatePanel>
<asp:Button ID="bOutsideButton" runat="server"  OnClick="bOutsideButton_Click"/>
```

Note how the `Button` control named `bOutsideButton` is not contained within the `UpdatePanel`'s `ContentTemplate`. However, the addition of the `Triggers` element with an enclosed `AsyncPostBackTrigger` that references the uncontained button through the trigger's `ControlID` property will provide the connection. This connection ensures that the clicking of that button will refresh the content within the `UpdatePanel`.

The default usage of the `UpdatePanel` should enhance usability of the site through the implementation of AJAX in the web page. This experience can be enhanced even further.

Enhancing the AJAX Experience

The experience that you have so far with the changes to the Notifications control have already increased usability. There are two more AJAX server controls that you can add that will increase usability even more. These controls, `UpdateProgress` and `Timer`, each take different approaches to helping enhance the user's experience when using your web application.

The `UpdateProgress` control is a communications tool for relaying information to the user; it provides the capability to notify the user when some work is happening on the page. In the example that you just worked through, it would be hard to identify a need for this control because everything tended to happen fast, and because the work was simple and everything resides on the same machine. However, in those cases where processing may take several seconds, it becomes very important for users to know that something is happening. If they clicked a button and the page just sat there, many users would click the button again. This could cause problems on the server, such as double-charging a user's credit card for an order.

The other control, the `Timer`, enables you to eliminate the need for user interaction to cause an update. Instead, you set a value whereby the template updates itself as configured, rather than requiring user input. This enables you to add functionality such as automatically scrolling through a list of items or replacing images on a regular basis.

In the next activity you will add both of these controls to the `UpdatePanel` with which you were just working.

TRY IT OUT Adding Controls to the Update Panel

In this activity, you enhance the Notifications control to display a message to the user when the content is being displayed, as well as add a timer to the panel so that the content refreshes itself on a regular basis.

1. Ensure that Visual Studio is running and your RentMyWrox solution is open. Open the `Controls\NotificationsControl.ascx` markup page.

2. Add the following code above the closing `ContentTemplate` element:

```
<asp:Timer runat="server" ID="tmrNotifications" Interval="5000"
        OnTick="Notifications_Tick" />
```

3. Open the code-behind page and add the following method:

```
protected void Notifications_Tick(object sender, EventArgs e)
{
    numberToSkip++;
    DisplayInformation();
}
```

4. Add the following lines to the `DisplayInformation` method, after the code that applies the filter on `DisplayType`. When added, the method should look like Figure 13-22.

```
// rolls over the list if it goes past the max number
if (numberToSkip == notes.Count())
{
    numberToSkip = 0;
}
```

```
private void DisplayInformation()
{
    hfNumberToSkip.Value = numberToSkip.ToString();

    using (RentMyWroxContext context = new RentMyWroxContext())
    {
        var notes = context.Notifications
            .Where(x => x.DisplayStartDate <= DateForDisplay.Value
                && x.DisplayEndDate >= DateForDisplay.Value);

        if (Display != null && Display != DisplayType.Both)
        {
            notes = notes.Where(x => x.IsAdminOnly == (Display == DisplayType.AdminOnly));
        }

        // rolls over the list if it goes past the max number
        if (numberToSkip == notes.Count())
        {
            numberToSkip = 0;
        }

        lbPrevious.Visible = numberToSkip > 0;
        lbNext.Visible = numberToSkip != notes.Count() -1;

        Notification note = notes.OrderByDescending(x => x.CreateDate).Skip(numberToSkip).FirstOrDefault();

        if (note != null)
        {
            NotificationTitle.Text = note.Title;
            NotificationDetail.Text = note.Details;
        }
    }
}
```

FIGURE 13-22: Updated DisplayInformation method

5.   Run the application and go to \Admin. Note how the content updates every five seconds, starting over at the beginning of the list when it hits the maximum number.

6.   Go back into the markup page and add the following code after the UpdatePanel. The finished control should look like Figure 13-23.

```
<asp:UpdateProgress ID="uprogNotifications" DisplayAfter="500" runat="server"
    AssociatedUpdatePanelID="upNotifications">
    <ProgressTemplate>
        <div class="progressnotification">
            Updating...
        </div>
    </ProgressTemplate>
</asp:UpdateProgress>
```

FIGURE 13-23: Updated control to include UpdateProgress method

7.   Add the following line of code anywhere within the Next_Click method:

```
System.Threading.Thread.Sleep(5000);
```

8.   Add the following selector to the RentMyWrox.css file:

```
.progressnotification {
    height: 30px;
    width: 500px;
    background-color: #FDE9EF;
    padding-left: 40px;
    line-height: 32px;
    color: #C40D42;
}
```

9.   Run the application and go to the \Admin page. Once the page renders, click the Next link under the notification. You should see a screen similar to Figure 13-24.

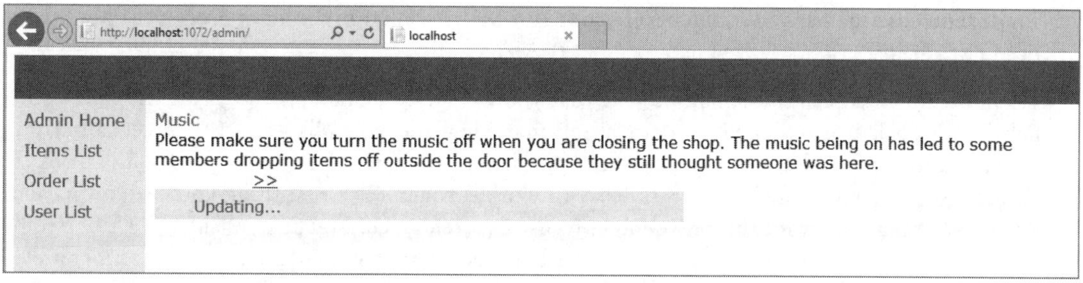

FIGURE 13-24: Update Progress message visible

10. Delete the line of code that you added in step 7.

How It Works

The first control that you added was the `Timer` control. By adding this to the page you have changed the experience such that users can view the various notifications without having to take any action. You set two key values: the `Interval` property and the `OnTick` event handler.

The `Interval` property sets the time, in milliseconds, before the timer goes off. You can set this interval as necessary, in this case you set it to five seconds. The timer automatically restarts itself after the previous call completes. This is an interesting item because you can put it inside the panel where it acts like the `LinkButton` controls, or you can put it outside of the panel and establish the relationship through the `UpdatePanel` `Triggers`, and restarting of the timer happens automatically, even if the results from the previous call have not been available on the screen for the set period. Once the timer has reached the set interval, a partial postback is fired and a call is made to the event handler for the `OnTick`, just like the event handlers were set up for the Previous and Next `LinkButtons`.

The `Timer` control added a new JavaScript file to the scripts on the page:

```
<script src="../Scripts/WebForms/MsAjax/MicrosoftAjaxTimer.js"
        type="text/javascript"></script>
```

It also added a new `<span>` element in the location where the `Timer` control was added in the markup:

```
<span id="ContentPlaceHolder1_BaseId_tmrNotifications"
    style="visibility:hidden;display:none;"></span>
```

However, this new HTML element is set to not display; it is simply a placeholder for the content. This element is never actually made visible, it is instead used as a placeholder so that the JavaScript that is running in the application has a DOM reference.

Using AJAX in MVC

The pattern of different implementation approaches between ASP.NET Web Forms and ASP.NET MVC continues when you consider bringing AJAX into your application. Web Forms implements support around the use of various server controls. MVC takes a different approach through the use of HTML helpers that are designed to support AJAX calls.

The most important of these, and the one that you will be using here, is the `@Ajax.ActionLink` helper. This helper is designed to create a link that when clicked, calls a controller, gets a partial view, and then puts what is returned from that partial view into a particular area on the page. While it seems complicated, it is pretty easy to work through. The first thing you need is an element on the page that you want the new content to use as a reference. You can consider this to be something like the `UpdatePanel` from Web Forms, but it is simply an HTML element (generally a `<div>` or a `<span>`) that you can uniquely identify, such as the following:

```
<div id="elementtobeupdated">content to be replaced</div>
```

Once you know where the content will be going, you can build the `Ajax.ActionLink`. There are quite a few different method signatures for this `ActionLink`, with each needing different sets of information. The various items that are part of a method signature are listed in Table 13-2.

TABLE 13-2: Potential Items for Populating an Ajax.ActionLink

VARIABLE	DESCRIPTION
`Action`	The `Action` is the method that is to be called when the item is clicked. This action needs to return a partial view in order for this to work correctly.
`AjaxOptions`	The `AjaxOptions` object is used to set the expectations for what will happen when the action is taken. The available properties include the following: HttpMethod: Indicates the HTTP method (GET or POST) to be used while making an AJAX request Confirm: Used to display a message to the user in a confirmation dialogue. If the user selects OK, then the call to the server is made. OnBegin: Defines the name of the JavaScript function that will be called at the beginning of the request OnComplete: Specifies the name of the JavaScript function that will be called when the request is completed OnSuccess: Specifies the name of the JavaScript function that will be called when the request is successful OnFailure: Specifies the name of the JavaScript function that is called if the request fails LoadingElementId: While an AJAX request is being made, you can display a progress message or animation to the end user. The value given to this property identifies an element in the page. This AJAX helper only displays and hides this element. UpdateTargetId: Specifies the ID of a particular DOM element. This particular element will be populated with the HTML returned by the action method. InsertionMode: Defines how the new content will be used in the screen when the call is completed. The possible values are InsertAfter, InsertBefore, and Replace.

VARIABLE	DESCRIPTION
Controller	The name of the controller containing the action that will be responding to the request. You do not include the "Controller" part of the string. If the controller is not provided, the referenced action is on the same controller that created the current view.
Route Values	The route values are the items that need to be added into the route for use within the action. These items will be either URL values or query string values, depending upon your setup and need.
Text to Display	This item is the text that should be displayed—the words that appear on the screen such that clicking on them causes the call to the action.

Thus, adding a section for which the content will be replaced as well as the part of the page that updates the section to be replaced would look like the following code:

```
<div id="elementtobeupdated">content to be replaced</div>
@AJAX.ActionLink("Click Me",
                "Details",
                "ClickMe",
                new { @Model.Id },
                new AJAXOptions
                {
                    UpdateTargetId = " elementtobeupdated",
                    InsertionMode = InsertionMode.Replace,
                    HttpMethod = "GET"
                })
```

The `<div>` element contains the content that will be replaced. Both of these references, the element with which to interact and what to do with the content (in this case replace), are set within the `AJAXOption` class.

If you compare this `ActionLink` to the `Html.ActionLink` that you worked with before, you will see that the only difference is this `AJAXOption` class; all the other parameters are the same as those you might use if you were building a simple `ActionLink`.

All the other work that is going on throughout this whole process is also work that you have done before; you are just wrapping all of this work into AJAX-based functionality. You will see this all in the next Try It Out.

TRY IT OUT Add AJAX Calls to Add Items to the Shopping Cart

In this activity you will add AJAX calls that add items to a shopping cart and display an updated summary of the cart. However, because there is not yet any functionality around the shopping cart, you will have to add all of the supporting functionality as you add the AJAX functionality. Be aware, there is a lot of this!

1. Ensure that Visual Studio is running and your RentMyWrox solution is open. Expand your Models folder. Add a new class called `ShoppingCart`. Add the using statements and properties listed here:

```
using System;
using System.ComponentModel.DataAnnotations;
```

```
namespace RentMyWrox.Models
{
    public class ShoppingCart
    {
        [Key]
        public int Id { get; set; }

        [Required]
        public Item Item { get; set; }

        [Required]
        public Guid UserId { get; set; }

        [Required]
        [Range(1,100)]
        public int Quantity { get; set; }

        [Required]
        public DateTime DateAdded { get; set; }
    }
}
```

2. Add a new class, ShoppingCartSummary. Add the following properties:

```
public int Quantity { get; set; }

public double TotalValue { get; set;}
```

3. Add a new class, OrderDetail. Add the following properties with attributes:

```
[Key]
public int Id { get; set; }

[Required]
public Item Item { get; set; }

[Required]
[Range(1, 100)]
public int Quantity { get; set; }

public Double PricePaidEach { get; set; }
```

4. Add a new class, Order. Add the following properties and attributes:

```
[Key]
public int Id { get; set; }

[Required]
public Guid UserId { get; set; }

public DateTime OrderDate { get; set; }
```

```
public DateTime PickupDate { get; set; }

public string HowPaid { get; set; }

public List<OrderDetail> OrderDetails { get; set; }

public double DiscountAmount { get; set; }
```

5. Open the `Models\RentMyWroxContext` file and add the following DbSets. When completed, your context file should look similar to Figure 13-25.

```
public virtual DbSet<ShoppingCart> ShoppingCarts { get; set; }

public virtual DbSet<Order> Orders { get; set; }
```

```
7  ⊟    public class RentMyWroxContext : DbContext
8       {
9  ⊟        // Your context has been configured to use a 'RentMyWroxContext' connection string from your application'
10           // configuration file (App.config or Web.config). By default, this connection string targets the
11           // 'RentMyWrox.Models.RentMyWroxContext' database on your LocalDb instance.
12           //
13           // If you wish to target a different database and/or database provider, modify the 'RentMyWroxContext'
14           // connection string in the application configuration file.
15           public RentMyWroxContext()
16  ⊟            : base("name=RentMyWroxContext")
17           {
18           }
19
20  ⊟        // Add a DbSet for each entity type that you want to include in your model. For more information
21           // on configuring and using a Code First model, see http://go.microsoft.com/fwlink/?LinkId=390109.
22
23           public virtual DbSet<UserDemographics> UserDemographics { get; set; }
24
25           public virtual DbSet<Hobby> Hobbies { get; set; }
26
27           public virtual DbSet<Item> Items { get; set; }
28
29           public virtual DbSet<Notification> Notifications { get; set; }
30
31           public virtual DbSet<ShoppingCart> ShoppingCarts { get; set; }
32
33           public virtual DbSet<Order> Orders { get; set; }
34       }
35  }
```

FIGURE 13-25: Updated context file

6. Build the solution (Build ⇨ Build Solution). Once complete, select Tools ⇨ NuGet Package Manager ⇨ Package Manager Console window. Type in the following line to create the new database migration and then click Enter:

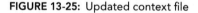

```
add-migration "order and shoppingcart"
```

7. Type in **update-database** to process the migration script and click Enter.

8. Right-click on the Views\Shared directory and add a new view named `_ShoppingCartSummary` using the settings shown in Figure 13-26.

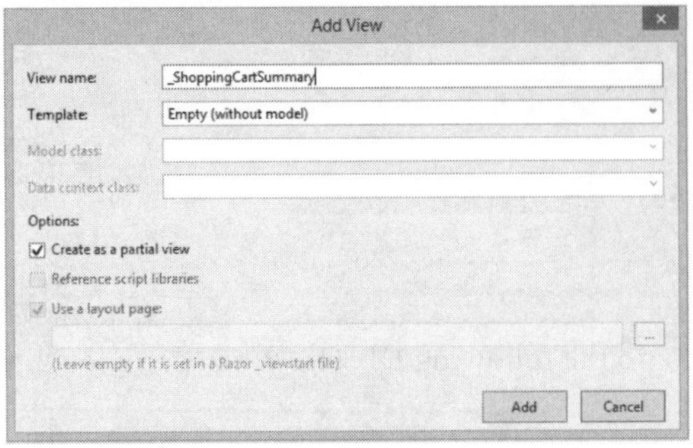

FIGURE 13-26: Configuration for a new partial view

9. Add the following to the new file. It should look like Figure 13-27 when completed.

```
@model RentMyWrox.Models.ShoppingCartSummary

@if(Model != null && Model.Quantity > 0)
{
    <span># in Cart: @Model.Quantity</span>
    <span class="moveLeft">Value: @Model.TotalValue.ToString("C")</span>
}
else
{
    <span>Your cart is empty</span>
}
```

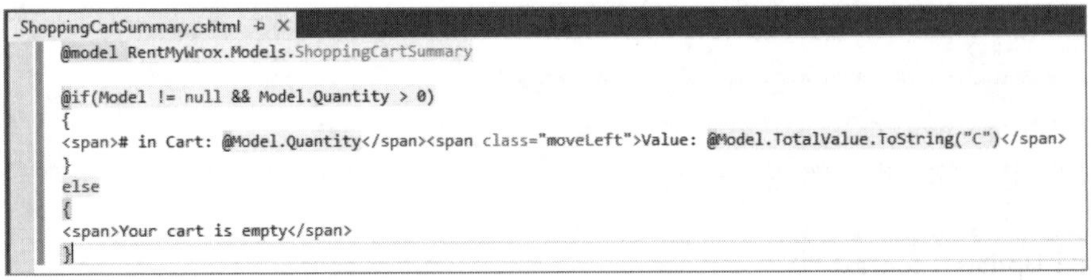

FIGURE 13-27: New partial view content

10. Right-click on the Controllers directory and add a new Empty Controller named **ShoppingCartController.**

11. Add the following using statement at the top of the page you just created.

```
using RentMyWrox.Models;
```

12. Add a new private property inside the ShoppingCartController class as shown in the following example. This part of your page should look similar to Figure 13-28.

```
private Guid UserID = Guid.Empty;
```

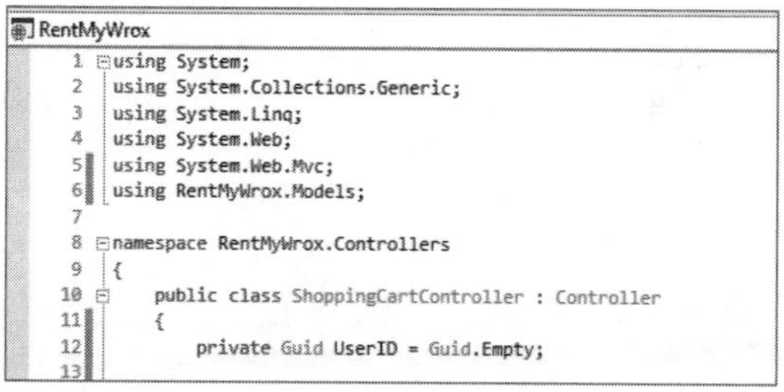

```
1  using System;
2  using System.Collections.Generic;
3  using System.Linq;
4  using System.Web;
5  using System.Web.Mvc;
6  using RentMyWrox.Models;
7
8  namespace RentMyWrox.Controllers
9  {
10     public class ShoppingCartController : Controller
11     {
12         private Guid UserID = Guid.Empty;
13
```

FIGURE 13-28: New Controller with private variable

13. Add a new private method:

```
private ShoppingCartSummary GetShoppingCartSummary(RentMyWroxContext context)
{
    ShoppingCartSummary summary = new ShoppingCartSummary();
    var cartList = context.ShoppingCarts.Where(x => x.UserId == UserID);
    if (cartList != null && cartList.Count() > 0)
    {
        summary.TotalValue = cartList.Sum(x => x.Quantity * x.Item.Cost);
        summary.Quantity = cartList.Sum(x => x.Quantity);
    }
    return summary;
}
```

14. Add a new action to the controller, above the method you just added:

```
public ActionResult Index()
{
    using(RentMyWroxContext context = new RentMyWroxContext())
    {
        ShoppingCartSummary summary = GetShoppingCartSummary(context);
        return PartialView("_ShoppingCartSummary", summary);
    }
}
```

15. Add a new method to the controller, above the private method:

```
public ActionResult AddToCart(int id)
{
    using (RentMyWroxContext context = new RentMyWroxContext())
    {
        Item addedItem = context.Items.FirstOrDefault(x => x.Id == id);

        // now that we know it is a valid ID
        if (addedItem != null)
        {
            // Check to see if this item was already added
            var sameItemInShoppingCart = context.ShoppingCarts
                .FirstOrDefault(x => x.Item.Id == id && x.UserId == UserID);
            if (sameItemInShoppingCart == null)
```

```
        {
            // if not already in cart then add it
            ShoppingCart sc = new ShoppingCart
            {
                Item = addedItem,
                UserId = UserID,
                Quantity = 1,
                DateAdded = DateTime.Now
            };
            context.ShoppingCarts.Add(sc);
        }
        else
        {
            // increment the quantity of the existing shopping cart item
            sameItemInShoppingCart.Quantity++;
        }
        context.SaveChanges();
    }
    ShoppingCartSummary summary = GetShoppingCartSummary(context);
    return PartialView("_ShoppingCartSummary", summary);
}
}
```

16. Right-click on your RentMyWrox project and select Manage NuGet Packages. Ensure that you are in the Online and Microsoft and .NET areas of the window and search for "unobtrusive." Your results should be similar to those in Figure 13-29.

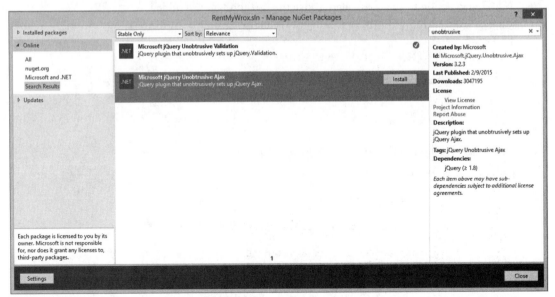

FIGURE 13-29: Search results in NuGet Package Manager

17. Click the Install button in the tile named Microsoft jQuery Unobtrusive AJAX and accept any license agreements that may appear.

18. Once the package installation is complete, open your `App_Start\BundleConfig.cs` file and add the following line:

```
bundles.Add(new ScriptBundle("~/bundles/jqueryajax").Include(
        "~/Scripts/jquery.unobtrusive-ajax*"));
```

19. Open your `Views\Item\Index.cshtml` file. Find the code `<a class="inlinelink" href="">Add to Cart</a>` and replace it with the following:

```
@Ajax.ActionLink("Add to Cart",
        "AddToCart",
        "ShoppingCart",
        new { @item.Id },
        new AJAXOptions
        {
            UpdateTargetId = "shoppingcartsummary",
            InsertionMode = InsertionMode.Replace,
            HttpMethod = "GET"
        },
        new { @class = "inlinelink" })
```

20. Make the same change in the `Views\Item\Details.cshtml` file, but use `{ @Model.Id }` in place of `{ @item.Id }`. The code should look like:

```
@Ajax.ActionLink("Add to Cart",
"AddToCart",
"ShoppingCart",
new { @Model.Id },
new AjaxOptions
{
    UpdateTargetId = "shoppingcartsummary",
    InsertionMode = InsertionMode.Replace,
    HttpMethod = "GET",
    OnBegin = "fadeOutShoppingCartSummary",
    OnSuccess = "fadeInShoppingCartSummary"
},
new { @class = "inlinelink" })
```

21. Open your `Views\Shared\_MVCLayout` file. Locate your header and add the following code immediately after the logo image:

```
<span id="shoppingcartsummary">@Html.Action("Index", "ShoppingCart")</span>
```

22. At the bottom of the file you will see some `@Scripts.Render` commands. Add the following to that same area:

```
@Scripts.Render("~/bundles/jqueryajax")
```

23. Open the `Content\RentMyCrox.css` file and add the following styles:

```
.moveLeft {
    margin-left: 15px;
}
```

```
#shoppingcartsummary {
    vertical-align: middle;
    text-align:right;
    margin-left: 100px;
}
```

24. Run the application and navigate to your home page. You should get a screen similar to the one shown in Figure 13-30.

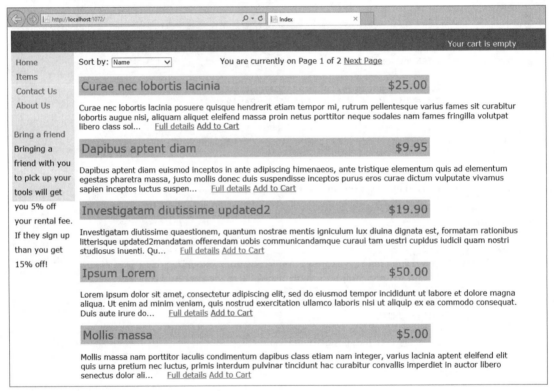

FIGURE 13-30: Screen with empty shopping cart

25. Click one of the Add to Cart links. The top part of your page should change without the entire page refreshing, as shown in Figure 13-31.

How It Works

Many different things happened within this activity. The first few steps were building out the object model that you need to manage a shopping cart for the user. You built the model classes, attributing them as necessary, and then added them to the context so that the Entity Framework understands that there is an expectation that those items will be persisted. Two classes were not directly added to the context, ShoppingCartSummary and OrderDetail, but they were not added for different reasons.

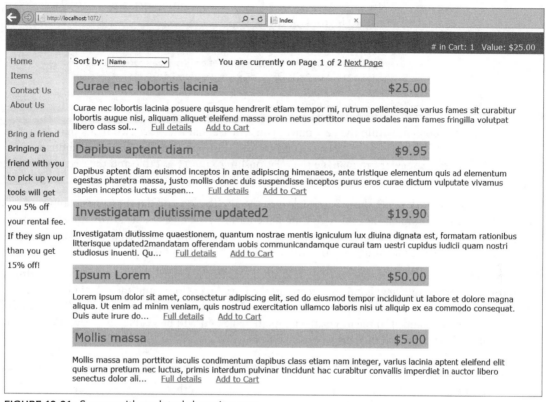

FIGURE 13-31: Screen with updated shopping cart

The `ShoppingCartSummary` class was not added because it is not intended to be something that is persisted; it is a class that is designed to pass information, in this case summary information, to the view. This approach is also known as using a ViewModel. The `OrderDetail` class was not added to the context file because, while it needs to be persisted, the class has no meaning outside of its parent `Order`. If you recall back to `Order`, that class has an `OrderDetails` property that contains a collection of `OrderDetail` objects. With the approach that you took, you can always access the `OrderDetail` from the `Order`, but you will not be able to access it directly because you don't have a property in the context.

The following code is part of the content from the migration script that was created to get these model changes into the database:

```
CreateTable(
            "dbo.OrderDetails",
            c => new
                {
                    Id = c.Int(nullable: false, identity: true),
                    Quantity = c.Int(nullable: false),
                    PricePaidEach = c.Double(nullable: false),
```

```
                        Item_Id = c.Int(nullable: false),
                        Order_Id = c.Int(),
                    })
                .PrimaryKey(t => t.Id)
                .ForeignKey("dbo.Items", t => t.Item_Id, cascadeDelete: true)
                .ForeignKey("dbo.Orders", t => t.Order_Id)
                .Index(t => t.Item_Id)
                .Index(t => t.Order_Id);
```

If you compare the content within the new object you will see that there are two items that do not appear in your model definition, the `Item_Id` and `Order_Id` properties. These table columns were added by the Entity Framework to manage the relationship to the `Item` table and the `Order` table respectively, and are what the Entity Framework uses to link to the various objects.

Once the necessary work to get the new models into the application and database was completed, you were able to start working on the real AJAX implementation. The business need you are solving is the capability to add an item to the shopping cart and see an area on the page display some information about the shopping cart, including the number of items in the cart and their total value.

The approach that you took to solve the business need was to use a partial view to manage the display of the content; the partial view is called directly in the initial page load, and then the HTML from that initial load of the partial view is replaced by the content of a response from an AJAX call to the server. This partial view was added to the top of the template page and will be visible on every MVC page in the application. The code that did this part is shown here:

```
<span id="shoppingcartsummary">@Html.Action("Index", "ShoppingCart")</span>
```

There are two parts to note. The first is the `Html.Action` method that is calling the partial view that was output from the `Index` method in the `ShoppingCartController`. This was added to ensure that the content is added to the page as part of the initial page download. The second is that the element containing the output from the partial view has an id so that it can be identified. This identification is important so that the browser can find the element that will have its content replaced by the output from the AJAX call. You'll learn more about this later.

The initial partial view that was being created is very simple. The controller action that performs the work is simple as well, and is shown here:

```
public ActionResult Index()
{
    using(RentMyWroxContext context = new RentMyWroxContext())
    {
        ShoppingCartSummary summary = GetShoppingCartSummary(context);
        return PartialView("_ShoppingCartSummary", summary);
    }
}

private ShoppingCartSummary GetShoppingCartSummary(RentMyWroxContext context)
{
    ShoppingCartSummary summary = new ShoppingCartSummary();
    var cartList = context.ShoppingCarts.Where(x => x.UserId == UserID);
    if (cartList != null && cartList.Count() > 0)
    {
        summary.TotalValue = cartList.Sum(x => x.Quantity * x.Item.Cost);
```

```
            summary.Quantity = cartList.Sum(x => x.Quantity);
        }
        return summary;
    }
```

The `Index` method calls another method that finds all of the items in the `ShoppingCart` table for a particular user and then counts the items and totals the `Costs` to create a single class with both of those values, a `ShoppingCartSummary`. This `ShoppingCartSummary` is then passed to the partial view as the model that will be used for display. Using the class like this is why you didn't have to add it to the context; it is not data that should be directly persisted in the database.

A note about the `UserId`: You are currently using an empty GUID, or a GUID that has zeroes (0s) in every position. This means that all of the items that you add to the shopping cart will be entered with a single value and will thus always be added and available. This is obviously not how you would want to go into production, but at this point you don't have users. You will change these when you get to the chapter on authentication, Chapter 15.

Now that you have your partial view you can add the AJAX that will do all the work of sending information to the server, getting a response, and then replacing a part of the downloaded page with that response. You did not directly add any AJAX code; you instead used an AJAX helper as shown here:

```
 1 @Ajax.ActionLink("Add to Cart",
 2      "AddToCart",
 3      "ShoppingCart",
 4      new { @item.Id },
 5      new AJAXOptions
 8      {
 7          UpdateTargetId = "shoppingcartsummary",
 8          InsertionMode = InsertionMode.Replace,
 9          HttpMethod = "GET" // <-- HTTP method
10      },
11      new { @class = "inlinelink" })
```

Lines 1–4 and line 11 of the preceding snippet build the link that becomes visible to the user, with line 1 adding the text that is being displayed, and lines 2, 3, and 4 adding the action, controller, and Url variables necessary for building the URL that will be called when the link is clicked. If this link is on an item with an Id of 10, the URL that will be built is \ShoppingCart\AddToCart\10. Line 11 assigns the CSS class to the element. All of those lines are common with the `Html.ActionLink` HTML helper.

Lines 5–10 are what sets this apart from the HTML helper, the `AJAXOptions`. Table 13-2 included the definitions of the various properties, but in this case you are using only three of them: `UpdateTargetId`, `InsertionMode`, and `HttpMethod`. The `UpdateTargetId` property is used to define the DOM element that is going to be affected by this AJAX call. The string value that is assigned here, `"shoppingcartsummary"`, is the same as the Id from the element that surrounds the partial view. The next property, `InsertionMode`, defines what is going to happen with the results from the AJAX request; in this case it is going to replace the content of the element that was just identified. The other options are to insert the results either immediately before or immediately after the identified element. The `HttpMethod` defines the method to be used in the AJAX call back to the server.

The HTML that was created by this control is shown here:

```
<a class="inlinelink"
   data-ajax="true"
```

```
data-ajax-method="GET"
data-ajax-mode="replace"
data-ajax-update="#shoppingcartsummary"
href="/ShoppingCart/AddToCart/5">Add to Cart</a>
```

If you remember back to the validation that you did in Chapter 12 you will see some commonalities, especially in the use of custom attributes to change the behavior of the item being clicked. If you removed all the attributes that are prefaced with `data-ajax` you would have a simple anchor element that causes a complete postback and page replacement. However, the addition of the attributes turns the click into an event that the jQuery Unobtrusive library is able to parse and understand. You can see the attributes in this element refer almost directly back to the values that you set in the `AJAXOptions`.

In order to get this functionality you had to add the new NuGet package, to get the JavaScript libraries that support this approach. You then needed to add the JavaScript libraries that were downloaded into your Scripts directory to a bundle, which was then added to the page. This ensured that the scripts you added to the project were downloaded to the client so that they were available for the client to use when conducting the AJAX calls.

Once the anchor element was created, a click on the visible text would fire off an asynchronous call to the server. Unlike the AJAX call that was performed by the Web Forms control, this is a GET call that contains no request body. This means that the size of the request is minimal. Compare that to the POST request that contained every form value on the page, including ViewState, that was sent by the Web Forms control.

Just as with the Web Forms call, the content being returned is minimal, as shown in Figure 13-32.

FIGURE 13-32: F12 Developer Tool showing the response body

The most complicated code that you had to add is the action that responds to this AJAX request. The process happening within this code is as follows:

1. The URL is parsed to identify the Id of the item being added to the shopping cart.

2. The database is queried to ensure that the Id being sent is valid.

3. The `ShoppingCart` collection is then queried to determine whether there is already an item in the shopping cart for this user that has this same Id. If so, this means that the item was already added to the cart. Rather than add the item again, thus loading two rows into the database with the same item, when the item is already in the shopping cart the action merely increments the quantity.

4. If there is not a matching `ShoppingCart` with that Id, then a new one is created and added to the context's collection.

5. Changes to the database are saved.

6. A call is made to determine the `ShoppingCartSummary`.

7. The `ShoppingCartSummary` is returned to the same partial view that was used when creating the initial page load, thus replacing the content with the output from a different action.

8. The partial view is rendered into HTML and then returned to the client, as shown in Figure 13-32.

In this activity you were able to take advantage of the built in ASP.NET MVC support for AJAX helpers that tie into the Unobtrusive JavaScript library to allow the simple coding to support AJAX-based requests.

In both of the instances that you have worked through in this chapter you have been sending HTML content back and forth and replacing preexisting content with the new information. There are other approaches than sending HTML when doing work with AJAX. In the next section, you will examine one of those other approaches.

USING WEB SERVICES IN AJAX WEBSITES

Sending HTML content through AJAX is a simple approach that requires minimal work on both the client and the server. However, there is redundancy in the information that is being transmitted back to the client. In the last activity, you created an AJAX call that returned an abbreviated set of information, shown here again:

```
<span># in Cart: 2</span><span class="moveLeft">Value: $50.00</span>
```

This is a total of almost 70 characters that would be downloaded every time a user added an item to the shopping cart. However, only six characters are actually important: the number of items (two in this case) and the value (50.00). You can make a change that will decrease the typical response size of adding an item to the shopping cart by a significant amount. While this may not seem important in the context of this application, imagine what this could mean to a company such as Amazon that handles thousands of these responses a minute; it could lead to a substantial savings in bandwidth usage, which could directly affect the profitability of the company.

Making this change requires that rather than download the HTML, you instead download the values that need to be displayed. This can be done by converting the information that you need, in this case the `ShoppingCartSummary` object, into a JSON string and returning that string, which is shown here in its default format:

```
{"Quantity":2,"TotalValue":50}
```

This transfer set is 30 characters, but you can modify it by shortening the property names on the class being converted to JSON to smaller property names, such as `Qty` and `Val`, which would remove an additional 12 characters from the download. The other change that you have to make is related to how you handle the item coming down. When using the HTML approach, you simply replace existing content with a new set of content. Obviously, you cannot take that same approach here because there is a lot of intermediate content that you will want to maintain, and instead just replace bits and pieces of the content.

But before getting into how you will manage that information once it gets to the client, first you will learn how to get an object from the server, rather than HTML snippets. The most common approach to getting an object from the server is through a web service.

Technically, a web service is generally defined as a method of communication between two computers over a network. However, that would mean that everything you have done so far has been based on web services because you are building a system that enables one computer, the client, to communicate with another computer, the server. That is why we are using a more specific definition whereby a web service is a method of communicating object information between two computers. This object is not HTML, but rather a serialized version of an object.

SERIALIZATION AND DESERIALIZATION

Serialization is the process of translating an object into a transferrable format. It is usually understood to mean the translation of an object into a string such that the string can be converted back into an object at the end of the transference. This is especially important when you are looking at web communications because the protocol is based upon sending strings back and forth between the client and the server.

When an object is serialized, the serializer (the software that does the work) generally goes through all the properties of the object and converts them into a series of key/value pairs, where the key is the name of the property and the value is the string version of the property value. If the property is not a simple type, then the serializer will serialize the property value into its own set of key/value pairs. The serializer does this same work for every property on the object, going as deeply as necessary into the object to get to the base values.

In deserialization the reverse happens. The object is constructed, then the list of key/value pairs is gone through and the string is parsed as necessary to get the appropriate type. The same happens with any complex types that are properties on the object; those auxiliary key/value pairs are gone through and those subordinate objects are created and the values populated.

In the current .NET environment there are three different ways to create a web service: Windows Communication Foundation (WCF), ASP.NET Web API, and ASP.NET MVC. Each of these approaches differs in terms of how it works and what it tends to be used for within a development project.

WCF is a complete framework for supporting communications between different computers. It provides a huge set of functionality and it supports many different protocols, including protocols other than HTTP. It is Microsoft's enterprise-level area of the .NET Framework that supports communication. As you can guess, there are a lot of different capabilities within WCF, and in some cases using WCF is mission critical. This is not one of those cases.

The next approach to creating a web service in .NET is through the use of ASP.NET Web API. Web API is a much slimmer web service management system; it supports only the creation of REST services, whereas WCF supports the creation of many different types of services. Using Web API enables developers to build URLs that are very similar to the URLs that you created when working with ASP.NET MVC.

Speaking of ASP.NET MVC, you can also create web services in MVC through actions on a controller. You can change an MVC action into a web service by changing the return value. Most of the actions that you have worked with up to this point have returned some type of view, either full or partial. However, you can just as easily return a serialized object rather than HTML from a View, as shown here:

```
public ActionResult Details(int id)
{
    using (RentMyWroxContext context = new RentMyWroxContext())
    {
        Item item = context.Items.FirstOrDefault(x => x.Id == id);
        return Json(item, JsonRequestBehavior.AllowGet);
    }
}
```

This code snippet should be familiar; the only difference is rather than return `View(item)`, the method instead returns the results of a method that converts an object into JSON. Also, the URL to get this object would be `\Item\Details\5` to get an Item with an Id of 5.

Web API also uses a controller and action process, with routing, just as MVC does. However, the naming process is different, as the URL and HTTP methods are fully integrated so that the intermediate descriptor that you tend to see in MVC URLs is left out. Thus, in a Web API application, the default URL that you would use is `\Item\5` because a `GET` against that URL means that you want to see the item. A `PUT` or a `POST` to that URL would be either creating or updating an `Item` object.

Web API is able to avoid this intermediate descriptor because it does not have to worry about creating HTML. If you look at MVC you will see that this intermediate descriptor is generally more about the view that you will be using by default (through convention) than it is anything else; thus the `\Item\Details\5` call would, by default, expect to call an Action named Details and return a view that is also named Details. Web API doesn't have to worry about that, so it takes a different approach.

The following snippet shows a complete controller that covers all of the available methods for an object, in this case an Item:

```
public class ItemsController : ApiController
{
    // GET api/items
    public IEnumerable<Item> Get()
    {
        using (RentMyWroxContent context = new RentMyWroxContent())
        {
            return context.Items.OrderBy(x => x.Name);
        }
    }

    // GET api/items/5
```

```
    public Item Get(int id)
    {
        using (RentMyWroxContent context = new RentMyWroxContent())
        {
            return context.Items.FirstOrDefault(x => x.Id == id);
        }
    }

    // POST api/item
    public void Post(Item item)
    {
        using (RentMyWroxContent context = new RentMyWroxContent())
        {
            var savedItem = context.Items.Add(item);
            context.SaveChanges();
        }
    }

    // PUT api/items/5
    public void Put(int id, [FormValues] values)
    {
        using (RentMyWroxContent context = new RentMyWroxContent())
        {
            var item = context.Items.FirstOrDefault(x => x.Id == id);
            TryUpdateModel(item);
            context.SaveChanges();
        }
    }

    // DELETE api/items/5
    public void Delete(int id)
    {
        using (RentMyWroxContent context = new RentMyWroxContent())
        {
            var item = context.Items.FirstOrDefault(x => x.Id == id);
            if (item != null)
            {
                context.Items.Remove(item);
                context.SaveChanges();
            }
        }
    }
}
```

One of the Web API default features that should leap out at you is how the names of the Actions correspond to an HTTP method. If you look at the comments, you can see how each of these methods relates directly to the typical action that you would take on an object:

➤ Get a list of objects.

➤ See a particular object.

➤ Create a new object.

➤ Update an existing object.

➤ Delete an object.

Thus, anything you would want to do with an object would be available on that controller.

Another difference between ASP.NET MVC and ASP.NET Web API is that using Web API to manage the process allows some flexibility out of the box. Because Web API is built solely to provide serialized objects, it handles the serialization process for you. There are multiple formats in which this object can be returned, with the most common being JSON and XML. When you are building this in ASP.NET MVC, you define the format of the item being returned. That means if you want to support both JSON and XML formats so that different requesters will get their preferred format, you have to code for both approaches. When you do the same in Web API, you don't need to worry about serializing into the appropriate format; Web API takes care of that for you based on the request headers; all you have to worry about is returning the correct object.

While Web API offers additional features that are not supported by default through MVC, most of those features do not matter in this case. Since you, as the site developer, are the one who is going to be consuming the services, a lot of the flexibility offered by Web API (and WCF for that matter) are not needed; the code that you will be writing on both the client and the server simply need to be able to talk together. In the next activity, you will be writing a web service that provides information to your client.

TRY IT OUT Add the Store Hours to Your Application

There is a popular feature on many brick-and-mortar store websites that informs visitors whether the store is open, and if not when it will next be open. In this activity you create a web service that returns such information as a serialized JSON object.

1. Ensure that Visual Studio is running and your RentMyWrox solution is open.

2. Expand your Models folder. Add a new class called `StoreOpen`. Add the properties shown here:

```
public bool IsStoreOpenNow { get; set; }

public string Message { get; set; }
```

3. Right-click on your Controllers folder and add a new Empty MVC controller named `StoreOpenController`.

4. Fill out the `Index` action as shown here:

```
// GET: StoreOpen
public ActionResult Index()
{
    StoreOpen results = new StoreOpen();
    DateTime now = DateTime.Now;
    if (now.DayOfWeek == DayOfWeek.Sunday ||
        (now.DayOfWeek == DayOfWeek.Saturday &&
                now.TimeOfDay > new TimeSpan(18,0,0)))
    {
        results.IsStoreOpenNow = false;
        results.Message = "We open Monday at 9:00 am";
    }
    else if (now.TimeOfDay >= new TimeSpan(9,0,0) &&
                now.TimeOfDay <= new TimeSpan(18,0,0))
```

```
    {
        results.IsStoreOpenNow = true;
        TimeSpan difference = new TimeSpan(18,0,0) - now.TimeOfDay;
        results.Message = string.Format("We close in {0} hours and {1} minutes",
            difference.Hours, difference.Minutes);
    }
    else if (now.TimeOfDay <= new TimeSpan(9,0,0))
    {
        results.IsStoreOpenNow = false;
        results.Message = "We will open at 9:00 am";
    }
    else
    {
        results.IsStoreOpenNow = false;
        results.Message = "We will open tomorrow at 9:00 am";
    }
    return Json(results, JsonRequestBehavior.AllowGet);
}
```

5. Run the application. Go to \StoreOpen. You should be prompted to download a file as shown in Figure 13-33.

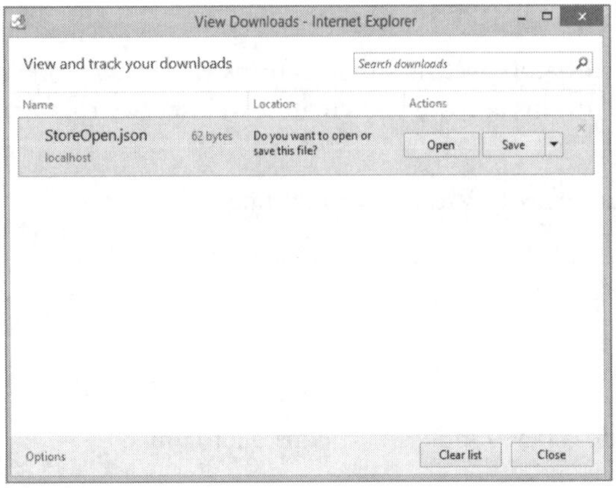

FIGURE 13-33: Downloading the StoreOpen.json file

6. Select Open, and if necessary choose to view the file in Notepad. You should get a response similar to the following snippet (your values may differ based on day and time):

```
{"IsStoreOpenNow":false,"Message":"We open Monday at 9:00 am"}
```

How It Works

You created a new model and controller just as you have done multiple times; nothing unusual about those steps. The Index action that you created in this controller constructs a new StoreOpen object and then populates the values based on the day and time of the request.

It is assumed that the store is open Monday through Saturday from 9:00 a.m. to 6:00 p.m. The logic checks for four different possibilities:

➤ After closing time on Saturday and Sunday the user gets a message that the store opens Monday morning.

➤ Between opening and closing times Monday through Saturday the user gets a message displaying the amount of time until the store closes.

➤ If it is after closing time but before midnight, then the user gets a message saying the store opens tomorrow morning.

➤ If it is after midnight but before opening time, then the user gets a message saying the store opens at 9:00 a.m.

All of this logic is used to populate the `StoreOpen` object that is returned to the user. The object is returned through the `Json` method, which serializes the object that was passed in as a parameter. The second parameter in the method is a `JsonRequestBehavior`. There are two potential behaviors, `AllowGet` and `DenyGet`. The default behavior is to disallow the return of a JSON object through a `GET` request. The reason why the default turns off the capability to retrieve a JSON object through a `GET` is because it is important for the developer to remember that information being passed through this approach is not secure, as demonstrated by the fact that you were able to download and open a file containing the JSON information. This default behavior forces you, as the developer, to consider the data you are exposing over the HTTP `GET` method and then make a conscious decision that it is OK to publicize. It is always OK to return JSON data from a `POST` or `PUT` method request because those HTTP verbs always assume that you have created or changed some information.

In this activity you created a controller and an action that returned a JSON-serialized object. What can you do with this object?

jQUERY IN AJAX

Creating a web service enables you to download information to a client application. However, at this point, the information is simply a string that represents an object. Using this item to affect the UI is where the power of jQuery comes into play. The next chapter provides a more in-depth look at the functionality available with jQuery. This section goes over only those parts that are necessary to support an object-based AJAX call.

One part in particular is necessary when using jQuery in AJAX, and that is the code that makes the server call. The jQuery method used to make a `GET` request that expects to get JSON back is the `getJSON` method, shown here:

```
$.getJSON("url to call")
```

One of the most important things that delineates jQuery is the $. This isn't a reference to all the money you can make if you are good at jQuery; it is similar to a namespace that defines the action that it precedes as being part of the jQuery library.

The $ can be confusing. In the previous example, it is used to represent jQuery mostly as a namespace. However, it is also used to identify a selection, such as the following:

```
$("#someDOMelement").html("some content");
```

In this example the $() represents a way to identify some content in the DOM, in this case an element with the id of "someDOMelement". The selector acts just like the selectors in CSS, so in this case you can tell that it is an id you are trying to match because of the "#" that is part of the selection identifier.

The only way to differentiate the usage is whether the $ immediately precedes a set of parentheses containing a selector or whether it precedes a period. When it precedes the period you know that the $ refers to a core method, in this case getJSON. What is not clear from the preceding usage is how to work with the data that is returned from the call.

The getJSON method has several different callbacks that you can use to manage the outcome of the call. The full definition is shown here:

```
$.getJSON("url to call")
    .done(function (data) {})
    .failure()
    .always();
```

These all take advantage of jQuery's Promise Framework (more on that in the next chapter), and you can actually chain as many of the different callbacks together as you need—whether it is multiple instances of the same callback, such as done, or one of each as you need it.

The done callback defines the work that you want done on the JSON object returned from the call. This work can be done in an anonymous function or in a well-defined function. The failure callback is designed to allow the client to manage problems in the request. If the server returned a server error, for example, the failure callback would be processed, as opposed to the done callback. The always callback is called every time the request is completed, whether it was a success and went through the done callback or whether it failed and went through the failure callback.

In this next activity you create jQuery code that will both call the server and manipulate items in the DOM. This means you will see both approaches that use the $ preface.

TRY IT OUT Calling the Server and Displaying Retrieved Information

In this activity you make the call to the server to get the information regarding store hours that you built in the last activity. After you download the information you will then display it in the UI.

1. Ensure that Visual Studio is running and your RentMyWrox solution is open.

2. Open your `Views\Shared\_MVCLayout.cshtml` file. In the `LeftNavigation` section, above the request for `"Notifications"`, add the following line. When you are done this section should look like Figure 13-34.

```
<div id="storeHoursMessage"></div>
```

```
<body>
    <div id="header">
        <img src="rentmywrox_logo.gif" />
        <span id="shoppingcartsummary">@Html.Action("Index", "ShoppingCart")</span>
    </div>
    <div id="nav">
        <div id="LeftNavigation">
            <ul class="level1">
                <li><a href="~/" class="level1">Home</a></li>
                <li>@Html.ActionLink("Items", "", "Items", new { @class = "level1" })</li>
                <li>@Html.ActionLink("Contact Us", "ContactUs", "Home", new { @class = "level1" })</li>
                <li>@Html.ActionLink("About Us", "About", "Home", new { @class = "level1" })</li>
            </ul>
            <br />
            <div id="storeHoursMessage"></div>
            @Html.Action("NonAdminSnippet", "Notifications")
        </div>
    </div>
```

FIGURE 13-34: Addition of area to display store hours message

3. Near the bottom of the page are some script elements containing the datepicker. Add the following within those script elements. When you are done it should look like Figure 13-35.

```
function getStoreHours() {
    $.getJSON("/StoreOpen")
        .done(function (data) {
            var message = data.Message;
            $("#storeHoursMessage").html(message);
            $("#storeHoursMessage").removeClass();
            if (data.IsStoreOpenNow == false)
            {
                $("#storeHoursMessage").addClass("storeClosed");
            }
            else {
                $("#storeHoursMessage").addClass("storeOpen");
            }
            setTimeout(function () {
                getStoreHours();
            }, 20000);
        });
};

$(document).ready(function () {
    getStoreHours();
});
```

```
40      @Scripts.Render("~/bundles/jquery")
41      @Scripts.Render("~/bundles/bootstrap")
42      @Scripts.Render("~/bundles/jqueryajax")
43      <script language="javascript" type="text/javascript" src="~/Scripts/jquery-ui-1.11.4.js"></script>
44      @RenderSection("scripts", required: false)
45      <script type="text/javascript">
46
47          $(document).ready(function () {
48              $(".editordatepicker").datepicker();
49          });
50
51          function getStoreHours() {
52              $.getJSON("/StoreOpen")
53                  .done(function (data) {
54                      var message = data.Message;
55                      $("#storeHoursMessage").html(message);
56                      $("#storeHoursMessage").removeClass();
57                      if (data.IsStoreOpenNow == false)
58                      {
59                          $("#storeHoursMessage").addClass("storeClosed");
60                      }
61                      else {
62                          $("#storeHoursMessage").addClass("storeOpen");
63                      }
64                      setTimeout(function () {
65                          getStoreHours();
66                      }, 20000);
67                  });
68          };
69
70          $(document).ready(function () {
71              getStoreHours();
72          });
73
74      </script>
75  </body>
```

FIGURE 13-35: JavaScript added to the page

4. Add the following styles to the RentMyWrox.css file:

```
.storeOpen {
    background-color:green;
    color:white;
    text-align:center;
    font-size: small;
    font-weight: bold;
    width:125px;
}

.storeClosed {
    background-color:#F8B6C9;
    color:red;
    text-align:center;
    font-size: small;
    font-weight: bold;
    width:125px;
}
```

5. Run the application and go to the home page. You should see a new addition on the left section of the screen. The content that you see will vary according to the day and time when you are running the app. Figure 13-36 shows the output on a Sunday.

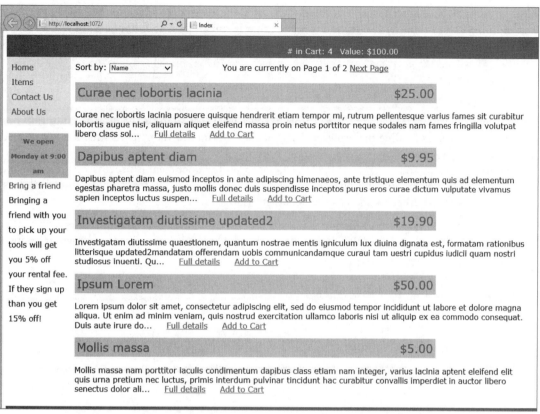

FIGURE 13-36: Running the new changes

How It Works

In this activity you performed two main activities. The first was adding some new HTML, including a new element to your left menu and a couple of new styles. The new element will be used to store content that comes from the server, while the styles will be used to display the message appropriately. Unlike the previous AJAX approach, however, you did not fill the content from the server; these `<div>` tags simply act as containers for when you make your independent server calls.

The second activity was to add some JavaScript code. In summary, the JavaScript that you added took the following steps:

1. Called the server using the URL for the controller that you added in the last exercise

2. Took the information that comes back and puts the message into the `<div>` tags

3. Evaluated the `IsStoreOpenNow` property to determine which style to apply to the message: either a style for when the store is open or a different style if the store is closed

4. Set a timer to query the server again in 20 seconds so that the value being displayed is frequently refreshed

Now consider how each step was performed. Two different items were added to the page. The first was a function, getStoreHours. The second was code that is run as soon as the engine got to the line. This code is shown again here:

```
$(document).ready(function () {
    getStoreHours();
});
```

The $() indicates that the content is a selector. In this case, the selector is the document, or the containing DOM. You are telling the browser that you want to run the anonymous function when the document is ready, or was finished loading into the browser. This processing occurs simultaneously with the loading of images and other downloadable items, after the document is processed. The anonymous function that you are running has one line, a call to the getStoreHours function. In a nutshell, this code runs the other method as soon as the document is loaded.

The getStoreHours JavaScript function performs the work of making the call to the server and then updating the UI based on the results. This code is repeated here with line numbers for easier reference:

```
1   function getStoreHours() {
2       $.getJSON("/StoreOpen")
3           .done(function (data) {
4               var message = data.Message;
5               $("#storeHoursMessage").html(message);
6               $("#storeHoursMessage").removeClass();
7               if (data.IsStoreOpenNow == false)
8               {
9                   $("#storeHoursMessage").addClass("storeClosed");
10              }
11              else {
12                  $("#storeHoursMessage").addClass("storeOpen");
13              }
14              setTimeout(function () {
15                  getStoreHours();
16              }, 20000);
17          });
18  };
```

Line #1 is the function definition. Note that there is no defined return type such as you may be used to with C#; instead this simply delineates a set of code that needs to be run. The contents of the function is a getJSON method that fetches a set of data from the URL defined in line 2.

Once the data is collected, the done callback is used to handle the data, as shown by the anonymous function defined on line 3. The data that is returned from the call is passed into the anonymous function where it is available as if it were a standard object (which it is, but more on that in the next chapter!). Lines 4 and 5 are getting a specific value, the Message property, from the returned data and setting the html content of the element that has an id of "storeHoursMessage", which coincidentally enough is the <div> element that you added in the left navigation panel.

After setting the message, line 6 clears the class that is currently assigned to that element. It is done this way because it is simpler to just remove the class and add a new class than to evaluate the class value to ensure that it is correct. You cleared the class value because the next few lines of the method are setting the appropriate style based on the value of the `IsStoreOpenNow` property. If the store is open, the green background with white text style will be displayed, highlighting that the store is open and indicating how long before it closes.

The last part of the method, in lines 14–16, uses the `setTimeout` method that is built into the window, or browser. This method acts like a timer that sets an amount of milliseconds before it goes off and an anonymous function that will be run when the timer expires. In this case the anonymous function is running the `getStoreHours` function, thus ensuring that every 20 seconds the method is called again so that the server is queried and the response is redisplayed.

One thing that you need to understand is that while you added this logic to an ASP.NET MVC view, you could just as easily have added the exact same information to a page that was created from a Web Forms response—especially because none of the information being displayed was added at the server, it was all defined based on the results of the call to the web service. Adding this same functionality would require the exact same client-side steps, but in an .aspx (or .ascx) page rather than the .cshtml page.

Hand-coding AJAX calls is certainly more work that using either Web Forms server controls or MVC AJAX helpers, but the capability to use the jQuery library in your ASP.NET application makes writing AJAX code in JavaScript very straightforward. Obviously there are more complex approaches to performing AJAX interactions, such as performing a POST with a populated object that is being passed into the action, but those are more differences in degree as opposed to significantly more work; jQuery makes your job easy, just like the other helpers you used previously.

PRACTICAL AJAX TIPS

The following tips will help you get the most out of using AJAX in your website:

➤ `UpdatePanels` may seem like functionality that you would want to add everywhere, but use them only when needed and not as a default approach. There is still a lot of communication going to the server, so using multiple `UpdatePanels` on a data entry page may be problematic, as every form element is submitted multiple times. It also means that you have to ensure when you write your code-behind that you do not reference those properties in such a way that these multiple posts cause a problem, perhaps by saving incomplete information to the database.

➤ When you use an `UpdatePanel` you should also use an `UpdateProgress` control as well. This helps your users understand that something is changing on the screen. It's especially important when the change is happening because of a user request. Because the page is not being posted back to the server, it is more difficult to determine when a button click did anything, as all the processing is happening in the background and is not automatically shown in the UI. This is where `UpdateProgress` controls help; they provide visual cues to the changes.

➤ When working with AJAX in an MVC application, using AJAX helpers is a time-saver. These helpers demonstrate the use of the Unobtrusive JavaScript libraries in support of AJAX. While this chapter described how to write AJAX interaction using JavaScript and jQuery, you could just as easily have added the appropriate attributes onto the element and included the Unobtrusive JavaScript libraries to get an AJAX experience.

➤ When you consider your approach to getting asynchronous information from the server, you have two real options. The first is bringing down HTML snippets that you can place into various areas of the UI. This is the solution that is used by both of the built-in AJAX supports. However, your particular need may steer you away from this approach and toward one in which it makes more sense to download the elements once and then update the values within the elements. Both of these are equally valid approaches; you need to weigh the extra effort of building the second approach against the limitations of the first approach.

SUMMARY

ASP.NET's support of AJAX makes it much easier to implement AJAX within your application. Whether you are implementing an AJAX approach in Web Forms or MVC, there is built-in functionality that makes your implementation process much cleaner and simpler. The capability to customize the AJAX process using jQuery and JavaScript makes the development process more uniform and supportable.

To use AJAX in Web Forms requires several different server controls. The most important control is the `UpdatePanel`, which contains the content that will be replaced during the AJAX call. The `UpdatePanel` is unusable unless there is also a `ScriptManager` server control. The `ScriptManager` is used to manage the JavaScript files that are downloaded to the client in order to support the client-side firing of the AJAX call.

If you are working in ASP.NET MVC and need to use AJAX then you will likely take advantage of the AJAX helpers that do the work of formatting the HTML so that the jQuery Unobtrusive AJAX library will properly work. The helper enables you to determine which HTML element will be affected by the results of a call. Typically this approach is used to display a partial view.

If the default helpers and server controls do not provide the behavior that you are looking for, you can still use jQuery and JavaScript to perform any kind of server call for any kind of response type with which you can pretty much do anything in the browser. This is certainly more effort than using one of the other approaches, but it is also completely customizable to solve your needs.

EXERCISES

1. What would you have to do differently if you wanted to put the functionality from the last activity, for store hours, on an ASP.NET Web Forms page?

2. What steps would you need to take if you wanted to implement the Unobtrusive AJAX jQuery library in an ASP.NET Web Form page?

3. What are some of the challenges with adding a timer to a web page for which the results from the call update a section of the page?

▶ WHAT YOU LEARNED IN THIS CHAPTER

AJAX	AJAX stands for Asynchronous JavaScript and XML and refers to a design where the browser does not necessarily replace the entire page every time there is a need for information from the server. The browser instead replaces a part of the page in such a way that the user can continue work.
AJAX.ActionLink	A helper method in ASP.NET MVC that builds out an element so that it can take advantage of the Unobtrusive AJAX library. This method helps the developer easily implement an AJAX approach to replacing HTML content.
AJAXOptions	A class that manages all the configuration of the AJAX part of the AJAX .ActionLink. There is a direct relationship between the properties in the class and the output in the element that is used for Unobtrusive AJAX.
AsyncPostBackTrigger	A setting on the UpdatePanel whereby you link a client-side action to the UpdatePanel and define that action as the one that will cause an asynchronous postback
ContentTemplate	An UpdatePanel does not actually hold the content that is going to be updated. It instead contains a ContentTemplate, which is the attribute containing the actual elements that are going to be updated.
Deserialization	The process of turning a string value back into the object that it represents
F12 Developer Tools	A toolkit that ships with Microsoft Internet Explorer. It provides developers with a lot of support, including CSS and styling support, and request and response information and details, including headers and body, and the speed of the server response.
getJSON	A utility method in jQuery that handles a GET call to a web service. By definition, the response that comes back from the server is expected to be in JSON format.
Json method	A method available on an ASP.NET MVC controller. It takes in an object and serializes it as it returns the serialized object back to the client.
Mozilla Firefox Developer Tools	Like the F12 Developer tools that ship with Internet Explorer, the Mozilla Firefox Developer Tools are available with every Mozilla Firefox installation. They provide much of the same support as the F12 tools.
PostBackTrigger	This is linked to an UpdatePanel, but rather than cause a partial page callback it instead causes a full page postback, just as if AJAX were not being used at all.

ScriptManager	A required part of using AJAX in ASP.NET Web Forms. Necessary whenever an UpdatePanel is present, it holds the links to the supporting JavaScript files.
ScriptManagerProxy	Enables you to put the ScriptManager on a master page and then handles the linking from an UpdatePanel on the content page to the ScriptManager on the master page.
Serialization	The conversion of an object to a string representation. This is necessary so that you can transfer the object over the Internet.
Single-Page Application	A single-page application is an approach to building a website whereby the user downloads the initial page and all of the JavaScript files necessary to manage all interaction between the user and the server. There is no full page request; all updates happen using AJAX.
Unobtrusive AJAX	A JavaScript and jQuery library that allows for the management of AJAX requirements through attribution on the affected elements. It eliminates much of the custom scripting that generally has to be done when using AJAX.
UpdatePanel	An ASP.NET Web Forms server control that defines a particular set of content as being available for replacement through an AJAX call. The content to be replaced is stored in the ContentTemplate.
UpdateProgress	This server control provides user feedback when an AJAX call is being processed. This is especially important when the user clicks a button and expects something to happen. If the effect were a full-page fetch, the user would know something is happening because a new page would be downloading; but because it is an asynchronous request, the updateProgress control provides that information.
Web Service	An approach in which the server handles a request and sends information back to the client. Technically a web service is just a way to allow two computers to communicate over the network, but we have modified that definition to mean the transmission of an object over the network.

14

jQuery

- ➤ The history of jQuery and why it is so important
- ➤ Features available in jQuery
- ➤ Using jQuery to work within your page
- ➤ Deeper integration of the jQuery framework

CODE DOWNLOADS FOR THIS CHAPTER:

The wrox.com code downloads for this chapter are found at `www.wrox.com/go/ beginningaspnetforvisualstudio` on the Download Code tab. The code is in the chapter 14 download and individually named according to the names throughout the chapter.

Earlier in the book, you were concentrating on other areas of the application that were not specific to jQuery, but you have come across some mentions of it in bits and pieces. There have been examples using jQuery to support client-side validation as well as support AJAX calls and displaying the results on the page. A jQuery UI widget was also pulled into the application so that you could invoke a date picker. This should give you an idea of how jQuery ends up being intertwined throughout the client side of a website. This chapter clarifies why jQuery is so prevalent in modern web development, and provides more exposure to the functionality that is available within the jQuery libraries.

AN INTRODUCTION TO jQUERY

jQuery is a JavaScript library that best estimates say is now used in about two out of three websites on the Internet. It is called a JavaScript library because it is completely written in JavaScript. This enables jQuery to be used within a JavaScript method just like a core

JavaScript method; it is simply an additional set of objects and methods that are made available in JavaScript, much like how the Entity Framework adds a separate set of functionality to .NET. In order to understand the history of jQuery, you need to understand the evolution of JavaScript.

Early JavaScript

Now on version 6, released in June 2015, JavaScript was first included in Netscape Navigator 2, shipped in late 1995. By 1996, Microsoft started including JavaScript in Internet Explorer, starting with IE 3. At this point, both implementations were different, which made it difficult to provide a dynamic experience across both browsers. This differentiation lead to those dreaded phrases such as "best viewed in Internet Explorer" or "best viewed in Netscape."

Even though the language itself was standardized in 1997 when Ecma International (an international standards organization) published ECMAScript, which was based on JavaScript, that did not mean that the same scripts would work the same way with different browsers. By itself, a JavaScript method is pointless; it only becomes useful when it is somehow interacting with the user. This was another major problem—each of the major browser companies had built its own enhancements to the DOM, and these enhancements were what JavaScript had to interact with, so different approaches to defining the DOM meant different code to interact with each. These DOM definitions were not part of the Ecma standardizations; they were defined in a separate standardization effort by the W3C. HTML 5, the newest version of HTML, was updated to better define the DOM and its interaction points, and it marks the best attempt to offer standardization across DOM elements so that the JavaScript standards will be able to consistently, and in a standard fashion, identify and interact with DOM elements regardless of the browser being used.

Even as browsers moved toward implementing both JavaScript and the DOM in a standardized fashion, there were some problems with the universal adoption of JavaScript.

➤ The language is sufficiently different from other common development languages that it's necessary to learn a second language when working with web applications.

➤ Because JavaScript typically relies on a runtime environment, such as the web browser, its behavior is still not completely 100% consistent between each environment.

➤ It is necessary to include some processing code (JavaScript) within the display code (HTML) to ensure that they work together.

The mixing of processing code and display code is the same problem that led to ASP.NET being created to replace classic ASP. Whereas ASP.NET Web Forms are a much cleaner approach than Classic ASP, they still had their own sets of problems related to the linking of processing and display, which led to the development of ASP.NET MVC. JavaScript has the same problem. In order for JavaScript to be the most efficient, it had to be bound to HTML elements so that events from the element would lead to running a set of JavaScript. This means that not only does the JavaScript implementation have to understand the DOM, the DOM has to understand the JavaScript method(s).

jQuery's Role

Released in 2006, jQuery is a library that was introduced to solve all three of the aforementioned problems. While at its core jQuery is a DOM-manipulation library, it also provides a completely new way to manage events and event handling by providing event assignment and event callback definition in a single step in a single location. That means that using the jQuery library makes it easy to add event handlers to the DOM by using JavaScript, rather than adding HTML event attributes throughout the page to call JavaScript functions. This completely eliminates the need for the circular reference, instead allowing the display code to be ignorant of the processing code.

Another advantage of jQuery is the level of abstraction that it offers compared to JavaScript. Much of the code that developers were writing on the client side was related to selecting a part of the screen and doing something with that area. jQuery provides a way to do the same thing while enabling the developer to avoid JavaScript for much of the work—instead, for example, using a one-line jQuery command to take the place of 15 lines of JavaScript. This means that developers do not necessarily have to become experts in JavaScript to be effective UI developers; understanding a few different commands in jQuery enables them to get much of their work done.

The last problem mentioned regarding JavaScript usage in the browser involves cross-browser incompatibilities. jQuery understands that the various JavaScript engines from the major browsers can be different, so as part of the abstraction just mentioned, the jQuery library handles all of these incompatibilities when it builds out its interfaces. This means that the functionality offered by jQuery is standardized across browsers in a way that straight JavaScript code is not.

The core jQuery library supports a lot of features:

➤ DOM element selection

➤ DOM element manipulation

➤ AJAX

➤ Events

➤ Animations and other effects

➤ Asynchronous processing (separate from AJAX)

➤ Data, especially JSON, parsing

➤ Additional plugins, extensibility

Some of the additional plugins have grown into significant libraries of their own. A selection of the more important libraries is listed in Table 14-1.

TABLE 14-1: Additional jQuery Modules

MODULE	DESCRIPTION
jQuery UI	A set of user interface components. These components include user interactions, effects, themes, and widgets. An example of a jQuery widget is the date picker that you added in Chapter 11.
jQuery Mobile	The growth of mobile devices being used to access the Internet has led to the need for HTML5- based UI systems that are both extremely small (data transfer to a mobile device can be expensive) and flexible—especially in terms of determining viewable space and scripting support.

continues

TABLE 14-1 *(continued)*

MODULE	DESCRIPTION
QUnit	A JavaScript unit testing framework. While not based on jQuery itself, it is used by the jQuery, jQuery UI, and jQuery Mobile projects for testing. QUnit is capable of testing any JavaScript code, not just jQuery. T can also be used to test itself.
jQuery Validation	This framework supports client-side validation. It makes standard validation trivial while also offering numerous options for customization. It includes multiple validation methods that validate against different types of data, including e-mail address or URL, as well as the capability to write your own validation methods.
Globalize	Content on the Internet is accessible to visitors anywhere in the world as long as they have an Internet connection. This has made globalization and internationalization increasingly important, as enterprises want to provide access and communication to people who don't speak the native language of the website.
jQuery Mouse Wheel Plugin	This is a very specialized library, but it solves a surprisingly complex problem: interacting with specialized hardware on the client that was not even imagined when JavaScript came out but soon became a standard piece of hardware.

Because jQuery is open source, you have also seen other implementations that take advantage of the functionality it provides. Microsoft, for example, provides the capability to install (as a package) many different parts of the jQuery framework as well as some customizations to it that are now built in to output generated in a project, such as Web Forms AJAX and validation. The scripts that are used by Microsoft in these cases use parts of the jQuery framework as well.

OPEN SOURCE

The term *open source* is generally used to refer to a set of functionality, either an application or a library, whereby the source code is available for download and usage by developer. Each set of functionality generally has a licensing agreement that instructs users as to what they can and cannot do with the project's source code. Some of the licenses are very open, allowing users to do almost anything they want, while other agreements are much more restrictive and limit how the application or library may be used.

Some of these licenses include the following:

➤   MIT license: Permits reuse within proprietary software provided that all copies of the licensed software include a copy of the MIT License terms and the copyright notice. jQuery uses an MIT license.

> ➤ GNU General Public license: In a GPL situation, users have the right to freely distribute copies and modified versions of a work with the stipulation that the same rights be preserved in derivative works. This means that a developer cannot sell a non–open source version of a product that uses a GPL licensed product or library.
>
> ➤ Apache license: This type of license gives users of the software the freedom to use the software for any purpose, to distribute it, to modify it, and to distribute modified versions of the software, under the terms of the license, without concern for royalties. This is the license under which ASP.NET is available.

Each of the different jQuery libraries is available for use within your ASP.NET application, be it Web Forms or MVC. Including these items in your application depends upon the library that you will be using, where it will be used, and other considerations regarding its usage. However, the mechanics of interacting with the libraries are the same across all the jQuery libraries, even the standard library.

Including the jQuery Library

Once you determine that the best way to fulfill a set of business requirements in your application is through the use of jQuery, you have to determine which jQuery parts you want and how you will make them available in your application. Because you are working within Visual Studio, the default way to add third-party libraries is through the use of NuGet packages, and indeed you have already added several jQuery packages using that approach. The items with the checkmark in Figure 14-1 are the jQuery items that are already installed in your sample application.

At this point you have installed the jQuery core libraries, the jQuery UI package, and the jQuery Validation framework, as well as several Microsoft-specific Unobtrusive jQuery libraries. As you discovered in earlier chapters, the Microsoft libraries are necessary so that the various ASP.NET helpers are available to handle creation of the appropriate HTML elements with the appropriate attributes. The attributes enable the JavaScript library to be called "unobtrusive."

These libraries are slightly misnamed in that they make it seem as if jQuery and unobtrusive are different. Unobtrusive is simply an approach to using JavaScript whereby the separation of functionality from the presentation layer is enforced. Using this definition means that jQuery is unobtrusive as well because that is one of the points of the jQuery library.

Although it has been mentioned several times, it may not be completely clear how JavaScript and the DOM can be mixed together and what this problem looks like. An example of this mixed-up approach is shown here:

```
<input type="text" name="date" onchange="validateThisDate()" />
```

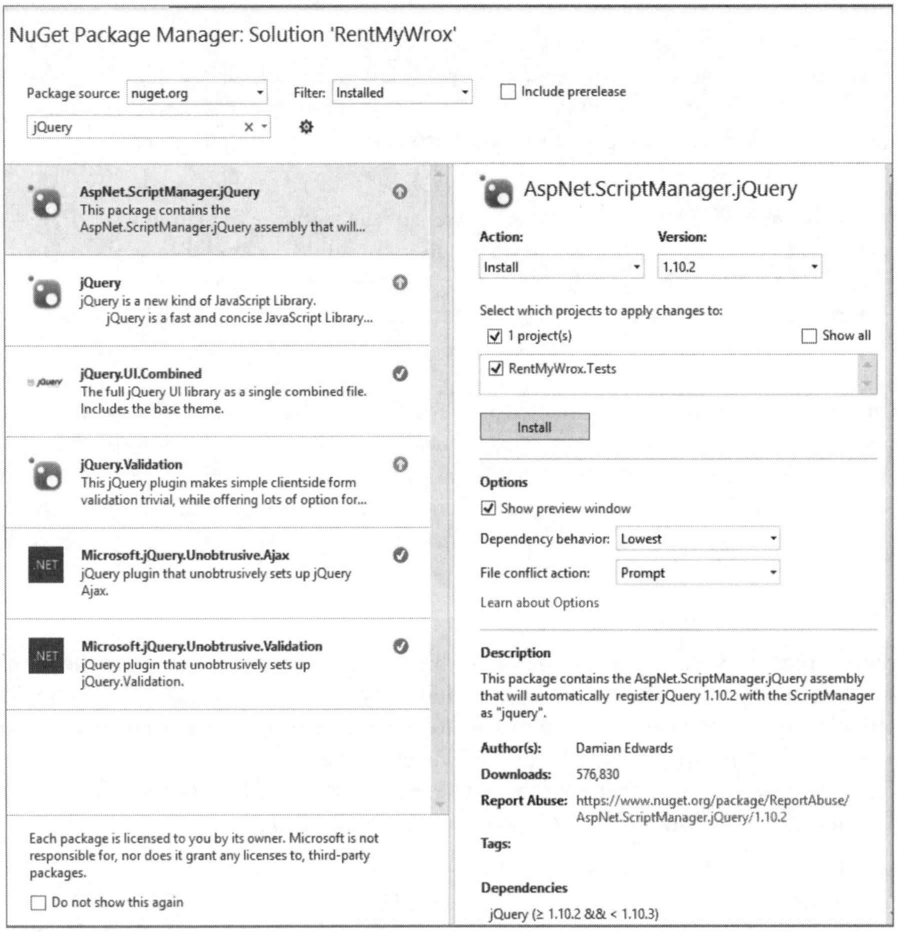

FIGURE 14-1: Installed jQuery packages

The onchange attribute is where the mix-up happens—where the code calls a JavaScript function from within the HTML element, forever linking these two items together. The unobtrusive solution is to perform the linking in code so that the HTML\ DOM content does not reference the JavaScript; instead, all references are from JavaScript to the DOM element. The unobtrusive approach enables any JavaScript changes, such as changing the name of a function, to be limited to occurring within JavaScript, without having to change any HTML.

This change in approach means that the linking would happen as follows:

HTML

```
<input type="text" name="date" id="date" />
```

JAVASCRIPT

```
window.onload = function() {
    document.getElementById('date').onchange = validateDate;
};
```

In short, all the default jQuery packages that you need are already attached to your solution. Therefore, your real concern is ensuring that the jQuery library files are available for download to the client's machine and that they are available to use within your UI code. There are a couple of different ways to ensure that the web page knows to download the script; either adding a reference directly to the page or using bundles to group multiple scripts together into a single reference.

The first approach is to add a reference directly to your page. This is the approach you took when you added the initial jQuery UI script to support the date picker. This code is an HTML script element whereby you set the `src` attribute to download the script file as shown here:

```
<script src="/Scripts/jquery-2.0.3.min.js" type="text/javascript"></script>
```

This simple approach ensures that the necessary script is downloaded. As you need other scripts you just add another reference link. Doing this in the `head` element of your page ensures that it is available for all the JavaScript and jQuery code that follows. If you are using a master or layout page, then you can add these references to the template page so they are available to all the content pages. This can result in the browser downloading files that won't be used during the visit, but because the browser caches these files locally, the user is only taking that initial hit in downloading the extra file(s); for the rest of the visit, and perhaps any subsequent visits, that file will not have to be downloaded.

There are several problems with this approach, however. The first is version management. The preceding code snippet references version 2.0.3 of the jQuery library. This means that when 2.0.4 comes out and you want to reference it in your website, you will have to manually change the code. Ideally, you would like a solution whereby the browser can get the script files without having to worry about the version. You could do this manually by changing the default filename, but this will cause all sorts of confusion with NuGet upgrades because files that it expects to be available no longer are.

Another problem is the number of separate files that may end up being downloaded. As you add different libraries to your site to support various pieces of functionality, you continue to add script references. As you start writing your own JavaScript libraries and including them in different files to support your custom business needs, the list gets even longer. The result is a lot of files being downloaded, many of which may end up unused.

You also have to be very careful about function naming conventions, as the more scripts that the browser runs through, the more likely it is that a conflict will result. Thus, while in general the hit of downloading an unused library may be acceptable, downloading many unused libraries that are all referenced together may not be.

Fortunately, ASP.NET has a way to solve these problems: adding an abstraction layer to the script download. This abstraction enables you to define the files that the abstraction references through wildcards or other replacement values. This way, you can set the abstraction to ignore the version number of the jQuery file, for example, and simply download whatever version of that file is in the directory. This abstraction also enables you to add scripts as a group, so if you have several scripts that have a dependency you can ensure that all those files are downloaded together, along with the file(s) on which they may be dependent. These abstractions, which are a part of the ASP.NET framework, are called bundles.

Bundles

Bundles provide support for grouping different files together. These files can be JavaScript or CSS, and the result of creating a bundle is the capability to merge different files into a single file for easy reference. In addition, modern browsers limit the number of simultaneous connections that they support to the same domain. Therefore, reducing the number of files to be downloaded enables the available connections to do less connecting and disconnecting from the server and instead spend that time on downloading larger files. Usually this causes an overall decrease in time spent downloading files. One additional side effect of bundling is that it incrementally decreases the amount of time spent looking for JavaScript functions across all the available scripts because there is a much greater chance that the needed function is included in the same file, or the same area of memory. Obviously this isn't going to save you seconds of response time, but every millisecond helps!

You can add bundling in the `App_Start\BundleConfig.cs` file. A good example of how bundling is built is demonstrated within the NuGet package you added:

```
// Order is very important for these files to work,
// they have explicit dependencies
bundles.Add(new ScriptBundle("~/bundles/MsAjaxJs").Include(
        "~/Scripts/WebForms/MsAjax/MicrosoftAjax.js",
        "~/Scripts/WebForms/MsAjax/MicrosoftAjaxApplicationServices.js",
        "~/Scripts/WebForms/MsAjax/MicrosoftAjaxTimer.js",
        "~/Scripts/WebForms/MsAjax/MicrosoftAjaxWebForms.js"));
```

The preceding snippet creates a bundle named `MsAjaxJs` that appears to be placed within the `bundles` directory. However, there is no actual "bundles" directory; instead, the framework reads that as a special routing call which responds with a single file that concatenates all the included files. You don't have to do anything special to reference the bundle, as the normal script reference would work as shown here:

```
<script src="/bundles/MsAjaxJs" type="text/javascript"></script>
```

When you are working within an ASP.NET view, you also have the additional capability to add the reference through a scripts helper:

```
@Scripts.Render("~/bundles/MsAjaxJs")
```

This is a shortcut, because the output from this command is the script reference tag listed previously.

In this next Try It Out, you adjust some of the scripts that have already been added and ensure that they are bundled, and called, correctly.

TRY IT OUT Bundling JavaScript Files

In this activity you make some changes to previously added jQuery functions by adding them into external sheets and referencing them as appropriate. You also ensure that your jQuery link is correct and without version problems.

1. Ensure that Visual Studio is running and your RentMyWrox solution is open. Open the `Views\Shared\_MVCLayout.cshtml` file. Scrolling down to the bottom of the file displays a section similar to what is shown in Figure 14-2.

```
_MVCLayout.cshtml  ⊣ ✕
    34       ⊟        <div id="specialnotes">
    35                    @RenderSection("SpecialNotes", false)
    36       └        </div>
    37       ⊟        <div id="footer">
    38                    footer content here
    39       └        </div>
    40                @Scripts.Render("~/bundles/jquery")
    41                @Scripts.Render("~/bundles/bootstrap")
    42                @Scripts.Render("~/bundles/jqueryajax")
    43                <script language="javascript" type="text/javascript" src="~/Scripts/jquery-ui-1.11.4.js"></script>
    44                @RenderSection("scripts", required: false)
    45       ⊟        <script type="text/javascript">
    46
    47       ⊟            $(document).ready(function () {
    48                        $(".editordatepicker").datepicker();
    49                    });
    50
    51       ⊟            function getStoreHours() {
    52                        $.getJSON("/StoreOpen")
    53       ⊟                    .done(function (data) {
    54                                var message = data.Message;
    55                                $("#storeHoursMessage").html(message);
    56                                $("#storeHoursMessage").removeClass();
    57                                if (data.IsStoreOpenNow == false)
    58       ⊟                        {
    59                                    $("#storeHoursMessage").addClass("storeClosed");
    60       └                        }
    61       ⊟                        else {
    62                                    $("#storeHoursMessage").addClass("storeOpen");
    63       └                        }
    64       ⊟                        setTimeout(function () {
    65                                    getStoreHours();
    66                                }, 20000);
    67                        });
    68                    };
    69
    70       ⊟            $(document).ready(function () {
    71                        getStoreHours();
    72                    });
    73
    74                </script>
    75       │  </body>
    76       │  </html>
```

FIGURE 14-2: Bottom of the _MVCLayout.cshtml page

2. Delete line 41, which references "bootstrap."

3. In the Solution Explorer, right-click on the Scripts directory and add a new item, a JavaScript file (found under Web) named MainPageManagement.js, as shown in Figure 14-3.

4. Cut the getStoreHours function and the ready method that calls the getStoreHours method and paste them into the new JavaScript file you just created. It should look like Figure 14-4 when completed.

5. Delete the script element that included jquery-ui, as well as the two @Scripts.Render lines. Add a new line in their place as shown in the following example. When completed, this area of the page should look like Figure 14-5.

```
@Scripts.Render("~/bundles/common")
```

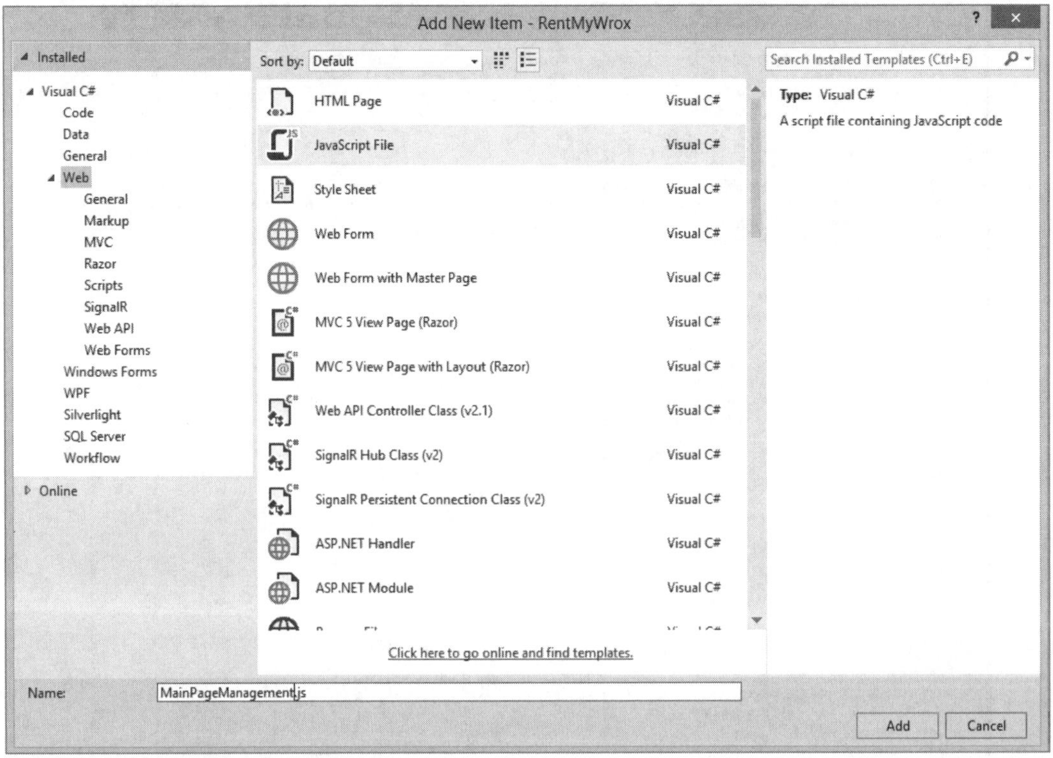

FIGURE 14-3: Adding a new JavaScript file

FIGURE 14-4: After moving some JavaScript from the layout file

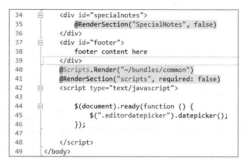

```
34        <div id="specialnotes">
35            @RenderSection("SpecialNotes", false)
36        </div>
37        <div id="footer">
38            footer content here
39        </div>
40    @Scripts.Render("~/bundles/common")
41    @RenderSection("scripts", required: false)
42    <script type="text/javascript">
43
44        $(document).ready(function () {
45            $(".editordatepicker").datepicker();
46        });
47
48    </script>
49  </body>
```

FIGURE 14-5: The updated layout file

6. Open the `App_Start\BundleConfig.cs` file and add the following lines:

```
bundles.Add(new ScriptBundle("~/bundles/common").Include(
            "~/Scripts/jquery-{version}.js",
            "~/Scripts/jquery-ui-{version}.js",
            "~/Scripts/jquery.unobtrusive-ajax*",
            "~/Scripts/MainPageManagement.js"
));
```

7. Run the application. Note that it all still works the same.

How It Works

During this exercise you cleaned up your layout page by removing some of the JavaScript that was entered directly into the page, instead creating a separate JavaScript file that is labeled appropriately to show the work going on within the script. Once the file was moved, however, you had to ensure that you still linked the script in to the page so that the store hours code was still able to function.

Rather than add a new link into the file, you instead created a single bundle that would take care of downloading all the configured scripts. The purpose of creating a single bundle is to enable the downloading of various scripts needed throughout your site in one fell swoop. In other words, if you viewed the source for the file, you should see a single link. The source that was created is shown in Figure 14-6.

As you can see, however, it appears that where there should only be one file, it instead looks like all the script files referenced in the bundle were referenced in the source. While that may not be quite what you anticipated, it's actually a good thing because you are running the application in debug mode, which means the bundle manager copied each script separately; that way, if necessary, you could debug a particular script, rather than the bundled script.

To make bundling happen as it would in production, you need to run the application in a non-debug fashion. This does not mean that you can simply run it in release mode and you will see the changes. You must instead set the compilation mode in the `web.config` file because it will currently be set to true, as shown in line 26 of Figure 14-7.

```
File  Edit  Format
 85    <span>Lorem ipsum dolor sit amet, consectetur adipiscing elit, sed do eiusmod
       laboris nisi ut aliquip ex ea commodo consequat. Duis aute irure do...</span>
 86         <a class="inlinelink" data-ajax="true" data-ajax-method="GET" data-aja
 87    </p>
 88  </div>
 89  <div>
 90      <div class="listtitle"><span class="productname">Mollis massa </span><span
 91      <p>
 92    <span>Mollis massa nam porttitor iaculis condimentum dapibus class etiam nam
       curabitur convallis imperdiet in auctor libero senectus dolor ali...</span>
 93         <a class="inlinelink" data-ajax="true" data-ajax-method="GET" data-aja
 94      </p>
 95  </div>
 96
 97
 98
 99      </div>
100      <div id="specialnotes">
101
102      </div>
103      <div id="footer">
104          footer content here
105      </div>
106      <script src="/Scripts/jquery-1.10.2.js"></script>
107  <script src="/Scripts/jquery-ui-1.11.4.js"></script>
108  <script src="/Scripts/jquery.unobtrusive-ajax.js"></script>
109  <script src="/Scripts/StoreHoursManagement.js"></script>
110
111
112      <script type="text/javascript">
113
114          $(document).ready(function () {
115              $(".editordatepicker").datepicker();
116          });
117
118      </script>
119
```

FIGURE 14-6: The newly created source

```
24 ⊟   <system.web>
25         <authentication mode="None" />
26         <compilation debug="true" targetFramework="4.5" />
27         <httpRuntime targetFramework="4.5" />
28 ⊟      <pages>
29 ⊟        <namespaces>
30            <add namespace="System.Web.Helpers" />
31            <add namespace="System.Web.Mvc" />
32            <add namespace="System.Web.Mvc.Ajax" />
33            <add namespace="System.Web.Mvc.Html" />
34            <add namespace="System.Web.Optimization" />
35            <add namespace="System.Web.Routing" />
36            <add namespace="System.Web.WebPages" />
37            <add namespace="Microsoft.AspNet.Identity" />
38          </namespaces>
```

FIGURE 14-7: Web.config file content

Setting the debug attribute to false enables you to see the rendered values for the bundled scripts; but once you set this debug value to false, you will see the warning dialog shown in Figure 14-8. This dialog appears when you turn debug off but run the application in debug mode.

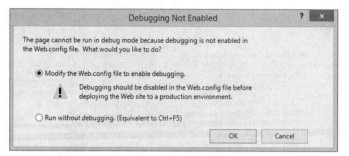

FIGURE 14-8: Debugging Not Enabled dialog

When you get this warning and you want to see the bundling, you need to select the second radio button, "Run without debugging." With this option you won't be able to hit any breakpoints or perform any debugging, but you will be able to see what happens when the bundle is rendered, as shown in Figure 14-9.

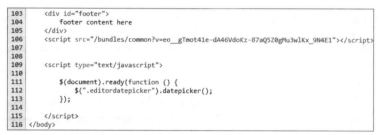

```
103    <div id="footer">
104        footer content here
105    </div>
106    <script src="/bundles/common?v=eo__gTmot41e-dA46VdoKz-87aQ5Z0gMu3wlKx_9N4E1"></script>
107
108
109    <script type="text/javascript">
110
111        $(document).ready(function () {
112            $(".editordatepicker").datepicker();
113        });
114
115    </script>
116 </body>
```

FIGURE 14-9: Source code with bundling

The `src` attribute that is set for the single script element includes the name that you set for bundle. It also contains a query string key\value pair, where the key is "v" and stands for version. The value used here, a long string, sets the version of the JavaScript scripts that it is referencing. If you don't change the script files, then this number will not change. However, changing the script files causes a new version number to be issued. This version is important because it enables the browser to download the script file locally and cache it. When the version string changes, the browser recognizes that a change has occurred and calls for the new files, rather than continuing to access the old, cached value. The version is necessary because the script filename itself has not changed; it still matches the name you originally configured.

If you examine the new JavaScript file you will see that it contains all the different script files. Note also that all the white space has been removed from the file, as shown in Figure 14-10.

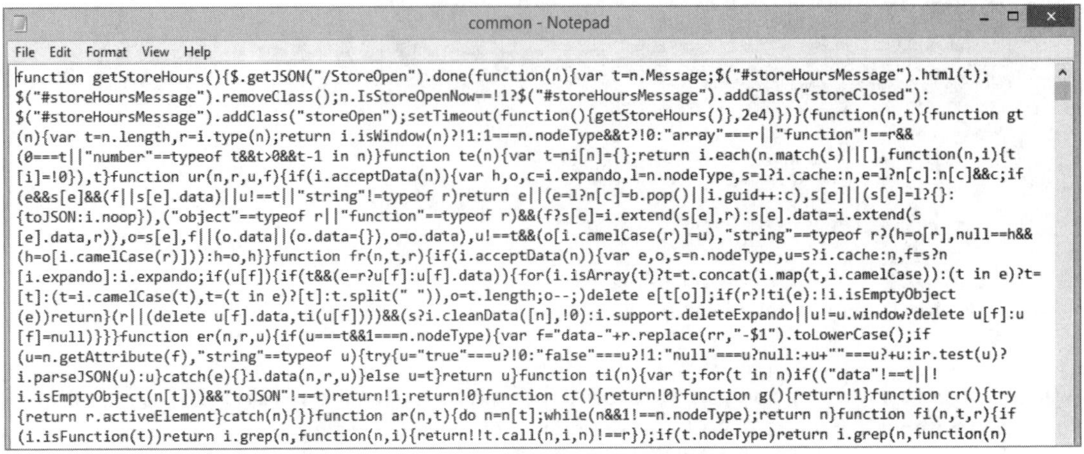

FIGURE 14-10: Bundled JavaScript output

The first line is the script that you created in the exercise. However, as you can see, all the line breaks and white space have been completely removed. This does not affect usage at all, it simply removes the extra spaces and makes the download a little bit smaller.

Getting the scripts into your page makes them available for use in the browser. In the next section you will learn more details about how to use jQuery and JavaScript to customize the user experience—in other words, to build more scripts that you could add to new bundles!

jQUERY SYNTAX

jQuery is a JavaScript object that you can reference through the $ function. The $ is not a direct reference to the object itself, as you are familiar with when you new a class in C#, but is instead a factory method. A *factory method* is a software design approach, or pattern, whereby you can create an object without specifying the exact class of the object that you are creating. This means you do not create a copy of the object yourself, but instead call a method on the factory class, which creates the object for you. This way, your code doesn't have to understand how to build an item; it can instead call some code that knows how the object should be built. This approach abstracts away the actual jQuery object and enables it to be referenced with a single character. You have used the $ function when you were building the jQuery selectors.

The other approach that you have used is the $. approach, or the utility functions. These items do not act upon the jQuery object directly but instead provide other supporting functionality. In Chapter 13 you used the $.getJSON method to make a call to the server and get back a JSON object. Both of these approaches to using jQuery features are part of the jQuery Core.

jQuery Core

The jQuery Core is the traditional set of jQuery functionality. It is the base on which all the other libraries and plugins build. A couple of requirements are part of making jQuery work within your application. First, you need to ensure that you have referenced the jQuery code before you reference any method that takes advantage of jQuery. Failure to provide the scripts in the appropriate order will result in JavaScript errors, because the code is trying to take advantage of an object that has not yet been substantiated.

Second, you need to ensure that all your scripts run only after the DOM has finished loading. Unless told otherwise, the browser will run JavaScript as soon as it comes upon it while parsing the down-loaded document. If you don't make the scripts wait until the DOM has loaded before running, then you run the risk of the DOM object not being loaded at the time the script is run. As a result, you might get a JavaScript error, at worst. At best, the behavior that you are hoping for won't take place because it will not be rerun when the DOM finishes with its loading process.

You have already used the check that ensures the DOM has completed loading in a previous chapter, so it should not be completely new. Adding a check to ensure that the DOM is loaded looks like this:

```
$(document).ready(function() {
    // The work you want performed when the document is ready
});
```

You can also use the following shortcut to perform the same action:

```
$(function() {
    // The work you want performed when the document is ready
});
```

In this case you have the exact same outcome, but rather than having to define the DOM element that you want to wait for, you instead use the function that you want run as the parameter. jQuery then knows to assign that function just as if you directly used the `ready` method.

jQuery also has the capability to queue up work. This enables you to easily create many different `ready` methods as needed, and each time the browser comes across a method it adds the function callback to the queue for that element. When the state of the element changes, such as when the document is loaded, the browser runs through the queue of callbacks for that change until all the expected actions have been taken. This enables you, as the developer, to maintain smaller, more discrete sets of functionality rather than having to maintain one large monolithic function, such as you would have to do if the queueing structure were not supported.

Before getting too deep into the selecting and changing of DOM elements using jQuery, you should first learn some of the various utility methods available from within the jQuery object that are designed to help provide support for manipulation.

Working with the jQuery Utility Methods

Some of these jQuery utility methods can be performed in lieu of using a selector approach, and you get the same outcome. Other methods provide true utility functionality by providing helpers that enable developers to build robust sets of functionality for the client side.

Many other different utility functions are available, as shown in Table 14-2. Each of these methods provides a useful set of functionality by abstracting out the JavaScript code that you would have to otherwise write in order to perform these common tasks.

TABLE 14-2: Useful jQuery Utility Methods

METHOD	DESCRIPTION
contains	Determines whether one DOM element is a descendent of another DOM element. Returns true if the contained element is within the container element, no matter how deep the nesting. Only element nodes are supported; if the second argument is a text or comment node, the function always returns false. `$.contains( container, contained )`
data	Enables you to attach data of any type to DOM elements. This same functionality can be achieved by using the selector approach, but if you don't necessarily have selector information the `data` method still gives you access to the DOM element. `$.data( element, key, value )`
each	A generic iterator function that enables you to go through the different elements in an array or array-like object and perform work on each item as it is iterated. `$.each( object, callback )`
extend	Merges two or more objects into one. Goes through the properties of the target object and replaces the values of the target from the source property's value. If the target doesn't have the property then it is added to the object. The deep variable is a Boolean, which indicates whether the replacement should be recursive or simple. `$.extend( [deep], target [, object1 ] [, objectN ] )`
inArray	Determines whether a value is in the array, returning the index if it is contained or a -1 if the array does not contain the value. `$.inArray( value, array [, fromIndex ] )`

METHOD	DESCRIPTION

is	There are many different is functions that determine the type of variable that it is given. This is necessary because JavaScript is dynamically typed, meaning the same variable can contain values of many different types, one after the other. Thus, if you need to do something specific to that type with the value, then you first need to confirm that it is appropriate. The is functions include the following:
	
	`$.isArray(value)`
	
	`$.isEmptyObject(value)`
	
	`$.isFunction(value)`
	
	`$.isNumeric(value)`
	
	`$.isPlainObject(value)`
	
	`$.isWindow(value)`

merge	Merges two different arrays together into the first array: `$.merge( first, second )`
parseHTML	Parses a string into a set of DOM nodes. A string representation of HTML, such as that returned from a controller action that returns a partial view, would need to be parsed into DOM elements before it can be properly inserted into an actual element. `$.parseHTML( data [, context ] [, keepScripts ] )`
trim	Removes the whitespace from the beginning and the end of a string: `$.trim( str )`
queue	Shows or manipulates the queue of functions to be executed on the matched elements; it provides a look into the actual code that is going to be run on a particular element. `$.queue( [queueName ] )`

Looking at the items in this table, you will see that there are several different types of utilities. The first is code-based, in that these methods provide support for processing. Whether this processing results in a change to a DOM element is irrelevant; this set of methods are helpers that provide support such as joining or enumerating through arrays, or evaluating the type of a variable, or even merging two objects into a single, new object.

The second type of utility method are those methods that scan the entire document body. These are the methods that can check whether one element contains another, or set any value on any attribute on any elements. Most of these can also be done with selectors and then interact with the element attributes at that point, but the utility methods give you another approach to solving the problem.

Selecting Items Using jQuery

The last chapter contained a brief explanation of jQuery selection, or using jQuery to find one or more DOM elements based on one or more characteristics of that element. As demonstrated in the previous chapter, the most common approach to selection within jQuery is to use the same selector pattern and approach that's supported in CSS selectors. However, there are some subtle differences in some of the selectors, and other, more flexible selectors that are available for use within jQuery. Table 14-3 lists some of the approaches to element selection that are available in jQuery.

TABLE 14-3: jQuery Selectors

NAME	DESCRIPTION

Attribute Contains Prefix Selector	Selects elements that have the specified attribute with a value either equal to the provided string or starting with that string followed by a hyphen (-).
	
	`<input name="the-news">` SELECTED
	`<input name="the">` SELECTED
	`<input name="thenews">` SELECTED
	`<script>`
	`$( "input[name|='the']").css( "border", "3px" );`
	`</script>`

Attribute Contains Word Selector	Selects elements that have the specified attribute with a value containing a given word, delimited by spaces. This expects a space on either (at least one) end of the string.
	
	`<input name="the-news">`
	`<input name="the news">` SELECTED
	`<input name="thenews">`
	`<script>`
	`$( "input[name~='the']" ).val( "" );`
	`</script>`

Attribute Ends With Selector	Selects elements that have the specified attribute with a value ending exactly, case sensitive, with a given string.
	
	`<input name="the-news">` SELECTED
	`<input name="the news">` SELECTED
	`<input name="thenews">` SELECTED
	`<script>`
	`$( "input[name$='news']" ).val( "" );`
	`</script>`

NAME	DESCRIPTION

Attribute Equals Selector	Selects elements that have the specified attribute with a value exactly equal to a certain value, including case.
	`<input name="the-news">`
	`<input name="the news">`
	`<input name="thenews">` SELECTED
	`<script>`
	`$( "input[name='thenews']" ).val( "" );`
	`</script>`

Attribute Not Equal ToSelector	Selects elements that either don't have the specified attribute or do have the specified attribute but not with a certain value.
	`<input name="the-news">` SELECTED
	`<input name="the news">` SELECTED
	`<input name="thenews">`
	`<script>`
	`$( "input[name!='thenews']" ).val( "" );`
	`</script>`

Class Selector	Selects elements that are labeled with this particular class, regardless of the type of element.

Even Selector	Selects even elements, zero-indexed.
	`<input name="the-news">` SELECTED
	`<input name="the news">`
	`<input name="thenews">` SELECTED
	`<script>`
	`$( "input:even" ).val( "" );`
	`</script>`

Greater Than Selector	Selects all elements at an index greater than the index within the matched set.
	`<input name="the-news">`
	`<input name="the news">`
	`<input name="thenews">` SELECTED
	`<script>`
	`$( "input:gt(1)" ).val( "" );`
	`</script>`

Id Selector	Selects all elements where the "id" attribute of an HTML element matches the provided value.

continues

TABLE 14-3 *(continued)*

NAME	DESCRIPTION

Less Than Selector	Selects all elements at an index less than the index within the matched set.
	
	`<input name="the-news">` SELECTED
	
	`<input name="the news">`
	
	`<input name="thenews">`
	
	`<script>`
	
	`$( "input:lt(1)]" ).val( "" );`
	
	`</script>`

Odd Selector	Selects odd elements, zero-indexed.
	
	`<input name="the-news">`
	
	`<input name="the news">` SELECTED
	
	`<input name="thenews">`
	
	`<script>`
	
	`$( "input:odd" ).val( "" );`
	
	`</script>`

Only Child Selector	Selects all elements that are the only child of their parent.
	
	`<div>`
	
	    `<input name="the-news">` SELECTED
	
	`</div>`
	
	`<div>`
	
	    `<input name="the news">`
	
	    `<input name="thenews">`
	
	`</div>`
	
	`<script>`
	
	`$( "div input:only-child" ).val( "" );`
	
	`</script>`

Only Of Type Selector	Selects all elements that have no siblings with the same element name.
	
	`<div>`
	
	    `<input name="the-news">` SELECTED
	
	`</div>`
	
	`<div>`
	
	    `<input name="the news">`
	
	    `<input name="thenews">`
	
	`</div>`
	
	`<script>`
	
	`$( "input:only-of-type" ).val( "" );`
	
	`</script>`

NAME	DESCRIPTION
Parent Selector	Selects all elements that have no siblings with the same element name.
Universal Selector	Selects all elements.

Determining the best approach to creating the selectors that you will use in your jQuery is going to depend on what you are trying to do. Each separate requirement may need a different selector. An element can be targeted by multiple selectors, based on different criteria that may match that particular element, including class, element type, id, and any of the other items that were discussed in the preceding table.

MODIFYING THE DOM WITH jQUERY

Once you have one or more elements selected, there are many different things that you can do with them. You can perform calculations or perform submissions with their values; you can ignore their values and change their appearance and display. After selecting the DOM element, you can perform any action supported by JavaScript on that element, its attributes, and its value.

Changing Appearance with jQuery

Changing the display of a DOM element using jQuery goes far beyond making the text bold or changing the background color, though you can certainly do those changes as well. Probably one of the first things you think of when someone mentions appearance and HTML pages is CSS, and jQuery supports a set of functions for manipulating the CSS on elements. Some of these methods are shown in Table 14-4.

TABLE 14-4: CSS Methods in jQuery

METHOD	DESCRIPTION
addClass	Adds the specified class(es) to each element in the set of matched elements. `$( "p" ).addClass( "myClass yourClass" );`
css	Gets the value of a style property for the first element in the set of matched elements *or* sets one or more CSS properties for every matched element. `var color = $( "p" ).css( "background-color" );`
hasClass	Determines whether any of the matched elements are assigned the given class. `$( "p" ).hasClass( "myClass" );`
height	Gets the current computed height for the first element in the set of matched elements or sets the height of every matched element. It returns a value in pixels, but without the attached unit, i.e., 400 instead of 400px. `$( "p" ).height( ) = 100;`

continues

TABLE 14-4 *(continued)*

METHOD	DESCRIPTION

position	Gets the current coordinates of the first element in the set of matched elements, relative to the offset parent. You cannot set these values, you can only get them as needed. These elements must be visible and the results do not account for borders, margins, or padding.
	
	`var selectedElement = $( "p:last" );`
	
	`var position = selectedElement.position();`
	
	`$( "p:first" ).val = position.left + position.top;`

removeClass	Removes a single class, multiple classes, or all classes from each element in the set of matched elements. `$( "p" ).removeClass( "myClass yourClass" )`
toggleClass	Adds or removes one or more classes from each element in the set of matched elements, depending on the presence of the class. If the class exists, it is removed. If the class is missing, it is added. `$( "p" ).toggleClass( "myClass" );`
width	Gets the current computed width for the first element in the set of matched elements or sets the width of every matched element. It returns a value in pixels, but without the attached unit, i.e., 400 instead of 400px. `$( "p" ).width( ) = 100;`

There are other ways to change the appearance of DOM elements after you have selected them. As just shown, changing the assigned styles is one approach to changing the display. Style changes, however, are generally static changes. You can also use JavaScript, thus jQuery, to provide simple animations or other visual effects to DOM elements. Table 14-5 describes the various animation and other effects methods available in jQuery.

TABLE 14-5: Animation and Other Effects in jQuery

METHOD	DESCRIPTION

animate	Performs a custom animation of a set of CSS properties. The typical usage is with the method signature of `animate( properties, options )`.
	
	`<input id="someelement">`
	
	`<input id="anotherelement">`
	
	`$( "#someelement" ).click(function() {`
	  `$( "#anotherelement" ).animate({`
	    `left: "+=50" // move it left everytime there is a click`
	  `}, 5000, function() {`
	    `// do something when the animation has completed`
	  `});`
	`});`

METHOD	DESCRIPTION

delay	Sets a timer to delay execution of subsequent items in the queue. This value is usually chained with other animation items.
	
	```<input id="someelement">```
	
	```<input id="anotherelement">```
	
	```$("#someelement").click(function() {```
	
	``` $("#anotherelement").slideUp(300).delay(800).fadeIn(400);```
	
	```});```

fadeIn	Displays the matched elements by fading them to opaque. The function takes a duration in milliseconds, defaulting to 400, or two string values of "slow" or "fast"; or 600 and 500 milliseconds, respectively.
	
	```<input id="someelement">```
	
	```<input id="anotherelement" hidden>```
	
	```$("#someelement").click(function() {```
	
	``` $("#anotherelement").fadeIn("slow");```
	
	```});```

fadeOut	Hides the matched elements by fading them to transparent. The function takes a duration in milliseconds, defaulting to 400, or two string values of "slow" or "fast"; or 600 and 500 milliseconds respectively.
	
	```<input id="someelement">```
	
	```<input id="anotherelement" hidden>```
	
	```$("#someelement").click(function() {```
	
	``` $("#anotherelement").fadeOut ("slow");```
	
	```});```

fadeToggle	Displays or hides the matched elements by animating their opacity. The function takes a duration in milliseconds, defaulting to 400, or two string values of "slow" or "fast"; or 600 and 500 milliseconds, respectively.
	
	```<input id="someelement">```
	
	```<input id="anotherelement" hidden>```
	
	```$("#someelement").click(function() {```
	
	``` $("#anotherelement").fadeToggle ("slow");```
	
	```});```

continues

TABLE 14-5 *(continued)*

METHOD	DESCRIPTION

`hide`	Hides the matched elements. There is no animation involved, nor any arguments that can be passed into the method.
	`<input id="someelement">`
	`<input id="anotherelement">`
	`$( "#someelement" ).click(function() {`
	  `$( "#anotherelement" ).hide();`
	`});`

`show`	Displays the matched elements There is no animation involved, nor any arguments that can be passed into the method.
	`<input id="someelement">`
	`<input id="anotherelement" hidden>`
	`$( "#someelement" ).click(function() {`
	  `$( "#anotherelement" ).show();`
	`});`

`slideDown`	Displays the matched elements with a sliding motion. This method animates the height of the matched elements. This causes lower parts of the page to slide down, making way for the revealed items. The function takes a duration in milliseconds, defaulting to 400, or two string values of "slow" or "fast"; or 600 and 500 milliseconds, respectively.
	`<input id="someelement">`
	`<input id="anotherelement" hidden>`
	`$( "#someelement" ).click(function() {`
	  `$( "#anotherelement" ).slideDown(1000);`
	`});`

`slideTog-`
`gle`
	Displays or hides the matched elements with a sliding motion. This method animates the height of the matched elements, acting as if `slideDown` were called if the element is hidden or `slideUp` if the element is visible. The function takes a duration in milliseconds, defaulting to 400, or two string values of "slow" or "fast"; or 600 and 500 milliseconds, respectively.
	`<input id="someelement">`
	`<input id="anotherelement" hidden>`
	`$( "#someelement" ).click(function() {`
	  `$( "#anotherelement" ).slideToggle(1000);`
	`});`

METHOD	DESCRIPTION

`slideUp`	Hides the matched elements with a sliding motion. This method animates the height of the matched elements. This causes lower parts of the page to slide up as the items are hidden. The function takes a duration in milliseconds, defaulting to 400, or two string values of "slow" or "fast"; or 600 and 500 milliseconds, respectively.
	
	`<input id="someelement">`
	
	`<input id="anotherelement">`
	
	`$( "#someelement" ).click(function() {`
	
	`  $( "#anotherelement" ).slideUp(1000);`
	
	`});`

`toggle`	Displays or hides the matched elements. This method can be thought of as running the `show` method when an item is hidden, or running the `hide` method if the item is visible.
	
	`<input id="someelement">`
	
	`<input id="anotherelement">`
	
	`$( "#someelement" ).click(function() {`
	
	`  $( "#anotherelement" ).toggle();`
	
	`});`

Animation enables you to move areas of the screen to grab the user's attention. Using animation, for example, to slide out old content and slide in new content informs the user that there has been a change in an area. This becomes more important as you use AJAX approaches whereby information on the screen can change at any time.

The changing of information is generally the result of a user activity, such as clicking a button or selecting an item in the drop-down box. However, many other actions can cause a programmatic reaction. These actions are known as JavaScript and jQuery events.

Handling Events

A lot of different events are occurring within JavaScript that you can take advantage of within jQuery. These events are different from the events that you interacted with when doing the code-behinds in ASP.NET Web Form controls and pages, but the concept behind them is the same. An event provides a way to interact with either the user of the system or the system itself in order to learn that a state has changed and that something may need to happen because of this change.

Once you recognize that acknowledgment of an action is required—whether it is a button click or a timer expiring—you need an event handler, or the action to be taken upon that action, which you can attach to that action. After you have completed the creation of the event handler and the linking of that event handler to that event, you have created a way to monitor, and react to, that particular action. You can then do this across all the actions you care about.

As shown in Table 14-6, there are many different potential events that you can interact with as needed. It's unlikely that you will need to interact with each, but if you do you have that capability. There is no limit to the number of events that you can handle; nor is there a limit to how many handlers are attached to an event.

Not only can you use JavaScript and jQuery to assign an event handler to an event so that the event handler will be called as necessary, you can also use jQuery to call an event on an element, thus enabling you to programmatically act as the user if necessary. This enables you to use exactly the same approach regardless of how you want to perform the work, rather than write one set of code for interacting with the user and a second set of code to support system interaction.

TABLE 14-6: Common JavaScript Events

EVENT	DESCRIPTION

change	Binds an event handler to the change JavaScript event, or triggers that event on an element.
	
	`<input id="someelement" type="text">`
	
	`<input id="anotherelement">`
	
	`$( "#someelement" ).change(function() {`
	`  $( "#anotherelement" ).toggle();`
	`});`

click	Binds an event handler to the change JavaScript event, or triggers that event on an element.
	
	`<input id="someelement">`
	
	`<input id="anotherelement">`
	
	`$( "#someelement" ).click(function() {`
	`  $( "#anotherelement" ).toggle();`
	`});`

dblclick	Binds an event handler to the dblclick JavaScript event, or triggers that event on an element. This event is triggered only after this exact series of events:
	The mouse button is depressed while the pointer is inside the element.
	The mouse button is released while the pointer is inside the element.
	The mouse button is depressed again while the pointer is inside the element, within a time window that is system-dependent.
	The mouse button is released while the pointer is inside the element.
	
	`<input id="someelement">`
	
	`<input id="anotherelement">`
	
	`$( "#someelement" ).dblclick(function() {`
	`  $( "#anotherelement" ).toggle();`
	`});`

EVENT	DESCRIPTION

focus	Binds an event handler to the `focus` JavaScript event, or triggers that event on an element. Elements with focus are usually highlighted in some way by the browser—for example, with a dotted line surrounding the element. The focus is used to determine which element is the first to receive keyboard-related events.
	
	`<input id="someelement">`
	
	`<input id="anotherelement">`
	
	`$( "#someelement" ).focus(function() {`
	`    $( "#anotherelement" ).toggle();`
	`});`

hover	Binds two handlers to the matched elements, to be executed when the mouse pointer enters and leaves the elements. The `hover` method binds handlers for both the `mouseenter` and `mouseleave` events. You can use it to simply apply behavior to an element during the time the mouse is within the element.
	
	`<input id="someelement">`
	
	`<input id="anotherelement">`
	
	`$( "#someelement" ).hover(`
	`    function() {`
	`        $( "#anotherelement" ).show();`
	`    }, function() {`
	`        $( "#anotherelement" ).hide();`
	`});`

keypress	Binds an event handler to the `keypress` JavaScript event, or triggers that event on an element. The `keypress` event is sent to an element when the browser registers keyboard input that is not a modifier or non-printing key such as Shift, Esc, and Delete.
	
	`<input id="someelement">`
	
	`<input id="anotherelement">`
	
	`$( "#someelement" ).keypress(function() {`
	`    $( "#anotherelement" ).toggle();`
	`});`

mousedown	Binds an event handler to the `mousedown` JavaScript event, or triggers that event on an element. This event is sent to an element when the mouse pointer is over the element, and the mouse button is pressed.
	
	`<input id="someelement">`
	
	`<input id="anotherelement">`
	
	`$( "#someelement" ).mousedown(function() {`
	`    $( "#anotherelement" ).toggle();`
	`});`

continues

TABLE 14-6 *(continued)*

EVENT	DESCRIPTION

mouseenter	Binds an event handler to be fired when the mouse enters an element, or triggers that handler on an element. This JavaScript event is proprietary to Internet Explorer; but because of the event's general utility, jQuery simulates it so that it can be used regardless of browser.
	
	`<input id="someelement">`
	
	`<input id="anotherelement">`
	
	`$( "#someelement" ).mouseenter(function() {`
	`    $( "#anotherelement" ).toggle();`
	`});`

mouseleave	Binds an event handler to be fired when the mouse leaves an element, or triggers that handler on an element. This JavaScript event is proprietary to Internet Explorer, but because of the event's general utility, jQuery simulates it so that it can be used regardless of browser.
	
	`<input id="someelement">`
	
	`<input id="anotherelement">`
	
	`$( "#someelement" ).mouseenter(function() {`
	`    $( "#anotherelement" ).toggle();`
	`});`

mousemove	Binds an event handler to the mousemove JavaScript event, or triggers that event on an element. This event is sent to an element when the mouse pointer moves inside the element.
	
	`<input id="someelement">`
	
	`<input id="anotherelement">`
	
	`$( "#someelement" ).mousemove(function() {`
	`    var msg = "Handler for .mousemove() called at ";`
	`    msg += event.pageX + ", " + event.pageY;`
	`    $( "#anotherelement" ).append("<div>" + msg + "</div>");`
	`});`

EVENT	DESCRIPTION

mouseout	Binds an event handler to the `mouseout` JavaScript event, or triggers that event on an element. This event is sent to an element when the mouse pointer leaves the element.
	
	`<input id="someelement">`
	
	`<input id="anotherelement">`
	
	`$( "#someelement" ).mouseout(function() {`
	`    $( "#anotherelement" ).toggle();`
	`});`

mouseover	Binds an event handler to the `mouseover` JavaScript event, or triggers that event on an element. This event is sent to an element when the mouse pointer enters the element.
	
	`<input id="someelement">`
	
	`<input id="anotherelement">`
	
	`$( "#someelement" ).mouseover(function() {`
	`    $( "#anotherelement" ).toggle();`
	`});`

mouseup	Binds an event handler to the `mouseup` JavaScript event, or triggers that event on an element. This event is sent to an element when the mouse pointer is over the element, and the mouse button is released.
	
	`<input id="someelement">`
	
	`<input id="anotherelement">`
	
	`$( "#someelement" ).mouseup(function() {`
	`    $( "#anotherelement" ).toggle();`
	`});`

ready	This event is executed when the DOM is fully loaded. It is fired when the DOM has been loaded but it doesn't wait for all the scripts and images to download, so there may be some conflict between using large scripts and `ready` functions. It is one of the most commonly used jQuery functions, and it can only be applied to the document element. This enables you to reference the `ready` function in multiple ways, as shown in the following examples. Each line is calling the same function as soon as the `ready` event is fired.
	
	`$( document ).ready( handler )`
	
	`$().ready( handler )`
	
	`$( handler )`

continues

TABLE 14-6 *(continued)*

EVENT	DESCRIPTION

submit	Binds an event handler to the `submit` JavaScript event, or triggers that event on an element. This event is sent to an element when the user is attempting to submit a form, and it can only be attached to a `form` element. The event handler function is called before the actual submission, so the form submission can be handled by calling the `preventDefault` method on the event.
	
	`<form id="thisForm" action="somePage.aspx">`
	
	   `<input id="someelement">`
	
	   `<input id="anotherelement">`
	
	`</form>`
	
	`$( "#thisForm" ).submit(function( event ) {`
	
	  `$( "#anotherelement" ).toggle();`
	
	  `Event.preventDefault();`
	
	`});`

The `ready` method is so important because of how jQuery links the code and the user interface, especially when using the unobtrusive approach. The expectation from this approach is that any relating of code and display would only happen in the code, meaning any time you care about a change of state in a DOM element, you need to map the relationship in code. Therefore, the most frequently used concept in jQuery is the capability to select an element; otherwise, how would you be able to instruct it to manage some specific event?

As you can see, there are many different interactions that you can work with on the client side to capture input, whether it be direct, such as clicking a button or a key, or indirect, such as through mouse movement. You can then create jQuery and JavaScript functions to respond to those interactions as needed.

In this Try It Out, you put together various selectors, events, and display changes to add interactivity to your sample application.

TRY IT OUT Adding jQuery to Your Application

In this exercise you use jQuery to enhance the user experience of interacting with your sample application.

1. Ensure that Visual Studio is running and your RentMyWrox solution is open. Open the `MainPageManagement.js` file that you created in the last activity.

2. Add the following functions:

```
function fadeOutShoppingCartSummary() {
    $("#shoppingcartsummary").fadeOut(250);
}
```

```
function fadeInShoppingCartSummary() {
    $("#shoppingcartsummary").fadeIn(1000);
}
```

3. Open the `Views\Item\Details.cshtml` page. In the `AjaxOptions` object within the `"Add to Cart"` `Ajax.ActionLink`, add the following properties. It should look like Figure 14-11 when completed. Ensure that you add a comma at the end of the property that appears before the ones you are adding.

```
OnBegin = "fadeOutShoppingCartSummary",
OnSuccess = "fadeInShoppingCartSummary"
```

```
23          @if (Model.IsAvailable)
24          {
25              @Ajax.ActionLink("Add to Cart",
26              "AddToCart",
27              "ShoppingCart",
28              new { @Model.Id },
29              new AjaxOptions
30              {
31                  UpdateTargetId = "shoppingcartsummary",
32                  InsertionMode = InsertionMode.Replace,
33                  HttpMethod = "GET",
34                  OnBegin = "fadeOutShoppingCartSummary",
35                  OnSuccess = "fadeInShoppingCartSummary"
36              },
37              new { @class = "inlinelink" })
38          }
```

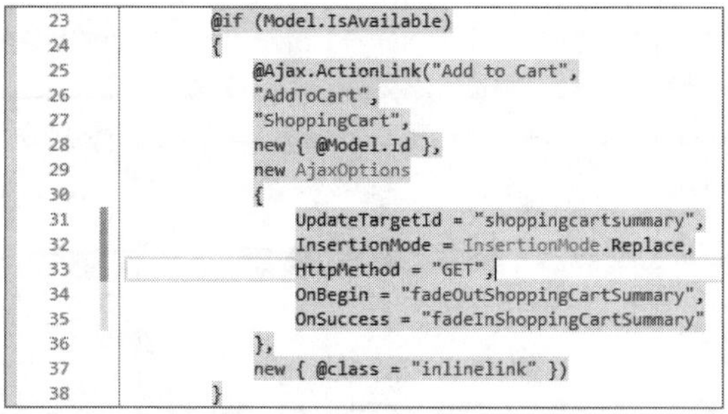

FIGURE 14-11: Updated Ajax.ActionLink

4. Add the following code at the bottom of the page:

```
@section Scripts {
    <script>
        var isLarge = false;

        $(".textwrap").click(
            function () {
                if (!isLarge) {
                    isLarge = true;
                    $(this).css('height', '500');
                    $(this).attr("title", "Click to shrink");
                }
                else {
                    isLarge = false;
                    $(this).css('height', '150');
                    $(this).attr("title", "Click to expand");
                }
            });
    </script>
}
```

5. Open the `View\Items\Index.cshtml` page. Update the `AjaxOptions` with the same changes that you made to the `Details.cshtml` page as shown here:

```
OnBegin = "fadeOutShoppingCartSummary",
OnSuccess = "fadeInShoppingCartSummary"
```

6. Add the class `"listitem"` to the `<div>` element that is within the `foreach` loop.

7. As shown in Figure 14-12, add the following at the bottom of the page:

```
@section Scripts {
    <script>
        $(".listitem").hover(
        function () {
            $(this).css('background-color', '#F8B6C9');
        }, function () {
            $(this).css('background-color', 'white');
        });
    </script>
}
```

```
44    <div class="listitem">
45        <div class="listtitle"><span class="productname">@item.Name</span><span class="listprice">@item.Cost.ToString("C")</span></div>
46        <p>
47            @if (item.Description.Length > 250)
48            { <span>@item.Description.Substring(0, 250)...</span> }
49            else { @item.Description }
50            @Html.ActionLink("Full details", "Details", new { @item.Id }, new { @class = "inlinelink" })
51            @Ajax.ActionLink("Add to Cart",
52                "AddToCart",
53                "ShoppingCart",
54                new { @item.Id },
55                new AjaxOptions
56                {
57                    UpdateTargetId = "shoppingcartsummary",
58                    InsertionMode = InsertionMode.Replace,
59                    HttpMethod = "GET",
60                    OnBegin = "fadeOutShoppingCartSummary",
61                    OnSuccess = "fadeInShoppingCartSummary"
62                },
63                new { @class = "inlinelink" })
64        </p>
65    </div>
66    }
67
68    @section Scripts {
69    <script>
70        $(".listitem").hover(
71        function () {
72            $(this).css('background-color', '#F8B6C9');
73        }, function () {
74            $(this).css('background-color', 'white');
75        });
76    </script>
```

FIGURE 14-12: Updating the Index page

8. Run the application and go to the home page. Mouse over items in the list and note how the background changes.

9. Add an item to the cart and note how the shopping cart area fades out and then fades back in with the new values.

10. Go into the details page of an item to which you have added a picture. Click the picture to see how it grows, and note how clicking on it again shrinks it back to the original size.

How It Works

In this activity you made several simple jQuery changes that improve the user's interaction with your sample application. One of the first items that you added is shown here:

```
function fadeOutShoppingCartSummary() {
    $("#shoppingcartsummary").fadeOut(250);
}
```

When this function is called, it runs a selector for an element with the `id` of `"shoppingcartsummary"` and then performs a `fadeout` method on it with a duration of .25 seconds. The other method makes the same selection but performs the opposite fading, a `fadein`, to change the element from transparent back to visible.

These new methods were hooked into the UI by the changes you made to the link that adds an item to the cart. The new `AjaxOption` that you updated is shown here:

```
new AjaxOptions
{
    UpdateTargetId = "shoppingcartsummary",
    InsertionMode = InsertionMode.Replace,
    HttpMethod = "GET",
    OnBegin = "fadeOutShoppingCartSummary",
    OnSuccess = "fadeInShoppingCartSummary"
}
```

The two methods that you created are linked by setting two different properties. The `OnBegin` property on the `AjaxOptions` object takes a string value that corresponds to the name of a JavaScript function that is run when that event is fired. The two that you wired up are `OnBegin` and `OnSuccess`. The `OnBegin` event is fired when the `Request` object is created but before it is sent to the server. The `OnSuccess` event is fired when the call is completed successfully. Two other events can be managed: `OnFailure` and `OnComplete` are fired if an exception is thrown during the AJAX call and when the entire experience is completed (even after `OnSuccess` or `OnFailure`), respectively.

The next set of jQuery that you added was an event handler for a `click` event. The selector that you chose used a class selector that looked for a class of `"textwrap"`. The selector is shown here:

```
$(".textwrap").click(...
```

The work going on in the method is dictated by the value of a separate JavaScript variable that is used to indicate whether the item selected is expanded. This variable was defined as `var isLarge = false`. Definition is different in JavaScript than it is in C# or VB.NET because JavaScript is not a type-safe language—the `var` represents a variant, or simply a container that could be of any type.

The function evaluates the value in the `isLarge` variable and branches based on the result. It then toggles `IsLarge` to the updated value. The function then updates the style height to either the large or the small height, and updates the `title` attribute, or value shown on hover, as necessary based on the image's size. The two lines of code are shown here:

```
$(this).css('height', '150');
$(this).attr("title", "Click to expand");
```

One thing to consider is the use of the `$(this)`, which, when used within a selector, refers to the item that is causing the event to be fired. Thus, when you use a selector that results in multiple items being wired up, it demonstrates how the event being called is specific to the individual item being affected, rather than the entire range of items matching that particular selector.

The two items that were run on the selected item are the `css` and `attr` functions. The `css` function overwrites a particular variable that is available for CSS styling—in this case, the `height` key. The `attr` method enables you to override an attribute on the element—in this case, the `title` attribute.

You added the last set of jQuery to use the `hover` event to change the background of an item. This could have been done just as easily in CSS, as done with the items in the left menu, but for many developers it's easy to understand, find, and maintain the simple jQuery code that was added, rather than manipulate complex CSS.

The capability to use jQuery to manage complex styling is an important consideration. One of the primary reasons to do this in jQuery instead is because it enables you to debug jQuery processing, whereas you can't do that in CSS.

DEBUGGING jQUERY

Debugging in jQuery is a little different from any of the debugging that you have done so far. It is different because it is pure client-side debugging, whereas the other debugging you have done has been all server-side. Even when you are debugging within a view, you are still debugging processing that is being done on the server. When you are debugging jQuery, you are debugging on the client, in the browser. This results in a completely different experience.

There are two different approaches to client-side debugging: One uses debugging tools in Visual Studio, whereas the other uses debugging tools that are part of the browser. In the next Try It Out, you practice each of these techniques for debugging JavaScript and jQuery code.

TRY IT OUT   Debugging JavaScript Code

In this exercise you configure your local browser to support debugging of your local JavaScript code. You also practice debugging the jQuery code that you already wrote. After that, you have the opportunity to add custom debugging code to the jQuery functions and see how that helps to support your debugging efforts. The following directions assume that you are using Internet Explorer for debugging.

1. Ensure that Visual Studio is running and your RentMyWrox solution is open. Open Microsoft Internet Explorer and ensure that it is set up to debug. In IE, select Tools ⇨ Internet Options ⇨ Advanced. Under the Browsing section, find Disable Script Debugging (Internet Explorer) and ensure that it is unchecked, as shown in Figure 14-13. Click OK or Apply when you are done.

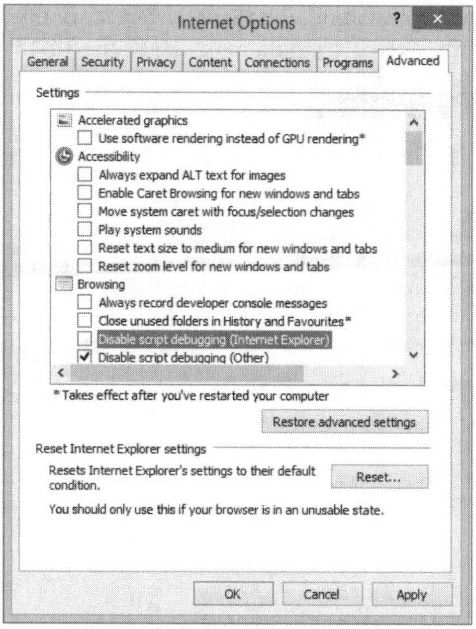

FIGURE 14-13: Enabling debugging in Internet Explorer

2. Stop debugging the application. Open the `MainPageManagement.js` file that you created earlier in the chapter. Add breakpoints to each of the named functions, as shown in Figure 14-14.

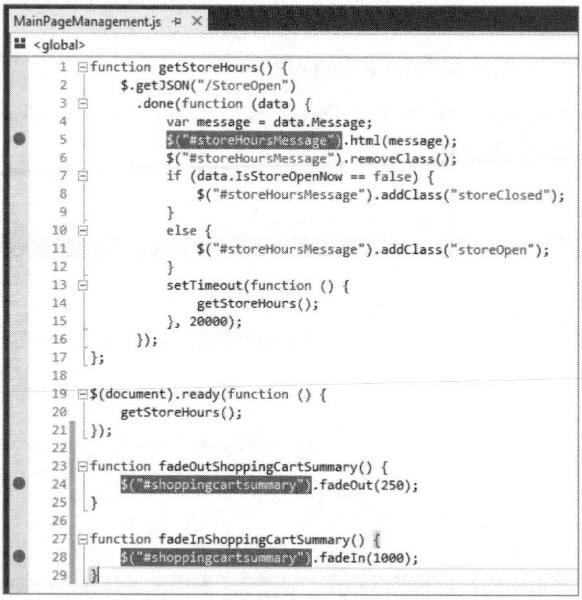

FIGURE 14-14: Adding breakpoints in jQuery/JavaScript

3. Run the application, noting how it stops at the first breakpoint and how the debugger is able to show the JSON value that was downloaded from the server. It should look like Figure 14-15.

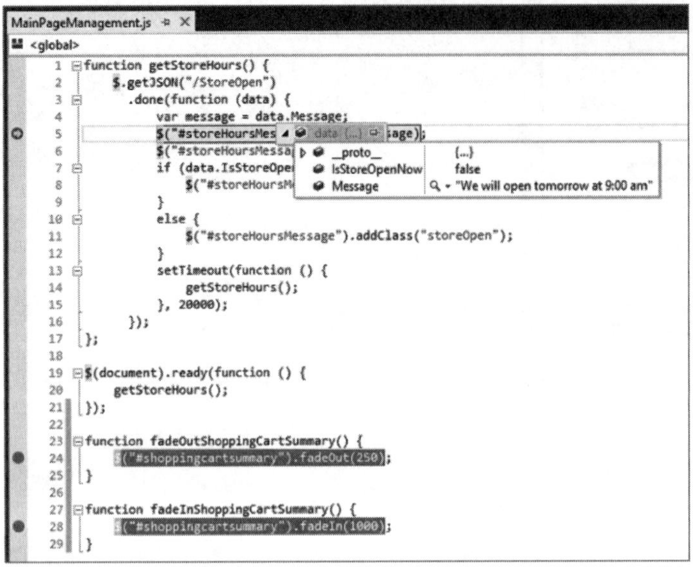

FIGURE 14-15: Hitting a breakpoint in JavaScript

4. Continue the application past the breakpoint and click the link to add an item. You should see the debugger stop at your breakpoint in the fadeOutShoppingCartSummary method. Close the browser and stop debugging the application.

5. Restart the application by using Ctrl+F5, or start without debugging.

6. Go to the home page in Internet Explorer and access the F12 Developer tools. From the Debugger tab, find the hover function at the bottom of the page.

7. Add a breakpoint as shown in Figure 14-16.

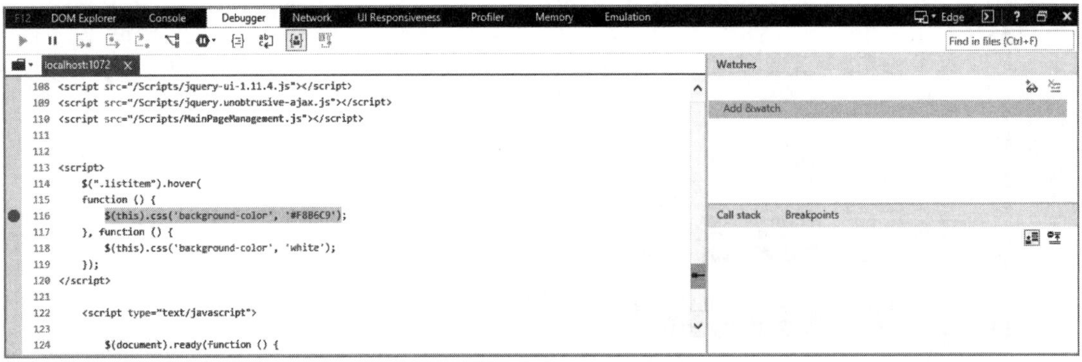

FIGURE 14-16: Setting a breakpoint in the browser tools

8.   Mouse over an item in the list. You should see the breakpoint hit, as shown in Figure 14-17.

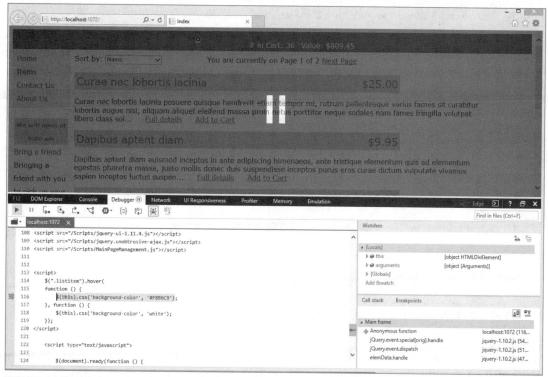

FIGURE 14-17: Hitting a breakpoint in the browser tools

9.   Expand the Watches window in the top right-hand corner of the Browser tools. Scroll down through the items in the window to get an idea of the information that is available to you through these tools.

10.   Close the browser and stop running the application.

How It Works

When JavaScript tools and jQuery first came out it was difficult to debug through the code. However, as JavaScript and jQuery became increasingly prevalent, development tools such as Visual Studio started to add more support for debugging client-side code. In Visual Studio 2015, the integration is complete. Debugging JavaScript and jQuery code in Visual Studio is virtually the same as debugging your C# code. You can set breakpoints, and when the code is stopped you can evaluate the values of variables and selections as desired, just as you can with C# and VB.NET code.

The biggest difference is the additional capability to debug in the browser. You have already seen how the F12 Browser tools enable you to get information about the HTML elements, including styling and layout affects. Another piece of functionality that is supported is the capability to debug through JavaScript. As you saw, when you hit a breakpoint, you have visibility into many different items. If you have selected an element, you can see everything about that element. You can see the values of its attributes, and you can access its value, even child elements. You can then examine those child elements and their attributes and values, including children, and so forth.

As you work with the F12 debugger, you will notice a few things. First, you cannot run the application in debug mode and debug within Internet Explorer. If you try to debug in the browser you will get an error, as shown at the bottom of Figure 14-18.

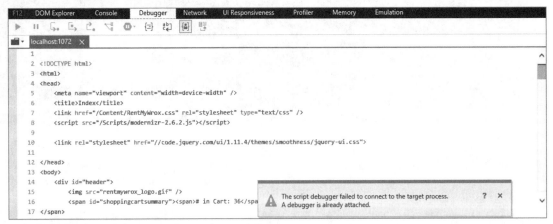

FIGURE 14-18: Error in browser when trying to debug

The easiest way to debug in the browser and still run the application locally is through the approach that you used, running the application but without debugging. You can do this by selecting Ctrl+F5 or the upper menu, using Debug ➪ Start Without Debugging. These approaches start the application without attaching the debugger. This enables the browser debugger to interact with the process.

Debugging is important when working with any programming language, and especially when you are just starting to work with it. This is particularly true when working with jQuery and JavaScript, simply because it is different from most of the other languages. This difference can cause you to make simple errors, such as incorrect selectors (using the hashtag when you should have used the period) or not setting up the functions correctly so that they are never run. Debugging will help you gather information about what you may be doing wrong.

PRACTICAL TIPS ON jQUERY

Working in jQuery can be an interesting experience for developers who are used to working in C# or VB.NET environments. The difference in approaches can be startling, especially the lack of type-safe variables and working with the results from a selector as opposed to a known, named variable. Following is a short list of tips that will help you when working with jQuery in your own applications:

➤ Practice your jQuery, especially something that you will be working with in the future. Getting the selectors correct, especially with more complex scenarios, can take some time to get right—especially because many of the differences are a single character.

➤ Don't be afraid to use multiple approaches to help you when debugging your client code. You may often be able to use the debugger when running locally, but at other times you may have to use other approaches.

➤ Use the jQuery.org website as a resource for understanding how to use jQuery. It contains full documentation about the various functions as well as multiple source code examples.

➤ Search out other jQuery learning tools. It has become so popular across the Internet that many different sites provide interesting and useful information about implementing jQuery in your web application.

SUMMARY

jQuery has quietly become the most frequently used client-side framework. It is an open-source framework that offers abstraction over JavaScript, or ECMAScript, which is available in nearly all client-side web browsers, be they desktop or mobile devices. Because jQuery is a JavaScript abstraction, it is "linked" to a web page as is a JavaScript file, so you don't need to do anything complicated to make it work with your application, just a simple tag.

Linking in jQuery is straightforward, as is the linking in of any custom scripts that you have written to support your application. However, there is a limit to the number of connections that a browser supports to a single server, so adding multiple images and script files can actually slow down the loading of your page because opening and closing the connection can be an expensive operation. ASP.NET provides a capability to help you: bundles.

Bundles are a built-in capacity for combining different JavaScript files into a single file. This enables you to create multiple scripts to support whatever work you are doing—even if it means creating a different script for each complicated function that needs to be performed. Using bundling, you can create a list of those files. Then, upon application startup, a single file with the contents from all the files in the list is used.

These files contain the code that does all the work, the jQuery code itself. There are two major approaches when using jQuery. The first uses a jQuery utility function. These functions enable you to step back from the DOM and take an approach to performing work on the DOM itself. These utilities also provide other special support, such as enumeration.

Whereas the utility approach enables you to work on the DOM from the outside, the other approach enables you to work on the DOM from inside, from within an HTML element. The difference between the two approaches is subtle; with the utility approach you reach into the HTML and change the value, whereas the selector approach allows you to select an element in the HTML, assign it as a variable, and then change one of its values. It enforces the selection of an item and the performance of work on that selected item.

There are many different things that you can do with this item once it is selected. You can change the value, the style, parts of the style—virtually anything related to the data within an element and the appearance of the element. You can add new elements, and move or delete existing elements. All of this is available through jQuery.

EXERCISES

1. Create the jQuery and HTML changes necessary to change the color of only this particular `<h1>` element when your mouse moves over the content of this specific `<p>` element:

    ```
    <h1>Title</h1>

    <p>Content</p>
    ```

2. What are some of the things that you need to take into account when you start considering adding bundling to your web application?

3. How do you add special jQuery code when using `Ajax.Helpers` in an ASP.NET MVC view?

▶ WHAT YOU LEARNED IN THIS CHAPTER

$	The $ is not a direct reference to the object itself but instead a factory method that, when used with a selector, returns one or more HTML elements that fit the criteria stated by the selector.
$.	The $. approach represents jQuery utility methods. It provides jQuery support by providing access to enumeration logic as well as other utility items such as type checking.
Bundles	Bundling is a feature in ASP.NET that makes it easy to combine or bundle multiple files into a single file. You can create CSS, JavaScript, and other bundles. Fewer files means fewer HTTP requests, and that can improve first page load performance. When creating bundles, a good convention to follow is to include "bundle" as a prefix in the bundle name. This prevents a possible routing conflict.
ECMAScript	A scripting language specification. The best-known implementation is JavaScript that is used for the scripting that happens within a web browser.
jQuery debugging	Visual Studio enables you to debug in JavaScript with a very similar experience to debugging your server-side code. You can set breakpoints, step through the code processing, and inspect the values of variables and other items as needed. You also have the capability to debug in the web browser, independently of Visual Studio. This enables you to debug even when you don't have local copies of the scripts, such as when linking to scripts hosted on other sites.
jQuery NuGet Package	This package copies all the necessary and most recent versions of the jQuery scripts into your scripts directory. If you add the scripts to your application using bundles, you can ensure that your code is using the most recently installed version of jQuery without having to make any changes other than copying in a new version of the scripts.
Open Source	A developmental model that promotes universal access and redistribution of an end product, generally software. The key aspect of open-source software is that the source code files are available for consumption and modification.
Unobtrusive	A general approach to the use of JavaScript in web pages. The key feature is supporting the separation of functionality from the user interface. jQuery supports an unobtrusive approach because it enables you to do all your linking of events or changes apart from the actual HTML. This in turn enables you to keep your HTML elements completely functionality free, other than providing a defining characteristic, such as a name, that enables the jQuery scripts to find the element.

Security in Your ASP.NET Website

WHAT YOU WILL LEARN IN THIS CHAPTER:

➤ The difference between authentication and authorization

➤ Implementing security in ASP.NET applications

➤ Security and the database

➤ How to secure your web application

➤ Adding roles into your security

➤ Using the user information

CODE DOWNLOADS FOR THIS CHAPTER:

The wrox.com code downloads for this chapter are found at www.wrox.com/go/
beginningaspnetforvisualstudio on the Download Code tab. The code is in the chapter 15
download and individually named according to the names throughout the chapter.

It seems like every week there is a news article about data breaches in online applications.
While your application does not have the same security needs as a major online company that
stores credit card numbers or banking information you do still have to enforce a certain level
of security to keep your users' information private. Also, because you care about your users as
individuals rather than simply as visitors, you need to have a way for them to uniquely identify
themselves. This is the responsibility of ASP.NET security.

Sometimes, not only do you care about who a user is, you also care about what that user can
do within your application. You can see this in your sample application—you created a place
where a special kind of user can add items and manage other information. Determining what
certain users can do, once you know who they are, is another area that is managed by ASP
.NET security.

Up until now you have separated some of the functionality so that you can easily control who can do what, in some cases even adding some unused information about a user. In this chapter, you will combine these considerations and implement security in your sample application, taking one of the last steps toward making it a usable system.

INTRODUCING SECURITY

Security is the concept of ensuring that only certain people can take certain actions. Consider, for example, a bank's security guard, who allows many different things to happen within the bank depending upon who is taking the actions. The guard would likely not even look twice if he saw the bank manager walk into the vault. Conversely, if someone in a clown mask walked into the vault, the guard would likely take some kind of action.

Your application will generally take the same kind of approach. It identifies who the user is and then evaluates what that user wants to do. In the previous example, the guard can identify the bank manager and understands that he is allowed to enter the vault. If, instead, the guard identifies someone entering the vault as the owner of the coffee cart outside the bank, that is likely to get more of a reaction, even if the guard recognizes the person. That's because although the person may be recognized, the act that he is trying to perform may not be expected or allowed.

Because your application is taking the same steps as the bank guard, several items are evaluated about the user. The first evaluation is determining "who are you?" The second evaluation is making that user "prove who you are." The third evaluation is a determination of what that user can do in the application based on who they are.

Identity: Who Are You?

The whole concept of security in the bank example is to ensure that only the appropriate person can take an action. If you apply that goal to your application, then the first thing you have to do is recognize someone who is interacting with your application as an identified user. This establishes the connection between your application and the person. You have almost certainly done this yourself on other websites, generally by going to a certain page on the site and "registering." This provided the initial introduction between the person visiting, you, and the site.

Your application needs to do the same. If you want an understanding of who the users are, then you have to provide a way for them to be introduced, a way for them to register with your site. This registration determines who they are in relationship to your site.

Authentication: How Can Users Prove Who They Are?

After visitors have been introduced to your site, you have an understanding of who and what they are. However, at some point users are going to leave your site, hopefully to return at another time. If you still care about who those users are when they next visit, and in conjunction with the introduction that they previously made, you need a way for them to prove that they are the same person who was registered earlier. It would be easy to do if they were at the bank: You could simply ask them for a picture ID and compare the name and picture to both the person holding the ID and to your records. If all the information seems correct, you let them proceed with their transaction.

Because it is important for visitors to prove that they are, indeed, a particular user, you have to provide them with a way to prove the relationship via your web application. Typically this would be through the use of a username and password that was configured during the introduction, or site registration. The more complex the combination of information, the more likely it is that the person who provides that same information is that identified user. The concept of verifying that visitors are who they say they are is called authentication—the user authenticates his or her identity.

Authorization: What Are You Allowed to Do?

In some cases, the actions that different users can take don't vary. If so, simple identification is all you need. However, your sample application has to make some determination about what the user can do. This determination is called authorization. This is why the bank guard would be suspicious of the coffee cart owner going into the bank vault. Although the guard has identified, or authenticated the cart owner, that person is not authorized to be in the bank vault.

Your application needs to make the same kind of determination. Is this authenticated user allowed to take a particular set of actions (mainly those that you have until now put into the Admin folder of your sample application)? If they are authorized to take the actions, then the system lets them proceed. If they are not allowed to take those actions, then the system stops them.

The most common way to determine authorization is to assign a specific role to a user and then determine whether that role is allowed to take an action. Different roles have different levels of authorization as needed. Users can have no roles or multiple roles, whatever is appropriate for ensuring that the application is secured correctly. You will be covering roles later in this chapter.

Logging in with ASP.NET

The most recent versions of ASP.NET Web Forms and MVC have made some significant changes in terms of how identity and security are managed. Web Forms and MVC used to take different approaches, but this has been changed and now both approaches use the same fundamental system. This is important because it means that a user can log into a Web Forms login page yet use that same authentication against MVC routes and views. This was not the case previously.

When working with an ASP.NET scaffold-created project, the initial configuration and management is all done within the `Startup.Auth.cs` file in the `App_Start` directory. This page is shown in Figure 15-1.

The first three lines from this method show some features of the ASP.NET login management process:

```
app.CreatePerOwinContext(ApplicationDbContext.Create);
app.CreatePerOwinContext<ApplicationUserManager>(
    ApplicationUserManager.Create);
app.CreatePerOwinContext<ApplicationSignInManager>(
    ApplicationSignInManager.Create);
```

```
public void ConfigureAuth(IAppBuilder app)
{
    // Configure the db context, user manager and signin manager to use a single instance per request
    app.CreatePerOwinContext(ApplicationDbContext.Create);
    app.CreatePerOwinContext<ApplicationUserManager>(ApplicationUserManager.Create);
    app.CreatePerOwinContext<ApplicationSignInManager>(ApplicationSignInManager.Create);

    // Enable the application to use a cookie to store information for the signed in user
    // and to use a cookie to temporarily store information about a user logging in with a third party login provider
    // Configure the sign in cookie
    app.UseCookieAuthentication(new CookieAuthenticationOptions
    {
        AuthenticationType = DefaultAuthenticationTypes.ApplicationCookie,
        LoginPath = new PathString("/Account/Login"),
        Provider = new CookieAuthenticationProvider
        {
            OnValidateIdentity = SecurityStampValidator.OnValidateIdentity<ApplicationUserManager, ApplicationUser>(
                validateInterval: TimeSpan.FromMinutes(30),
                regenerateIdentity: (manager, user) => user.GenerateUserIdentityAsync(manager))
        }
    });
    // Use a cookie to temporarily store information about a user logging in with a third party login provider
    app.UseExternalSignInCookie(DefaultAuthenticationTypes.ExternalCookie);

    // Enables the application to temporarily store user information when they are verifying the second factor in the two-factor authentication process.
    app.UseTwoFactorSignInCookie(DefaultAuthenticationTypes.TwoFactorCookie, TimeSpan.FromMinutes(5));

    // Enables the application to remember the second login verification factor such as phone or email.
    // Once you check this option, your second step of verification during the login process will be remembered on the device where you logged in from.
    // This is similar to the RememberMe option when you log in.
    app.UseTwoFactorRememberBrowserCookie(DefaultAuthenticationTypes.TwoFactorRememberBrowserCookie);
```

FIGURE 15-1: Startup_Auth page

Here, three items are being created and added to the Owin context. Think of the Owin context as being the memory space that manages the running application, so loading an item into the Owin context means you are getting that item ready to be accessed—in this case to support the authentication process.

OWIN

OWIN, or Open Web Interface for .NET, defines a standard interface between .NET web servers and web applications. The goal of the OWIN interface is to add a layer of abstraction between the web server and the application. The purpose of this approach is to end the requirement that ASP.NET applications always have to be run in Microsoft IIS, enabling them instead to be executable in other OWIN containers, including Windows Services. Using OWIN you can even run ASP.NET applications on other operating systems, such as Linux or iOS.

Three different items are being added to the context: the `ApplicationDbContext`, the `ApplicationUserManager`, and the `ApplicationSigninManager`. Each of these classes manages a part of the authentication process. The `ApplicationDbContext` is the connection to the database. This is especially interesting because it shows how the information necessary for authentication is stored in the database using the Entity Framework's Code First approach, just like the rest of your database application.

The second class that had its `Create` method called and then added to the Owin context was the `ApplicationUserManager`. This class handles the creation and management of the user. It contains many different useful methods, including, but not limited to, `Create`, `Find`, `ChangePassword`, `Update`, and `VerifyPassword`—all methods that are necessary when working with users. The `ApplicationUserManager` uses the `ApplicationDbContext` to access the database in order to work with the user information.

The last item added to the Owin context was the `ApplicationSigninManager`. As you can probably tell by the name, this object handles the sign-in, or login, process. It does not have a lot of different methods and properties to it; the main thing it does is evaluate the passed-in information. The method signature that you will be using is shown here:

```
public SignInStatus PasswordSignIn(string userName, string password,
    bool isPersistent, bool shouldLockout);
```

As you can see, four different values are passed into the evaluation method. The first two are the username and password entered by the user. The third value, `isPersistent`, tells the framework whether or not the response sent to the user will set a cookie that remembers the username that was entered. The last value, `shouldLockout`, tells the framework whether it should lock the account if there is a matching username in the system but the password is incorrect.

The item returned from this method is a `SignInStatus` enum. Table 15-1 describes the different enum values.

TABLE 15-1: SignInStatus Values

VALUE	DESCRIPTION
Success	The username and password that were passed in matches the information stored for the user. The user has been authenticated.
LockedOut	The account that matches the username passed in has been locked out. The account could have been previously locked out or could be locked out if the results of this call caused it, i.e., the `shouldLockout` value is true. If the account is locked then a user cannot login for a defined period of time.
RequiresVerification	The account that matches the username requires validation. This is based on a configuration value that is set on the `ApplicationUserManager`. The user is recognized but not authenticated. The user will not be able to log into the application until he or she is verified.
Failure	This value is returned when the system is not able to log in the user. This could be because the username doesn't match an account or the password does not match the expected value for the account that matches the passed-in username. The framework does not differentiate between these two because it is not good practice to inform a possible hacker that the entered username is correct, which provides an advantage to someone trying to break into the system.

You may be wondering how everything is being managed when you only get an enum value back from a login. This is all hidden from you by the Identity framework, but the framework takes care of everything. It does this by setting an authentication cookie. The setup for this cookie is also done in the `Startup_Auth` file. The area that handles this configuration is shown here:

```
// Enable the application to use a cookie
// to store information for the signed in user
// and to use a cookie to temporarily store information
// about a user logging in with a third party login provider
// Configure the sign in cookie
app.UseCookieAuthentication(new CookieAuthenticationOptions
{
    AuthenticationType = DefaultAuthenticationTypes.ApplicationCookie,
    LoginPath = new PathString("/Account/Login"),
    Provider = new CookieAuthenticationProvider
    {
        OnValidateIdentity = SecurityStampValidator
            .OnValidateIdentity<ApplicationUserManager, ApplicationUser>
            ( validateInterval: TimeSpan.FromMinutes(30),
              regenerateIdentity: (manager, user) =>
                  user.GenerateUserIdentityAsync(manager))
    }
});
```

The system uses a cookie to allow the browser to send token-based information back and forth between the server and the client so that users do not have to re-enter login credentials on every call. When the framework processes a successful login attempt, the next step is to add a cookie to the `Response` object. This cookie is then available on each subsequent call.

The ASP.NET Identity framework also supports third-party managed logins. The out-of-the-box experience supports logins from Google, Twitter, Microsoft, and Facebook. In these cases, you set up a relationship between your application and the authentication provider. Users then log into the provider, using their familiar and trusted credentials, and the provider sends a token with the user that the Identity framework knows it can trust. The Identity framework understands that the token is valid because of the relationship you set up between your application and the provider. Once you have set up the relationship in the provider's website, they provide the information (such as the client id and client secret) that you need to develop the trusting relationship on your side. The following example shows how to set up one of these relationships:

```
app.UseMicrosoftAccountAuthentication(
    clientId: "",
    clientSecret: "");
```

This relationship is a trust relationship. Your user trusts the third-party provider to maintain his or her authentication information. You trust the third-party provider to authenticate the user properly. The third-party provider trusts you with the information that the user is known to them. This circle of trust enables all parties to provide the appropriate level of service to their customers. The relationship is shown in Figure 15-2.

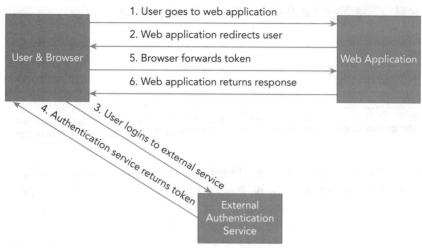

FIGURE 15-2: Interaction with third-party authorizer

While a lot of the authentication functionality is provided by the ASP.NET Identity framework, it requires a certain amount of configuration. When you use the project scaffolding to create the project, as you did, many of those configuration items are set to a default value, which may or may not be the values that you need to support your requirements. The next section covers the configuration of security in ASP.NET.

Configuring Your Web Application for Security

Configuring your web application requires some decisions. The easiest is identifying the database server in which you are going to save the user information. Some of the more difficult decisions are related to your security expectations, especially the rules that you are going to put into place for username and passwords, as you have control over those requirements and will be able to evaluate the trade-off between strong security and user convenience.

In this Try It Out, you set up your sample application to enable users to register with and log into the site.

Adding Registration Capability

Changing your sample application so that it supports user account management require that you update some of the files that were copied in during project creation.

1. Ensure that Visual Studio is running and you have the RentMyWrox application open.

2. Open your `web.config` page. Look for the section labeled `connection strings` (see Figure 15-3). Copy the `connectionString` value from the `RentMyWroxContext` element to the `DefaultConnection` value.

FIGURE 15-3: Current Web.Config file

3. Open the `Site.Master` file in your root directory. Find the `head` section and remove the "My ASP .NET Application" section from the title element. Add the following lines within the `head` section (see Figure 15-4):

```
<link href="~/Content/RentMyWrox.css" rel="stylesheet" type="text/css" />
<script src="/bundles/common"></script>
```

```
4  <head runat="server">
5      <meta charset="utf-8" />
6      <meta name="viewport" content="width=device-width, initial-scale=1.0" />
7      <title><%: Page.Title %></title>
8      <asp:PlaceHolder runat="server">
9          <%: Scripts.Render("~/bundles/modernizr") %>
10     </asp:PlaceHolder>
11     <webopt:bundlereference runat="server" path="~/Content/css" />
12     <link href="~/favicon.ico" rel="shortcut icon" type="image/x-icon" />
13     <link href="~/Content/RentMyWrox.css" rel="stylesheet" type="text/css" />
14     <script src="/bundles/common"></script>
15 </head>
```

FIGURE 15-4: Updated head section of the Master page

4. Find the `ScriptManager` server control and the `ContentPlaceHolder` with the `Id` of `MainContent`. Delete everything in between them.

5. Below the closing tag for the `ContentPlaceHolder`, delete everything to the closing form element. It should look like Figure 15-5 when you are done.

6. Add the following code between the `ScriptManager` control and the `ContentPlaceHolder`:

```
<div id="header">
    <img src="rentmywrox_logo.gif" />
</div>
<div id="nav">
    <div id="LeftNavigation" style="height:400px;">
        <ul class="level1">
            <li><a href="/" class="level1">Home</a></li>
            <li><a href="/" class="level1">Items</a></li>
            <li><a href="/Contact" class="level1">Contact Us</a></li>
            <li><a href="/About" class="level1">About Us</a></li>
        </ul>
        <div id="storeHoursMessage"></div>
    </div>
</div>
<div id="section">
```

```
16 ⊟<body>
17 ⊟    <form runat="server">
18 ⊟        <asp:ScriptManager runat="server">
19 ⊟            <Scripts>
20                  <%--To learn more about bundling scripts in ScriptManager see http://go.microsoft.com/fwlink/?LinkID=301884 --%>
21                  <%--Framework Scripts--%>
22                  <asp:ScriptReference Name="MsAjaxBundle" />
23                  <asp:ScriptReference Name="jquery" />
24                  <asp:ScriptReference Name="bootstrap" />
25                  <asp:ScriptReference Name="respond" />
26                  <asp:ScriptReference Name="WebForms.js" Assembly="System.Web" Path="~/Scripts/WebForms/WebForms.js" />
27                  <asp:ScriptReference Name="WebUIValidation.js" Assembly="System.Web" Path="~/Scripts/WebForms/WebUIValidation.js" />
28                  <asp:ScriptReference Name="MenuStandards.js" Assembly="System.Web" Path="~/Scripts/WebForms/MenuStandards.js" />
29                  <asp:ScriptReference Name="GridView.js" Assembly="System.Web" Path="~/Scripts/WebForms/GridView.js" />
30                  <asp:ScriptReference Name="DetailsView.js" Assembly="System.Web" Path="~/Scripts/WebForms/DetailsView.js" />
31                  <asp:ScriptReference Name="TreeView.js" Assembly="System.Web" Path="~/Scripts/WebForms/TreeView.js" />
32                  <asp:ScriptReference Name="WebParts.js" Assembly="System.Web" Path="~/Scripts/WebForms/WebParts.js" />
33                  <asp:ScriptReference Name="Focus.js" Assembly="System.Web" Path="~/Scripts/WebForms/Focus.js" />
34                  <asp:ScriptReference Name="WebFormsBundle" />
35                  <%--Site Scripts--%>
36              </Scripts>
37          </asp:ScriptManager>
38          <asp:ContentPlaceHolder ID="MainContent" runat="server">
39          </asp:ContentPlaceHolder>
40      </form>
41 </body>
```

FIGURE 15-5: Post-deleted section of the Master page

7. Add a closing `</div>` tag after the `ContentPlaceHolder`.

8. Open the `Views\Shared\_ShoppingCartSummary.cshtml` page. Add the following code into the area that's displayed when there is information in the shopping cart. When you are done it should look like Figure 15-6.

```
<a class="checkout" href="\shoppingcart\checkout">Check Out</a>
```

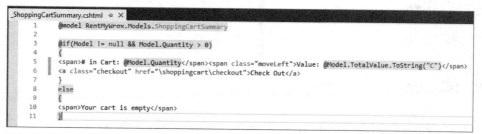

```
_ShoppingCartSummary.cshtml + X
 1   @model RentMyWrox.Models.ShoppingCartSummary
 2
 3   @if(Model != null && Model.Quantity > 0)
 4   {
 5   <span># in Cart: @Model.Quantity</span><span class="moveLeft">Value: @Model.TotalValue.ToString("C")</span>
 6   <a class="checkout" href="\shoppingcart\checkout">Check Out</a>
 7   }
 8   else
 9   {
10   <span>Your cart is empty</span>
11   }
```

FIGURE 15-6: New Shopping cart summary partial view

9. Open the `Content\RentMyWrox.css` file and add the following style:

```css
.checkout {
    margin-left: 15px;
    color:white;
    font-size: small;
}
```

10. Open `ShoppingCartController.cs` and add a new method:

```
[Authorize]
[HttpGet]
```

```
public ActionResult Checkout()
{
    using (RentMyWroxContext context = new RentMyWroxContext())
    {
        return null;
    }
}
```

11. Open the Server Explorer window (View ➪ Server Explorer). In the Data Connections section, expand your RentMyWrox connection, and expand the Tables section. It should look like Figure 15-7.

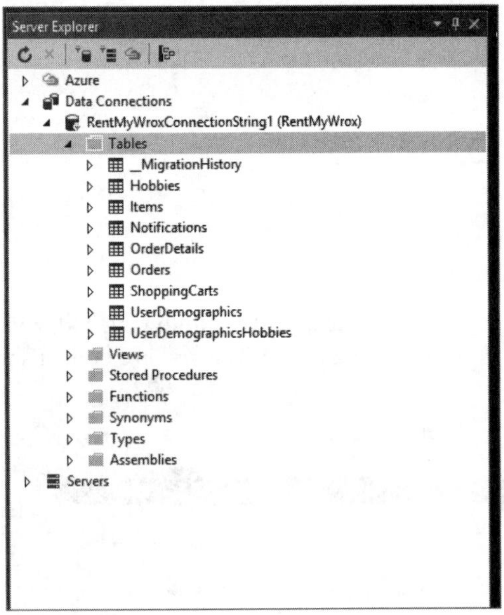

FIGURE 15-7: Initial tables in database

12. Run the application. If there's nothing in the shopping cart, add an item so you can see the Check Out link. Then click the link. You should be transferred to a login screen (see Figure 15-8).

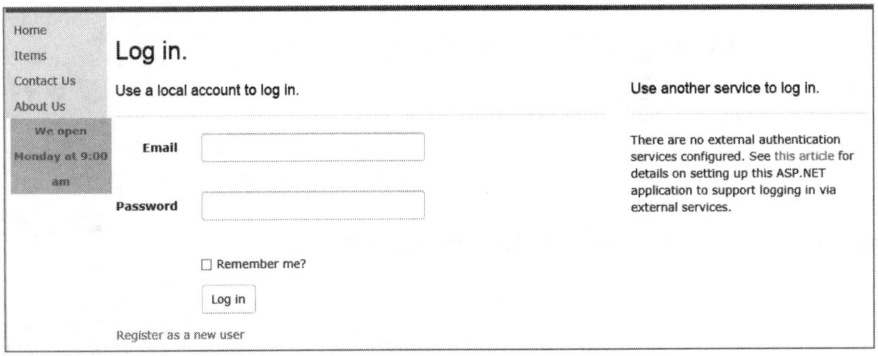

FIGURE 15-8: Login page

13. Click the Register as a New User link on the bottom of the page. You will be taken to a Register page, as shown in Figure 15-9.

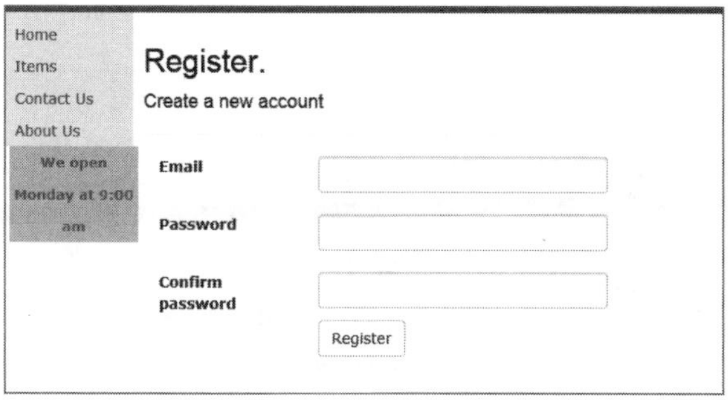

FIGURE 15-9: Register page

14. Enter an e-mail address, such as admin@rentmywrox.com, and a simple password, such as "password," in the two password boxes. Clicking the Register button will display the message shown in Figure 15-10.

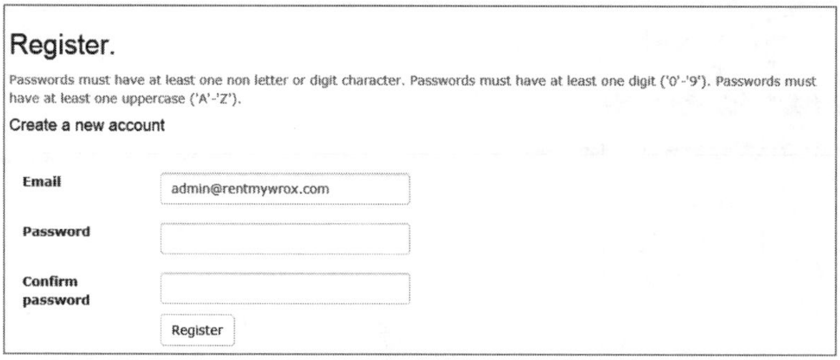

FIGURE 15-10: Validation failure page

15. Enter a password that meets the required criteria, such as "Password1!" and click Register.

16. You should get a blank page with the URL of "ShoppingCart\Checkout," as shown in Figure 15-11.

17. Go back to Server Explorer and expand the Tables section (see Figure 15-12).

How It Works

In many ways, the actions that you just took were more about editing already existing security measures, which you created at the beginning of the project, than implementing them. Before this could all work properly, however, you had to make the appropriate changes so that the registration pieces created during project creation would visually fit into the rest of the application. If you didn't make the changes to the Site.Master file, all the created registration files would look out of place.

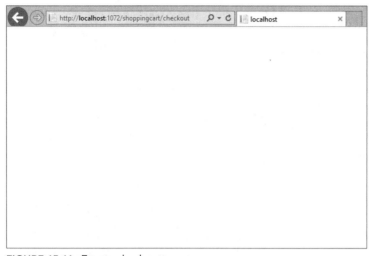

FIGURE 15-11: Empty checkout page

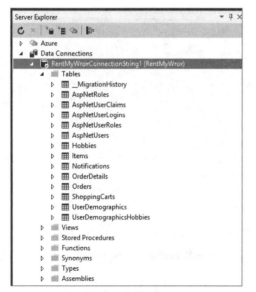

FIGURE 15-12: Updated database

After updating the master page so that the account management pages look more like the site, you next created an additional link on the shopping cart section that takes users to the checkout process. You then created a simple Checkout method on the ShoppingCartController page. This method is really just a stub at this point because it doesn't do anything within the method itself. However, you added an attribute to this action (that you'll learn more about later) that tied it to the entire Identity system.

The Identity system was created during creation of your project. At that time you could make an authentication selection, and you chose Individual User Account. When selecting that approach, the project scaffolding is created with several different sets of code. The first is the various set of models that are found in the `IdentityModels` file within the Models directory. These models are the same regardless of whether you use an MVC or Web Form project. Within this file are two different classes within the `Models` namespace: `ApplicationUser` and `ApplicationDbContext`. Each of these classes inherits other classes, with `ApplicationUser` inheriting from `IdentityUser`, and `ApplicationDbContext` inheriting from `IdentityDbContext`.

That these classes inherit from base classes is important, as it enables you to customize them as desired. The `ApplicationUser`, for example, does not have any additional properties other than those provided by the `IdentityUser`. These default properties are listed in Table 15-2.

TABLE 15-2: IdentityUser Properties

PROPERTY	TYPE	DESCRIPTION
AccessFailedCount	int	Specifies the current number of failed access attempts for lockout
Claims	ICollection<TClaim>	The collection of claims that the user has assigned
Email	string	User's e-mail address
EMailConfirmed	bool	Specifies whether the e-mail has been confirmed by the user responding to an e-mail from the system
Id	TKey	The user identifier. It defaults to a GUID, but the system can be configured to use other types as well.
LockoutEnabled	bool	Indicates whether lockout is enabled for this user
LockoutEndDateUtc	DateTime?	The date-time value (in UTC) when lockout ends; any time in the past is considered not locked out.
Logins	ICollection<TLogin>	The collection of logins for the user. This is an interesting concept, as it means that a particular e-mail address/login name has multiple logins. This happens when a user has a login for your site as well as a login through a trusted third party. Thus, no matter how a user logs into your site, that user is recognized as a single user.
PasswordHash	string	The salted/hashed form of the user password

continues

TABLE 15-2 *(continued)*

PROPERTY	TYPE	DESCRIPTION
PhoneNumber	string	The user's phone number
PhoneNumberConfirmed	bool	Specifies whether the phone number has been confirmed
Roles	ICollection<IRole>	The collection of roles to which the user has been assigned
SecurityStamp	string	A random value that changes when a user's credentials change. The primary purpose of this property is to enable "sign out everywhere." The idea is that whenever something security related is changed on the user, such as a password, your application should automatically invalidate any existing sign-in cookies. This ensures that if the user's password/account was previously compromised, the attacker no longer has access because the SecurityStamp is compared each time a token-based login is performed.
TwoFactorEnabled	bool	Specifies whether two-factor authentication is enabled for this user
UserName	string	The UserName is the online identity of the visitor.

As you can see from the list of properties, many features can be enabled by default and supported by the system out of the box. These features include confirmation (both e-mail and phone) as well as two-factor authentication.

Confirmation is the process in which the system sends a code through the selected approach that is being confirmed, either e-mail or phone, and the user must enter the code that was sent through that process into the application. By entering this code, the system verifies that there is a relationship between that selected approach and that user. In other words, the system knows that that person has access to that particular e-mail address or phone number. Typically, as soon as a user registers for your application, you would send that person the applicable confirmation(s). The registration process that was created by the project scaffolder shows how this could be done, though it is commented out in the actual page:

```
string code = manager.GenerateEmailConfirmationToken(user.Id);
string callbackUrl = IdentityHelper
        .GetUserConfirmationRedirectUrl(code, user.Id, Request);
manager.SendEmail(user.Id, "Confirm your account",
        "Please confirm your account by clicking
        < a href =\"" + callbackUrl + "\">here</a>.");
```

After the user registration has been confirmed, the application creates a random value that it uses as a confirmation token. This token is then part of an e-mail that is sent to the e-mail address provided during registration. The user is then expected to click the URL that was assigned—the URL that contains the confirmation token. This request is received by the application, which attempts to match the confirmation token to an account. If the attempt is successful, then the application marks that e-mail as being confirmed.

Two-factor authentication provides an additional layer of security: It expects a user to provide login information through multiple components. An ATM uses two-factor authentication in that it expects users to provide a physical item, their ATM card, as well as an identifying number. Obviously this won't work when authenticating for a website, so another approach was taken whereby the user uses mobile phone two-factor authentication.

In mobile phone two-factor authentication, users install a special application on their phone. A user securely logs in to the authenticating system with this application. This syncs the phone to the user's login account. Going forward, once two-factor authentication is enabled, the user has to get a value from their phone and use that value as part of the login process to the application. This makes it like the ATM in that users must have something—namely, their phone—as one authentication factor, as well as the traditional login/password combination for the second factor.

While all of this is provided with the Identity framework, because your application is not accepting a credit card or doing any online processing other than reserving equipment that the user would have to pick up in person, none of this functionality has been implemented in your application.

It was mentioned earlier that all the identity efforts were actually "turned on" by an attribute that was added to an action. This action is shown again here:

```
[Authorize]
[HttpGet]
public ActionResult Checkout()
{
    using (RentMyWroxContext context = new RentMyWroxContext())
    {
        return null;
    }
}
```

The `Authorize` attribute is the important attribute because it adds a requirement that users visiting this URL must be authenticated. That is why after adding this attribute, clicking the link to this URL took you immediately to the login page instead. The system was able to evaluate whether you were logged in because it looked in the request's cookie collection to see if an authentication cookie was present. Failing that check would take you to the login page that was configured in the `Startup.Auth.cs` file within the `App_Start` directory. When configuring the cookie authentication process, you can set the `LoginPath` property as shown here:

```
app.UseCookieAuthentication(new CookieAuthenticationOptions
{
    AuthenticationType = DefaultAuthenticationTypes.ApplicationCookie,
    LoginPath = new PathString("/Account/Login"),
    Provider = new CookieAuthenticationProvider
```

```
        {
            OnValidateIdentity = SecurityStampValidator
                .OnValidateIdentity<ApplicationUserManager, ApplicationUser>(
                    validateInterval: TimeSpan.FromMinutes(30),
                    regenerateIdentity: (manager, user)
                        => user.GenerateUserIdentityAsync(manager))
        }
    });
```

This setting ensured that the login page created by the project scaffolding is called when necessary. Because you didn't have an account, you had to click the "Register for an account" link. This brought you to the account registration page. Registering for your application was straightforward, and already handled by the defaults set during project creation, including the default settings for password validation. Password validation ensures that the password is as secure as possible. The available validation settings are shown in Table 15-3.

TABLE 15-3: Password Validation Configuration Properties

PROPERTY	DEFINITION
RequireDigit	Specifies whether the password requires a numeric digit (0–9)
RequiredLength	Contains the value for the minimum required password length
RequireLowercase	Specifies whether the password requires a lower case letter (a–z)
RequireNonLetterOrDigit	Specifies whether the password requires a non-letter or digit character
RequireUppercase	Specifies whether the password requires an uppercase letter (A–Z)

1. The default settings that were created can be found in the `App_Start\IdentityConfig.cs` file, and are shown here:

```
// Configure validation logic for passwords
manager.PasswordValidator = new PasswordValidator
{
    RequiredLength = 6,
    RequireNonLetterOrDigit = true,
    RequireDigit = true,
    RequireLowercase = true,
    RequireUppercase = true,
};
```

As you saw when you created your initial login, the validator expects a minimum of six characters in the password, of which at least one needs to be a non-letter or digit (i.e., a special character), one needs to be a number, one needs to be lowercase, and another needs to be uppercase. Enabling each of these validations helps to ensure that the password will not be easy to break.

The validation against these password characteristics does not happen until the form is submitted upon user creation. The registration method is shown here:

```
protected void CreateUser_Click(object sender, EventArgs e)
{
    var manager = Context.GetOwinContext().GetUserManager<ApplicationUserManager>();
    var signInManager = Context.GetOwinContext().Get<ApplicationSignInManager>();
    var user = new ApplicationUser(){UserName = Email.Text, Email = Email.Text};
    IdentityResult result = manager.Create(user, Password.Text);
    if (result.Succeeded)
    {
        signInManager.SignIn( user, isPersistent: false, rememberBrowser: false);
        IdentityHelper.RedirectToReturnUrl(Request.QueryString["ReturnUrl"],
                Response);
    }
    else
    {
        ErrorMessage.Text = result.Errors.FirstOrDefault();
    }
}
```

The `ApplicationUserManager.Create` method returns an `IdentityResult` object that contains a `Succeeded` flag. If there is any problem in creating the user, then the `Succeeded` flag is set to false and the `Errors` property is updated, including the reason(s) for the failure. In the case of password validation the message would contain a list of the validation requirements that failed.

Successfully creating a user account did one more thing: It created the database tables necessary to persist the default user information. This was possible because the Identity framework uses the Code-First Entity Framework approach just like the rest of your application. While it is taking a similar approach, it is doing it in a different database context, the `ApplicationDbContext`. You could have changed it so that it was using the same context as the rest of your application, but keeping them in two different contexts enables them to be accessed and maintained separately. In many companies that have different applications, it is common for user information to be shared across multiple applications. Keeping this a separate context makes that easier. While you do not have to worry about this with your sample application, it is a best practice to separate your security information from your business information. You are doing that here by using a second context.

Figure 15-13 shows a screen shot of the data that was created as part of the registration process.

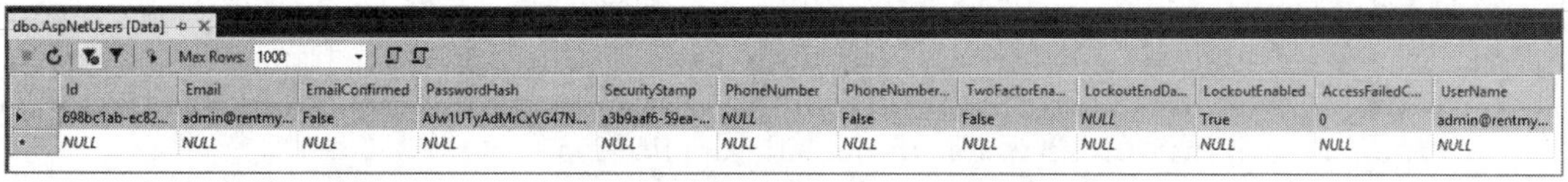

FIGURE 15-13: AspNetUsers data

As you can see, all the properties in Table 15-3 are present in the table. Note in particular the value in the `PasswordHash` column. This is not the password that was entered in the registration screen. It is instead hashed and salted.

Hashing is the process of applying a formula to a string of text; it produces a return value of fixed length that cannot be decrypted back into the original value. If you repeat the same hash on the same text, you will get the same result. Matching hash results indicates that the data has not been modified.

Salting is a process that strengthens encryption and hashes, making them more difficult to break. Salting adds a random string to the beginning or end of the input text prior to hashing or encrypting the value. When attempting to break a list of passwords, for example, hackers have to account for the salt as well as possible password information before being able to break into the application. If each value being salted is assigned a different salt value, the ability to create a table of potential password values for a password-cracking program becomes exceedingly complex and difficult.

The results of the hashed password are what is stored in the database. When users attempt to log in to the application, the password that they enter into the login screen is salted, or has a string value added, and then hashed. This value is compared to the value stored in the database. If the hashed values are the same, then the password is correct. This enables the application to validate a password without actually having to save the password itself anywhere. It is impossible for the application to recover the actual password itself.

As this example shows, configuring the Identity framework for use in your application is mainly an exercise in defining the database connection and then setting values for items such as password validation expectations. The Identity framework, especially in conjunction with the scaffolded project files, does the rest of the work for you.

After configuring the Identity framework for use within your application, the next step is to start taking advantage of actually knowing who the users are.

Working with Users within Your Application

Knowing who your users are is great, once you have the code written to take advantage of the user information. The main pieces of information to which you currently have access are as follows:

➤ Username

➤ E-mail address

➤ Phone number

➤ Unique identifier or Id

As mentioned earlier, once a user is logged into your application, an authentication cookie is created that is used going forward for identifying and validating the user. After the framework has validated the token, it is able to create a true identity for that user. Once the framework gets that information, it can store it such that it is accessible through the application.

There are two approaches to getting the user information, and the approach that you take depends on the object making the call; making it from the view or the controller requires one approach, while getting the user information in another class—even a Web Form code-behind—requires another approach.

Accessing the user information from within a controller is simple, as the base controller class from which all controllers inherit has a `User` property. This property is of type `System.Security.IPrincipal`, which is the default type for security within Windows. If you were working with a desktop application, when looking for the logged-in user it would also be an `IPrincipal`.

Note that this doesn't do you any good in terms of trying to get an `ApplicationUser` that you can use, as the `User` property is not convertible to something that you can use. Instead, you have to use a method on the `Identity` property of the `Principal` to get the user's `Id`, and then use that to get the `ApplicationUser`, as shown here:

```
string userId = User.Identity.GetUserId();
ApplicationUserManager aum = HttpContext.GetOwinContext()
        .GetUserManager<ApplicationUserManager>();
ApplicationUser appUser = aum.FindById(userId);
```

Once you have the `ApplicationUser` from the `ApplicationUserManager` you can then access the properties as desired. In the next Try It Out, you start to use the `ApplicationUser` information within your application.

TRY IT OUT | Update Shopping Cart Based on Real User

In this activity you use the user information that was created during user registration. Specifically, you update the shopping cart management so that the shopping cart works appropriately when a user is logged in.

1. Ensure that Visual Studio is running and the RentMyWrox application is open.

2. Right-click on your Controllers directory, and add a new item. Create a class file called **UserHelper.cs**.

3. In your new file, add the following `using` statements:

```
using Microsoft.AspNet.Identity;
using Microsoft.AspNet.Identity.Owin;
using Microsoft.Owin.Security;
using RentMyWrox.Models;
```

4. Inside the class definition add the following line of code:

```
private const string coookieName = "RentMyWroxTemporaryUserCookie";
```

5. As shown in Figure 15-14, add the following method:

```
public static Guid GetUserId()
{
    Guid userId;
    if (HttpContext.Current.User != null)
    {
        string userid = HttpContext.Current.User.Identity.GetUserId();
        if (Guid.TryParse(userid, out userId))
        {
            return userId;
        }
    }
}
```

```
    if (HttpContext.Current.Request != null
            && HttpContext.Current.Request.Cookies != null)
    {
        HttpCookie tempUserCookie = HttpContext.Current.Request.Cookies
                .Get(coookieName);
        if (tempUserCookie != null && Guid.TryParse(tempUserCookie.Value,
                out userId))
        {
            return userId;
        }
    }

    userId = Guid.NewGuid();
    HttpContext.Current.Response.Cookies.Add(
            new HttpCookie(coookieName, userId.ToString()));
    HttpContext.Current.Request.Cookies.Add(
            new HttpCookie(coookieName, userId.ToString()));
    return userId;
}
```

```csharp
using System;
using System.Collections.Generic;
using System.Linq;
using System.Web;
using Microsoft.AspNet.Identity;
using Microsoft.AspNet.Identity.Owin;
using Microsoft.Owin.Security;
using RentMyWrox.Models;

namespace RentMyWrox.Controllers
{
    public class UserHelper
    {
        private const string coookieName = "RentMyWroxTemporaryUserCookie";

        public static Guid GetUserId()
        {
            Guid userId;
            if (HttpContext.Current.User != null)
            {
                string userid = HttpContext.Current.User.Identity.GetUserId();
                if (Guid.TryParse(userid, out userId))
                {
                    return userId;
                }
            }

            if (HttpContext.Current.Request != null && HttpContext.Current.Request.Cookies != null)
            {
                HttpCookie tempUserCookie = HttpContext.Current.Request.Cookies.Get(coookieName);
                if (tempUserCookie != null && Guid.TryParse(tempUserCookie.Value, out userId))
                {
                    return userId;
                }
            }

            userId = Guid.NewGuid();
            HttpContext.Current.Response.Cookies.Add(new HttpCookie(coookieName, userId.ToString()));
            HttpContext.Current.Request.Cookies.Add(new HttpCookie(coookieName, userId.ToString()));
            return userId;
        }
```

FIGURE 15-14: UserHelper.cs

6. Add the following method:

```
public static ApplicationUser GetApplicationUser()
{
    string userId = HttpContext.Current.User.Identity.GetUserId();
    ApplicationUserManager aum = HttpContext.Current.GetOwinContext()
            .GetUserManager<ApplicationUserManager>();
    return aum.FindById(userId);
}
```

7. Add the following method:

```
public static void TransferTemporaryUserToRealUser(Guid tempId, string userId)
{
    using (RentMyWroxContext context = new RentMyWroxContext())
    {
        if (context.ShoppingCarts.Any(x => x.UserId == tempId))
        {
            Guid newUserId = Guid.Parse(userId);
            var list = context.ShoppingCarts.Include("Item")
                    .Where(x => x.UserId == tempId);
            foreach (var tempCart in list)
            {
                var sameItemInShoppingCart = context.ShoppingCarts
                    .FirstOrDefault(x => x.Item.Id == tempCart.Item.Id
                            && x.UserId == newUserId);
                if (sameItemInShoppingCart == null)
                {
                    tempCart.UserId = newUserId;
                }
                else
                {
                    sameItemInShoppingCart.Quantity++;
                    context.ShoppingCarts.Remove(tempCart);
                }
            }
            context.SaveChanges();
        }
    }
}
```

8. Open the `ShoppingCartController` file and delete the following line:

```
private Guid UserID = Guid.Empty;
```

9. As shown in Figure 15-15, add the following line to the top of the `AddToCart` action:

```
Guid UserID = UserHelper.GetUserId();
```

```
public ActionResult AddToCart(int id)
{
    Guid UserID = UserHelper.GetUserId();
    using (RentMyWroxContext context = new RentMyWroxContext())
    {
        Item addedItem = context.Items.FirstOrDefault(x => x.Id == id);

        // now that we know it is a valid ID
        if (addedItem != null)
        {
            // Check to see if this item was already added
            var sameItemInShoppingCart = context.ShoppingCarts.FirstOrDefault(x => x.Item.Id == id && x.UserId == UserID);
            if (sameItemInShoppingCart == null)
            {
                // if not already in cart then add it
                ShoppingCart sc = new ShoppingCart
                {
                    Item = addedItem,
                    UserId = UserID,
                    Quantity = 1,
                    DateAdded = DateTime.Now
                };
                context.ShoppingCarts.Add(sc);
            }
            else
            {
                // increment the quantity of the existing shopping cart item
                sameItemInShoppingCart.Quantity++;
            }
            context.SaveChanges();
        }
        ShoppingCartSummary summary = GetShoppingCartSummary(context);
        return PartialView("_ShoppingCartSummary", summary);
    }
}
```

FIGURE 15-15: UserHelper.cs

10. Expand the Accounts directory. Click the arrow to the left of Register.aspx to expand the other files. Open Register.aspx.cs. Update the method by adding the highlighted lines from the following code:

```
protected void CreateUser_Click(object sender, EventArgs e)
{
    var manager = Context.GetOwinContext().GetUserManager<ApplicationUserManager>();
    var signInManager = Context.GetOwinContext().Get<ApplicationSignInManager>();
    var user = new ApplicationUser() { UserName = Email.Text, Email = Email.Text };
    Guid oldTemporaryUser = Controllers.UserHelper.GetUserId();
    IdentityResult result = manager.Create(user, Password.Text);
    if (result.Succeeded)
    {
        Controllers.UserHelper.TransferTemporaryUserToRealUser(oldTemporaryUser,
                user.Id);
        signInManager.SignIn( user, isPersistent: false, rememberBrowser: false);
        IdentityHelper.RedirectToReturnUrl(Request.QueryString["ReturnUrl"],
                Response);
    }
    else
    {
        ErrorMessage.Text = result.Errors.FirstOrDefault();
    }
}
```

11. Open the `Login.aspx.cs` file. Update the `Login` method by adding the highlighted areas shown here:

```
protected void LogIn(object sender, EventArgs e)
{
    if (IsValid)
    {
        var manager = Context.GetOwinContext()
                .GetUserManager<ApplicationUserManager>();
        var signinManager = Context.GetOwinContext()
                .GetUserManager<ApplicationSignInManager>();
        Guid currentTemporaryId = Controllers.UserHelper.GetUserId();

        var result = signinManager.PasswordSignIn(Email.Text, Password.Text,
                RememberMe.Checked, shouldLockout: false);
        switch (result)
        {
            case SignInStatus.Success:
                var user = signinManager.UserManager.FindByName(Email.Text);
                Controllers.UserHelper.TransferTemporaryUserToRealUser(
                        currentTemporaryId, user.Id);
                IdentityHelper.RedirectToReturnUrl(
                        Request.QueryString["ReturnUrl"], Response);
                break;
            case SignInStatus.LockedOut:
                Response.Redirect("/Account/Lockout");
                break;
            ...
        }
    }
}
```

12. Run the application and add an item to the shopping cart.

13. When the shopping cart summary refreshes, click the checkout link. You should go to the login page.

14. Log in with the user information that you created in the last activity. You will end up at a blank Checkout screen.

15. Change the URL to go to the home page and you will see that the shopping cart summary still shows the same summary information.

How It Works

Most of the new functionality that you added was in a new class, `UserHelper`. This class is designed, as the name says, to help when working with users. You added three different methods to `UserHelper`. The first method, `GetUserId`, manages getting the user's Id from a logged-in user, where possible. If the user is not logged into the application, this method assigns the person a temporary user identifier that can be used to manage items put into the shopping cart. The second method, `GetApplicationUser`, gets an `ApplicationUser` object that corresponds to a particular user Id. The third method,

`TransferTemporaryUserToRealUser`, merges a shopping cart that users may have started using a temporary ID with the shopping cart that uses their real Id value.

As mentioned earlier in this chapter, user information is sent back and forth between the client and the server in an authentication cookie. The `GetUserId` method adds to that by creating a cookie, passed back and forth between the client and server, that contains the temporary user Id number that was created. This creates a unique identifier for visitors, regardless of whether they are logged into the application.

The method first determines whether a valid user is attached to the `HttpContext`. The following code snippet includes this check:

```
if (HttpContext.Current.User != null)
{
    string userid = HttpContext.Current.User.Identity.GetUserId();
    if (Guid.TryParse(userid, out userId))
    {
        return userId;
    }
}
```

Because the class is not a controller, you don't have access to a `User` property. Instead you have to go through the `HttpContext` to get to the `Identity`. Once you get the `Identity` you can call the `GetUserId` method, which returns a string representation of the user's Id. There will always be an `Identity` if the `User` exists, but if the user is not logged into the application the `GetUserId` will return a null string. This is why the application does a `TryParse`, just in case the value returned cannot be converted into a `Guid`.

The following example shows more of the method, specifically the part that handles reading the temporary identifier:

```
if (HttpContext.Current.Request != null
        && HttpContext.Current.Request.Cookies != null)
{
    HttpCookie tempUserCookie =
                HttpContext.Current.Request.Cookies.Get(coookieName);
    if (tempUserCookie != null && Guid.TryParse(tempUserCookie.Value, out userId))
    {
        return userId;
    }
}
```

The first section checks whether a cookie was already set with the same key. If so, the value is evaluated; and if the value can be converted to a `Guid`, then it is returned as the value. When no cookie has been set with the key, the user has not yet been assigned a temporary value, so the next few lines enable the system to create the appropriate cookie:

```
userId = Guid.NewGuid();
HttpContext.Current.Response.Cookies.Add(
        new HttpCookie(coookieName, userId.ToString()));
HttpContext.Current.Request.Cookies.Add(
        new HttpCookie(coookieName, userId.ToString()));
```

Typically you would only need to set the cookies on the `Response` object, as those are the ones that the browser picks up to return to the server on the next request. However, you are also setting the `Request` cookies because there may be another call to the method later in the process, so setting it in both `Response` and `Request` ensures that it will be available no matter when the call is made.

Whereas this method ensures that there is always a unique identifier, whether or not the user is logged in, the next method, `GetApplicationUser`, is only responsible for getting the `ApplicationUser`. This code is shown again here:

```
public static ApplicationUser GetApplicationUser()
{
    string userId = HttpContext.Current.User.Identity.GetUserId();
    ApplicationUserManager aum = HttpContext.Current.GetOwinContext()
            .GetUserManager<ApplicationUserManager>();
    return aum.FindById(userId);
}
```

This simple method is responsible for looking up the `ApplicationUser` based on an Id. However, due to the nature of ASP.NET, it can do this without having to pass any parameters into the method because it can get all the needed information itself. First, it can get the user's Id from the `HttpContext`, just as you can do from within a controller. However, because you don't have all the built-in functionality of a controller, you instead have to access a "real" `HttpContext` instance by going through the `HttpContext` class's `Current` property, which is a wrapper for the active `HttpContext` for this request. Once you have the user's `Identity`, you can call the `GetUserId` method to get their Id as a string.

The next line in the method demonstrates the approach to getting instantiated versions of various managers. If you remember the `Startup.Auth.cs` file, there are several lines of code that create various authentication items and add them to the `OwinContext`. These lines are displayed here:

```
app.CreatePerOwinContext(ApplicationDbContext.Create);
app.CreatePerOwinContext<ApplicationUserManager>(ApplicationUserManager.Create);
app.CreatePerOwinContext<ApplicationSignInManager>(ApplicationSignInManager.Create);
```

An `ApplicationUserManager` was already created and added to the `OwinContext`, so all you need to do is fetch the object from the `OwinContext`. This fetch is what you are doing with the `GetUserManager` method with the type of `ApplicationUserManager`. You can take a similar approach to getting an instantiated `ApplicationSignInManager` by using that type in the method call, rather than the `ApplicationUserManager` type.

Once you have the user manager, you simply need to call the `FindById` method with the Id that you previously determined. You could have added this code into those methods but following the best practice of putting code that is repeated in multiple places into a single method that can be called anywhere, it made sense to extract the method to a class that can be accessed from all other code within the application.

The last method in this class is `TransferTemporaryUserToRealUser`. This method is responsible for transferring items that may have been added to a shopping cart before the user is logged in to the logged-in user's cart. Unfortunately, it is not quite as simple as updating the database with the new `UserId` value, as users may already have items in their shopping cart from a previous visit, so the items in both carts (temporary and "real user") have to be evaluated to determine whether the quantity should be updated or the line item updated with the user's id.

Note something interesting in this method:

```
var list = context.ShoppingCarts.Include("Item").Where(x => x.UserId == tempId);
```

The `Include` method is necessary in this case because the system will only return with the base data and not load any related entities. You might realize that this is the first time you are pulling a `ShoppingCart` item out of the database and needing to do anything with the Item; in every other case you were including a property on the `ShoppingCart.Item` as a query value so that the Entity Framework already knew that it had to deal with the item as a related entity.

If you did not have the `Include` method in the query, then the `Item` property would always be null. Also, because the `Item_Id` database column added by the Entity Framework to manage this relationship is not part of the `ShoppingCart` model, you cannot even access that value for the comparison.

Once the `UserHelper` class was added, the other changes that you made were to take advantage of the `UserHelper` methods you added. The `ShoppingCartController`, for example, will now use the appropriate id, temporary or real, and remember it between calls to the server, while the code that handles the login and registration work both call the method that moves shopping cart items as soon as the user logs in (or registers).

At this point, you have added authentication to the application, or the capability to confirm that someone is who they say they are. You also added a little bit of authorization by using the `Authorize` attribute to ensure that a specific method can only be called when the user is logged in, as that single action is what starts all the authentication that has been defined so far.

However, you don't yet have a capability to discern anything beyond whether a user has been authenticated. That's why there were no changes to the administrative pages yet. Managing access to those pages requires more than a simple check for authentication; it also needs an approach to determine if a user is authorized to view those specific pages. That's where roles come into the picture.

ROLES

A traditional approach to determining authorization is through the use of roles. A role provides a way to define a set of responsibilities, much like a list of things that can be done by someone within that role. When you look at it in security terms, a role can be used to lock down an action such that "only users that have this specific role" can take the action. Typically, roles are delineated by the type of work that a user can do, and then users are assigned one or more roles as necessary to define their actual responsibilities. In our previous example about the bank, the guard was able to identify a person because of the role that they played, that of manager.

In the ASP.NET Identity framework, a collection of roles is available on the `ApplicationUser`. A role is a separate item within the context of the Identity framework, which translates into them having their own database table, `AspNetRoles`, and another table that joins the user to one or more roles, `AspNetUserRoles`. This join table is necessary because a role may be assigned to more than one person, and a person may have more than one role.

Using roles provides a much more granular level of authorization, as you can be as specific as necessary when you are grouping responsibilities. In the sample application, you really only need one role that will be used to ensure that a user going into the Admin section is both logged in and authorized to take that action, but it is easy to conceive of cases in which the grouping of responsibilities may lead to many different, more granular roles.

Creating a project with authentication does not create any role-management screens. Any role creation and configuration has to be either coded or entered directly into the database. There's really nothing special that you have to do with a role, however, to create it; a default role has only two properties: Id and Name.

Configuring Your Application to Work with Roles

Creating and linking roles are straightforward tasks, so getting roles onto a User object is easily and automatically done once linked in the database. However, getting the application to understand the roles is a bit different, and varies, of course, between ASP.NET Web Forms and ASP.NET MVC applications. You saw how MVC uses an attribute to ensure that a user is authenticated, which makes sense because everything that happens in MVC is happening to code. Web Forms are different in that everything there is file-based. Thus, an approach using attributes is more difficult to implement.

Instead, when working with an ASP.NET Web Forms application, you can manage authorization in configuration files. There hasn't been much discussion about configuration files other than when you have accessed one to manage the connection strings; however, configuration files can manage much more than just database connection information. You can also have more than one configuration file in an application, as you can place one in nested directories as well. By convention, code in a directory looks first for configuration files in that directory. If none is found in that directory, the code then looks up a level (while still in the context of the running application) until a configuration file is located and referenced.

Configuration files are important because they provide a simple way to handle authorization for ASP.NET Web Forms pages. An abbreviated version showing how this can work is displayed here:

```xml
<?xml version="1.0"?>
<configuration>
    <system.web>
      <authorization>
        <allow roles="Role1, Role2" />
        <deny users="*"/>
      </authorization>
    </system.web>
</configuration>
```

Putting this code in any directory with Web Forms files ensures that the application is locked down and only accessible for those users who have been assigned either Role1 or Role2. In those cases where the user is not logged in, or is logged in but does not have the appropriate role and tries to access a page in this directory the framework will instead forward the user to the login page. If the user can log in and has the appropriate roles, then he or she will be allowed to visit any of the pages in the directory.

The preceding approach can limit access to every page in the directory, but you also can limit access to specific pages through configuration as well. Recall the example when you created the scaffolded project, in the Account directory that contains all the scaffolded user interaction. The `web.config` file included for this change is shown here:

```xml
<?xml version="1.0"?>
<configuration>
  <location path="Manage.aspx">
    <system.web>
      <authorization>
        <deny users="?"/>
      </authorization>
    </system.web>
  </location>
</configuration>
```

In this case, the configuration specifies that anyone who is logged in can go to the `Manage.aspx` file, which makes sense when you look at the content of the Account directory and evaluate what each page is expected to do. The only one that is expected to work with an authenticated user is `Manage .aspx`, which maintains login information—valid only for authenticated users.

TRY IT OUT   ADDING ROLES

In this activity, you lock down the administrative portion of your application based on a role that you create. You will have the opportunity to check several different settings and how they impact security.

1. Ensure that Visual Studio is running and the RentMyWrox application is open. Run the application and go to \Admin, as shown in Figure 15-16.

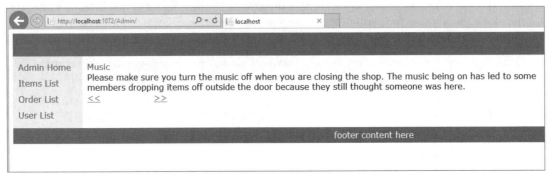

FIGURE 15-16: Default page in the Admin directory

2. Right-click on the Admin directory and select Add New Item. Make sure you are in the Web section on the left, and select Web Configuration File, as shown in Figure 15-17. Click the Add button.

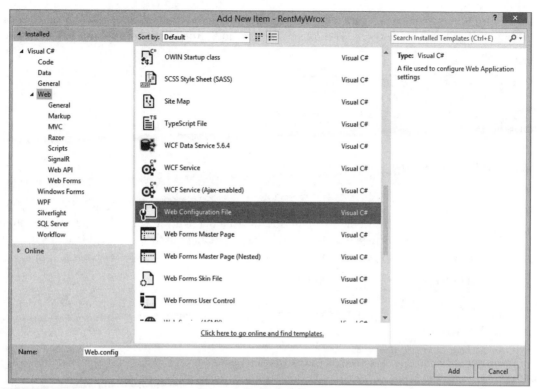

FIGURE 15-17: Creating a web.config file for the Admin directory

3. Update the new file so that it has the following content:

```xml
<?xml version="1.0"?>
<configuration>
  <system.web>
    <authorization>
      <deny users="?"/>
    </authorization>
  </system.web>
</configuration>
```

4. Run the application again and try to go to the Admin page. It will take you directly to the login page. Enter your credentials, which you created earlier. If you entered the login information correctly, you should be taken back to the default admin screen.

5. Change the "?" in `<deny users="?"/>` to "*" so that the line looks like `<deny users="*"/>` instead.

6. Run the application again and try to go to the Admin page (/Admin). It will take you directly to the login page. Enter your credentials. If you entered the login information correctly, note that you are not taken to the admin screen, but back to the login page, without any validation errors.

7. Open Server Explorer, and select Database and then Tables. Right-click on the AspNetRoles table and select Show Table Data. When the grid opens, add "Admin" to both columns as shown in Figure 15-18.

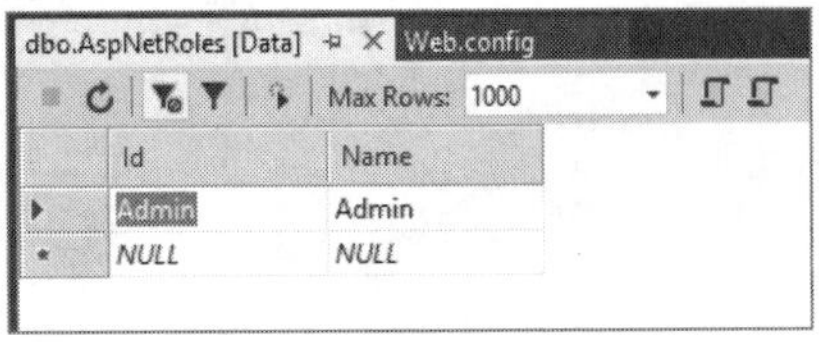

FIGURE 15-18: Adding a role to the database

8. Show the Table Data for both the AspNetUsers table and the AspNetUserRoles table. Copy the Id of the user who will become an administrator from the AspNetUsers table and paste it into the UserId column of the AspNetUserRoles table. Type "**Admin**" in the RoleId column. It should look like Figure 15-19 when you are done.

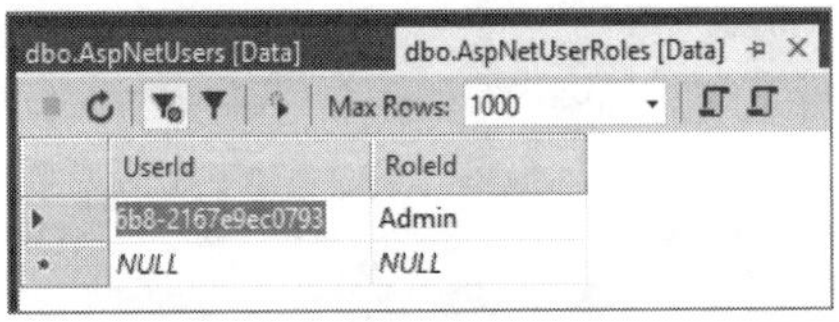

FIGURE 15-19: Assigning a role to a user in the database

9. Update the web.config file that you added as follows:

```xml
<?xml version="1.0"?>
<configuration>
  <system.web>
    <authorization>
      <allow roles="Admin" />
      <deny users="*"/>
    </authorization>
  </system.web>
</configuration>
```

10. Run the application and go to the Admin page. You should be redirected to the login page.

11. Log in with the user whose Id was assigned the role. Upon entering the correct credentials you will be taken to the Admin page.

How It Works

The Identity framework supports the use of roles in authorization by default, so all you had to do to populate roles was create one or more roles and then assign them to a user. You did this without any UI, instead entering them directly into the database. However, once you did this, they became immediately available on the user, as shown in Figure 15-20.

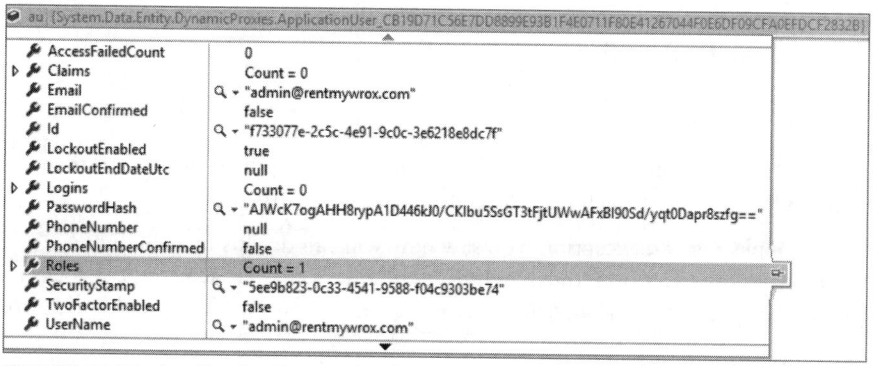

FIGURE 15-20: ApplicationUser with roles collection populated

Once you added the role and linked it to a user, you could use the web.config approach to lock down a complete directory. You actually took it through three different steps. The first, whereby you used a "?" in the deny element, denied access to the directory if the user was not logged in. However, once the user was logged in, the use of the "?" granted them access to the files. This result is comparable to the Authorize attribute that you used on the MVC action.

The next step changed the "?" to a "*". This completely changed the meaning because this step denies any user access to the pages in the directory, regardless of login status. Any directory that has this configuration, and only this configuration, can never be accessed, as there is no exception to a simple "Deny All" approach.

You can override this "Deny All" approach by adding another configuration, in this case the allow element. By adding an allow element with a role (or list of roles), you changed the authorization for this directory to be "no user, logged in or not, is allowed to access this directory unless they have an allowed role." This progression of authorization is what allowed your role-bearing user to access the pages within the directory while other users were still kept out.

This shows how you can lock down ASP.NET Web Forms and limit access to a subset of roles. You can do the same in ASP.NET MVC. The Authorize attribute that you worked with before has an override that accepts a list of roles. This override would be used as follows:

```
[Authorize(Roles = "Admin")]
public ActionResult SomeAction()
```

The outcome of this attribute is the same as when you used the configuration approach on the Admin directory, only those logged-in users that have a role of Admin are allowed to access this URL and thus call this action. Any other type of user would be sent directly to the login screen, as happened during the exercise.

Also, just as the web.config approach can secure either an entire directory or a single page (through the use of the location element), you can do the same with the Authorize attribute. The current example locks down a single action, much like the web.config in the Account directory locks down a single page; remember that the closest correspondence between the two approaches is an .aspx page to an action on a controller.

Although you have used the `Authorize` attribute only on a controller action, it can also be used at the controller level. This would look like the following:

```
[Authorize(Roles = "Admin")]
public class SomeAdminController : Controller
```

It results in every action on that controller acting as if that attribute were applied directly to them. This approach is more like the web.config approach that locks down an entire directory.

When considering giving a single page an exception, you saw how you can do this by including a `location` element that manages the exception; thus, with the configuration approach, you can lock out the directory and then create a special exception, using the `location` element, for a particular file or files.

You have a similar capability through attributes in MVC:

```
[Authorize(Roles = "Admin")]
public class SomeAdminController : Controller
{
    [AllowAnonymous]
    public ActionResult Index()
    {
    }
}
```

The `AllowAnonymous` attribute enables you to configure an action to be accessible even when the controller itself has been attributed with an `Authorize` element. The combination of `Authorize` and `AllowAnonymous` enables you to define authorization at a high level but also allows exceptions.

A lot of the simple authorization needs can be managed through the judicious use of web.config authorization for Web Forms as well as the use of `Authorize` attributes in MVC. However, sometimes you will need to determine whether a user is authorized or within a role.

Programmatically Checking Roles

You can't always make your decisions about how to handle different considerations regarding authentication and authorization at the page level. Perhaps you only want to show a section of a page a user is logged into; or if the user has a particular role, the page itself may have a different requirement for authorization than a particular section. Thus, working with this section will require a different way to manage that determination. This is where programmatic checking of roles comes into play.

The advantage of checking on roles and login status in code is that the approach is generally similar in both MVC and Web Forms, as shown here:

IN CONTROLLER OR VIEW

```
User.IsInRole("Admin")
```

EVERYWHERE ELSE

```
HttpContext.Current.User.IsInRole("Admin");
```

Both of these return a simple Boolean value that indicates whether the user has been assigned the input role. This method returns false if the user is not authenticated or the user is authenticated but does not have the role.

In the next Try It Out, you add functionality to the application that is dependent upon accessing identity information programmatically.

TRY IT OUT   Changing Menu Options Based on Role

In this activity, you update your application to add additional menus to it. In some cases, the menus are displayed only if the user is logged in, while in others the menus are displayed only if the user has a specific role.

1. Ensure that Visual Studio is running and you have the RentMyWrox application open. Open the `Views\Shared\_MVCLayout.cshtml` file.

2. Find the `<ul>` element for the left menu. As shown in Figure 15-21, replace everything within the `<ul></ul>` elements with the following code:

```
<li><a href="~/" class="level1">Home</a></li>
<li><a class="level1" href="~/Contact">Contact Us</a></li>
<li><a class="level1" href="~/About">About Us</a></li>
@if (!User.Identity.IsAuthenticated)
{
    <li><a class="level1" href="~/Account/Login">Login</a></li>
}
else
{
    <li> </li>
}
@if (User.IsInRole("Admin"))
{
    <li><a class="level1" href="/Admin/Default">Admin Home</a></li>
    <li><a class="level1" href="/Admin/ItemList">Items List</a></li>
    <li><a class="level1" href="/Admin/OrderList">Order List</a></li>
    <li><a class="level1" href="/Admin/UserList">User List</a></li>
}
```

3. Open the `Site.Master` in the root directory. Find the `<div>` with the id of "LeftNavigation." Replace it with the following:

```
<ul class="level1">
    <li><a href="/" class="level1">Home</a></li>
    <li><a href="/Contact" class="level1">Contact Us</a></li>
    <li><a href="/About" class="level1">About Us</a></li>
    <li runat="server" id="loginlink">
        <a class="level1" href="~/Account/Login">Login</a>
    </li>
    <li runat="server" id="loggedinlink"> </li>
</ul>
<asp:Menu ID="AdminMenu" runat="server" DataSourceID="SiteMapDataSource1"
        IncludeStyleBlock="false"></asp:Menu>
<asp:SiteMapDataSource ID="SiteMapDataSource1" runat="server"
        ShowStartingNode="False" />
<div id="storeHoursMessage"></div>
```

```
<body>
  <div id="header">
    <img src="rentmywrox_logo.gif" />
    <span id="shoppingcartsummary">@Html.Action("Index", "ShoppingCart")</span>
  </div>
  <div id="nav">
    <div id="LeftNavigation">
      <ul class="level1">
        <li><a href="~/" class="level1">Home</a></li>
        <li><a class="level1" href="~/Contact">Contact Us</a></li>
        <li><a class="level1" href="~/About">About Us</a></li>
        @if (!User.Identity.IsAuthenticated)
        {
        <li><a class="level1" href="~/Account/Login">Login</a></li>
        }
        else
        {
          <li> </li>
        }
        @if (User.IsInRole("Admin"))
        {
          <li><a class="level1" href="/Admin/Default">Admin Home</a></li>
          <li><a class="level1" href="/Admin/ItemList">Items List</a></li>
          <li><a class="level1" href="/Admin/OrderList">Order List</a></li>
          <li><a class="level1" href="/Admin/UserList">User List</a></li>
        }
      </ul>
      <br />
      <div id="storeHoursMessage"></div>
      @Html.Action("NonAdminSnippet", "Notifications")
    </div>
  </div>
```

FIGURE 15-21: Updating the menu in the _MVCLayout.cshtml file

4. Open the `Site.Master.cs` code-behind. Add the following code to the `Page_Load` method:

```
AdminMenu.Visible = HttpContext.Current.User.IsInRole("Admin");
loginlink.Visible = !HttpContext.Current.User.Identity.IsAuthenticated;
loggedinlink.Visible = !loginlink.Visible;
```

5. Run the application and go to the home page. Click the Login button and log in with a user who has the Admin role (see Figure 15-22).

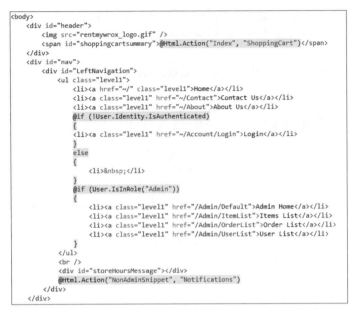

FIGURE 15-22: Home page with Admin menu

6. Click the Admin Home link to go to the Admin home page.

How It Works

In this activity, you added links to your application so that users who were not authenticated would be sent to a login screen. You did this by adding a new list item to the layout view. However, to ensure that the link is only available when the user isn't authenticated, you added a check in the view, as shown again here:

```
@if (!User.Identity.IsAuthenticated)
{
    <li><a class="level1" href="~/Account/Login">Login</a></li>
}
```

You can access the User property in your view just as you can in your controller, so by accessing the User.Identity you have access to the IsAuthenticated property, which tells you whether the current user has logged into your site. In this case, you are checking to see if the user is not authenticated, in which case you display the login link.

Later in that same page, you also do a check to determine whether the user is assigned a particular role:

```
@if (User.IsInRole("Admin"))
{
}
```

If the user has been assigned the Admin role, then additional menu items are available, which take them to the Admin section. If not, they won't even know those menu options are available.

In the Site.Master page you took a different approach. This is because of the simple capability to convert an HTML element into a server control that you can access in code. The markup and code-behind lines of code are displayed here:

MARKUP

```
<li runat="server" id="loginlink">
    <a class="level1" href="~/Account/Login">Login</a>
</li>
<li runat="server" id="loggedinlink"> </li>

<asp:Menu ID="AdminMenu" runat="server" DataSourceID="SiteMapDataSource1"
        IncludeStyleBlock="false"></asp:Menu>
```

CODE-BEHIND

```
AdminMenu.Visible = HttpContext.Current.User.IsInRole("Admin");
loginlink.Visible = !HttpContext.Current.User.Identity.IsAuthenticated;
loggedinlink.Visible = !loginlink.Visible;
```

The logic that you use in the code-behind is the same as you used in the view. This is because the security system is not MVC or Web Forms; it is part of ASP.NET, so it is available in both. The only difference is that controllers and views have a slightly different access point because they both have the User exposed as a property, whereas in non-controller and view files you have to access that same User through the HttpContext.Current.

You have now added authentication and authorization to the sample application. Because the Identity framework is based in ASP.NET, rather than in either of the two framework technologies, you were able to use the same approach in evaluating and working with users and their credentials.

PRACTICAL SECURITY TIPS

The items below are a few things you need to keep in mind when you work with security within your application.

➤ Although you did not work with security until close to the end of the book, you should actually consider security from the beginning of the application development process. You want to determine at the outset what kind of authentication and authorization needs you will have because this may affect many different aspects of the development process.

➤ Determining roles can be one of the more complicated processes of adding security. A common mistake is to simply use job titles as a role. This means that a piece of functionality may need to support many different roles, and tracking functionality to the list of roles becomes very problematic. Instead, take an approach whereby roles define a common set of job requirements. This likely means that a user will have multiple roles, but it is a lot easier to change the role assignment for a user than it is to change the code to add a new job-title type role to a controller. This is especially true because you will need to build a UI to manage user-role assignment, so managing more roles becomes a lot simpler while still remaining very flexible.

➤ The most secure approach to take is a *white-list* approach, which means that the default is to deny all actions to a user unless otherwise specified. Permission is assigned on an as-needed basis. This keeps your application more secure than taking the opposite approach whereby you start off allowing the user to do anything and secure functionality as needed.

➤ The importance of security cannot be overstated. Obviously, the effect of a security breach will be based on what you are doing; but whenever you make the decision to add authentication, any breach will, at minimum, rupture the trust that users may have in your company and application.

SUMMARY

Adding security to your ASP.NET web application is not as scary as it could be. The Identity framework was redesigned to make it very developer friendly. You can see this from the very beginning in terms of how the framework uses Entity Framework Code First to manage database access. This fits perfectly into how your own application accesses the database. It means that everything you already do to manage your own database you can extend to manage the database part of your security system.

The most complex aspect of working with the Identity framework is how it is instantiated into the Owin context and how you may need to pull various objects out of the Owin context so that you can use them for interaction with the system. However, by working with the Owin context, you have access to all the different security aspects, from authenticating a user from the username and password they entered into your system, to evaluating users to determine whether they have the necessary roles to access specific pages or perform actions within pages.

Configuring the usage of authentication is dependent upon the framework that you are using. If you are configuring ASP.NET Web Forms pages, you can maintain security expectations through the use of configuration files in which you define those expectations—either for all files in a directory or for individual files. If you are working in MVC you don't have the capability to use web.config files for security because MVC uses a different, non-file-system-based approach. Instead, you put authorization attributes on actions and/or controllers. The attributes define the authorization expectations.

Because the Identity framework is an ASP.NET approach, working with the framework in code is virtually the same regardless of which framework you are using. This means the methods are the same and the way that you get the information is the same whether you are working with MVC or Web Forms.

EXERCISES

1. Whenever the application starts, what two files are responsible for setting configuration items such as minimum length for a password?

2. What is the difference between authentication and authorization?

▶ WHAT YOU LEARNED IN THIS CHAPTER

`ApplicationDbContext`	A class created at the same time that the project is created. It acts as the database context file for all the tables that are part of the Identity framework. It is completely comparable to the `DbContext` that you have been using throughout the application.
`ApplicationSigninManager`	Handles the management of signing in
`ApplicationUser`	The user class that is created during the scaffolding process. It acts as the definition of what constitutes a user.
`ApplicationUserManager`	A scaffold-created class that performs many user-management tasks
Authentication	The process of verifying that users are who they say they are. At a minimum, it requires the user to provide a username and password that must be identical to the information provided when the account was created.
Authorization	The process of determining whether the user is allowed, or authorized, to take an action. Authorization can be managed at any level. In the ASP.NET framework, it is usually managed by the roles that have been assigned to a user.
authorization attribute	An MVC feature that enables you to define authentication and authorization requirements. This attribute can be applied at either a controller or action level.
authorization element	A component used when configuring authentication and authorization for Web Forms in a `web.config` file
Hash	A process that takes a value and creates a one-way conversion to another value. The beauty of a hash is that it is impossible to go back to the original value, and no other value can be hashed and match the hash from the first value. Therefore, it is ideal for matching passwords without the system ever having to know what that password is.
Identity framework	A .NET system that manages authentication and authorization. It provides a facility for defining the user and storing information about this user, as well as any affiliated roles.
`IdentityResult`	The result of an identity operation, such as a login. It includes a property for `Succeeded`, so you can tell whether the login worked; and a property for `Errors`, which provides a list of strings describing the encountered problems.

`IsInRole`	A method on the Identity. You can pass in a role name and get a Boolean indicating whether the logged-in user has been assigned that role.
`OwinContext`	A container used to store security information. It is initialized upon application startup; and if you need various Identity components, you generally fetch them from the OwinContext.
`PasswordValidator`	A class used to validate passwords upon user registration or password change. It enables you to set minimum length and the type of characters that are required.
Role	An item used to describe the relationship between the user and the kinds of actions that they can perform. The application is coded to validate a role for a set of functionality, and the user is assigned one or more roles that determine what they can do in the application.
Salt	A value added to a hash. It is used in Identity to further obfuscate the hashed value of the password.
`SignInStatus`	An enum that is returned from an attempt to sign in. It describes the outcome, such as success or failure.

16

Personalizing Websites

WHAT YOU WILL LEARN IN THIS CHAPTER:

➤   Adding personal information to ASP.NET Identity

➤   Managing your security database

➤   Different approaches to website personalization

➤   How to implement personalization in your website

CODE DOWNLOADS FOR THIS CHAPTER:

The wrox.com code downloads for this chapter are found at `www.wrox.com/go/beginningaspnetforvisualstudio` on the Download Code tab. The code is in the chapter 16 download and individually named according to the names throughout the chapter.

Implementing security in your web site means that you now have the ability to identify your users. Once you can do that, you can start gathering information about them—everything from their name and address, to date of birth, to favorite color—whatever information you can use to make their experience with your site more welcoming, memorable, and special. The more welcome your users feel, the more comfortable they will be when working with your application, and the more likely that they will come back.

Once you have identified users, you can also monitor other aspects about them, including what pages they visit, how often they visit, what items they may click on most, and other interesting information. With that kind of data you can build directed marketing efforts, or remember users and take them directly to given product pages—benefits that aren't possible when you don't have the capability to recognize a user or you don't have information about that user.

Any of this information can be considered for, and used in, personalization, which is simply the concept of having your application recognize a user and take specific actions based on the information you have about that user. It could be as simple as displaying their name or as complex as building an entire preference catalog specifically for them.

UNDERSTANDING THE PROFILE

Previous versions of ASP.NET had a complete profile manager, a special ASP.NET component that was tacked onto the login manager; and although it was flexible, in that you could add any kind of data to it, it was also complicated because it kept the information separate from the user. While the storage mechanism was complicated, however, the manager hid most of that from you and made it almost transparent to use.

The main reason why this approach was taken was because the previous version of user management was not flexible. The design was extremely rigid so that the framework always understood each row in the various identity tables (those tables were very much like the default tables that were created in the sample application) because this was before the Entity Framework was completely melded into the framework. Any changes to those tables could break the system.

Now that ASP.NET Identity uses the Entity Framework in general, and Code First specifically, the personalization approach that you use is more manageable; it's directly integrated with the user, rather than kept separately and accessed through a separate manager. In the next section you will learn the steps necessary to add personalization support information to the default user.

Creating the Profile

Several steps are necessary to add profile information to the default ASP.NET Identity setup. The first step is determining what additional information you want to gather. This information could be a simple type, such as a string for first name, or a complex type, such as an address. Second, after you have determined the additional information that you want to add, you must then consider how you will be accessing the information. The last step is to implement the data changes and update the database.

Determining the additional information is usually the simplest part of the process. You may need to consider how to build out complex types if you need those, but there is nothing new about determining the additional information and that information's specific types.

You should also spend some time considering how you will be accessing the information; think about extra information are you adding as well as how you want to combine the user and profile information. The recommended approach is to use a different database context for your security information (so that it can have different database access rights). Doing so enables you to identify the interaction between the two, which in turn determines how you define the personalization information.

Lastly, after determining that it makes the most sense to put the additional information into the security database, you add the information to the models and then update the database. All these steps are part of the next Try It Out.

TRY IT OUT   Initial Configuration for Personalization

In this exercise you add various personalization features to the application, including new information that will be part of the same database context as the rest of the security system, as well as personalization data that will be saved with traditional application data.

1. Ensure that Visual Studio is running and you have the RentMyWrox application open.

2. Open the `Model\IdentityModels.cs` file, and add a new using statement for `System .ComponentModel.DataAnnotations`.

3. As shown in Figure 16-1, add the following class to the file:

```
public class Address
{
    public string Address1 { get; set; }

    public string Address2 { get; set; }

    public string City { get; set; }

    [StringLength(2)]
    public string State { get; set; }

    [StringLength(15, MinimumLength = 2)]
    public string ZipCode { get; set; }
}
```

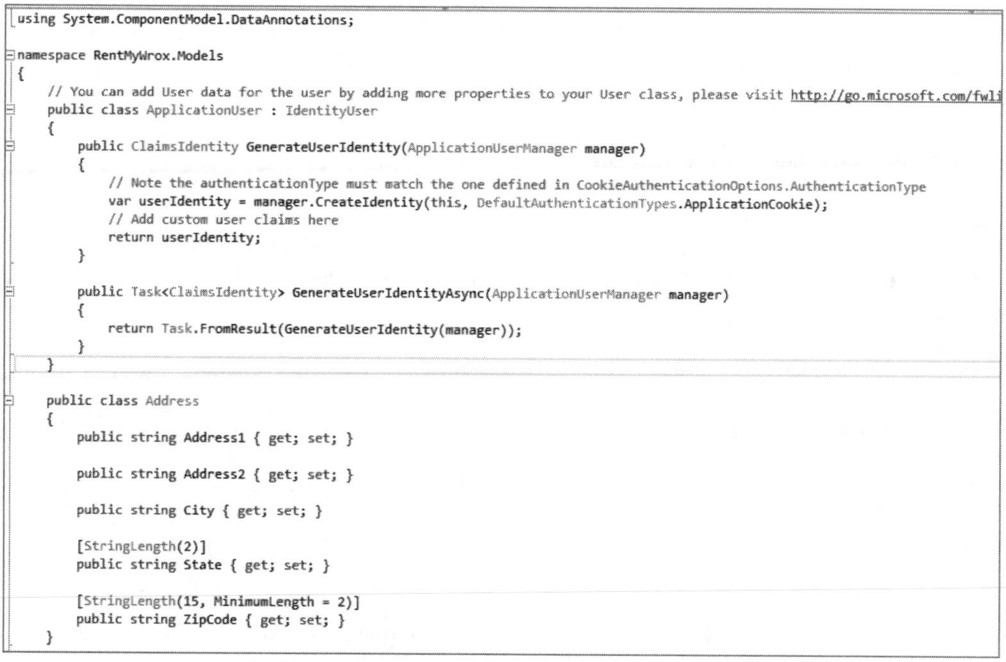

```
using System.ComponentModel.DataAnnotations;

namespace RentMyWrox.Models
{
    // You can add User data for the user by adding more properties to your User class, please visit http://go.microsoft.com/fwli
    public class ApplicationUser : IdentityUser
    {
        public ClaimsIdentity GenerateUserIdentity(ApplicationUserManager manager)
        {
            // Note the authenticationType must match the one defined in CookieAuthenticationOptions.AuthenticationType
            var userIdentity = manager.CreateIdentity(this, DefaultAuthenticationTypes.ApplicationCookie);
            // Add custom user claims here
            return userIdentity;
        }

        public Task<ClaimsIdentity> GenerateUserIdentityAsync(ApplicationUserManager manager)
        {
            return Task.FromResult(GenerateUserIdentity(manager));
        }
    }

    public class Address
    {
        public string Address1 { get; set; }

        public string Address2 { get; set; }

        public string City { get; set; }

        [StringLength(2)]
        public string State { get; set; }

        [StringLength(15, MinimumLength = 2)]
        public string ZipCode { get; set; }
    }
```

FIGURE 16-1: New class for addresses

4. Add the following properties to the `ApplicationUser` class (see Figure 16-2):

```
public string FirstName { get; set; }
```

```
public string LastName { get; set; }

public Address Address { get; set; }

public int UserDemographicsId { get; set; }

public int OrderCount { get; set; }
```

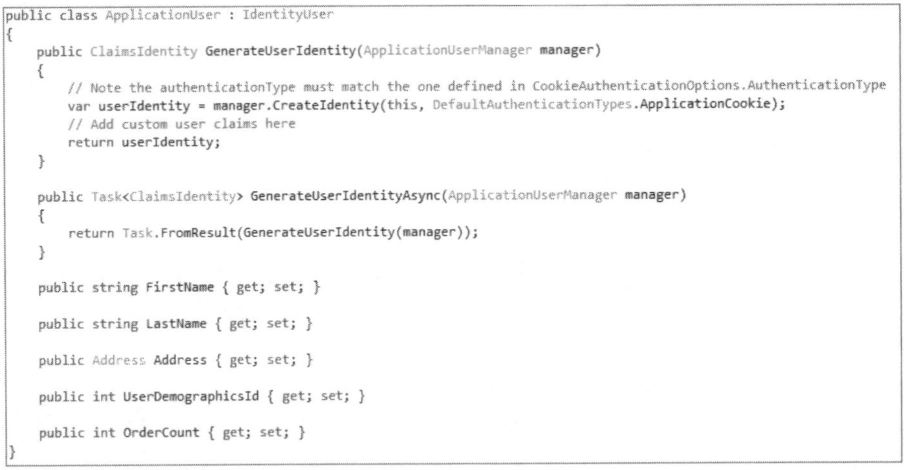

```
public class ApplicationUser : IdentityUser
{
    public ClaimsIdentity GenerateUserIdentity(ApplicationUserManager manager)
    {
        // Note the authenticationType must match the one defined in CookieAuthenticationOptions.AuthenticationType
        var userIdentity = manager.CreateIdentity(this, DefaultAuthenticationTypes.ApplicationCookie);
        // Add custom user claims here
        return userIdentity;
    }

    public Task<ClaimsIdentity> GenerateUserIdentityAsync(ApplicationUserManager manager)
    {
        return Task.FromResult(GenerateUserIdentity(manager));
    }

    public string FirstName { get; set; }

    public string LastName { get; set; }

    public Address Address { get; set; }

    public int UserDemographicsId { get; set; }

    public int OrderCount { get; set; }
}
```

FIGURE 16-2: Additional user properties

5. Right-click the Models directory and add a new class called `UserVisit`. Add the following properties (don't forget to add a new using statement for `System.ComponentModel.DataAnnotations`):

```
[Key]
public int Id { get; set; }

[Required]
public Guid UserId { get; set; }

[Required]
public int ItemId { get; set; }

[Required]
public DateTime VisitDate { get; set; }
```

6. Open the Models\RentMyWroxContext and add the following line with the other DbSets:

```
public virtual DbSet<UserVisit> UserVisits { get; set; }
```

7. Open the Package Manager Console by selecting Tools ➪ NuGet Package Manager ➪ Package Manager Console. Create a new migration script by entering the following command and clicking Enter:

```
add-migration "regular personalization"
```

8. Open the new file in the Migrations folder that includes the string "regular personalization." It should look like Figure 16-3. Note that the new migration file does not contain any of the new properties added to the user area.

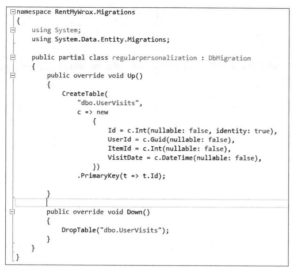

```
namespace RentMyWrox.Migrations
{
    using System;
    using System.Data.Entity.Migrations;

    public partial class regularpersonalization : DbMigration
    {
        public override void Up()
        {
            CreateTable(
                "dbo.UserVisits",
                c => new
                    {
                        Id = c.Int(nullable: false, identity: true),
                        UserId = c.Guid(nullable: false),
                        ItemId = c.Int(nullable: false),
                        VisitDate = c.DateTime(nullable: false),
                    })
                .PrimaryKey(t => t.Id);

        }

        public override void Down()
        {
            DropTable("dbo.UserVisits");
        }
    }
}
```

FIGURE 16-3: Initial migration script

9. Back in the Package Manager Console window, enter the following command in a single line and click Enter:

```
enable-migrations -ContextTypeName RentMyWrox.Models.ApplicationDbContext
        -MigrationsDirectory:ApplicationDbMigrations
```

10. Go to your Solution Explorer. You will notice a new directory was added, ApplicationDbMigrations, as shown in Figure 16-4.

FIGURE 16-4: New migrations directory

11. Enter the following command in the Package Manager Console window, in a single line:

```
add-migration -configuration:RentMyWrox.ApplicationDbMigrations.Configuration
        Personalization
```

12. Go to the ApplicationDbMigrations folder and open the file that contains "Personalization" in the title (see Figure 16-5).

```
public partial class Personalization : DbMigration
{
    public override void Up()
    {
        AddColumn("dbo.AspNetUsers", "FirstName", c => c.String());
        AddColumn("dbo.AspNetUsers", "LastName", c => c.String());
        AddColumn("dbo.AspNetUsers", "Address_Address1", c => c.String());
        AddColumn("dbo.AspNetUsers", "Address_Address2", c => c.String());
        AddColumn("dbo.AspNetUsers", "Address_City", c => c.String());
        AddColumn("dbo.AspNetUsers", "Address_State", c => c.String(maxLength: 2));
        AddColumn("dbo.AspNetUsers", "Address_ZipCode", c => c.String(maxLength: 15));
        AddColumn("dbo.AspNetUsers", "UserDemographicsId", c => c.Int(nullable: false));
        AddColumn("dbo.AspNetUsers", "OrderCount", c => c.Int(nullable: false));
    }

    public override void Down()
    {
        DropColumn("dbo.AspNetUsers", "OrderCount");
        DropColumn("dbo.AspNetUsers", "UserDemographicsId");
        DropColumn("dbo.AspNetUsers", "Address_ZipCode");
        DropColumn("dbo.AspNetUsers", "Address_State");
        DropColumn("dbo.AspNetUsers", "Address_City");
        DropColumn("dbo.AspNetUsers", "Address_Address2");
        DropColumn("dbo.AspNetUsers", "Address_Address1");
        DropColumn("dbo.AspNetUsers", "LastName");
        DropColumn("dbo.AspNetUsers", "FirstName");
    }
}
```

FIGURE 16-5: ApplicationDbMigration migration file

13. Try to update the database using the standard command in the Package Manager Console: update-database. You should get the "migrations failed" esponse shown in Figure 16-6.

```
Package Manager Console
Package source: nuget.org        ▼  ⚙  Default project: RentMyWrox          ▼  ⊠ ▪
PM> update-database
Specify the '-Verbose' flag to view the SQL statements being applied to the target database.
More than one migrations configuration type was found in the assembly 'RentMyWrox'. Specify the name of the one to use.
PM> |
```

FIGURE 16-6: Failed database update

14. Enter the following command in the Package Manager Console:

    update-database -configuration:RentMyWrox.ApplicationDbMigrations.Configuration

15. Enter this command into the Package Manager Console:

    update-database -configuration:RentMyWrox.Migrations.Configuration

16. Validate that the databases have been properly updated by going into Server Explorer. You should see an additional table for UserVisits and additional columns in the AspNetUsers that match the properties that you added to the ApplicationUser table.

How It Works

Adding properties to an existing model, as well as adding completely new classes, is something that you have done before, so the initial parts of this activity should be something you can soon do routinely. However, the output and the changes that you have to start making because of these additions are something that you have not seen yet in this project.

First, you can no longer run a simple update-database command as you have been able to until this point. The error message returned was quite specific about why the error occurred: mainly because the system found two different configuration files and was confused about what tables should actually be updated.

You haven't really reviewed the migration configuration file before. Each database context file needs a Configuration class file that defines the process for managing database migrations. These files are created when you enable migrations for a specific DbContext. The content of the file that you created in this activity is displayed here:

```
internal sealed class Configuration :
        DbMigrationsConfiguration<RentMyWrox.Models.ApplicationDbContext>
{
    public Configuration()
    {
        AutomaticMigrationsEnabled = false;
        MigrationsDirectory = @"ApplicationDbMigrations";
        ContextKey = "RentMyWrox.Models.ApplicationDbContext";
    }

    protected override void Seed(RentMyWrox.Models.ApplicationDbContext context)
    {
        //  This method will be called after migrating to the latest version.

        //  You can use the DbSet<T>.AddOrUpdate() helper extension method
        //  to avoid creating duplicate seed data. E.g.
        //
        //     context.People.AddOrUpdate(
        //       p => p.FullName,
        //       new Person { FullName = "Andrew Peters" },
        //       new Person { FullName = "Brice Lambson" },
        //       new Person { FullName = "Rowan Miller" }
        //     );
        //
    }
}
```

One constructor and one method, Seed, were created during the process of enabling migrations. The constructer sets several properties that were inherited from the DbMigrationsConfiguration class. These properties are described in Table 16-1, along with other properties that can be managed in the Configuration class.

TABLE 16-1: Database Migration Configuration Properties

Property	Description
`AutomaticMigrationDataLossAllowed`	Specifies whether data loss is acceptable during automatic migration. If set to false, an exception is thrown if data loss may occur as part of an automatic migration.
`AutomaticMigrationsEnabled`	Specifies whether automatic migrations can be used when migrating the database. If so, manual migrations are no longer necessary and the system handles the migration as needed. This value is set to false by default.
`ContextKey`	Distinguishes migrations belonging to this configuration from migrations belonging to other configurations using the same database. This property enables migrations from multiple different database contexts to be applied to a single database. This value is set by default, generally with the fully qualified type name from the context. In the configuration file created earlier, you can see that the value "RentMyWrox.Models.ApplicationDbContext" was used, the type name for the context.
`MigrationsDirectory`	The subdirectory in which code-based migrations are stored. This property must be set to a relative path for a subdirectory under the Visual Studio project root; it cannot be set to an absolute path. The default version, for the first DbContext where migrations were enabled, is "Migrations." Each subsequent context that you want to use will have to have a directory set when you enable migrations.
`TargetDatabase`	This property is of type `DbConnectionInfo` and is provided to enable the developer to override the connection of the database to be migrated. This means you don't use the setting that is set for the context being migrated.

Setting these values gives you some additional control over migrations and how they happen. Automatic migrations represent an interesting group of these configuration settings. The approach that you have used so far is manual migration. Automatic migrations enable you to skip the step in which you run the `Add-Migration` command in the Package Manager Console. Instead, the system automatically runs the migration whenever you run the `update-database` command.

It would seem that the system could simply check migrations whenever you run the upgrade, updating the database if there are any changes. However, if you consider that approach more closely, you will see that you lose control over the update process; it is better to wait until someone tells the system to run the update rather than doing it on its own.

If you are running with automatic migrations enabled, you can also determine whether or not losing data is allowed during the migration process. When you run the manual migration you don't have this option; instead, you can add code to the `Up` and `Down` methods (in the migration file that was created when the `add-migration` command was run) to manage these special cases.

When every update you do with your database is simple, it makes sense to pursue an automatic migration process. However, it is very difficult to predict that at the beginning of the project. In those cases where your database update is very simple and/or straightforward, you can change this value. Therefore, for some changes you can run with automatic migrations enabled, and for others you can switch that flag off and require manual migrations. While a case-by-case approach may make the process of updating unpredictable, it is certainly supported within all database contexts that may be updated.

The method that was created in the new `Configuration` class, `Seed`, is run on every update, as it enables you to add or update data in the database. Typically this would be used for lookup tables, such as if the sample application had shipping types that were stored in a database. It can also be run on existing data to change the data as needed to support the migration that is being performed on the database tables. In this case there was no need to pre-create or update any data.

As you can see, each database context you are going to migrate needs to be defined. In your case, one is defined as the default because it is stored in the "Migrations" directory. This is the only configuration in which you can add a migration without specifying a configuration by name; however, you always need to add the configuration when you are running the `update-database` command with multiple configurations, even if you are doing the update with the default configuration.

Note that having multiple configurations only became an issue when you added extra personalization-based information to the `ApplicationUser` class. You could have continued handling migrations and updates without specifying configuration information, but once you needed to update the security information in the second context you had to create the second configuration file.

There was one more interesting item as part of this migration that is outside of the change in how you migrate the database going forward, and that is how the new `Address` class was handled by the system when you defined the new class and added it as a new property to the `ApplicationUser` class. The table that stores the user information is shown in Figure 16-7.

FIGURE 16-7

As you can see, the information specific to the address was not put into its own table. These fields were instead added directly into the table, prefaced by the class name "Address" and an underscore character before the property name. The framework made this decision not because the `Address` class was in the same physical file as the `ApplicationUser` class, but because of how the `Address` was defined.

If the information stored in the address were important as a discrete item, such as a scenario in which you want multiple people who live at the same address to share the same information, then you could have effected that by adding an `Id` property to the `Address` class and attributing it with the `key` attribute. You would then also add the address to the list of DbSet values defined in the

`ApplicationDbContext`. By adding it to the context file you ensure that you can access it independently of the user.

Although you could have taken this approach, there was no need because in this particular case you only care about the address as a set of unique values on the user. In fact, you would have a very similar database design if you added them as simple properties on the `ApplicationUser` class, but by pulling those data fields out into their own class you can perform special work on them, as shown later in the book.

You added one other additional class as part of this activity, the `UserVisits` class, which contains information about items that a user interacts with, as well as the date and time that this interaction occurs. However, this class was added to the `RentMyWroxContext` class, rather than the user context. This reflects the consideration regarding how information should be stored, with the options being as attributes of the user or as a stand-alone item.

As you think about how to best capture information, consider it in terms of a separation of concerns. In other words, although there are many things that you need to know about the user, such as orders, shopping cart items, etc., there are very few things that a user has to know about. An order is pointless without a user who placed it, but a user without an order is a valid item in itself. With that in mind, you can see why the decision was made to put the `UserVisit` table in a separate context from the security information. The user doesn't care about the items that he or she visited, but the system does; therefore, that information should be kept with the rest of the non-user information.

The work that you just performed is as complicated as it gets when configuring your application to support personalization and additional user information. You need to determine the properties that you want to add to your application, and you need to evaluate how you can best access the information. These two considerations together will help you understand how to construct your object models.

Once you have your object models constructed, the next step is to update the database to support the additional information. When using more than one context in a file, you have an additional level of complexity for this step, but it is still a relatively simple process. After you have the models defined and the database properly updated, the next step is to use this information.

Using the Profile

Now that you have whatever personalization information that you want to capture added to the models in your application and to the database, the next thing to do is actually use the information. In this next Try It Out, you make the necessary changes in your application to capture and use all of this information.

TRY IT OUT   Capturing and Applying Data

In this exercise you update your application to capture data and take advantage of that data. As you go through the various steps, consider how they enhance your visitors' experience as they interact with your application. You can see many of these features in major eCommerce sites.

1.   Ensure that Visual Studio is running and you have the RentMyWrox application open.

2. Open the `Account\Register.aspx` page. Because you will be adding multiple rows to the file, it may be easiest to create one and copy/paste the rest, ensuring that you name everything correctly.

```
<div class="form-group">
    <asp:Label runat="server" AssociatedControlID="FirstName"
        CssClass="col-md-2 control-label">First Name</asp:Label>
    <div class="col-md-10">
        <asp:TextBox runat="server" TextMode="SingleLine" ID="FirstName"
            CssClass="form-control" />
        <asp:RequiredFieldValidator runat="server" ControlToValidate="FirstName"
            CssClass="text-danger"
            ErrorMessage="The first name field is required." />
    </div>
</div>
<div class="form-group">
    <asp:Label runat="server" AssociatedControlID="LastName"
        CssClass="col-md-2 control-label">Last Name</asp:Label>
    <div class="col-md-10">
        <asp:TextBox runat="server" TextMode="SingleLine" ID="LastName"
            CssClass="form-control" />
        <asp:RequiredFieldValidator runat="server" ControlToValidate="LastName"
            CssClass="text-danger"
            ErrorMessage="The last name field is required." />
    </div>
</div>
    <div class="form-group">
    <asp:Label runat="server" AssociatedControlID="Address1"
        CssClass="col-md-2 control-label">Address Line 1</asp:Label>
    <div class="col-md-10">
        <asp:TextBox runat="server" TextMode="SingleLine" ID="Address1"
            CssClass="form-control" />
        <asp:RequiredFieldValidator runat="server" ControlToValidate="Address1"
            CssClass="text-danger"
            ErrorMessage="The Address Line 1 field is required." />
    </div>
</div>
<div class="form-group">
    <asp:Label runat="server" AssociatedControlID="Address2"
        CssClass="col-md-2 control-label">Address Line 2</asp:Label>
    <div class="col-md-10">
        <asp:TextBox runat="server" ID="Address2" CssClass="form-control" />
        <asp:RequiredFieldValidator runat="server" ControlToValidate="FirstName"
            CssClass="text-danger"
            ErrorMessage="The address line 2 field is required." />
    </div>
</div>
<div class="form-group">
    <asp:Label runat="server" AssociatedControlID="City"
        CssClass="col-md-2 control-label">City</asp:Label>
    <div class="col-md-10">
        <asp:TextBox runat="server" ID="City" CssClass="form-control" />
        <asp:RequiredFieldValidator runat="server" ControlToValidate="FirstName"
            CssClass="text-danger" ErrorMessage="The city field is required." />
    </div>
</div>
```

```
<div class="form-group">
<asp:Label runat="server" AssociatedControlID="State"
        CssClass="col-md-2 control-label">State</asp:Label>
<div class="col-md-10">
    <asp:TextBox MaxLength="2" runat="server" ID="State"
        CssClass="form-control" />
    <asp:RequiredFieldValidator runat="server" ControlToValidate="FirstName"
        CssClass="text-danger"
        ErrorMessage="The state field is required." />
</div>
</div>
<div class="form-group">
    <asp:Label runat="server" AssociatedControlID="ZipCode"
        CssClass="col-md-2 control-label">Zip Code</asp:Label>
    <div class="col-md-10">
        <asp:TextBox MaxLength="10" runat="server" ID="ZipCode"
            CssClass="form-control" />
        <asp:RequiredFieldValidator runat="server" ControlToValidate="FirstName"
            CssClass="text-danger"
                ErrorMessage="The zip code field is required." />
    </div>
</div>
```

3. Open the `Register.aspx.cs` file and change the `CreateUser_Click` method as follows:

```
protected void CreateUser_Click(object sender, EventArgs e)
{
    var manager = Context.GetOwinContext().GetUserManager<ApplicationUserManager>();
    var signInManager = Context.GetOwinContext().Get<ApplicationSignInManager>();
    var user = new ApplicationUser()
    {
        FirstName = FirstName.Text,
        LastName = LastName.Text,
        UserName = Email.Text,
        Email = Email.Text,
        OrderCount = 0,
        UserDemographicsId = 0,
        Address = new Address
        {
            Address1 = Address1.Text,
            Address2 = Address2.Text,
            City = City.Text,
            State = State.Text,
            ZipCode = ZipCode.Text
        }
    };
    Guid oldTemporaryUser = Controllers.UserHelper.GetUserId();
    IdentityResult result = manager.Create(user, Password.Text);
    if (result.Succeeded)
    {
        Controllers.UserHelper.TransferTemporaryUserToRealUser(oldTemporaryUser,
                                user.Id);
        signInManager.SignIn( user, isPersistent: false, rememberBrowser: false);
        Response.Redirect(@"~\UserDemographics\Create?" +
```

```
                    Request.QueryString["ReturnUrl"]);
        }
        else
        {
            ErrorMessage.Text = result.Errors.FirstOrDefault();
        }
    }
```

4. Open the `Models\ShoppingCartSummary.cs` file and add a new property:

```
public string UserDisplayName { get; set; }
```

5. Open the `Controllers\ShoppingCartController.cs` file. As shown in Figure 16-8, add the following lines in the `GetShoppingCartSummary` method:

```
var appUser = UserHelper.GetApplicationUser();
if (appUser != null)
{
    summary.UserDisplayName = string.Format("{0} {1}", appUser.FirstName,
            appUser.LastName);
}
```

```
private ShoppingCartSummary GetShoppingCartSummary(RentMyWroxContext context)
{
    ShoppingCartSummary summary = new ShoppingCartSummary();
    Guid userId = UserHelper.GetUserId();
    var cartList = context.ShoppingCarts.Where(x => x.UserId == userId);
    if (cartList != null && cartList.Count() > 0)
    {
        summary.TotalValue = cartList.Sum(x => x.Quantity * x.Item.Cost);
        summary.Quantity = cartList.Sum(x => x.Quantity);
    }
    var appUser = UserHelper.GetApplicationUser();
    if (appUser != null)
    {
        summary.UserDisplayName = string.Format("{0} {1}", appUser.FirstName, appUser.LastName);
    }
    return summary;
}
```

FIGURE 16-8: Updated GetShoppingCartSummary method

6. Open `Views\Shared\_ShoppingCartSummary.cshtml`. Update the UI to the following code:

```
@model RentMyWrox.Models.ShoppingCartSummary
@{
    string display;
}
@if (Model != null && Model.Quantity > 0)
{
    display = string.Format("{0}{1}you have {2} items in your cart with a
                value of {3}",
        Model.UserDisplayName,
        string.IsNullOrWhiteSpace(Model.UserDisplayName) ? " Y" : ", y" ,
        Model.Quantity,
        Model.TotalValue.ToString("C")
        );

<span>@display</span>
<a class="checkout" href="\shoppingcart\checkout">Check Out</a>
```

```
    }
    else
    {
        display = string.Format("{0}{1}your cart is empty",
            Model.UserDisplayName,
            string.IsNullOrWhiteSpace(Model.UserDisplayName) ? " Y" : ", y"
            );
    <span>@display</span>
    }
```

7. Open the `UserDemographicsController` and find the `Create` method that handles POST requests. Update the method as follows:

```
[ValidateInput(false)]
[HttpPost]
public ActionResult Create(UserDemographics obj)
{
    using (RentMyWroxContext context = new RentMyWroxContext())
    {
        var ids = Request.Form.GetValues("HobbyIds");
        if (ids != null)
        {
            obj.Hobbies = context.Hobbies.Where(x => ids.Contains(x.Id.ToString()))
                .ToList();
        }
        context.UserDemographics.Add(obj);
        var validationErrors = context.GetValidationErrors();
        if (validationErrors.Count() == 0)
        {
            context.SaveChanges();

            ApplicationUser user = UserHelper.GetApplicationUser();
            user.UserDemographicsId = obj.Id;
            context.SaveChanges();

            return Redirect(Request.QueryString["ReturnUrl"]);
        }
        ViewBag.ServerValidationErrors =
                ConvertValidationErrorsToString(validationErrors);
        return View("Manage", obj);
    }
}
```

8. Run the application and go to the registration screen, shown in Figure 16-9.

9. Register a new user, ensuring that you fill out all the necessary fields.

   a. Click the Register button.

   b. Go to the UserDemographics page, where you can fill out the questionnaire.

   c. Saving will take you back to the page from which you accessed the login page.

10. Open the `Controllers\UserHelper.cs` file. Find the `TransferTemporaryUserToRealUser` method and add the following code above the `context.SaveChanges` method:

```
foreach(var tempUserVisits in context.UserVisits.Where(x=>x.UserId == tempId))
{
    tempUserVisits.UserId = newUserId;
}
```

FIGURE 16-9: Updated registration page

11. Add the following new method to the `UserHelper` class:

```
public static void AddUserVisit(int itemId, RentMyWroxContext context)
{
    Guid userId = GetUserId();
    context.UserVisits.RemoveRange(context.UserVisits.Where(x => x.UserId == userId
            && x.ItemId == itemId));
    context.UserVisits.Add(
                    new UserVisit
                    {
                        ItemId = itemId,
                        UserId = userId,
                        VisitDate = DateTime.UtcNow
                    }
    );
}
```

12. Go back to the `ShoppingCartController.cs` file and locate `context.SaveChanges` in the `AddToCart` method. As shown in Figure 16-10, add the following code above it:

```
UserHelper.AddUserVisit(id, context);
```

```
public ActionResult AddToCart(int id)
{
    Guid UserID = UserHelper.GetUserId();
    using (RentMyWroxContext context = new RentMyWroxContext())
    {
        Item addedItem = context.Items.FirstOrDefault(x => x.Id == id);

        // now that we know it is a valid ID
        if (addedItem != null)
        {
            // Check to see if this item was already added
            var sameItemInShoppingCart = context.ShoppingCarts.FirstOrDefault(x => x.Item.Id == id && x.UserId == UserID);
            if (sameItemInShoppingCart == null)
            {
                // if not already in cart then add it
                ShoppingCart sc = new ShoppingCart
                {
                    Item = addedItem,
                    UserId = UserID,
                    Quantity = 1,
                    DateAdded = DateTime.Now
                };
                context.ShoppingCarts.Add(sc);
            }
            else
            {
                // increment the quantity of the existing shopping cart item
                sameItemInShoppingCart.Quantity++;
            }
            context.UserVisits.Add(
                new UserVisit
                {
                    ItemId = id,
                    UserId = UserID,
                    VisitDate = DateTime.UtcNow }
            );
            context.SaveChanges();
        }
        ShoppingCartSummary summary = GetShoppingCartSummary(context);
        return PartialView("_ShoppingCartSummary", summary);
    }
}
```

FIGURE 16-10: Updated AddToCart method

13. Open the `ItemController.cs` file and update the `Details` action as follows:

```
[OutputCache(Duration = 1200, Location = OutputCacheLocation.Server)]
public ActionResult Details(int id)
{
    using (RentMyWroxContext context = new RentMyWroxContext())
    {
        Item item = context.Items.FirstOrDefault(x => x.Id == id);
        UserHelper.AddUserVisit(id, context);
        context.SaveChanges();
        return View(item);
    }
}
```

14. While still in `ItemController.cs`, add a new action:

```
public ActionResult Recent()
{
    using (RentMyWroxContext context = new RentMyWroxContext())
```

```
    {
        Guid newUserId = UserHelper.GetUserId();
        var recentItems = (from uv in context.UserVisits
                            join item in context.Items on uv.ItemId equals item.Id
                            where uv.UserId == newUserId
                            orderby uv.VisitDate descending
                            select item as Item).Take(3).ToList();
        context.SaveChanges();
        return PartialView("_RecentItems", recentItems);
    }
}
```

15. Right-click on Views\Shared and add a new view. Name it **_RecentItems** and ensure that it is a partial view, as shown in Figure 16-11.

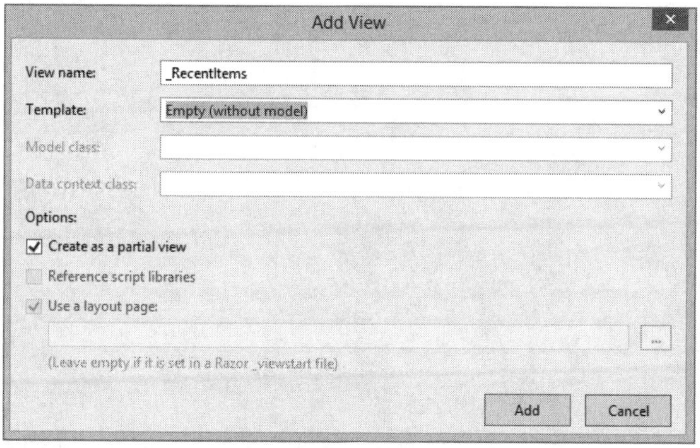

FIGURE 16-11: Adding a new view

16. Add the following content to the new view:

```
@model List<RentMyWrox.Models.Item>

@if (Model != null && Model.Count > 0)
{
    <div id="recentItemsTitle">Items you have recently reviewed</div>
    foreach (var item in Model)
    {
        <span class="recentItem">
            <div class="recentItemsName">@item.Name</div>
            <span class="recentItemsDescription">
                @if (item.Description.Length > 250)
                { <span>@item.Description.Substring(0, 250)...</span> }
                else
                { @item.Description }
            </span>
        </span>
    }
}
```

17. Open your `RentMyWrox.css` file and add the following styles:

```
#recentItemsTitle{
    background-color:#F8B6C9;
    color:white;
    font-weight:800;
    width: 900px;
    margin-top: 15px;
    display:block;
    padding: 10px;
    float:left;
}

.recentItemsName {
    color:#C40D42;
    font-size: 16px;
    font-weight:600;
}

.recentItem{
    padding: 10px;
    width:275px;
    float:left;
}

.recentItemsDescription {
    color:#C40D42;
    float:left;
    font-size: 12px;
}
```

18. Open the `Views\Shared\_MVCLayout.cshtml` page. Find the `@RenderBody` method and add the following line below it, while still in the same `<div>` tags (see Figure 16-12).

```
<span>@Html.Action("Recent", "Item")</span>
```

FIGURE 16-12: Updated layout page

19. Run the application. Go into several detail pages and then back to the home page. It should look like Figure 16-13.

How It Works

In this activity you added several pieces of functionality that will provide a more welcoming and useful experience to users. They will feel more welcome because the site now remembers them by name, and it will be more useful as well as remembering and displaying some of the things that they viewed and/or purchased on previous visits. Personalization items include using the visitor's name when they log in, and adding it to text related to their shopping cart (whether it is empty or not), as shown in Figure 16-14.

Home	Sort by: Name ▾	You are currently on Page 1 of 2 Next Page

Contact Us
About Us
Login

Curae nec lobortis lacinia $25.00

Curae nec lobortis lacinia posuere quisque hendrerit etiam tempor mi, rutrum pellentesque varius fames sit curabitur lobortis augue nisi, aliquam aliquet eleifend massa proin netus porttitor neque sodales nam fames fringilla volutpat libero class sol... Full details Add to Cart

Dapibus aptent diam $9.95

We open
Monday at 9:00 am

Bring a friend

Bringing a friend with you to pick up your tools will get you 5% off your rental fee. If they sign up than you get 15% off!

Dapibus aptent diam euismod inceptos in ante adipiscing himenaeos, ante tristique elementum quis ad elementum egestas pharetra massa, justo mollis donec duis suspendisse inceptos purus eros curae dictum vulputate vivamus sapien inceptos luctus suspen... Full details Add to Cart

Investigatam diutissime updated2 $19.90

Investigatam diutissime quaestionem, quantum nostrae mentis igniculum lux diuina dignata est, formatam rationibus litterisque updated2mandatam offerendam uobis communicandamque curaui tam uestri cupidus iudicii quam nostri studiosus inuenti. Qu... Full details Add to Cart

Ipsum Lorem $50.00

Lorem ipsum dolor sit amet, consectetur adipiscing elit, sed do eiusmod tempor incididunt ut labore et dolore magna aliqua. Ut enim ad minim veniam, quis nostrud exercitation ullamco laboris nisi ut aliquip ex ea commodo consequat. Duis aute irure do... Full details Add to Cart

Mollis massa $5.00

Mollis massa nam porttitor iaculis condimentum dapibus class etiam nam integer, varius lacinia aptent eleifend elit quis urna pretium nec luctus, primis interdum pulvinar tincidunt hac curabitur convallis imperdiet in auctor libero senectus dolor ali... Full details Add to Cart

Items you have recently reviewed

Ipsum Lorem
Lorem ipsum dolor sit amet, consectetur adipiscing elit, sed do eiusmod tempor incididunt ut labore et dolore magna aliqua. Ut enim ad minim veniam, quis nostrud exercitation ullamco laboris nisi ut aliquip ex ea commodo consequat. Duis aute irure do...

Curae nec lobortis lacinia
Curae nec lobortis lacinia posuere quisque hendrerit etiam tempor mi, rutrum pellentesque varius fames sit curabitur lobortis augue nisi, aliquam aliquet eleifend massa proin netus porttitor neque sodales nam fames fringilla volutpat libero class sol...

Investigatam diutissime updated2
Investigatam diutissime quaestionem, quantum nostrae mentis igniculum lux diuina dignata est, formatam rationibus litterisque updated2mandatam offerendam uobis communicandamque curaui tam uestri cupidus iudicii quam nostri studiosus inuenti. Qu...

FIGURE 16-13: Home page with recent items displayed at the bottom

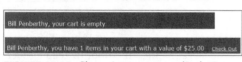

Bill Penberthy, your cart is empty

Bill Penberthy, you have 1 items in your cart with a value of $25.00 Check Out

FIGURE 16-14: Shopping cart area displaying name

You were able to capture this information by first adding the new data entry fields on the registration page. Once the UI was updated, you then updated the code-behind so that the `ApplicationUser` that you were creating had the additional fields. This change was very limited, as you simply needed to add the data captured in your new data entry fields to their appropriate properties in the model.

You also made a change so that rather than simply return to the page that requested the login, the user was then taken to the `UserDemographics` entry screen, with the requesting URL being passed to that screen as a query string value. After the user fills out their `UserDemographics` screen, they are taken to the page from which they started the registration process—the value of which was passed via query string through each one of the requests.

While they might not seem like much, these few changes are a huge step in personalization. That's because you can now display the user's name, which is significant because it gives users the sense of a relationship. For example, imagine how users would react to seeing someone else's name on the screen after they logged in. They would certainly lose confidence in your application and its ability to keep their information safe. Feeling safe is an important part of personalization, and it is enhanced by the building of a relationship.

Adding the user's name to the UI required a change to the object that is used to populate the shopping cart, the `ShoppingCartSummary` class, where you added a property that would "carry" the user's display name. Once the name was added, you could change the text displayed so that it included the user's name in a proper sentence.

The other set of changes that you made were all related to providing a list of recently viewed items. You can see this type of functionality on many eCommerce sites, such as Amazon.com. You capture the relationship in two different instances: whenever the user goes to the details page for an item and whenever an item is added to the shopping cart. Because you are capturing this in more than one place, it makes sense to pull that code out and put it in a shared location. In this case that's the `UserHelper` class, to which you already added various helper methods that support interacting with user information.

The method that is capturing this information is shown again here:

```
public static void AddUserVisit(int itemId, RentMyWroxContext context)
{
    Guid userId = GetUserId();
    context.UserVisits.RemoveRange(context.UserVisits.Where(x => x.UserId == userId
            && x.ItemId == itemId));
    context.UserVisits.Add(
                new UserVisit
                {
                    ItemId = itemId,
                    UserId = userId,
                    VisitDate = DateTime.UtcNow
                }
    );
}
```

Note two things about this example. First, the method is taking a context as a parameter. This means that the method does not have its own place where it runs the `SaveChanges` method, instead expecting the calling code to manage that aspect. If the calling code doesn't take this action, then the method call would be in vain. The other option would be to create a context within the method and use that to manage the database access, but that would mean a second connection open to the database in the same method call. Since a limited number of database connections are available, it simply doesn't make sense to consume two of them for the same call when you can pass the context into a method. Therefore, by convention, whenever you use a context as a method parameter, that method could be making changes in that context; so if you call another method and pass in a context, then you should also assume the responsibility of saving those changes.

The second interesting item in the `AddUserVisit` method is that the first thing you do is remove any other visits by that same user to a particular item. If you don't take this approach, you may well present a view in which the same product is listed multiple times, and that would be an unpleasant user experience.

COORDINATED UNIVERSAL TIME (UTC)

UTC is the primary time standard used throughout the world to regulate clocks and coordinate time zones. It is the mean solar time at 0 degrees longitude, and is defined by the International Telecommunications Union and based on International Atomic Time, which also adds leap seconds at irregular intervals to compensate for the changes in earth's rotation. All the other time zones are defined in relation to UTC. You may see time notations such as UTC–8, which corresponds to Pacific Standard Time, the time on the West Coast of the U.S.

UTC is commonly used to store times in a database because it standardizes them, enabling a database to gather date and time information from multiple time zones and store them in a single time zone where you can easily use the standard offsets, such as –8 for Pacific Time, in order to display the correct time for users based on their particular system time. This ensures that all of the times are saved relatively, for everyone across the world, rather than in a single time zone.

You were capturing this information so that you could display it to the user. This display is being handled by a partial view that presents a horizontal list of items that the user has already visited. If the user has not visited any items, then nothing is displayed, not even the section header.

The controller action that builds this list is shown again here:

```
public ActionResult Recent()
{
    using (RentMyWroxContext context = new RentMyWroxContext())
    {
        Guid newUserId = UserHelper.GetUserId();
        var recentItems = (from uv in context.UserVisits
                           join item in context.Items
on uv.ItemId equals item.Id
                           where uv.UserId == newUserId
                           orderby uv.VisitDate descending
                           select item as Item).Take(3).ToList();
        context.SaveChanges();
        return PartialView("_RecentItems", recentItems);
    }
}
```

continues

---

continued

This is the first time you have done a LINQ join in which you are linking information from two different collections. You are taking a value from the first collection of objects, `UserVisit.ItemId`, and using that value to join to the second collection. You are able to do this join because the `ItemId` value from the `UserVisit` has a corresponding value in the `Id` property of the `Item` collection. The `join` statement that you built does exactly that—it joins the second collection (`Items`) to the first collection (`UserVisits`) by using the `on` keyword and defining the relationship between the two properties as `equal`.

After adding the join for the two collections, you were able to sort it in descending order by the time visited. In the next line you took the first three items from the list using the `Take` extension method. This ensures that the list is never more than three items long, the maximum number of items that would nicely fit in the UI.

Once you had the application updated to capture and display the additional information, the last thing you had to do was add a few styles to the style sheet so that the new section of the screen you added looks like a regular part of the site.

Adding personalization information and displaying it is no different than any other data that you capture and use. The only reason it is special is because the data doesn't necessarily fit any business purpose per se; its entire purpose for existing is to build a better and more comfortable relationship between users and your application, with the hope that they spend more time with it, and even consider it the primary solution for whatever problem your application is meant to solve. In the case of the sample application, you want users to consider your lending library first whenever they need a tool—even before they would consider going to a hardware store and purchasing a new one. The steps that you took here will incrementally increase the likelihood of that happening because users feel that you understand them and their desires; you have demonstrated that you know them personally because you implemented personalization in your application.

PRACTICAL PERSONALIZATION TIPS

The following list contains some tips to keep in mind when you are implementing personalization:

➤ You can't immediately access the user information that is stored in the authentication cookie immediately after logging in. The system automatically loads the information into the response cookies, but the default user management tools expect to read from the request cookies, so you won't be able to access the user until the next time that user visits the site. This is why successful logins redirect the user to a different page; at that point, the page to which the user was redirected can access the user information.

➤ When you are considering whether information should be stored in the Identity database or in your own application database, a key consideration is whether the information you are saving describes your user or the interaction between your user and your site. If the information is specific to, and about, the user, then that is personalization data stored with the user.

When the information is not specifically about and describing the user, then that information should probably be stored in your application's database context.

➤ Try to keep your personalization data as flat as possible. In other words, avoid any approach that creates a lot of database tables and stores a lot of information—that's probably not something you want to attach to your user. Keep in mind that because the goal is personalization, you will likely be accessing the user upon every request for which the user has logged in. Therefore, you want something very performant by ensuring that the number of tables being managed is minimized.

SUMMARY

Personalization is when a system, such as your web application, can recognize users and provide information specific to their needs. A system can provide personalization by gathering information about the person, whether through direct questions or through tracking their movement through the site. As creepy as this might sound, it is a critical part of being able to predict your user's wants and needs so that your application can better support them and makes information available to them without the user having to take any special action. Personalization is used on all the major eCommerce sites, which analyze their visitors' habits in order to determine what to present to them, with the goal of driving more sales.

In the current world of ASP.NET, implementing personalization is no big deal. It has been made easy because of the way in which the Identity framework uses Entity Framework Code First to manage creation of the security database. Using EF Code First enables you to customize the data tables that store user information. With this level of customization you can add any number of properties on a user account, of any type—from simple C# types to complex objects.

EXERCISES

1. Your e-commerce site sells women's clothing. What kind of information would you gather if you wanted to get an understanding of the color palette that the user preferred?

2. What could you do with the information that you just gathered?

▶ WHAT YOU LEARNED IN THIS CHAPTER

Automatic Migration	The capability of Entity Framework Code First to perform a database migration in a single step, rather than requiring you to first create a migration and then update the database. Using an automatic migration may be worth it if you find that you rarely, if ever, customize your migration files. Any time you need to customize the migration script by altering database types or adding indexes or other database-specific items (that you can't define in the model using an attribute) you need to use a manual migration. Automatic migration is managed by a value in the `Configuration` class in your Migration directory.
`-configuration`	A new keyword used when either adding a migration or updating a database. It is necessary when the application contains more than one database context.
`Configuration.cs`	A class created when you enable migrations in more than one database context for your application. It contains all the configuration information that defines the Migration directory, whether to use automatic migration, etc. It also contains the `Seed` method, whereby you can define data that will be created every time a deployment happens for the database context.
Migration Directory	The directory that contains a `Configuration.cs` class and all the migration scripts for a database context. It is created when you run the `enable-migration` command in the Package Manager Console, and it requires that you pass in the name of the directory as a parameter in the command.
Personalization	The concept of recognizing users and providing special information to them based on this recognition. It can be as simple as using their name in the site or as complex as tracking their preferences and always using these preferences when displaying content to them.

17

Exception Handling, Debugging, and Tracing

WHAT YOU WILL LEARN IN THIS CHAPTER:

➤ The different types of exceptions

➤ How to handle exceptions

➤ Debugging your application

➤ How to use the Page Inspector

➤ Using standard tracing in ASP.NET

➤ Logging

CODE DOWNLOADS FOR THIS CHAPTER:

The wrox.com code downloads for this chapter are found at `www.wiley.com/go/beginningaspnetforvisualstudio` on the Download Code tab. The code is in the chapter 17 download and individually named according to the names throughout the chapter.

Unfortunately, the more time you spend as a developer, the greater the variety of errors you will encounter, as errors are a common part of the development process. However, as your application evolves, the burden is on you to find these errors and resolve them, because they demonstrate some kind of problem in either your software or the data with which you are working.

You have already had some exposure to exceptions throughout the book, but your software can experience other types of problems that don't throw exceptions. Because of this lack of exceptions, these problems can be difficult to track down; instead, you have to follow through the code and examine what is happening with the data, rather than analyze an exception to get this information. This process can be very complicated, especially in larger applications, because a request could travel through many different classes and objects between the request being received and the response being returned.

In this chapter you will learn different ways to watch your application so that you can understand the cause of different types of problems. This chapter also covers debugging and introduces other tools in Visual Studio that enable you to get up close and personal with the processing of your application.

Because your application runs outside of Visual Studio, such as after you put it into a production environment, you will also learn about various ways to capture information without the application running in debugging mode. These approaches may not give you an immediate understanding of the problem, but they provide you with a way to evaluate it so that you can still try to remedy it.

ERROR HANDLING

In many ways error handling is a process as much as a set of specific techniques. It is virtually impossible to get everything right the first time you write the code for an application because so many things can go wrong. You can mistype a variable name, put a method call in the wrong place, run across bad data during the running of the application, or even something completely out of your hands such as the database server going down during the running of the application. You need to anticipate these kinds of failures and design your application to deal with them.

The process of managing errors is called debugging. Visual Studio includes a rich set of tools to help you debug your application. These tools range from checks during the compilation of your code, to the ability to watch your application as it runs, checking the values of different variables along the way. There is a much more detailed discussion of debugging later in this chapter.

Different Types of Errors

You might run into three different types of errors during the application development process:

➤   **Syntax errors:** Errors caused when the code itself is incorrect, either because of typos or missing language. These types of errors throw compile-time errors and you will not be able to run the application.

➤   **Logic errors:** Errors that cause an incorrect outcome. These could be as simple as subtracting a value when it should be added, or using the wrong value for a calculation, or any number of different possibilities where the code is just wrong. The application will still compile and most likely run, but it won't return the results you may be looking for.

➤   **Runtime errors:** Errors that cause the application to crash or throw exceptions while running. Sometimes a logic error may demonstrate as a runtime error, but not always.

Each of the preceding errors is explained in detail in the following sections.

Syntax Errors

Syntax errors, also known as *compile-time errors*, are caused when the code that you write is incorrect. You may have already run into these when working with the sample application if you missed a line of code or mistyped a variable name. These errors are generally caught during compilation time—or even earlier than that, as Visual Studio understands the compilation rules and reevaluates the area of code that you are working on with every keystroke. This reevaluation is what enables the IntelliSense auto-complete dropdown to be populated. However, as shown in Figure 17-1, it also populates the Error List pane with all the current syntax errors, repopulating this view after each keystroke.

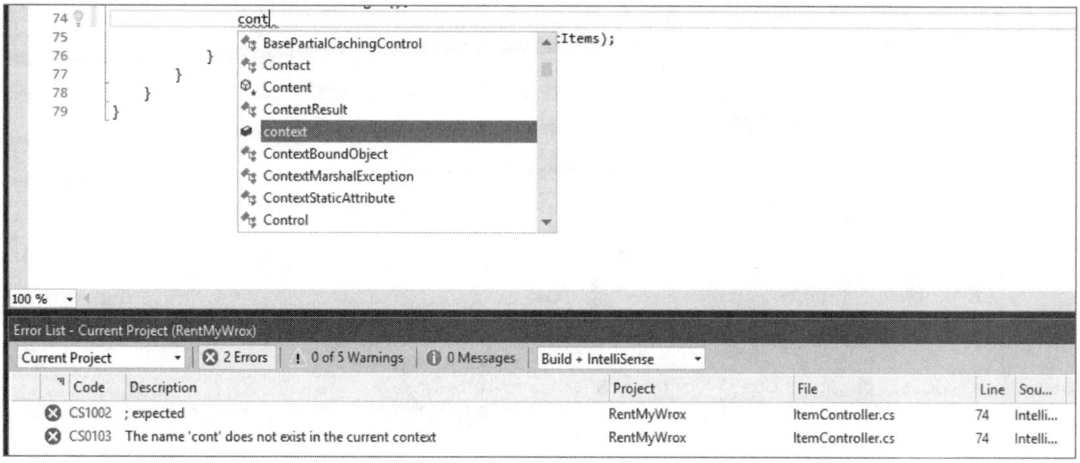

FIGURE 17-1: Error List in Visual Studio

The error list displayed in Figure 17-1 lists all the syntax errors found across the application. As you can see, two different errors were found on line 74, the line where the cursor is located; the first indicates that a semicolon (;) is missing, while the second error states that the keystrokes already typed in are not a value. This second error will disappear once the typing is completed and Visual Studio recognizes the action that you are trying to take, while the first will go away once you type the semicolon character at the end of the line of code.

The presence of any errors in this list will prevent the application from compiling, so it should become second nature to take a quick look at the Error List to see if there are any outstanding errors before you try to run the application. However, it is possible that there are errors present in the application that the reevaluation hasn't caught. The larger your application, the greater the chance that syntax errors in other parts of the system will not be displayed until after you try to compile the application.

Items listed in the Error List are easy to find and fix. Not only does the list display the filename and line number, double-clicking on the row with the error also takes you directly to the line in that file and the description explains the nature of the problem.

Logic Errors

Whereas syntax errors stop your application from compiling, much less running, logic errors are much more subtle. They won't cause a problem with compilation and may not even throw a runtime exception; instead, you simply won't get the expected output. These are the most common errors by far, as there is no automatic notification when they happen; they instead rely on something, or some-one, recognizing that the behavior is unexpected.

Consider the following snippets that have been taken from the sample application and slightly altered:

MIS-ASSIGNMENT ERROR

```
using (RentMyWroxContext context = new RentMyWroxContext())
{
    var item = context.Items.FirstOrDefault(x => x.Id == itemId);
    tbAcquiredDate.Text = item.DateAcquired.ToShortDateString();
    tbCost.Text = item.Cost.ToString();
    tbDescription.Text = item.Name;
    tbItemNumber.Text = item.ItemNumber;
    tbName.Text = item.Description;
}
```

COMPARISON ERROR

```
using (RentMyWroxContext context = new RentMyWroxContext())
{
    Notification note = context.Notifications
    .Where(x => x.DisplayStartDate >= DateTime.Now
        && x.DisplayEndDate <= DateTime.Now)
    .FirstOrDefault();

    return PartialView("_Notification", note);
}
```

Each of these snippets contains one or more logical errors that will compile without a problem yet negatively affect your application's ability to run correctly. Can you find them just by examining the code?

The error in the first snippet is noticeable when you look for a problem, but if you aren't expecting a problem it would be easy to miss that you are assigning the value of the item's Name property to the value of an object named tbDescription, and the value of the item's Description property to an object named tbName. Identifying this is made even more difficult because it may actually be correct; perhaps the TextBox controls were poorly named or the terms "Description" and "Name" mean different things in the different contexts (business interface vs. user interface).

The error in the second snippet is much more subtle and thus harder to track down. The require-ment that this snippet is trying to fulfill is to display those notifications that are currently active; today's date falls between the DisplayStartDate and DisplayEndDate properties of the notifica-tion. Therein lies the problem. The code snippet returns a notification only if the DisplayStartDate is greater than or equal to the current DateTime and the DisplayEndDate is less than the current DateTime. Thus, the only items that will be returned are those whose DisplayEndDate is before their DisplayStartDate or those items that are malconfigured. The comparison operators for the DisplayStartDate and DisplayEndDate are reversed.

Later in the chapter you will look at the support Visual Studio offers you for tracking these errors down.

Runtime Errors

An error that you are not able to see until the application is actually running is a runtime error. Obviously, because the application is running, this error is not a syntax error but instead means that something in your application did something unexpected that the application cannot handle. One of the more problematic concerns about runtime errors is that they may only happen occasionally, especially when they are related to log errors.

Consider the following conditions (again taken from the sample application and altered):

```
protected void SaveItem_Clicked(object sender, EventArgs e)
{
    if (IsValid)
    {
        Item item;
        using (RentMyWroxContext context = new RentMyWroxContext())
        {
            item = new Item();
            UpdateItem(item);
            context.Items.Add(item);

            context.SaveChanges();
        }
        Response.Redirect("~/admin/ItemList");
    }
}

private void UpdateItem(Item item)
{
    item.Description = tbName.Text;
    item.Name = tbDescription.Text;
}

public class Item
{
    [Key]
    public int Id { get; set; }

    [MaxLength(50)]
    public string Name { get; set; }

    [MaxLength(250)]
    public string Description { get; set; }
}
```

There is a close replication of the logical error that you saw earlier, but in this case you are building the object that will be saved to the database. This means that it is a logical error, although sometimes it will cause a runtime exception. If you look at the data attributes for the item you will see that the maximum length for the Name property is 50 characters, while the maximum length for the Description property is 250 characters.

These MaxLength attributes are what's causing the problem. You correctly built the client-side validation so that both properties will be validated before returning to the server, so it's easy to assume that it all will work correctly. Indeed, when you run some simple tests it seems to work—there are no exceptions. However, the first time a user types a value longer than 50 characters into the tb Description textbox, a runtime error is thrown because that large value was incorrectly assigned to the Name property, therefore failing validation when the SaveChanges method is run on the context. This error causes an exception to be thrown.

A parser error is another type of runtime error that does not throw an exception. Rather, it throws an error that you can see in the browser as opposed to automatically in the debugger. Figure 17-2 shows one of these parser errors.

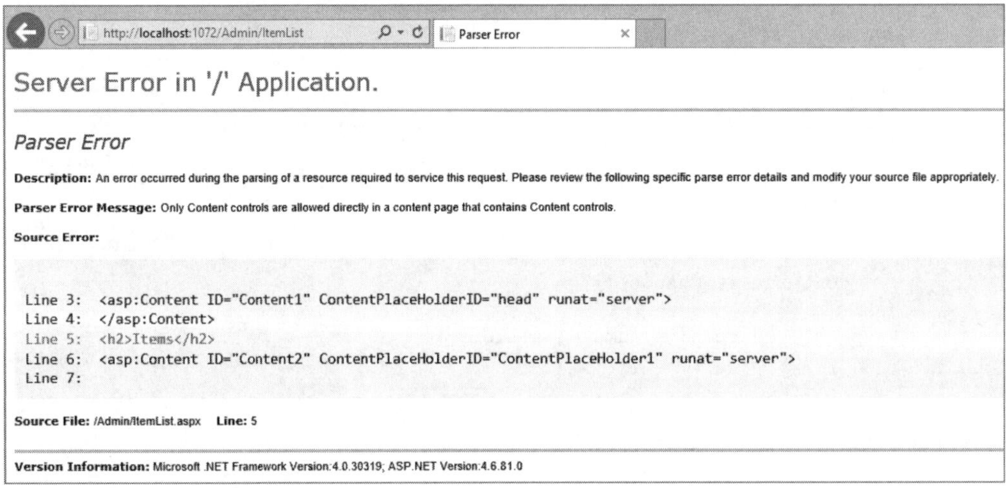

FIGURE 17-2: ASP.NET Web Forms parser error

Parser errors can happen when "non-code" elements are run. For ASP.NET Web Forms, this would likely mean that controls are incorrectly configured in the markup page, as shown in the figure. With ASP.NET Web Forms markup pages, even items that you would expect to create syntax errors will successfully compile yet throw an error during runtime. Figure 17-3 shows an example of this: The server control name is spelled incorrectly yet the application still compiles and runs until it gets to that page. Note that Visual Studio understands that something is wrong with the syntax because the markup page has a squiggly line under the misspelled control name, indicating a problem.

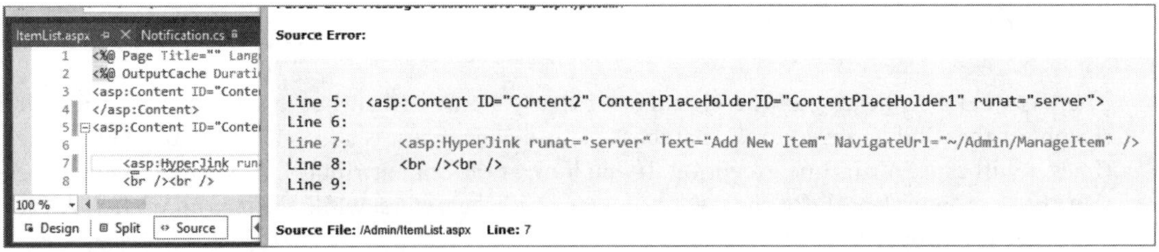

FIGURE 17-3: ASP.NET Web Forms server error with VS

Unfortunately, you have some of the same possibilities when working with ASP.NET MVC views, as shown in Figure 17-4, even though there is a problem with the code. In this case the highlighted line, line 9, references an invalid property named "Bame" on the Item object.

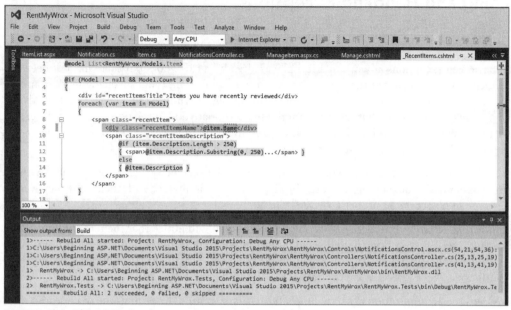

FIGURE 17-4: This MVC view has syntax error yet compiles.

That name is not a valid property, and Visual Studio indicated that with the squiggly line under the property name. However, it compiles successfully.

The primary difference between ASP.NET Web Forms and ASP.NET MVC is that this problem throws a runtime exception in MVC that you can examine in Visual Studio, rather than the server error thrown in Web Forms. Running this view as shown causes the exception shown in Figure 17-5.

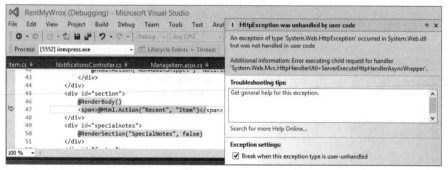

FIGURE 17-5: Runtime error caused by MVC view syntax error

One of the key outputs from a runtime error is an exception. In the next section you will learn how to catch and work with .NET exceptions.

Catching and Handling Exceptions

There are many different default .NET exceptions, all of which inherit from the base `Exception` class. This inheritance creates a set of common properties that are available on all .NET exceptions.

You have seen exceptions at work in a few places already in this book, but there has not been a lot of in-depth discussion about them, other than that you don't want them surfacing in your application. In a nutshell, exceptions are errors that occur during the runtime of a program. The advantage of using exceptions is that the program doesn't terminate due to the occurrence of the error; it instead "throws" an exception. This enables you to understand the error condition by analyzing the exception, while giving the application the opportunity to continue its processing.

When .NET throws an exception you will see that it is of a specific type and always ends with the term "Exception." These exceptions are objects, and you can interact with them as if they were any other type of object if you properly "catch" them.

If you peruse different Internet articles on exceptions, you will notice that the terminology differs from that used when working with a regular custom object. Exceptions tend to be "thrown" or "tossed"; and when handled appropriately, they are said to be "caught," "captured," or "handled." In many ways these verbs are appropriate.

Consider how an application runs. In simple terms it steps through the first line of code and then goes to the next line. It processes in this way until it gets to the final line of the code, at which time the application ends. Many different method calls and work may occur in between, but this is generally how the program flows. However, when an error is encountered the application stops what it is doing, identifies and wraps the error in an exception, and then throws it out of the method in which it is running.

This is done through each level of the application (or each of the methods in which the error may happen) until it gets to a point where there is a handler for the exception, where the exception is caught. If there is no handler for the exception, then the application stops running.

Three keywords support the exception system: `try`, `catch`, and `finally`. Each of these keywords references a specific part of the exception system, as shown here:

```
try
{
    // take a series of actions that may cause an exception
    // this may be one method in particular or a whole set of
    // steps.
}
catch(Exception ex)
{
    // if an exception is thrown the code in this section
    // will be run
}
finally
{
```

```
        // code in this section will be run regardless of
        // whether or not an exception was thrown
}
```

The `try` keyword defines the wrapper; or the block of code where you are ready to capture an exception. An exception happening inside this block will be directed to the code block defined by the `catch` keyword. An exception happening outside of a `try` block will propagate up the call stack until either it is caught or it surfaces in runtime, causing the application to crash.

CALL STACK

The call stack is a data structure that stores information about the active routines of a software application. Also known as the execution stack or run-time stack, the primary responsibility of the call stack is to keep track of which active functions should return control when they finish executing. An active function is a method that has been called but has not yet completed. It is called a stack because these method calls can be nested as shown:

```
public void TopMethod()
{
    MiddleMethod();
}

public void MiddleMethod()
{
    BottomMethod();
}

Public void BottomMethod()
{
    // processing
}
```

The call stack for your application varies according to where you examine it. If you looked at the call stack in the `TopMethod`, you would see that it only contains `TopMethod`. If you examined the call stack while in the `MiddleMethod` you would see that both `TopMethod` and `MiddleMethod` were in the call stack. Examining the call stack while in the `BottomMethod` would show all three methods.

The call stack shrinks and grows as the application proceeds. Just as the call stack becomes three deep when in the `BottomMethod`, after processing is completed in that method and it returns to the `MiddleMethod` the call stack will unwind, or back up one level, and only show the `TopMethod` and `MiddleMethod`. The same happens when the `MiddleMethod` returns.

Later in this chapter you will learn how to navigate the call stack in Visual Studio so that you can monitor the entire range of calls happening within that current processing stack.

The `try` keyword defines the code block that is going to be managed for exceptions. The `catch` keyword defines the code block that will run when an exception is thrown from code being managed within the `try` block. Typically, the work being performed in this area evaluates the exception to determine whether execution can resume or should be stopped, and to take some action to publicize that an error occurred.

You can use the catch keyword without the parameters:

```
try
{
    // some work
}
catch
{
    // some other work
}
```

If you use the `catch` block without the parameters, however, you will never be able to do anything with the exception, so cases in which you will want to use this approach are very limited.

You can also use multiple `catch` blocks for a single `try` block, each capturing a different kind of exception:

```
try
{
    // some work
}
catch(ArgumentNullException ex)
{
    // some other work
}
catch(Exception ex)
{
    // some other work
}
```

If you chain your `catch` blocks in this way the order is important. The framework evaluates the parameter of the first `catch` block to see if the exception that was thrown matches. If it doesn't match, it goes on to the second `catch` block and tries again, through the entire chain of `catch` blocks until it finds one that matches. If there is no match, then the exception keeps going up the call stack. This is why when you see multiple catch blocks, you may see the last one as a very generic type such as an `Exception`, which is the base class for every exception, so it catches all exceptions that reach that point.

Once you catch the exception you have to determine what your application will do. First, you need to evaluate the type of exception that is thrown. Table 17-1 describes the most common exceptions that you will run into when you are working with ASP.NET applications.

TABLE 17-1: Common Exceptions

EXCEPTION	DESCRIPTION
`AmbiguousMatchException`	Thrown when binding to a member results in more than one member matching the binding criteria. This is common in ASP.NET MVC when two different actions can respond to a single request. Because the system can't determine which is the appropriate value, it throws this exception. This exception is very rarely deliberately thrown by a developer.
`ArgumentNullException`	Thrown when a null reference is passed to a method that doesn't accept it as a valid argument. This exception is commonly thrown by developers when they write a method that is accepting arguments of a complex type and they cannot handle a null object.
`ArgumentOutOfRangeException`	Thrown when the value of an argument is outside the allowable range of values as defined by the invoked method. This is different from an `ArgumentNullException` in that the object is not null, but instead has some invalid data. An example here could be a function that includes taking the square root of a value. This means that the value cannot be negative, so passing in a negative value should throw an `ArgumentOutOfRangeException`.
`DBConcurrencyException`	Thrown by a `DataAdapter` during an insert, update, or delete operation if the number of rows affected equals zero. This exception could be thrown when using ASP.NET Web Forms data controls for direct access to the database. It is rarely thrown by a developer.
`FileNotFoundException`	Thrown when the system tries to access a file on the file system that does not exist. This exception can be thrown by developers when they determine that an expected resource does not exist. It can also be thrown by the framework when the attempt to access the file happens.
`HttpRequestValidationException`	Thrown when a potentially malicious input string is received from the client as part of the request data. This type of exception is generally not thrown by the developer but when Request Validation fails.
`IndexOutOfRangeException`	Thrown when an attempt is made to access an element of an array or collection with an index that is outside its bounds. This exception is rarely thrown by a developer. It's typically seen when working with arrays or other types of collections and there is an attempt to access an item outside the collection, e.g., trying to access item 21 when there are only 20 items in the collection.

continues

TABLE 17-1 *(continued)*

EXCEPTION	DESCRIPTION
InvalidCastException	Thrown when the conversion of an instance of one type to another type is not supported. For example, attempting to convert a Char value to a DateTime value throws this exception. It is virtually never thrown by a developer, but by the framework.
KeyNotFoundException	Thrown when the key specified for accessing an element in a collection does not match any key in the collection. This is much like an IndexOutOutRangeException in that it works on collections, but it requires one of the collections types that use a key/value approach, such as a Dictionary.
NoNullAllowedException	Thrown when you try to insert a null value into a column where AllowDBNull is set to false. This exception could be thrown when using ASP.NET Web Forms data controls for direct access to the database. It is rarely thrown by a developer.
NullReferenceException	One of the most common exceptions, this is thrown when you try to access a member on a type whose value is null. A NullReferenceException exception typically reflects developer error, with the most common reasons being that you've forgotten to instantiate a reference type or you get a null return value from a method and then call a method on the returned type. This exception may be thrown by a developer, but most developers would use ArgumentNullException to manage null values being passed into a method.
OutOfMemoryException	Thrown when there is not enough memory to continue the execution of a program. This exception represents a catastrophic failure. The most common way to have this problem in a web application is to try to load too much dynamic information into memory, such as loading all the rows of a database into memory and then working with them in memory. This exception is a default system exception and is never thrown by a developer.
StackOverflowException	Thrown when the execution stack overflows because it contains too many nested method calls. This is another fairly common exception and is generally called when using recursion, when a method calls itself.

One of the most common mistakes that new developers make is deciding that they should probably use try and catch keywords in every method so that all exceptions can be caught and dealt with.

You should only do this if you know that you can actually handle the exception; and you should never have an empty catch block, as shown here:

```
try
{
    // some work
}
catch
{}
```

These empty catch blocks may be convenient in that using them stops the exception from rising any higher up the call stack, but it does nothing to help you actually fix the problem. You should catch the error when you have a chance to either fix the problem or to mitigate the issue that caused the error, such as using a default value or retrying a database call; whatever failed.

When you get exceptions that you can't handle, instead, allow these exceptions to continue up the stack. Later in this chapter you will learn how to configure the application to handle these unhandled exceptions in a way that enables you (as the developer) to gather information about the problem yet still provide a consistent experience to the user even though the work that they were trying to do failed.

While I have so far been emphasizing the errors thrown by the framework, it is important to realize that as a developer you will sometimes be creating and throwing exceptions yourself, in your own code. An example of this would be a method that you create that accepts an object as one of the properties. Would you be able to perform the work that you need to when the object is null? If not, what would you do? How would you handle it? In many cases you will throw an exception, as shown here:

```
public void AlphabetizeList(List<ApplicationUser> list)
{
    if (list == null)
    {
        throw new ArgumentNullException("list");
    }

    list  = list.OrderBy(x=>x.LastName)
                .ThenBy(y=>y.LastName).ThenBy(z=>z.MiddleInitial);
}
```

By throwing the exception you are telling the calling code that the argument passed in is problematic. Doing the check also ensures that your method doesn't try to do any work on the null object, as doing that would cause the framework to throw a `NullReferenceException`. You may wonder why you don't just let the framework go ahead and do that; but if you did, you would be making it more complicated for the developer of the calling method to determine what happened. Instead, you are passing back an `ArgumentNullException` that includes information about the argument causing the problem. This makes it very easy to determine both what the problem is and the steps necessary to remedy it.

So far you have seen how to catch an exception and how to throw an exception. Sometimes you need to do both: catch an exception, do something with it, and then turn around and rethrow the exception so that it can continue up the call stack. Here is the appropriate way to handle such a case:

```
try
{
    // some work
}
catch(Exception ex)
{
    // log the exception in your logging system
    throw;
}
```

This is different from the earlier snippet when your method was throwing an exception, because at that point you used the `throw` keyword along with the exception that you were going to throw. In this case you are using just the keyword itself without an exception, but because the keyword is within a catch block it can determine its context. Make sure that you do not do this:

```
try
{
    // some work
}
catch(Exception ex)
{
    // log the exception in your logging system
    throw ex;
}
```

This approach will break the link between the exception and its originator, making the exception look like it was thrown from this method rather than the method that actually threw it. The throw that sends the exception becomes the owner, regardless of whether you just created the exception yourself or are passing it through from another area.

It is easy to get the impression that exceptions are bad so you should never write code that throws them. However, exceptions enable you to communicate problems back to consuming code; you are throwing an exception because it is giving you incorrect or broken information. If you don't tell the calling code (by throwing the exception), the problem won't be understood. Ideally, your code throws the exception to the calling code, which is then fixed so that it can start calling your code correctly. A well-constructed exception policy helps to ensure quality.

When you get an exception, your responsibility is to fix the calling code so that the exception disappears. If you were calling the `AlphabetizeList` method from the earlier example and you received an `ArgumentNullException`, then you would know that you have to fix your code so that you are not passing in a null list. Thus, you may have to make a change from

```
try
{
    using (ApplicationDbContext context = new ApplicationDbContext())
    {
        var userList = context.ApplicationUsers;
        AlphabetizeList(userList);
        return View(userList);
    }
```

```
    }
    catch(Exception ex)
    {
        // log the exception in your logging system
        throw;
    }
```

to

```
    try
    {
        using (ApplicationDbContext context = new ApplicationDbContext())
        {
            var userList = context.ApplicationUsers.Where(x=>x.State == state);
            if (userList != null)
            {
                AlphabetizeList(userList);
            }
            return View(userList);
        }
    }
    catch(Exception ex)
    {
        // log the exception in your logging system
        throw;
    }
```

This ensures you are not calling the method with the incorrect item. You can start to see how there may be chains of these types of methods. Perhaps the method calling the `AlphabetizeList` message was called from other code that passes in the filter criteria, and the only way that the code can call the `AlphabetizeList` method with a null object is if calling methods send information that causes the list to be null, such as sending filter criteria that no item in the list will match. In that case you may want to set up the code as follows and throw an exception when incoming data causes an improper state:

```
    try
    {
        using (ApplicationDbContext context = new ApplicationDbContext())
        {
            var userList = context.ApplicationUsers.Where(x=>x.State == state);
            if (userList != null)
            {
                throw new ArgumentException("state returns null list",
                    state);
            }
            AlphabetizeList(userList);

            return View(userList);
        }
    }
    catch(Exception ex)
    {
        // log the exception in your logging system
        throw;
    }
```

Unfortunately, this means that there is no hard-and-fast rule about when you should throw exceptions. It is instead a step-by-step evaluation. The key thing to remember is that your code needs to be able to tell calling code about any problems it may have, especially when interacting with information that was provided by the calling code.

Once you have caught an exception you need to understand where it came from and what caused it so that you can fix the problem. Remember that although exceptions are not bad, that doesn't mean you want them hanging around in your application. Ideally, your application will ship and never throw a single exception, even if every method that you write has at least one `throw new Exception` line, because you have written your code so that they simply don't happen.

Every exception in .NET inherits from the `Exception` class, which means that is a set of common properties that give you information about the nature of the exception. These common properties are listed in Table 17-2.

TABLE 17-2: Properties on the Exception Class

PROPERTY	DESCRIPTION

`Data`	This property is a dictionary containing a collection of key/value pairs that provide additional user-defined information about the exception. The interesting thing about the `Data` property is that you can continue to add information to it as it goes up the call stack.
	
	`catch (Exception e) {`
	`        e.Data.Add("RequestedState", state);`
	`        throw;`
	`}`

`HelpLink`	The `HelpLink` property is intended to contain a link to information about that exception. The information available from that link generally describes the conditions that caused the exception to be thrown and may describe how to identify and fix the problem.
`InnerException`	The `Exception` instance that caused the current exception. When an exception X is thrown as a direct result of a previous exception Y, the `InnerException` property of X should contain a reference to Y. You can create a new exception that catches an earlier exception. The code that handles the second exception can make use of the additional information from the earlier exception to handle the error more appropriately. Suppose there is a function that reads a file and formats the data from that file. In this example, as the code tries to read the file, an `IOException` is thrown. The function catches the `IOException` and throws a `FileNotFoundException`. The `IOException` could be saved in the `InnerException` property of the `FileNotFoundException`, enabling the code that catches the `FileNotFoundException` to examine the cause of the initial error.

PROPERTY	DESCRIPTION
Message	A string value that describes the current exception. Error messages target the developer who is handling the exception. The text of the Message property should completely describe the error, and when possible also how to correct it. Top-level exception handlers may display the message to end users, so you should ensure that it is grammatically correct and that each sentence of the message ends with a period.
Source	The name of the application or the object that causes the error. If the Source property is not explicitly set, the name of the assembly where the exception originated is returned instead.
StackTrace	A string representation of the immediate frames on the call stack. This listing provides a way to follow the call stack to the line number in the method where the exception occurs. It provides details of the bottom-most area where the exception was thrown all the way to the top where the method that called that code is defined. This is the most useful property for determining exactly where the error occurred. Remember that if you throw an exception again (something you should not do), then the StackTrace property is reset and you lose the StackTrace from that point forward.
TargetSite	The method that throws the current exception. If the method that throws this exception is not available and the stack trace is not a null reference, TargetSite obtains the method from the stack trace. If the stack trace is a null reference, TargetSite also returns a null reference.

The most important properties that you will use are the exception type itself (ArgumentNullException, NullReferenceException), Message and the StackTrace. These give you an understanding of the type of problem and where it occurs. You will learn more details about analyzing exceptions later in the chapter.

With the recommendation to let exceptions flow up through the call stack, you have to be wondering when (or if) they finally are caught. Again, the answer depends. If an exception is thrown, one of two things will happen: You will catch the exception and attempt to recover. The second is that you won't recover and you have to decide on a course of action. In some cases you can parse the error to give the user some information that may be of use, but for other unexpected errors you cannot do that. Also, at some point you have to decide whether a generic error-handling approach is best.

The next section demonstrates how ASP.NET helps you display errors and globally manage exceptions when they happen without alerting the user, even though the application just experienced an error.

Global Error Handling and Custom Error Pages

You have already seen instances of the "Yellow Screen of Death," the default screen that appears when ASP.NET encounters an error. It is not the most welcoming screen for a user. However,

ASP.NET provides a way to prevent users from ever getting to that screen, through its support for custom error pages.

A custom error page is a page you create that is displayed to the user in lieu of the standard error screen. Typically this page is styled like the rest of the application and provides a reassuring message to the user. You can enable custom error pages in the web.config file by adding a new element to the system.web node:

```
<customErrors mode="On" defaultRedirect="~/Errors/Error500.aspx"
              redirectMode="ResponseRewrite">
    <error statusCode="404" redirect="~/Errors/Error404.aspx" />
    <error statusCode="500" redirect="~/Errors/Error500.aspx" />
</customErrors>
```

By adding this customErrors element you have enabled custom error pages. You can turn this on or off through the mode attribute, with on meaning that custom error pages will be used, and off meaning the opposite. You can also use RemoteOnly, which means that the custom error page will only be returned to users calling the server from a different machine. This setting enables you to see the error message when debugging, yet show the custom error page when anyone calls it from a different machine. The other primary attributes in the customErrors element are defaultRedirect, which provides the default redirect page if no specific error page is available for the exception, and redirectMode, which has two options:

➤ ResponseRedirect: Specifies that the URL to direct the browser to must be different from the original web request URL

➤ ResponseRewrite: Specifies that the URL to direct the browser to must be the original web request URL

The other part of the configuration is the error nodes within the customErrors element. These nodes provide the mapping between a specific HTTP status code (such as 404) and a web page. You can create maps as detailed as needed, one per status code if that is required; any items not explicitly mapped will be sent to the defaultRedirect value.

It's important to realize, however, that this behavior does not capture any information about the exception that caused the redirect to the custom error page (as opposed to a 404 Page Not Found error). However, ASP.NET provides a facility to capture information about those exceptions through the support of a *global error handler*.

This global error handler is part of the global.asax page that resides in the root directory of the application.

```
void Application_Error(object sender, EventArgs e)
{
}
```

When an exception is thrown and not handled, it ends up reaching the Application_Error event handler. At that point you can work with it as necessary so that you will always know when there was an exception.

The following activity gives you some hands-on experience with these error-handling concepts.

TRY IT OUT | Adding Error Pages

In this activity you will be adding global error handling and custom error pages to your application.

1. Ensure that Visual Studio is running and you have the RentMyWrox application open. Open the Global.asax file. Add the following new method (see Figure 17-6).

```
void Application_Error(object sender, EventArgs e)
{
    if (HttpContext.Current.Server.GetLastError() != null)
    {
        Exception myException = HttpContext.Current.Server.GetLastError()
            .GetBaseException();
    }
}
```

```
Global.asax.cs  ⊕ ✕
⊞ RentMyWrox                                              ▼  ⁺≡ RentMyWrox.Global
    1    ⊟using System;
    2     using System.Collections.Generic;
    3     using System.Linq;
    4     using System.Web;
    5     using System.Web.Mvc;
    6     using System.Web.Optimization;
    7     using System.Web.Routing;
    8     using System.Web.Security;
    9     using System.Web.SessionState;
   10
   11    ⊟namespace RentMyWrox
   12     {
   13    ⊟    public class Global : HttpApplication
   14         {
   15    ⊟        void Application_Start(object sender, EventArgs e)
   16             {
   17                 // Code that runs on application startup
   18                 AreaRegistration.RegisterAllAreas();
   19                 RouteConfig.RegisterRoutes(RouteTable.Routes);
   20                 BundleConfig.RegisterBundles(BundleTable.Bundles);
   21             }
   22
   23    ⊟        void Application_Error(object sender, EventArgs e)
   24             {
   25                 if (HttpContext.Current.Server.GetLastError() != null)
   26                 {
   27                     Exception myException = HttpContext.Current.Server.GetLastError().GetBaseException();
   28                 }
   29             }
   30         }
   31     }
```

FIGURE 17-6: Application_Error event handler

2. Right-click the Project name in Solution Explorer. Select Add ⇨ New Folder, and name it **Errors**.

3. Right-click the folder you just added and select Add ⇨ New Item. Select to add a "Web Form with Master Page." Name the file **Error404** and select the Site.Master file as shown in Figure 17-7.

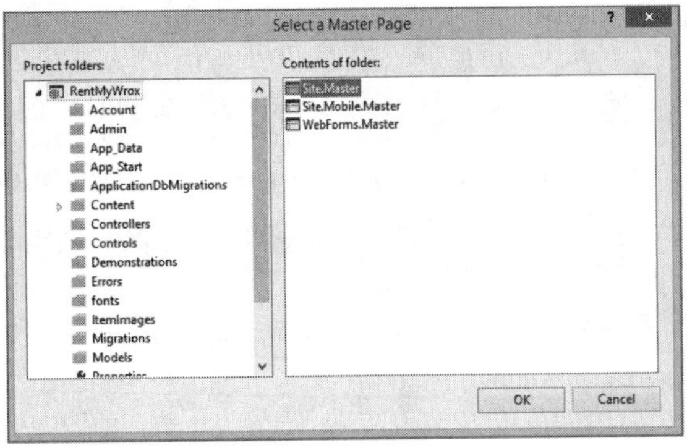

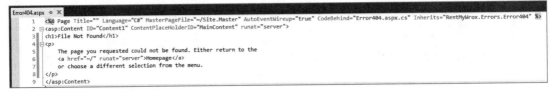

FIGURE 17-7: Master page selected

4. Open the markup page that you just added, and add the following content within the Content tags (see Figure 17-8):

```
<h1>File Not Found</h1>
<p>
    The page you requested could not be found. Either return to the
    <a href="~/" runat="server">Homepage</a>
    or choose a different selection from the menu.
</p>
```

```
Error404.aspx  ⊕ ×
   1     <%@ Page Title="" Language="C#" MasterPageFile="~/Site.Master" AutoEventWireup="true" CodeBehind="Error404.aspx.cs" Inherits="RentMyWrox.Errors.Error404" %>
   2   ⊟ <asp:Content ID="Content1" ContentPlaceHolderID="MainContent" runat="server">
   3     <h1>File Not Found</h1>
   4   ⊟ <p>
   5         The page you requested could not be found. Either return to the
   6         <a href="~/" runat="server">Homepage</a>
   7         or choose a different selection from the menu.
   8     </p>
   9     </asp:Content>
```

FIGURE 17-8: Error404 content

5. Add another a page, the same way, named **Error500**.

6. Add the following content to the markup page:

```
<h1>Other Error</h1>
<p>
    There was an error on the server. Either return to the
    <a href="~/" runat="server">Homepage</a>
    or choose a different selection from the menu.
    We have been notified about the problem and will work
    on it immediately.
</p>
```

7. Open the web.config file and find the system.web node. Add the following code right below the opening tag. It should look similar to Figure 17-9 when completed.

```
<customErrors mode="On" defaultRedirect="~/Errors/Error500.aspx"
        redirectMode="ResponseRewrite">
    <error statusCode="404" redirect="~/Errors/Error404.aspx" />
    <error statusCode="500" redirect="~/Errors/Error500.aspx" />
</customErrors>
```

```
20 ⊟   <connectionStrings>
21        <add name="DefaultConnection" connectionString="data source=ASP-NET\SQLExpress;initial catalog=Rent
22        <add name="RentMyWroxContext" connectionString="data source=ASP-NET\SQLExpress;initial catalog=Rent
23        <add name="RentMyWroxConnectionString1" connectionString="Data Source=ASP-NET\SQLEXPRESS;Initial Ca
24      </connectionStrings>
25 ⊟   <system.web>
26 ⊟     <customErrors mode="On" defaultRedirect="~/Errors/Error500.aspx" redirectMode="ResponseRewrite">
27          <error statusCode="404" redirect="~/Errors/Error404.aspx" />
28          <error statusCode="500" redirect="~/Errors/Error500.aspx" />
29        </customErrors>
30      <authentication mode="None" />
31      <compilation debug="true" targetFramework="4.5" />
32      <httpRuntime targetFramework="4.5" />
```

FIGURE 17-9: Custom error configuration in the web.config file

8. Run the application and go to the home page.

9. Append a term to the URL so that the system returns a 404 error (the example uses "New Item").
You should get a screen similar to that shown in Figure 17-10.

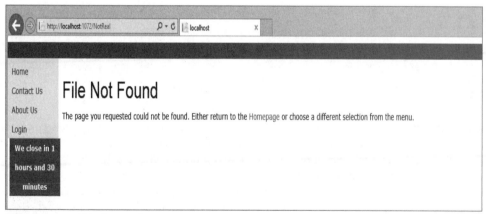

FIGURE 17-10: Displaying the Error404 page

How It Works

In this activity you took several steps to introduce custom error pages and global error handling into
your application. First, you added the event handler that will respond to any exceptions not handled
in your code. The exception is not as straightforward to access as it is in your typical try \ catch
block. Instead, this is really a last chance exception handler, as it captures an error at the last possible
opportunity while the framework still has control of the request, but after it has completed the page
processing phase.

Because it has completed processing, the exception is accessible only on the HTTPContext—the base object that is available throughout the entire request-response process. The code that you have to use is shown here:

```
HttpContext.Current.Server.GetLastError()
```

What this code does is access the server information in the current HttpContext. The Server property is a HttpServerUtility object and contains methods that help manage information about the server. One of these is the GetLastError method, which pulls the last exception that happened during this request. The returned type is an Exception, so you can now access the properties of that exception just as you would in a traditional catch block.

The code you added contained an additional method: GetBaseException. This method returns the Exception that is the root cause of the exception stream, enabling you to always see the initial Exception that was thrown. This becomes important in a case like the following:

```
public void ExternalMethod
{
    try
    {
        CallSomeMethod();
    }
    catch(Exception ex)
    {
        throw new SecondException("Top exception", ex);
    }
}

public void CallSomeMethod
{
    throw new Exception("This is the bottom exception");
}
```

As mentioned earlier in the chapter, if you "rethrow" the same exception, you break the stack trace. However, you can throw other exceptions and nest the previous exception as just shown. This creates a chain of exceptions whereby each exception becomes nested in the next exception. This chain of exceptions consists of a set of exceptions such that each exception in the chain was thrown as a direct result of the exception referenced in its InnerException property. For a given chain, there can be exactly one exception that is the root cause of all the other exceptions in the chain. This exception is called the *base exception* and its InnerException property always contains a null reference.

This becomes important because of the rule to capture only those exceptions that you can handle. However, in a long method chain it is hard to determine exactly what you may be able to solve and whether the exception is called updated by work that happens in that method or by the information passed into your method from the calling code. In those cases you can see the exception wrapping as shown in that last code snippet. Unfortunately, this means that in order to get to the base exception, you would have to go into an exception and then access its InnerException property until you get down into the exception where the InnerException is null. The GetBaseException does that recursive check for you. You should get into the habit of using the GetBaseException for any code where you do not know how the exception stack is built. It may not be as necessary in an application over which you have full control, but if you consume third-party applications or controls, then you really don't have control over what is going on inside those areas. Rather than take any chances, simply get the base exception all the time.

You didn't yet do anything with the exception that was thrown; you will get to that later in the chapter. Also, accessing the exception in this event handler does not affect the next part of the changes you made when you added the custom error pages. You added one page to manage any 404 errors that may happen on your web site and another that captures any exceptions and displays a page which is much friendlier than the Yellow Screen of Death.

Even though you interact with the exception in your Global.asax page, the framework still calls the custom error page. With these two items together, you can find and do work with the exception at the highest level, as well as automatically provide a user-friendly custom error message. In addition, even though the error pages that you created were ASP.NET Web Form pages, you could have just as easily used MVC to make the error pages—all you would need to do is change the redirectMode attribute to ResponseRedirect, rather than ResponseRewrite. The ResponseRedirect is much like the redirect process covered in Chapter 8 whereby the server responds to the client with a Redirect status code so that the browser requests the redirected page. A ResponseRewrite is like the Server .Transfer whereby it requires a physical file to be present on the server that the framework uses to create the response. It is because the ResponseRewrite requires a physical file that you cannot redirect with that mode to an MVC URL.

The custom error pages and global error pages work regardless of the ASP.NET framework that you are using. However, an additional approach is supported in ASP.NET MVC to manage exceptions that are thrown from a controller. The next section describes how that process works and how it differs from the global error handling approach that you just added to the application.

Error Handling in a Controller

The custom errors and global error handling that you just worked with were part of the earliest forms of ASP.NET Web Forms and have evolved to support MVC as well. ASP.NET MVC has its own specific way to manage exceptions that may happen within a controller or within the code that it calls. This MVC approach uses an attribute that can be applied at the action, controller, and application level: the HandleError attribute.

When applying the HandleError attribute you have the option to set the different properties shown in Table 17-3.

TABLE 17-3: HandleError Properties

PROPERTY	DESCRIPTION
ExceptionType	Defines the type of exception to which the attribute should be applied. If the value isn't set, then the attribute defaults to be set to handle the base class Exception.
Master	Defines the master view for displaying exception information
View	Defines the page view that will be used for displaying the exception

Adding a `HandleError` attribute to a controller looks something like the following:

```
[HandleError(ExceptionType=typeof(NullReferenceException),
        View="NullReferenceView")]
[HandleError(View = "ExceptionView")]
public class ItemController : Controller
```

The preceding snippet defines two different views that are responsible for displaying your error message. These error views are expected to be in the Views\Shared directory and look like all the other views, except there is no matching controller because the error framework acts as a controller in this case; that's why the `HandleError` attribute also allows you to set the `Master` page property.

You have seen how to add the attribute to a controller, but you can also add the attribute so that it covers the entire application. This is a bit more work, as you have to make a couple of changes at the core of the application. First, you need to add a new class that will add the `HandleError` attribute as a filter. This class is shown here:

```
public class FilterConfig
{
    public static void RegisterGlobalFilters(GlobalFilterCollection filters)
    {
        filters.Add(new HandleErrorAttribute());
    }
}
```

Once you have created the class that manages registration of the filter (MVC attributes are also called filters), you have to wire this into the application. You do this in the `Global.asax` class by adding a line (highlighted below) to the `Application_Start` method:

```
void Application_Start(object sender, EventArgs e)
{
    // Code that runs on application startup
    AreaRegistration.RegisterAllAreas();
    FilterConfig.RegisterGlobalFilters(GlobalConfiguration.Configuration);
    RouteConfig.RegisterRoutes(RouteTable.Routes);
    BundleConfig.RegisterBundles(BundleTable.Bundles);
}
```

When you are considering using the `HandleError` attribute, you should be aware of a few limitations. The first is that the error won't be logged anywhere, as there is no code that is handling the exception. Second, exceptions raised outside of controllers, such as within a view, are not handled. Third, 404 errors are not handled, so if you want Page Not Found errors to be handled, you still need to use the `customErrors` method covered in the previous section.

The MVC approach offers less support out of the box than the `customErrors` approach. What it does offer is customizability. ASP.NET Web Forms took an approach whereby it would try to provide everything that the user would need. It opted for functionality over customizability. ASP.NET MVC chose the other route. In MVC you can replace or extend the `HandleError` attribute.

Therefore, you can write code that enables you to solve some of the limitations, such as interacting with the exception.

You have been introduced to several different approaches to creating and catching exceptions. The next section describes how you can manage interacting with these exceptions, and your code in general, as it is running, as many times as you need to see the problem in action before you understand how to fix it.

THE BASICS OF DEBUGGING

Debugging is the process of finding problems in your code and fixing them. These problems can be caused by many different things, and determining the root cause can sometimes be a challenge. Many times you have to trace the execution of your program to watch what is happening to the data so that you can determine what is actually causing the error.

Luckily, Visual Studio provides a lot of different tools that are designed to give you insight into the flow of your application. You have seen how you can use breakpoints to stop the flow of your application, giving you access to the state of the various objects in the system. You can add these anywhere and you can evaluate the status of almost any kind of object. You can stop at a point in the application and then go through it line by line to watch how information changes on each line.

Tools Support for Debugging

In Visual Studio there are many different ways to see the values of the various objects within your application. Not only can you see the values, you also have multiple ways to move through the code as your application executes. The first thing you will do is examine the various ways that you can move through the execution of your application.

Moving Around in Debugged Code

Before you can move through your code, you have to consider how you enter it. You always have the option to run your application without debugging (Ctrl+F5), but if you are going to run in debug mode there are several different ways that you can start. One is the way that you have started up until this point, using F5, or Start. This enables you to run in debug mode. Running in debug mode enables you to add breakpoints, stopping the code at any point during its processing; and it will take you directly to any unhandled exception when it is thrown.

Once you have stopped the execution flow with a breakpoint you can restart the code execution. You can use F5 to restart the application, which allows the program to execute until it hits the next breakpoint. You can also select F11 to restart the application and then step to the next line of code that is executing. This process, going from one line to the next line of executing code, is called *stepping through*. Table 17-4 describes several other combinations of keystrokes that help you move around once program execution has been paused.

TABLE 17-4: Keystrokes That Support Debugging

KEYS	DESCRIPTION
F5	Starts the application in debug mode. If code execution is stopped, F5 will restart execution and allow it to run until the next breakpoint is hit or execution has completed.
F11	Starts the application in debug mode. If code execution is stopped, such as at a breakpoint, then F11 restarts execution, runs the next line of code, and then pauses again as if it had hit a breakpoint. If you select F11 on a method call you are taken into the method, where you can continue to step through execution.
F10	Starts the application in debug mode. When code execution is stopped, F10 restarts execution, runs the next line of code, and then pauses again as if it had hit a breakpoint. F10 differs from F11 in that if you select it on a method call, the execution flow does not go into the method; instead, it continues to the line after the method call. It does not allow you to trace into the method.
Shift + F11	This combination of keys enables you to complete the execution within your current code block. It is generally used after you have used the F11 key to enter into a method and determined that you do not need to continue through the processing within that method. Using this combination of keystrokes enables you to move to the next line after the call that took you into that code block.
Shift + F5	Stops debugging and closes the browser window
Ctrl + Shift + F5	This combination of keys stops debugging, closes the browser window, and restarts debugging.
F9	Toggles breakpoints on and off. If you are doing this while running in debug mode, you can only do it when execution is stopped. This means that you are either turning it off once you get to a breakpoint or you are turning it on once you have stepped into a line of code. You can also perform this when the application is not running to toggle a breakpoint on the line of code that has focus.
Ctrl + Shift + F9	Deletes all the breakpoints. You have to confirm that you want to take this action. You can do this just as you would with F9, either while the application is running and execution has stopped, or simply when in the IDE.

You can manage movement through the code using the keystrokes shown in Table 17-4 or through buttons on the Debugging toolbar (see Figure 17-11.)

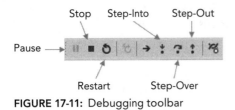

FIGURE 17-11: Debugging toolbar

The Debugging toolbar should be displayed in your Visual Studio toolbars when in debug mode. If it isn't, you can right-click an existing menu item and ensure that Debug is checked, as shown in Figure 17-12.

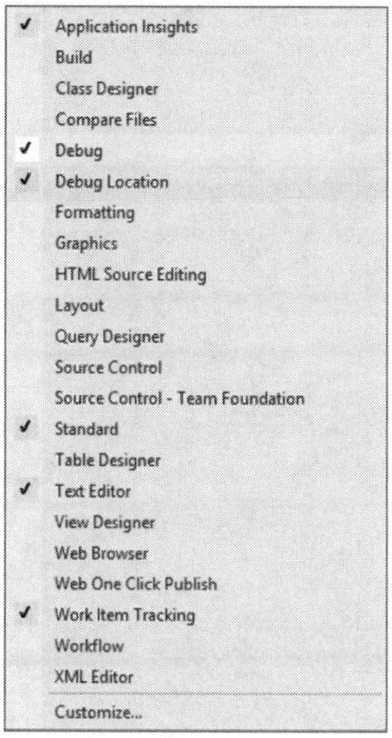

FIGURE 17-12: Debugging toolbar

Understanding how to move through the code when in debugging mode is the first part of being able to understand what is going on with your application. The next is accessing the information so that you can analyze it. You have seen how you can move your mouse over an object when execution has stopped and then drill down into that object and its assigned values. This is effective, but it can be a little awkward, especially if you want to do something such as compare values in different objects. Fortunately, Visual Studio provides different forms of support to help you get the information you need.

Debugging Windows

Visual Studio has various windows that are designed to support debugging. The first set is related to monitoring the values of different variables within your code. The following sections look at those first.

Watch Windows

The most important and flexible debugging window is the Watch window. A Watch window enables you to enter one or more variables and monitor the values of the variable. You can open the Watch window when execution is stopped by selecting Debug ⇨ Windows ⇨ Watch. Note that there are multiple Watch windows, as shown in Figure 17-13.

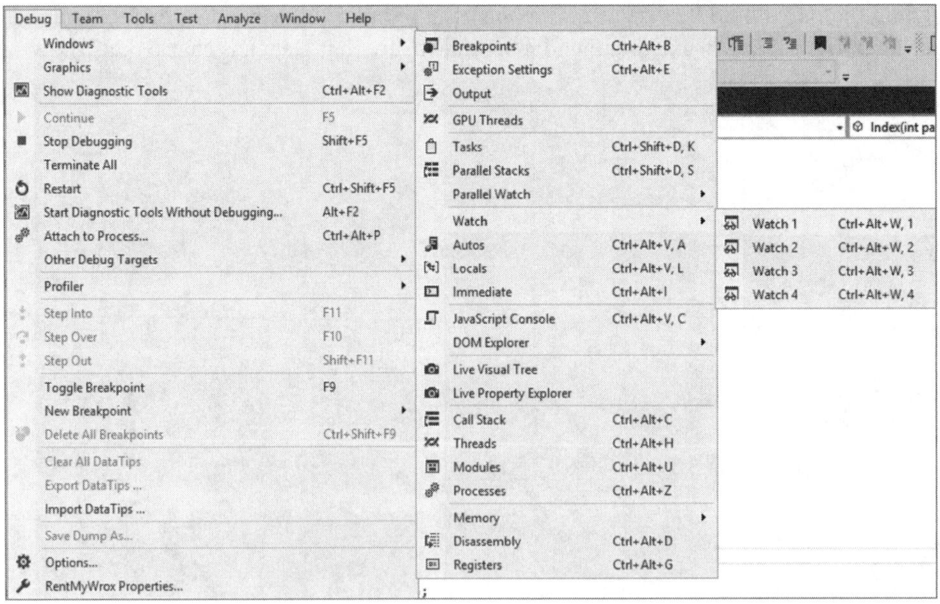

FIGURE 17-13: Watch windows

A Watch window is a simple grid with three column headings: Name, Value, and Type. Using the Watch window is simple: Double-click into the grid and type the names of the variable(s) that you want to watch into the Name column, and the Value and Type column will populate as appropriate. As the program execution continues, you can watch the values change in the Watch window. Figure 17-14 shows the Watch window in use while running through the default page of the sample application.

Three different values are being watched in this figure: `ViewBag.PageSize`, `ViewBag.PageNumber`, and `items.Count()`. You can see that execution is paused on line 28, and the value for each of the items listed in the Name section has a value displayed. You can also perform calculations in the window, so content in that column is calculated and the values displayed:

```
items.Count() * ViewBag.PageSize
```

Although you can do some calculations in the Watch window, you cannot do everything. Things such as LINQ statements will not be run, nor will some of the different casting approaches. However, most other calculations can be performed and their answer displayed.

Autos Window

Another window that supports debugging is the Autos window. It is available in the same area of the menu as the Watch window and offers some of the same functionality. The display of the Autos window is the same as the Watch window too, a grid with three columns. The primary difference is whereas the Watch window requires you to enter the variables that you want to watch, the Autos window simply displays all the active variables (see Figure 17-15).

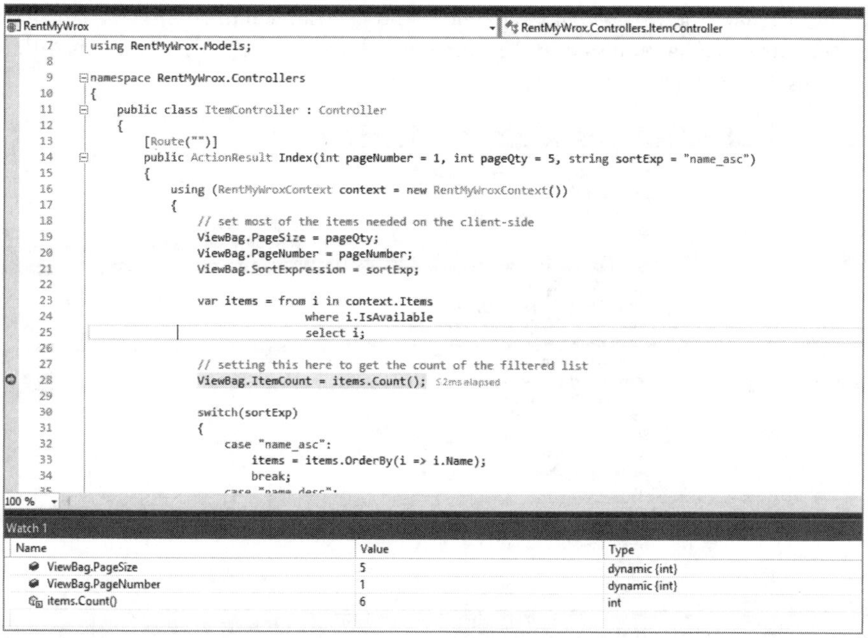

```
RentMyWrox                                                    RentMyWrox.Controllers.ItemController
   7    using RentMyWrox.Models;
   8
   9    namespace RentMyWrox.Controllers
  10    {
  11        public class ItemController : Controller
  12        {
  13            [Route("")]
  14            public ActionResult Index(int pageNumber = 1, int pageQty = 5, string sortExp = "name_asc")
  15            {
  16                using (RentMyWroxContext context = new RentMyWroxContext())
  17                {
  18                    // set most of the items needed on the client-side
  19                    ViewBag.PageSize = pageQty;
  20                    ViewBag.PageNumber = pageNumber;
  21                    ViewBag.SortExpression = sortExp;
  22
  23                    var items = from i in context.Items
  24                                where i.IsAvailable
  25                                select i;
  26
  27                    // setting this here to get the count of the filtered list
  28                    ViewBag.ItemCount = items.Count();  ≤2ms elapsed
  29
  30                    switch(sortExp)
  31                    {
  32                        case "name_asc":
  33                            items = items.OrderBy(i => i.Name);
  34                            break;
  35                        case "name_desc":
100 %
```

Watch 1		
Name	Value	Type
ViewBag.PageSize	5	dynamic {int}
ViewBag.PageNumber	1	dynamic {int}
items.Count()	6	int

FIGURE 17-14: Working Watch window

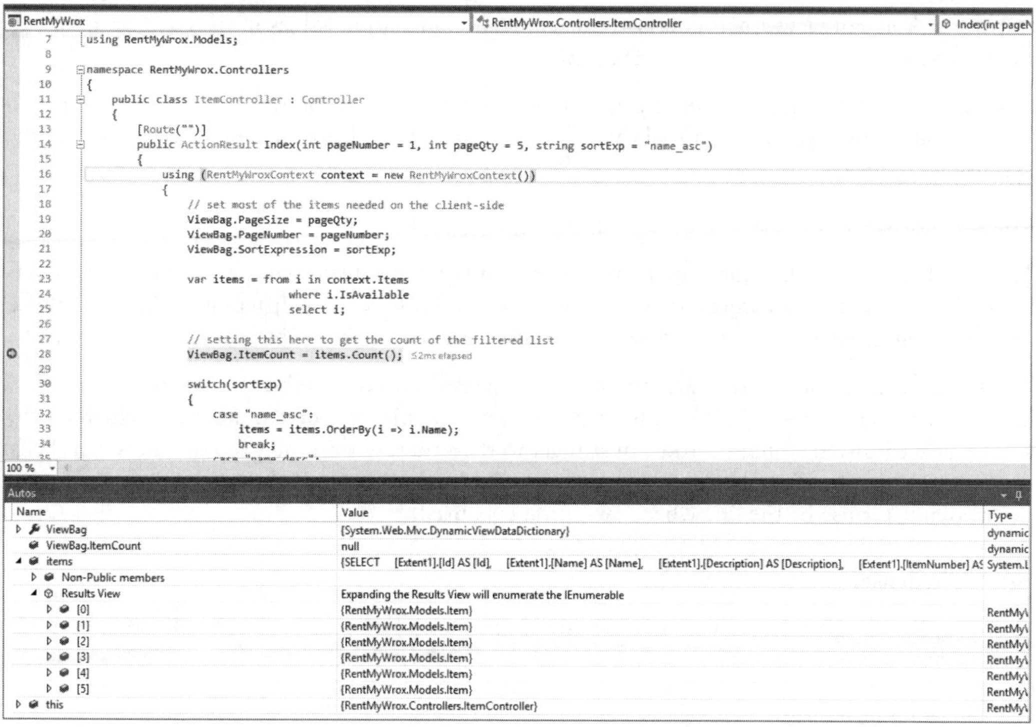

```
RentMyWrox                                          RentMyWrox.Controllers.ItemController                        Index(int pageN
   7    using RentMyWrox.Models;
   8
   9    namespace RentMyWrox.Controllers
  10    {
  11        public class ItemController : Controller
  12        {
  13            [Route("")]
  14            public ActionResult Index(int pageNumber = 1, int pageQty = 5, string sortExp = "name_asc")
  15            {
  16                using (RentMyWroxContext context = new RentMyWroxContext())
  17                {
  18                    // set most of the items needed on the client-side
  19                    ViewBag.PageSize = pageQty;
  20                    ViewBag.PageNumber = pageNumber;
  21                    ViewBag.SortExpression = sortExp;
  22
  23                    var items = from i in context.Items
  24                                where i.IsAvailable
  25                                select i;
  26
  27                    // setting this here to get the count of the filtered list
  28                    ViewBag.ItemCount = items.Count();  ≤2ms elapsed
  29
  30                    switch(sortExp)
  31                    {
  32                        case "name_asc":
  33                            items = items.OrderBy(i => i.Name);
  34                            break;
  35                        case "name desc":
100 %
```

Autos		
Name	Value	Type
▷ 🔧 ViewBag	{System.Web.Mvc.DynamicViewDataDictionary}	dynamic
ViewBag.ItemCount	null	dynamic
⊿ ● items	{SELECT [Extent1].[Id] AS [Id], [Extent1].[Name] AS [Name], [Extent1].[Description] AS [Description], [Extent1].[ItemNumber] AS AS	System.L
▷ ● Non-Public members		
⊿ ⊙ Results View	Expanding the Results View will enumerate the IEnumerable	
▷ ● [0]	{RentMyWrox.Models.Item}	RentMyW
▷ ● [1]	{RentMyWrox.Models.Item}	RentMyW
▷ ● [2]	{RentMyWrox.Models.Item}	RentMyW
▷ ● [3]	{RentMyWrox.Models.Item}	RentMyW
▷ ● [4]	{RentMyWrox.Models.Item}	RentMyW
▷ ● [5]	{RentMyWrox.Models.Item}	RentMyW
▷ ● this	{RentMyWrox.Controllers.ItemController}	RentMyW

FIGURE 17-15: Working Autos window

Here you can see the `ViewBag`, the variable named `items`, and a variable named `this`. The `ViewBag` and the `items` are the same as what you saw in the Watch window, but the "this" value is different. Figure 17-16 shows this variable when fully expanded.

▲ ⊘ this	{RentMyWrox.Controllers.ItemController}
▷ ⚡ ActionInvoker	{System.Web.Mvc.Async.AsyncControllerActionInvoker}
▷ ⚡ AsyncManager	{System.Web.Mvc.Async.AsyncManager}
▷ ⚡ Binders	{System.Web.Mvc.ModelBinderDictionary}
▷ ⚡ ControllerContext	{System.Web.Mvc.ControllerContext}
⚡ DisableAsyncSupport	false
▷ ⚡ HttpContext	{System.Web.HttpContextWrapper}
▷ ⚡ ModelState	{System.Web.Mvc.ModelStateDictionary}
▷ ⚡ Profile	{System.Web.Profile.DefaultProfile}
▷ ⚡ Request	{System.Web.HttpRequestWrapper}
▷ ⚡ Resolver	{System.Web.Mvc.DependencyResolver.CacheDependencyResolver}
▷ ⚡ Response	{System.Web.HttpResponseWrapper}
▷ ⚡ RouteData	{System.Web.Routing.RouteData}
▷ ⚡ Server	{System.Web.HttpServerUtilityWrapper}
▷ ⚡ Session	{System.Web.HttpSessionStateWrapper}
▷ ⚡ TempData	{System.Web.Mvc.TempDataDictionary}
▷ ⚡ TempDataProvider	{System.Web.Mvc.SessionStateTempDataProvider}
▷ ⚡ Url	{System.Web.Mvc.UrlHelper}
▷ ⚡ User	{System.Security.Principal.GenericPrincipal}
⚡ ValidateRequest	true
▷ ⚡ ValueProvider	Count = 6
▷ ⚡ ViewBag	{System.Web.Mvc.DynamicViewDataDictionary}
▷ ⚡ ViewData	{System.Web.Mvc.ViewDataDictionary}
▷ ⚡ ViewEngineCollection	Count = 2
▷ ⚙ Static members	
▷ ● Non-Public members	

FIGURE 17-16: Expanded this variable in the Autos window

The "`this`" keyword is a synonym for the overall class that is being handled, in this case a controller. You can view any property of the controller, including values in the base `Controller` class such as the `User` and even the `HttpContext`.

In short, the Watch window enables you to select which variables you want to watch, whereas the Autos window gives you access to all the values that are currently available in the area where the execution is paused.

Locals Window

The Locals window is like the Autos window in that the items displayed are automatically determined by the window. However, the scope of the variables selected is different in that only those variables that are in scope at the point of the paused execution are visible, as shown in Figure 17-17.

The Locals window shows the variables that were passed into the method, whereas the Autos window doesn't. The `ViewBag` isn't locally scoped (defined within the current method), which is why you don't see it listed by name. You can still get to the values within the `ViewBag`, however, because they are contained within the `this` keyword, which like the Autos window contains all the properties available for use by the line where execution is paused.

Other Windows

In addition to the variable monitoring windows, there are other windows available to help support your debugging requirements.

Breakpoint Window

The Breakpoint window displays all of the breakpoints that you have set throughout the application, as shown in Figure 17-18.

FIGURE 17-17: Working Locals window

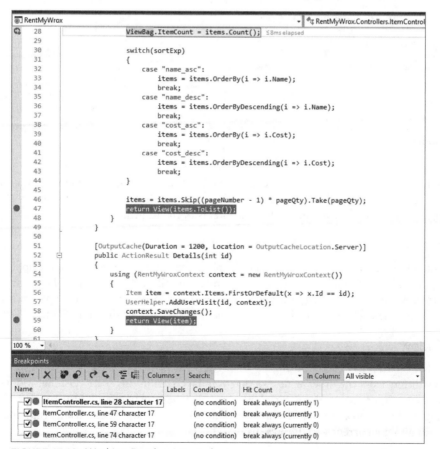

FIGURE 17-18: Working Breakpoint window

It contains the page and line information as well as any condition that has been set for a breakpoint, and the amount of times that breakpoint has been hit during the current phase of execution.

You have seen how you can set a regular breakpoint, but you can also add a condition. A condition is a rule (or set of rules) that determines when the breakpoint will stop the execution of the application. The default behavior is for execution to stop every time the application hits that breakpoint, but using a condition you can specify when to break, such as only when the value of a variable exceeds a set amount. You can add conditions to a breakpoint by right-clicking on it and selecting "Conditions." You can also add a condition by right-clicking on the breakpoint from the Breakpoint window. The Conditions selection window is shown in Figure 17-19.

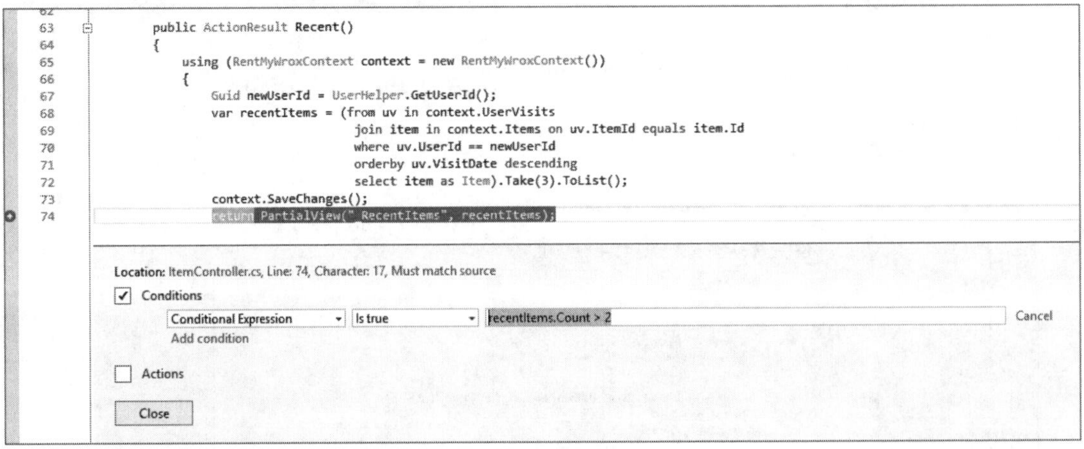

FIGURE 17-19: Window for selecting a condition

In this case, a condition is set for the breakpoint `recentItems.Count > 2`. As shown in the figure, `recentItems` is the result set from a database query, so the condition displayed ensures that the execution will break only when there are more than two items in the returned list.

Call Stack Window

Whereas the Breakpoint window gives you a view into the places where you are set to stop the application's execution, the Call Stack window gives you a view into the call stack for the line of code at which you are paused. As you move through the application, you can easily get back to the parent calling method simply by double-clicking on the base item in the call stack list, as shown in Figure 17-20.

Immediate Window

Another window that is extremely useful during the debug process is the Immediate window. The Immediate window differs from the other windows that you have seen in this section in that it does more than simply display information about variables available when debugging; it also enables you to execute code. Figure 17-21 shows two different approaches—in the first, a method was run, and in the second, details about a current variable are displayed.

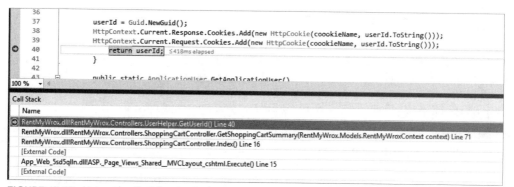

FIGURE 17-20: Using the Call Stack window

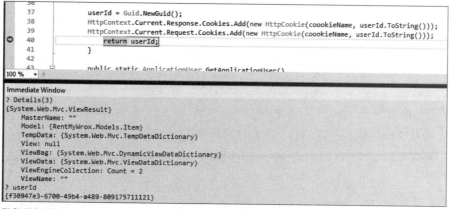

FIGURE 17-21: Using the Immediate window

The key to working in the Immediate window is the `?` character, which tells the system to write the results out. The first line of the Immediate window is `? Details(3)`, where the `?` tells the window to output the results to itself. The window then runs the `Details` method of the controller, passing in the value of 3. The results of the method are shown below that line.

The next instance of the `?` is with `? userId`, where the window outputs the value of the variable named `userId`. You can also do work with those values, such as use the command below, which would return `false` to the Immediate window:

```
? userId == Guid.Empty
```

You can do many more things with the Immediate window. For more information about its functionality, go to `https://msdn.microsoft.com/en-us/library/f177hahy.aspx`.

Debugging Client-Side Script

You have spent some time debugging server-side code so that you can get an understanding of the code that is processed on the server to create the HTML and other content sent to the user's browser. However, this debugging functionality that you have seen so far seems to end once the content has been sent to the client. Fortunately, you can perform additional debugging of JavaScript running on the client side using many of the same tools that you have just worked with.

This means that you can add breakpoints in JavaScript. If you are using inline JavaScript, you can do this simply by putting a breakpoint onto the line of JavaScript code on that page that you want to debug. If you want to debug JavaScript code that you wrote, such as the methods in `MainPageManagement.js`, you can just add a breakpoint as you did in the C# code. In the following Try It Out activity, you're going to be given some error-causing code and walk through the process of finding and resolving the issue.

TRY IT OUT   Debugging Faulty Code

In this exercise you will use the debugging that you just reviewed as you finish your sample application by completing the order process. As part of this effort you are given code that causes some kind of error. You will then walk through the code, tracking the error and fixing the problem. Some of the windows that were just described are used as part of this process. A lot of changes will be coming in, with extra steps to walk through the debugging process, so make sure you have plenty of time!

1. Ensure that Visual Studio is running and you have the RentMyWrox application open.

2. Open Controllers\ShoppingCartController.cs and find the `Checkout` method. Replace the content with the following:

```
Guid UserID = UserHelper.GetUserId();
ViewBag.ApplicationUser = UserHelper.GetApplicationUser();
ViewBag.AmCheckingOut = true;
using (RentMyWroxContext context = new RentMyWroxContext())
{
    var shoppingCartItems = context.ShoppingCarts
                            .Where(x => x.UserId == UserID);
    Order newOrder = new Order
    {
        OrderDate = DateTime.Now,
        PickupDate = DateTime.Now.Date,
        UserId = UserID,
        OrderDetails = new List<OrderDetail>()
    };
    foreach (var item in shoppingCartItems)
    {
        OrderDetail od = new OrderDetail
        {
            Item = item.Item,
            PricePaidEach = item.Item.Cost,
            Quantity = item.Quantity
        };
        newOrder.OrderDetails.Add(od);
    }
    return View("Details", newOrder);
}
```

3. Right-click the Views\ShoppingCart directory and add a new view. Name it **Details,** use the Empty (without Model) template, and make it a Partial View.

4. Add the following content to the new page you just created:

```
@model RentMyWrox.Models.Order
@{
    RentMyWrox.Models.ApplicationUser au = ViewBag.ApplicationUser;
}
<h1>Checkout</h1>
@using (Html.BeginForm())
{
    <div>@au.FirstName @au.LastName</div>
    <div>@Html.DisplayFor(user => au.Address)</div>
    <br />
    <span>Enter your pickup date: </span> @Html.EditorFor(model => model.PickupDate)
    <br />
    <table class="table" width="600">
        <tr>
            <th>Quantity</th>
            <th>Name</th>
            <th>Price</th>
        </tr>
    @foreach (var item in Model.OrderDetails) {
        <tr>
            <td align="center">
                <input type="text" value="@item.Quantity"
                    id="@item.Item.Id" name="@item.Item.Id"
                    style="width:25px"/>
            </td>
             <td>@Html.DisplayFor(modelItem => item.Item.Name)</td>
            <td align="right">@item.PricePaidEach.ToString("C")</td>
        </tr>
    }
    </table>
    <p><input type="submit" value="Complete Order" class="btn btn-default" /> </p>
}
```

5. Right-click the Views\Shared\DisplayTemplates directory and add a new view. Name it **Address,** use the Empty (without Model) template, and make it a Partial View.

6. Add the following content to the new page you just created:

```
@model RentMyWrox.Models.Address
<div>
    @Model.Address1
</div>
<div>
    @Model.Address2
</div>
<div>
    @Model.City, @Model.State @Model.ZipCode
</div>
```

7. Open the Views\Shared_MVCLayout.cshtml file. Add the following code directly under the @Model definition. It should look like Figure 17-22 when completed.

```
@{
    bool userIsCheckingOut = ViewBag.AmCheckingOut == null ? false
        : ViewBag.AmCheckingOut;
}
```

```
_MVCLayout.cshtml  ⊕ ✕
    1    @using RentMyWrox.Models;
    2    @{
    3        bool userIsCheckingOut = ViewBag.AmCheckingOut == null ? false : ViewBag.AmCheckingOut;
    4    }
    5    <!DOCTYPE html>
    6  ⊟<html>
    7  ⊟<head>
```

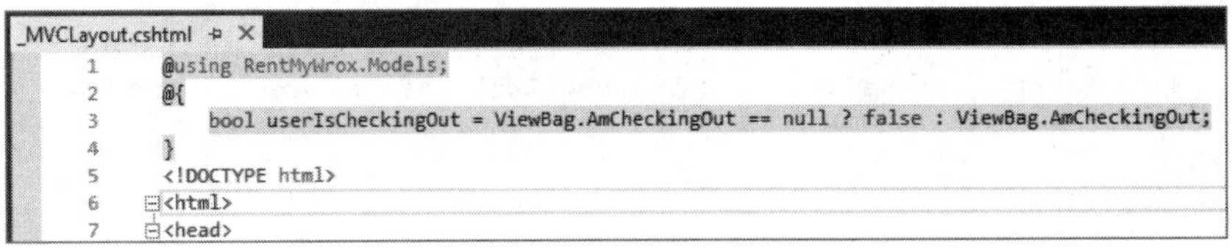

FIGURE 17-22: _MVCLayout content

8. Find the `div` element with an id of `"header"`. Wrap the span with the id of `"shoppingcart summary"` by adding the highlighted text shown here:

```
@if (!userIsCheckingOut)
{
    <span id="shoppingcartsummary">
        @Html.Action("Index", "ShoppingCart")</span>
}
```

Do the same in the `div` element with the id of `"section"` for the unnamed span. It should look like Figure 17-23 when completed.

```
_MVCLayout.cshtml*  ⊕ ✕
    4    }
    5    <!DOCTYPE html>
    6  ⊟<html>
    7  ⊟<head>
    8        <meta name="viewport" content="width=device-width" />
    9        <title>@ViewBag.Title</title>
   10        <link href="~/Content/RentMyWrox.css" rel="stylesheet" type="text/css" />
   11        @Scripts.Render("~/bundles/modernizr")
   12        <link rel="stylesheet" href="//code.jquery.com/ui/1.11.4/themes/smoothness/jquery-ui.css">
   13
   14    </head>
   15  ⊟<body>
   16  ⊟    <div id="header">
   17          @if (!userIsCheckingOut)
   18          {
   19          <span id="shoppingcartsummary">@Html.Action("Index", "ShoppingCart")</span>
   20          }
   21      </div>
   22  ⊞ <>...</>
   49  ⊟    <div id="section">
   50          @RenderBody()
   51          @if (!userIsCheckingOut)
   52          {
   53              <span>@Html.Action("Recent", "Item")</span>
   54          }
   55      </div>
   56  ⊞ <>...</>
   59  ⊞ <>...</>
   62      @Scripts.Render("~/bundles/common")
   63      @RenderSection("scripts", required: false)
   64  ⊞ <>...</>
   71    </body>
   72    </html>
```

FIGURE 17-23: Addition of checks

9. Run the application. Log in, ensure that you have items in your shopping cart, and select the Checkout link. You should get the exception shown in Figure 17-24.

```
[HttpGet]
public ActionResult Checkout()
{
    Guid UserID = UserHelper.GetUserId();
    ViewBag.ApplicationUser = UserHelper.GetApplicationUser();
    ViewBag.AmCheckingOut = true;
    using (RentMyWroxContext context = new RentMyWroxContext())
    {
        var shoppingCartItems = context.ShoppingCarts.Where(x => x.UserId == UserID);
        Order newOrder = new Order
        {
            OrderDate = DateTime.Now,
            PickupDate = DateTime.Now.Date,
            UserId = UserID,
            OrderDetails = new List<OrderDetail>()
        };
        foreach (var item in shoppingCartItems)
        {
            OrderDetail od = new OrderDetail
            {
                Item = item.Item,
                PricePaidEach = item.Item.Cost,
                Quantity = item.Quantity
            };
            newOrder.OrderDetails.Add(od);
        }
        return V
    }
}
```

⚠ NullReferenceException was unhandled by user code   ✕

An exception of type 'System.NullReferenceException' occurred in
RentMyWrox.dll but was not handled in user code

Additional information: Object reference not set to an instance of an object.

FIGURE 17-24: Error thrown when checking out

10. Open the Debug ⇨ Windows ⇨ Locals window. Expand the shoppingCartItems and Results view (see Figure 17-25).

```
38              foreach (var item in shoppingCartItems)
39              {
⇨ 40                OrderDetail od = new OrderDetail
41                {
42                    Item = item.Item,
43                    PricePaidEach = item.Item.Cost,
44                    Quantity = item.Quantity
45                };
46                newOrder.OrderDetails.Add(od);
47              }
48              return View("Details", newOrder);
49          }
```

100 % ▾

Locals

Name	Value
▷ ● $exception	{"Object reference not set to an instance of an object."}
▷ ● this	{RentMyWrox.Controllers.ShoppingCartController}
▷ ● context	{RentMyWrox.Models.RentMyWroxContext}
⊿ ● shoppingCartItems	{SELECT [Extent1].[Id] AS [Id], [Extent1].[UserId] AS [UserId],
▷ ● Non-Public members	
⊿ ◎ Results View	Expanding the Results View will enumerate the IEnumerable
⊿ ● [0]	{RentMyWrox.Models.ShoppingCart}
▷ ♪ DateAdded	{10/5/2015 8:40:39 AM}
♪ Id	5040
♪ Item	null
♪ Quantity	1
▷ ♪ UserId	{f733077e-2c5c-4e91-9c0c-3e6218e8dc7f}
▷ ● newOrder	{RentMyWrox.Models.Order}
▷ ● item	{RentMyWrox.Models.ShoppingCart}
● od	null
▷ ● UserID	{f733077e-2c5c-4e91-9c0c-3e6218e8dc7f}

FIGURE 17-25: Locals window when stopped by error

11. Go back into ShoppingCartController and find the code that is accessing the database. Update it as shown here:

```
var shoppingCartItems = context.ShoppingCarts
    .Include("Item")
    .Where(x => x.UserId == UserID);
```

12. Run the application.

13. Log in, ensure that you have items in your shopping cart, and select the Checkout link. You should get a screen similar to that shown in Figure 17-26.

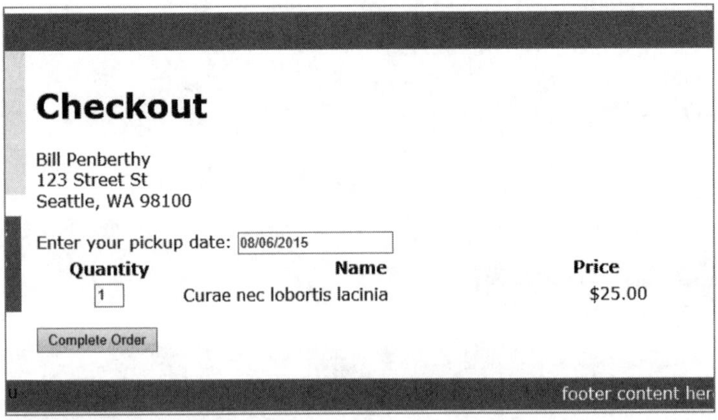

FIGURE 17-26: Successful Checkout window

14. Stop the application. While still in the ShoppingCartController, add the following action:

```
[Authorize]
[HttpPost]
public ActionResult Checkout(Order order)
{
    Guid UserID = UserHelper.GetUserId();
    ViewBag.ApplicationUser = UserHelper.GetApplicationUser();
    using (RentMyWroxContext context = new RentMyWroxContext())
    {
        var shoppingCartItems = context.ShoppingCarts
                .Include("Item")
                .Where(x => x.UserId == UserID);
        order.OrderDetails = new List<OrderDetail>();
        order.UserId = UserID;
        order.OrderDate = DateTime.Now;
        foreach (var item in shoppingCartItems)
        {
            int quantity = 0;
            int.TryParse(Request.Form.Get(item.Id.ToString()),
                    out quantity);
            if (quantity > 0)
            {
                OrderDetail od = new OrderDetail
                {
                    Item = item.Item,
                    PricePaidEach = item.Item.Cost,
                    Quantity = quantity
                };
```

```
                order.OrderDetails.Add(od);
            }
        }
        order = context.Orders.Add(order);
        context.ShoppingCarts.RemoveRange(shoppingCartItems);
        context.SaveChanges();
        return RedirectToAction("Details", "Order",
                new { id = order.Id });
    }
}
```

15. Add a breakpoint at the highlighted line in the preceding snippet.

16. Run the application.

17. Log in, ensure that you have items in your shopping cart, and select the Checkout link. Click the Complete Order button. Execution should stop at the breakpoint you just added.

18. Open the Debug ➪ Windows ➪ Autos window (see Figure 17-27).

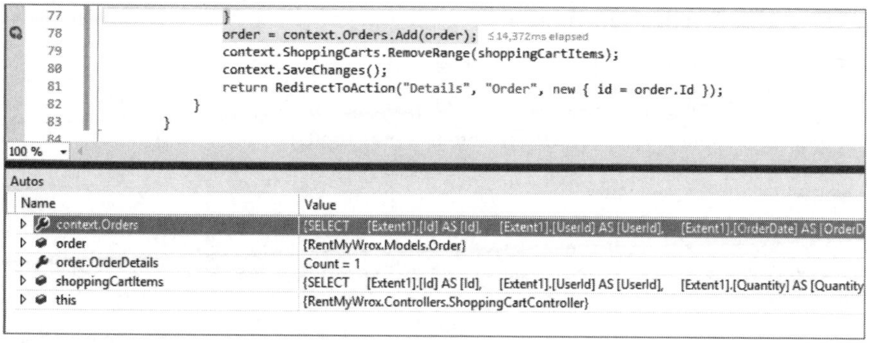

FIGURE 17-27: Autos window

19. Expand the `order` and `order.OrderDetails` areas. You can see values populated as expected in the order, but note that `order.OrderDetails` has 0 items listed (see Figure 17-28).

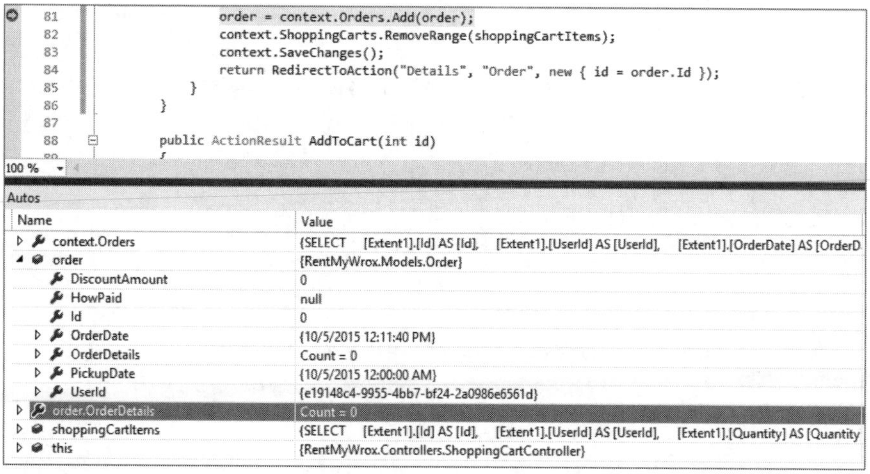

FIGURE 17-28: Autos window with details displayed

20. Update the method that you just added, replacing the following code:

OLD

```
int.TryParse(Request.Form.Get(item.Id.ToString()), out quantity);
```

NEW

```
int.TryParse(Request.Form.Get(item.Item.Id.ToString()), out quantity);
```

21. Run the application.

22. Log in, ensure that you have items in your shopping cart, and select the Checkout link. Click the Complete Order button. Execution should stop again at the breakpoint.

23. Hover your mouse over the `order` object on that line, and expand the dropdown. You should be able to see that there are now items in the `OrderDetails` property.

24. Stop the application. Right-click on the Controllers directory and add a new controller, MVC 5 Controller - Empty, named **OrderController**.

25. Add the following method to this new controller:

```
public ActionResult Details(int id)
{
    Guid UserID = UserHelper.GetUserId();
    ViewBag.ApplicationUser = UserHelper.GetApplicationUser();
    using (RentMyWroxContext context = new RentMyWroxContext())
    {
        var order = context.Orders
            .Include(p => p.OrderDetails.Select(c => c.Item))
            .FirstOrDefault(x => x.Id == id && x.UserId == UserID);
        return View(order);
    }
}
```

26. Right-click on the Views\Order directory and add a new view. Name it **Details**, use the Empty (without Model) template, and make it a Partial View.

27. Add the following to the new view:

```
@model RentMyWrox.Models.Order
@{
    RentMyWrox.Models.ApplicationUser au = ViewBag.ApplicationUser;
}
<div>
    <h4>Order #@Model.Id</h4>
    <hr />
    <div>@au.FirstName @au.LastName</div>
    <div>@Html.DisplayFor(user => au.Address)</div>
    <br />
    <div>
        <span class="leftside">
            @Html.DisplayNameFor(model => model.OrderDate)
        </span>
        <span class="rightside">
            @Html.DisplayFor(model => model.OrderDate)
        </span>
    </div>
    <div>
```

```
            <span class="leftside">
                @Html.DisplayNameFor(model => model.PickupDate)
            </span>
            <span class="rightside">
                @Html.DisplayFor(model => model.PickupDate)
            </span>
        </div>
        <br />
<table class="table" width="600">
    <tr>
        <th>Quantity</th>
        <th>Name</th>
        <th>Price</th>
    </tr>
    @foreach (var item in Model.OrderDetails)
    {
        <tr>
            <td  align="center">
                @Html.DisplayFor(modelItem => item.Quantity)
            </td>
            <td>
                @Html.DisplayFor(modelItem => item.Item.Name)
            </td>
            <td align="right">
                @item.PricePaidEach.ToString("C")
            </td>
        </tr>
    }
</table>
```

28. Run the application and complete the order process. You should get a screen similar to the one shown in Figure 17-29.

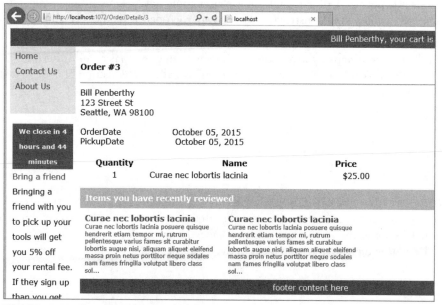

FIGURE 17-29: Completed order detail screen

How It Works

The first set of changes that you added to the application were related to displaying the screen to manage the checkout process. In the `Checkout` method you created a new `Order` object and copied the `ShoppingCartItems` to the `OrderDetails` of the new order. You also added a couple of items to the `ViewBag`.

The first part of the addition to the `ViewBag` was adding a Boolean value, `AmCheckingOut`. This tells the views that it is in "checkout mode." The other change you made, to the `Checkout` method, was adding the `ApplicationUser` to the `ViewBag`. You did this so that the name and address information would be available for display in the UI.

You made a couple of different changes to the existing layout page to take advantage of the `AmCheckingOut` value in the `ViewBag`. Because you only wanted to manage this special condition in a few places (during the checkout process) you had to add some code to the view that enables it to handle when a `ViewBag` value is not present, as shown here:

```
bool userIsCheckingOut = ViewBag.AmCheckingOut == null
    ? false
    : ViewBag.AmCheckingOut;
```

The only time this value is added to the `ViewBag` is when the special considerations need to be made, so the absence of the value is defined as false so that there is no change in the UI.

Another UI change that you made was adding a display template to manage the display of the address. You did this the same way that you created the previous shared templates, by creating a view in the correct directory with the same name as the type being displayed.

Once you ran the application after the initial changes it threw an exception. This is one of the exceptions that you do *not* want to catch; instead, you want to know that it occurred so you can resolve it. As soon as the exception was thrown, you were able to see that it was a `NullReferenceException`, and where in the code it happened. Unfortunately, however, it could have been multiple items in that area of code because it is a compound constructor. That's why you opened the Locals window, which gives you access to all the local variables.

As you go through the Locals window, you are looking for something that has a null value but shouldn't. In addition, this object has one of the properties being called. The section of code that threw the exception is shown here:

```
OrderDetail od = new OrderDetail
{
    Item = item.Item,
    PricePaidEach = item.Item.Cost,
    Quantity = item.Quantity
};
```

You know that a property had to be called, so the problem is that either `item` or `item.Item` is null. After expanding the `shoppingCartItems` you can see that there are items in the list, so you know that the `item` is not null. This leaves the `item.Item`, which is indeed shown with a null value. That's the problem you fixed by adding the `Include` statement in the database query.

Once you got the UI working to display the checkout screen, the next action that you added was supporting the submission from that checkout screen. This action takes the order that is returned and converts it into an order that is persisted to the database. However, as the Autos window showed, there was a problem with the initial set of code; you were able to see that the OrderDetails property did not have any items. The problem was that all of the quantities were coming through as 0, so the items were not being added to the list. Knowing that the quantities were present in the UI, you would look at how the quantity is being determined. The problem was that the attempt to get the quantity was looking for the incorrect Id; it was using a value that didn't match the value used in the UI (where the view was defined using the Id of the Item to create the name of the textbox). After you fixed that the system populated the order correctly.

The last parts of the application that you worked on were the order controller and the order confirmation view that will be used to display the details for an order. The selection of the order to send to the view is no different from any of the other actions that you have created—with one exception. This exception is shown here:

```
var order = context.Orders
            .Include(p => p.OrderDetails.Select(c => c.Item))
            .FirstOrDefault(x => x.Id == id && x.UserId == UserID);
```

The use of the Include is different from anything that you have used before. That's because this is the first time you have needed to use a grandchild object. A *grandchild* object is an object, in this case an Order, that has a child, the OrderDetail, which has its own child, in this case an Item. The previous approach to using the Include was different in that you identified the child object to include by passing in a string value that matched the name of the property to include. In this case, because you also wanted to include the grandchild, you needed to use a different Include, one that enabled you to include both the child, p.OrderDetails as defined in the preceding code, and its child, added by using the Select method and defining the Item property.

Using debugging while writing your code is invaluable. Unfortunately, it doesn't provide any support when running the code independently of your Visual Studio debugger. In the next section you will learn how to capture error information in the running application regardless of its environment.

TRACING YOUR ASP.NET WEB PAGES

Tracing is the ability to get information output about the running of an application and is built into ASP.NET, and it provides a lot of support for understanding how your application is behaving while running. In addition, because it is built into ASP.NET, it does not require any special coding to access the information. When you enable tracing, you ensure that the system captures information about the complete processing of each request. The default items that are displayed in a trace's details are listed in Table 17-5.

TABLE 17-5: Sections Available in Trace Output

TRACE SECTION	DESCRIPTION
Request Details	Displays general information about the current request and response. Some of the interesting information displayed in this section includes the time of the request, the request type, such as GET or POST, and the returned Status Code.
Trace Information	Displays the flow of page-level events. If you have created custom trace messages (next section), the messages are displayed here as well.
Control Tree	Displays information about ASP.NET server controls that are created in the page. This section is only filled by ASP.NET Web Forms pages and controls.
Session State	Displays information about values stored in session state, if any.
Application State	Contains information about values stored in application state, if any. Application state is a data repository available to all classes in an ASP.NET application. Application state is stored in memory on the server and is faster than storing and retrieving information in a database. Unlike session state, which is specific to a single user session, application state applies to all users and sessions. Therefore, application state is a useful place to store small amounts of often used data that does not change from one user to another. You did not do anything that uses application state.
Request Cookies Collection	Displays the cookie information that was sent from the browser to the server. You used Request Cookies to hold the temporary user information, so you should see those values listed in this section.
Response Cookies Collection	Displays the cookie information that was returned from the server to the client
Headers Collection	Displays information about request and response message header name/value pairs, which provide information about the message body or requested resource
Form Collection	Displays name/value pairs that show the form element values (control values) submitted in a request during a POST operation. You need to be very careful with this because all information is visible, including values that may have been entered into a Password box.
Querystring Collection	The values that are passed in the URL. In a URL, query string information is separated from the path information by a question mark (?); multiple query string elements are separated by an ampersand (&). Query string name/value pairs are separated by an equals sign (=).
Server Variables	Displays a collection of server-related environment variables and request header information. This includes the requested URL, information about where the request came from, local directories, and so on.

Before you can access any of this information, you need to enable tracing. You do this by adding a configuration item into the `system.web` element within the `web.config` file.

A common version of this configuration is shown here:

```
<trace mostRecent="true" enabled="true" requestLimit="100"
       pageOutput="false" localOnly="true" />
```

The available configuration attributes are listed in Table 17-6.

TABLE 17-6: Trace Configuration Attributes

ATTRIBUTE	DESCRIPTION
Enabled	You can set this to true or false and it enables tracing across the entire application. To override this setting for individual pages, set the `Trace` attribute in the @Page directive of a page to true or false.
PageOutput	When `PageOutput` is true, trace information is put at the bottom of every page sent to the browser. Trace information is also available from the trace viewer. When this value is false, the trace information is available only on the trace viewer.
RequestLimit	A value specifying the number of trace requests to store on the server. The default is 10.
TraceMode	The order in which trace information is displayed. Set to SortByTime, the default value, to sort by the order in which information was processed. Set to SortByCategory to sort alphabetically by a user-defined category.
LocalOnly	Makes the trace viewer available only when being called from a browser on the host Web server. The default value is true.
MostRecent	Specifies whether to display the most recent trace information as tracing output. When the RequestLimit is exceeded, then detail is discarded. If this value is set to false, the newest data will be discarded.

You will be able to see this trace information at an address that became available once tracing was enabled, `Trace.axd`. Figure 17-30 shows this initial page.

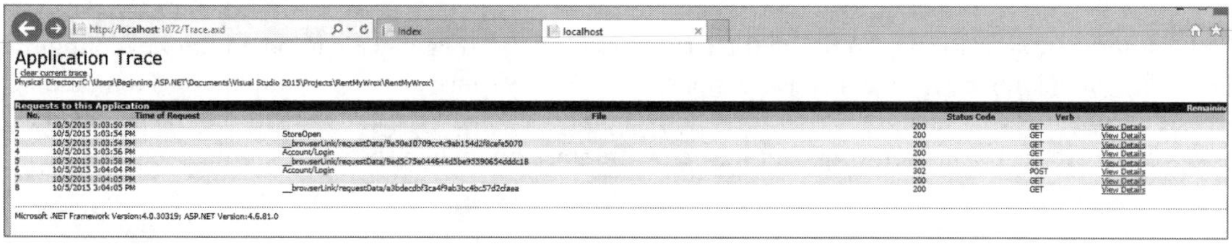

FIGURE 17-30: Trace listing page

This shows you the list of requests that have been traced. The list is refreshed every time the server is restarted, so accessing traces from previous runs is not possible. The list only displays the list of requests, but it provides access to the trace details from the link on the right side of the page. Clicking one of these links gives you the trace details, as shown in Figure 17-31.

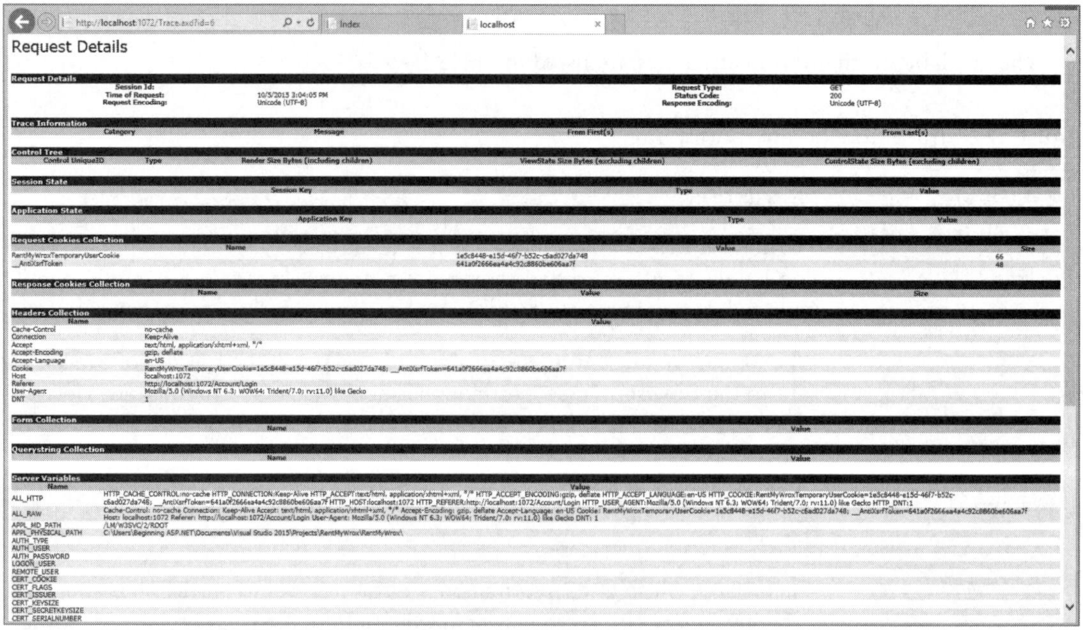

FIGURE 17-31: Trace details page

Adding tracing to your application enables you to gather information about its behavior as it is being used. However, while the default information can provide some interesting information, adding custom information makes tracing even more effective.

Adding Your Own Information to the Trace

Every application that uses ASP.NET has different requirements, which means that each of them has different items that could be important. This is why you have the capability to add information to the trace.

Adding custom information to the trace requires two different steps: adding additional configuration, and adding additional code to support the trace, because although you don't need to add any additional code to support a default trace, you do need to add the calls to tell the tracing engine what custom information you want added to the trace and when the trace should occur.

Adding configuration requires adding one more configuration value to the system.diagnostics element. In the system.diagnostics element of the web.config file you need to configure a listener:

```
<trace>
  <listeners>
    <add name="WebPageTraceListener"
         type="System.Web.WebPageTraceListener, System.Web,
         Version=2.0.3600.0, Culture=neutral,
         PublicKeyToken=b03f5f7f11d50a3a"/>
  </listeners>
</trace>
```

Once you have added the listener, you have to add the code to add the additional information to the trace. The primary approach is using the System.Diagnostics.Trace class. The methods are shown in Table 17-7.

TABLE 17-7: Trace Methods

METHOD	DESCRIPTION
TraceError	Writes an informational message to the trace. If this method is used the message is displayed in red.
TraceInformation	Writes an informational message to the trace
TraceWarning	Writes an informational message to the trace. If this method is used the message is displayed in red.
Write	Writes an informational message to the trace
WriteIf	Writes an informational message to the trace if a specific condition is met
WriteLine	Writes an informational message to the trace

In the next Try It Out activity you enable tracing in your application, and make some changes to include custom trace information.

TRY IT OUT Configuring Tracing in Your Application

In this activity you will configure tracing in your application and add some custom debugging information.

1. Ensure that Visual Studio is running and you have the RentMyWrox application open. Open the web.config file.

2. Insert the following line in your system.web element (see Figure 17-32).

```
<trace mostRecent="true" enabled="true" requestLimit="1000"
       pageOutput="false" localOnly="true" />
```

```
Web.config  ▣  X
    7 ☐    <configSections>
    8          <!-- For more information on Entity Framework configuration, visit http://go.microsoft.com/fwlink/
    9          <section name="entityFramework" type="System.Data.Entity.Internal.ConfigFile.EntityFrameworkSectio
   10          <section name="glimpse" type="Glimpse.Core.Configuration.Section, Glimpse.Core" />
   11        <!-- For more information on Entity Framework configuration, visit http://go.microsoft.com/fwlink/?L
   12
   13 ⊞    <appSettings>...</appSettings>
   20 ⊞    <connectionStrings>...</connectionStrings>
   25 ☐    <system.web>
   26          <trace mostRecent="true" enabled="true" requestLimit="100" pageOutput="false" localOnly="true" />
   27 ☐        <customErrors mode="On" defaultRedirect="~/Errors/Error500.aspx" redirectMode="ResponseRewrite">
   28            <error statusCode="404" redirect="~/Errors/Error404.aspx" />
   29            <error statusCode="500" redirect="~/Errors/Error500.aspx" />
   30          </customErrors>
```

FIGURE 17-32: Web.config file after enabling trace

3. Run the application. Click through a couple of pages in the site to build up some history. After a few clicks, go to \Trace.axd. You should see a trace list.

4. Click into one of the detail pages by selecting the View Details link at the far right of each row.

5. Stop debugging.

6. Add the following element after the closing tag for system.web. It should look like Figure 17-33 when completed.

```
<system.diagnostics>
  <trace>
    <listeners>
      <add name="WebPageTraceListener"
           type="System.Web.WebPageTraceListener, System.Web,
                 Version=2.0.3600.0, Culture=neutral,
                 PublicKeyToken=b03f5f7f11d50a3a"/>
    </listeners>
  </trace>
</system.diagnostics>
```

7. Open your Global.asax file. Add the following lines in the Application_Error method, after you define the myException object:

```
Trace.TraceError(myException.Message);
Trace.TraceError(myException.StackTrace);
```

8. Run your application. Go to Order\Details. You should be taken to your error page. If so, go to \Trace.axd.

9. Click the View Details link where the file column has the value of "order/details." You should see a page similar to Figure 17-34 where you see the stacktrace from an error displayed in the body of the trace.

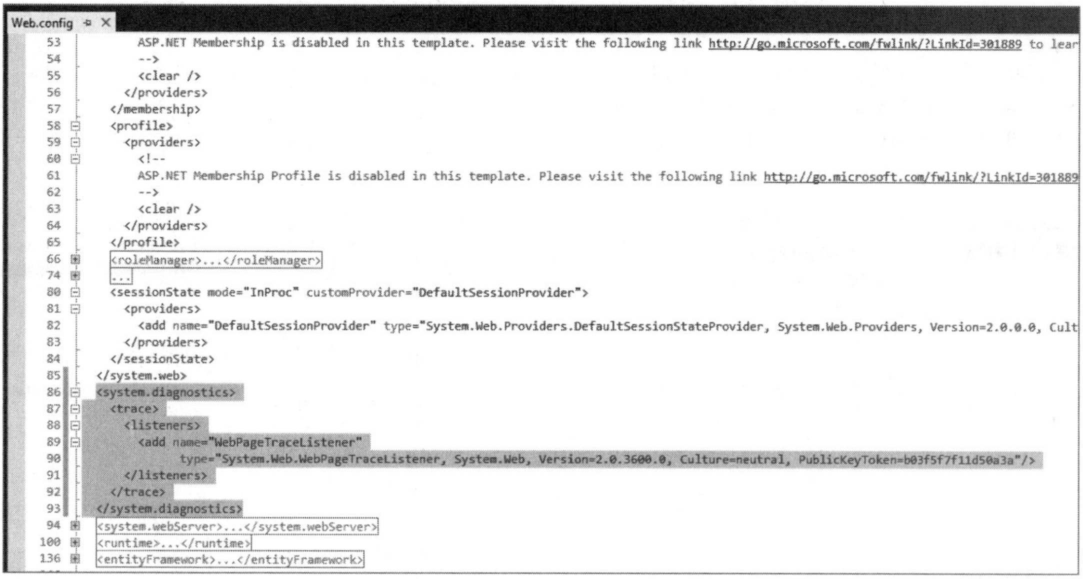

FIGURE 17-33: Web.config file after enabling listeners

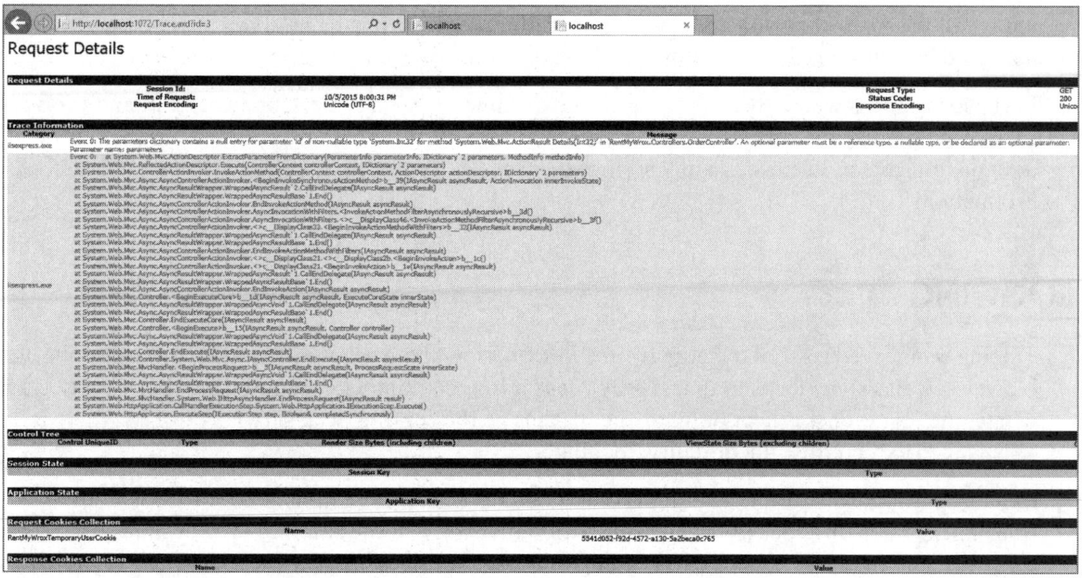

FIGURE 17-34: Trace details page with error

How It Works

You added the configuration necessary to support both default trace and custom trace information. You set it up so that it would automatically be on, and that the system stores the 1,000 most recent traces. You then added the configuration that sets up the trace listener so that you could write code that would write to the trace system.

Once the configuration was completed, you added the trace to the global error handler that you set up earlier in the chapter. By going to a page that would throw an exception (the `Details` action on the `Order` controller requires an integer `id` parameter to be sent in the call), you were able to create a trace that included the exception.

You made two different calls to write the trace. The first was to send just the exception message to the trace, and the second was to send the complete stack trace. Those two pieces of information should provide you with a good idea about where to look in order to understand any exceptions that may occur in the production environment.

Tracing and Performance

As you might guess, tracing incurs some performance overhead, because extra work must happen on the server to save this information. Therefore, it may not always be in your best interest to keep tracing on all the time when you are running in a production environment. Typically, because tracing is managed by configuration, you can turn it on or off as needed.

In those instances where there are separate environments, such as development, test, and production, tracing is usually turned on in both development and test because these environments are designed to have problems—mainly so that there are no problems left when your application gets to production!

LOGGING

Tracing is an excellent tool to get real-time information about what is going on in your application. However, it has some flaws in that it only keeps a limited number of requests; and, probably even worse, the request list is kept only for the lifetime of the running web site. Fortunately, there is an easy way to extend this functionality: logging.

In its most simple definition, logging is the capability to maintain data about or from your application. This data is different from the information necessary in the running of your application, as it generally contains data about what is going on inside your application. This data can be stored as text in local file storage, in a database, by calling a remote web service, or a variety of different ways that enable you to store and consume this kind of information.

There is no .NET built-in facility for creating logs, but a plethora of third-party tools are available. In this section you will be working with one of those third-party tools, an open-source tool called nLog.

nLog provides a lot of different functionality, but the only part of it that you will be working with at this point is its text logging capability. For more information about the complete set of functionality, visit http://www.nlog-project.org.

Downloading, Installing, and Configuring a Logger

Adding logging to your application is made easy through the use of NuGet packages, which enable you to integrate additional functionality. The logging system you will be integrating, nLog, is a single library file that NuGet automatically makes available within your application. In this next Try It Out you will install, configure, and implement logging within the sample application.

TRY IT OUT Adding nLog to Your Application

The following steps will add logging to your sample application so that you have long-term storage of activity going on within it.

1. Ensure that Visual Studio is running and you have the RentMyWrox application open.

2. In the Solution Explorer, right-click the project and select Manage NuGet Packages.

3. Search for nLog. You will get a result set with the top item being nLog. Select this top result and click the Install button.

4. Accept any licensing screens that appear.

5. Open your `web.config` file. Find the `configSections` element contained in the configuration node. Add the following code within that node:

   ```
   <section name="nlog" type="NLog.Config.ConfigSectionHandler, NLog"/>
   ```

6. Immediately below the closing configSections, add the following code. When completed, your configuration should be similar to Figure 17-35.

   ```
   <nlog xmlns:xsi="http://www.w3.org/2001/XMLSchema-instance">
     <targets>
       <target name="logfile" xsi:type="File" fileName="${basedir}/Logs/log.log"
           layout="${longdate}  ${message}
           Trace: ${stacktrace}"  />
     </targets>
     <rules>
       <logger name="*" minlevel="Info" writeTo="logfile" />
     </rules>
   </nlog>
   ```

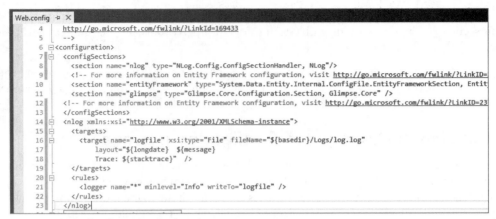

FIGURE 17-35: Configuration for logging

7. Open the `global.asax` file. Add the following code within the `Application_Error` message, underneath the trace lines:

```
ILogger logger = LogManager.GetCurrentClassLogger();
logger.Error(myException, myException.Message);
```

8. Right-click the project solution, select Add ⇨ New Folder, and name it **Logs**.

9. Run the application. Go to \Order\Details (to cause an error).

10. Open your Logs directory by right-clicking the folder and selecting Open Folder in File Explorer. You should see a file named `Log.txt`.

11. Open this file. The contents should look similar to Figure 17-36.

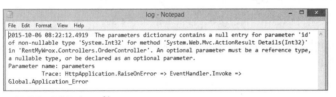

FIGURE 17-36: Log file content

How It Works

Integrating nLog into your ASP.NET MVC application is simple. The key task is ensuring that the proper configuration is added to your application. There are two different approaches for configuring nLog. The first is by using a special nLog configuration file that contains the configuration items. The second is by adding the configuration to your `web.config` file. In this activity, you added it to your `web.config` file so that you have only one place to manage configuration of your application.

There are two parts to adding any special configuration to the `web.config` file. The first is adding the `configSection`. By doing this you are telling the configuration manager how to manage the configuration section defined in the `configSection`, the second part of configuration.

You need to set up two different items for nLog to work. The first is the target. The target refers to how the log information will be persisted. It defines the destination, the format, and how the log entry will be written. In this case, you set it to be a text file that is saved in a named file. You could have set up a target that would have saved the information into a database or made a call to a web service.

The second configuration item for nLog is the rule. Whereas the target defines how the log entry will be persisted, the rule defines what kind of log entries will be sent to which target. This is managed by the `minLevel` attribute. Various values can be set here, each one relating directly to a specific error severity level. The various log levels are described in Table 17-8.

TABLE 17-8: nLog Logging Levels

LEVEL	DESCRIPTION
Fatal	The highest level, it means that there is a serious problem such as system being down or unavailable.
Error	Application crashed or exception thrown
Warn	Incorrect behavior but the application can continue. An example of this could be an invalid URL was requested.
Info	Any kind of interesting, but normal, information. This could include failed logins, new users registering, and so on.
Debug	Information that is useful when debugging your application. This could include anything, such as values being passed into methods.
Trace	A lower level than debug, perhaps including items such as times in and out of a method to support performance logging.

Configuring the log level is what provides a lot of customization because it enables you to determine what kind of information is logged. You can put the `minLevel` to a low level when working in local, development, or test, and ratchet it up so that only errors and above are logged in production.

Once you have logging configured, the last task is to add the actual logging calls. The code that you used is shown again here:

```
ILogger logger = LogManager.GetCurrentClassLogger();
logger.Error(myException, myException.Message);
```

The first line creates the logger itself. It is important to realize that you cannot create a new logger; you have to instead use one of the factory methods. The `GetCurrentClassLogger` is recommended because it gives you a specially constructed logger that configures itself based on the class that is calling the logger. In this case (in the global exception handler) it may be unnecessary, but if you were going to add logging anywhere else in your application this would be the appropriate method.

After the logger is created, the last thing you need to do is actually log the information. There is a method for each of the logging levels. When logging the data, you need to determine the appropriate logging level for that information. This is used to route the information to the appropriate target, if it even needs to be routed based on the rule setting.

Logging enables you to maintain a record of what is going on within your application. This supports your error management strategy by putting the error information in a place where you can use it to determine causation. If there is a flaw in your application, logging enables you to determine where it occurs and the state of the data. This in turn enables you to fix the problem, as every problem in your application can lead to decreased user satisfaction, and potentially cause loss of revenue.

SUMMARY

Writing software is not a perfect art. As a developer, you will likely spend a lot of time tracking down problems in software, whether you wrote it or someone else did. There are three different types of errors that you will run into; syntax, runtime, and logic. Syntax errors are the easiest to determine because they prevent the application from compiling and the compiling will give you information about the problem.

Runtime errors cause exceptions to be thrown by the .NET framework. An exception is a notification that an error has been detected. Rather than automatically crashing your code however, it gives you an opportunity to interact with the problem through using the keywords `try`, `catch`, and `finally`. The `try` keyword wraps around the code that may throw an exception, while the `catch` is one or more code blocks that allow you to handle the exception.

Exceptions tend to give you information about the problem that occurred. The last kind of error is much more subtle, the logic error. This error means that you wrote code that worked; it just didn't work as you were expecting it to. These errors are the hardest to find. However, there are multiple tools, windows, provided by Visual Studio that allow you to access and watch data as it flows through your application. Between these windows and the debugger, you are able to monitor all of the data in your application to understand where the issues come from.

All of this helps you manage problems during the development cycle; however, they do not do much to help you if the application is not running in the debugger. There are a couple of additional tools that will support those, tracing and logging.

Tracing is a process where you can have your web server remember information about the processing that has occurred over the most recent count of requests. This processing is then available via a web page so that you can examine what happened during that request. If you or some other user is testing your application and experiences a problem you can simply look up the trace based on the part of the application that they were visiting and the time of the error.

Logging is very similar to tracing, except you have to add code to write information to the logger. The logger also supports writing information out to a physical file so that you review it at any point, regardless of whether the server was restarted; tracing will lose its information if the web server is restarted.

EXERCISES

1. What is the problem with the following code snippet?

```
try
{
    // call the database for information
}
catch(Exception ex)
{
    // handle the exception
}
catch (ArgumentNullException ex)
{
    // handle the exception
}
```

2. Can you use trace or logging to get an understanding of your application's performance?

▶ WHAT YOU LEARNED IN THIS CHAPTER

Call Stack	A list of the working code elements. As each method calls another method, that new method is added to the call stack. The primary responsibility of the call stack is to return the executing code to a defined place, but it also provides you with an understanding of the code flow during the debugging process.
Custom Error Pages	Custom error pages enable you to create pages that fit the look and feel of your web site, in this case to display errors to the user. You can make the pages as specific or general as needed to best suit your needs.
Debugging	The process of running through the execution of your code and determining if it is providing the expected results
Debugging Windows	Various windows provided with Visual Studio to help support your debugging efforts. They are designed to give you access to the various variables and values that are being used within the executing code.
Exception	A special .NET object that contains information about errors that have occurred, including the type of error and where it happened. It can be caught and dealt with or allowed to surface through the application as it goes up through the stack until it is caught or the application stops working.
Global Error Handling	An approach to error handling whereby it is handled in a single spot within the application. This allows for a standard approach in a single place. However, it can also allow for some lost context, as the actual calling point may no longer be known.
HandleError Attribute	A global error handling approach that is specific to ASP.NET MVC. You can assign specific exceptions to specific approaches and handlers at the action level, at the controller, or application-wide.
Logging	The process of writing information about an application's processing to a central repository such as a database or a text file
Logic Error	Occurs when the code builds and runs but is not getting the expected outcome. It can range from something simple, such as using > rather than >=, to very complex, depending on expected outcome.
Runtime Error	Occurs when code compiles and runs, but at some point an exception is thrown that can stop the application's execution
Stacktrace	The call stack, attached to a thrown exception. It shows the call stack as of the method that threw the exception.
Tracing	The process of keeping a running list of data about the activity within your application. It is different from logging in that it is built into ASP.NET and captures the internal processing that is generally unreachable for logging.
Syntax Error	An error in which the code is incorrect and thus can't be compiled

18

Working with Source Control

WHAT YOU WILL LEARN IN THIS CHAPTER:

➤ What source control is and why you should use it

➤ Using Team Foundation Services as your source code repository tool

➤ How to check in and check out code

➤ Merging and branching your source code

CODE DOWNLOADS FOR THIS CHAPTER:

The wrox.com code downloads for this chapter are found at `www.wiley.com/go/beginningaspnetforvisualstudio` on the Download Code tab. The code is in the chapter 18 download and individually named according to the names throughout the chapter.

Source control is aptly named, because it is the process of controlling the source code that makes up your application. Source control is not about how you should name your files or directories, but rather about how you can back up and version your code. Called *development operations*, or *DevOps*, there is an entire discipline around this process, but this chapter touches on only those aspects that directly impact a developer during the process of creating and maintaining an application.

If you were going to build a business application, rather than a learning application as you are doing here, you would have planned to use source control from the very beginning, especially if multiple developers would be working on the project.

INTRODUCING TEAM FOUNDATION SERVICES

Team Foundation Services (TFS) is Microsoft's source control product. It is available as a server product for on-premises use, as well as being available as a cloud-based version called Visual Studio Online. Both versions of the application can be used to manage multiple projects across multiple users. TFS is a complete Application Lifecycle Management (ALM) system, because it can manage the tracking of requirements, tasks, and defects, as well as handle many other features that help team members interact with one another. This system is quite powerful, but the only part of this set of functionality you will be using is the source control. The other aspects of TFS are considerably more function-rich than you need here and would take another book to describe!

Why Use Source Control

One of the primary features of source control is that it acts as a version management system for your source code. Think of it as a way to back up all the source code files for your application. More important, it gives you access to every version of your file. As you have likely already noticed, every time you compile and run your web application, Visual Studio automatically saves any files that you may have changed. This means that the previous version of your work is overwritten each time you build your code. Once that happens, you no longer have a previous version of your code unless you manually copied it elsewhere.

Perhaps the most obvious reason for source control is that you can access previous versions of your source code, as long as you have taken the step of telling the system to remember these changes. However, versioning is not the only reason to have source control systems. Imagine working in a team. When one of your teammates is fixing a defect in one section of the application while you are working on another area, you will quickly find another reason for source control: allowing the sharing of code between different users. You can do the same thing with a shared network folder, perhaps, but that does not provide the version management features.

There are several different advantages offered by a system such as TFS. The first is the code repository, or versioning system, for your code as just discussed. Second is the capability to label your code, giving a specific version of it a name that is meaningful—for example, something like "Production 1.0 – Release," rather than use the system's vaguely named default version, something along the lines of "0.9.754." The third powerful advantage is branching, which describes the source control system's capability to make a complete copy of your code, enabling you to work on both in parallel.

Branching, especially in an enterprise environment, is very important. Consider an application that has been developed and released. Typically, two different types of work need be done on that application moving forward: maintenance and bug fixes on the released version, and larger, more significant changes such as new functionality. Branching enables you to handle both of these types of work. A branch of code that contains the released version can have work done that supports the necessary changes but won't be affected by the work being done on the larger set of changes.

This enables work to happen in parallel—small incremental fixes to an application, say version 1.1, and larger, more long-term changes that may be called version 2.0. As long as the smaller incremental fixes are merged back into the branch with the larger changes, the version 2.0 branch will contain both sets of changes to the application, whereas the version 1.1 branch contains only the short-term changes and is completely unaffected by work being done, in parallel, on the version 2.0 branch. You read much more about branching and merging later in this chapter.

Setting Up a Visual Studio Online Account

You will use Visual Studio Online as your source code repository. It is available in a free version that supports up to five users per account. Sign-up requires a Microsoft Live account. If you do not have a Microsoft Live account, you can sign up for one at http://www.live.com.

If you already have a Microsoft Live account, or after you have created one, log into Visual Studio Online at `http://www.visualstudio.com`. When you do, you will get a notice that informs you that "you are not the owner of any accounts," as shown in Figure 18-1.

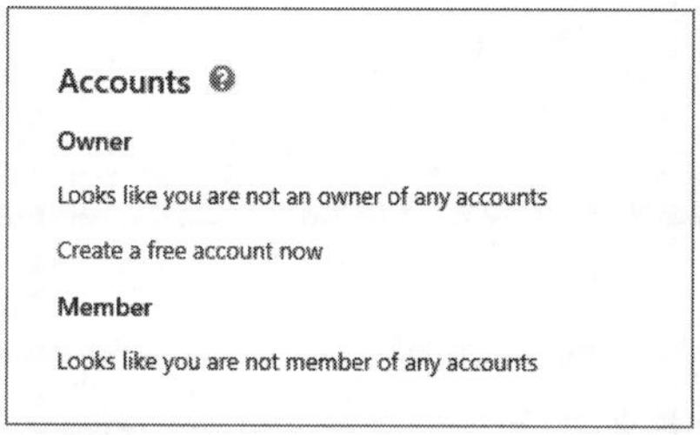

FIGURE 18-1: Visual Studio Online initial login message

Clicking the "Create a free account now" link will open the Create a Visual Studio Online dialog shown in Figure 18-2. Here you will need to determine and input the URL you want to use to access your online account. This URL will be used later when you configure Visual Studio to access your repository. It is possible that the URL you select may already be taken by a different user. In that case, select another name until you find one that is not already being used.

FIGURE 18-2: Creating a Visual Studio Online account

Creating your account opens a page where you can create your first project, as shown in Figure 18-3. Think of your project as being the first directory that you will use to store files. The project name you select should give users some idea of what is contained within that project. While this might not be critical in your personal work, it is very important when working with professional projects, as other developers and teammates should be able to quickly locate the files they need in order to do their work. Choosing meaningful project names is a good best practice to adopt.

Other options in this dialog include the type of version control and the process template that you want to use. There are two version control options: Team Foundation Version Control and Git. The former is a centralized schema whereby all files are kept on the server in Azure. Git is a more distributed version whereby version management is on your machine, including all copies of the files. For this exercise, select Team Foundation Version Control.

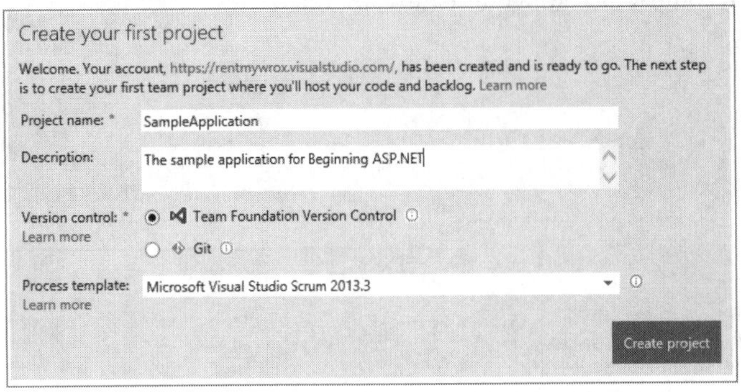

FIGURE 18-3: Creating a project in Visual Studio Online

The process template enables you to configure the project management process that you want to use during development. TFS provides the capability to manage your entire software development life cycle. It can manage all of the requirements that a system may need through its ability to create and manage user stories (a way of defining the functions a business system must provide). TFS also supports the creation and assignment of tasks; or the actual work needed to complete those software requirements, and track any defects that may be found during a quality assurance and testing process, as well as provide reports that show the project's status at any time during the process. TFS supports various types of project management processes; each of them has a process template you can select. Because you won't be using any of the aforementioned features, it doesn't matter what you select here.

Click the Create Project button. When you get the confirmation screen, you have successfully set up your Visual Studio Online TFS repository. The next step is to connect your local Visual Studio to the repository. Every time you have a new Visual Studio installation, or any time there is a change in the TFS server that you use, you need to go through this exercise.

TRY IT OUT Connecting Visual Studio to Team Foundation Server

1. This process is started in Visual Studio by selecting Team ➪ Connect to Team Foundation Service from the top menu in Visual Studio. This brings up the Team Explorer - Connect dialog shown in Figure 18-4.

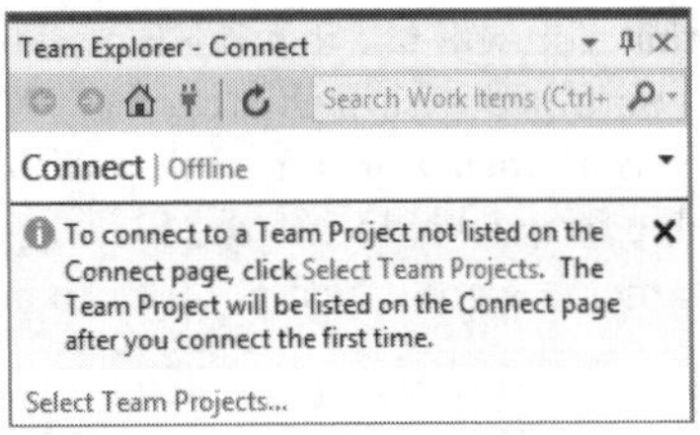

FIGURE 18-4: Team Explorer - Connect dialog

2. Clicking the Select Team Projects link brings up the Connect to Team Foundation Server dialog shown in Figure 18-5.

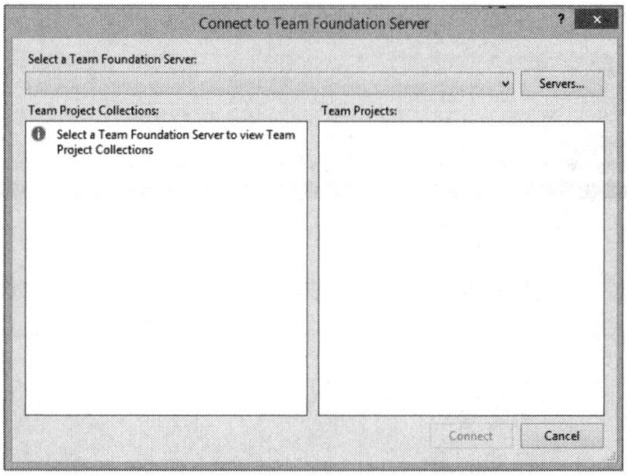

FIGURE 18-5: Connect to Team Foundation Server dialog

3. Because your server is likely not already available in the server dropdown at the top of the page, click the Servers button to add a Team Foundation Server. This brings up the dialog shown in the background of Figure 18-6.

4. Clicking the Add button brings up the foremost dialog in Figure 18-6, Add Team Foundation Server.

5. Input the URL that you used when creating your Visual Studio Online account. All the options in the Connection Details section should be grayed out as you complete the URL.

6. Clicking OK brings up a login screen where you need to enter the same credentials that you used to create the Visual Studio Online account. This ensures that you have the authority to access this account.

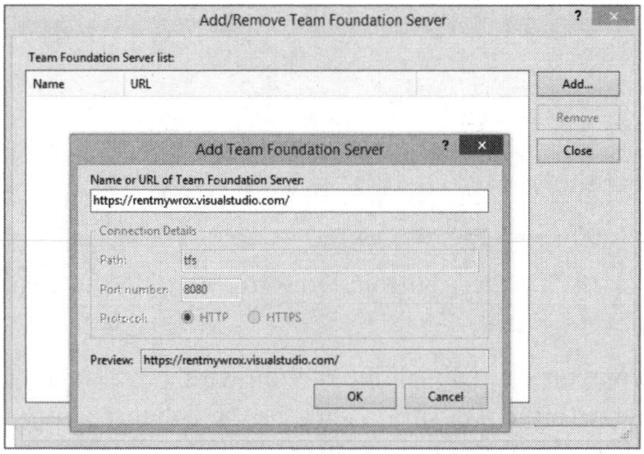

FIGURE 18-6: Adding a Team Foundation Server

7. Ensure that the Add/Remove Team Foundation Server window is active. Once you have completed the login process, your account is listed in the Team Foundation Server list, as shown in Figure 18-7.

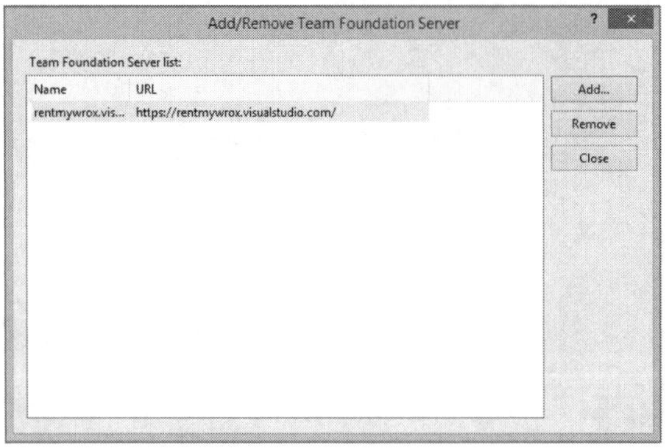

FIGURE 18-7: Team Foundation Server list

8. Clicking the Close button brings back the Connect to Team Foundation Server dialog again, but with your Visual Studio Online project available in the dropdown. Select your account to fill out the Team Project Collections and Team Projects panes, as shown in Figure 18-8.

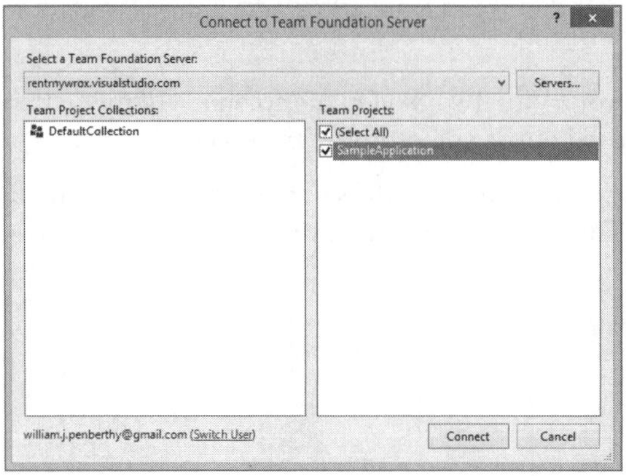

FIGURE 18-8: Selecting projects to use as a repository

9. Selecting your project will enable you to click the Connect button. Do so to bring up the Team Explorer pane shown in Figure 18-9.

10. Once configured, the Team Explorer pane controls virtually all interaction with TFS. To configure Visual Studio to be able to share source code with the repository, click the "Configure your workspace" link. This opens the editing pane shown in Figure 18-10.

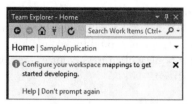

FIGURE 18-9: Team Explorer pane before workspace mapping

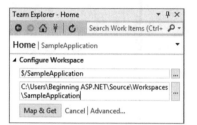

FIGURE 18-10: Configuring the workspace

11. Select the directory that you want to use to store the code. After selecting Map & Get, you will see a message that says "The workspace was mapped successfully."

12. Go back into Solution Explorer, right-click on the solution, and select Add Selection to Source Control. The dialog that opens will be similar to the one shown in Figure 18-11.

FIGURE 18-11: Adding your solution to Source Control

13. Click the OK button. Now you can go to the Source Control Explorer from either your Team Explorer window or by selecting Views ⇨ Other Windows ⇨ Source Control Explorer from the top menu bar in Visual Studio. Your Source Control Explorer window should look something like Figure 18-12. You won't see colors in the image, but this book will address color in the text, assuming it will help you as you follow along on your own screen.

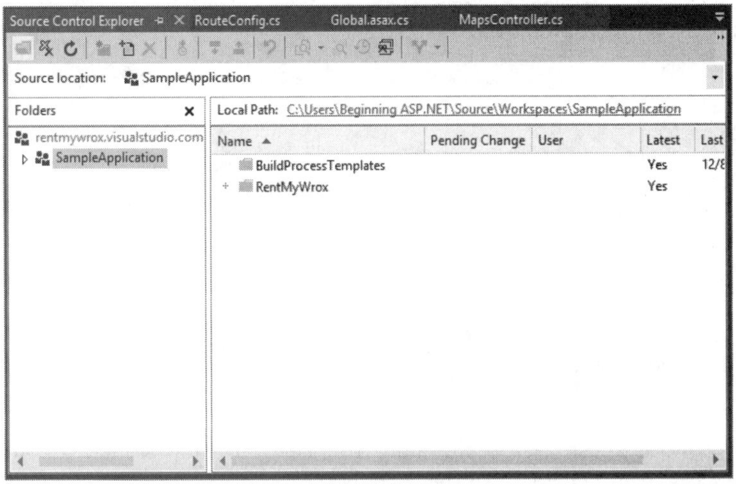

FIGURE 18-12: Source Control Explorer window after adding the solution

14. The solution you just added appears in the pane on the right, as shown in the figure. Note also the green plus (+) sign to the left of the RentMyWrox folder. This is significant because it indicates that something was added to the local directory but it has not yet been saved to the server. If your hard drive were to crash right now, the next time you looked at your online account you would notice that this new directory and files were not available within your project. Ensuring that your files are available is the next step.

How It Works

Step 11, where you map a local directory to the online directory, is the key to tying your local system to the TFS system. This creates a workspace. A workspace is your local copy of the code base with which you will be working. This is where you develop and test your code in isolation until you are ready to check in your work. In most cases, the only workspace you need is created automatically for you, and you don't have to edit it. If you are doing the mapping before you have a version of the code on the computer, such as when installing on a second machine, then select the directory that you want to use to store the code to create the mapping.

Linking Visual Studio to your TFS account enables you to take full advantage of the features of TFS and the source code repository. You are giving Visual Studio immediate access to two different versions of your source code: the one on the server and the one on your local machine. By having this access, Visual Studio can analyze your code to determine if there are changes; and as mentioned later in this chapter, it gives you the opportunity to compare these two versions side-by-side.

An added bonus of this setup is that if you have logged into Visual Studio, you can also access your TFS account using other installed versions of Visual Studio where you are logged in. You will still have to link the online directory to a local directory as you did in steps 10 and 11.

Checking Code In and Out

Getting copies of source code to and from the server is accomplished through the process of "checking in," which copies code from your machine to the server; "getting," which copies the files from the server to your local machine; and "checking out," which is the process of notifying the server that you are going to modify one or more files. While checking out isn't really necessary from a workflow perspective when working as a solo developer, it is useful when working on a team because it enables your teammates to know which files you are changing. This is important because it can help identify potential conflicts whereby your changes may impact a teammate's changes. It is also how Visual Studio determines which files it needs to track for check-ins.

Once you completed the linking between the source control server and your local machine, you were left in a state in which you still had some files that were not copied to the server (those files with the green plus sign). To do your first check in, go to the Pending Changes view in Team Explorer (see Figure 18-13).

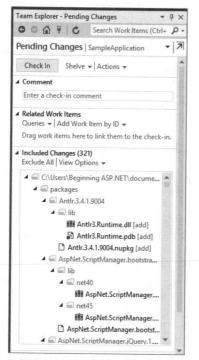

FIGURE 18-13: Pending changes before a check-in

As you can see, this view contains several sections. The first section, Comment, enables you to provide some useful information about changes that will be incorporated with this set of changed files. Even if you are the only developer in the project, this is important because you may need this information later. Perhaps a change you made as part of this check-in affects a different set of functionality. Having a useful comment enables you to easily find this set of changes, known as a changeset, if you ever have such a need. A *changeset* is a set of changes which should be treated as an indivisible group (i.e. an atomic package); the list of differences between two successive versions in the repository

The Related Work Items section does not really have any bearing on what you are doing here. It's a way to link a check-in to a task, user story, or defect.

The last two sections are Included Changes and Excluded Changes (not shown in Figure 18-13). They represent every file in your local copy of the project that has been checked out from the TFS system. These are files that the system has identified as having been changed. The difference between the files in the Included and Excluded sections is whether a given file will be part of this particular check-in. You will not always want to check in every file that has been changed, such as a configuration file containing a local database connection string, so moving files between the Included and Excluded changes gives you control over every file.

When you are ready to check in your changes, click the Check In button. You will get a confirmation dialog asking if you wish to continue the check-in process. Click Yes to start the file copy process. When the upload is completed, you get a confirmation message that a changeset has been successfully checked in, and the Included Files section in your Team Explorer window will be empty.

> **NOTE** The first time you check in, it might take a while because a lot of files need to be uploaded.

Undoing Changes

When working in a source control system, you may come across problems that need to use special source control features for resolution. One example of this is when you are working on a set of changes to the application but you get to a point where you just want to start over. TFS and Visual Studio provide the capability to undo changes. This means that you can select one or more files and have them revert to the version that you previously downloaded from the server. It will not copy to your local directory the most recent version of that file, but rather find the specific version of the file that was checked out prior to editing. This is an easy way to go back to "how it was before." In order for this approach to be most useful, however, you must do regular check-ins once you believe that your code is correct and performs as expected.

Performing undo on changes is simple. In the Team Explorer – Pending Changes window, select the file or files that you want to undo and right-click to bring up the context menu shown in Figure 18-14.

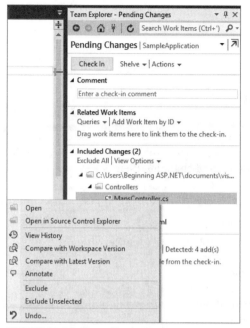

FIGURE 18-14: Team Explorer context menu

The bottom option in the popup menu is Undo. Selecting this option opens the confirmation window shown in Figure 18-15.

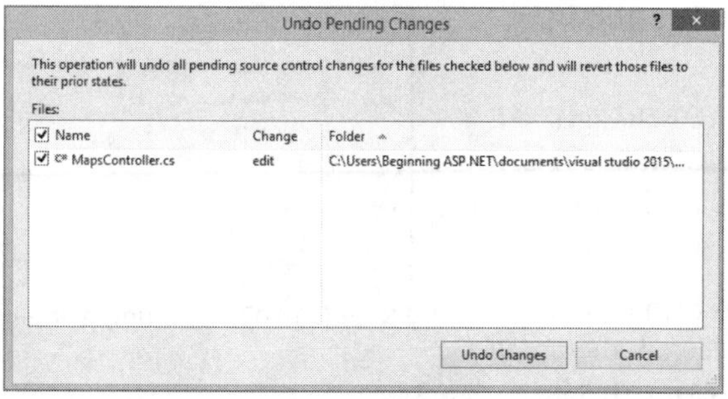

FIGURE 18-15: Undo Pending Changes confirmation

Click the Undo Changes button to bring up one more confirmation dialog (see Figure 18-16). Visual Studio wants to be really, really sure that you want to revert your changes because there is no way to undo this action; it doesn't keep multiple versions of your files in the local workspace.

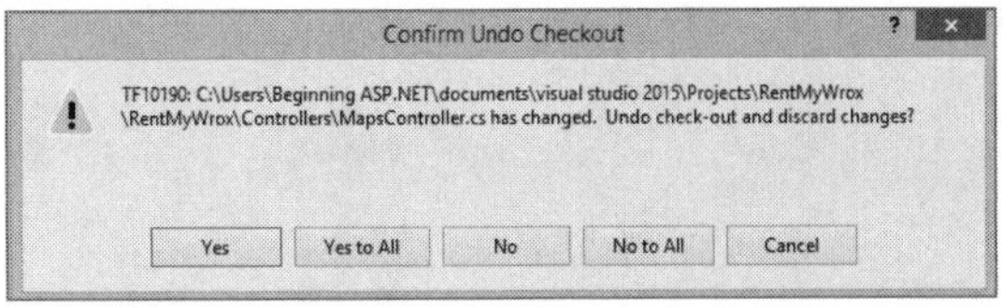

FIGURE 18-16: Final confirmation dialog before undoing changes

Be aware that once you have undone your changes, TFS has no record of what those changes were, so be sure that you want to take this step. After you have completed the undo process you will have the same version of those files that you had before you started changing them.

Shelvesets

While running Undo on a set of changes completely reverts any work that you have done on your application, TFS provides a way to store changes in the system without them overwriting the current version of the source code files. Called a *shelveset*, you can think of this stand-alone collection of files as a change-set that is not checked into the base solution but is instead put in a separate "cupboard." This enables you to take advantage of the backup capability of the source control system without affecting the application. An additional benefit is that other developers can locate and download that shelveset. This enables you to still share code with other developers without the risk of overwriting the code for everyone. This is useful when two developers are working on larger features that may affect the rest of the code base.

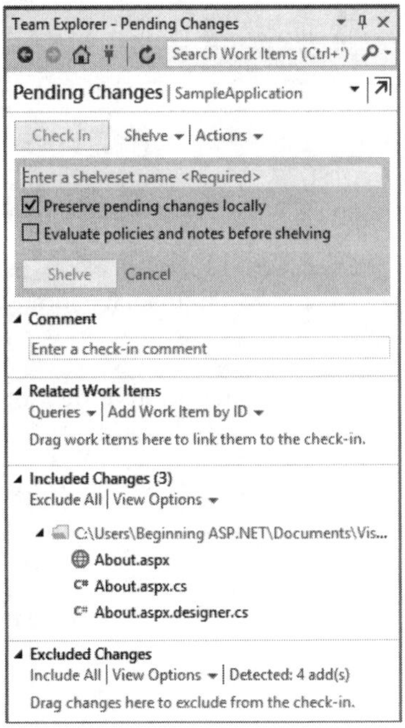

Creating a shelveset is much like checking in your changes. At the top of the Pending Changes dialog is a Shelve link, as shown in Figure 18-17. Selecting this link expands a pane in which you can create the name for the shelveset.

You can also select whether you wish to "Preserve pending changes locally." If you leave this checkbox selected, there will be no changes to your local workspace. Unchecking this box

FIGURE 18-17: Creating a shelveset

saves the Included Changes files to the server as a shelveset and then runs an undo on those files. In the example described earlier, in which you work on a set of changes for a while and decide to start over, this would be a perfect way to safely save your changes in case you need to refer back to them as you move forward again.

Getting a Specific Version from the Server

There may also be times when you need to get a previous version of your source code. Perhaps you have spent a few fruitless hours going down a rabbit hole with a change, and you just want to start over again. However, you did some check-ins during that time, so undoing changes will not give you the results you want. Instead, you can go back to a previous version of the code—perhaps the last check-in last week. You can do this by getting a specific version of your code.

One way to do this is through the Solution Explorer. Right-clicking the solution will bring up a context menu that contains an option for Source Control. Selecting this menu item brings up the context menu shown in Figure 18-18.

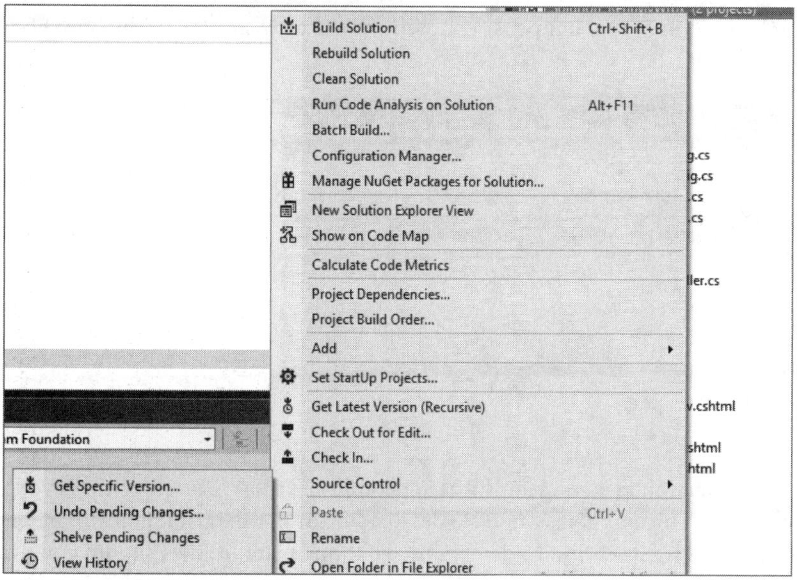

FIGURE 18-18: Source Code menu from Solution Explorer

From this submenu you can select Get Specific Version. That brings up the Get dialog shown in Figure 18-19.

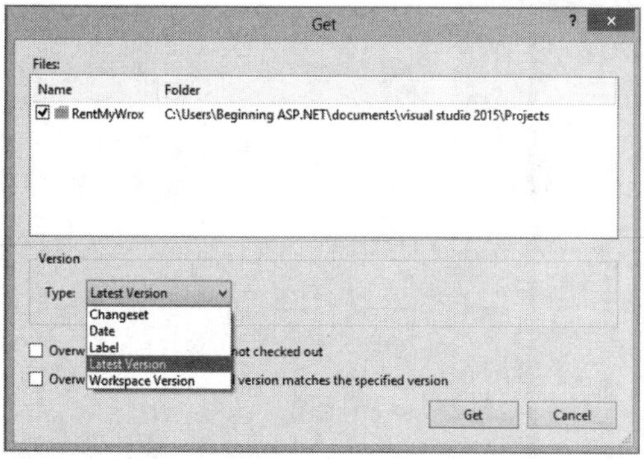

FIGURE 18-19: Get dialog, for retrieving a specific version

This enables you to determine what version you would like to go back to in your local development workspace. You can go back to a particular changeset, a date, or a particular label. Select whichever is appropriate and continue through the process. When it completes, you will have downloaded a different version of the source code.

Before reverting to a previous version, undo any changes that you may already have pending. Otherwise, Visual Studio may identify conflicts between the file being downloaded from the server and the current file on your local machine. The system will try to merge the changes, but it is possible that it may not be able to do it. If this happens, you will get a dialog similar to the one shown in Figure 18-20.

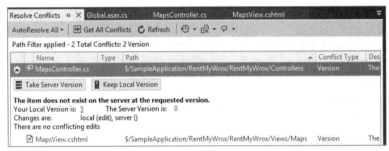

FIGURE 18-20: Conflict found

You can choose to take server version or keep your local version as necessary. In other cases you may be asked to merge changes. This happens when Visual Studio cannot determine how a merge should happen and needs manual intervention to determine what one or more files should contain.

If you have a saved shelveset, the process is slightly different. Figure 18-21 shows how you need to work through the menu structure.

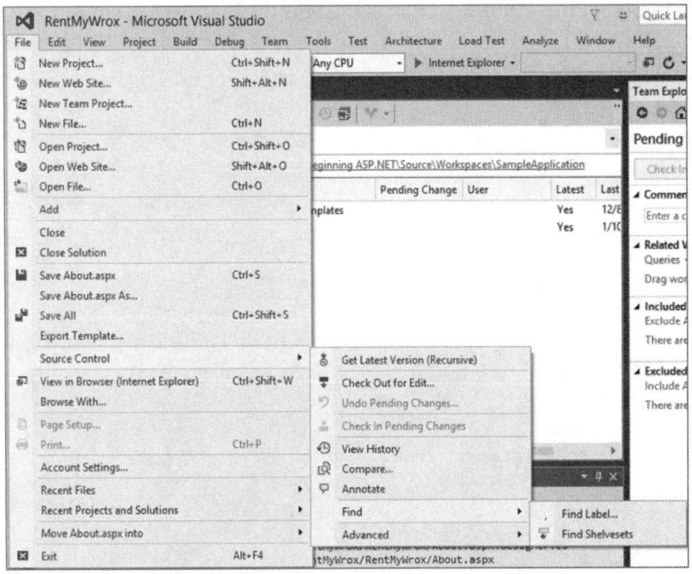

FIGURE 18-21: Finding a shelveset

Selecting Find Shelvesets brings up a list of shelvesets that you have checked in. Click one to display its contents, as shown in Figure 18-22.

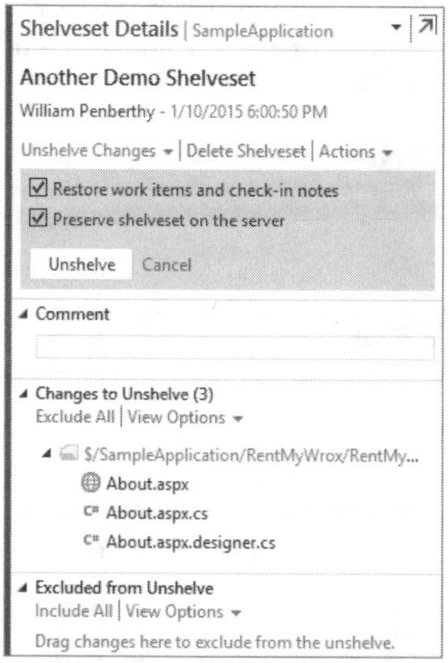

FIGURE 18-22: Unshelving a shelveset

By selecting to restore work items and clicking the Unshelve button, the files in the Changes to Unshelve section will be copied back to your local workspace.

Seeing Changed Items in Solution Explorer

You can always get a list of your changed files by going to Pending Changes in the Team Explorer window. You can also get an overview of each file's status in Solution Explorer. Figure 18-23 shows an example. The following list describes what the various icons mean. Note that the image won't show color in the book, but the descriptions include color references to help if you're following along on your own computer:

FIGURE 18-23:
Visualizing file status in Solution Explorer

➤ The About.aspx file has a red check next to it. This indicates that the file has been checked out from TFS, either by your editing of the file or by manually checking the file out.

➤ The AboutUs.aspx file has a green plus sign next to it, indicating that the file was added to source control locally but has not yet been checked in to the server.

➤ Lastly, the Bundle.config file has a blue lock next to it. This lock indicates that the local version of this file is the same as the version of the file on the server.

Looking at History and Comparing Versions

As you perform your day-to-day work, you may need to see what kind of changes have been made to a file. Visual Studio enables you to look at a file's history of check-ins, which not only supports the need to get a list of changes, it provides the capability to compare two different versions of the same file to be able to evaluate the changes.

To find the history of the page, select that file in your Solution Explorer window and right-click to get the popup context menu. Select Source Control ⇨ View History. This opens a window that displays a list of the check-ins for a file. An example is shown in Figure 18-24.

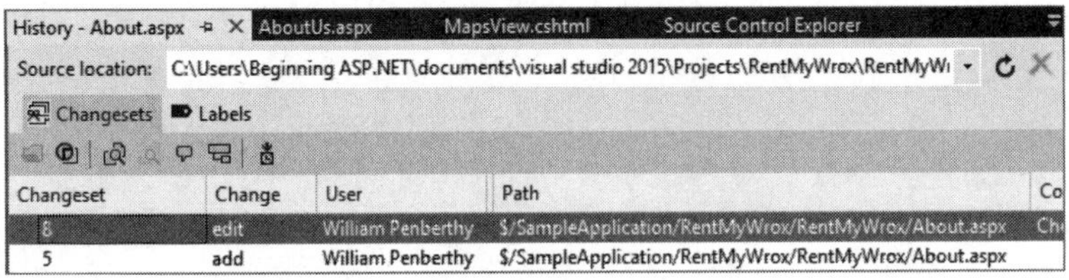

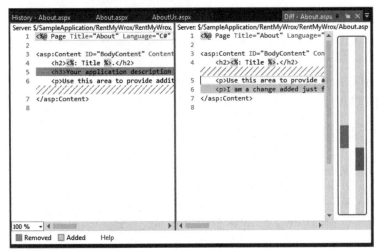

FIGURE 18-24: History window for a file

To see what changed between any two versions, simply highlight the two versions, right-click the selection, and select Compare. This will bring up a screen similar to the one shown in Figure 18-25.

FIGURE 18-25: Comparing two versions of a file

This shows a simple comparison screen. The two different versions of the file are side-by-side. Text highlighted in red has been removed, while the text highlighted in green has been added. The area on the right side of the screen provides a high-level view of where the changes are located in relationship to the visible pane. This is a very simple file, but a larger, more complex page might contain many different areas of red and green that may need to be reviewed.

Labeling

Labeling is the capability to give a useful name to a version of the code. It doesn't change the version of the source code that is on either your machine or the server, but rather gives it a more human-readable name. Creating and applying a label can be done in Source Control Explorer by right-clicking the directory that you want to label and selecting Advanced ⇨ Apply Label. This brings up a New Label dialog similar to that shown in Figure 18-26.

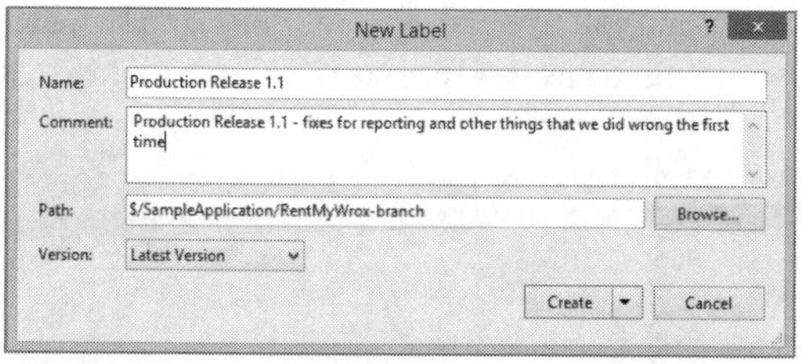

FIGURE 18-26: Creating and applying a label

After creating the label, you can refer to this particular version of the source code by that label. Whenever you are looking for a particular version, you will always have the capability to search by label. Typically, a label is added whenever a milestone event is reached, such as a release.

Interacting with a Team

Working with a team is inevitable in the life of any professional developer. This is good in that you get the opportunity to work on large applications with a group of intelligent people; but it has its own set of potential problems, such as the opportunity for multiple developers to step on each other's work. TFS does what it can to help ensure that this doesn't happen, but there are other steps you can take to ensure that you don't negatively impact the team:

1. Always get the latest version of code, compile, and validate that the application works correctly before you check in your changes.

2. If you need to merge a new version from the server with one of the files that you have changed, ensure that you do not break the other person's changes.

3. Only check in code that compiles and runs unless it has been prearranged with the team.

4. Ensure that your check-in comments are accurate and succinct. They may be looked at by others, who need to understand those changes and how they might impact their work.

5. Lock a file if you are making significant changes. This will prevent other developers from checking in changes that may affect the changes you are making. However, when locking a file, you need to ensure that you are doing it for a brief time only. Many developers have returned from vacation to a very upset team because they locked one or more files right before they left.

Changing Default Source Control Behavior in Visual Studio

Checking out code is another task that becomes more important when working with a team. Checking out code does several things. It notifies others that a file is being edited. It also acts to ensure that your locally running Visual Studio knows that it should track that file for changes. This is especially important when you are editing a file outside of Visual Studio, such as copying a different version of an image file in your application. If you take this action through the file system, then Visual Studio will not recognize that a change was made. However, manually checking out the file alerts Visual Studio that something needs to be tracked.

By default, Visual Studio automatically checks out files that you are editing, but you can change this behavior if desired. These settings are available by selecting Tools ➪ Options ➪ Source Control, as shown in Figure 18-27.

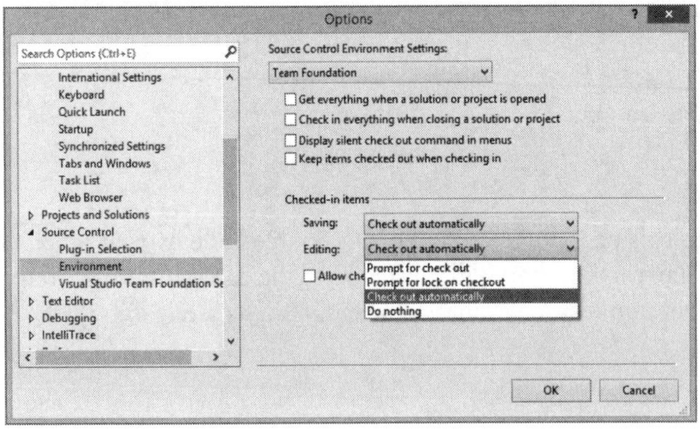

FIGURE 18-27: Changing default settings when working with a file in source control

The following options are available:

➤ **Check out automatically:** This is the default. Every time you edit and/or save a file, Visual Studio will check out the file.

➤ **Prompt for check out:** Visual Studio will ask whether it should check out the file.

➤ **Prompt for lock on checkout:** Visual Studio will ask whether it should lock the file on the server because of the check-out.

➤ **Do Nothing:** Visual Studio will do nothing—i.e., will not track any changes.

Something to consider as you go through those options is that you cannot check in a changed version of a file unless you have checked it out. That is why the system is initially set up to check out on save and edit; so that the system knows that there may be changes and Visual Studio will allow check-ins.

BRANCHING AND MERGING

As mentioned previously, branching is the duplication of an object under revision control (such as a source code file or a directory tree) so that modifications can happen in parallel in both versions. When you get to the point where you need to support two different versions of the code, you need to create a TFS branch.

To do so, go to the Source Control Explorer and right-click on the workspace name. This brings up the context menu. Select Branching and Merging ⇨ Branch. This will display the Branch dialog shown in Figure 18-28.

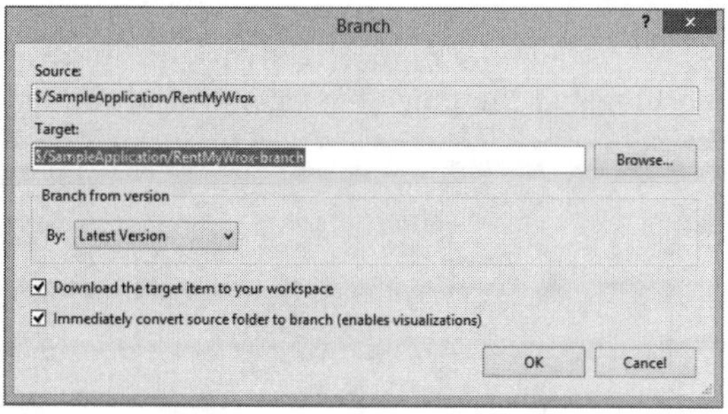

FIGURE 18-28: Branch dialog

This dialog enables you to determine where the new files should go, as well as from which version of the software you want to branch. In this case you are going to branch from the latest version. Click the OK button to bring up a dialog that shows you the status of the branching. You will spend some time watching the blue line go across the screen until the branching is completed. Once completed, your Source Control Explorer will look something like Figure 18-29.

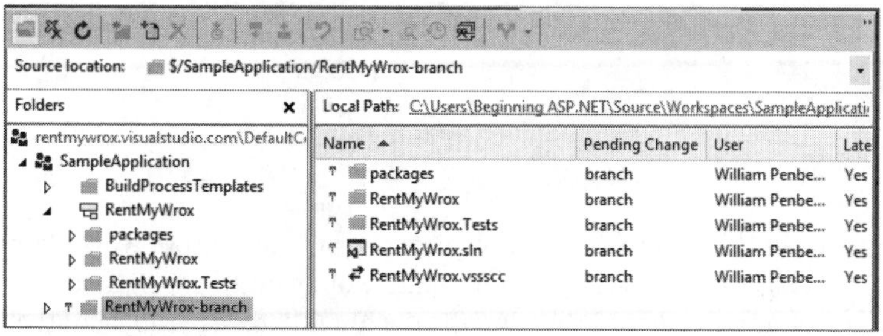

FIGURE 18-29: Source Control Explorer after branching

There is a purple icon to the left of each folder and file (while you can't see the colors in the book, it might be useful if you're following along on your machine). This indicates that it is a branch that has not yet been checked in. Also note that the icon next to the RentMyWrox folder has changed from a folder to a branch. The folder icon that is next to the RentMyWrox branch folder will change to the same branch icon after the changes are checked in. While the icons will be the same, these two directories will have a unique relationship. The directory that was copied is known as the trunk, while the copied directory will be a branch off that trunk.

After the new branch has been created you can now work in each version of the code as desired. Typically, the cut branch—in this case, RentMyWrox-branch—is the one that has the smaller, more incremental changes, while the already existing directory, the trunk, continues to have the larger, more time-intensive, longer-running changes. At regular intervals changes in the cut branch should be merged into the trunk. This ensures that the short-term fixes and changes are included in the next major release. The more often this merge is performed, the easier each merge will be because there will likely be fewer differences within the same set of source code.

Using Visual Studio and TFS to perform merges is fairly straightforward. Right-click the folder from which you want to merge and then select Branching and Merging ➪ Merge, which brings up a dialog similar to that shown in Figure 18-30.

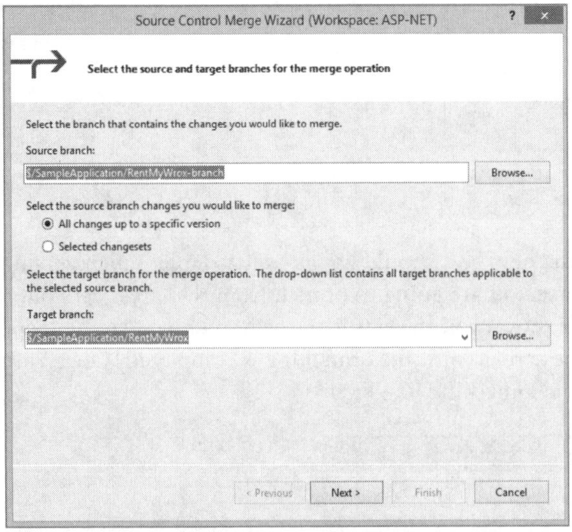

FIGURE 18-30: Merging branches

There are three areas of importance in this screen. The source branch is the area from which you want to copy the changes, and the target branch is the area to which you want to copy changes. Generally, the source is the branch that was cut and the target is the area that was branched, the trunk. The system supports going the other way too; that type of approach is generally called a *reverse merge* because it is much more unusual to be merging items from the trunk to the branch.

Merging the two can be problematic in cases for which both the branch and the trunk have had a lot of work going on and they were not frequently merged. The more work that happens in each directory between merges means the more complex the merge will end up being. Visual Studio will likely be unable to resolve many of these differences, so it ultimately requires human intervention to determine what the merged code should look like.

If the branch is never merged back into the trunk, then that work will not be available in the trunk. This means that defects that were resolved by work in the branch may reappear when code from the trunk is released. Frequent merging ensures that this doesn't happen, and that changes in the branch are always reflected and available in the trunk.

SUMMARY

This chapter has attempted to condense an entire book's work of information into some useful points and suggestions that will help you keep your ASP.NET application backed up and versioned. You have used Visual Studio Online, a version of Team Foundation Services (TFS), to act as a source code repository.

Visual Studio Online and TFS are complete application lifecycle management solutions, because they offer more than source code repository functionality. TFS also supports the gathering and capturing of requirements, tasks, and defects, and it also has a powerful reporting infrastructure that can support many different project management methodologies.

When dealing with only the source code repository capability, you can check in code, get code, and check out code. Copying code from your local directory to the server is checking in. A group of changed files are put together into a changeset, and that changeset is merged into the server. After this merge, the complete directory is given a new version number that represents the state of every file at that particular point in time. Each check-in results in the creation of a new version on the server.

Getting code is the process of copying files from the server. The most common behavior is Get Latest, whereby you copy to your local system all the files that have changed since the last time you did a Get, but you can also get specific versions of the files as necessary.

Checking out is a way of notifying the server that you are going to be making changes to a file. By default, Visual Studio checks out a file whenever you make a change. This is important because these checked out files are the ones that Visual Studio tracks for check-in. You will not be able to check in files that have not been checked out. You may check out files in several different ways. The first way flags the file on the server so that other developers know that you may be making changes. The second way actually locks the file so that other developers cannot check in changes to that file. You need to be careful with locking a file because doing so may impact other developers trying to do their work.

Working in a team requires more discipline than working alone. You have to be responsible for ensuring that your changes do not overwrite or break other changes made by other developers. You also have to ensure that you do your best to keep the application in a workable and functional state.

Source control is a critical part of development. Even a developer working alone will find it very useful, especially the versioning part of the system because it provides more than simple backup functionality. It is also imperative that anyone working professionally as a developer understand how source control works and how to interact with the system.

EXERCISES

1. What is a changeset, and why does it matter in source control?

2. What happens during a checkout?

3. What does TFS offer to enable a developer to determine who may have changed a file?

▶ **WHAT YOU LEARNED IN THIS CHAPTER**

Branching	The duplication of an object under revision control (such as a source code file or a directory tree) so that modifications can happen in parallel in both versions
Check in	The process of putting changed files into source control and creating a new version of the source code
Check out	The process of notifying the source control system that a file is being worked on
Labeling	The process of naming a version of the software. Labeling enables a complete version to be retained and accessed as needed.
Merging	The process of synchronizing two different branches. Changes in one branch are merged into the other branch to ensure that edits are available in both branches.
Repository	The online set of source controlled items
Shelveset	The group of files that make up a single check-in
TFS	Team Foundation Server, Microsoft's version of source control used during this chapter
Workspace	The area on a local machine containing the source control files that were checked out

19

Deploying Your Website

WHAT YOU WILL LEARN IN THIS CHAPTER:

➤ How to get your application ready for deployment

➤ Using values stored in configuration files

➤ Managing multiple environment settings

➤ Introduction to Windows Azure, Web Apps, and Azure SQL

➤ Publishing your application

➤ The importance of validating your deployment

Eventually, it is hoped that your application gets to a point where other people want to use it as well. The easiest way to do that is to deploy it to another server where other people can look at it themselves. Also, at some point you will need to deploy the application to a production environment so that it can interact with the public—doing the job that it was designed for.

Moving it from your local development machine to a remote server is a big step. It means you have to ensure that your application can handle multiple environments, and these multiple environments generally require different configurations, including SQL Server connection strings, so you have to manage those different values as part of your deployment strategy.

Part of this whole process is ensuring that you have a remote system to which you can deploy. Once that system is appropriately configured, your application can be deployed, or published.

PREPARING YOUR WEBSITE FOR DEPLOYMENT

Doing the work of building your application is the hard part, but deploying it to a different system is not necessarily the easiest part. When you build and run the application on the same machine, things tend to work a lot better than when you move it to a different machine. Numerous things can go wrong and render your application inoperable after deployment. These problems can stem from many different sources, such as the installed software being different so dependencies are missing on the server, or being unable to write a file because your running application does not have the security rights.

This section covers all the little details that you have to handle to ensure that your application is ready to be run on a different machine and connected to different machines in different environments. You will also learn how to add flexibility to your application by removing hard-coded settings that would require code changes if something about your business changes, turning those into configuration items.

Avoiding Hard-Coded Settings

A hard-coded setting is a value that you have defined within code that may change during the life span of your application. Unfortunately, because the value is defined in code, you have to deploy a brand-new version of the application to change that value. Typically these values are items such as external web links (links to a different website), e-mail addresses, and other text that is either displayed to the user or used in business logic somewhere within your application.

You have an example of this built into the sample application, as shown here, where the store hours are hard-coded:

```
public ActionResult Index()
{
    StoreOpen results = new StoreOpen();
    DateTime now = DateTime.Now;
    if (now.DayOfWeek == DayOfWeek.Sunday
            || (now.DayOfWeek == DayOfWeek.Saturday
                    && now.TimeOfDay > new TimeSpan(18,0,0)))
    {
        results.IsStoreOpenNow = false;
        results.Message = "We open Monday at 9:00 am";
    }
    else if (now.TimeOfDay >= new TimeSpan(9,0,0)
            && now.TimeOfDay <= new TimeSpan(18,0,0))
    {
        results.IsStoreOpenNow = true;
        TimeSpan difference = new TimeSpan(18,0,0) - now.TimeOfDay;
        results.Message = string.Format(
                "We close in {0} hours and {1} minutes",
                difference.Hours, difference.Minutes);
    }
    else if (now.TimeOfDay <= new TimeSpan(9,0,0))
    {
        results.IsStoreOpenNow = false;
        results.Message = "We will open at 9:00 am";
    }
    else
```

```
        {
            results.IsStoreOpenNow = false;
            results.Message = "We will open tomorrow at 9:00 am";
        }
        return Json(results, JsonRequestBehavior.AllowGet);
    }
```

Fortunately, ASP.NET has a way to manage this through the use of the `Web.config` file. You have done some work in the `Web.config` file already by managing database connection strings and adding other configuration settings to the file. The `Web.config` file can also maintain information that you can use within your application.

The Web.config File

You have been in and out of the `Web.config` file several times over the course of this project. One of the areas in which you have not spent much time is the `appSettings` element. The `appSettings` element is a child element of the `configuration` element, which is the base element in the file. The `appSettings` element offers programmatic access to sets of information such as the snippet shown here where values are given a unique key:

```
<appSettings>
    <add key="OpenTime" value="9" />
</appSettings>
```

There are a couple different ways you can access this information, through code and an approach known as expression syntax.

Expression Syntax

Expression syntax enables you to bind control properties directly to values in your configuration file. When you are working in ASP.NET Web Forms server controls, you use the following format to bind in a value from the `Web.config` file:

```
<%$ AppSettings:KeyName %>
```

This means that if you wanted, for example, to add a footer control that displayed some brief legalese, you would need to first add the information to your `Web.config` file using the the following code:

```
<add key="FooterDisclaimer"
        value="Copyright RentMyWrox, 2015, All Rights Reserved" />
```

You would then reference this value in a control:

```
<asp:TextBox ID="Disclaimer" runat="server"
        Text="<%$AppSettings:FooterDisclaimer %>" />
```

When working with ASP.NET Web Forms you can also directly link the control to a configuration value after you have added the value to the `Web.config` file. You can do that when you are creating the server control that contains the configuration value by using the Expression Editor.

To open the Expression Editor dialog, select the server control to which you want to add the configurable value and go to the `Properties` window. Look for the major section called Data. It should contain an `Expressions` subsection, as shown in Figure 19-1.

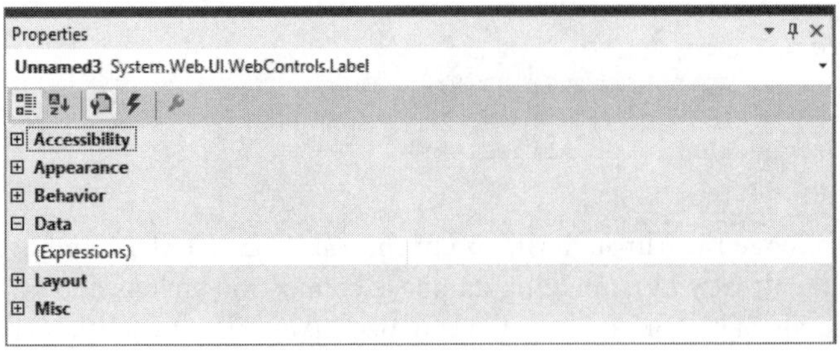

FIGURE 19-1: Properties window

If you do not see the Expressions section, you may need to ensure that you have selected the control in either the Split or Design modes; it is not always available when selecting your control in the Source (markup) window. Once you have the Expressions section available you can click the ellipses button on the right to open the Expressions dialog (see Figure 19-2).

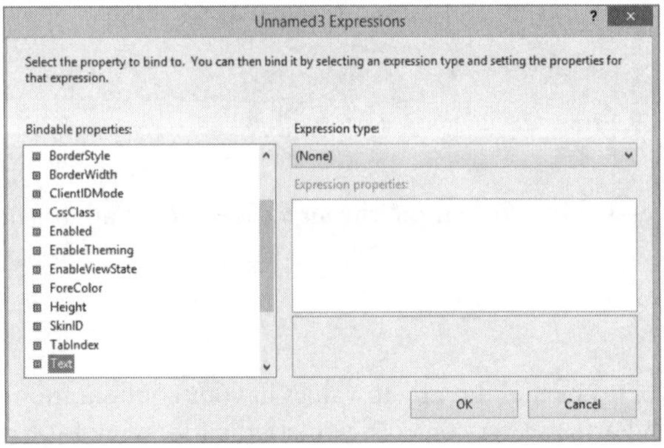

FIGURE 19-2: Expressions dialog

Selecting Text from the Bindable Properties pane and AppSettings from the Expressions Type dropdown, as shown in Figure 19-3, brings up a dropdown containing all the keys that have been added to the appSettings.

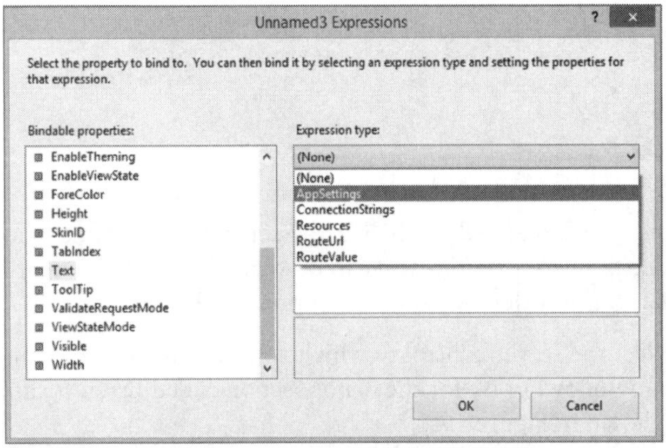

FIGURE 19-3: AppSettings in the Expressions dialog

Selecting one of these values fills out the property, as shown in the earlier examples.

The Web Configuration Manager Class

The Expression Editor only works when you are working in ASP.NET Web Forms pages. It is not supported when in a code-behind page or when working in any ASP.NET MVC components. For those other instances when you need to access configuration-based values in code (whether Web Forms code-behind or MVC), you have the `System.Web.Configuration.WebConfigurationManager` to help support working with configuration values.

Using this class is very simple and it can be used whenever C# execution is supported. The complete class and approach is shown here:

```
@System.Web.Configuration.WebConfigurationManager
        .AppSettings.Get("TestConfigurationValue")
```

This method call returns a string, so if the information is actually a different type then you need to cast or convert it as necessary.

In this next Try It Out activity, you convert some of the hard-coded information that you have scattered around the application into values that can be managed within the `Web.config` file.

TRY IT OUT   Adding Configuration

In this activity you will be doing several different things. The first is to create `Web.config` `appSettings`. You then abstract out access to the `Web.config` file into a class containing static properties that map to configuration values. Lastly, you update those areas of code to use configuration values rather than the hard-coded values they are currently using.

1. Ensure that Visual Studio is running and you have the RentMyWrox application open. Open the `Web.config` file.

2. Find the `appSettings` element in the `Web.config` file and add the following items:
```
<add key="AdminItemListPageSize" value="5" />
<add key="StoreOpenTime" value="9" />
<add key="StoreCloseTime" value="18" />
<add key="StoreOpenStringValue" value="9:00 am" />
<add key="ViewNotifications" value="true" />
```

3. Right-click on the Models directory and add a new class named **ConfigManager.cs**.

4. Add the following property to the new file:
```
public static int AdminItemListPageSize
{
    get
    {
        int answer = 5;
        string results = WebConfigurationManager.AppSettings
                .Get("AdminItemListPageSize");
        if (!string.IsNullOrWhiteSpace(results))
        {
            int.TryParse(results, out answer);
        }
```

```
        return answer;
    }
}
```

5. Add the following items:

```csharp
public static int StoreOpenTime
{
    get
    {
        int answer = 9;
        string results = WebConfigurationManager.AppSettings.Get("StoreOpenTime");
        if (!string.IsNullOrWhiteSpace(results))
        {
            int.TryParse(results, out answer);
        }
        return answer;
    }
}

public static int StoreCloseTime
{
    get
    {
        int answer = 18;
        string results = WebConfigurationManager.AppSettings.Get("StoreCloseTime");
        if (!string.IsNullOrWhiteSpace(results))
        {
            int.TryParse(results, out answer);
        }
        return answer;
    }
}

public static string StoreOpenStringValue
{
    get
    {
        string results = WebConfigurationManager.AppSettings
            .Get("StoreOpenStringValue");
        if (string.IsNullOrWhiteSpace(results))
        {
            results = "9:00 am";
        }
        return results;
    }
}

public static bool ViewNotifications
{
    get
    {
        bool answer = false;
        string results = WebConfigurationManager.AppSettings
```

```
              .Get("ViewNotifications");
    if (!string.IsNullOrWhiteSpace(results))
    {
        bool.TryParse(results, out answer);
    }
    return answer;
}
}
```

6. Open the `StoreOpenController.cs`. There are three instances of `TimeSpan(18,0,0)`. Replace the "18" with `ConfigManager.StoreCloseTime` to get the following:

```
TimeSpan(ConfigManager.StoreCloseTime,0,0)
```

7. Replace the "9" in `TimeSpan(9,0,0)` with `ConfigManager.StoreOpenTime` to get this:

```
TimeSpan(ConfigManager.StoreOpenTime,0,0)
```

8. Wherever you see the phrase "9:00 am" make the following change. The completed page should look like the one shown in Figure 19-4.

From:
```
results.Message = "We open Monday at 9:00 am";
```

To:
```
results.Message = "We open Monday at " + ConfigManager.StoreOpenStringValue;
```

```
public ActionResult Index()
{
    StoreOpen results = new StoreOpen();
    DateTime now = DateTime.Now;
    if (now.DayOfWeek == DayOfWeek.Sunday || (now.DayOfWeek == DayOfWeek.Saturday && now.TimeOfDay > new TimeSpan(ConfigManager.StoreCloseTime,0,0)))
    {
        results.IsStoreOpenNow = false;
        results.Message = "We open Monday at " + ConfigManager.StoreOpenStringValue;
    }
    else if (now.TimeOfDay >= new TimeSpan(ConfigManager.StoreOpenTime, 0,0) && now.TimeOfDay <= new TimeSpan(ConfigManager.StoreCloseTime, 0,0))
    {
        results.IsStoreOpenNow = true;
        TimeSpan difference = new TimeSpan(ConfigManager.StoreCloseTime, 0,0) - now.TimeOfDay;
        results.Message = string.Format("We close in {0} hours and {1} minutes", difference.Hours, difference.Minutes);
    }
    else if (now.TimeOfDay <= new TimeSpan(ConfigManager.StoreOpenTime, 0,0))
    {
        results.IsStoreOpenNow = false;
        results.Message = "We will open at " + ConfigManager.StoreOpenStringValue;
    }
    else
    {
        results.IsStoreOpenNow = false;
        results.Message = "We will open tomorrow at  " + ConfigManager.StoreOpenStringValue;
    }
    return Json(results, JsonRequestBehavior.AllowGet);
}
```

FIGURE 19-4: Updated StoreOpenController

9. Open your View\Shared_MVCLayout.cshtml file. Find and update the following code as shown:

From:
```
<span>@Html.Action("Recent", "Item")</span>
```

To:
```
@if (ConfigManager.ViewNotifications)
```

```
    {
        @Html.Action("NonAdminSnippet", "Notifications")
    }
```

10. Open Admin\ItemList.aspx. In your GridView, replace the value in the PageSize attribute with the following (see Figure 19-5):

```
<%$ AppSettings:AdminItemListPageSize %>
```

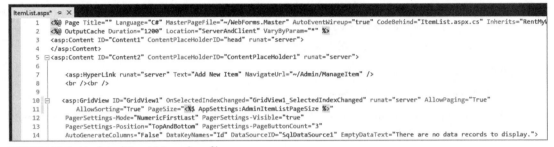

FIGURE 19-5: Updated ItemList markup file

11. Run the application and confirm that everything works as expected such as the store hours section showing up properly including logging in as an administrator and checking the Item list.

How It Works

The ConfigManager class that you built is designed to look in the Web.config file and make the configuration values available for common use. These properties are doing more than simply getting a value from the configuration file, however, because they also manage a default value, as well as handling cases where the value is missing from the configuration file. Each property even ensures that the string value is converted or parsed to the appropriate type. Imagine how much code you would have to write if you had to do all this each time you wanted to get the value from the file rather than putting this all in one place!

The code you added set a default value, but sometimes this isn't ideal and you would instead throw an exception if the configuration item was missing. That approach would be similar to this:

```
get
{
    string results = WebConfigurationManager.AppSettings.Get("SomeValue");
    bool answer;

    if (string.IsNullOrWhiteSpace(results) || !bool.TryParse(results, out answer);)
    {
        throw new KeyNotFoundException("config error for SomeValue");
    }

    return answer;
}
```

Using this approach ensures that if no value is set, or if the value that is returned cannot be parsed into the appropriate type, then the method will throw an exception rather than try to use a default value.

One more thing to consider is that you can also write to the `Web.config` file, if necessary, by using the `Set` method (rather than the `Get` method to retrieve information from configuration). This is common when you want to be able to do some configuration of the site through the UI, perhaps by adding a page that enables you to change the values for these fields as desired.

You have converted some of your hard-coded values to configuration values and ensured that you are calling them correctly. You had to do this so that you can easily support changes that may happen when your application is deployed to another computer. Now that your code is updated to support this, you can get ready for the deployment.

PREPARING FOR DEPLOYMENT

All of your work so far has been local, using a web server running on your local machine that connects to a SQL database server that is also running on your machine. You have then been accessing that web server from a browser that is also, you guessed it, on your machine. Once you deploy your application, this will all be different. The new web server will be running on one machine, while the new SQL Server will be running on a different machine; and while your browser will still be running locally, it won't be running locally on the same machine as the web server or the database server.

Because these will all be different machines, your new SQL Server will not be the same as your development SQL Server, so you know that the connection strings will be different. In this section you will set up both your deployment environment and the process to manage changes that are needed for handling these configuration differences based on environment.

You will be using Microsoft Azure as your web hosting system, as well as to manage your online data store. For those of you who are unable to access Azure, you will also walk through a file-based deployment process so that you can still follow along with the publishing process.

Microsoft Azure

Microsoft Azure is a collection of different cloud services, including analytics, computing, database, mobile, networking, storage, and web. Here you will be working with two services in specific: App Services and SQL Database.

The App Services offering from Azure enables you to host web applications built on multiple languages—from .NET to PHP to Java. This offering is especially powerful because it enables you to easily scale the resources dedicated to managing your application; as your user base grows, so can the resources that are handling the work.

The SQL Database service is basically your SQL Server instance hosted in the cloud. The Azure-based system has an even higher performance and reliability factor than your local SQL Server; and like the App Services, you can scale your resources up or down as necessary.

Microsoft Azure offers a 30-day free trial, which is what you will be using for the deployment. Note some caveats about working with Microsoft Azure:

➤ Not all areas and countries have access to Azure services depending on local or international agreements.

➤ You are required to enter a credit card number when signing up for Azure. They won't charge it unless you give them permission after the 30 day period, but you will not be able to set up an account without providing a credit card number.

If you can't access or sign up for Azure services, feel free to skip this next step and go directly to publishing your site. File-based instructions are also provided as you walk through the publishing steps.

 **TRY IT OUT**   Registering for Microsoft Azure

In this activity you create an account with Microsoft Azure. It is recommended that you use the Windows Live account that you have used previously to download Visual Studio and set up the source control from Chapter 18.

1. Open a web browser and go to `http://azure.microsoft.com`. You should get a welcome screen similar to the one shown in Figure 19-6.

FIGURE 19-6: Azure home page

2. Click the Try for Free button in the middle of the screen. There is also a Free Trial link at the top right. This brings up the Free Trial page (see Figure 19-7).

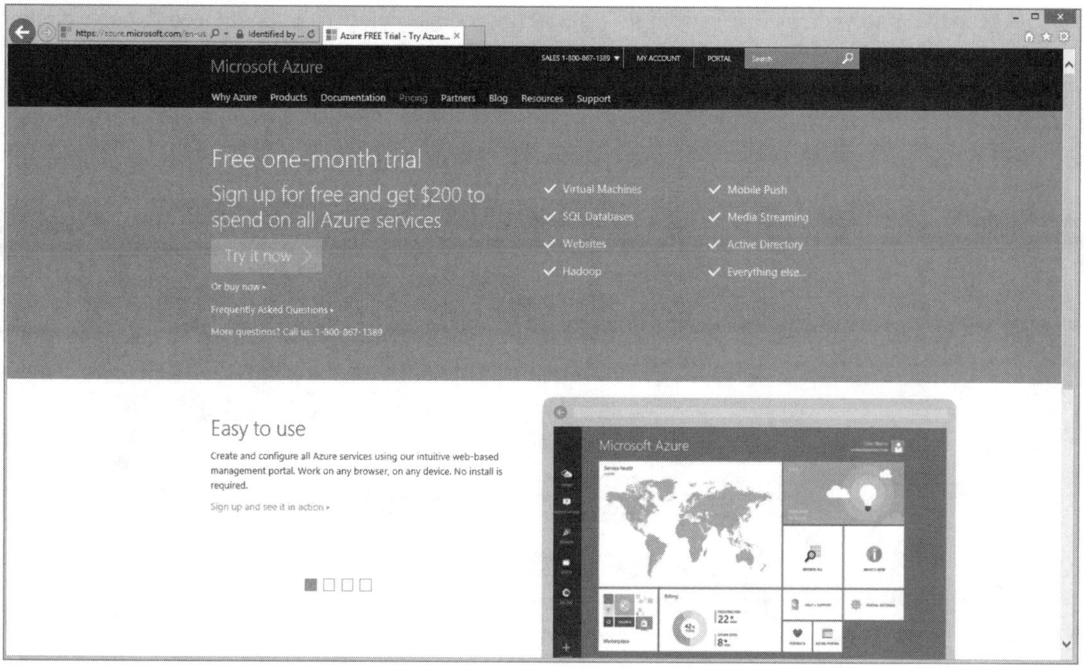

FIGURE 19-7: Azure free trial page

3. Click the Try It Now link. Log in using your Windows Live account. This brings up the sign-up page shown in Figure 19-8.

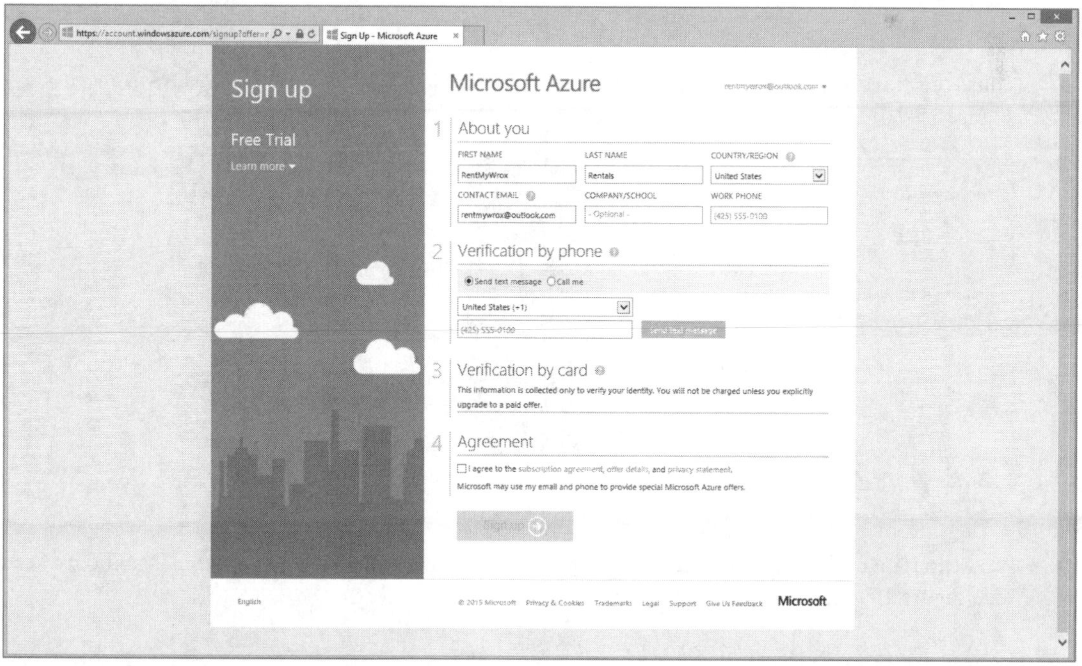

FIGURE 19-8: Azure sign-up page

4. Create your account as directed on the page. This is the point at which you need to enter credit card for confirmation. Click Sign Up when your information has been added and the button has been enabled. After some processing you will be presented with the Subscription Is Ready page (see Figure 19-9).

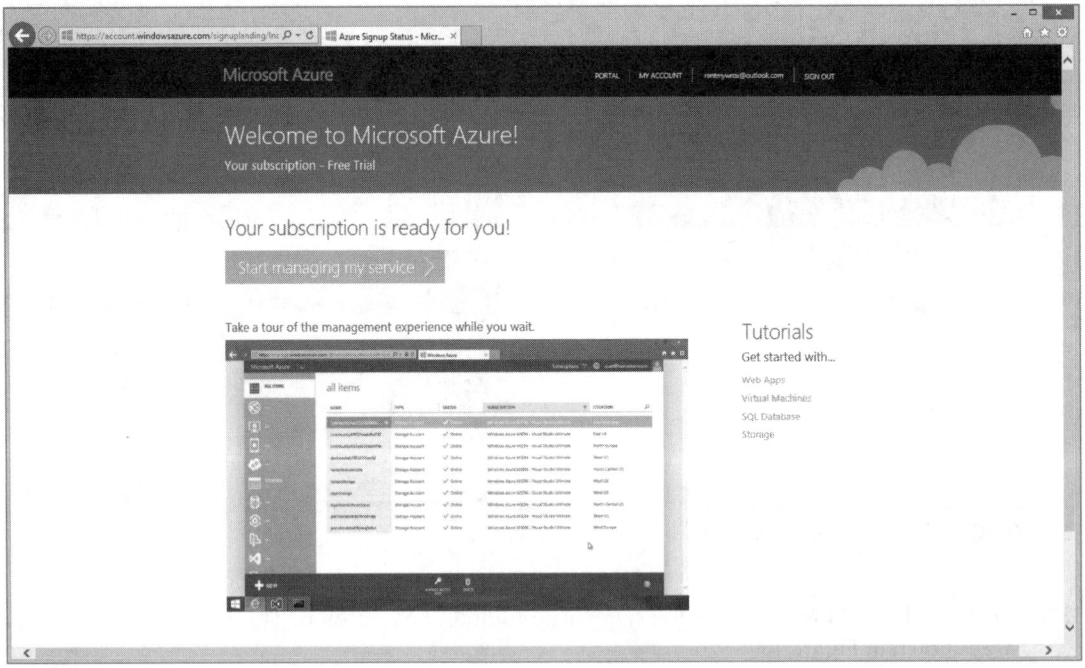

FIGURE 19-9: Subscription is ready page

5. Click the Start Managing My Service button. You will get a dialog offering a short tour (see Figure 19-10).

WINDOWS AZURE TOUR

Hi RentMyWrox!

Take this 30 second tour to see how the management portal makes creating and managing your cloud resources easy.

→   2   3   4   5

FIGURE 19-10: Azure tour page

6. You can either click through the tour (very brief) or close the popup to get your Dashboard screen (see Figure 19-11).

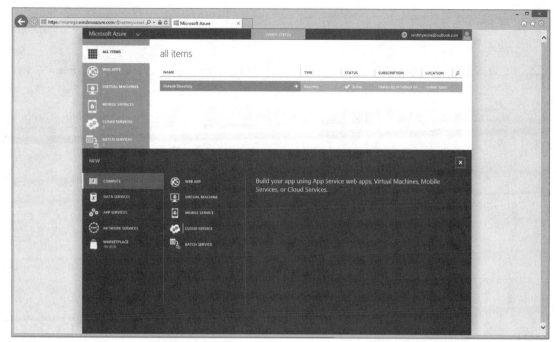

FIGURE 19-11: Azure dashboard page

How It Works

In this activity, you created a free Azure subscription that enables you to deploy your application to another system over the Internet and test how successful that deployment was. Up until now all you have done is create the initial subscription, you have not signed up for any specific services. Don't forget that this subscription expires in 30 days!

Now that you have a new system to which you can deploy your application, the next step walks you through the publishing process.

PUBLISHING YOUR SITE

You have set up your application to support multiple environments by putting information into the configuration file. You have also set up the destination system to which you will publish your site. The next step is to publish it, which is demonstrated in the following Try It Out.

TRY IT OUT   Publishing Your Site

In this activity you publish your website to either Microsoft Azure or your local system (or both), depending on your capability to access this third-party system.

1. Ensure that Visual Studio is running and you have the RentMyWrox application open. Build your application and double-check your Error List window to ensure that there is nothing wrong with the application.

2. In the Solution Explorer window, right-click the RentMyWrox project and select Publish. This opens the Publish Web dialog shown in Figure 19-12.

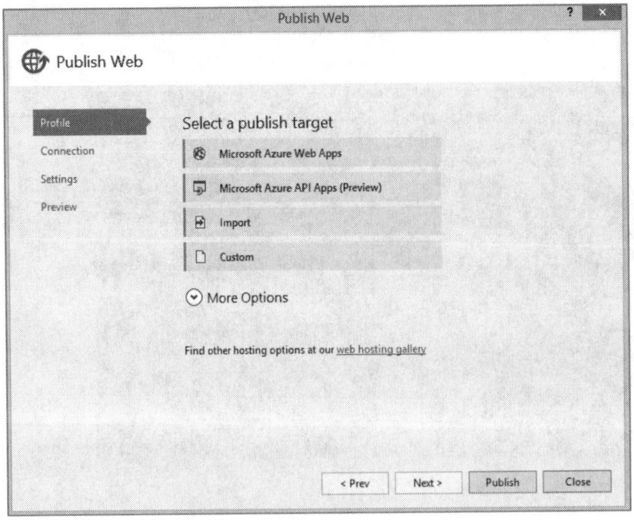

FIGURE 19-12: Publish Web dialog

3. If you are going to publish to Azure, continue from here. If not, you may want to instead go directly to Step 20.

4. Under the "Select a publish target" section, click the Microsoft Azure Web Apps button. This should bring up the dialog shown in Figure 19-13.

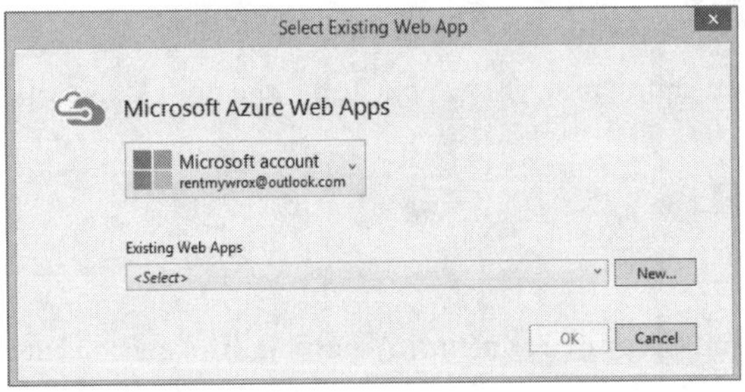

FIGURE 19-13: Select Existing Web App dialog

5. If your account doesn't appear under the Web Apps section, you will have a link to log in to your account. Click this link and ensure that you use the same credentials you used in the last activity.

6. Click the "New…" button. This brings up the Create Web App on Microsoft Azure dialog shown in Figure 19-14.

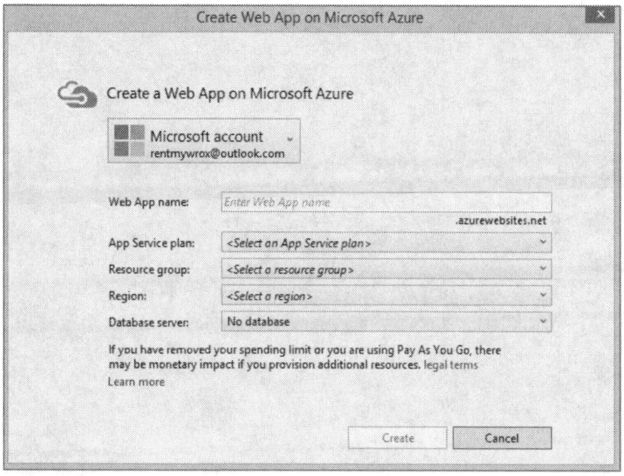

FIGURE 19-14: Create Web App on Microsoft Azure dialog

7. Enter your preferred Web App name. It may take several attempts before you find one that is not already being used because the Web App name has to be unique within the Azure system.

8. Select "Create new App Service plan" and enter a value that identifies your site in the textbox that appears.

9. Do the same with the Resource group.

10. Select a Region that makes the most sense for your location. When completed, your Create Web App screen should look similar to Figure 19-15.

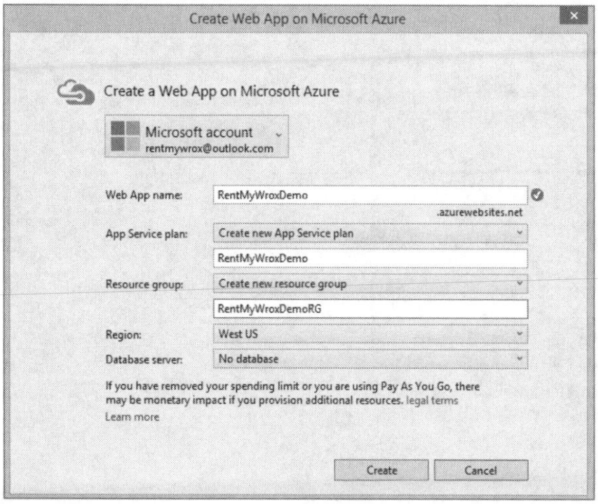

FIGURE 19-15: Completed Create Web App on Microsoft Azure dialog

11. Click the Create button. The system will process for a while, as shown by the progress bar in the lower-left corner of Figure 19-16.

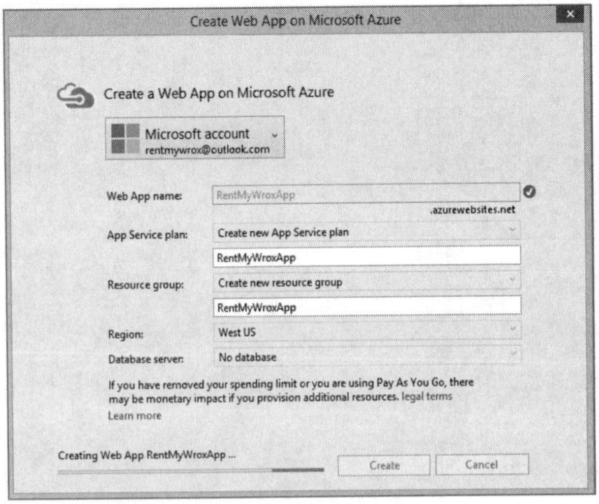

FIGURE 19-16: Creating the new Web App

12. When completed, you should be back on the Publish Web screen. Click the Validate Connection button. The dialog shown in Figure 19-17 should appear.

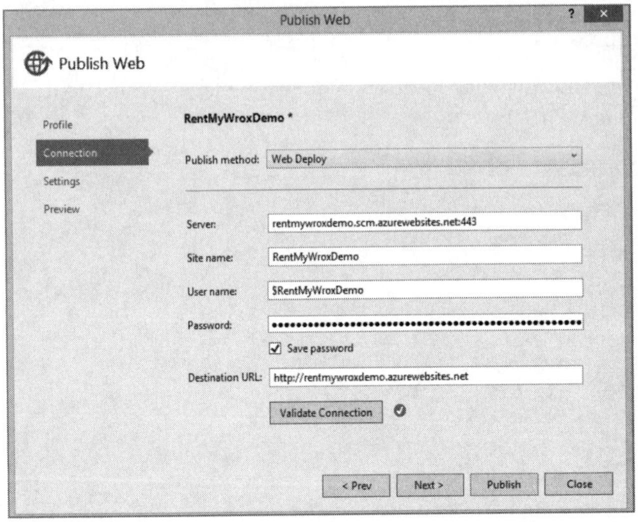

FIGURE 19-17: Creation screen with connection validated

13. Click the Publish button. You should be able to see an Azure App Service Activity tab in the lower part of the IDE, where the Output and Error List tabs are located. When the process is finished, it should open your website on the server.

14. Log in to your Microsoft Azure account, which opens the dashboard dialog.

15. Click the Web Apps link on the left. This opens the Web Apps page, with the Web App that you added listed (see Figure 19-18).

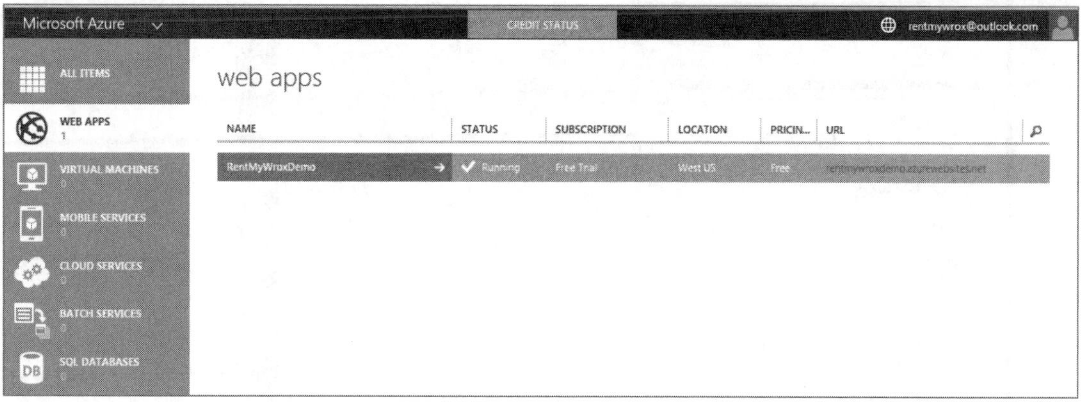

FIGURE 19-18: Web Apps listing in Azure

16. Select the SQL Database link from the menu on the left. This opens the dialog shown in Figure 19-19.

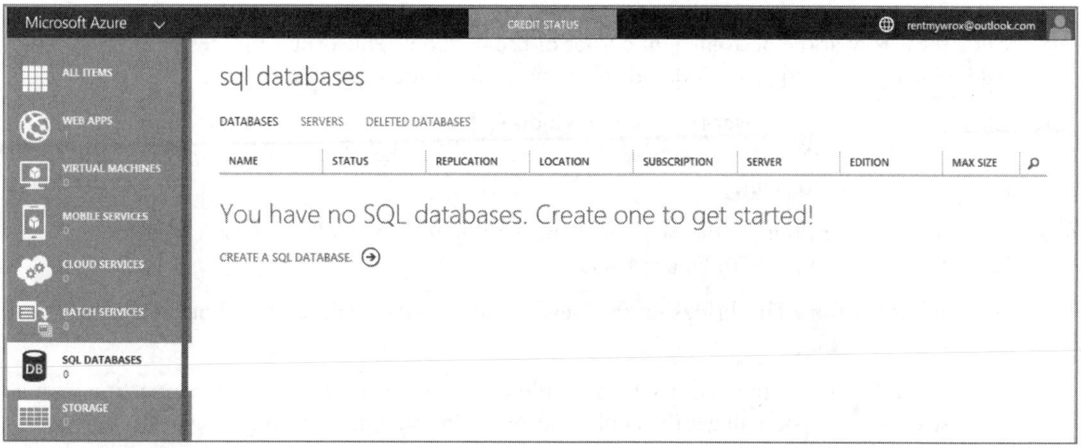

FIGURE 19-19: SQL Database listing in Azure

17. Select the Create a SQL Database link. This opens a Custom Create dialog. Add a database name, as shown at the bottom of Figure 19-20.

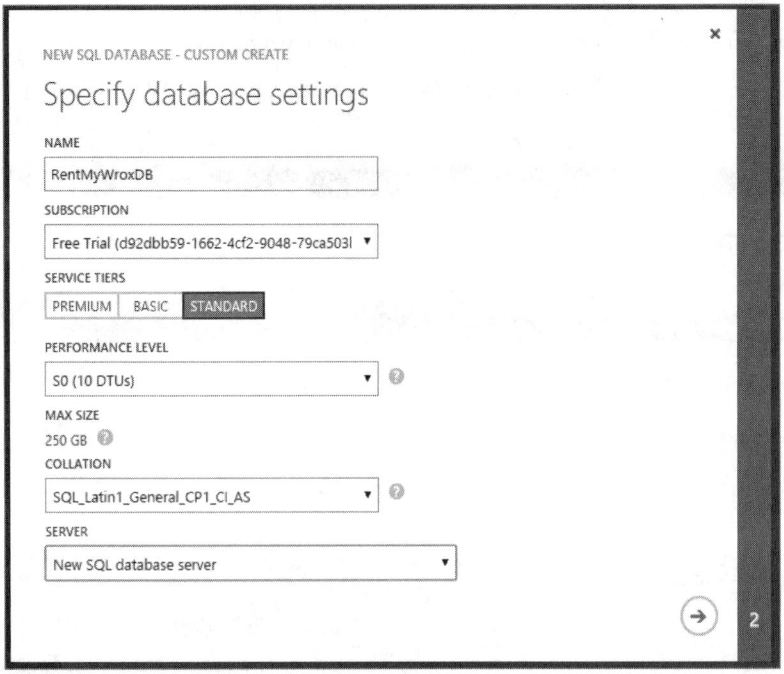

FIGURE 19-20: Creating a SQL Database

18. Click the arrow at the bottom-right corner of the window. This brings up the Create Server dialog. Add a login name and password and select the appropriate region (see Figure 19-21).

19. Click the check on the lower right of the window. This takes you back to the Azure SQL Database listing (see Figure 19-22). It may take several minutes for the creation to complete. This is the last step to publishing to Azure.

20. The following steps outline the process for publishing to a local file directory. You should be at the Publish Web screen (refer to Figure 19-12).

    a. Select Custom. This brings up the New Custom Profile dialog. Enter **LocalToFile** as shown in Figure 19-23.

    b. Click the OK button. Your screen should change so that the left-hand Connection item is selected, and you will get the configuration dialog shown in Figure 19-24.

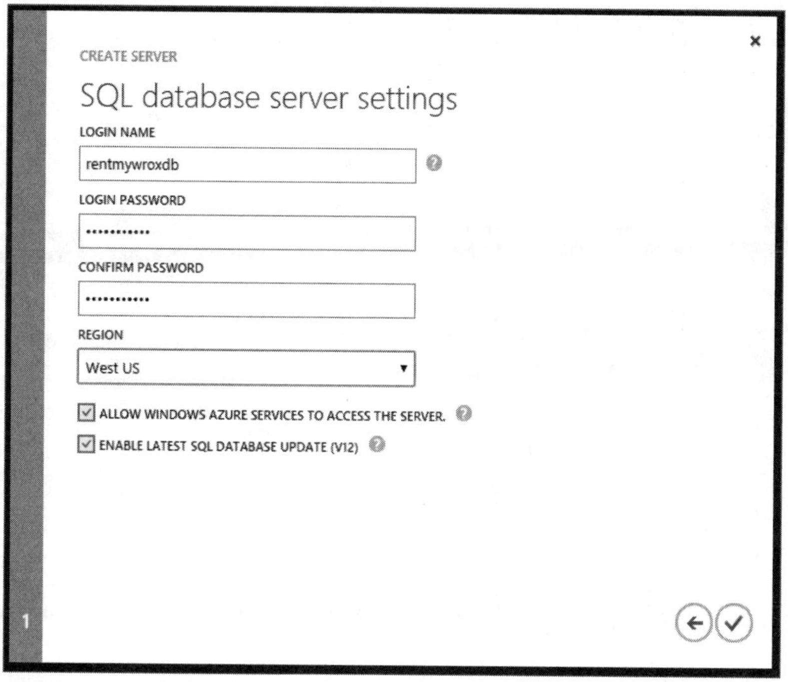

FIGURE 19-21: Create Server dialog in Azure

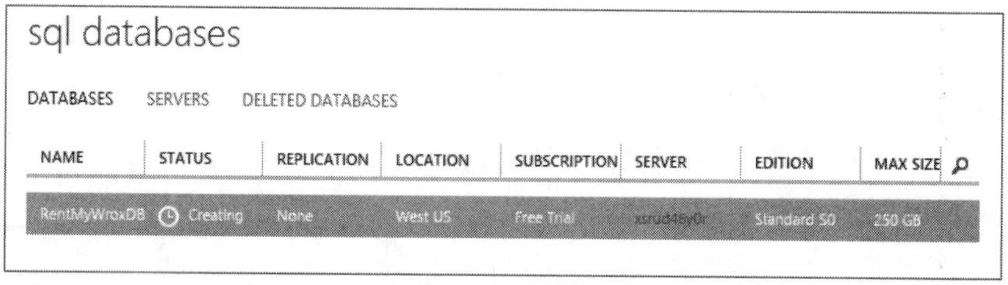

FIGURE 19-22: Database being created in Azure

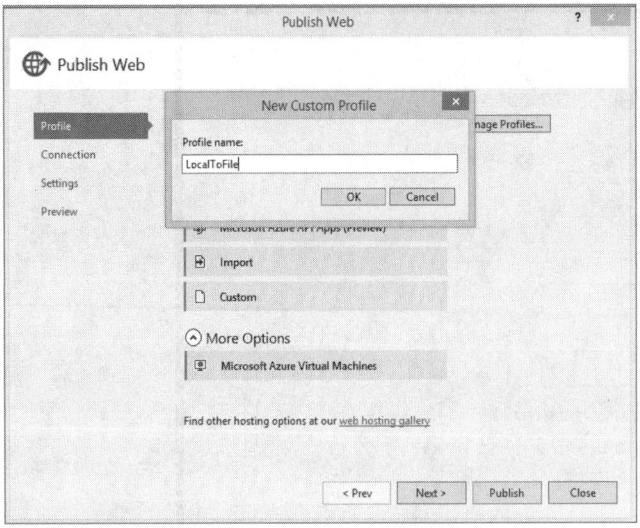

FIGURE 19-23: Adding a custom publish profile

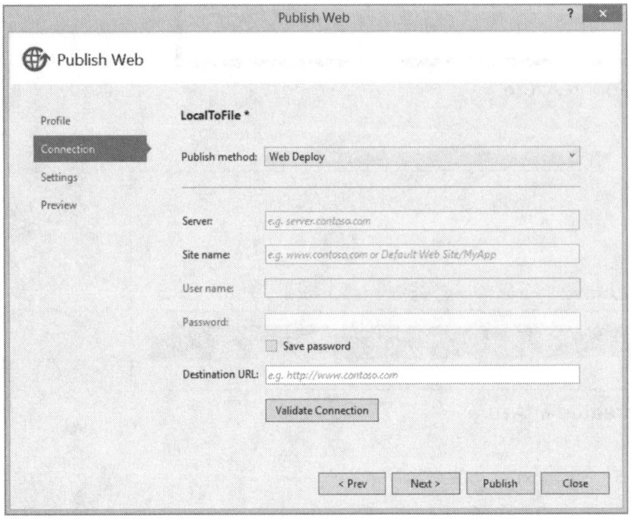

FIGURE 19-24: Configuration screen for a custom profile

c.   Select File System from the Publish method dropdown. This will bring up the Target Location dialog shown in Figure 19-25.

d.   Click the ellipses button to open a file system explorer window. Choose the directory where you want to publish the files. If you need to add a directory, click the small Create New Folder button above the directory list.

e.   Click the Publish button. You should see lines of information describing what is being copied being listed in your Output window. When it is completed, open the directory to which you published. You'll see a list similar to the one shown in Figure 19-26.

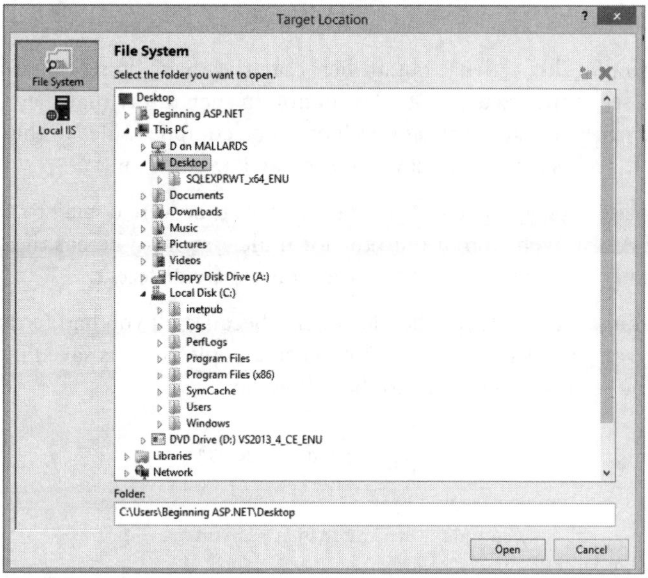

FIGURE 19-25: Selecting a target location for a custom profile

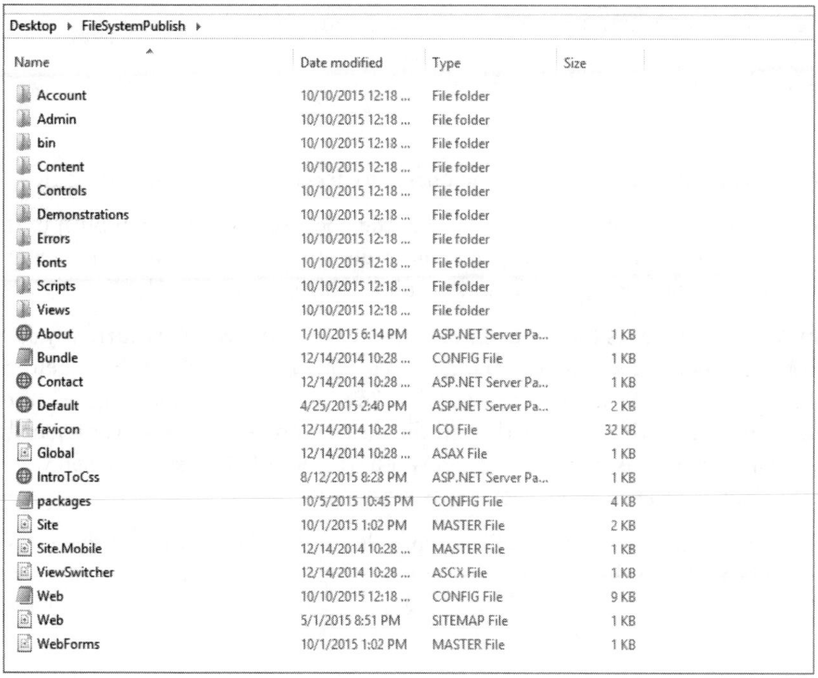

FIGURE 19-26: Published files

How It Works

Two different publishing processes occurred in this activity, but at their core they were doing the same thing. The goal of publishing is to copy a set of files to a remote destination in such a way that they work; therefore, the class files and all the necessary supporting files have to be compiled, files in the References have to be copied to the server, necessary folders have to be created, and so on.

When you ran the publishing process for either profile you created a set of files that were copied to the destination—either onto a Microsoft Azure Web App or onto the local file system. Whereas the publishing part of the process was the same, setting up the profiles was completely different.

The simple approach was creating the publishing profile for the file system, because all you had to do was select the directory where you will write the output. This profile, when completed, was saved into a .pubxml file. If you look inside that file you see content similar to the following:

```
<Project ToolsVersion="4.0"
         xmlns="http://schemas.microsoft.com/developer/msbuild/2003">
  <PropertyGroup>
    <WebPublishMethod>FileSystem</WebPublishMethod>
    <LastUsedBuildConfiguration>Release</LastUsedBuildConfiguration>
    <LastUsedPlatform>Any CPU</LastUsedPlatform>
    <SiteUrlToLaunchAfterPublish />
    <LaunchSiteAfterPublish>True</LaunchSiteAfterPublish>
    <ExcludeApp_Data>False</ExcludeApp_Data>
    <publishUrl>
        C:\Users\Beginning ASP.NET\Desktop\FileSystemPublish
    </publishUrl>
    <DeleteExistingFiles>False</DeleteExistingFiles>
  </PropertyGroup>
</Project>
```

If you recall the setup screens, you can see that each of the questions asked has a corresponding element.

The good thing about that is that you no longer have to answer the questions when you publish in the future, as they will already be filled out. However, if you want to do something special when during an application publish, you can change the setting for that particular publish.

One of the most frequently changed items is the DeleteExistingFiles node, which is currently set to false. When this is set to true, the publishing process first deletes all the files from the website before it writes the new ones. The process always writes the updated files and replaces those files on the server; however, the DeleteExistingFiles setting ensures that all the files are copied to the server regardless of whether they have been changed. This is important when you have a lot of changes, or when you make changes that remove or rename the current .aspx pages.

It was a lot more complicated to set up the Azure publishing profile, so it makes sense that the .pubxml file would be a lot more complicated as well—and it is, as shown in Figure 19-27.

FIGURE 19-27: Web App .pubxml file

Note, however, that a lot of information filled out during the process is not included in this file. This missing information is not part of the publish process and was instead used to create the Azure Web App to which the application will be published. You could have just as easily set up a Web App from the Azure dashboard, just as you did to create the SQL Database, and then select that Web App when publishing.

Deploying your application using the publish process in Visual Studio is very straightforward, even the first time when you have to ensure everything is correctly configured. After that, publishing is even easier, requiring just a few mouse clicks, because all the information has already been gathered.

You may have noticed that one specific part of the publish process was incorrect: connecting to the database. You have a new database but you have not done anything to add those specific configurations to the deployed application. There is support for this within Visual Studio as part of the publishing process, called Web.config transformations.

Introducing Web.config Transformations

Something you may not have noticed about your `Web.config` file is that it has an arrow next to it, indicating that it can be expanded. Doing so shows that two more files are available, `Web.Debug.config` and `Web.Release .config` (see Figure 19-28).

FIGURE 19-28: Multiple configuration files

These additional files are important because they are the ones that manage your environment-specific information. In this case, two are currently defined: Release and Debug. When you are running locally, you are running in Debug mode, so you would use the settings in this version of the file. When you published the application to the server, you published it in Release mode, which means that the Release version of the configuration would have been copied to the server.

You can do more than simply change values between different environments as the configuration files are run through a process called *transformation* when they are deployed. The `Web.config` file has the `Web.Release.config` file applied against it, much like a template, with the result of this template application being copied to the server. This transformation can do many things. It can manage the change of values for different configuration items in the `appSettings` and `con- nectionString` elements as well as alter other attributes in different elements throughout the configuration file.

You can see an example of this if you published your application to a local directory. The `Web.config` file that you have been working with contains the following element:

```
<compilation debug="true" targetFramework="4.5" />
```

However, if you look at the `Web.config` file that was deployed to your local directory, you will see this element is instead:

```
<compilation targetFramework="4.5" />
```

This means that particular element was transformed.

The transformation rules are configured in the different versions of `Web.config` files. In this instance, if you look into the `Web.Release.config` file, you will see the following code (comments removed for brevity):

```
<configuration xmlns:xdt="http://schemas.microsoft.com/XML-Document-Transform">
  <system.web>
    <compilation xdt:Transform="RemoveAttributes(debug)" />
  </system.web>
</configuration>
```

Compared to the basic `Web.config`, there are two things going on in this page. The first is the `xmlns:xdt=""`, which defines the `xdt` preface as defining a transform attribute. If you don't have this section, then you will not be able to use the `xdt:Transform` attribute shown in the contained elements as the configuration system will display errors.

This `xdt:Transform` attribute defines the rules. Here, the transformation is going to be run on the `compilation` element, as that is the name of the element that includes this transformation attribute. In this specific instance, the transform that was set up by default is called `"RemoveAttributes"` and contains `"debug"`, or the name of the attribute to be removed. This one line of code in the `.Release.config` file ensured that the `Web.config` file was altered during the publishing process.

XPATH

Your `Web.config` files are XML files. This means that when you are working with them as XML files (as opposed to accessing them through the application), you can use XPath. XPath is a language that enables you to select nodes within an XML file. Because transformation happens outside of the application running, the .NET Framework supports using XPath to define items that you want to change during the `Web.config` transformation process. You will see some simple XPath statements in this section. For a more thorough overview, go to `https://msdn .microsoft.com/en-us/library/ms256115(v=vs.110).aspx`.

Table 19-1 describes other options available during the transformation process.

TABLE 19-1: Transformation Items

NAME	DESCRIPTION
`Locator = Condition(XPath expression)`	Specifies an XPath expression that is appended to the current element's XPath expression. Elements that match the combined XPath expression are selected.
`Locator = Match(attribute names)`	Selects the element or elements that have a matching value for the specified attribute or attributes. If multiple attribute names are specified, only elements that match all the specified attributes are selected.
`Transform="Replace"`	Replaces the selected element with the element that is specified in the transform file. If more than one element is selected, only the first selected element is replaced.
`Transform="Insert"`	Adds the element that is defined in the transform file as a sibling to the selected element or elements. The new element is added at the end of any collection.
`Transform="Remove"`	Removes the selected element. If multiple elements are selected, the first element is removed.
`Transform="RemoveAttributes (comma-delimited list of one or more attribute names)"`	Removes specified attributes from the selected elements
`Transform="SetAttributes(comma-delimited list of one or more attribute names)"`	Sets attributes for selected elements to the specified values. The `Replace` transform attribute replaces an entire element, including all of its attributes. In contrast, the `SetAttributes` attribute enables you to leave the element as it is but change selected attributes. If you don't specify which attributes to change, all attributes present in the element in the transform file are changed.

Each of the attributes does one of two things. It either identifies the element that needs to be changed (the Locator attributes) or defines the kind of change that needs to happen (the Transform attributes). There will always be a Transform attribute, as otherwise there wouldn't be a transformation; but the Locator attribute is optional, as demonstrated in the default Release configuration file. If you don't specify a Locator attribute, the element to be changed is specified by the element that contains the Transform attribute. In the following example, the entire system.web element from the Web.config file is replaced, because no Locator attribute is specified to indicate otherwise:

```
<?xml version="1.0"?>
<configuration xmlns:xdt="http://schemas.microsoft.com/XML-Document-Transform">
  <system.web xdt:Transform="Replace">
    <customErrors defaultRedirect=" ~/Errors/Error500.aspx " mode="RemoteOnly">
      <error statusCode="500" redirect="~/Errors/Error500.aspx" />
    </customErrors>
  </system.web>
</configuration>
```

This means that all the content you already have in the system.web node, such as your trace setup and your other customError pages (such as Error404.aspx), would not be included in the Release-version transformed configuration file. Thus, you have to be careful when setting up your transforms because it is easy to transform your configuration files in such a way as to break your application.

While the Release and Debug versions of the configuration file are included automatically, you actually have much better control over transformation now that you have created publish profiles, as you can set the transformation for each of those profiles rather than rely on the default types to manage these. In many cases you will have different systems all running in Release mode, such as your test system and your production system. Each of those will likely have different values that need to be configured differently from the other environments, regardless of whether those other environments are Debug or Release versions.

In this next Try It Out, you add Web.config transformations to your application.

TRY IT OUT Adding Transformations to Your Application

In this activity you manage some of the environment-specific changes that you need to handle for the different versions of your applications. You will be creating different versions of these for each of the publishing methods that you worked on in the previous exercise.

1. Ensure that Visual Studio is running and you have the RentMyWrox application open. Expand the Properties section and the PublishProfiles folder, as shown in Figure 19-29.

2. Right-click one of the .pubxml files, in this case the RentMyWroxDemo.pubxml file, and select Add Config Transform. After doing that, check your Web.config file. It should contain an additional item (Web.RentMyWroxDemo.config or whatever name you used for your .pubxml file), as shown in Figure 19-30.

FIGURE 19-29: Publish-Profiles directory

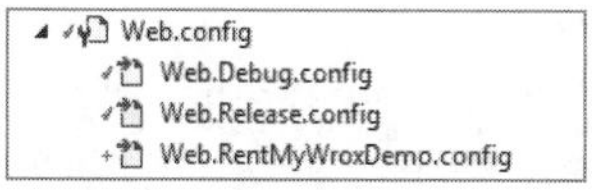

FIGURE 19-30: New PublishProfiles-based configuration

3. Right-click the new file and select Preview Transform. You should get a screen similar to the one shown in Figure 19-31. The left side is the original Web.config file, while the right side is the transformed file. You should see the checked areas highlighted.

FIGURE 19-31: Previewing the transformation

4. Close the preview window. Open your PublishProfile.config file, in this case the Web .RentMyWroxDemo.config file. Add the following content to the configuration element:

```
<appSettings>
    <add key="StoreCloseTime" value="19"
            xdt:Transform="SetAttributes" xdt:Locator="Match(key)" />
    <add key="StoreOpenTime" value="10"
            xdt:Transform="SetAttributes" xdt:Locator="Match(key)" />
    <add key="StoreOpenStringValue" value="10:00 am"
            xdt:Transform="SetAttributes" xdt:Locator="Match(key)"/>
</appSettings>
[
```

5. Right-click this updated file and select Preview Transform. You should see additional changed areas, as shown in Figure 19-32.

```
<appSettings>
  <add key="webpages:Version" value="3.0.0.0" />
  <add key="webpages:Enabled" value="false" />
  <add key="PreserveLoginUrl" value="true" />
  <add key="ClientValidationEnabled" value="true" />
  <add key="UnobtrusiveJavaScriptEnabled" value="true" />

  <add key="AdminItemListPageSize" value="5" />
  <add key="StoreOpenTime" value="9" />
  <add key="StoreCloseTime" value="18" />
  <add key="StoreOpenStringValue" value="9:00 am" />
  <add key="ViewNotifications" value="false" />
</appSettings>
```

```
<appSettings>
  <add key="webpages:Version" value="3.0.0.0" />
  <add key="webpages:Enabled" value="false" />
  <add key="PreserveLoginUrl" value="true" />
  <add key="ClientValidationEnabled" value="true" />
  <add key="UnobtrusiveJavaScriptEnabled" value="true" />

  <add key="AdminItemListPageSize" value="5" />
  <add key="StoreOpenTime" value="10" />
  <add key="StoreCloseTime" value="19" />
  <add key="StoreOpenStringValue" value="10:00 am" />
  <add key="ViewNotifications" value="false" />
</appSettings>
```

FIGURE 19-32: Transformed store hours change

6. Close the preview window. Back in the configuration file, add the following code. It should look like Figure 19-33 when done.

```
<connectionStrings>
    <add name="DefaultConnection" connectionString=""
            xdt:Transform="SetAttributes"  xdt:Locator="Match(name)"
            providerName="System.Data.SqlClient" />
    <add name="RentMyWroxContext" connectionString=""
            xdt:Transform="SetAttributes"  xdt:Locator="Match(name)"
            providerName="System.Data.SqlClient" />
    <add name="RentMyWroxConnectionString1" connectionString=""
            xdt:Transform="SetAttributes"  xdt:Locator="Match(name)"
            providerName="System.Data.SqlClient" />
</connectionStrings>
```

```
<configuration xmlns:xdt="http://schemas.microsoft.com/XML-Document-Transform">
  <connectionStrings>
    <add name="DefaultConnection" connectionString="" providerName="System.Data.SqlClient" />
    <add name="RentMyWroxContext" connectionString="" providerName="System.Data.SqlClient" />
    <add name="RentMyWroxConnectionString1" connectionString="" providerName="System.Data.SqlClient" />
  </connectionStrings>
  <appSettings>
    <add key="StoreCloseTime" value="19" xdt:Transform="SetAttributes" xdt:Locator="Match(key)" />
    <add key="StoreOpenTime" value="10" xdt:Transform="SetAttributes" xdt:Locator="Match(key)" />
    <add key="StoreOpenStringValue" value="10:00 am" xdt:Transform="SetAttributes" xdt:Locator="Match(key)"/>
  </appSettings>
  <system.web>
    <compilation xdt:Transform="RemoveAttributes(debug)" />
    <!--
      In the example below, the "Replace" transform will replace the entire
      <customErrors> section of your web.config file.
      Note that because there is only one customErrors section under the
      <system.web> node, there is no need to use the "xdt:Locator" attribute.

      <customErrors defaultRedirect="GenericError.htm"
        mode="RemoteOnly" xdt:Transform="Replace">
        <error statusCode="500" redirect="InternalError.htm"/>
      </customErrors>
    -->
  </system.web>
</configuration>
```

FIGURE 19-33: Transformed store hours change

7. Log in to your Microsoft Azure account. Click the SQL Database link on the left, and then click the name of your SQL Database. This brings up the detail screen shown in Figure 19-34.

8. Under the Connect to your Database section is a link called "View SQL Database Connection strings for ADO .NET, ODBC, PHP, and JDBC." Click this link to go to a Connection Strings dialog similar to that shown in Figure 19-35.

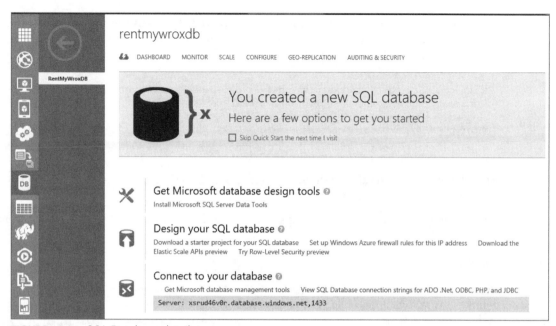

FIGURE 19-34: SQL Database details screen

FIGURE 19-35: Connection Strings dialog

9. Copy the top connection string, in the box labeled ADO.NET. Paste this value into the three connection strings that you added in Step 6. One of your connections would look like the following snippet. You need to replace the highlighted value with your own password.

```
<add name="DefaultConnection"
    connectionString="Server=tcp:xsrud46v0r.database.windows.net,1433;
    Database=RentMyWroxDB;User ID=rentmywroxdb@xsrud46v0r;
    Password={your_password_here};Trusted_Connection=False;
    Encrypt=True;Connection Timeout=30;"
        xdt:Transform="SetAttributes"  xdt:Locator="Match(name)"
        providerName="System.Data.SqlClient" />
```

10. Right-click this updated file and select Preview Transform. You should see that your connection string section has been updated as well.

11. Right-click the `Web.Debug.config` file and select Preview Transform. You should see your original `Web.config` values.

How It Works

The transformation process that is run when you publish a profile can also be run through the Preview Transform link. This process applies the rules you defined against the default `Web.config` file to create the file that you are previewing.

When you were working with the `appSettings` values, you used a `Locator` attribute that matched by the `name` attribute. Therefore, when this locator is applied, it will find an element in the base configuration file with the same name. If there is no element with the same name, then the process does nothing. When the name is matched, the `Transform` attribute is examined to determine what needs to happen.

When you were working with the connection string data, you were not able to use the `Locator` with the name attribute, as the element definition was different. You instead had to use the `Locator` with the key attribute to ensure that you were able to find the appropriate elements. In all cases you selected the `SetAttribute` transformation.

The `SetAttribute` transformation takes the value of every attribute that is set in the transformation file and sets the result attribute to that value. When an attribute is not in the source file, the transformation ensures that it is added to the output. If the attribute is in the source file but not in the transformation file, then the attribute is copied to the output without being changed.

Note that you had to ensure that the parent elements were included in the transformation file. This is because the transform process works its way through the file, matching the various elements based on parent node and the `Locator` attribute that you selected. Without that complete relationship there would be no way to perform the match.

You have now configured your application so that configuration values will be set according to the publish profile.

Moving Data to a Remote Server

One of the first things that you likely noticed when running your application is how empty it looks, as shown in Figure 19-36.

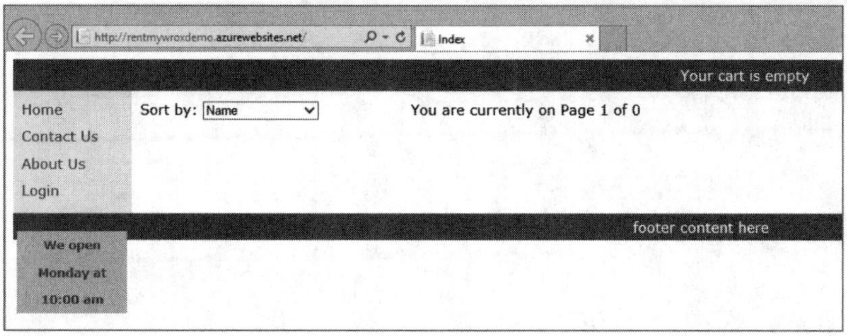

FIGURE 19-36: Deployed, but empty, web server

There are two different approaches to getting data into the database. The first is to copy information from your development database to the online database. The second is to simply add all the information directly to the online application. In this next Try It Out activity you copy some of the information from your local database to the Azure database.

TRY IT OUT   Copying Data to the Remote Server

In this activity, you copy some of the local information to your Azure database in the cloud. If you were unable to create an Azure account, you should still read through this exercise and perform as many steps as possible.

1.   Log in to your Azure dashboard.

2.   Click the SQL Databases menu item on the left of the screen.

3.   Go into the details of your database by clicking on the name.

4.   Find the menu item "Set up Windows Azure firewall rules for this IP address" and click it. This should bring up a screen like that shown in Figure 19-37. Note the bar at the bottom showing the IP address.

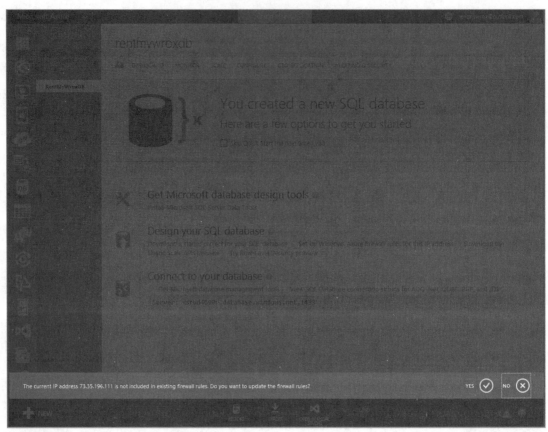

FIGURE 19-37: Confirmation screen to add IP address

5. Open SQL Server Management Studio and ensure that you are connected to your RentMyWrox database.

6. Right-click the database name and select Tasks ➪ Generate Scripts as shown in Figure 19-38. This brings up the dialog shown in Figure 19-39.

7. Click the Next button, which brings up the Choose Objects dialog. "Select specific database objects" should be enabled. Select the following objects as shown in Figure 19-40.

    ➤ dbo.AspNetRoles

    ➤ dbo.Hobbies

    ➤ dbo.Items

    ➤ dbo.Notifications

    ➤ Stored Procedures

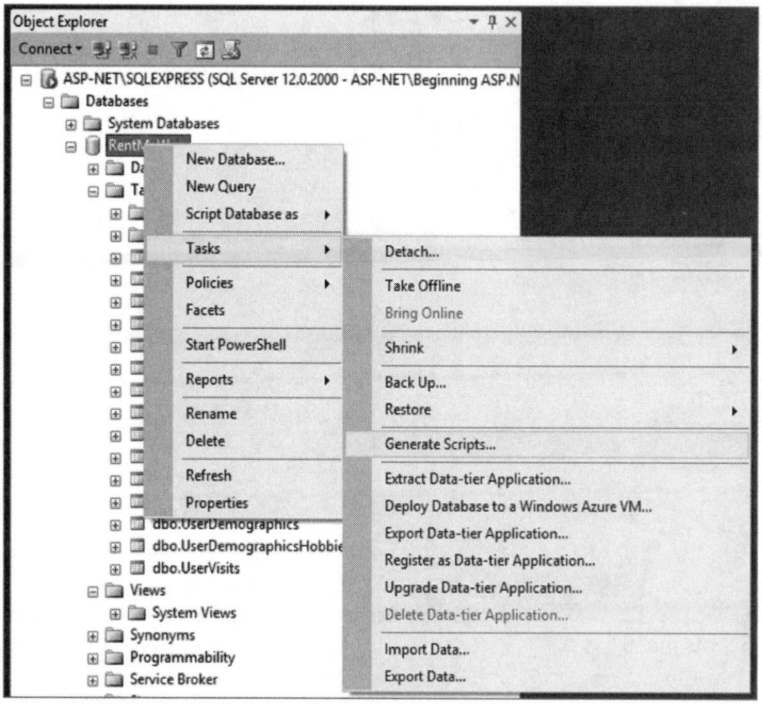

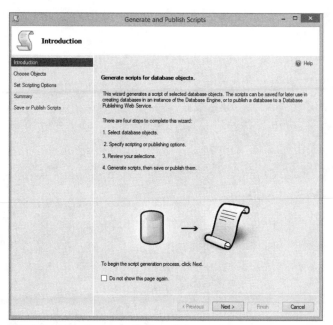

FIGURE 19-38: Generate Scripts menu

FIGURE 19-39: Generate Scripts dialog

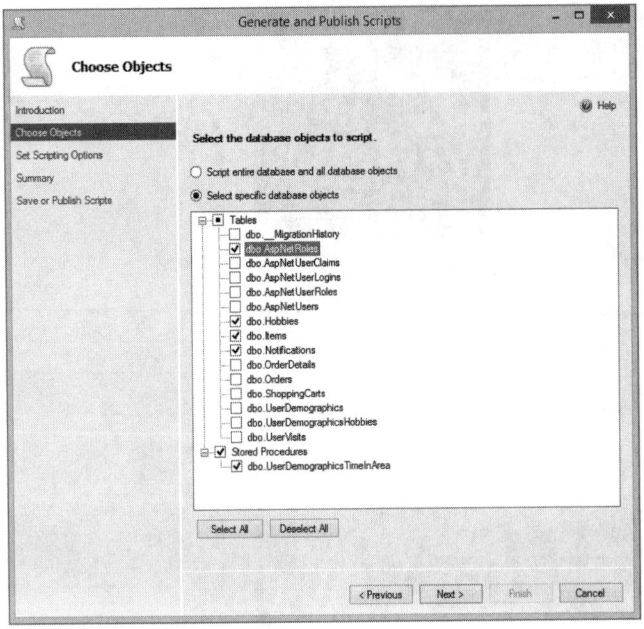

FIGURE 19-40: Generate Scripts menu

8. Click the Next button, which brings up the Set Scripting Options dialog. Ensure that "Save to new query window" is selected, as shown in Figure 19-41.

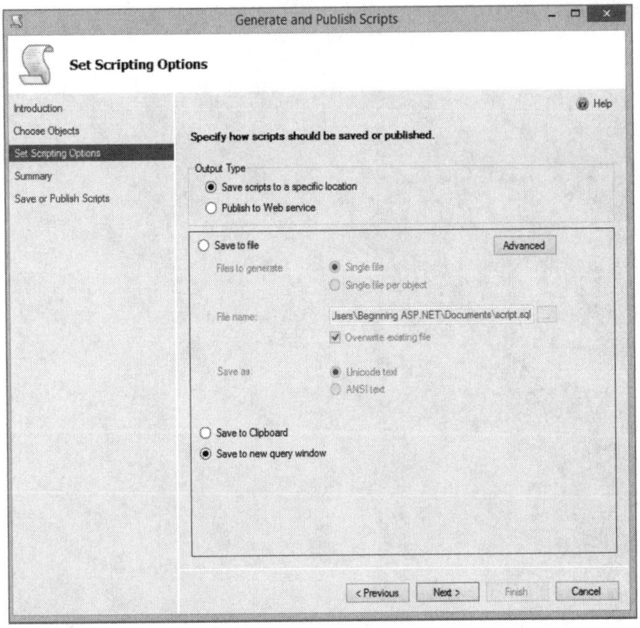

FIGURE 19-41: Specifying script output

9. Click the Advanced button, which brings up the Advanced Scripting Options dialog. Change the following settings. When completed it should look similar to Figure 19-42.

    ➤ Script USE DATABASE - false

    ➤ Type of data to script - Data only

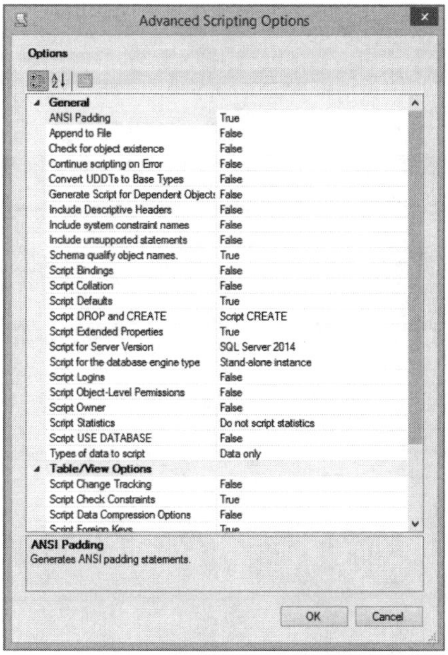

FIGURE 19-42: Advanced Scripting Options

10. Select OK in the Advanced Scripting Options dialog.

11. Select Next to get the Summary screen, and then Next again to complete the process. This brings you to the Save or Publish Scripts dialog shown in Figure 19-43.

12. Click the Finish button. You should see a long SQL script. In the Object Explorer of SQL Server Manager, click the Connect button.

13. In the connection window, enter the information from your Azure connection string. It should look similar to Figure 19-44 when completed.

14. Click the Connect button. You should see your Azure SQL database appear in the Object Explorer window.

15. Ensuring that you are still on the query window that was created, select Query ➪ Connection ➪ Change Connection. This brings up the Connect to Database Engine dialog.

16. Your Azure connection should be available in the dropdown for server name. Select that connection and click Connect.

17. Select the appropriate database in the dropdown as shown in Figure 19-45.

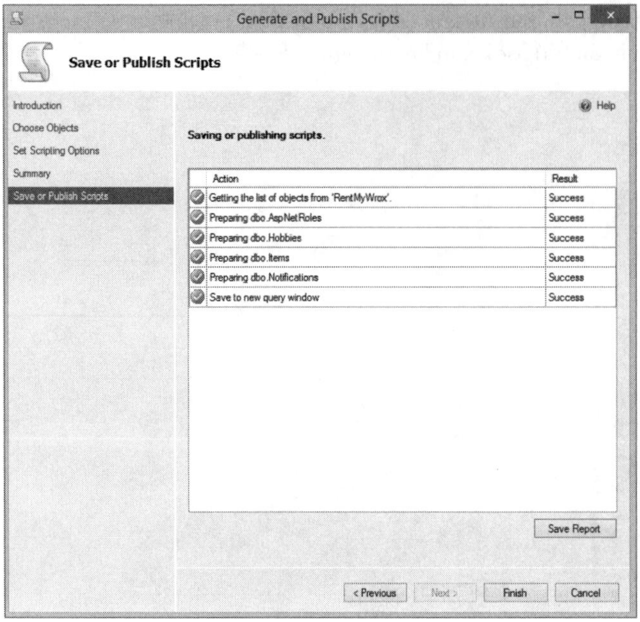

FIGURE 19-43: Finished creating items

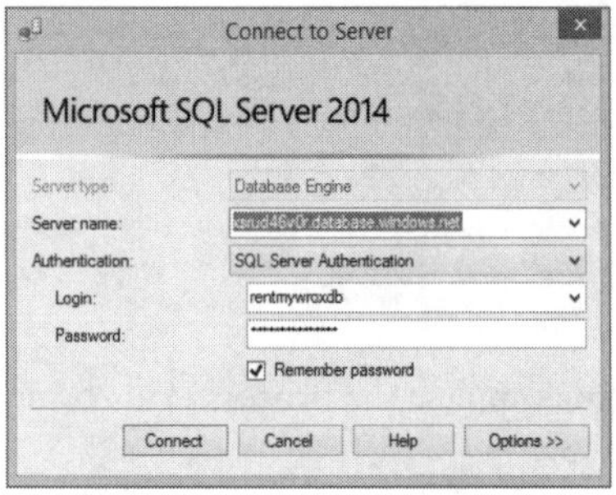

FIGURE 19-44: Connecting to Azure SQL

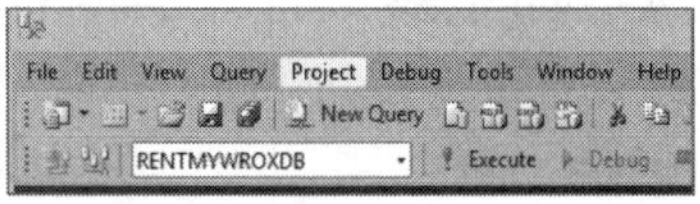

FIGURE 19-45: Selecting the appropriate database

18. Click the Execute button. You should see output similar to that shown in Figure 19-46.

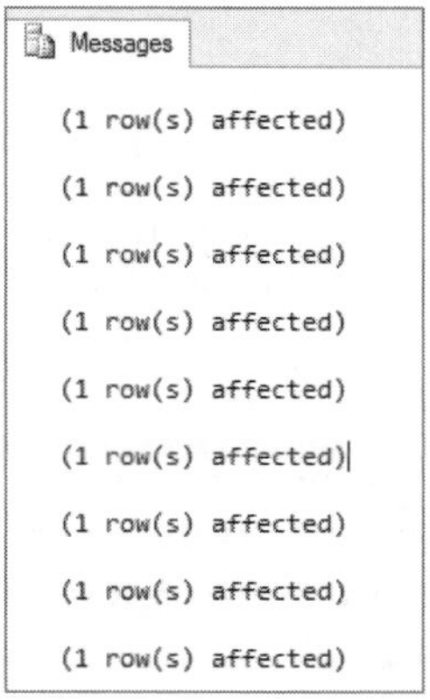

```
 Messages
  (1 row(s) affected)

  (1 row(s) affected)

  (1 row(s) affected)

  (1 row(s) affected)

  (1 row(s) affected)

  (1 row(s) affected)|

  (1 row(s) affected)

  (1 row(s) affected)

  (1 row(s) affected)
```

FIGURE 19-46: Output of database-seeding

19. Go to your online application. It should now appear properly, as shown in Figure 19-47.

FIGURE 19-47: Populated online application

How It Works

In this activity you copied data from your development environment and added it to the remote version of your application. You were able to do this through SQL Server Manager Studio by going through a series of options that set up a process to write out the SQL scripts necessary to remove only the data from the selected tables. You did not select all the tables to transfer over, but rather those tables that contain business information as opposed to user information. This enables you to keep the user information separated between the deployed application and your local application.

The scripts that were created copy the data from one system to the other. Three steps happen for each batch of data, with the first and third steps turning on and turning off functionality in the table, respectively, and the middle step actually inserting the data. The following snippet shows these steps:

```
SET IDENTITY_INSERT [dbo].[Hobbies] ON
GO
INSERT [dbo].[Hobbies] ([Id], [Name], [IsActive]) VALUES (1, N'Gardening', 1)
GO
INSERT [dbo].[Hobbies] ([Id], [Name], [IsActive]) VALUES (2, N'Cooking', 1)
GO
SET IDENTITY_INSERT [dbo].[Hobbies] OFF
GO
```

The functionality that is being flipped, IDENTITY_INSERT, enables you to enter in the value for the Id column. The whole point of an Identity column is to generate the value for you upon insertion, so you need to turn off the functionality to allow input of the value. Once you have inserted the data, you then need to ensure that you turn it back on; otherwise, all of your regular your data entry through the application will fail.

Now that you have completed copying your application and data, it would be easy to assume that you are finished with deployment. However, there is one more thing that you must do on a deployment, and that is to ensure that the application is working as expected.

SMOKE TESTING YOUR APPLICATION

The phrase "smoke test" comes from the process of testing new electronic hardware when you plug in a new board and turn on the power. If you see smoke coming from the board, you don't have to do any more testing; you know that it failed. Unfortunately, while it is still called smoke testing, your application will never smoke after a failed deployment. Instead, you have to actually do some testing to ensure that your application works as desired.

It is important that you perform this testing after each deployment. Many things can go wrong during a deployment—a file isn't properly copied, the configuration transformation doesn't provide the expected outcome, a database migration failed, or, even worse, the application just doesn't work on the server even though it did locally.

The only way to ensure that the application is working correctly on the server is to test it after deployment. That means going through the application and trying all the major functionality. This should usually be a pretty quick process—even enterprise applications can be smoke tested in just a couple of hours. Applications like the sample application can be smoke tested in just a few minutes. The following Try It Out walks through a smoke test.

TRY IT OUT Smoke Testing Your Application

In this activity, you smoke test your application to ensure that the deployment was successful.

1. Open a web browser and go to your deployed application.
2. Check the color of the background and ensure that the hours are displaying correctly.
3. While on the front page, click the Next Page link to ensure that you can move to the second page.
4. Click the Full Details link. Ensure that you see the details for that item.
5. Ensure that the Recently Reviewed area shows the item that you clicked on.
6. Click the Add to Cart link. Review the shopping cart area at the top of the screen to ensure that it shows up appropriately.
7. Click the Checkout link. You should go to the Login screen.
8. Click the "Register as a new user" link and ensure that you are taken to the Register screen.
9. Register a new user to confirm that you are taken to the User Demographics screen.
10. Fill out and submit the User Demographics screen. You should be taken to the Checkout screen.
11. Click the Complete Order button. You should be taken to the Order confirmation screen (see Figure 19-48).

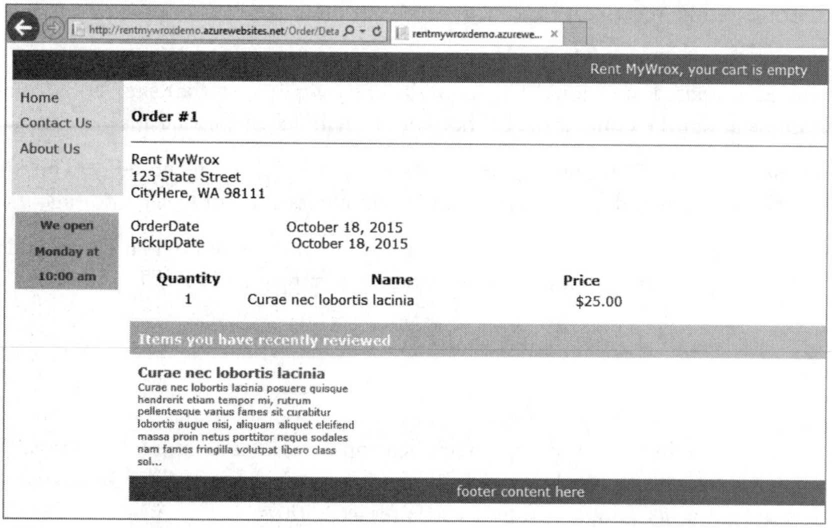

FIGURE 19-48: Completed smoke test order

How It Works

This was a simple walk-through of the main functionality of the application. By performing this walk-through, you were able to verify that all the major components are performing as expected.

Congratulations, you have completed the deployment of your website!

GOING FORWARD

Now that you have worked through a beginning ASP.NET application, you may be curious to learn more about various topics that could only be briefly covered during the course of this project. Fortunately, Wrox has a complete line of books that go over these different aspects of a web application in much more detail. Here are just a few:

➤ *Beginning Visual C# 2015 Programming* (ISBN: 978-1-119-09668-9)

➤ *Beginning Visual Basic 2015* (ISBN: 978-1-119-09211-7)

➤ *Beginning JavaScript, 5th Edition* (ISBN: 978-1-118-90333-9)

➤ *Web Development with jQuery* (ISBN: 978-1-118-86607-8)

➤ *Professional Visual Studio 2015* (ISBN: 978-1-119-06805-1)

➤ *Beginning HTML and CSS* (ISBN: 978-1-118-34018-9)

Of course, books are not your only source of information about developing ASP.NET web applications. Following are some online resources that may also be of interest:

➤ `http://p2p.wrox.com`: The public discussion forum from Wrox where you can go for all your programming-related questions. This book has its own link on that site. You can ask specific questions about the content of this book and I will do my best to answer them.

➤ `http://www.asp.net`: The Microsoft community site for ASP.NET technology. This site provides additional downloads, a support forum, documentation, and user tutorials.

➤ `http://msdn.microsoft.com/asp.net`: The official home for ASP.NET, it contains documentation, sample applications, and other resources that support ASP.NET.

SUMMARY

The last thing that you have to do after building an application is make it available to others. When your application is a web application, "making it available" means that you will be deploying it to an accessible location so that other people can find and interact with it.

A few different things have to be managed as you deploy an application from your local machine. One of these tasks is handling database connection strings that will be different because of the new environment, because you will no longer be connecting to the same database server. Another task is ensuring that you are not deploying in debug mode; you are not in development anymore!

Obviously, when you are ready to deploy, you need a destination for your application. In this case you deployed to Microsoft Azure. Microsoft Azure is a set of products that includes Web Apps and SQL databases, the two products that you used to host your Internet application. You used the publishing functionality that is built into Visual Studio to push the compiled software application to the web.

Not only does Visual Studio enable you to publish the application, it also saves these publish settings so that you can use them going forward. Rerunning the publishing process is simple once it has been configured the first time, as you have already filled out the settings. You can change them at any time, of course.

Moving data from development to the remote environment can be a little more tedious, however, if you choose to do this movement manually as you did here. It gave you complete control over the information that was copied to the remote system and was simplified due to the support that is built into SQL Server Management Studio. You could also elect to not add any data and instead completely configure the information through the UI that you created.

Once the application has been physically moved to the server, you always need to ensure that it has been correctly deployed. The best way to do this is to perform a quick smoke test whereby you click through the application and validate that it works as necessary. This should be a very simple and straightforward process, and it should be done every time you make a change to a remote application.

EXERCISES

1. You went through a process to copy information from your development environment to your remote application. Could you use the same approach to copy data from the server back to your local system?

2. What would be a reason to copy data from the server?

3. One of the changes that you did not do is to turn tracing on at the remote server. What code in the transformation file would be necessary to ensure that the following code is available to anyone who goes to the appropriate `trace.axd` page, regardless of from where that user is making the request?

```
<trace mostRecent="true" enabled="true" requestLimit="1000"
       pageOutput="false" localOnly="true" />
```

▶ **WHAT YOU LEARNED IN THIS CHAPTER**

Azure SQL Database	A relational database-as-a-service that is part of the Azure product offerings
Azure Web Apps	Web Apps in Azure App Service provide a scalable, reliable, and easy-to-use environment for hosting web applications.
Expression Binding	A technique that enables you to bind control properties to different resources, such as application settings defined in `Web .config`
Microsoft Azure	A collection of different cloud services, including analytics, computing, database, mobile, networking, storage, and web
Smoke Test	The process of doing a quick evaluation of an application to ensure that it is working as expected. It should always be run after any deployment.
Publishing Profile	Enables you to save the configuration information that was captured during the process of deploying the application
Transformations	A built-in ASP.NET feature that manages the maintenance of configuration files. You can add information, remove information, or change information in the configuration.
`WebConfigurationManager`	A class that provides access to data stored in configuration files

Answers to Exercises

CHAPTER 1

1. The difference between HTML and HTTP is that HTML is a markup language used to define content that is transmitted over the Internet, whereas HTTP is the transfer protocol that manages the transmittal of HTML over the Internet.

2. ViewState is how ASP.NET Web Forms manages state even though HTTP is, by definition, stateless. This is important because it enables your website to determine when something changes, and allows your application to support many built-in events.

3. The three architectural components that make up ASP.NET MVC are models, views, and controllers. A view is what the users see in the browser. Models represent the data that is displayed within the view. The controller is the part that manages the interaction between the two—it handles getting the model and making it available to the view.

4. Microsoft Visual Studio is the primary integrated development environment (IDE) used to create ASP.NET sites and applications. We are using this product throughout the book because it is the de facto standard for Microsoft Windows–based software development.

CHAPTER 2

1. The two approaches to building a web-based application are Web Site and Web Application. A web site does not pre-compile the source code, but instead deploys the source code to the server. When an application is started, there is JIT compilation. A Web Application is compiled and then copied to the server where it is run. Web Forms can be either approach, but MVC applications are only available within Web Applications.

2. Project templates are Visual Studio's way of creating projects that are designed for a specific need. Visual Studio includes numerous project templates, but the two that concern us most are ASP.NET Web Forms and ASP.NET MVC.

3. Compared to a Web Form project, two additional folders are created in an ASP.NET MVC application: the View folder and the Controller folder. They are not created in Web Form projects because a Web Form project does not embody the concepts of controllers or views.

CHAPTER 3

1. `.intro p` will match those items of type `<p>` that are completely contained within any kind of element that has a class named `intro`. The style `p.intro` will select all elements with class `intro` that are fully contained within a type element of `<p>`. The style `p, .intro` will select those elements that are either of type `<p>` or have their class set to "intro."

2. To stretch the "box" of an element you would use the `padding` property. The `padding` property extends the visible box of the element, while the `margin` property pushes the visible box away from the adjacent element. If, for example, you set the background-color of an element containing some text, `padding` would extend the background-color past the text, extending the colored area. Using `margin` will move the colored box without changing its size.

3. To allow the content of a web page to access styles contained in an external stylesheet you need to create a link between the web page and the external stylesheet. That link is created through the use of a link element that is placed in the header of the web page. A link looks like `<link href="styles.css" rel="Stylesheet" type="text/css" />`.

4. Some of the various Visual Studio aides include the following:

   ➤ **Design mode:** Enables the developer to see the rendered version of the HTML source code

   ➤ **Visual aids:** Provides different views of the rendered output in Design mode, including tags, borders around elements, etc.

   ➤ **Formatting toolbar:** Visible when in Design mode, the formatting toolbar enables developers to assign and/or create styles directly from within the window.

CHAPTER 4

1. The string `resultsAsAString` would be "What is my result? 12" because the `&` and the `+`, in this context, are concatenation operators.

2. The very last iteration of this loop would cause an exception because you are trying to access an item in the list that is not present. The loop definition should have been `i < collection.Count` for C# and `0 To collection.Count - 1` for VB.

3. The `foreach` construct is specifically designed to iterate through a collection. If you were going to use a `Do` loop, you would also have to add code that evaluates whether the list is completed, whereas the `foreach` provides that automatically.

CHAPTER 5

1. Not every property can be set in the code-behind, as the capability to access the properties in the code-behind depends on the `runat` property in the markup. Without that value set in the markup, there is nothing that you can do with it in code-behind.

2. The Text in a textbox can be retrieved simply by accessing the `Text` property. Understanding the selected checkbox items is different in that a list contains one or more items, each of which may have been selected. You need to go through the list and determine which of the item have their `IsSelected` property set to true. This creates a short list of those items that were selected.

3. Adding the `runat="server"` attribute makes a traditional HTML element an HTML control. This enables the value and some of the other attributes to be available for use in the code-behind.

4. ViewState is how the server is able to keep track of previous versions of information. It acts as a container for the default server control values that are being sent to the client. When the form is posted back to the server, the state management server analyzes the information in the ViewState and the information that was submitted with the form to determine its next step.

CHAPTER 6

1. The `TextboxFor` helper specifically binds a property on the model to an HTML element. This binding is achieved through a lambda expression that helps the system identify which property on the model should be used for the binding. The `Textbox` element typically takes a string name rather than a direct model binding. The name given to the helper is the name given to the HTML element that it creates. However, as long as the name that is passed into the helper is the same as the property name with which you want it to be related, the model binder can interpret which property should get the returned value.

2. The primary way that the Razor view engine knows the difference between code that it should process and text that needs to simply be passed through straight into the HTML is through the use of the @ character and curly brackets, {}. If C# (or VB) code is after the @ character or contained within a set of curly brackets, then the view engine knows to run the code.

   The view engine is also smart enough to realize when you start an HTML element, so it switches back into text-reading mode. However, if you want it to return to code processing mode, you need to preface it with the @ character again; thus, you may have @ code within other @-labeled constructs.

3. No, views do not always have to match the name of the action. If you return a `View()`, then it is expecting a one-to-one correlation; however, you also have the capability to add the

name of the view to be returned. This enables you to return any view from a controller action as long as you appropriately define the view method that is returned.

4. The model binder is able to determine nested object properties by using dot notation. For example, suppose you have an object structure like the following:

```
public class Parent
{
    public Child Child { get; set; }
}

public class Child
{
    public GrandChild GrandChild { get; set; }
}

public class GrandChild
{
    public string SomeProperty { get; set; }
}
```

A textbox would be able to set the property on the grandchild by ensuring that the name of the textbox element is "`Child.GrandChild.SomeProperty`" where the model that was passed to the view is a parent.

CHAPTER 7

1. Controllers and web pages are traditional OO classes, so even though they are already inheriting other classes, it is easy to add an intermediate class as long as that intermediate class extends the class that the page was already inheriting. However, views are a different kind of approach; they do not have a class definition or anything that enables you to create an inheritance scheme. They are instead a value that is processed.

2. The advantage of using the `Layout` command in the ViewStart file is that you do not need a hard link between your views and your layout. If you did not have the ViewStart and you wanted to change the layout to point to another file, you would have to go into every page to make the change. The ViewStart enables you to specify your primary layout page and then assign it by default.

CHAPTER 8

1. They would end up at `http://www.servername.com/Admin/~/default`, where they would most likely get a 404 error for Page Not Found. If the anchor tag were given the extra attribute for `runat="server"`, then the system would know to replace the ~ with the application root directory. However, without the `runat="server"`, the HTML from an HTML element turns into an HTML control, so the system does not do any additional interpretation of the code.

2.	There are two main approaches to finding the code that responds to a request to `http://www.servername.com/results`. The first is to look through the project to see if there is a folder with the name of "results." If there is, then there is a good chance that the default file in the directory responds to that request. This means that it is being served by an ASP.NET Web Forms page. If this does not provide a result, the next step would be to look into the Controllers directory to determine whether there is a controller that would be used to handle requests to this URL, most likely "ResultsController." If this controller does exist, look in the actions to find the one that would serve a get request to the base URL. If you are unable to find anything there, you need to check the `RouteConfig.cs` file to evaluate whether it contains a hard-coded route that will handle this approach. If so, then follow this routing suggestion to find the appropriate handler.

3.	Friendly URLs were implemented for several reasons. The first is that it makes addresses easier to remember, as the user doesn't have to include the extension on the URL. This makes URLs used for advertising much more effective. Another reason is that it makes other URLs more predictable and guessable. This gives users confidence that they can find information on your site. The last big reason is search engine optimization, which is better supported because friendly URLS allows the elimination of query strings in favor of URL variables, turning `http://www.servername.com/product.aspx?id=8` to `http://www.servername.com/product/8` or even `http://www.servername.com/product/Product_Name`.

CHAPTER 9

1.	The _MigrationHistory table keeps a record of every time the update database command was run in that database. It stores the name of the migration that was created by the developer, the context to which the migration was assigned, and information on the model(s) that were used. If you looked in the table, you would be easily able to determine the first two items, but the model information is stored in a binary format and is not intended to allow reverse migration outside the context of the Entity Framework.

2.	Attribute routing enables developers to define the URL that an action will respond to directly on the action, as opposed to a standard template. One of the primary problems with the template approach is that there always seemed to be at least one route in an application that could not be easily managed through the template approach. The developer would have to either hard-code a route in the `RouteConfig` file or otherwise manipulate how the action is named and called to ensure that it could be managed in the "one size fits all" approach of template-based routing. With attribute routing, however, you can determine at the action level what URL that action would respond to.

3.	Using the `using` statement ensures that the item being created, in this case the `DbContext`, is disposed of upon completion. Taking this step ensures that the .NET Garbage Collector will be able to pick this item out of memory the next time the collector runs. Otherwise, this item would likely linger in memory for a longer period and have a more long-term effect on memory usage, perhaps affecting the user experience.

CHAPTER 10

1. If you create a new item, there is a chance that the item will not be displayed in the list page, especially if you had recently visited the list page. This is because the cache was set to 20 minutes, so visiting the list page, creating or editing an item, and then immediately going back to the list page will likely result in the list itself being cached; therefore, the new list will not be called until after expiration of the previous cache. This is a perfect example of when caching can cause stale data to be presented to the user.

2. If you are not going to pass information to a view through the use of a `ViewBag`, then best approach is to create a `ViewModel`, which in this case is a class with two properties: the list of hobbies and the UserDemographics item that is currently being used as the model.

3. There are multiple reasons why you might want to use a more direct approach to the database, including response time and performance, complicated queries, integration with other applications that are using database access, and the need to keep consistent behavior between the applications.

CHAPTER 11

1. Yes, you can use a user control to solve the same kind of problem. While you will not get the automatic translation for `DisplayFor` or `EditorFor`, that's OK because neither concept is supported in the ASP.NET Web Forms world. You would instead create a user control that has a parameter of the model, or object, that you wanted to display. The code-behind could take that object and do the necessary work, whether it is simply displaying the item or doing business logic with that item. While the instantiation of the control is slightly more awkward, you can create a user control that is very similar to an MVC template.

2. You do not have to include the controller name in an `Html.Action` method call when the action that you are calling is on the same controller. If the action is on a different controller, you need to ensure that you include the appropriate controller name.

3. When you are working with attributes in the markup, it is important to remember that *everything is actually a string*, so putting an integer into a property defined as a string will not cause any problems; the property will be populated with the string version of the integer. It is going the other way that's a problem. When you are putting a string value into a non-string attribute, you must ensure that the string value can be parsed into the appropriate type. *If you don't* do this correctly, such as by putting the value "two" into an integer field, you will get several warnings. First, a validation error will be displayed in the markup page. Second, when you try to run the application, you will get an exception page because the system was not able to do the necessary conversion.

CHAPTER 12

1. Request validation has been turned on based on the attribute on the controller, so the only way any HTML would be allowed through the process is if it were turned on at the model level. If you examine the model, however, you will see that the `Description` property has the appropriate attribute to allow HTML. Thus, any HTML in the Title would cause an exception to be thrown, while any HTML in the Description would be allowed through the request process.

2. The order in which validation controls are added to the page does not affect anything about the actual validation.

3. Yes, it is certainly possible to set up a scenario in which a model can never be valid. Even ruling out such obvious errors as using a "less than" when you should have used a "greater than," it is easy to set up these kinds of cases, especially when using validation approaches that compare the values of one controller to another. If you followed the suggestion of ensuring that you always have a valid and complete message, then you should be able to understand and manage scenarios in which you have validated yourself into a corner.

CHAPTER 13

1. You would not have to do anything different as long as you added both the same `<div>` tags and scripting. This will work regardless of the type of ASP.NET that you used to create the page as long as all of the proper elements are within the page.

2. Using the Unobtrusive AJAX jQuery library in a Web Form application can be done in several ways. Perhaps the easiest is to include the script references to the JavaScript libraries, just as you did in the example. You can then manually add the attributes to the element that will be firing the change, typically an anchor link. An example would be the following:

    ```
    <a  data-ajax="true"
        data-ajax-method="GET"
        data-ajax-mode="replace"
        data-ajax-update="#thelementToReplace"
        href="/URL TO CALL">Displayed Text</a>
    ```

    The expectation is that you have a URL that will return some HTML that is appropriate to display in the element identified in the attributes.

3. There are several potential problems with using a timer to refresh content. The first of these is the bandwidth and processing that may be used unnecessarily. The browser will continue to make those calls as long as the page is open. The user could have gone to the page, looked around for a few minutes, and then decided to do something else without closing the browser. The page will continue making calls even though the user is not present. Another

problem that may be experienced could result from transient network outages or server problems; rather than getting the expected content part of the page, the user will instead be trying to deal with an error.

CHAPTER 14

1. This change is only supposed to work on these particular elements, so the first thing you should do is add an id to each so that your jQuery work can select the correct item. After adding ids, you can set the hover function of the <p> element to change the css color value of the <h1> element. All code is shown here:

    ```
    <h1 id="colorchange">Title</h1>
    <p id="hoverover">Content</p>

    $(document).ready(function () {
        $("#hoverover").hover(
            function () {
                $("#colorchange").css('color', 'yellow');
            }, function () {
                $("#colorchange").css('color', 'green');
            });
    });
    ```

2. Bundling enables you to combine multiple files of the same type, such as CSS or JavaScript, into a single file for download. Bundling becomes important when you want to get multiple scripts to the client side but the browser only supports a certain number of connections to a single domain. As the page is rendered, each call to a server may end up being queued. Therefore, bundling is a great benefit once you have more than five or six items being downloaded. These items can include images, CSS files, JavaScript files, and any other item that could be downloaded from the server.

    The size of the items that you are bundling is important as well. Putting multiple large files into a single bundle may slow the load time down because your users are getting a very large file over a single channel as opposed to two smaller files that can be downloaded at the same time.

    Lastly, the amount of change that happens in your scripting is important. Each change to the underlying scripts causes a new bundle to be downloaded to the client. Thus, if you are doing a lot of work on one script, you may want to move it out of the bundle and keep it separate; otherwise, the browser sees the bundle containing multiple files as new, although only one file has actually changed.

3. The Ajax.Helper class has four different events that you can add to a JavaScript function: OnBegin enables you to know when a call is getting ready to happen, but before the call to the server; OnComplete is called after the call to the server has completed but before the page is updated; OnFailure handles any error conditions; and OnSuccess is called after the page is updated. Each of these enables you to add a JavaScript function to the workflow.

CHAPTER 15

1.   These two files are the `Startup.Auth.cs` and `IdentityConfig.cs`. The `Startup.Auth.cs` file creates the `UserManager` and `SignInManager` as well as configures the way that cookies are going to be used for authentication. `IdentityConfig.cs` sets up the password validation requirements as well as other default user login details such as lockout periods and maximum attempts.

2.   Authentication is when a user confirms who they are, generally through the combination of username and password. Authorization comes after the user has been authenticated and is the determination about whether the user can take a particular action or set of actions.

CHAPTER 16

1.   There are a couple of different ways that you can gather this kind of information. One would be to simply ask users what colors they prefer. While not very sophisticated, it tends to get relatively accurate information. The other, and more subtle, approach is to track the various colors that users view during their shopping visits, perhaps also tracking search terms in case they also regularly contain colors.

2.   There are a lot of different things that you can do with this kind of information. For example, you can shade the background of the pages that you display to that user with a color. Another simple personalization would be displaying the user's preferred color(s) automatically so the user doesn't have to make the selection.

CHAPTER 17

1.   When you have multiple catch statements, the framework evaluates the exception against the catch parameters in order from the top down. Because it takes this approach, you need to ensure that the most general exception is at the bottom of the list. In this case, no exception will ever hit the second catch block because they all would be caught by the generic, first catch block.

2.   You can use either tracing or logging to provide information about anything going on within your application. This includes the capability to add tracing and/or logging code that will provide information about the time spent in each method. One approach would be to use code such as the following:

```
public ActionResult Details(string id)
{
    DateTime enterDate = DateTime.Now;

    // do lots of work that could take a long time

    string message = string.Format(
```

```
            "Details methods took {0} milliseconds",
            (DateTime.Now - enterDate).Milliseconds);
    System.Diagnostics.Trace.TraceInformation(message);

    return View();
}
```

CHAPTER 18

1. A changeset is the complete set of changes that is checked in at one time. It is important because it identifies the files that were changed, enabling those changes to be compartmentalized and removed (rolled back) if necessary.

2. A checkout describes when a user notifies the system, either deliberately or through editing a file, that he or she is going to make changes to a particular file. The checkout can be either locking or non-locking. When a file is locked, the system will not allow a different user to check the file out. Checking out is important because a user is not allowed to check in changes if that file has not been checked out.

3. TFS has the functionality to enable users to the view the history of a file. Also, if needed, users can display these different history versions side-by-side in order to compare specific changes within each version.

CHAPTER 19

1. Yes, you could use the exact same approach to copy data from the remote server. Note one caveat, however, with that approach. Because work would be happening both on the server and locally (developers working on features and real users signing up in production), there will be contradictory data. You would have no problems bringing remote data to a brand-new, empty database, but merging two different databases doesn't work as well.

2. The main reason that you would copy data from the server is because an error is occurring that seems to be based on the data in use. Generally, this kind of problem is hard to replicate because of this dependence on a specific piece of data; if none of your test data has that same error, then you will have problems finding it.

3. You would need to add the following code within the `system.web` element of the `web.RentMyWroxDemo.config` file:

```
<trace mostRecent="true" enabled="true" requestLimit="1000"
       pageOutput="false" localOnly="false"
       xdt:Transform="SetAttributes" xdt:Locator="Match(key)" />
```

INDEX

G

H

W